Microeconomics
The Freedom to Choose

Anthony I. Negbenebor
Gardner-Webb University

James F. Willis
San Jose State Universtiy

 *CAT Publishing Company*

Acknowledgements

Quotations in text from John Maynard Keynes, *The General Theory of Employment, Interest, and Money*, Harcourt, Brace & World, New York, 1936. Reprinted by permission of Harcourt Brace Jovanovich, Inc., and Macmillan, London and Basingstoke.

Quotation in text from John G. Gurley, "Maoist Economic Development" (from *America's Asia*, edited by Edward Friedman and Mark Selden, Random House, New York, 1971) in *Economics, Mainstream Readings and Radical Critiques*, 2nd ed., edited by David Mermelstein, Random House, New York, 1973. Reprinted by permission of the author and Random House, Inc.

In the text, "First Steps in Banking," from *Punch*, April 3, 1957, pp. 440-441. © 1972 by McGraw-Hill, Inc.

ISBN 1-56226-485-0

To Nicole, Diane and my Parents.
A.I.N.

To Marianna, Jim, and my mother.
J.F.W.

Table of Contents

Preface xvii

Chapter 1: Introduction to Economics 1
The Aims of Economics 2
    Solving Specific Economic Problems 3
What Is Economics? 4
Scarcity: Source of Basic Economic Questions 4
The What? How? and For Whom? 5
    Is Scarcity Meaningful Today? 6
Macroeconomics and Microeconomics: Economic Principles From Two Perspectives 6
What Is The Economist's Method? 7
The Citizen and Economic Policy 9
Applications: Concrete Examples of Abstract Ideas 9
End-of-Chapter Summaries 9
Mathematics and Economics 10
Positive Versus Normative Economics 11
A Word About Words 13
Application: Self-Interest—The Key to a More Productive Future? 14
    Self-Interest: Key to All Characters 14
Summing Up 15
Key Terms 17
Questions 17
Suggested Readings 18

Chapter 2: Introduction to the World's Economic System 19
The Economic Problem 20
The Economics of Change—A Brief History of the Evolution of the American
    Economy 20
    Feudalism—The Traditional Economy 21
    The Evolution of Capitalism 21
    The Enclosure Movement 21
    Emergence of Nations 22
    Development of the Protestant Ethic 23
    Inventions and Innovations 23
    The Birth of Capitalism—1776 23
    The Law of the Market 24
    Law of Accumulation 24
    Thomas Malthus 25
    1860 to 1910 25
    1929 to 1939 26
    1946—The Employment Act and the GI bill 26
    Today's Economy 27
Five Basic Characteristics of Capitalism—Market Efficiency, Role of Government and
    Market Failure, Consumer Sovereignty, Self-interest, Private Ownership 27
    Market Efficiency 27
    Role of Government and Market Failure 28
    Consumer Sovereignty 29
    Self-interest 29

Capitalism—The Market Economy 29
How Much is One Trillion Dollars? A Brief Digression on $1,000,000,000,000 30
    Private Ownership 30
Socialism..32
Mixed Economic System 32
Communism—A Theoretical Economic System 32
Factors of Production 33
    Land, Labor, Capital and Entrpreneurship 33
Cost Benefit Analysis..35
Opportunity Cost 35
Viewing the Choices: The Production-Possibilities Curve 36
    The Production Possibilities Table 36
    Graphing the Production Possibilities Curve 37
Economic Growth: Shifting the Production-Possibilities Curve 38
A Word of Caution 39
Increasing Opportunity Costs: Why Is The Curve Shaped That Way? 39
    What Is the (Positive) "Cost of the Lunch"? 39
    Resources Are Specialized 40
Mental Reservations 42
A Classical Explanation of Growth: Shifts in Production Possibilities 42
Summing Up 43
Key Terms 44
Questions 44
Suggested Readings..45

Chapter 3: Supply and Demand: The Market Economy 47
Price Determination in Competitive Markets 48
What is Competition? 48
How Are Prices Set? Supply And Demand..49
Demand 49
Demand versus Need or Want 49
Determinants of Demand..50
    Elaboration on TINPEA 50
An Individual Demand Curve 51
Veblen Goods and Giffen Goods—Two Exceptions to the Law of Demand 54
    Veblen Goods 54
    Giffen Goods 55
    Normal Goods versus Inferior Goods 55
Changes in Quantity Demanded Versus Changes in Demand..56
Demand: Summing Up 57
Market Demand 58
Supply..59
What Is Supply? 59
Determinants of Supply—TIPET 59
Supply Curve 60
    What Do Supply Data and the Supply Curve Tell Us? 61
Why Do Supply Curves Slope Upward? 62
Why Do Supply Curves Shift? 63
Adding Up To Market Supply 63
Summing Up: Difference Between Movements Along and Shifts In Demand and
    Supply Curves..64
Equilibrium Pricing 65

Conditions for Competitive Pricing 67
Application: Should We Let Supply and Demand Work? Rent Controls and the Price
   of Housing 69
      Government Determined Prices: The Arguments 69
      Are Rent Controls Effective? (The Best Case)..70
      Are Rent Controls Effective? (The Worst Case) 71
      The Dynamics of Rent Controlled Housing 72
      Illegal or "Black Markets" 73
      The Future of Rent Controls 73
Other Applications of Supply and Demand 74
      Supply and Demand for Clerks..74
      Supply and Demand for Doctors 76
California's Crowded Parks Problem 76
Summing Up 78
Key Terms 81
QUESTIONS 81
Suggested Readings..84

Chapter 4: Demand Side of the Market—Utility and Elasticity 87
Income and Substitution Effects 89
Theoretical Exceptions to the Law of Demand 90
Utility: Another Way to Explain Demand 93
      The Law of Diminishing Marginal Utility 94
      Making Choices that Maximize Utility 94
      Equilibrium in a World of Many Goods 96
      Utility Maximizing Behavior: an Arithmetic Illustration 96
Deriving a Demand Curve 97
Independent Utilities: A Simplifying Assumption 99
Market Demand 99
Elasticity: Estimating Consumer Responses to Price and Other Changes 100
Price Elasticity of Demand...101
Elasticity of Demand and the Slope of a Demand Curve 101
Computing Price Elasticities of Demand..102
Differing Elasticities of Demand 103
Determinants of the Elasticity of Demand 105
Some Selected Price Elasticities of Demand 106
Why Do Elasticities Matter? 107
Elasticities and Total Revenue 107
      Prices Go Up, Some Industries Prosper, Some Suffer 108
      Prices Go Down, Some Industries Suffer, Some Prosper 108
      Prices Go Up or Down, Revenues Remain the Same 108
Elasticities and Total Revenue: A Summation..108
Why Do Elasticities Matter? An Automobile Industry Example 109
Elasticities and Excise Tax Incidence 110
Price Elasticity and Straight-Line Demand Curves: A Final Note 111
An Implication: Where to Set Price 112
Other Demand Elasticities 112
Income Elasticity of Demand 112
Cross Price Elasticities of Demand 114
      Cross Price Elasticity Signs 115
      Why Do Cross Price Elasticities Matter? An Illustration 115
Application: Will Redistributing Income Make People Happier? 116

The Distribution of Satisfaction 116
The Distribution of Income 116
Governments and Income Distribution 117
Summing Up 118
Key Terms 122
Questions 122

Chapter 5: Supply Side of Markets—Production Costs **125**
What is Supply? 126
What Determines a Firm's Costs? 126
Explicit and Implicit Costs 127
Profit 128
Better Burger Company: An Illustration of Accounting Profit and Normal Profit vs.
Economic Profit and Economic Loss 128
Is Better Burger Profitable? 129
Summing Up Profits and Losses 130
The Influence of Time on Supply: Four Periods 130
Market Period 130
Short-Run Period 131
Long-Run Period 132
Historical Period 132
Costs and Supply in the Market Period 133
Costs and Supply in the Short-Run Period 133
The Law of Diminishing Returns or Variable Proportions 133
Short-Run Supply 134
An Example: Some Average and Marginal Costs for Better Burger 137
The Role of Fixed Cost 139
Costs and Supply in the Long-Run Period 139
Supply Curves for a Whole Industry 142
Elasticity of Supply 143
Some Final Words About Supply 144
Application: Markets for Illegal Goods 144
Pricing Illegal Goods: Alcohol and Narcotics 145
Effect of Illegality on Demand 146
Effect of Legalization on Supply 147
Reverse Price Discrimination Plus Strict Enforcement: An Alternative? 148
Effects of Strict Law Enforcement 149
Reverse Price Discrimination: An Alternative? 149
Illegal Drug Markets: A Summing Up 150
Summing Up 150
Key Terms 153
Questions 154
Suggested Readings 155

**Chapter 6: Market Equilibrium: Do Private Markets Always Produce What is Socially
Desirable** **157**
Equilibrium Price 158
Private Equilibrium 160
Social Equilibrium 161
Effects of Externalities 162
A Tax to Create Public Equilibrium 163
Can Externality be Internalized? 164

Common Property Resources 164
Government and Property Rights 165
How Much Government Intervention is Enough? 166
Spillovers and Government Intervention... 167
Application: How Much Clean Air Do We Want to Buy? 168
Dire Predictions and How to Live with Them 168
The Price of Breathing 169
Enforcing Limits on Air Pollution: Hard Choices.. 170
Summing Up 171
Key Terms 174
Questions 174
Suggested Readings 175

Chapter 7: Pure Competition **177**
Market Classifications 179
Characteristics of Pure Competition 179
        Pricing Decisions 180
        Output Decisions 181
Pure Competition in the Short Run.. 181
Total Revenue and Total Cost 181
Profit Maximization: Marginal Cost Equals Marginal Revenue 184
        The Competitive Firm's Market Situation 185
        The Competitive Firm's Conjectural Demand Curve 186
        Situation 1: Economic Profit... 186
        Situation 2: Normal Profit 188
        Situation 3: Economic Loss with Production... 189
        Situation 4: Economic Loss with Shut Down 190
Pure Competition, Short Run: A Summary 191
Marginal Cost: The Competitive Firm's Short-Run Supply Curve 193
Pure Competition in the Long Run 194
Increasing-Cost, Constant-Cost, and Decreasing-Cost Industries............................. 195
        Increasing-Cost Industries.. 196
        Constant-Cost Industries 197
        Decreasing-Cost Industries 198
The Advantages of Pure Competition 199
Most Technically Efficient Level of Cost 200
Most Allocatively Efficient Combination of Products... 201
Welfare of Buyers and Sellers: Consumers' and Producers' Surplus 202
        Benefits to Consumers: Consumers' Surplus 202
        Benefits to Producers: Producers' Surplus 203
        Competitive Equilibrium: Maximum Benefits to Consumers and Producers..........204
The Disadvantages of Pure Competition... 206
The Relevance of Pure Competition... 207
Application: Do We Really Want Competition? 208
Origins of the Government Intervention 209
No Bed of Roses: Agricultural Economic Problems... 210
        Demand... 210
        Supply: Short Run 211
        Supply: Long Run.. 212
        Continuity of Production... 213
        Technological Change.. 214
The Agricultural Support Program 214

Efforts to Reduce Direct Government Intervention 217
Back to Government Intervention: 1976 through 1989 217
Government Intervention on the Demand Side 217
    Has Intervention Worked? 218
Did the Agricultural Support Program Help All Agriculture? 219
    Exports 219
U.S. Agricultural Policy: A Reprise 220
Summing Up 220
Key Terms 224
Questions 225
Suggested Readings 227

Chapter 8: Monopoly 229
Pure Monopoly: A Definition 230
Barriers to Entry 232
Pure Monopoly: MR, AR, and D 234
Elasticity of Demand 236
Pure Monopoly: Short Run 237
Pure Monopoly: Long Run 241
Pure Competition Versus Pure Monopoly 241
Monopolies and Supply Decisions 244
Utilizing Technology Effectively: Natural Monopoly 245
Monopoly and the Creation of Technology 245
Technology: Dynamics Versus Statics 246
Regulated Monopoly 248
    Cost Overstatement Under Regulation: An Example 249
    Regulation of (Multi-firm) Monopolistic Industries: An Airline Example 250
Price Discrimination 250
    Conditions Necessary for Price Discrimination 251
    Graphic Analysis of Price Discrimination..252
Welfare Effects: A Comparison of Monopoly and Competition..253
The Welfare Effects of Price Discriminating Monopoly 255
Application: Regulation Versus Deregulation—When are Airline Markets
    Contestable? 255
Transportation Regulation: Public Interest or Industry Captured? 256
The Industry Under Regulation..256
What to Expect from Deregulation: A Brief Review...257
Deregulation: The Short Run...257
Deregulation: The Long Run and Reconcentration 258
Airline Mergers 258
Contestability and the Number of Firms 258
Barriers to Entry 259
Reregulation? 259
Summing Up 260
Key Terms 263
Questions 263
Suggested Readings 265

Chapter 9: Monopolistic Competition..267
What is Monopolistic Competition?..269
Sources of Product Differentiation 270
Advertising 271

Product Differentiation and the Price Elasticity of Demand 271
Monopolistic Competition: The Short Run 273
 Competition: A Reprise 274
 The Four Short-Run Profit and Loss Positions of a Typical Monopolistically
  Competitive Firm 275
Monopolistic Competition: The Long Run 277
 An Exception to Normal Profit 277
Monopolistic Competition: The Excess Capacity Argument 279
Monopolistic Competition: A Caveat 281
A Policy Question: Is Monopolistic Competition Often as Close as We Can Get and
 Want to Get to Pure Competition? 281
 Forms of Differentiation: A Reminder..281
Conclusions About Monopolistic Competition...283
SUMMING UP 284
Key Terms 285
Questions 285
Suggested Readings 287

Chapter 10: Oligopoly **289**
Definition of Oligopoly 290
 Number of Firms: Small 291
 Product: Both Homogeneous and Differentiated 291
 Barriers to Entry: Substantial 292
Behavior of the Oligopolistic Firm 292
How May Interdependent Firms React? Organization and Collusion 293
Class I Oligopolies: Organization and Collusion 293
 Efficiency Effects of Class I Oligopolies 294
 Social Reaction to Class I Oligopolies: The Antitrust Laws 294
Class II Oligopolies: Unorganized But Collusive..295
 Efficiency Implications of Class II Oligopoly 296
Class III Oligopolies: Unorganized, Non-Collusive 298
 The Kinked Demand Assumptions 299
 Kinked Demands, Sticky Prices, and Sluggish Output: Is This the Worst of
  Oligopoly? 300
 Relevancy of Kinked Demand Oligopoly 301
Nonprice Competition Among the Few 301
 Styling 301
 Services 302
 Quality 302
 Advertising 302
Profit Maximization: Fact or Fancy? 307
Profit Maximization: Summing Up 309
Oligopoly: Summing Up 310
 But are Costs Lower in Competitive Industries? 311
Application: Some Cases of Oligopoly Behavior 311
Class I Oligopoly: 311
Class II Oligopoly: Unorganized But Tacit Collusion in the Steel Industry..............314
Class III Oligopoly: No Dominant Firm in the Soft Drink Industry 317
 The Edgeworth Model of Duopoly 317
Summing Up 319
Key Terms 324
Questions 325

Suggested Readings 327

Chapter 11: Government and the Modern American Economy; 329
Government and Antitrust: The Rule of Reason 331
Mergers and Antitrust 332
Are Big Firms Bad for the Economy? 333
How Important is Static Pure Competition? 333
How Competitive is the U.S. Economy? More Antitrust or Less? 334
Why the Increased Competition from 1958 to 1987? 336
Antitrust Laws: Changes in the Future? 337
Public Choice: Can Economic Principles Explain Government Decisions? 337
The Economy: The Name of the Game and the Rules 338
    What is a Fair Game? 338
    Can All Players Be Made Better Off? 339
    Rules and Rule Changes 339
Public Choices in American Democracy: Whose Tastes Count Most? 340
    The Median-Voter Model 340
    Denying the Median Voter: Logrolling 341
    No Clear Winners: Cyclical Majorities 342
Representative Versus Direct Democracies 343
    What are the Objectives of Public Choice Makers? 343
    Rational Ignorance 344
Public Choices: How are Costs and Benefits Distributed? 344
    When Special Interests Seek Rents 346
    How To Seek Rents: Political Action Committees 348
    How Does Rent Seeking Affect Efficiency? 348
Resources Going Underground: The Role of Government 349
Is Public Choice Anti-Government? 350
Application: The Dairy Lobby—Are Both Consumers and Cows Milked? 351
A Model of the Milk Market 351
The Experience of Milk Price Supports 352
How Much Does the Program Cost? 353
Why Not a Competitive Milk Industry? 354
Why Don't Consumers Resist? 354
Summing Up 355
Key Terms 359
Questions 359
Suggested Readings 361

Chapter 12: Factor Markets—Capital and Natural Resources 363
What are Factor Markets? 364
Factors: Supply and Demand 364
What Determines the Demand for Factors? 365
An Example of Factor Demand 366
To Maximize Profit, Minimize Cost 370
Demand for a Resource by the Market as a Whole 370
Elasticity of Demand for a Resource 371
Income Distribution: "Fair" or "Unfair?" 372
Demand for Resources Among Monopolistic Firms 373
Product Monopoly: Is it a Problem in Factor Markets? 375
Application: How Much Education Should We Buy? 376
Society's "Purchase" of Education 380

Summing Up 382
Key Terms 385
Questions 386
Suggested Readings 388

Chapter 13: How Wage Rates and Other Factor Prices are Set **389**
Wages: Competitive Versus Noncompetitive...390
Why Not a Single Wage Rate? 393
    Different Skills and Different Supplies of Skills..393
    Different Wages and Same Skills 394
How Wages are Set: Competitively Priced Labor 395
How Wages are Set: Noncompetitively Priced Labor 397
Situation A: Monopsony in the Labor Market, Competition in the Product Market 398
    How Many Jobs to Offer: MRP = MRC 400
Situation B: Monopsony in the Labor Market, Monopoly in the Product Market 402
    Monopsony and Competition Compared in Labor Markets 403
    Monopsony: A Summary Point 405
    Professional Sports and Monopsony 405
Situation C: Bilateral Monopoly 406
    An Important Point About Bilateral Monopoly 407
    Exclusive and Inclusive Unions 408
    Other Strategies: Ways to Increase Jobs and Wages 408
The Government Steps In: Minimum-Wage Laws 409
    The Past and Future of Minimum-Wage Laws 411
The Evidence: Monopsony Versus Competitive Labor Markets 412
More About Wage Discrimination 413
What is Economic Discrimination? 413
Understanding Discrimination 414
    What are the Consequences of Crowding? 414
    Unequal Wages for Equal Jobs 416
A Note of Caution 417
What Can Be Done About Discrimination? 418
    Public Action 418
    Private Action 418
    Unions 419
    Creating Entrepreneurs 419
Other Factors of Production: Land, Capital, and Entrepreneurship 419
    Land and its Rent..419
    Rents as Signals: Valid or Not? 420
    Quasi Rents or Common Rents..422
    Capital and Interest Rates 424
    Government and the Capital Market...425
    Entrepreneurship and Profit 426
    Is Profit Earned? 427
Application: Comparable Worth—Market Distortion or Sensible Correction for
    Discrimination? 427
Two Views About the Earning Gap 428
Discrimination or Voluntary Choice: The Evidence 429
Choice of Occupation 430
Group A Versus Group B: A Policy Synopsis...430
    Group A: Policy Recommendation 430
    Group B: Policy Recommendation 431

Comparable Worth: More Fairness or Fewer Jobs? 431
    The Argument Against Comparable Worth 432
    The Case for Comparable Worth 433
    What are Large or Small Costs and Benefits? 433
    Comparable Worth: Its Future 434
Summing Up 434
Key Terms 441
Questions 441
Suggested Readings 443

Chapter 14: Patterns of International Trade 445
What Makes Up Trade? 446
How Important is Trade to America? 447
America's Balance of Trade and Net Foreign Trade 447
But is Trade as Important to Us as to Others? 449
The Gains from Trade 450
Trade and Comparative Advantage 451
The Terms of Trade 453
Gains from Trade 453
What Determines Comparative Advantage? 455
Demand Considerations 456
Increasing Costs and Other Cautions 456
The Means of Protection 458
    Tariffs 458
    Elasticity and the Burden of the Tariff 460
    Import Quotas 462
    Export Quotas: Rational Ignorance by Consumers? 463
Arguments in Favor of Protection 464
    The Infant-Industry Argument 464
    The National-Security Argument 465
    The Cheap-Foreign-Labor Argument 465
    The Macroeconomic-Employment Argument 465
    Retaliation for "Unfair" Trade Practices 467
    The Rustbelt: Protecting Declining Industries 467
International Trade Policy Since World War II 468
Regional Trade Agreements 468
Current Regional Trade Arrangements 469
Multilateral Free Trade: Its Future 469
Free Trade: A Reprise 470
Application: Does Trade Create Development? 470
The Relation Between Trade and Development 471
    The Classical View 471
    Reservations About the Traditional View 473
    Those With Reservations: Modify Free Trade 475
Debt Problems of the LDCs and NICs 475
Implications for Trade Policies 476
Summing Up 477
Key Terms 482
Questions 483
Suggested Readings 485

Chapter 15: International Trade: Exchange Rates and the Balance of Payments 489

An Example of Trade Involving Different Domestic Currencies..490
A Workable International Monetary System 491
Foreign Exchange Markets: Determining Equilibrium Exchange Rates.......................493
    Freely Floating Exchange Rates...493
Advantages and Disadvantages of Floating Exchange Rates.......................................495
    Fixed Exchange Rates..496
Exchange Rate Market Intervention..497
Adjusting Economies to Fluctuations in the Exchange Rate 498
    Means of Adjustment...499
The Gold Standard..500
Postwar International Exchange Arrangements 503
The Managed or "Dirty" Float: Whither the Future?...504
The Mexican Peso and the December 1994 Debt Crisis...504
The Balance of Payments 506
    The Balance-of-Payments Statement 506
    The Balance of Payments in Summary 508
    Deficits to be Financed: Current and Capital Account Balances 508
Application: Politics and the Balance-of-Payments Problem 510
Reasons Behind Import Restraints 510
Protectionism: Costs and Benefits 511
America's Trade Problem: The Myths 512
Protectionism: Will It Triumph or Fail?..513
Lessons to Be Learned 513
Summing Up 514
Key Terms 518
Questions 518
Suggested Readings..520

Chapter 16: Economic Systems - How Many In The Twenty-First Century? 523
Basic Economic Choices: A Reminder 524
Evaluating an Economic System...525
    Static Efficiency 525
    Dynamic Efficiency...526
Property Rights: Should They be Vested in Individuals or in the State? 526
    Private Property Rights 526
    Public Property Rights..526
Why Do Property Rights Matter? 527
Market Capitalism 527
Economic Advantages of Market Capitalism 528
Economic Criticisms of Capitalism 529
Planned Socialism 529
What is Planned Socialism?..530
    Advantages of Planned Socialism 530
    Criticisms of Planned Socialism 530
Marx and Socialism..530
Dialectical Materialism...531
Class Conflict 531
Falling Profits and the Reserve Army of the Unemployed..532
Recurring Business Cycles 533
Marx's Prediction: The Collapse of Capitalism 533
What Happened to the Collapse? 534
Efficiency of Central Planning: The "Fatal Conceit" Problem 534

The End of Planned Socialism? 535
Transition from Planned Socialism to Market Capitalism: How Long and How
    Difficult? 536
Key Reforms 536
        Secure Private Property Rights 537
Prices that Reflect Relative Scarcity 537
A Monetary System that Permits Price Stability 537
        Institutional Reform 538
Mixed Economies: A Third System? 538
The End of Socialism: A Disclaimer 538
Economic and Political Freedom: Are They Related? 539
Faster Growth 539
Political Freedom: Does it Follow from Economic Freedom 539
China: A Test Case? 540
Summing Up 540
Key Terms 544
Questions 544
Suggested Readings..545

Glossary 547

Index 577

Preface

An educated person is one who has finally discovered that there are some questions to which nobody has the answers. Also, who voluntarily does more thinking than is necessary for his own survival.

Anonymous

To the Students

Writing an economic textbook is a very demanding undertaking, especially when we know that there are literally scores of good economic textbooks already on the market. Why, then, spend literally hundreds of hours writing yet another economic textbook? After several years of teaching basic economics, we have come to the very real conclusion that there is not a textbook on the market that is designed to present the basic economic theory as a guide to successful living and explain the complex theories in a language that the first-time economic students can understand.

Economics, like other academic disciplines, has its own vocabulary. Unlike the physical sciences, however, where the student is encountering terms for the first time, much of the vocabulary of economics (terms such as efficiency, capital, stock, labor) has a common usage that is already familiar to the student. Economists, however, use the vocabulary of economics in a very exact way, and often the common usage of a term is not the same as the economic usage.

Economics is valuable only if it explains the real world. Economics should be able to answer very specific questions like: Why are there three major domestic producers of automobiles and hundreds or even thousands of producers of textiles? Why is there a positive association between growth of the money supply and inflation? Why do interest rates rise when people expect the inflation rate to increase? The successful student will be able to apply the knowledge he or she gains of real-world economic behavior to explain any number of events that have already occurred or are yet to occur.

This book is useful to the degree that students can apply this theory to their lives. It is critical that the student see the tremendous advantage that the economic way of thinking affords them. Economics becomes exciting when students become aware that this book is directly preparing them for personal success.

Knowing that you are studying for life-long success, not for an economic final exam only brings a new perspective to this course. At the end of many chapters there is a section entitled "Application." This section will illustrate how you can apply the material presented in the chapter to enhance your personal success.

Economics, although admittedly not an easy subject, can be very rewarding if you apply yourself to the material. We have tried to present only information that will remain important to you long after the final exam is over. Hopefully this book and the course will help you achieve this objective.

To the Instructor

Why is it that what we teach have such a half-life? Are we trying to teach too much? Is our basic principles course getting away from being an analysis of basic principles? Are our textbooks more plumbers' manuals on technique than analysis of a social science subject? What do we want our students to know? We wrote this textbook with these questions in mind. It is written for the students, not for the professor.

We have tried to do two things. First, we have reduced the complexity found in basic principles of economics books to the point at which first-time students can grasp (and, we hope, retain) them. Second, we have applied the basic principles to problems that these students can recognize.

We realize, however, that different instructors may wish to delve more deeply into an issue or expand on a problem in a particular chapter. Therefore, we have listed, at the end of chapters, a number of additional sources.

We feel that this principles of economics text has several distinct advantages over many others in the field:

1. It is not an encyclopedia of economics but rather contains enough theory to equip the student with a permanent level of economic literacy.

2. Most theoretical chapters contain extended applications that use the economic principles just covered to analyze practical economic problems.

3. Every attempt has been made to communicate in the everyday language of the student rather than in the technical language of the economic journal.

4. Special attention has been given to chapter summaries, end-of-chapter materials, and the glossary in order to help the student

review and to reinforce the concepts presented in each chapter. An important feature of this text is the use of margin notes in which key terms are highlighted. These notes, plus the list of key terms at the end of each chapter, are helpful learning aids.

Acknowledgments

This text has undergone several reviews both by students (in formal class) and by instructors of economics from numerous Colleges and Universities. We are indebted to many individuals although we alone assume responsibility for any errors or inconsistencies.

The following economists have provided specific comments and material which we have incorporated into this text.

Kirk Blackerby – San Jose State University
Glenn Bottoms – Gardner-Webb University
Richard Cebula – Emory University
Joseph Domitrz – Western Illinois University
Jonathan Elimimian – Johnson C. Smith University
Steve Kaifa – City University of New York
James Koch – Illions State University
Anthony Ostrosky – Illinois State University
R.D. Peterson – Colorado State University
Joseph Perry – University of North Florida
Martin Schwartz – State University of New York
Richard Vonburg – Eastern Wyoming College
Mark Weglarski – Macomb Community College

A special thanks to James L. Gilbertie of Shasta College and Martin Primack of San Jose State University for their major contributions throughout the text.

The most important acknowledgment and thanks goes to the thousands of students we have had the privilege to have in our classes over many years of teaching. Without the enthusiasm, encouragement and support that these students gave, this text would not have become a reality. Also thanks to the following individuals for their direct and indirect support—M. Christopher White, Frank Bonner, Gil Blackburn, and Broyhill School of Business faculty.

The management and staff of CT Publishing have been exceptionally accommodating and helpful in the lengthy process of preparing and publishing this manuscript. While that has been true of all at CT, we want to express our particular gratitude to our publisher, Leslie Winegar.

I. Anthony Negbenebor
James F. Willis

CHAPTER 1

Introduction to Economics

Every individual endeavors to employ his capital so that its product may be of greatest value. He generally neither intends to promote the public interest, nor knows how much he is promoting it. He intends only his own security, only his own gain. And he is in this led by an invisible hand to promote an end which was no part of his intention. By pursuing his own interest he frequently promotes that of society more effectually than when he really intends to promote it.

Adam Smith, Wealth of Nations (1776)

OBJECTIVES

After studying this chapter you will be able to:

- Define and explain economics.
- Explain economic scarcity.
- Explain the difference between Macro and Micro economics.
- Describe the role of the entrepreneur in a capitalistic economic system.
- What economic questions face any given society?
- Have a working knowledge of the following terms and concepts:

Dependent variable	Macroeconomics	Positive economics
Economics	Microeconomics	Resources
Economist's method	Normative economics	Scarcity
Independent variable	Opportunity cost	Wants
Inverse		

Introduction to Economics

The Aims of Economics

Economics has had a bad press ever since the nineteenth-century Scottish essayist Thomas Carlyle referred to it as "the dismal science." Carlyle had in mind the gloomy predictions about the future welfare of the human race that many economists were making at the time. This was about a hundred years ago, when economists were still being referred to as "political economists"—an apt name for them, calling to mind Lenin's remark that "political institutions are a superstructure resting on an economic foundation."

Economics has changed in the hundred years since Carlyle called it a dismal science. It has become more scientific and less dismal. The subjects that economists deal with—for example, prices, jobs, the distribution of Income, the growth of output and Real Income, the prevention of Inflation—have remained the same, but what has changed are the methods we use to investigate them, and the amounts and kinds of information we have. Our view of the future has also changed: most economists today are optimistic about the ability of people to solve economic problems.

Frequently, we hear it said that economists seem unable to agree on solutions to economic problems. Since economics is a way of thinking about such problems, and is designed to identify alternative solutions, the disagreement is understandable. For a long time, it was common to find economists divided on ideological grounds between those who favored systems of private enterprise and individual initiative and those who favored systems of collective activity and public control. A major convergence among those concerned with economic policy in the late twentieth century has occurred on the questions of which of these two systems should be given emphasis by society's seeking economic growth. Economists on the "left" now seem willing to grant the necessity for a society to appeal to human acquisitiveness and self-interest. Generating incentives to work, to take risks, and to innovate seem to be an increasing priority in all parts of the world. We will say more about these developments in the application in this chapter.

Solving Specific Economic Problems

Though most economists agree about the nature of economic behavior by individuals, there is room for disagreement about specific measures to solve particular economic problems. Should government intervene to prevent mergers and takeovers of firms? Will the United States fall into a recession next year and, if so, should interest rates be raised now to fight inflation? Are foreign manufacturers increasing their share of key U.S. markets and, if so, should the American government intervene? These are but a few of the many economic policy questions that arise constantly and about which economists may have different opinions. In short, when you complete your course in economics you will not have a set of policy conclusions to carry with you but a way of examining the alternatives and formulating your own views about policy questions as they arise. Nonetheless, certain tools and methodology, such as quantitative methods and model building, are accepted by nearly all economists. Most economists accept a basic procedure for looking at aggregate economic problems, like unemployment, and a t nonaggregate market problems as well.

The fact that today's economists, in the mainstream, are optimistic about the future, should not seem strange. Most of the increase in goods and services, the real income that improves the material well being of people, has occurred in the last century and a half. While economic problems remain for all nations, we now know that improvement in economic organization and institutions combined with the enormous potential of further technological change make possible continued advance in standards of living. This is true not only for the relatively wealthy industrial nations but for the newly industrializing nations and less developed nations as well. Can economic problems, then, be eliminated? Few economists would go so far as to say yes. However, the most famous economist of this century, John Maynard Keynes (rhymes with *gains*), writing in 1930 and looking ahead to the next hundred years, put his view in this way:

> I draw the conclusion that, assuming no important wars and no important increase in population, the *economic problem* may be solved, or at least be within sight of solution, within a hundred years. This means that the economic problem is not — if we look into the future — *the permanent problem of the human race.*

Keynes expressed this very optimistic view in the early years of the Great Depression of the 1930's. He was wrong, of course, in assuming that there would be no major wars after 1930, but his assumption about no major increase in population may turn out to be correct, at least for the more developed industrial countries. Keynes's statement illustrates two things: (1) economists of the twentieth century are no longer dismal about the future, and (2) economists develop economic principles not for the sake of abstract exercise, but to be able to analyze and propose solutions to problems constantly confronted by the human race. Economists are, in short, deeply concerned with *people* and their material well-being.

What Is Economics?

Economics is the study of how people can allocate scarce resources to satisfy their **wants**. Wants are defined as all things that people would consume if they had unlimited resources. In other words, economics is the social science that identifies the various means by which people can satisfy their desires for goods and services by using the limited resources available to produce those goods and services. This is a very general definition, but a useful one, because it points out certain basic features of economics.

Economics
The study of how people can allocate scarce resources to satisfy their wants.

Wants
All things that people would consume if they had unlimited resources.

1. *Economics, as a social science,* deals with the actions of groups of people in relation to society. Economics differs from physical science, which has laws established in the laboratory where conditions can be controlled. The laboratory of economists is the world, in which nothing is certain and nothing can be controlled with surety. Economists base their principles on what they observe about people—their willingness to spend money or to save it, for example—and on what they observe about the economic institutions that people have created, such as private property rights, government planning, and economic institutions such as banks that bring savers and investors together.

2. *Economics is analytical.* Economists use the principles of economics to diagnose various problems, such as unemployment and poverty, and propose solutions to them. Instead of choosing one solution and saying, "Here's what to do," economists set forth the available alternative solutions to a given problem and point out the costs and benefits of each.

3. *Economics is concerned with the material well-being of people.* Economists measure current economic activity and project figures for the future. This does not mean that they feel it is *only* material well-being that counts, but they do insist that it takes the use of limited material resources (land, labor, capital, and entrepreneurship) to solve social problems. Solving economic problems, thus, is closely tied to efforts to solve other kinds of problems.

Scarcity: Source of Basic Economic Questions

Why do societies need to find answers to economic questions? For that matter, why do economic questions arise at all? To understand the answers to these questions, consider two important facts:

Resources
The inputs that are used to make consumer and producer goods.

1. At any given time, the **resources** available to a society are limited. There is only so much oil, gold, timber, or wheat; just so much capital, just so much labor. **Resources**—the inputs used to make consumer and producer goods—are limited.

2. People—individuals, families, or larger groups—have needs, wants, and desires which have to be satisfied, as much as they can be, by the goods and services produced by employing the society's limited resources. However, wants and desires—unlike resources—appear to be virtually unlimited. History and psychology show us that they may never be satisfied, since satisfaction of some wants only seems to lead people to acquire new wants.

Scarcity
The relationship between limited resources; and unlimited wants which results in the inability to satisfy all human wants for goods and services.

As we move along, we shall look at each of these considerations in greater detail. For now, let's stress the fact that resources are *limited,* human wants are *unlimited,* and this means that our society, and every other society, no matter how rich or how poor, has to face the problem of **scarcity**—the inability to satisfy all people's wants for goods and services at zero price. In other words, if someone has to pay for it, with money or effort, it is scarce.

Consider the vast array of goods and services to be produced in the United States this year. Will there be ten or eleven million automobiles? How many video cassette recorders (VCRs) and how many color television sets? Will automobile production be even more automated this year than last? Who will "consume" the automobiles and television sets? These are the kinds of questions each resource-using society must ask. The basic economic questions that result from scarcity are shown in the following section.

The What? How? and For Whom?

Scarcity results in the following basic questions: 1) what shall be produced, 2) how shall goods be produced, and 3) for whom shall output be produced.

1. *What* shall be produced? Out of all the combinations of goods that present technology makes possible, what combinations of cars, television sets, vacations, medical services, and so on, shall we choose?

2. *How* shall the goods be produced? There are many questions contained within this big question, which encompasses not only the technology of production, but also the *system* by which production is organized. Will markets be publicly or privately controlled? Will there be competition? How much consolidation of producers will there be? (That is, large firms, as opposed to small, mom-and-pop producer units.)

3. *For whom* shall output be produced? In other words, who is going to have the satisfaction of consuming the goods? This is the basic *distributive* question. Will the income of the society be distributed equally, or will there be a few who are rich and a majority who are poor? Or will there be some other distribution?

Are the solutions to these questions interdependent? Clearly they are. The technology and organizational structure of a society heavily influence who will receive satisfaction as consumers. When a society's industries tend toward monopolistic firms, the markets that result are likely to create a more unequal distribution of income. Why this is so will become clear later.

Is Scarcity Meaningful Today?

In many of the chapters, we'll talk about debates in the United States that involve scarcity and its effects on choice making. As we will see, in many ways the debates have centered on differences in definitions and ideologies. In spite of these differences of opinion, it is clear that, in the sense of unlimited wants pursuing limited resources, scarcity exists even for supposedly well-off Americans, and that even this affluent society must make choices about how to use its limited resources.

The concept of scarcity is one of the cornerstones of **Economics.** The problem of allocating scarce goods is what economics is all about.

Macroeconomics and Microeconomics: Economic Principles From Two Perspectives

Macroeconomics
The study of the forces that determine the level of income and employment in a society.

Macroeconomics is the study of the forces that determine the level of income and employment in a society. Macroeconomics gives us the big picture of a society, or what economists call its aggregate performance. In this text, that perspective focuses first on the origins of economic scarcity, the problems of economic development, and how households and business firms make economic decisions. Going beyond that, we build a simple model of aggregate economics, gradually adding the components that make up our complex economic world: government spending, gross domestic product, business cycles, the level of employment, the level of income, the money supply, banking, and expansion and growth.

Microeconomics
The study of disaggregated economic activities, or how a market economy allocates resources through prices.

Microeconomics is the study of disaggregated economic activities. Beginning with scarcity, economic development, and basic decisions by households and firms, microeconomics seeks to provide an understanding of a market economy and, in particular, the role of prices in such an economy. It examines the various ways product and factor markets may be organized and how their performance may be understood both privately and socially.

While macroeconomics and microeconomics differ in focus, each deals with the same basic subject matter of economic activity. It is not surprising, therefore, that some areas of study are taught in both micro and macro, though from a different perspective. Two areas that may be included in both halves of this book are international trade and finance and comparative economic systems.

What Is The Economist's Method?

Even though economics is a social science, rather than a physical science, its method is scientific and based on facts and logic. An economist's starting point, like a chemist's or physicist's, is a hypothesis, or an assumption about a relationship between two things (or ten or twenty things). At this point, however, the economist steps outside the safety of the laboratory into the less predictable realm of the real world. We can best demonstrate the three stages of the economist's job with an example.

Suppose that you are a young economist, a consultant to the President's Council of Economic Advisors, and are called to a meeting of the council. Everyone looks grave. The chairman explains that the country's economy is showing some alarming tendencies. Personal incomes in the last year have risen, but for some reason, consumer spending has fallen. People just aren't buying, and business is beginning to hurt. The President is deeply concerned, and so is Congress. You are to find out what has happened and tell the government what to do about it.

Now you begin on stage 1 of the economist's three-stage process (see Figure 1-1). First you gather all the data you can that might explain what has happened. Exactly how much did incomes grow in the past year? Did spending on consumer goods change in any way, and if so, how? How do the figures for the past three-month period compare with the figures for the same quarter a year ago? Has there been a change in the relationship between income and spending? What have people been doing with all the money they haven't been spending? Have they been saving it? Have they been using it to pay taxes?

Figure 1-1
The Three Basic Stages in Economic Analysis

Stage 1	Stage 2	Stage 3
Gathering facts	*Formulating and testing theory*	*Making economic policy*
The economist gathers data that are relevant to the hypothesis or statement (this is called *descriptive* economics).	On the basis of the data, the economist sets forth a theory about economic behavior and tests the theory (this is the *theorizing* stage).	The policy maker, who is not necessarily the same person as the economist, formulates measures to deal with economic behavior and its consequences (this is the *policy-making* stage).

After you have finished this fact-finding or *descriptive* stage, you embark on stage 2, the *theorizing* stage. You try to formulate a theory that will explain the way behavior changes as income changes. You want to express not only what is happening now, but also what is likely to happen a year from now, two years, or five years from now, given certain incomes, populations, and supplies and prices of goods. The theory you evolve may be a simple one (people have lost faith in material things and are giving all their money to churches), or very complex (people are more afraid of inflation and at the same time distrustful of anything modern, so they are putting all their money in gold, Renaissance paintings, and pre-1914 Rolls-Royces). In any event, you spend days writing up your version of the situation, using all the facts you have gathered and expressing your opinion in the clearest manner possible.

On the basis of the data you have collected, you form the hypothesis that short-term changes in consumer spending depend not only on changes in income but also on changes in other factors such as taxes and expectations about the future. You can use various statistical techniques to isolate the effect of one factor (short-term income changes) on another (consumer spending).

When you are setting up these theoretical interrelationships, you construct a *model*, a systematic analogy to real consumer behavior. This model enables you to interpret the statistical results.

Suppose you find that there is a weak (perhaps nearly zero) correlation, during any six-month period, between changes in people's incomes and changes in their spending habits. In other words, even if their incomes go up, their spending changes little, or perhaps not at all. Then you must explain the decline in consumer spending in terms of changes in other factors.

Your model may include the expectations people have about future changes in prices and in taxes (income taxes, excise taxes). Suppose your data show that taxes (and other important factors that might offer some explanation) have not changed in the past six months. Then you conclude that the decline in spending must be due to *expectations* about the future. People are putting off buying things until later in the year. They're waiting for inventory-reduction sales, for the crops to come in, for an expected drop in interest rates. For many reasons, they're just holding onto their money and waiting. You incorporate all these ideas in your report to the chairman of the President's Council of Economic Advisors.

The third stage is the *policy-making* stage. This stage is out of your hands, because the people who decide on the economic policy act on their own, although they may base their decisions on the economists' recommendations. The policy maker may be Congress, or the President, or the President and the Cabinet acting together. But bear in mind that a nation's economic policy is part of its overall social policy (including diplomatic, military, and political policies). Your role as an economist has been only to identify to the policy makers the nature of the problem, tell them how serious it is, and point out alternative solutions, with the costs and benefits of each.

(For a fascinating discussion of public policy decisions, read *America's Hidden Success*, by John E. Schwartz, published by Norton in 1988 as a paper back. This book provides a reassessment of public policy from Kennedy to Reagan.)

The Citizen and Economic Policy

The above example is fairly simple and clear-cut. The policy maker here may decide on the basis of reports prepared by you and others that no change in economic policy is required. It appears in this case that consumer spending is going to rise in the long term, as prices fall and as people adjust to their higher incomes.

From this illustration, you might conclude that economic investigation and policy making are processes reserved for experts in politics and economics. This is not so. Whether the issue is local or federal taxes, or local or national economic policies, the United States needs an enlightened public. The *non*economist, *non*politician, just plain citizen can review, criticize, and in the long run even change economic policy. People can do this by discussion with others and by the way they vote.

We write this book with the conviction that (1) the economic principles a person needs to know to make intelligent decisions on economic issues are simple, and that (2) such positions should be founded in fact and logic.

Applications: Concrete Examples of Abstract Ideas

Much of economics consists of abstractions, theories, and discussions of curves and trends. But, as we pointed out at the beginning of this chapter, it isn't all just theories; you already know a lot about economics. So we have tried to use the knowledge you already have to illustrate the theoretical part of economics. You will find sections near the end of chapters called "applications" throughout this book. They show you one or more practical applications of the theory or principle that has just been explained. For example, in the chapter that introduces the theory of supply and demand, there is an application that discusses a concrete example of supply and demand: rent controls and the price of housing. These applications can serve as beacons to help you fix your position in unfamiliar surroundings as you explore the economic way of thinking.

End-of-Chapter Summaries

At the end of each chapter, you'll find a section titled "Summing Up." These sections repeat, in condensed form, what the chapter or application is about. Even if you feel you understand the chapter as you read it, read "Summing Up" carefully. The repetition will help to imprint the material in your mind. Also, after the Summing Up sections to each chapter, there is a list of "Key Terms," concepts that are important to understand and remember. These terms and their definition can be checked by (1) rereading the margin notes in that chapter as well as by (2) checking the glossary at the end of the book.

Mathematics and Economics

One reason why economics has a reputation for being a tough subject is that many people are afraid of mathematics, and they associate economics with it. However, as you work your way through this book, you will realize that it contains very little mathematics. When economists write articles in professional journals, they may use advanced mathematics, but you do not need to know advanced mathematics to learn the basic principles of economics.

This book does contain a number of graphs and tables of data. The data serve to ensure that we are using facts as the basis for our discussions, and the graphs are simply devices to help you visualize abstract ideas. Figure 1-2 is an example of a graph.

Independent Variable
In a set of relationships, this is the variable that changes first.

All the graphs we use are two-dimensional. That is, they measure the relationships between two factors. They have *height* (measured along the vertical axis) and *length* (measured along the horizontal axis). The measure of the first factor to change (called the **independent variable**) comes from the vertical axis. The measure of the factor whose value depends on that of the first factor (the **dependent variable**) comes from the horizontal axis.[1]

Dependent Variable
In a set of relationships, the variable whose value depends on the value of the independent variable.

As we go along, we will use graphs to chart the progress of a number of dependent and independent variables: prices of goods, quantities sold, demand for goods and services, jobs, wages, and so forth. In each case, the rule about reading graphs will remain the same.

Now look at Figure 1-2 and we'll discuss some of the kinds of relationships that may occur between dependent and independent variables. The lines drawn on this diagram are called *curves*, even though in this case they are straight lines.

Inverse
The relationship between independent and dependent variables is inverse if the dependent variable changes in the opposite direction from the independent variable.

1. Curve A is a case in which the relationship between the independent and dependent variables is **inverse**. This means that as the independent variable increases (moves up the vertical axis), the dependent variable decreases (moves toward zero). As the independent variable decreases, the dependent variable increases. We say that curve A is *negatively sloped*, or that it *slopes downward*.

---

[1]Note that this is a convention adopted in economics with supply and demand diagrams. In mathematics, though, the reverse is usually the case with the dependent variable on the vertical axis and the independent variable on the horizontal axis.

Figure 1-2
An Illustration of Graphing

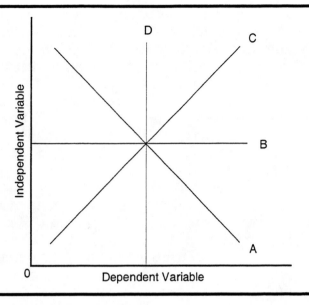

2. Curve B is a case in which the independent variable doesn't change at all. All change occurs in the dependent variable. The dependent variable responds almost without limit at the given value of the independent variable.

3. Curve C is a case in which the relationship between the independent and dependent variable is **direct**. As the independent variable increases, so does the dependent variable. As the independent variable decreases, so does the dependent variable. We say that curve C is *positively sloped*, or that it *slopes upward*.

4. Curve D is a case in which the dependent variable doesn't change at all. All change in D takes place in the independent variable. The independent variable responds almost without limit at the given value of the dependent variable.

　　If you keep these four cases in mind, you won't be confused by the graphs in this book. Indeed, the graphs will help you to visualize and understand relationships that might otherwise be hard to grasp.

Direct
The relationship between the independent variable and the dependent variable is direct if the dependent variable changes in the same direction as the independent variable.

Positive Versus Normative Economics

A person starting out in a first course in principles of physics or chemistry usually does so with no preconceived notions. Since we don't feel at home talking about subnuclear particles, we're willing to leave that subject to the physicists and take anything they say as the truth. However, most people approach economics with a considerable amount of built-in expertise. We have biases about economics, as we do about any social science. We cannot avoid having them, since from an early age we have all had considerable experience as members of the economic society. For example, we get jobs, spend income, pay taxes, and watch the government spend.

But we do not simply leave economic issues to the economists and the politicians. Citizens who are *not* economists, who are *not* politicians, are the ones who must in the long run make choices, through voting or in other ways. Citizens must choose among alternative solutions to economic problems, and they often have to approve or turn down choices that have already been made by some governing body. To be a good citizen, to make intelligent choices on voting day, one needs an understanding of economic principles, backed up by a knowledge of how those principles work out in actual application.

Normative Economics Consists of making judgments about what should be.

Positive Economics Consists of deter- mining what is.

When you come to the point of choosing among alternative solutions, you enter the area of **normative economics**, or making judgments about what *should* be. **Positive economics**, on the other hand, consists of determining what *is*. It involves stating facts. We have pointed out that when you gather facts and apply economic principles in an attempt to find a solution to a problem, you do not find just one answer, one unique "right" way; you find that there are several alternative solutions. Normative economics involves looking at these various solutions and applying personal or collective value judgments, to decide what *should* be. (Generalizing about economic behavior naturally has some normative aspects. Therefore, in writing a book about economics, we cannot avoid a few judgments here and there. We have tried to keep them to a minimum. When they do appear, we try to point them out and you're free to agree or disagree.)

To be sure that you understand the difference between positive and normative statements, let's take an example. You go to a party and find an economist who is talking about food stamps and their economic impact. The following conversation takes place:

Economist: The United States spent $6 billion in 1994 on the food stamp program. *(Positive)*

You: But a lot of people were still going hungry because they had to present the food stamps at stores in person, and many elderly or disabled people were too feeble to go to the store. It wasn't fair. *(Normative)*

Economist: A family of four with an income of $6,000 a year or less can qualify for $150 a month in food stamps. *(Positive)*

You: A family of four can't *live* on $6,000 a year—not what *I'd* call living. *(Normative)*

See how hard it is to keep from being normative? *(Normative)*

A Word About Words

Economists sometimes speak what seems to be a language all their own. In fact, someone once defined an economist as a person who states the obvious in terms of the incomprehensible. When economists speak of contrived versus natural scarcities, implicit factor returns, and maximum-profit monopoly equilibrium, you may wonder if they're really speaking English. Throughout this book, we have tried to avoid speaking "economese," or what William F. Buckley calls "econospeak." However, we could not weed out *all* the economese, because economics is a complex subject, full of precise language. When we introduce a term, we put it in italics and define it. Boldface type means that you can find the word defined and highlighted in the margin of the text page on which it appears as well as in the Glossary at the back of the book. As you go along, whenever you are not certain of the meaning of something, don't look back through the book for the definition. Just turn to the Glossary and look it up. Definitions are important in economics, because often a word means one thing in everyday usage and another in the language of economists. This book is designed to help you learn economics in the clearest and most painless way possible.

ECONOMIC NEWS

Atomic Test Raises India's Clout; Poor Remain Hungry

Lincoln Evening Journal, May 29, 1974

In May of 1974 the Indian government announced to its people that it had successfully detonated an atomic bomb. Millions of Indians woke up hungry each morning and their immediate concern is where the next meal for their family is going to come from.

A typical Indian response was noted in the Lincoln Evening Journal. A 40-year-old laborer was told of the atomic test blast and asked his opinion of this historic event. "It's beyond my intelligence to know anything about a bomb, my only ambition is to feed my children and my wife."

The elite of India tended to have a different perspective of this event, which put India in the exclusive nuclear club along with the United States, the Soviet Union, Britain, France and China. Using such phases as "India comes of age," and "India joins the major industrial nation" the political leaders exalted this event as a major triumph for the Indian people.

Statistics are hard to come by, but of the 585 million people in India, it is estimated that 32 percent live in dire poverty earning less than 35 U.S. dollars a year. In addition, an incredible 80 percent of the nation's children are said to be malnourished and 71 percent of the population is illiterate. In light of these statics, it is hard to understand how one of the largest papers in India, the Hinduston Times, could boast about this event.

The Hinduston Times said the nuclear test proves "India has the talent, the resources and the infrastructure that makes for high achievement capability. Our knowledge in nuclear science has raised our status not only in Southeast Asia but in the whole world."

The exact cost of building an atomic bomb was not given by the Indian government, which government officials insists will not be used to develop nuclear weapons. But experts say the cost of equipping the country with a modest nuclear retaliatory force would range from $8 billion over 10 years.

APPLICATION:
Self-Interest—The Key to a More Productive Future?

The public is merely a multiplied "me."

Mark Twain

There is only one class in the community that thinks more about money than the rich, and that is the poor. The poor can think of nothing else.

Oscar Wilde

These quotations illustrate two points: (1) what happens to the economy as a whole depends on the economic actions of individuals, and (2) economic forces vitally affect and concern each of us. Economists and noneconomists alike have long sought to understand the basic motivations that determine how we play our roles as consumers or producers on the economic stage. In this application we are going to examine some views on this subject.

Self-Interest: Key to All Characters

One of the first people to theorize about economic motivation was Adam Smith, author of *The Wealth of Nations* (1776), who is often considered the founder of modern economics. Smith contended that people were not moved primarily by love of their fellow humans; they ordinarily acted in their own self-interest. Smith said, "It is not from the benevolence of the butcher, the brewer, or the baker that we expect our dinner, but from their regard to their own interest." He said that he never knew business people to get together in the social interest. Rather, they sought some "nefarious purpose."

If Adam Smith were alive today and could see laborers banding together to form unions, co-ops, and consumer-protection societies or business executives getting together to discuss common concerns, he would probably attribute the same motives to these groups. Such ventures, he'd probably say, would result in conspiracies against the public interest. This view of human nature led Smith to argue that the economic role government should perform is to create conditions under which the individual's pursuit of self-interest results in maximizing the public welfare. But Smith did not make clear what *kind* of political system would do this. What would prevent public officials from acting in their own interest rather than in the public's? This problem of self-interested people making public choices comes up again and again.

> Samuel Butler wrote in his notebooks: "The world will always be governed by self-interest. We should not try to stop this; we should try to make the self-interest of cads a little more coincident with that of decent people."

SUMMING UP

1. Economics has acquired the reputation of being difficult, abstract, and mathematical. This book attempts to make the difficult understandable, to give concrete examples to demonstrate the abstractions, and to explain the mathematics so that people without an extensive mathematics background can readily grasp the ideas.

2. In the nineteenth century, people referred to economists as "political economists." They also called economics "the dismal science," because of the pessimistic views of the future many economists held. We have come a long way in the past hundred years. Technology and improved economic organization have caused many modern economists to have an optimistic view of the ability of people to improve their material well-being.

3. Adam Smith, considered by many to be the founder of modern economics, argued that self-interest and acquisitiveness were the primary economic motivations of people. Smith thought that the appropriate economic role of government was to provide a system within which individual self-interest could be harnessed to accomplish the public good.

4. Most modern economists, beginning with Alfred Marshall, assume that people are motivated in their economic actions primarily by a desire for monetary gain and a desire to achieve maximum satisfaction. They are not able, however, to measure satisfaction or pain precisely, even though they can measure profit.

5. Most orthodox economists regard the idea of the economic citizen (the profit- and satisfaction-maximizing person) as the most useful long-term view of human behavior, and believe that this view explains and predicts people's economic actions more accurately than any other single assumption.

6. Economists differ greatly among themselves about how to *solve* economic problems, but less about how to *study* them. While there is room for disagreement about alternative solutions to specific economic problems, there is increasing agreement that economic growth is enhanced by a system of incentives to individual initiative that encourages work, risk taking, and innovation.

7. *Economics* may be defined as the social science that study the ways people allocate scarce resources in order to satisfy their wants.

Economists perform their functions by identifying alternative means through which people can provide for their material well-being.

8. Economics differs from physical science, in that physical science proves its principles by means of controlled and repeatable experiments. The laws of economics are derived from observations of human behavior. As behavior changes, so must economists' rules.

9. When economists identify the alternative solutions to economic problems, they also point out the costs and benefits of each.

10. Economists are not necessarily more materialistic than other people. They do, however, insist that solutions to noneconomic questions require material resources (land, labor, capital, and entrepreneurship). Thus, these solutions are based in economic reality.

11. Economic Analysis is done in three stages: (a) gathering facts, (b) theorizing and testing theory, and (c) making economic policy.

12. Gathering of facts is necessary to ensure that concrete information (not hearsay or superstition) is the basis for economic investigation and decisions. Theorizing is necessary to enable the economist to construct a systematic analogy to real life (a *model*), since reality itself is too complex to be described fully. Policy making, though frequently based on economic advice, is often out of the economist's hands.

13. This book is written with the following convictions: (a) people need to know economic principles in order to understand economic issues and these principles *can* be stated in a clear, understandable way; and (b) discussions about economic issues should be founded in logic and fact.

14. In *normative economics*, value judgments form the basis for choosing solutions to economic problems. Normative economics states what *should be. Positive economics* states what *is*; no value judgments are made. This book tries to avoid making normative statements. When they do occur, we have identified them, and the reader is free to agree or disagree.

15. The book makes a strong effort to avoid the use of "economese," or complex ways of wording economic principles. When more technical terms first occur, they are highlighted and defined in margin notes. They are defined again in the Glossary at the end of the book.

Key Terms

Dependent Variable
Economics
Economist's method
Independent variable
Inverse
Macroeconomics
Microeconomics

Normative economics
Opportunity cost
Positive economics
Resources
Scarcity
Wants

QUESTIONS

1. Give two examples for each of the following: (a) a free good, (b) an economic good. Explain why the examples you gave are considered a free good and or an economic good.

2. The U.S. is considered a rich country because Americans have an abundance of goods and services to choose from. How can there be scarcity in a land of abundance?

3. Consider the following statements and decide whether each is normative or positive:
   a) There are too many homeless in the United States today.
   b) Unemployment among black teenagers in the United States is almost 50 percent.
   c) A federally guaranteed annual income is a good idea.
   d) Federally guaranteed annual incomes involve a transfer of income from one group to another.
   e) The distribution of wealth in the United States is not equal.
   f) The distribution of wealth in the United States should be equal.

4. What is an economic model? Why do economists construct models rather than just trying to describe reality?

5. Why do economists differ on solutions to specific economic problems when they differ relatively little on the way to analyze these problems?

6. Suppose that you are the personal assistant to the President of the United States on economic matters. The President calls you in and says: "For my main campaign plank this year, I am going to promise to solve the nation's economic problems in my next term of office. I want your advice, though, on whether this is a realistic promise." What advice would you offer?

7. What are the three basic stages in economic analysis? What is the role of the economist in the third stage?

8. Using Figure 1-1, do the following things:
   a. Label the axes on which one measures changes in the dependent variable and the independent variable.
   b. Draw "curves," showing (1) an inverse relationship between the two variables; (2) a direct relationship between them; (3) a curve that is positively sloped; (4) a curve that is negatively sloped; (5) a curve in which all change is in the dependent variable; and (6) a curve in which all change is in the independent variable. Label the curves 1,2,3, and so on.

Figure 1-1 Graph for problem 8

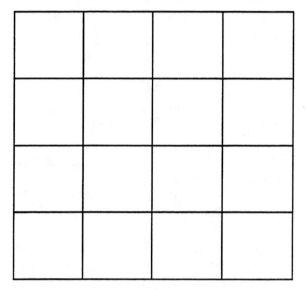

9. Why are more and more societies relying on self-interest as the basis for incentives to economic activity?

Suggested Readings

Dolan, Edwin G. and John C. Goodman. *Economics of Public Policy, Fourth Edition.* St. Paul, Minn., West Publishing Co. 1989 (Chapter 1, "Thinking about Public Issues and Policy")

Miller, Roger Leroy, Daniel Benjamin, and Douglass C. North. *The Economics of Public Issues.* New York, Harper Collins, 1993 (Chapter 15, "The Social Costs of Drug Wars")

CHAPTER 2

Introduction to the World's Economic System

Whoever you are, wherever you live, whatever your ancestry, and however you spend your time and money, one thing is certain—you are an expert—inveterate game player.

True, you may never feed a slot machine or roll dice. You may be blissfully unaware of the odds of drawing a worthless poker hand (50-50) or a perfect bridge hand (nearly 160 million to 1). Monopoly, Clue, and Go may bore you. You may visit Atlantic City often—to see your aunt. And you may believe that Pac-Man is a shipping clerk. Nonetheless, you play games—tough competitive games with high stakes. You have little choice. Not to play is not to live.

Across the Board, September, 1984

OBJECTIVES

After studying this chapter you will be able to:

- Describe the main characteristics of: capitalism, mix capitalism, socialism, feudalism, and communism.
- Explain why the law of accumulation is so important to the growth and prosperity of an economic system.
- Describe the five major characteristics of capitalism.
- Use the production-possibilities curve to illustrate the concepts of scarcity and opportunity cost, and to explain why individuals and countries have to make choices.
- Have a working knowledge of the following terms and concepts:

Consumer sovereignty	Market economy	Production-possibilities curve
Efficient markets	Market failure	Role of government
Externalities	Mixed system	Self-interest
Law of accumulation		

Introduction to the World's Economic System

The Economic Problem

Throughout history, every society has had to find a way to answer the following questions: What goods and services will be produced? How shall they be produced? Who gets the goods and services once they are produced by society? Today the world has evolved three basic ways of answering these age-old questions—three types of economic systems (Feudalism, Capitalism, and Socialism).

The Economics of Change—A Brief History of the Evolution of the American Economy

Any economic system is always in a state of change. This is true today, as it was 1,000 years ago. The rate of change can be extremely fast—as the countries of the former Soviet Republic are currently experiencing, or it can be agonizingly slow—as was the experience of European economies during the middle ages. This section will take you on a whirl wind tour of the last 1,000 years of economic history.

The tour begins in England in the year 1000. The economic system was known as feudalism, the economic system that existed before the advent of capitalism or socialism. Feudalism is a simple farm-based economic system where tradition and authoritarian command are the guiding forces. Tradition dictated that if your father was a farmer, then you would also be a farmer. The goods and services produced in this simple economic system are very basic—food, shelter and clothing. There are not a lot of decisions to be made, as life is a reflection of the past, and production techniques are passed on from generation to generation with little change. Parts of South America, Africa, and Asia still produce and trade goods and services, as they have for many generations. Typically, production involved very simple materials, intensive labor, and little, if any, capital equipment. There is usually no separation of politics, religion and economics—they are typically all mixed together in a feudalistic economic system.

Feudalism—The Traditional Economy

Feudalism
A simple farm-based economic system where tradition and authoritarian command are the guiding forces.

Feudalism—the economic system that existed in England 1,000 years ago—was, in many ways, the opposite of capitalism. **Feudalism -** is a simple farm-based economic system where tradition and authoritarian command are the guiding forces. The concepts of profit or material acquisition were not part of this system. The early merchant had a precarious existence in that if a church official visited the merchant and found that they were making a profit—a concept that was arbitrarily defined—they could be fined, imprisoned and even executed in some cases. Even as late as 1639 in Boston, records show that numerous merchants were prosecuted for the horrible crime of making a profit. The concept of banking was labeled as usury, something that no honest man would be associated with.

Change was not tolerated, tradition was to be maintained at all cost. Even the simplest of changes in the production process were strongly resisted. In France, around 1540, in the town of Valence, over 70 merchants were hanged for the crime of importation of calico cloth.

The wealth of a nation was defined as the amount of gold and silver stored in the cellars of the nobility and the church. There was no reinvestment of capital, and money was not set aside for development of new and innovative products—this was not a part of the feudalistic system.

The Evolution of Capitalism

Capitalism
An economic system in which private property is emphasized.

In 1776, Adam Smith published his book, *The Wealth of Nations*, in which he described the emergence of a new economic system called capitalism (an economic system in which private property is emphasized). How did this new economic system, which was so different from feudalism, come into existence? It was not by the creative edict of a great leader or statesman, rather capitalism slowly developed over hundreds of years. There were several major and countless lesser events that occurred, which fostered the evolution of capitalism.

The Enclosure Movement

The birth of capitalism was a most painful process. The enclosure movement, which started in the fifteenth century, illustrates just how painful this transition was for the citizens of Europe. With the increased demand for wool, some of the nobility who controlled the land decided it would be more profitable to raise sheep instead of crops. The lord of the manor would enlist the aid of the kings solders and inform the peasants that the land upon which their families had raised crops for countless generations was to be enclosed within a hedge so that sheep could graze. Often the peasant families were given just 24 hours to vacate the land, after which time the soldiers returned to destroy the buildings and slaughter anyone still on the land. The peasants wandered into the nearest village hoping, most often in vain, to find work. This was a gradual process that became increasingly popular with the nobility, so that armies of vagrant families roamed the countryside by the end of the sixteenth century.

The enclosure movement eventually became enormous in scope, and the horror it inflicted on the people of Europe created a very dark legacy for the birthing of capitalism. By the middle of the sixteenth century, riots were a common reaction. In one riot, over 3,500 peasants were killed. This process continued into the nineteenth century. One of the largest enclosures occurred in 1820, when the Duchess of Sutherland threw 15,000 peasant families off their land as she enclosed 794,000 acres to graze 130,000 sheep.

The enclosure movement indirectly supported early manufacturers by creating a large pool of surplus workers which would push wages down to bare subsistence levels for hundreds of years in Europe. The low wages encouraged industrial growth as the corporate owners reinvested profits that the low wages helped create.

ADAM SMITH (1723 – 1790)

The First Capitalist Economist

In 1776, two great events took place. In North America, the Declaration of Independence articulated a belief in political freedom. In Europe, a book written by a professor at the University of Glasgow was published that established the science of economics. Entitled *An Inquiry into the Nature and Causes of the Wealth of Nations*, the lengthy book represented a thorough examination of questions which are now called economics: questions about labor, prices, income distribution, rent, profit, capital accumulation, and public finance.

Adam Smith was born in the village of Kirkaldy along the east coast of Scotland in 1723. His father had died before he was born. A peculiar incident of his childhood was his kidnapping by a band of gypsies when he was 4 years old; the gypsies abandoned him along the road when they realized that they had been traced and were being pursued.

He studied at the University of Glasgow during his teens and entered Oxford University on a scholarship at the age of 17, specializing in literature and philosophy.

After completing his studies at Oxford, he returned to Glasgow and in 1751 was appointed to a professorship in logic and moral philosophy, which included subjects such as natural theology, ethics, jurisprudence, and political economy. Smith was 28 years old at the time.

In 1764 he was employed as a tutor and companion to the son of the Countess of Dalkeith, and the salary included a life-time pension, although his duties ended by 1766. The major activity of his work with the young nobleman consisted of traveling in France, where he became acquainted with Voltaire and Quesnay.

By 1759, he had written and published his first

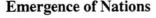

book, *The Theory of Moral Sentiments.* Seventeen years later he had written *The Wealth of Nations.*

In 1778, Smith was appointed Commissioner of Customs for Edinburgh, a sinecure which provided him with income that enabled him to live comfortably with his aged mother as a serene and contented bachelor.

Smith, one of the most creative thinkers of all time, identified a number of basic principles which he believed should guide us in our economic activity.

In explaining the sources of wealth, Smith first concentrated on the primary importance of labor rather than of money or of land. The principle of division of labor, he said, causes "the greatest improvement in the productive power of labor, and the greater part of the skill, dexterity, and judgment with which it is anywhere directed or applied."

Another principle set forth by Adam Smith was that of economic liberty. He asserted that individuals know what is best for them. If left alone, free of government control or private monopoly, people will be motivated by the desire for profit to produce the goods and services that society wants. Self-interest will bring about the greatest amount of common good.

Smith attacked legally protected monopolies and called for free trade in international commerce. His ideas became the basis for laissez-faire economics. His great book created a new science.

Emergence of Nations

The emergence of the strong nation state throughout Europe was essential to the emergence of capitalism. The centralized monarchies created a level of stability that would encourage early businessmen to take the risk involved in creating new industries. The nation states also created a common currency, a common language and a stable system of laws and courts—all important prerequisites in the evolution to a capitalistic economy. These governments also encouraged exploration of the establishment of foreign trade. The voyage of Columbus—as every school child knows—was financed by Isabella of Spain, and the voyage of Sir Francis Drake—one of the most lucrative in exploration annals—was financed by Queen Elizabeth of England.

Development of the Protestant Ethic

Feudalism was dominated by two strong forces—tradition and command of the state. The monarchs during much of this period shared governance of the people with the Church of Rome. The pope and clergy had tremendous sway over the minds of the people. The church had always questioned the ethics of early merchants and businessmen, and did not hesitate to have them imprisoned, or even executed, for making a profit. Banking—the lending of money—was a sin or usury. Life on earth was not for the acquisition of material wealth or for establishing the good life in materialistic terms. The Protestant reformation gradually replaced the church of Rome and created an ethic that was supportive of capitalism. Under the Protestant ethic, one had the responsibility to use the talents that God had given them, even in the business world. Thus, success and material wealth became signs of being blessed and, with some exaggeration, rich men were viewed as saintly

Inventions and Innovations

The industrial revolution occurred after the birth of capitalism, but the 500 years prior to this paved the way for the industrial revolution. Feudalism fought change and punished those who were bold or reckless enough to try to circumvent tradition. Yet, change did occur, often at great risk to the innovator. Some of the more significant inventions were the windmill, the map and a host of other navigational aids, the printing press, the paper mill, and the mechanical clock.

The Birth of Capitalism—1776

The birth of capitalism occurred because people were dissatisfied with life under feudalism. They may not have known what economic system was being created with their insistence on change, but the desire for change did create a system that was different than any the world had ever known. People wanted the ability to chose their own destiny, to be freed of the bond of church and state. Economists mark the official start of capitalism as 1776—the year Adam Smith published his famous book, *The Wealth of Nations*, which describes the new economic system. In its day, this book was considered revolutionary. The concept, for example, that the wealth of a nation was all it produced, not the amount of gold in the king's treasury, was a radical assertion. The book was not an economic textbook, but rather an explanation of capitalism and the role of government in this new economic system.

The Law of the Market

The Law of the Market
States that individuals
interacting in a
competitve market,
would promote their
own self-interest and in
the process, promote the
self interest of society as
a whole.

What held society together, and why did this new economic system function so effortlessly in the absence of tradition and the iron fisted rule of the state that had created order in feudalism? The answer Smith reasoned was "self interest." There was no need for the state to direct the lives of individuals as long as self interest was allowed full expression. This concept, he summarized in **the law of the market**, which states that individuals interacting in a competitive market, would promote their own self interest and, in the process, promote the self interest of society as a whole. The businessperson produces a new product that, if successful, will indeed create wealth for the businessperson, but society will also benefit from the new good or service. It is assumed that the market is competitive and that competition will protect the consumer from the greed of the businessperson. In order to stay competitive, the producer must constantly search for ways to produce more efficiently and to improve the quality of the product. The producer is, in a sense, at the mercy of the consumer, in that they must produce products that the consumer wants and, because of intense competition, must constantly seek ways to lower the price while improving the quality of the product.

The computer industry is a good example of how the market works for the consumer. In the 1970s, IBM, with over 350 thousand employees, dominated the computer industry. Then a couple of college drop-outs introduced the "Apple" computer, a much more user-friendly computer. Apple quickly took a percentage of this market, leaving IBM scrambling to bring out its own user-friendly computer. In the early 1980s, another college student changed the computer industry by innovating the custom computer, allowing the customer to decide what components would go into their computer. Michael Dell became a billionaire, the consumer got a better product, and IBM again had to change to meet the new competition.

Competition will also assure society that the good is produced in the correct quantity. If there are too few pizza restaurants, the market will signal this by the existing restaurants making profits. These profits will attract others to open pizza restaurants until the optimal number of restaurants are open. Prices are determined in the market through the interaction of supply and demand. Smith saw that capitalism functioned best with the least amount of government involvement. The concept market failure was used to justify government involvement in the economy. A market failure exists when the consumer wants a good or service and the business sector fails to provide it.

Law of Accumulation

Law of Accumulation
Individual business
owner will invest profits
when they occur, back
into their business.

Smith noted that capitalism is growth oriented, because of the law of accumulation. Each individual business owner will invest profits, when they occur, back into their business. This investing of profits back into the business is in the self interest of the business owner who believes that the expansion of the business will result in even larger profits in the future. Thus, by each owner following their self interest, the interest of society is also served, in that the investment results in more jobs and more goods produced.

Thomas Malthus

In 1798, Thomas Malthus shocked the intellectual elite of Europe with his book entitled, *An Essay of the Principles of Population as it Affects the Future Improvement of Society*. Adam Smith had noted that economic conditions were very difficult for the worker in the early stages of capitalism, but, because of the law of accumulation and the law of the market, economic conditions would, in time, improve greatly for the entire society. The economic pie was initially small, but would eventually grow dramatically. Malthus agreed that over time the output, or the economic pie, would get bigger; however, he noted that the population would grow at an even faster pace—thus, you would get a larger pie, but the individual slices would still be small, because there would be more people to divide the pie among. Adam Smith assumed that the population would grow at a very modest rate, while the studies of Malthus indicated that the population actually grew at a rather rapid rate, doubling every 25 years. Malthus said that population would grow at a rate that would always outpace production of food; thus, regardless of how efficient the economic system was, if population was not held in check, society would never advance beyond the subsistence level. In his day, since there was no easy way to control population growth, Malthus concluded that society would never advance beyond subsistence level. This bleak prediction resulted in economics becoming known as the dismal science. To this day, some students still refer to the study of economics as the dismal science. Obviously, these students are not in this class reading this great text!

The Malthusian theory on population sparked a debate, over the role that population plays in the wealth of nations, which is still going on today. However, there are some observations that seem to validate this theory—the nations of the world that have stabilized their population growth rates have the highest standards of living in the world, while the nations that have the highest population growth rates are the poorest countries of the world. In 1981, China—with over one billion people on a land mass slightly larger than the U.S. and only one-third the farmland—instituted its one-child policy, declaring that each family would only be allowed one child. The reason for this drastic measure was that, with the current rapid population growth rate, mass starvation was predicted within twenty-five years, if the growth rate was not curtailed.

China's goal is to maintain the "one child" policy for 100 years. Then the population of China will be reduced to 600 million citizens from its current 1,000 million. As the population is reduced and the economic output is expanded, the materialistic standard of living should increase dramatically for the average Chinese citizen.

1860 to 1910

In 1860, the U.S. economy consisted mostly of farmers with very limited industrial production. Europe was the industrial center of the capitalistic world. By 1910, the U.S. emerged as the largest industrial nation of the world. There were many reasons why the U.S. economy was able to make such a rapid transformation from a developing nation to the leading industrial nation of the world in just 60 years. The five most important factors were: government, labor, capital, natural resources, and the type of economic system, capitalism.

The two most important elements for this rapid industrial growth was the type of economic system, capitalism and the role of the federal government during this period of time. The federal government facilitated the growth of the economic system, not by what it did, but rather by what it did not do. The presidents and congresses of that period of time were content to allow corporate America to function on its own. They believed in the concept of laissez faire, which is French for "let it be." Government intervention in the economy was to be avoided. The only time the government intervened was to assist corporate America by supplying the infrastructure needed by business. The government contented itself with delivering the mail; building roads, bridges, and communication lines; and subsidizing the expansion of the railroads. Thus capitalism, with a laissez faire government, in combination with the other three factors, resulted in the dynamic growth that the U.S. economy experienced during the period from 1860 to 1910.

1929 to 1939

The year 1929 marked the end of capitalism as described by Adam Smith. The depression of the 1930s was so severe that, for the first time in our economic history, the federal government rejected the concept of *laissez faire* and became actively involved in just about every facet of the U.S. economy. The government directly regulated the financial markets, including the banking industry. It provided jobs for some of the unemployed, and created the welfare, social security and unemployment programs. The agricultural and business sectors also received direct aid from the federal government. Many of these programs are still in place, even though the great majority of these programs were only supposed to last through the end of the depression. Thus, this ten year period of time ushered in the economics of mixed capitalism for the U.S. economy. The dominant aspect of our economic system is still capitalism; however, a growing part of our economy is socialistic.

1946—The Employment Act and the GI bill

The year 1946 saw two pieces of legislation enacted that would be instrumental in bringing about further changes in our economic and social structure. The .ib.Employment Act of 1946; basically stated that congress and the president had a responsibility to the American people to intervene in the economy, during recessions, to bring the economy back to full employment. This legislation brought the economist from the classroom to the halls of congress. A council of economic advisors was created for the president and the congress, with the intent that these economic advisors would keep the president and members of the congress informed as to the current health of the economy, and, in times of economic turmoil, would advise them of the appropriate action the government should take.

The GI bill was enacted to ease the return of 16 million soldiers back to civilian life. One of its major provisions provided free education and training to all returning soldiers. Before WWII, college was reserved for the wealthy. There were basically two groups in the U.S. economy—the workers, with no college education, and the wealthy elite, with their college degrees. The GI bill resulted in millions of soldiers getting college degrees and technical training that not only increased their earning capacity but also the productivity of the entire nation. This opening of higher education laid the foundation for the middle class and the entry of our economy into the new industrial age.

This bill also provided veterans with the ability to own their own home. Ten years after the passage of this legislation, close to 70 percent of the American people owned their home, compared to 30 percent before the GI bill.

Today's Economy

The U.S. economy continues to evolve, for change is a part of life. The rest of this text will examine, in some detail, the current U.S. economy and how it has changed since the 1950s.

Five Basic Characteristics of Capitalism—Market Efficiency, Role of Government and Market Failure, Consumer Sovereignty, Self-interest, Private Ownership

Market Efficiency

The concept of *market efficiency* is one of the most important aspects of our capitalistic system. How *efficient* are the goods and services, demanded by consumers produced. Adam Smith noted that capitalism would produce goods and services in the most efficient manner, because of competition. This concept was illustrated as we read how competition forced Mr. Lowe to improve his product and keep his cost to a minimum in order to maintain his market share. Every competitive producer is constantly striving to improve the quality and lower the production cost in their search for profits.

The more efficient the markets, the more difficult it is to make a profit. If the market is "perfectly efficient" then all producers would have equal access to information eliminating any chance for profit over a long period of time. Profits are therefore rewards for more efficiently gathering information and the willingness to take risk based on the data you gathered. Mr. Lowe acquired the information about his new product and then risked his time and money in producing this product. After his initial success, his ability to continue making profits now depended on his ability to efficiently produce this product, relative to his competition and his ability to improve the product faster than his competitors.

It should be evident now why our market economy tends to foster efficient markets. The U.S. economy is the most competitive economic system in the world and it is this intense competition that is critical for market efficiency. The concept of TANSTAAFL is also illustrated in this concept. Profits are possible, but for most producers they tend to be very difficult to maintain over time.

Role of Government and Market Failure

According to Adam Smith, government should play a minimal role in a capitalistic economic system. Government protects private property, enforces a legal system, and provides national defense. Today most economists rely on the concept of *market failure* to analyze the validity of government involvement in the economy. Market failure occurs when one or more of three conditions exist.

1. The absence of competition, which results in inefficient use of resources (markets become inefficient). The consumer is no longer assured that the good or service will be produced at the lowest price and highest quality.

2. When externalities occur. Externalities (positive or negative) are costs or benefits that are not properly assigned by the market. An example of a negative externality is industrial pollution. Without governmental enforcement, business would pollute, avoiding the cost of properly disposing of their industries waste while imposing costs on the rest of society.

   Another example of a negative externality is when your neighbor decides to burn his old car tires in his back yard, while you are having a wedding reception in your adjacent backyard. Your neighbor receives the benefit of disposing of his old tires, while imposing cost on you. Thus, you incur some of the cost of the tire disposal, while receiving none of the benefits. Your neighbor is imposing a negative externality on you. A positive externality occurs when you receive a benefit without incurring any of the cost involved in producing the benefit. If your neighbor plants a flower garden in the front yard that you view everyday, you have received a positive externality.

3. A market failure also occurs when the market fails to provide a good or service that consumers demand. Shasta Dam, the second largest dam in the U.S., was built by the federal government to meet the demands of consumers in Northern California. The consumers wanted flood control, irrigation water, cheap electricity, and an expanded recreation base. Private enterprise would not build the dam. The market failed to give the consumers of Northern California what they wanted, so it was logical that the federal government step in and build the dam.

   Thus, the U.S. government was following the dictates of Adam Smith when it broke up Rockefeller's trust, Standard Oil in 1914, when it promotes international trade; builds lighthouses, dams, and national parks; and restricts industrial pollution.

   The *role of government* in a capitalistic system is very controversial at best. A socialistic definition of the role of government would be very large, from socialized medicine to stronger controls if not ownership of our large corporations. The conservative economist would advocate government intervention only in very limited situations, where clear and obvious market failures occurred.

   Even if you limit the role of the government to market failures, there is still considerable controversy. For example it is clear that the market fails to protect the environment. The question then becomes "What form should the government intervention take and what degree do we want to protect the environment?" Should logging be prohibited to protect the spotted owl? The role of government will continue to be debated by economists and the general public, as long as economic systems exist.

Consumer Sovereignty

Consumer Sovereignty
Consumer demand determines what will be produced.

Adam Smith noted that capitalism made the consumer king. According to Smith, it was the consumer who holds the power in a capitalistic system. If a business is to succeed it must produce a product that will entice the consumer to spend his limited income on it. If the consumer rejects the product, then the entrepreneur will be driven from the marketplace. If the businessperson is successful in producing and marketing a new product, any profits will typically be short lived, as other businesses enter this profitable market.

Self-interest

Adam Smith made the observation that self-interest was the glue that held this new (1770s) economic system together. He noted that with the removal of the government and traditions as the controlling elements in people's lives, that for the first time in history, people were free to choose. People made their choice about where to work and how to spend their limited income on the basis of self-interest. Adam Smith called it the "invisible hand" that directs people in a capitalistic economy. We are all guided in the hundreds of daily decisions we make on the basis of what will be best for the individual. This is why Mr. Lowe and Mr. Walton created their businesses. It allows people to maximize their individual talents. Self-interest is also great for society, for when individuals promote their own self-interest, they usually also promote the welfare of the general society. Students are promoting their own self interest by earning a degree. This college degree will allow the student to earn a higher income. However, students are also benefiting society by earning a degree. The skills they now have allow them to contribute more to society. The doctor is able to give more to society than the registered nurse. The RN contributes more than the floor nurse, who contributes more than orderlies. Each worker is providing society with valuable work skill, but the more training one has, the greater value their work is to society and the greater the financial rewards to the individual. This is a win-win situation. The individual, by promoting their self interest, also promotes the welfare of society.

Capitalism—The Market Economy

Capitalism can be described as an economic system that has an efficient market, where consumer sovereignty exists and people (the private sector) own the means of production. In this economy, self-interest is allowed expression in the production process and the government role is limited to market failure.

Table 2-1. GDP in Billions of Dollars

This data illustrates the tremendous growth in the U.S. economy from 1923 to 1999

Year	Actual Dollars
1950	$ 286
1955	400
1960	506
1970	992
1975	1,549
1980	2,633
1982	3,057
1987	4,200
1992	6,039
1993	6,374
1994	6,887
1995	7,297
1996	7,629
1997	8,125
1998	8,610
1999	9,072

How Much is One Trillion Dollars? A Brief Digression on $1,000,000,000,000

In 1923, the U.S. economy produced $103 billion worth of goods and services. Seventy-one years later, in 1999, the U.S. economy will produce close to 9 trillion dollars of goods and services.

To really appreciate the accomplishment of the U.S. economy over the last 76 years, you must understand the enormity of a trillion dollars. Here's an example that will give some meaning to this number. It would take you 19 years to spend a trillion dollars if you spent it at the rate of $100,000 a minute, 24 hours a day, 7 days a week for the entire 19 years. Now you will also have a better understanding of the tremendous effort that the federal government must make in spending close to $2 trillion this year, and the fact that our national debt will exceed $4.5 trillion at the end of 1997.

Private Ownership

In a socialist economy such as Cuba and North Korea, all the means of production—factories, farms, and mines—are all owned by the state. Capitalism emphasizes that the people, not the government, own the production facilities. General Motors is owned by the stockholders. Individuals in a capitalistic society have the ability to become owners of a business by either starting their own business or by buying shares of stock in an established business.

Spotlight on Self-interest

A key part of the Economic way of thinking (EWOT) is the knowledge that people always behave in a way that promotes their own self-interests. If you want to change an individual's or society's behavior pattern, all you have to do is find a way to make it in their self-interest to do what you want to happen.

In 1984, Sheldon Bissell's teenage son was killed by a drunk driver. Mr. Bissell declared war on drunk drivers. He created a program that would greatly reduce the incidence of drunk driving.

The program was simple. He deposited an initial $2,000 in a special bank account and then advertised in a local newspaper, promising $100 to any person who spotted a drunk driver and called 911. The $100 would be paid only if the traffic stop resulted in a drunk-driver arrest. To ensure anonymity, tipsters who called were given a secret number by the dispatcher, who notified the bank. The bank in turn paid the $100 when the tipster produced the number and claimed the money.

"The thing is, this program works," said Highway Patrol Inspector Irwin Cantieri of the California Highway Patrol's San Andreas Office. "When Mr. Bissell first came in here, I was skeptical. But after 6 months, it was clear that his program is very effective." This program has now been instituted in ten other counties in California.

Mr. Bissell's program works so well because it provides a safe way for citizens to promote their own self interest.

KARL MARX (1818 - 1883)

"The communist disdain to conceal their views and aims...they openly declare that their ends can be attained only by the forcible overthrow of all existing social relations. Let the ruling classes tremble...the proletarians have nothing to lose but their chains. They have the world to win."

This excerpt from the *Communist Manifesto* established Karl Marx as an economic radical, a force to be dealt with. History will note what lasting force Marx will have on future economic systems. China, and Cuba are just two of the countries of the world that have claimed that their political, social, and economic structures are based on Marxist theory. During the 20th century, the ideas of Karl Marx have had a larger impact on human history than the thoughts of any other economist.

Marx was born in Treves, Germany in 1818, the son of a successful lawyer. He was educated at the Universities of Bonn and Berlin, and received his doctorate in philosophy at the University of Jena in 1841, when he was only 23 years old. brilliant student, he became an adherent of the British economist, David Ricardo, who emphasized the importance of the labor theory of value—the idea that the primary component of value and therefore of price is the amount of labor that goes into the production of a good or service. This was the position of Adam Smith. Marx, however, came to the conclusion that the system of capitalism was unjust and full of contradictions, and should therefore be destroyed. He believed that since labor is the primary source of value, workers ought to receive the entire product of the economy, and that the other factors of production were actually taking benefits which rightfully should go only to workers. Adam Smith and David Ricardo saw the labor theory of value as a description of how part of the economy works. Marx saw it as a call for revolution.

Marx believed that the capitalist system had to give way to a new economic system which would involve worker domination. Although he believed in an inevitable breakdown to be followed by a socialist economy, he gave little thought to the details of the new system except that planning would replace "market anarchy."

Marx worked with various revolutionary groups throughout his lifetime, and the successful communist revolutions in Russia and China both consider him to be their guide, even though their revolutions took place long after his death.

Many economists who disagree with Marx's conclusions consider that parts of his critical analysis of capitalism are valid. What he did not envisage is that capitalism had the potential for solving many of its problems without violence or revolution; and that 20th century capitalism actually would provide that working class with the benefits he believed they deserved but did not have in the 19th century.

Socialism

Socialism
An economic system in which property and the means of production are collectively owned or controlled.

Socialism is an economic system in which property and the means of production are collectively owned or controlled. Decision-making is in the hands of the community and the government. This economic system encompasses the idea that the government should play a major role in the production and distribution process. The government will make many of the decisions that individuals make in a capitalistic economic system.

Mixed Economic System

One of the major contributions of Karl Marx is his theory of economic evolution. Basically, he noted that every economic system (except for pure communism, which is only a theoretical-economic system) is in a process of constant change. Capitalism in 1776 would be different 50 years later and much different in 1997. He predicted that all capitalistic countries would eventually evolve into socialism and then communism. History will be the judge of that. But today, our economic system has changed so much from 1776 that it would be misleading to classify it as capitalistic. Thus, the term *mixed capitalism*, a mixture of capitalism and socialism, is a more accurate description of our economic system, with the predominant element still being capitalism.

Communism—A Theoretical Economic System

Communism
A system of government in which the state controls the means of production and a single, often authoritarian party holds power with the intention of establishing a higher social order in which all goods are equally shared by the people.

Communism is a system of government in which the state controls the means of production an da single, often authoritarian party holds power with the intention of establishing a higher social order in which all goods are equally shared by the people. According to Karl Marx, who popularized the concept of communism, all economic systems were in a state of evolution eventually evolving to the utopia economic system of communism. Marx gave no indication as to how long this evolutionary process would take, only that feudalistic economies would evolve into capitalistic economies, and then capitalistic economies would evolve into socialism. During the socialistic state of evolution, the state will own and operate the means of production, distribution and all markets. Labor is free to work where they

choose and enjoy the fruit of their productivity. When the economy is able to provide abundance for all, the stage is set for the final evolution to a communist economic system. Under this economic system, government will eventually disappear and workers will work according to their ability and receive according to their needs. When communism has matured, machines will do most, if not all, the work, and the people of this society will have all the material goods they desire. People will then live in harmony, free of the rule of any government. Most economists see communism as a fanciful utopia. Today when a country labels themselves as communist, what they are stating is that their current economic system is a form of socialism, they are followers of the Marx economic theory and one day hope to obtain the utopia state of communism.

Factors of Production

Land, Labor, Capital and Entrpreneurship

Production
The process of converting resources into finished and useful goods.

Production is the process of converting resources into finished and useful goods. Economists refer to four categories of resources: **land, labor, capital,** and **entrpreneurship**. These resources, when combined with current technology, result in the production of goods for a society.

1. *Land*: Economists use this term in a very general sense to consist of all natural resources, including raw land, minerals, lakes, rivers, climate and forests.

2. *Labor* or *Human Resources*: You are currently improving the human resource base of the U.S. by attending college. People are a country's most valuable resource; the standard of living in any country is a reflection of the level of human resource development.

3. *Capital*: Tools, buildings, computers, etc., are used in the production process. When a farmer uses a tractor, it becomes part of the country's capital. Do not be confused by the fact that a truck is a capital good when bought by a corporation, but a consumer good when purchased by a student. Just as a computer can be either a capital good or a consumer good depending on its usage. Capital can also mean financial capital, the money to pay for land, labor or tools and buildings.

4. *Entrepreneur*: This is probably the most important element in the production process. It is again the human element, the risk taker, the decision maker. It is the person who has an idea and is willing to risk his or her own money and others' in combining the other three input factors to create and market a finished product. It is to the entrepreneur that we as a society owe a debt. For these are the people who have the creative genius to develop a new product, the managerial talent to combine raw material, labor, and capital to efficiently manufacture a product. They have fortitude to take the risks necessary to promote a new product, often in the face of initial rejection. Without the entrepreneur, capitalism could not exist.

Edward Lowe's story is a classic example of entrepreneurship. After reading "Before Kitty Litter" you should have a better understanding of this concept and its importance to the American economy.

"Before Kitty Litter"

Before 1946, people who kept cats in the house usually dealt with the problems of nature with a common sandbox or a hole in the screen door. At this time Edward Lowe worked at his father's garage where one of his nightly tasks was to clean the garage floor of the day's deposit of car oil and grease. Over time he came to favor a ground-up version of local clay for an absorbent. One night after finishing up his usually duties at the garage, he took a bag of the clay home to use in his cat box instead of sand. He was so taken by the results that he felt other cat owners might also be appreciative of the absorbent features of the clay. He also found that clay was superior to sand because sand tended to stick to the cat's feet and would track through the house.

It's important to keep in mind that at this time there was no cat litter on the market. Mr. Lowe packed the ground-up clay into paper sacks, wrote the name "Kitty Litter" on them and took them to the local pet store. The pet store owner clearly questioned who would pay good money (65 cents) to buy these bags of clay when sand had worked for hundreds of years. Mr. Lowe was not to be denied, he demonstrated the superior qualities of his product by pouring a shot glass of water into a bowl of clay to show why clay worked better than sand. The store owner agreed to shelve the product and to explain how it worked to cat owners.

Initially no one seemed willing to pay even 65 cents for this new product. At this point many of us would probably have given up the project, especially with our friends questioning our sanity, but Mr. Lowe knew the value of his product. If he could get the consumer to try it he was sure that they would become as hooked on it as he and his neighbors were. With this in mind he told the store owner to give the bags away as free samples.

The rest of the year our entrepreneur—who today is a multi-millionaire—visited pets store with free samples and attended cat shows where he went from booth to booth offering to clean out cat boxes if he could replace their sand with his new product. Sometimes he literally cleaned out hundreds of cat boxes a day, always replacing it with his product and leaving his order forms with the cat owner. In time, the stores reported that cat owners who had taken samples came back and asked to buy the product. At the end of his first year total sales were a little over $400.

Mr. Lowe's energy and persistence gradually paid off as orders steadily increased. In the early 1960s several supermarkets agreed to carry "Kitty Litter" or its cheaper version called "Tidy Cat." The rest is history—a new industry was created.

There is another lesson to be learned from Mr. Lowe. As orders poured in, Mr. Lowe concentrated his energies on expanding his factories to try to meet the tremendous flood of new orders. There was no plan developed to deal with the competition that would soon appear. Whenever a new industry is born and profits are being made, competition is sure to follow. It did. Dozens of new cat litter brands appeared of the market, and not just plain clay. Everything from green deodorizing specks to pellets made of alfalfa were quickly brought on the market.

Thus, Mr. Lowe learned what every freshman economic student learns, that if profits are being made, competition will quickly enter (assuming no barriers to entry). In order to remain the leader in this market Mr. Lowe hired a consumer marketing firm and started a research department to try to keep his product the best in the industry.

Today Mr. Lowe lives on his large Michigan estate and writes poetry as he walks through the surrounding forests.

SAM WALTON (1908 – 1992)

A Tribute to One of the Greatest American Entrepreneurs

Sam Walton embodied the spirit of capitalism. In 1953, with $5000 of his own savings and $20,000 borrowed from his father-in-law, Walton and his family bought their first retail store, a little, run-down 5-and-10 Ben Franklin store in a rural southern town in Arkansas, with a population of 5,500. From this humble start Sam Walton became the richest man in the United States.

The driving force in Mr. Walton's success was a desire to provide his customers with a better product at a lower price. He knew that to succeed in the competitive retail market, he had to constantly innovate: do it differently, better than his competitors. The key to his enormous success was based on three ideas. First, you could take a smaller markup than the competition, and increase your revenues through higher volume. Second, compete by keeping the operating cost lower, being more efficient. Third, he would open his discount stores, Wal Marts, in small towns, with populations of less than 50,000. Places that his toughest competitors, like K-Mart and Target, view as too small.

Pursuing this basic strategy, he expanded to become the largest retail chain in America. Along the way, he changed the way retail markets operate, saved American consumers hundreds of billions of dollars in their purchases of goods, directly employed over 400,000 and has provided the opportunity for many to become wealthy by buying Wal Mart stock. A $1,500 investment in this stock in 1971 is now worth over $3 million. It is probably safe to say that there is not one person in this country who has not benefited from the creative energies of Sam Walton, the entrepreneur.*

*See "Sam Walton: Made in America" by DoubleDay, 1992.

Cost Benefit Analysis

One of the main points of this chapter is that studying economics is important because it provides you with a mechanism to make better decisions. Every decision you make is based on **cost benefit analysis**. Simply stated, you make decisions by weighing the perceived cost of an action versus the perceived benefits to be obtained from the expenditure. You might not recognize this as the way you make decisions, but it is. For example, the decision to take this course was made by considering what costs were involved and what benefits you would get from this course. Since you are taking the course, the expected benefits must have been greater than the expected cost of this course. This is the way you make all your decisions, from how many units or hours to take per semester to what to buy for lunch. Literally hundreds of decisions a week are made on the basis of cost benefit analysis. What is the cost versus what are the benefits?

Opportunity Cost

Opportunity Cost
The cost associated with the highest valued alternative you have to give up in order to obtain a good or service.

An economic tool that is a great aid in cost benefit analysis is the concept of **opportunity cost**. Opportunity cost is the cost associated with the highest valued alternative you have to give up in order to obtain a good or service; it is the opportunity foregone. The cost to you of reading this wonderful text right now is what else you might be doing with your time. You might be reading a history text, watching TV, or entertaining a friend. Thus, the concept of opportunity cost helps you understand the cost of an activity. Often, wrong decisions are made because the full costs or benefits are not known. If students realized the real cost (the opportunity cost) of their education, their behavior might be different. For many college

students, the cost of attending college is thought of in terms of the cost of tuition, room and board, books, etc. These are part of the cost of attending college, but students not versed in the economic way of thinking are apt to leave out what can be the biggest cost, the opportunity cost of your time. Most students would be working full time if they were not attending college. This cost, usually well over $10,000 a year, is important to include in your cost benefit analysis. The point is that this concept helps clarify the cost of an action, thus improving your decision-making ability.

In a business, the concept of opportunity cost also helps in the decision-making process. If you allow space in your showroom to be taken up by slow-moving merchandise, you are incurring a cost that may be greater than the benefits of displaying the product. The cost is defined by the revenue you could be generating if you displayed another product in its place. Hopefully, the benefits of displaying the current item are greater than its opportunity cost.

Viewing the Choices: The Production Possibilities Curve

At this point a numerical example will help. Suppose that a hypothetical society, Shelby, must economize, that is, choose between producing two goods: beef and all-purpose machines. (These all-purpose machines do many things such as produce television programs, build roads, churn ice cream, dry wet hair, dig wells, light buildings, type letters, sew shoe uppers to soles, and drive people to work.) Obviously, this is a great simplification of choice making. In the real world, two things are obvious: (1) choices are in *many* dimensions, with thousands of alternatives among which to choose, and (2) choices change almost continuously as technology changes. But in order to simplify the description of the process and make it easier to visualize what we mean by choices, we chose just two commodities. Let these two represent, in microcosm, the more complex process of choice making in the real world.

One way to visualize Shelby's choices is to look at the *production-possibilities curve*, a useful device derived from the *production-possibilities function*, which is defined as follows:

Production-Possibilities Function
Shows the combinations of goods that a society's resources can produce at full employment in a particular period of time (using the best technology).

The **production possibilities function** *shows those combinations of goods that the full-employment use of a society's resources can produce during a particular period of time (using the best available technology).*

In other words, this represents for a society a kind of frontier, or outer limit to the capacity both to produce and to make choices among goods.

The Production Possibilities Table

Suppose that Table 2-2 represents the various combinations of beef and all-purpose machines available to Shelby at a given time, within the limitations set out above (full employment and the best use of existing technology).

What does this table show? Let's look at it as a set of tradeoffs; that is, it's like a menu, except that the diner can't buy *all* the items on it. Consider combination A. This shows that when Shelby produces no beef, it can produce 20,000 machines. If it wants to use some of its resources to produce beef, it must give up (produce less of) machines. This is illustrated at point E where it can produce 2,000 tons of beef, but only 18,000 machines. In the second case, it must give up 2,000 machines for 2,000 tons of beef; in other words, the marginal rate of transformation (MRT) is $\frac{2}{-2} = -1$. The MRT is the rate at which one good is traded off for another. More on this later. These tradeoffs may continue until the situation evolves into combination E. At this point, Shelby, employing all its resources and the best technology, can produce 8,000 tons of beef, but can't manufacture any machines. In making choice E, Shelby gives up 8,000 machines for the additional 2,000 tons of beef and incurs a MRT of $\frac{2}{-8} = -\frac{1}{4}$. The key point is that the MRT continually decreases, reflecting a growing opportunity cost, which will be explained shortly.

Which of these various combinations will (or should) Shelby

produce? There is no way for us to find out from this table. Answering this question is very complex, and the mechanisms by which societies make such choices vary greatly. Remember that we assumed that Shelby is a private-enterprise capitalist society, and so the decision is largely made in its marketplaces. But we don't know which decision its producers and consumers will make. The data in Table 2-2 simply indicate the possibilities. (In some societies, these decisions might be made by both markets and government. In others, the decision may be made only by government fiat.)

Graphing the Production Possibilities Curve

Graphs, being pictures, not only adorn, but also tell stories. For many people, a graph—in this case a picture of certain economic relationships—can be worth a thousand words. For clarification, refer back to the basic data which it portrays. Figure 2-1 is a visual image of the data in Table 2-2.

Point C in Figure 2-1, for example, represents a combination that is a maximum attainable output: 4,000 tons of beef and 14,000 all-purpose machines. Each of the combinations, A, B, C, D, and E is possible for Shelby. The curve that has been drawn through these points is the production possibilities curve (PP curve).

Why are points F, G, H, and I not on the 1995 PP curve? Point F represents less production of *both* beef and machinery than some combinations that are on the curve. In other words, F does not represent a maximum attainable output. To see this, follow the dashed line that goes through point F. If Shelby chose to produce 3,000 machines (possible at F), it could produce approximately 7,400 tons of beef, much more than the 4,000 indicated at F. In other words, if Shelby picked combination F, it would not be maximizing output, and it would not be employing its resources fully.

Table 2-2
Production Possibilities for Beef Versus Machines, Shelby, 1995

Product	Production Rates				
	A	**B**	**C**	**D**	**E**
Beef (thousands of tons)	0	2	4	6	8
Machines (thousands)	20	18	14	8	0
Marginal Rate of Transformation (MRT)	$\frac{2}{-2} = -1$	$\frac{2}{-4} = -\frac{1}{2}$	$\frac{2}{-6} = -\frac{1}{3}$	$\frac{2}{-8} = -\frac{1}{4}$	

Figure 2-1
Production-Possibilities Curve, Shelby, 1995

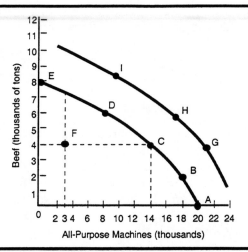

We could apply the same logic to all such points (combinations) below or to the left of the production-possibilities curve. On the other hand, points such as G, H, and I which lie beyond or to the right of the current PP curve, are by definition not attainable. They would involve Shelby turning out more of *both* products than it possibly could, given its current technology and endowments of resources. Since we are assuming full employment and best use of existing technology, points G, H, and I are clearly unattainable.

Economic Growth:
Shifting the Production-Possibilities Curve

While points G, H, and I are not attainable for Shelby in 1995, they may be reached if one or more of the following things happen:

1. Resources available to the nation (land, labor, capital, and entrepreneurship) increase, or

2. There is an improvement in the technology with which Shelby employs its resources, or

3. Shelby engages in trade with other nations, allocating its resources to their most productive uses and importing goods from Boiling Springs and other nations who can produce them with greater efficiency. This means producing goods in which Shelby has a comparative advantage and importing goods in which it does not have such an advantage. This very important source of growth will be explained more fully in chapters which deal with international trade and finance.

Any one or all of these happenings will make it possible to produce more of both beef and machines. They will, in other words, shift the PP curve outward or to the right. We should note that although the two curves—(A, B, C, D, E) and (G, H, I)—are parallel, it is by no means sure that the economic growth that the shift reflects will involve simply larger quantities of the same goods as before. As we shall see later in this chapter, economic growth is likely to change the composition of output (what can be produced, as well as what is produced) since it is likely to change both the costs of production and the tastes and preferences of those who consume it.

A Word of Caution

Resist the temptation to read too much into a picture or graph. When we look at a Picasso painting, we may each read into it something different if we wish. On the other hand, what one may legitimately see in a graph is determined by the definitions and assumptions underlying the graph. In Table 1-1, we can see what the production alternatives are (at full employment and using the best technology). We do not, however, know which choice Shelby will make. There are social, political, moral, cultural, and legal aspects to be taken into account.

One thing is evident: What Shelby produces today will influence what it can produce in the future. Let us assume that Shelby is a less developed (low-income) country. Shelby, let us suppose, has a ten-year objective to increase productivity from point C (in 1995) to point H (in 2005). Refer again to Figure 1-2. This means that Shelby has to shift its production-possibilities curve to the right. To do this, it must have more productive capacity, which means more all-purpose machines. Thus politico-economic objectives in 1995 may dictate more machines (at the cost of less beef) to increase capacity for tomorrow's output. We say that movement from C to H is Shelby's planned growth path.

Increasing Opportunity Costs: Why Is The Curve Shaped That Way?

Refer again to Table 2-2. Each time Shelby chose to produce more of one good (beef or machines) it had to produce less of the other (remember that it has no unemployed resources with which to produce more of the desired good). We define what the nation gives up of the one good to produce more of the other as its opportunity cost. This is a very fundamental concept that underlies the entire study of economics. With all economic goods, there is a (positive) opportunity cost. Put another way, we shall assume that there is no "free lunch" (zero opportunity cost) in using resources. The real or opportunity cost of using any resource, thus, is what we give up of other things in order to do so.

What Is the (Positive) "Cost of the Lunch"?

You have of course noticed that the PP curve is concave to the origin of the diagram. This is so because there is a hidden assumption underlying the choosing of the numbers and the construction of the curve. The assumption is that of *increasing opportunity cost*. To define this concept, let us go back to Shelby and its twin industries, beef and all-purpose machines.

Figure 2-2 represents the production-possibilities curve for Shelby in 1995. The solid line (A, B, C, D, and E) represents the full-employment choices available to the nation if resources are specialized in producing either beef or all-purpose machines. The dashed line (A and E) represents the choices that would be available if resources were equally productive in either employment. With A, B, C, D, and E the opportunity cost of producing more of either good grows larger. With A and E, the opportunity cost is constant.

We can illustrate *opportunity cost* by referring to movements along the PP curve. Suppose that the Farmer's Party gains power in Shelby, and the government decides to produce fewer machines (producer goods) and more beef (consumer goods). It decides to move from the machine-beef ratio at point C on the PP curve to the ratio at point D. This means that Shelby gives up 6,000 machines in order to get 2,000 more tons of beef. The machines it gives up (six thousand) are the *real opportunity cost* of the additional beef (two thousand).

Now suppose that Shelby decides to produce *no* all-purpose machines and instead uses its resources to produce *only* beef. The effect is that Shelby moves to point E from point D on the PP curve. What has Shelby given up? As you can see, the 2,000 additional tons of beef cost 8,000 machines. In other words, the real opportunity cost—as measured by the increasing slope of the PP curve —is becoming larger (the marginal rate of transformation is getting smaller). This would also be true if Shelby chose to produce more machines instead of more beef. In moving down the PP curve, Shelby would be forced to give up more and more beef for each additional machine produced, or would face **increasing opportunity cost**.

Increasing Opportunity Cost
The assumption that as a nation chooses to produce more of one good, it must (ultimately) give up increasing amounts of the other good.

Resources Are Specialized

The Shelby example we are considering is hypothetical. Consideration of opportunity cost as well as benefits is always important in reality in making private or public choices. Suppose that the United States is considering a public choice involving speed limits on its highways (as it did in the 1970s and again in the late 1980s). If a law is enacted lowering the speed limit to 55 mph, it will presumably have some social benefits, especially the saving of human lives as well as the saving of automotive fuels. What, though, are the (opportunity) costs? Some are obvious such as the added cost of law enforcement, but these are relatively small. The most significant cost to both individuals and to society is the cost of people's time. Driving more slowly, of course, results in more time being used in transportation; that additional time could have been used to produce goods and services and their value is the major real opportunity cost of lowering the speed limit.

Why does relative cost ultimately increase as a full-employment society chooses to reallocate its resources? Why aren't resources completely *substitutable* in all uses, so that the PP curve looks like the straight dashed line AE in Figure 2-2? There are complex factors involved. We shall examine some of these later in this chapter. Fundamentally, the reason is this:

Resources are relatively more productive in some uses than in others.

Marginal Rate of Transformation
The rate at which one good is traded off for another.

Diminishing Marginal Rate of Transformation
The rate at which one good may be traded off or transformed into another ultimately decreases. In other words, the real opportunity cost ultimately rises.

Imagine what would happen in Shelby as it tried to produce more beef. Beyond some point, Shelby farmers would have to start turning their cows out into pasture land that is less well suited for cattle raising. Of course, if resources were equally adaptable to any use, all land could be used just as well for one thing as for another, and the **marginal rate of transformation**—the rate at which the one good is traded off for the other—would be constant. In other words, it would be technically homogeneous in application. In such a case, the curve would be a straight line, such as the dashed line AE in Figure 2-2. But in real life this is not usually the case, though occasionally one does find either perfect substitutability or perfect lack of it. In fact, sometimes resources gain in efficiency as they are reallocated from one use to another. However, we want our economic models to clarify reality. Therefore, if models are to help us analyze general economic problems, they must be based on valid assumptions. For this reason, we shall assume a **diminishing marginal rate of transformation**, which means that the rate at which one good may be traded off or transformed into another *ultimately* decreases—for a single firm, for an enterprise, or for an industry. In our illustration, this rate is shown as always decreasing (Table 2-2) from 1 (A to B) to $1/4$ (D to E).

Obviously, increasing efficiency, tied to growth, is an important aspect of economic development. Nonetheless, for the society as a whole, with existing technology, moving resources from one activity or industry to another (moving along the PP curve) ultimately decreases efficiency. This is so because, beyond some point (and with given technology and resources), people use inputs that are less and less well adapted to the new employment. Thus the industry will ultimately experience increasing relative cost. People will have to sacrifice more and more of one good to obtain a greater output of another.

Figure 2-2
Production-Possibilities Curve, Shelby, 1995

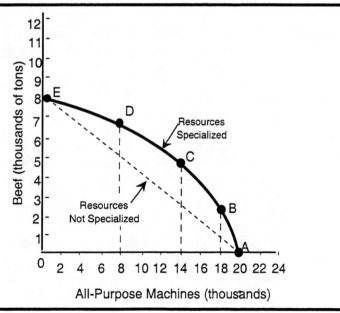

Mental Reservations

You may have some mental opposition to these working assumptions about scarcity and increasing relative cost and may ask why you should accept them. In your own experience with producing something or your reading of economic history, you may have observed the following cases: (1) Sometimes, as a production process is speeded up or modernized—that is, as more inputs are used—output increases more rapidly than input. Consider automobile production after 1914 and the emergence of the modern assembly line; (2) In the twentieth century, U.S. resources have become much more productive, thus shifting the PP curve. Actually, both these observations may be correct, and yet neither invalidates the law of increasing opportunity costs. The reasons why both factors above do *not* invalidate the concept of increasing opportunity costs are: (1) larger scale activities require new plants and equipment which can only be accomplished in a long run time frame *within* an industry not in terms of moving resources from one industry to another, and (2) most of the increase in resource productivity in the twentieth century has resulted from changes (improvements) in technology which are not incorporated into a particular production-possibility curve. Improving technology shifts the *entire* production-possibility curve to the right.

A Classical Explanation of Growth: Shifts in Production Possibilities

Consider case 1. Efficiency does increase as a result of specialization of resources and division of tasks, as markets expand and firms produce more and on a larger scale. This improvement of technique, which means more output from the same inputs, results in the shifting of the PP curve, not in movements along it. Economists have noted such growth in efficiency ever since Adam Smith, who published *The Wealth of Nations* in 1776. Smith wrote about a pin factory in England in which, as specialization increased, labor became much more productive and output increased accordingly, just as it has in twentieth-century automobile-assembly plants.

In the same way, steel output has increased. In the 1950s and 1960s the use of automation and improved techniques expanded greatly within the steel industry, resulting in increased production in the 1980s. Steel productivity throughout the world grew in the 1970s and 1980s as the result of new technology such as the oxygen process and continuous rolling mill. This has enabled the steel industry in the United States to prove that it was more than cost-competitive with foreign producers in the mid 1990s.

As for case 2, twentieth-century economic history does show this observation. Resources have indeed become much more productive since 1900. On the other hand, the static assumptions of the PP curve about fixed supplies of resources and given technology clearly do not hold true. Since 1900, the PP curve has shifted dramatically to the right. Except during depressions, especially that of the 1930s, the shifts have been fairly continuous. We can conclude from the assumptions of our production-possibilities model that the shifts have resulted from two factors:

1. Productivity has increased as a result of technological changes (new tools, new processes, and larger-scale activities). These changes have resulted, at least in part, from (a) increased economic integration, (b) market growth,

and (c) specialization and division of use of resources.

2. Amounts and varieties of resources have increased. Our producers today possess many resources not even considered potential inputs in 1900 (including a labor force that is much more productive, partly as a result of investment in education).

SUMMING UP

1. Throughout history, every society has had to find a way to answer the following questions: What goods and services will be produced? How shall they be produced? Who gets the goods and services once they are produced by society? Today the world has evolved three basic ways of answering these age-old questions - three types of economics systems (Feudalism, Capitalism, and Socialism).

2. Feudalism is a simple farm-based economic system where tradition and authoritarian command are the guiding forces. Feudalism was dominated by two forces - tradition and command state.

3. Capitalism is an economic system in which private property is emphasized. Economists mark the official start of capitalism as 1776 - the year Adam Smith published his famous book, The Wealth of Nations, which described the new economic system.

4. Socialism is an economic system in which property and the means of production are collectively owned or controlled. This economic system encompasses the idea that the government should play a major role in the production and distribution process.

5. What held society together, and why did capitalism function so effortlessly in the absence of tradition and iron fisted rule of the state that had created order in Feudalism? The answer Adam Smith (the first capitalist economist) reasoned was "self interest." This concept, he summarized in the Law of the market. It states that individuals interacting in a competitive market, would promote their own self-interest and in the process, promote the self interest of society as a whole.

6. Thomas Malthus in his book entitled - An Essay of teh Principles as it Affects the Future Improvement of Society - argued that population would grow at a rate that would always outpace production of food; thus, regardless of how efficient the economic system was, if population was not held in check, society would never advance beyond the subsistence level. This theory came to be known as the Malthusian theory.

7. Five basic characteristics of capitalism are maket efficiency, role of government and market failure, consumer sovereignty, self-interest, and private ownership.

8. Production is the process of converting resources into finished and useful goods. The factors of production and land and natural resources, labor or

human resources, capital and entrpreneurship.

9. Opportunity cost is the cost associated with the highest valued alternative you have to give up in order to obtain a good or service.

10. Production possibility function shows the combination of goods that a society's resources can produce at full employment in a particular period of time (using the best technology).

KEY TERMS

Capitalism
Consumer sovereignty
Efficient markets
Externalities
Factors of production
Fuedalism
Law of accumulation
Malthusian theory
Market economy
Market failure
Mixed system
Opportunity cost
Production possibilities function
Role of government
Self-interest
Socialism

QUESTIONS

1. Explain the economic questions that every society must answer. What three ways have the world evolved in answering these questions.

2. Describe the main characteristics of capitalism, mix capitalism, socialism, feudalism, and communism.

3. Explain why the law of accumulation is so important to the growth and prosperity of an economic system.

4. Explain the five major characteristics of capitalism.

5. What contributions did Thomas Malthus made to society. Explain the Malthusian theory. How does this theory relate to today's economy?

6. What contributions did Adam Smith made to society? Explain the "self-interest" theory. What did he mean by "the invisible hand" theory?

7. Use the production-possibility curve to ilustrate the concepts of scarcity and opportunity cost, and to explain why individuals and countries have to make choices.

8. What is the opportunity cost or real cost to the American economy of the present all-volunteer armed forces of the United States? Would it be lower with a return to the military draft?

SUGGESTED READINGS

Ahluwalia, M. S., N. Carter, and H. Chenery, "Growth and Poverty in Developing Countries," *Journal of Development Economics 6* (September 1979)

Easterlin, Richard, "Why Isn't the Whole World Developed?," *Journal of Economic History 61* (March 1981)

Gillis, Malcolm, Dwight Perkins, Michael Roemer, and Donald R. Snodgrass, *Economics of Development*, 2nd Ed. New York: W.W. Norton & Company, 1987

Hailstones Thomas and Frank Mastriana, *Contemporary Economic Problems and Issues*. Cincinnati: South-Western Publishing Co., 1988 (Chapters 12, 13, 14, and 15)

Hogendorn, Jan S., *Economic Development*, Second Edition. Harper Collins Publishers, 1992

Schnitzer, Martin C., *Contemporary Economic Systems*. Cincinnati: South-Western Publishing Co., 1987

Stein, Herbert. "Remembering Adam Smith." *Wall Street Journal*, March 21, 1994

Wilcox, Clair, Willis D. Weatherford, Jr., Holland Hunter, and Norton S. Baratz, *Economies of the World Today*. New York, Harcourt, Brace, Jovanovich, 1976

World Bank, *World Development Report 1992*

CHAPTER 3

Supply and Demand: The Market Economy

There are broad markets, thin markets, stable markets, big ones.
There are fish markets, flea markets, gem markets and then some;
Golf markets, money markets, flesh markets, gyrating ones;
Free markets, illegal markets, controlled markets, sloppy ones.
What a lot of markets there are!

OBJECTIVES

After studying this chapter you will be able to:

- Explain how supply and demand determine prices in a market economy. You will understand why water, a good that is critical to sustain life, is relatively cheap, and why those small crystals we call diamonds are so expensive.

- Use supply and demand to analyze and project future price trends. For example, if you invest $4,000 in a llama today, will the price go up in the future?

- Explain why it is better for society to have the market, and not governments, determine prices of the goods we buy.

- Understand why economists do not worry about the world running out of resources such as oil.

- Describe the determinants of supply and demand.

- Explain the difference between a change in demand and a change in the quantity demanded, and the difference between a change in supply and a change in the quantity supplied.

- Use supply and demand curves to illustrate problems and then to illustrate possible solutions.

- Have a working knowledge of the following terms and concepts:

Absolute and nominal price	Determinants of demand	Relative price
Ceteris paribus	Determinants of supply	Role of price
Change in demand	Giffen good	Shortage
Change in quantity demanded	Income effect	Substitute
Change in quantity supplied	Law of demand	Substitution effect
Change in supply	Law of supply	Supply and demand equilibrium
Complement	Market or equilibrium price	Supply curve
Demand curve	Normal good	Surplus
		Veblen good

Supply and Demand: The Market Economy

Price Determination in Competitive Markets

The operation of society necessarily involves making choices and these choices derive from three basic queries common to all societies: (1) *What* should be produced? (2) *How* should output be produced? (3) *For whom* should it be produced?

Let us now examine the means by which such choices—implicit in the production-possibilities curve—are made in a competitive private-enterprise system.

Economic reality is so complex that it cannot be described completely. What we can do, though, is establish principles and build models in order to draw analogies to reality. First we are going to set forth some building-block principles that will serve to explain a few things about a competitive market economy. Who is in control? Who or what sends out the signals that determine how we are going to use our resources?

Any economy, including one based on competition, is very complex. For the moment, we will not discuss the influence that big institutions—government, business, labor—have on making economic decisions. We will focus on competition and then, as we go along, add in the complexities introduced by big institutions and measure their effects by comparing them to the effects of competition.

What Is Competition?

Competition
The market form in which no buyer or seller has influence over the price at which the product is sold.

Price Rivalry
The contest in which sellers watch what prices others charge and then react to those prices.

A single word can have many different meanings. Take the word **competition**. If you think of competition as a contest between rivals (as the dictionary defines it), then it describes how the rivals interact. For economists, such a definition has two defects: (1) It is too general to use in analytical questions. (2) It contradicts real life, in which **price rivalry**—the contest in which sellers watch what prices others charge, and then react to those prices—*frequently is inversely related to the number of contestants*. If you are one seller among ten thousand others and you raise your prices, it affects the others little or not at all. If you are one seller among four and you raise your prices, the others may follow suit. Thus, for economists:

Competition *is the market form in which no individual buyer or seller has influence over the price at which the product is sold.*

Unorganized single buyers bid for the available goods, and this determines demand. Unorganized single sellers make offers to sell, and this determines supply. While we will have much more to say about competition in the microeconomics section of this book, this general definition will permit us to set forth some basic concepts of supply and demand.

How Are Prices Set? Supply And Demand

If no single seller can set prices and no single buyer can either, how do prices become set, and how are resources allocated in competitive markets? The answer is that there are two independent influences—supply and demand—that determine prices in a competitive market. Let's look at these two components separately.

DEMAND

Demand
A set of relationships showing the quantity of a good that consumers will buy at each of several prices within a specific period of time.

Demand is another word that has many meanings. For one thing, demand is not only a desire, but a desire plus the purchasing power to back up that desire. The newspapers may say that the demand for cars is expected to reach 11 million cars. A worried business executive may say that demand for the firm's product is "not good" or is "weak." Both of these statements mean something to the person making them. To economists, however, they lack one or both of the ingredients needed for analyzing markets: (1) the timing of the demand and (2) the range of prices for which the demand is expected to hold. The statement about automobile demand does not indicate the time period (this year) or the price range for which this estimate will hold. The worried executive, on the other hand, is summing up his or her judgment about the state of the market, rather than analyzing the general demand for the product. So let's define demand in a way that includes both necessary ingredients.

Demand *is a set of relationships showing the quantity of a good that consumers will buy at each of several prices within a specific period of time.*

Demand versus Need or Want

Demand is a very specific term. To have a demand for a product implies that you are capable of, and willing to, purchase an item within a range of prices (your demand schedule). You have a demand for Pepsi, so you go to the store and make the purchase. You might have a demand for Pepsi at the current range of prices, but if the price increased, the quantity demanded would decrease and at some point, as the price continued to rise, the quantity demanded might decrease to zero. Demand is not to be confused with words like *need* or *want*. These are vague terms that are not used by the economist. Most students want a 450 SL Mercedes, but probably few have a demand for one.

Determinants of Demand

What factors determine whether you will be in the market for Pepsi, that is, whether you have a demand for Pepsi, or any good? There are many *determinants of demand*, but the most important ones are summarized by TINPEA:

T	Tastes and preferences
I	Income
N	Number of people in market or population
P	Price of complements and price of substitutes
E	Expectations
A	Advertisement

Elaboration on TINPEA

T*astes and preferences*—If you think Pepsi tastes like a drain cleaner, does it matter what the price is? No, regardless of price, the quantity you demand will be zero. Tastes and preferences are general factors affecting demand that are strongly influenced by such diverse factors as family, gender, religion, peer group, age, etc.

I*ncome*—If your income and savings are $0, so is your demand. As your income changes, from the poverty level of a student, to $50,000+ of a young married couple (double income),   your demand for many products will also change.

N*umber of people in market or population*—The total market demand for a product is a reflection, to a large extent, of its population base. This is one reason so many businesses supported the NAFTA trade agreement—it expanded the population base from Canada through Mexico.

P*rice of complements and price of substitutes*—It is important to remember that *P* does not stand for the price of the product, but rather the price of substitutes and the price of complements. For example, when the price of eggs goes up this would cause the demand for bacon, a complement of eggs, to decrease (see Table 3-2).

E*xpectations*—The demand for a product is, to a large extent, based on our expectations of the product. Our expectations can be affected by any number of factors, from friends telling us of their experiences with the products, to reading about it in the paper, or seeing it advertised on television.

A*dvertisement*—The reasons why some producers spend huge sums of money on advertising their products is that it can greatly increase sales—increase the demand. General Foods spends more money advertising Cheerios than it spends on the production of the product. When advertising is successful, the result is a shift in the demand for the product. A shift in the demand for a product means that a new demand curve has been created. For example, General Foods is expecting to increase the demand for Cheerios by a new advertising campaign. If this campaign is successful, a greater quantity of Cheerios will be demanded at each possible price level. The top four cereal producers have raised their prices significantly over the last five years, and have been able to prevent sales from falling through the use of advertising.

Make sure you understand each of the determinants of demand and how they affect the demand for a product.

Let's take as an example a good that most people consider desirable: T-bone steak. What will be the quantity of T-bone steaks that you demand this year? You'll probably say, "That depends on what happens to the price of T-bones." Exactly! The price of a product—and changes in that price— are the main factors that determine how much of that product the public will buy. For example, an upswing in car sales followed the offer of price rebates by car manufacturers in 1988.

Of course, there are other factors that influence an individual's demand as we have seen earlier. For our example, we will consider the following:

1. Income of buyers.

2. Tastes and preferences of buyers.

3. Prices of other products, both **complements** (products used in conjunction with T-bone steaks, such as potatoes) and **substitutes** (products used in place of T-bone steaks, such as fish or chicken).

4. Consumers' expectations about future prices and market conditions.

Complements
Products used in conjunction with each other.

Substitutes
Products that may be consumed in place of each other.

These factors determine how many T-bones you or any other individual will buy or numbers bought by all buyers, within any given price range. So when you say that your demand for T-bones depends on what happens to the price, you are saying that this is true for your present income and tastes, given prices of other products and given your expectations about future prices and market conditions. In addition, there is a fifth factor that influences the total or market demand for a product, or for all products. That factor is *population*, or the number of consumers. (Remember that a problem of underdeveloped countries is that some have such small populations that there is inadequate demand to justify large-scale industries.) Let's hold these factors (income, tastes, other prices, and expectations) constant and establish demand for T-bone steaks in terms of the relationship solely between their price and quantity demanded. This amounts to the same thing as holding certain variables constant and permitting a *key* variable to change. This is called the **ceteris paribus** ("other things being equal") condition. It is an assumption that is common to much economic analysis, and in fact to analysis in other fields, too.

Ceteris Paribus
The "other things being equal" assumption that involves holding other factors constant while permitting a key variable to change.

An Individual Demand Curve

Let's take a week as the time period for which we're going to analyze your demand for T-bone steaks. Table 3-1 is a demand schedule which shows the number you will buy at various prices (holding constant your income, tastes, prices of other products, and your expectations about the future).

What do these data on demand tell us?

Table 3-1
Individual Demand Schedule for T-bone Steaks

Price Per Pound	Quantity Bought Per Week
$5.00	0
4.50	1
4.00	2
3.50	3
3.00	4
2.50	5
2.00	6
1.50	7

1. The quantity of T-bones you buy increases as the price falls and decreases as the price rises.

2. There is a price ($5.00) above which you will buy no T-bones; in other words, above that price you will be excluded from this market (or you will exclude yourself).

Now we are ready to transform the numbers of Table 3-1 into a more usable form, a **demand curve.** The first step in creating a graph from a demand schedule is to label the vertical axis as the price line and the horizontal axis as the quantity line. (In economics, prices are always put on the vertical axis and quantity is on the horizontal axis.)

The second step is to plot the demand data. Point A of Figure 3-1 represents two pieces of information - a price of $4.50 and a quantity of 1 unit. Point B represents $4.00 and a quantity of 2 units. After putting in points C, D, E, F, and G, you are ready for the fun part of graphing - going "dot to dot" and completing the demand curve of Figure 3-1. It should look like Figure 3-2.

Figure 3-1
Plot of Data in Table 3-1 (Practice graphing the supply data in Table 3-1.)

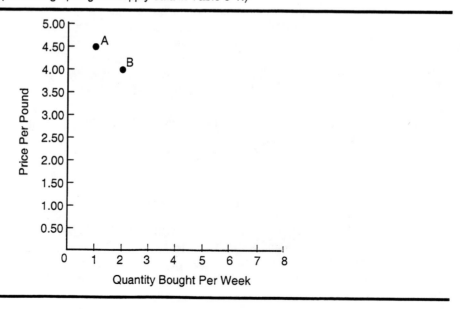

Now it's your turn. Draw a demand curve based on the information in the demand schedule of the table below.

Demand Schedule	
Price of T-shirts	Quantity demanded
$10.00	22
9.00	34
8.00	43
7.00	54
6.00	71

Demand Curve

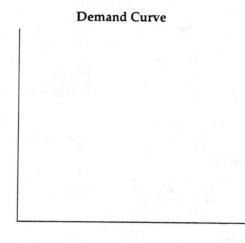

Demand Schedule
Indicates the quantity demanded at each of several prices.

Demand Curve
Represents that schedule when plotted on a two dimensional graph.

When we plot the **demand schedule** in Table 3-1, we obtain the **demand curve** shown in Figure 3-2, which shows price on the vertical axis and quantity on the horizontal axis. (Remember that economists call a diagonal line of this sort a curve, even though it is a straight line.)

Point A (price = $4.50, quantity = 0) is the upper limit to your demand. For you, $5.00 is the price at which (or above which) you will stop buying. Point B represents two T-bone steaks per week (price, $4.00); and point G, seven T-bone steaks (price, $1.50). As price falls, quantity demanded increases.

Figure 3-2
Demand Curve for T-bone Steaks

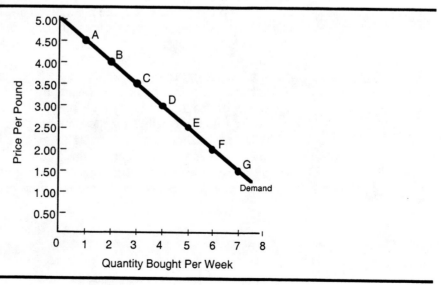

Law of Demand
Consumers buy more of a product at (relatively) low prices than at (relatively) high prices (ceteris paribus).

Income Effect
The change in quantity demanded of a good due to a change in real income caused by a change in the price of a good.

Substitution Effect
The change in quantity demanded of a good as its relative price changes and it becomes relatively less or more expensive leading to its substitution.

Veblen Goods
As the price increases, the quantity demanded also increases.

The fact that demand curve D in Figure 3-1 slopes down or to the right reflects the **law of demand**. *Consumers buy more at relatively low prices than at relatively high prices* (ceteris paribus). There are two reasons why:

1. As the price of a good falls, the purchasing power of your income increases, which ordinarily causes you to buy more of that good (the **income effect**). As the price of the good rises, your purchasing power declines, which ordinarily causes you to buy less of the good.

2. As the price of a good falls (other prices being unchanged), the good becomes relatively cheaper than other goods and you substitute the good for other, now more expensive, goods (the **substitution effect**). As the price of the good rises, you substitute other, now less expensive, goods for the one in question.

Each effect tends to reinforce the other. Under normal conditions, both tend to cause consumers to demand a greater quantity of a desirable good as its price goes down.

Veblen Goods and Giffen Goods— Two Exceptions to the Law of Demand

Veblen Goods
Consumers sometimes value a good just *because* it is expensive and because people with high social status consume it. This may sound crazy, but it is true for a limited number of products. If, for instance, Beluga caviar or imported perfumes sold for $1.00 a quart, people might not believe they were worth much. These goods could after all be bought by the masses. Such goods, which some people buy more of at a higher price than at a lower price, are called **Veblen goods**, after Thorstein Veblen (1857–1929), an American economist who wrote a stinging analysis of the motives behind the consumption habits of rich people. (Veblen's *The Theory of the Leisure Class* caused a sensation when it was published in 1899.) The demand curve for a Veblen good slopes up to the right. (This is an exception to the law of demand.)

Buying more of a product as its price increases might seem like weird behavior, but conspicuous consumption, if we're all honest, is not just a disease of the rich. Most of us buy a variety of items not for their utilitarian value, but rather for the statement they make. In the inner city, $200.00 tennis shoes are a popular form of conspicuous consumption. Meanwhile in suburban America, the forms of conspicuous consumption seem endless, from the expensive car to the size and location of your house. Remember, Veblen goods are minor exceptions to the law of demand.

THORSTEIN VEBLEN (1857–1929)

Economists always refer to the role of rationality in economic decisions, based on the idea that buyers will tend to spend limited incomes in the manner calculated to get the maximum of utility from the purchase. Thorstein Veblen looked at this assumption and came to the conclusion that psychological and social factors played as important a role in economic decisions as economic rationality.

Born in a farm community (Cato Township, Wisconsin) of Norwegian born parents, Veblen developed a mistrust of the accepted economic "laws" of his day. His education at Johns Hopkins, Cornell, and Yale, where he earned a Ph.D. in 1884, brought out his then unique perspective which gave relevance to the importance of society's culture and institutions in economic analysis.

His major work is *The Theory of the Leisure Class* (1899) in which he asserted that people at the upper end of the income spectrum set the consumption standards that lower economic levels tend to emulate. Further, he wrote, the economic elite are strongly motivated to display their affluence by conspicuous indication of their purchasing power by buying and displaying expensive and ostentatious items.

"Conspicuous consumption of valuable goods is a means of reputability to the gentlemen of leisure," wrote Veblen, thereby coining the purchase, "conspicuous consumption," which has entered the English language. The high income group ("the leisure class") spends its money conspicuously largely in order to call attention to its ability to indulge in lavish spending. It is then copied by lower level groups to the extent that they can afford at least some conspicuous purchasing ("the bandwagon effect").

In economic terms, Veblen expanded the concept of utility (the enjoyment or pleasure we get from consumption). Utility, he pointed out, comes from psychological satisfaction as well as from satisfaction in use; evidence of wealth is itself a source of utility.

Giffen Goods

Giffen Goods
Goods that consumers buy less of as the price of the good decreases.

Sometimes people have to spend a large part of their income on certain inexpensive goods simply because they have low incomes that permit them few choices. For example, basic food staples such as rice in some low-income countries, or corn, wheat, or potatoes in other parts of the world (including low-income areas of the U.S.). If the price of one of these staples falls, consumers have considerably more purchasing power and the income effect becomes potentially more important than the substitution effect (you can only consume so many potatoes, regardless of price.) If the price of rice falls in India, the income effect may move in the same direction as price, because people may spend less on rice and spend their newly freed purchasing power on milk, meat, and other high-protein foods and thus consumed less rice. Conversely, when rice goes up in price, because people have to spend more on rice, they have to do without the diversified diet. Goods with an income effect that moves in the same direction as price and outweighs the substitution effect—that is, goods that people buy less of as their price falls—are called **Giffen goods**, after Sir Robert Giffen, a 19th-century English economist.

Normal Goods versus Inferior Goods

Veblen and giffen goods are two odd exceptions to the law of demand. Most goods and services are classified as **normal goods**.

Normal Goods
As your income increases, so does your consumption of this good.

Inferior Goods
As your income increases, your consumption decreases.

Normal goods are products for which demand increases as your income increases. The demand for restaurant meals, cars, and theater tickets are examples of normal goods. As your income increases, you will normally buy more of these goods, even though the price of these goods remain constant. **Inferior goods** are the opposite of normal goods. The demand for inferior goods decreases as your income increases. Examples of inferior goods are powered milk, generic beer, Laundromats, bus rides, and hamburger helper. Remember, normal goods and inferior goods are goods for which demand changes as income changes. Veblen and Giffen goods are goods for which the quantity demanded changes in the same direction as the price of the good—as the price increases, so does the quantity demanded. Veblen and Giffen goods are examples of exceptions to the law of demand.

Changes in Quantity Demanded Versus Changes in Demand

Change in Quantity Demanded
A movement along a good's demand curve that can be caused only by a change in the price of that good.

Change in Demand
A shift of a good's demand curve that may be caused by a change in any factor other than the price of that good.

So far, we have been talking about a single demand curve, a curve charting the demand schedule for a desirable good and showing that *movements along* that curve are the result of changes in the price of that good. The only thing that can cause a **change in quantity demanded** (such as A to B in Figure 3-3), therefore, is a change in the price of the good. Remember that we are holding four factors constant: income, tastes of the consumer, prices of other goods, and the consumer's expectations of the future (plus population, for total demand). If even one of these factors changes, the entire demand curve will *shift*. There will be a **change in demand** itself (such as B to C in Figure 3-3).

Figure 3-3
Demand for T-Bone Steaks

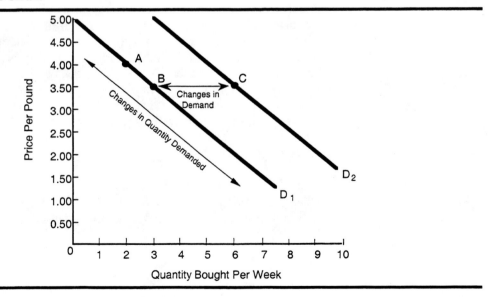

But people's incomes and tastes often do change, and so do the other factors. If we are to analyze the operations of markets and the pricing of goods and services, we must account for variations in these aspects, in addition to variations in price. Figure 3-3 shows the difference between a change in quantity demanded and a change in demand. The movement from A to B along demand curve D_1 (caused solely by a reduction in price from $4.00 to $3.50) is called a *change in quantity demanded*. The movement from B to C is from demand curves D_1 to D_2 and may be caused by a change in consumers' incomes or tastes, prices of other goods, or consumers' expectations for the future (or all of these). This movement involves a shift in the entire demand schedule.

First let's see what effect a change in income will have on changing demand. In Figure 3-3, D_1 is a curve showing your original demand for T-bone steaks. All points on it represent the original price-quantity relations. Now suppose you receive a raise in pay. Since we are assuming that T-bone steaks are a good you want, your demand curve will shift to D_2. Now that you have more income, you buy approximately three more steaks per week, at any price per pound between $1.50 and $5.00. Of course, if you were to have a pay cut, your demand curve would shift to the left as your income decreased. If we now take your income increase away, we expect that you will buy approximately three fewer steaks per week. In other words, your demand curve will shift back to D_1—unless, at the same time, your tastes or your expectations of the future, or the prices of other goods, change to offset the decrease in income.

Change in Other Prices. Suppose that the price of chicken doubles. Since T-bone steaks and chicken are to some extent substitutes for each other, your demand for the now relatively cheaper T-bone steaks will increase, perhaps to D_2. But if the price of chicken falls, your demand for the now relatively more expensive T-bones will decrease, perhaps from D_2 to D_1. The same thing might happen if potatoes suddenly went up to $2.00 per pound: since potatoes are a complement to steak, you might consume less steak along with fewer potatoes.

Change in Tastes. Suppose that your demand for T-bone steaks is at D_2 and you develop a yen for pizza, which weakens your taste for T-bones. Your demand for T-bones will shift to the left (perhaps to D_1).

Changes in Expectations About Future Prices. Suppose that you read in the newspaper that there is a failure in the grain crop and that there will soon be big increases in the price of steak because of a jump in the price of feed grains. Your demand curve for T-bones may shift to the right (you may decide to buy a dozen steaks and freeze them). In other words, D_1 is your demand curve only as long as your current expectations about prices remain the same.

Demand: Summing Up

There are four main things to remember about demand:

1. Demand curves slope downward, to the right. In other words, consumers buy more of a good at (relatively) lower prices than they buy at (relatively) higher prices (the *law of demand*).

2. Only changes in the price of a good can cause changes in the *quantity*

demanded of that good. Such changes result in *movements along* a demand curve.

3. The only demand factor that *cannot* cause a change in the demand for a good is a change in its own price.

4. Factors that may singly or jointly change the demand for a good are changes in income or tastes, changes in prices of other commodities, and changes in expectations about the future. These factors shift the entire demand curve and result in *changes in demand*.

Market Demand

So far, we have looked only at one person's demand. But competitive markets are made up of many unorganized buyers expressing their individual demands. How, theoretically, do we figure the total market demand? We must add up the demand schedules of many individuals, assuming that there are no interdependencies of demand, such as a desire to keep up with the Joneses.

Figure 3-4 illustrates the principle involved, since it shows the sum of your and my demand curves at each price, which gives a picture of market demand. My demand schedule is plotted from the same kind of data as in Table 3-1. Thus, when T-bone steaks are selling at $4.00 a pound, you buy three and I buy two. Let's assume for simplicity that we are the only two consumers who are buying them. Market demand at this price is then five T-bones per week. Similarly, when T-bones are selling at $2.00 a pound, you demand six per week and I demand five, making market demand eleven T-bones per week.

Figure 3-4
Market Demand for T-Bone Steaks

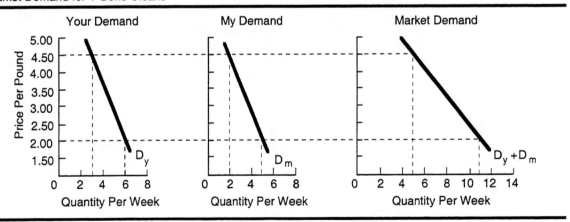

Here are some general things to remember about market demand:

1. People's demand curves are not the same, since individuals have different incomes, tastes, and expectations for the future.

2. Market demand curves, like the demand curves of individuals, slope downward or to the right, since they derive their slope from the slopes of the demand curves of individuals. Of course, the market demand curve represents a larger quantity of a given thing, because many people buy more than one person does.

3. *Number of buyers* (market population) is a determinant of market demand. As the number of buyers increases, so does demand.

SUPPLY

There are two sides to a market: demand and supply. We will now turn from the demand side to the supply side. Consumers who demand the output that the firm produces have a goal to maximize their satisfaction. Likewise, the firms who supply these products seek to maximize their profits. More on these will be discussed in the microeconomic section.

What Is Supply?

Supply
The set of relationships showing the quantity of a product that a firm will offer for sale at each of several prices within a specific period of time.

Supply *is the set of relationships showing the quantity of a product that a firm will offer for sale at each of several prices within a specific period of time.*

We set up the picture of the supply situation on the assumption that certain other factors are constant or unchanged—the *ceteris paribus* or other-things-being-equal assumption mentioned earlier.

Determinants of Supply—TIPET

There are five major determinants of supply. A change in any one of these determinants will result in a shift in the supply curve. **Remember**, a shift in the curve means a different quantity is being supplied at every price. TIPET, the determinants of supply, are the counterpart of TINPEA, the determinants of demand.

Technology—A supply curve is drawn assuming a certain level of technology. When better technology becomes available, the curve moves to the right. An increase in this technology normally means that the producer becomes more efficient, or more productive, at a lower per unit cost. This results in more profits, thus more production. With the discovery of the cotton gin, the supply of cotton textiles increased—the supply curve shifted to the right.
Input prices or resources—When we draw a supply curve, we assume that resource prices are constant. If the price of cotton falls, the supply curve for blue jeans will increase, as it is now more profitable to produce blue jeans.

Price expectations—If producers anticipate that prices for the product they are selling will be higher in the near future, they will probably increase inventories and decrease the amount available to consumers today. Oil producers expected a decontrolling of domestic oil prices in 1974, therefore they capped some of their wells in anticipation of being able to sell oil at higher prices in the near future. The supply curve for oil moved to the left.

Entry and exit of firms—As the number of firms in the industry decreases, the supply curve for the industry will move to the left.

Taxes and subsidies—If the government imposes a tax, such as the sales tax, the supply curve will decrease or shift to the left. Subsidies result in increased production—a shift to the right of the supply curve. When the government paid a subsidy to farmers for planting cotton, the production of cotton increased dramatically. Large amounts of cotton were even planted in southern California, in very arid lands that normally would never support such a thirsty crop.

In addition, the *number of firms* in the industry will affect total or market supply.

Who is the source of supply? In our competitive market, many relatively small firms do the supplying. Enough firms participate in the market so that no one firm can influence the price of a good in the market as a whole.

Law of Supply
A firm will offer more for sale at (relatively) higher prices than at (relatively) lower prices (ceteris paribus).

To illustrate, let's go back to T-bone steaks. Table 3-2, the supply schedule of the ABC Meat Market, sums up the quantities supplied at each price for T-bone steaks. See what happens to quantity as price goes down. The firm offers more for sale at (relatively) high prices than at (relatively) low prices (the **law of supply**).

Table 3-2
ABC Meat Market: Supply Schedule of T-bone Steaks

Price Per Pound	Quantity Supplied Per Week
$5.00	60
4.50	50
4.00	40
3.50	30
3.00	20
2.50	10
2.00	0
1.50	0

Supply Curve

Now that you know how to graph a demand curve, graphing a supply curve should be easy. But just to be safe, let's go through it once again. Let's start by transferring the supply schedule information of Table 3-2 to the graph of Figure 3-5. Point A represents a willingness on the part of ABC Meat Market to supply sixty pounds per week when the price is $5.00, point B represents 50 pounds supplied at $4.50 per pound. Figure 3-5 is a plot of all the data of Table 3-2. Connect the dots of Figure 3-5 to complete the graphing of the supply schedule of Table 3-2.

Supply Curve
Represents a firm's or industry's supply schedule plotted on a two dimensional graph.

The **supply curve** of a firm or industry shows the relationships between the various prices of a product and the quantities of it the firm or industry offers for sale. A change in the price of a product is the only thing that can cause a change in the quantity supplied. Such changes are reflected in movements along the supply curve, as shown by the arrows parallel to S in Figure 3-6, which shows the relationship between price per pound and quantity supplied. Note that the supply curve goes up, to the right. The vertical bar at the upper right of the graph means that a given firm—here the ABC Meat Market—eventually reaches its capacity, it runs out of storage space, counter space, or sales clerks to sell all those steaks. In other words, after a certain maximum is reached, it becomes impossible for the supplier to supply any more.

Changes in Quantity Supplied
Movements along a supply curve that are caused only by changes in the price of that product.

Suppose that the price of T-bone steaks goes up from $3.00 to $3.50 per pound. The ABC Meat Market will increase the quantity it supplies from twenty to thirty T-bone steaks per week. All such price changes are reflected in movements along a given supply curve, and are called **changes in quantity supplied**.

Figure 3-5
Supply Curve (Practice graphing the supply data in Table 3-2.)

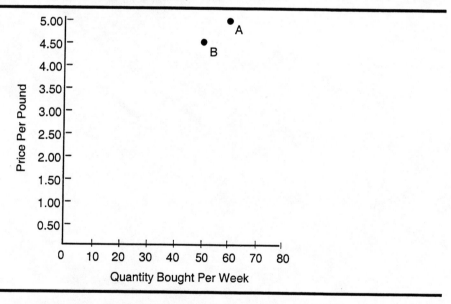

Changes in Supply
Shifts in a supply curve that may be caused by changes in any factor affecting supply other than a change in the price of that good.

What happens when there is a change in one or more of those "other factors" we mentioned? An improvement in the technique of production (a new meat-slicing machine), a lower resource price (price of feed grains goes down), a change in the firm's expectation (a rumor that meat prices may go down), or a change in price of other goods (a drop in the price of chickens)—all these factors, or just one of them, can cause the *entire* supply curve to shift. For example, in Figure 3-6, the movement from F to G reflects an increase in supply from level S to level S_1. Such shifts are called **changes in supply**.

What Do Supply Data and the Supply Curve Tell Us?

1. The number of steaks supplied per week rises as price rises and falls as price falls (the *law of supply*).

2. There is a price below which the firm will supply *nothing*. Reason: The firm that seeks to maximize profit likewise seeks to minimize losses. It will produce nothing if it cannot make a profit, or at least cover production expenses that cease if it ceases to produce. (More about this in the microeconomics section.)

3. Although, for a given firm with given physical facilities, the number of steaks supplied rises as the price rises, the number of steaks finally reaches a maximum, because the firm reaches its capacity.

Why Do Supply Curves Slope Upward?

There are two easily identifiable reasons why an individual firm's supply curve—unlike its demand curve—slopes upward or to the

Figure 3-6
ABC Meat Market: Supply Curve

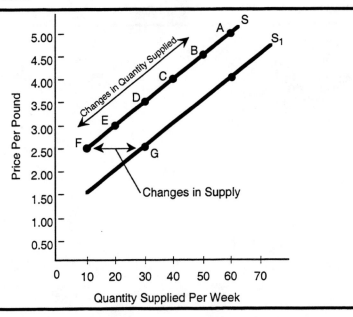

right. 1. A firm's resources can be used to produce more than one good. If, for instance, the price of beef increases (ceteris paribus), it becomes relatively more profitable to use resources to produce beef than to devote those resources to some other product such as pork. 2. The reverse occurs with price decreases; as a good's price falls, relative profitability declines and the firm reduces quantity supplied and shifts resources to other products. In addition, a firm producing larger rates of output will ultimately experience decreasing efficiency as it utilizes existing plant and equipment more intensively (the effect of bottlenecks, and the like).

Market Supply
The quantity supplied by
all firms in a market at
each of several prices.

Market supply or the supply curve of an industry is obtained by adding the supply curves of individual firms, and also slopes upward. An additional reason for variations in quantities supplied is that firms have *different* costs of production. As product price falls, those with higher costs may stop offering it for sale at all (industry quantity supplied will decrease). As the price rises, such firms will again offer it for sale (industry quantity supplied will increase).

Why Do Supply Curves Shift?

The factors discussed above explain why a firm or industry will have an upward sloping supply curve and also what *can cause a shift in supply or, in other words, cause supply to increase.* Quantity-supplied changes (such as the movement from E to F in Figure 3-6) vary directly with price. What, though, causes changes in supply, such as the shift from S to S_1 (such as the movement from F to G) in Figure 3-6? The factors that can cause such shift are:

1. *Improvements in Technology.* Technological changes increase productivity and reduce cost. Firms find it profitable to offer more of a product for sale at each price as a result.

2. *Reductions in factor prices.* As factor (labor, capital, land) prices fall, costs of firms are lowered and, again, firms find it profitable to offer more of a product for sale at each price.

3. *Changes in the prices of other products.* These prices determine the opportunity costs of a firm's resources. If the price of alternative product falls, the opportunity costs to ABC Meat Market decrease and cause the firm to offer more meat for sale at each price.

4. *Changes in price expectations.* If a firm expects its prices to fall in the future, it will offer more for sale at each present price. The reverse occurs for expected future price increases.

5. *Changes in the number of firms in an industry.* Industry or market supply, unlike the firm supply in Figure 3-6, also depends on the number of firms. As new firms enter an industry, industry supply grows; as firms exit the industry, industry supply decreases or shifts to the left.

Adding Up To Market Supply

We can chart supply the same way we chart demand. Figure 3-7 shows the process of adding up, or *aggregation*.

For simplicity, we have assumed that there are only two firms operating in the market. But the adding-up process is the same, even if there are thousands of firms. When steak is selling at $3.00, the ABC Meat Market will supply twenty steaks per week and the XYZ Meat Market will supply ten. Total market quantity supplied at this price is thirty per week. At $4.00 per pound, ABC will supply forty per week and XYZ thirty; total market quantity supplied at this price is seven per week.

The market supply curve takes its shape from the curves of the individual firms, so it slopes upward to the right. Remember that the number of firms helps to determine market supply. Naturally, more firms make a greater supply.

Before we go any further, let us sum up the distinctions between *movements along* demand and supply curves and *shifts in* them.

Summing Up: Difference Between Movements Along and Shifts In Demand and Supply Curves

1. The only thing that can cause a *movement along* the demand curve for a product is a change in price of that product. Such movements are called changes in *quantity demanded.*

2. Factors that can cause a *change in demand* or *shift in* an individual's demand curve for a product are things other than the price of that product: (a) changes in consumers' incomes, (b) changes in prices of other products, (c) changes in consumers' tastes, and (d) changes in consumers' expectations about future prices.

Figure 3-7
Market Supply of T-bone Steaks

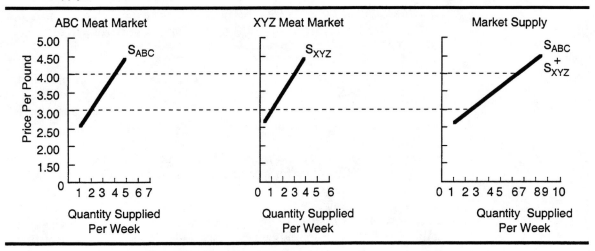

3. The only thing that can cause a *movement along* the supply curve for a product is a change in the price of that product. Such movements are called changes in *quantity supplied.*

4. Factors that can cause a *change in supply* or *shift in* an individual firm's supply curve for a product are things other than the price of that product: (a) changes in techniques of production, (b) changes in prices of other products, (c) changes in prices of inputs or resources, and (d) changes in firms' expectations about future prices and market conditions.

5. Changes in the number of consumers can also cause changes in market demand. Changes in the number of firms can also cause changes in market supply.

EQUILIBRIUM PRICING

Now let's return to our original question: How is the price of T-bone steaks, or of any product, determined? The answer is that their price tends toward an equilibrium price, one that clears the market.

Equilibrium Price
The price at which quantity demanded equals quantity supplied. It is a market-clearing price.

An **equilibrium price** or market clearing price is the price at which the quantity demanded is equal to the quantity supplied. It is the price that tends to prevail unless the factors (supply and demand) operating in the market change.

Let's see how such an equilibrium price comes into being in a competitive market through the joint influences of supply and demand. Table 3-3, shows price versus demand and supply for our minimarket, which—just to keep things simple—consists of only two consumers and two meat markets.

Table 3-3 shows that the equilibrium price—the price that prevails in this market—is $3.60 per pound. It is at this price that quantity demanded equals quantity supplied, or the market is cleared. Because it is sometimes easier to understand relationships visually, Figure 3-8 shows these demand and supply schedules combined on the same graph. (D represents columns (1) and (2) in Table 3-3, while S represents columns (1) and (3).)

As you can see, $3.60 is the equilibrium price—the price that clears this competitive market. This is so because any other price would create either shortages or surpluses.

Table 3-3
Market Demand and Supply Schedules for T-bone Steaks

Price Per Pound	Quantity Demanded Per Week	Quantity Supplied Per Week
$5.00	0	9
4.80	1	9
4.20	3	7
3.60	5 = Equilibrium =	5
3.00	7	3
2.40	9	2
1.80	11	1
1.20	13	0

Excess Demand
The amount consumers are unable to obtain of a good at a non-equilibrium price.

Suppose that for a while one of the meat markets cuts its price to $2.40 per pound. From Figure 3-8, we can see that the consumers would like to buy nine steaks per week at that price, while the firms would supply only two. The difference—seven steaks—is **excess demand**; or, from the consumer's point of view, a shortage of steaks. (Other examples of excess demand are long lines of drivers waiting for gas when a small gas station offers gas at cut-rate prices and the rush to get cheap balcony seats for a concert.)

Since the demand curve (D) reflects consumers' tastes, incomes, and the like, it indicates that the consumers are willing to pay more than $2.40 to obtain more than those two steaks they can buy at that price. As the consumers offer to pay more, the meat markets offer more steaks for sale. Only when steaks sell for $3.60 per pound is there no difference between the two sets of interests, quantity supplied and quantity demanded. Neither of the consumers is willing to pay more than $3.60 to buy the additional steaks that the meat markets would supply if the price were higher.

Figure 3-8
Market Demand and Supply: Equilibrium Pricing of T-bone Steaks

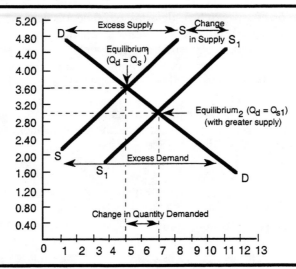

Excess Supply
The quantity of a good firms are unable to sell at a non-equilibrium price.

What's the matter with prices higher than $3.60? At a price of $4.80, the meat markets will gladly supply nine steaks per week. But at that price, one consumer will not buy *any* steaks, and the other consumer will buy only *one*. The difference—eight steaks—is **excess supply** or the quantity of a good firms are unable to sell at a non-equilibrium price. In order to sell steaks and clear the market, the meat markets lower their prices until the market is cleared at $3.60. (Other examples of excess supply are new cars left on the showroom floor after a price increase and new textbooks left on a bookstore's shelves after a price hike.)

Equilibrium at a price of $3.60 lasts as long as the set of forces defining supply and demand holds. If supply changes, as in the shift to S_1 (more supplied at all prices), a new market-clearing price (or equilibrium price) comes into being, in this instance at $3.00, where $Q_d = Q_{s_1}$.

Note that a *change in supply cannot cause a change in demand, and a change in demand cannot cause a change in supply.* In a competitive market, demand and supply are independent of each other. Thus, a change in the supply from S to S_1 results in a change in quantity demanded (see the bottom of Figure 3-8 between 5 and 7 on the horizontal axis).

It follows that (1) any change in supply or demand changes price, (2) any change in supply changes the quantity demanded, and (3) any change in demand changes the quantity supplied. The only exception occurs when equal and offsetting changes (either increases or decreases) of supply and demand occur simultaneously. We see this illustrated in Figure 3-9.

In Figure 3-9, the competitive market initially tends toward price $\overline{P}_E$ with demand, D_1 and supply, S_1. A market-clearing equilibrium quantity of Q_e is established and there is neither excess demand nor excess supply. If there are equal increases in both demand (D_1 to D_2) and supply (S_1 to S_2), there is a larger market with equilibrium quantity increasing from Q_e to Q_e' but the equilibriating price remains $\overline{P}_E$. The reverse can happen with a declining market size. Had demand and supply both decreased (D_2 to D_1, S_2 to S_1), the equilibrium quantity would have fallen (Q_e' to Q_e) but the equilibriating price would have remained $\overline{P}_E$.

Figure 3-9
Competitive Market Equilibrium With Equal Changes in Supply and Demand

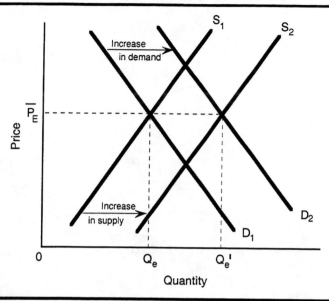

In Figure 3-9, the initial market equilibrium with demand, D_1, and supply, S_1, is with price, $\overline{P}_E$ and quantity, Q_e. When demand increases to D_2 and there is a proportional increase in supply to S_2, equilibrium price remainse $\overline{P}_E$ and equilibrium quantity increases to Q_e'.

Conditions for Competitive Pricing

Let us summarize the conditions that are necessary for competitive pricing to exist.

1. *Completely flexible prices.* If the government (or some other agency) had set the price of meat at $2.40, there would have been excess or unsatisfied demand. Black markets might have developed—as they did during World War II—to fill this unsatisfied demand at unregulated prices. In the following application, we will see the effect of inflexible prices in the case of price ceilings established by rent control laws.

2. *Full information.* In order for prices to be bid up or down to equilibrium, buyers and sellers obviously need to be aware of their alternatives, such as other prices.

3. *Expectation of constant prices.* If consumers think that today's $1.80 price will come down to $1.50 tomorrow, they may not buy any steak today. If producers think the same way, they may want to supply more steaks today than they would have otherwise.

4. *Free entry to and exit from markets.* Both buyers and sellers must be free to participate in the market or withdraw from it. In other words, there must be complete mobility of resources.

5. *Maximization of satisfaction and profits.* Buyers and sellers seek to maximize their satisfaction or profits, respectively, and always act to do so.

6. *Absence of collusion.* There must be no collusion between single buyers

or sellers or between groups of buyers and sellers. Otherwise, prices might be pegged rather than being competitively flexible.

Figure 3-10
Examples of Supply and Demand Shifts for Product X

A. DEMAND SHIFTS

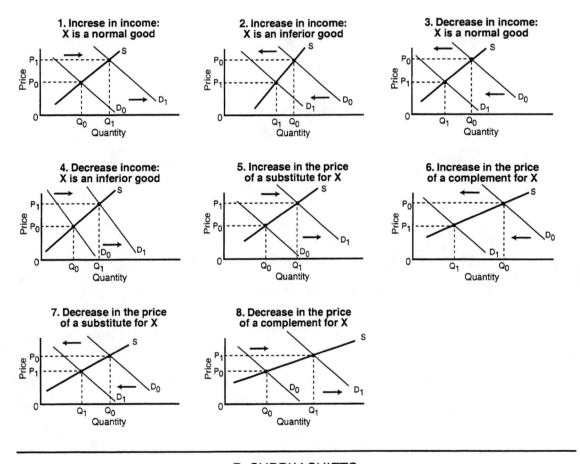

B. SUPPLY SHIFTS

APPLICATION:
Should We Let Supply and Demand Work?
Rent Controls and the Price of Housing

Friend and foe alike concede that market prices can be efficient devices for bringing the interests of buyers and sellers together and, ultimately, for making the two sets of interests consistent. The alternative in a world of scarcity, where resources must be allocated and products and services rationed, is for someone to set prices. The someone is *usually* (but not always) government.

We may presume that governments intentionally set prices at non-equilibrium, non-market clearing levels. There is no reason for governments to intervene in determining prices (other than an ideological reason) if prices are set at the same level as markets would tend to establish. As we have seen, actual prices can be above or below equilibrium levels and tend, *in free markets*, to create self-correcting responses to either excess demand (shortages) or excess supply (surpluses).

There are many examples of government intervention in price determination in the history of the United States. Indeed, such controls go back as far as the American revolution. Sometimes, as in that instance, these controls have occurred during periods of grave crisis and have consisted of direct establishment of "ceiling" prices. Such ceilings, for example, were created for many products (sugar, flour, gasoline, etc.) during World War II by the Office of Price Administration (O.P.A.). At times, intervention has taken the form of "floors" or efforts to keep prices from moving below pre-established levels or targets. Since 1929, the federal government has established target prices for a broad range of agricultural products (wheat, corn, tobacco, etc.) and has undertaken various activities to achieve those prices.

Government Determined Prices: The Arguments

Throughout history, governments have expressed their dissatisfaction with prices established in markets by either setting prices directly or by mandating the limits within which prices are permitted to (legally) move. As we indicated above, this has happened even in private enterprise economies such as that of the United States. What is the main non-ideological argument for this kind of activity? Generally, governments, whether local or national, have assumed authority over prices because of concern that markets would price and ration goods in a manner that is "unfair" or "inequitable." Concern, in other words, is over the availability of the good at the market price or over the effect on real income distribution of buying (or selling) it at that price. Here, let's concentrate on concerns of public officials that market prices will be "too high," and, as a result, decide to impose price ceilings. For the sake of specific illustration, we will focus on the price of housing and efforts especially at local government levels, to impose rent controls. Such laws have been enacted in many American cities and the question about them is not *whether* they work; rather, it is *how* do they work, *who* do they benefit, and *who* bears their costs. The question is especially meaningful given the numbers of people who can neither find nor afford housing and who show up in the data on homeless persons as the economy continues into the late 1990s.

Are Rent Controls Effective? (The Best Case)

Since we argued that there is always scarcity or, in other words, "no free lunch," you might suppose that the above question is needless. While that may be true, answering the question does illustrate the futility of trying to make resource allocation decisions without incurring opportunity costs.

In Figure 3-11, we see a hypothetical example of the imposition of rent controls in a situation in which the supply of

Figure 3-11
Rent Controls When the Housing Supply is Fixed

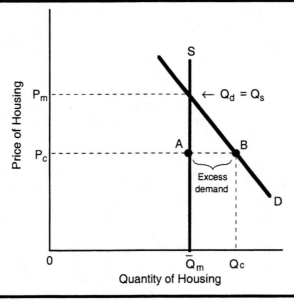

In Figure 3-11, the demand for housing (D) is downward sloping while the fixed supply of housing (S) is represented by a vertical line (from $\bar{Q}_m$) parallel to the axis on which the price of housing is measured. A market equilibrium price would tend to be established at P_m where the quantity demanded of housing equals the quantity supplied of housing or $\bar{Q}_m$. If government sets a price below equilibrium such as P_c (ceiling price), the equilibrium will still be at $\bar{Q}_m$ but there will be excess demand of $Q_c - \bar{Q}_m$ or AB.

housing (S) is $\bar{Q}_m$ and quantity supplied does not vary with housing prices. $\bar{Q}_m$ housing units, in other words, will be offered for rent at any of the prices represented on the vertical axis. With demand for housing, D, a free-housing market would tend to establish a market-clearing price, P_m, and the quantity demanded of housing (Q_d) would equal the quantity supplied (Q_s). All those looking for housing at that price would find it. Now let us suppose that a local government (New York City or one of the numerous others with rent control laws) imposes a ceiling price of P_c on housing units. The number of housing units offered for rent ($\bar{Q}_m$) does not change but there is a cost imposed on would-be renters. The quantity of housing demanded at P_c, $0Q_c$, is greater than

the quantity supplied, $0\bar{Q}_m$. The difference ($0Q_c - 0\bar{Q}_m$), or the distance AB, represents excess demand—the number of units renters cannot find at the controlled price. The costs of searching for housing that is unavailable are a significant part of this burden.

The costs above are only a part of the reason why many economists are skeptical of the argument that rent controls are effective tools of public policy whose objectives (housing availability and equity) are accomplished at low cost. Still, cities such as New York, which has had rent controls since World War II, show little inclination to repeal such controls.

Are Rent Controls Effective? (The Worst Case)

In the hypothetical case illustrated in Figure 3-10, renters didn't suffer a reduction in the number of housing units available because of rent controls. Instead, they incurred costs because at a below-equilibrium price, they searched fruitlessly for more housing than was available. The crucial assumption upon which that conclusion rested, that housing units offered for rent do not vary with rental prices, seems unrealistic. In Figure 3-12, we see what economists would expect (and data suggest) is more likely, a housing market with an upward sloping supply. A free housing market would tend to create a market equilibrium in Figure 3-12 with price P_m and quantity Q_m ($Q_d = Q_s$). Government now sets ceiling price P_c with the following effects: (1) the quantity supplied of housing declines from $0Q_m$ to $0Q_{c_1}$, creating an excess demand of ($0Q_m - 0Q_{c_1}$), or the distance; (2) at the lower ceiling price, renters try to increase the quantity demanded of housing from $0Q_m$ to $0Q_{c_2}$ creating additional excess demand of $0Q_{c_2} - 0Q_m$ or the distance BC; (3) the total excess demand resulting from the rent control is the sum of the two effects, or ($0Q_m - 0Q_{c_1}$) + ($0Q_{c_2} - 0Q_m$), or AB + BC = AC.

Are *any* renters made better off by the rent control (as city officials apparently intended)? *Yes.* Those who are able to rent housing ($0Q_{c_1}$) at the legislated price, P_c. They expend on housing $0P_cAQ_1$ whereas to obtain that amount of housing at the market price (P_m), they would have had to spend $0P_mDQ_{c_1}$. The difference, P_mP_cAD, represents an income transfer to renters which political decision-makers apparently intended.

Are renters as a *whole* made better off by the rent control? Economists are doubtful. Renters lose $0Q_m - 0Q_{c_1}$ of housing as a direct consequence of the price control because they have fewer units of housing that are offered for rent. Beyond this "supply effect," there is a "demand effect" as well; the quantity demanded of housing in Figure 3-12 increases from Q_m to Q_{c_2} as the legal price ceiling of P_c is imposed. The legally contrived shortage of housing, thus, at the controlled price is $0Q_{c_2} - 0Q_{c_1}$ or the distance AC. While some people are made better off, others are made worse off, and it is by no means clear that, on balance, rent controls improve the welfare of the general populace.

Figure 3-12
Rent Controls With a Variable Supply of Housing

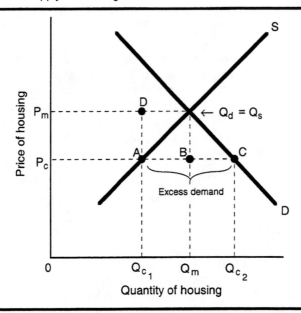

In Figure 3-12, the demand for housing (D) is downward sloping and the supply of housing (S) is upward sloping. A market equilibrium price would tend to be established at P_m where the quantity demanded of housing (Q_d) equals the quantity supplied (Q_s), or Q_m. If government sets a ceiling price such as P_c, the quantity supplied will be $0Q_{c_1}$, while the quantity demanded will be $0Q_{c_2}$; there will be excess demand of ($0Q_{c_1} - 0Q_{c_2}$) or AC.

The Dynamics of Rent Controlled Housing

The hypothetical housing market represented in Figure 3-12 is pictured at a point in time or in a static situation. Over time, or in a dynamic sense, the situation would likely get worse in terms of the costs of controlling housing prices. Since resources are required to maintain or expand housing, fixing its price lowers the returns on housing relative to the returns on other (non-controlled) uses of resources. In New York City, for instance, prices of co-ops, condominiums, and expensive apartments are not controlled. Neither are the prices of most goods other than housing. As the (relative) rate of return on housing for low and middle income renters declines, buildings may no longer be maintained adequately. In fact, buildings may even be abandoned and/or converted to other uses. A leftward shift of the supply curve from S to S' in Figure 3-13 would normally result in housing prices rising from P_e to P_e'; since this cannot (legally) occur, the quantity supplied at P_c will continue to decline further. Whereas excess demand at the controlled price would have equalled BC, the excess (people searching and working for housing) increases to ABC.

New York City has seen all of these effects. Landlords sometimes do not pay taxes on or adequately maintain buildings. There are entire blocks of buildings that stand vacant (at least for *legal* activities) and are unfit for housing. The city has, through tax arrears, become the owner of thousands of apartment buildings but is unwilling or financially unable to provide the housing that private landlords find unprofitable to provide.

Figure 3-13
The Dynamics of Rent Controlled Housing With a Declining Supply

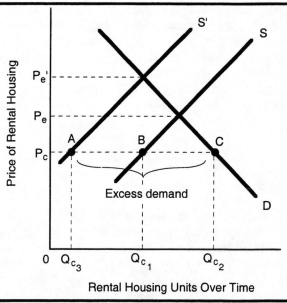

In Figure 3-13, a free housing market with demand D and supply S would be equilibriated at price P_e. If the supply of housing declined from S to S', the market would re-equilibriate at P_e'. In neither case would there be excess demand. If housing prices are controlled at P_c, the decline will increase the excess demand from BC to ABC.

Finally, many buildings have been converted to condominiums or to other uses whose prices are uncontrolled.

Illegal or "Black Markets"

Faced with the shortage of housing shown in Figure 3-12, renters, who cannot wait for months or years to obtain housing at the controlled price, resort to bribes or "side payments." People who have apartments at controlled prices sublet them out for higher prices or landlords accept non-rental payments in lieu of rents. New York City and other cities with stringent rent-control laws not only have to spend resources enforcing the laws but also to revise them often in order to prevent the voluntary exchanges in which renters and landlords would otherwise engage.

The Future of Rent Controls

Economists, even those on opposite ends of the political spectrum, agree that rent-control laws have perverse effects on those they seek to benefit. Assar Lindbeck characterizes them as "the most efficient technique so far known for destroying cities." Why are such efforts to stymie the operation of free-housing markets (ones in which landlords and renters make voluntary and mutually beneficial exchanges) not repealed? It seems unlikely that their continuation results from ignorance of their effects. Robert Thomas suggests instead that it is because the benefits of control are concentrated in the hands of a relatively small group (those who occupy rent-controlled housing) while the costs are spread over a much larger group (landlords, who are few, and many who seek better housing or who are new to the housing market). Says Thomas: "Politicians, attempting to win or to stay in office have found it necessary to pay attention to the private interests of tenants even at the cost of continued urban decay."

Other Applications of Supply and Demand

Supply and Demand for Clerks

In Figure 3-14, P_1 represents the equilibrium price that would be arrived at in an open market for store clerks. The union is able to get a higher wage (P_2) for the employees; but the employer will hire less workers (Q_2). There will also be a surplus of workers who want to work as represented by the difference between Q_2 and Q_3.

When unions are able to negotiate a higher wage for their members, the initial reaction from the employer is that at the higher wage there will be less demand for that type of employee. The demand has not shifted, rather the quantity demanded will

Figure 3-14
Supply and Demand for Union Labor

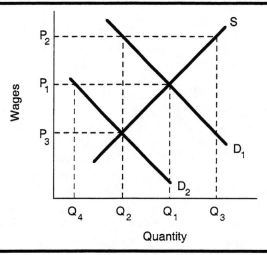

S and D_1 show how a union can achieve a wage above what a free market would set. D_2 illustrates the decrease in demand for labor that has occurred in the U.S. during the past few years as automation and lower-priced labor from developing countries such as Mexico have resulted in a decrease in demand for U.S. union labor.

decrease, as noted, as employment goes down to Q-2 in Figure 3-14. The only way that employees can negotiate a higher wage and still maintain the quantity demanded is for worker productivity to increase in line with the wage increase. Often workers will receive wage increases while the quantity employed stays constant. A decrease in the quantity demanded often occurs with a significant time lag (possibly even 5 or 10 years). Historically, if workers consistently receive wage increases greater than the increase in their productivity, eventually the quantity demanded will decrease.

Table 3-4 shows how some unions have been particularly successful in temporarily raising wages above the market equilibrium. Steel workers in the late 1970s and early 1980s were paid roughly 67 percent more than non-union steel workers. However, since the mid-1980s, because of the pressures of increased domestic and international competition, these union workers have accepted large pay cuts. In addition, the high wage resulted in many steel workers being laid off as management accelerated bringing in automated equipment to cut operating costs.

ECONOMIC NEWS

Boats Boycott New Crab Season

Commercial fishermen from three Northern California fishing ports, dissatisfied with the price offered for their catches, have boycotted the opening of the Dungeness crab season, industry officials said yesterday.

It is estimated that 250 to 300 fishermen whose boats are berthed in Eureka and Trinidad in Humboldt County and Crescent City in Del Norte County have not put to sea, although the Dungeness crab season opened in Northern California and Oregon on Saturday.

"We are offering $1.25 a pound, and they want $1.60 a pound," Thomas said. "We don't say the fishermen are asking too much, we just say, try to fish for a few days to find out how much crab is out there. Let the market set the price."

Table 3-4
1985 Pay Premiums that Can be Attributed to the Power of Labor Union

Industry	Production Worker Annual Pay	Market Pay for Comparable Skill Mix	Excess Over Market (%)
Cigarettes	$40,952	$21,217	93
Steel	37,635	22,485	67
Autos	36,418	21,935	66
Petroleum Refining	39,251	25,868	52
Paper	32,079	21,770	47
Organic Chemicals	35,372	25,764	37
Aircraft	31,930	23,827	34
Plastics	30,517	23,070	32

Supply and Demand for Doctors

Doctors are paid very high wages because they have been able to control the supply of doctors by the power of their union, the American Medical Association (AMA). See Figure 3-15. The AMA has been given the power by Congress to license all medical schools in the U.S. By restricting the number of medical schools, they have in effect reduced the supply of doctors and assured themselves of a very high income. Evidently, the medical profession has a firm grip on economic way of thinking.

California's Crowded Parks Problem

Long before every big holiday weekend the State Department of Parks and Recreation issues a public warning: "Unless you have reservations please stay away from state beach and mountain campgrounds. There is no more room."

The rate at which the state buys parks has slowed to almost a standstill in the last decade.

This year is no improvement. The state isn't planning on buying any complete park units, although it has approval to expand a handful of existing facilities.

"The money to buy parks has just dried up in recent years," said Lee Litz, chief of administrative services for the state agency.

The State Department of Parks and Recreation has traditionally been at the tail end of funding priorities. It receives about $20 million a year for operating costs, and while it raises some $7 million a year from entrance fees, it still has nothing left over for park acquisition.

For the most part, the department has relied on bond issues to raise money for parks. But in its 50-year history it has had only three of these.

Figure 3-15
Supply and Demand for Doctors

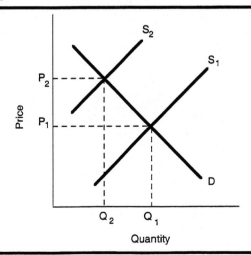

Illustrates how doctors, working with the force of supply and demand, have achieved very high wages.

ECONOMIC NEWS

Soviets 'Dump' Gems, Apparently to Buy Grain

September 1988

The Soviet Union "dumped" about $160 million in polished diamonds on the international market in 1986, apparently to help raise money to pay for the increased grain imports that followed its fifth straight poor harvest, according to diamond industry officials in the U.S. and abroad.

The heavy Soviet sales reportedly were at 5 to 10 percent—and sometimes more—below market prices, according to Lloyd Jaffee, president of the American Diamond Industry Association. He said the sales, which continued at least through July, also raised concerns at the recent World Congress of Diamond Bourses and Manufacturers in Antwerp, Belgium.

"I don't like to use the word 'dumping,' because it has a (bad) connotation," Jaffee said. "But we do know that at least twice before, the Soviets put a lot of diamonds on the market in a short period, and it depressed prices. This happened a third time this year, affecting prices in the U.S. as well as in Europe."

After one of the earlier incidents, several European nations—including Belgium, a major diamond polishing center—imposed temporary limits on the amount of Soviet diamonds allowed in their countries. Other nations with major diamond polishing industries include the U.S., Israel, and India.

The precise amount of Soviet sales was not known, and estimates varied considerably—but it appeared that the Soviets were selling polished diamonds at twice or more their normal rate for at least the first half of the year.

Earlier reports, quoting American and foreign diamond industry officials, have stated that about $160 million in the gems were dumped, and Jaffee confirmed the thrust of the earlier accounts, broadcast by Radio Liberty, a U.S. government funded station, and published in the *Economist* magazine.

One jewelry magazine reported this month that the below-market sales had stopped and that normal sales levels had resumed, but Jaffee said he could not confirm the story.

Intelligence analysts had tended to discount the initial accounts of Soviet gem dumping on the grounds that the Soviets generally export rough diamonds rather than the cut and polished stones that were being sold. Dumping diamonds on world markets would reduce prices for normal Soviet sales, they argued.

These analysts also said that despite the Soviet's propaganda against South African apartheid policies, they sell rough diamonds—polished diamonds are not covered—through 5-year contracts with the Central Selling Organization in London, run by De Beers Ltd. of South Africa. The De Beers organization has a virtual monopoly on the world's rough diamonds, handling about 80 percent of the market, according to the U.S. Department of Mines.

"With prices depressed for their oil and gold, the Soviets have turned to selling their diamonds in record numbers," the council official said. "The Soviets don't follow the diamond market that closely—they sell diamonds when the government says to do so. And if they can't sell at market prices, they sell under them, which they are doing now and hurting our industry."

In June 1992, the Russian republic of the former Soviet Union will allow the ruble to be traded on the world market. This is another vital step in bringing the republics of the former Soviet Union into a market economy. One of the largest roadblocks to Western corporations investing in the former Soviet republics was their inability to take their profits out of the country by converting the ruble to their currency. As of June 1992, this is now possible. This was one of the major reasons that Exxon in the spring of 1992 signed a partnership agreement with the Russian republic. Exxon has agreed to invest over $20 billion to help Russia modernize its oil industry.

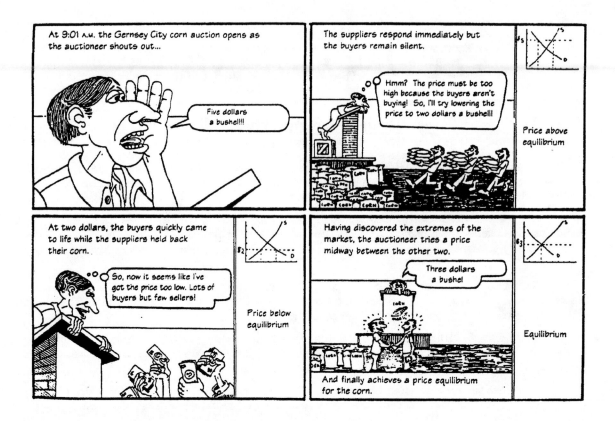

SUMMING UP

1. Studying the operation of a market system helps us to answer three basic questions about the use of resources: (a) *what* goods are produced (composition), (b) *how* goods are produced (technique), and (c) *for whom* goods are produced (distribution).

2. To understand the market system, one needs to begin with conditions of *competition*: the market form in which no buyer or seller has influence over the price at which the product sells.

3. Since each participant in a competitive market acts independently, *prices*—the signals for action in the market—are determined by independent movements of demand and supply.

4. There are two sides to every market: the demand side and the supply side. *Demand* is a set of relationships showing the quantity of a good that consumers will buy at each of several prices within a specific period of time.

5. One draws a demand curve for a good on the assumption of *ceteris paribus* (other things being equal). In other words, one assumes that the price, and only the price, of that good changes, not any of the other factors of demand.

6. We expect a demand curve to slope downward to the right, which means that people buy more of a good at low prices than at high prices (the law of demand).

7. The *law of demand* is based on (a) the income effect and (b) the substitution effect. The *income effect*: As the price of a good falls, the consumer has more purchasing power and ordinarily buys more of that good as a result. The *substitution effect*: As the price of a good falls, it becomes relatively cheaper than those goods for which it is a substitute. Thus people buy more of it because it is cheaper.

8. There are exceptions to the normal case, such as *Veblen goods* (perhaps diamonds, caviar, sable coats), and, especially in poor countries, *income-inferior goods* (certain basic staple goods, such as beans and rice).

9. For a given good, a *change in quantity demanded* is a movement along a demand curve. It can result only from a change in the price of the good. A *change in demand* is a shift of the demand curve, and can result from a change in any of the other factors affecting demand: income, tastes, the prices of substitutes and complements, and expectations.

10. Basic factors that can change demand are (a) consumers' incomes, (b) consumers' tastes and preferences, (c) prices of other products, (d) consumers' expectations about future market conditions and prices, and (e) the number of consumers.

11. One can calculate the market demand curve by adding individuals' curves, given that consumers buy independently of each other. Curves for market demand get their shapes from the demand curves of individuals, but measure larger quantities.

12. *Supply* is the set of relationships showing the quantity of a product that a firm will offer for sale at each possible price within a specific period of time.

13. Factors that can change supply are (a) changes in technology, (b) changes in prices of factors of production, (c) changes in prices of other goods, (d) changes in firms' expectations about future prices, and (e) changes in the number of firms.

14. A *supply curve* shows that (a) firms supply more of a given product at higher prices than at lower prices, and (b) there is a price below which firms supply nothing to the market.

15. Supply curves that slope upward to the right are based on the assumption that ultimately firms run into decreasing efficiency and increasing costs as they expand output, either because of fixed physical facilities or difficulty in managing a larger operation. Also, the relative profitability of supplying a product increases as its price increases.

16. One can estimate the curve for market supply by adding supply curves of individual firms, assuming that each firm behaves independently of the others. Changes in the number of firms cause changes in market supply.

17. Market prices, including competitive prices are *equilibrium prices*. That is, they are market-clearing prices. When there are equilibrium prices, quantity demanded and quantity supplied are equal and there is neither excess demand nor excess supply.

18. If prices are *above* equilibrium, there is *excess supply*—a market surplus or excess. If prices are *below* equilibrium, there is *excess demand*—a market shortage. In either case, demand and supply are not in equilibrium.

19. Conditions necessary to ensure competitive prices are (a) completely flexible prices; (b) possession of full information by both buyers and sellers; (c) expectation of constant prices; (d) free entry into and exit from markets; (e) consistent effort of firms to maximize profits and of consumers to maximize satisfaction; and (f) no collusion between buyers and sellers—all must behave independently of each other.

20. In a market economy, as long as resources are scarce, prices must be used to allocate resources and ration output. If markets are not permitted to establish equilibrium, prices must be set, usually by government, at non-equilibrium levels.

21. Non-equilibrium prices in markets set in motion self-correcting movements of price and quantity that eliminate excess demand or excess supply. Non-market determined disequilibrium prices have no corresponding mechanisms of self-correction.

22. Governmentally established non-equilibrium prices may consist of price floors or price ceilings. There have been numerous examples of both in American history and there are many such examples today.

23. Government intervention in market pricing is most often based on "fairness" in pricing, rationing, and income distribution. In this application, the focus is on local government control over housing prices, which usually leads to rent-control ordinances.

24. Free housing markets will establish equilibrium through prices that equate quantity demanded and quantity supplied. Housing prices that are set below equilibrium will result in excess demand.

25. Even if the quantity supplied of housing does not vary as housing prices are lowered by rent controls, there will be an excess demand at the legal price ceiling. Those seeking housing will not be able to obtain all (including the quality of housing) they wish at the ceiling price (Figure 3-10).

26. Economists are skeptical of the argument that rent controls make housing available at equitable prices. This is especially the case with a downward-sloping demand for housing combined with an upward sloping supply of housing (Figure 3-11).

27. When rent controls are imposed, those who benefit are the individuals who obtain the amount and quality of housing desired at the controlled price. Those who lose include landlords, but also renters who see a decline in the quantity supplied of housing (the direct effect of rent control) and renters who seek more housing at the lower price than they would have sought at the equilibrium price (the indirect effect of rent control).

28. The indirect effect, plus the direct effect above, constitute the total excess demand for housing at the controlled price.

29. Over time, stringent rent controls are likely to result in a decline in both the quantity and quality of rental housing available. Incentives are created (through changes in relative prices and returns on resource usage) to convert housing units to other uses, to decrease maintenance outlays and even to abandon buildings rather than pay taxes on them.

30. Rent controls continue in spite of the view of economists that they have unintended ill effects on those they seek to benefit. One explanation for their popularity is that their benefits are concentrated in politically active small groups, while their costs are spread over a much larger group (landlords but also those who suffer from urban decay and inability to find better housing.) One effect of rent controls is in the illegal housing markets they tend to create.

KEY TERMS

Absolute and nominal price
Ceteris paribus
Change in demand
Change in quantity demanded
Change in quantity supplied
Change in supply
Complement
Demand curve
Determinants of demand
Determinants of supply
Giffen good
Income effect
Law of demand
Law of supply
Market or equilibrium price
Normal good
Relative price
Role of price
Shortage
Substitute
Substitution effect
Supply and demand equilibrium
Supply curve
Surplus
Veblen good

QUESTIONS

1. Review the basic questions about use of resources, questions that are common to all societies. Be sure that you not only understand these questions but also realize why all societies must find answers.

2. Define *competition*, as economists use the word. How does the economist's way of looking at competition differ from your familiar usage of the word?

3. What is *demand*? Does the economist's meaning of demand differ from your usual meaning? If so, what do you think accounts for the differences? What is the *ceteris paribus* assumption?

4. Why do demand curves usually slope downward or to the right? What would it mean if one sloped *up* or to the right? List the five basic factors that influence demand. Which of these factors, in addition to price, do you think will be most influential in determining the demand for (a) cars? (b) safety matches? Why?

5. Define the *income effect* and the *substitution effect*. For a small change in the price of a good, which of the two effects would you expect to be more important? What are *inferior* goods? Can you think of some possible examples beyond those given in the chapter?

6. What is the *law of demand*? How is it explained? What can cause a change in demand? A change in quantity demanded?

7. How does one derive a market demand curve? What assumption(s) does one use to do so?

8. What is the *supply curve*? How do competitive suppliers behave toward each other? Why do supply curves usually slope up to the right?

9. What factors determine supply? What can cause a change in supply? A change in quantity supplied?

10. How does one derive a market supply curve? What assumption(s) does one use to do so?

11. How is *price* determined in a competitive market? What does *equilibrium* mean, in relation to the operation of a market? What conditions must exist in a market for competitive prices to be established? Are they hard to establish? Do you know any markets in which these conditions exist, or are closely approximated?

12. Suppose that you are chief economist for an automobile industry council. You are asked to forecast industry sales for next year. You know that in the coming year personal income is expected to rise by 3 percent, that mass transit is going to be heavily subsidized by government, and that the population and its average age are expected to remain fairly constant. What influences will each of these factors have on your forecast?

13. What determines the availability of housing to individuals in a free market?

14. What is meant in saying that there is no "free lunch" in imposing ceiling prices in housing markets?

15. Who benefits from rent-control laws? Who bears the costs?

16. How is the supply of housing related to the costs of rent-controls?

17. Does the area in which you live have a rent-control ordinance? If so, what costs and benefits are created by its enforcement?

18. Why do rent-control laws tend to foster the development of "black" (illegal) markets?

19. Is it likely, in a dynamic sense, that rent-control laws accomplish their objectives of making housing generally available at "affordable" prices? Why or why not?

20. If your answer to (7) above is negative, why do we continue to see rent-control laws passed and enforced?

21.   a. Illustrate the problem of a shortage of campsites using a hypothetical supply and demand graph. In illustrating a shortage, remember that the initial price must be **below** the market equilibrium price.
        b. Analyze this problem of campsite shortages from an economist's point of view, and present two possible solutions to this problem. Illustrate your solutions with a graph for each solution. Remember to start each graph with the basic X with the four key components clearly labeled.

22. Complete the supply and demand schedules below.
        a. What is the equilibrium price and quantity?
        b. What would happen if government set a price of $8.00? (The government decrees that it would be unlawful to charge less.)

Supply and Demand Schedules					
Price	Quantity Supplied	Quantity Demanded	Shortage	Surplus	Direction of Pressure on Price
$9.00	100	0	0	100	down
8.00	90	15			
7.00	80	30			
6.00	70	45			
5.00	60	80			
4.00	50	85			
3.00	40	90			

23. Draw in the new demand or supply curve, whichever is appropriate, on the graphs provided, based on the following changes. Indicate what happens to the equilibrium price and quantity in each case. The answers to question (a) is given as an example.
        a. The price of a factor of production increases.
        b. Income increases; assume the good is a normal one.
        c. Income increases; assume the good is an inferior one.
        d. The commodity becomes more fashionable.
        e. A new and more efficient method of production is invented.
        f. The price of a complementary good increases.

24. Can you think of a situation in which the price of the product increases and the amount demanded also increases? (Assume a normal good.)

25. Most people have some form of hospitalization insurance that substantially reduces the cost of staying in a hospital. Does this affect hospital usage?

26. How does the existence of traffic school, which keeps your first speeding ticket off the record, (insurance companies) actually increase the number of people speeding?

27. There are only 15 lockers available for the male faculty at Shasta College. Explain why allocating these lockers on a first-come basis is an inefficient way to allocate this resource.

28. How could the state use the pricing mechanism to eliminate 98 percent of all drunk drivers?

29. Why has the price of lumber increased so rapidly? Grphically illustrate your answer.

30. Washington and Oregon have a combined population that is similar to that of Massachusetts. Can you explain why the people of Washington and Oregon consumed three times the amount of electricity as Massachusetts this past year? Graphically illustrate your answer.

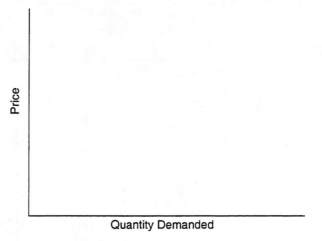

SUGGESTED READINGS

Cheung, Stephen N. S., "The Stated Intents and Actual Effects of a Rents Ordinance," *Economic Inquiry*. March, 1975

Egan, John J.; John Carr, Andrew Mott, and John Roos. *Housing and Public Policy: A Role for Mediating Structures,* Washington, D.C. American Enterprise Institute, 1981

Rand Corporation, "The Effects of Rent Control on Housing in New York City," In *Contemporary Issues in Economics: Selected Readings*. R. W. Crandall and R. S. Eckhaus, Eds. New York, Little Brown, 1972
Schuettinger, Robert F. and Eamonn F. Butler, *Forty Centuries of Wage and Price Controls*. Washington, D.C. The Heritage Foundation, 1979 (Chapter 19)

Thomas, Robert Paul, *Microeconomic Applications: Understanding the American Economy*. Belmont, Calif: Wadsworth Publishing Co., 1981 (Chapter 24)

Wall Street Journal. "Home Free: Some Rich and Famous of New York City Bask in Shelter of Rent Law." March 21, 1994

Demand Side of the Market—Utility and Elasticity

In 1985 more oranges were destroyed by USDA orders than by severe frost in Texas and Florida.

OBJECTIVES

After studying this chapter you will be able to:

- Explain the concept of elasticity
- Distinguish between the three types of elasticity.
- Explain how a business person would use this concept.
- List the determinants of the price elasticity of demand.
- Discuss the issue of cross elasticity.
- Have a working knowledge of the following terms and concepts:

Determinants of the price elasticity of demand	Price inelastic demand
Diminishing marginal utility	Role of price
Information	Short-run vs long-run elasticity curve
Marginal utility	Speculator
Middleman	Unitary elasticity
Price elasticity of demand	Utility
Price elasticity of supply	

Demand Side of the Market - Utility and Elasticity

What is Demand?

Demand
A set of relationships representing the quantities of a good that consumers will buy over a given range of prices in a given period of time.

Demand is a schedule representing the quantities of a good (a commodity or service) that consumers are able and willing to buy over a given range of prices in a specific period of time.

The demand schedule, in other words, reflects the way consumers react when faced with variations in the price of a good. Explanations or models of individual demand—like all models—depend on certain assumptions. Our examination of demand in this chapter will be based on the following: (1) Consumers know about, and can choose freely among, alternatives. (2) Consumers seek the maximum satisfaction from the goods they can buy with their limited incomes. (3) Things other than a good's price that might affect consumers' spending for that good—such as people's incomes and tastes, their expectations about future prices, and the prices of other goods, are assumed *not* to vary during the given time period.

With these assumptions in mind, look at Figure 4-1, which is a hypothetical individual demand curve for hamburgers. The demand curve (D) shows the relationship between prices of hamburgers in a given week and the quantity one person will buy at each possible price. Note that the person will not buy any hamburgers if their price goes as high as $1.70 each, and will buy an increasing number as their price falls. If the price goes to $1.20 a piece, that person will buy 10 per week. The important thing to remember is that there is a relationship between price and quantity demanded. That relationship is called the **law of demand**. This law states that the price of a good and the quantity demanded of that good are inversely related. (An increase in price results in a decrease in quantity demanded; a decrease in price results in an increase in quantity demanded.)

Law of Demand
The general rule that consumers buy more at low prices than they do at high prices.

Figure 4-1
Hypothetical Demand Curve for Hamburgers

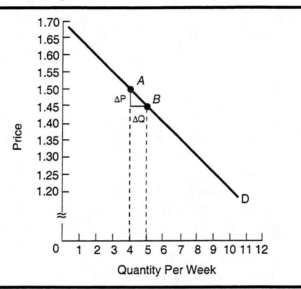

In Figure 4-1, D is a hypothetical demand curve for hamburgers. As price falls from $1.50 to $1.45, the quantity demanded increases from 4 to 5 per week.

Utility Theory
A theory of consumer behavior in which people buy goods based on the satisfaction they expect to derive from those goods.

When a demand schedule is plotted graphically, it is referred to as a demand curve. According to the law of demand, such curves are downward sloping. We will explain this inverse relationship, this downward-sloping demand curve, in two ways: (1) in terms of income and substitution effects, and (2) in terms of a theory of demand, called **utility theory**, the theory that people buy goods based on the satisfaction they expect to derive from those goods.

Income and Substitution Effects

Look at Figure 4-1. Price (vertical axis), the independent variable, is the factor that originally changes. Quantity sold (horizontal axis) is the dependent variable and responds to changes in price. Now suppose that the price of a hamburger falls from $1.50 (point A) to $1.45 (point B). According to the law of demand, this 5¢ decrease in price should result in an increase in the quantity demanded. In other words, the negative ΔP (where the Greek letter delta, or Δ, means a finite change) should result in a positive ΔQ, in this instance from 4 to 5.

Income Effect
The change in quantity demanded of a good due to a change in real income caused by a change in the price of a good.

First, the ΔQ (the greater number of hamburgers bought) is the result of the **income effect**—the change in quantity demanded caused by a change in consumer purchasing power resulting from a variation in the price of a good. With the same money income, a person can now buy more hamburgers (and/or other things, such as

Cokes, french fries, or fried chicken), so that person is in effect richer than before. Since, by assumption, hamburgers are a desirable good, part of the positive change in quantity is attributable to this income effect, the strength of which depends on what percentage of income an individual spends on hamburgers. If that individual hardly ever buys 1, a price drop for hamburgers has little or no effect on his or her purchasing power.

Whatever the strength of the effect, however, the income effect usually acts in a direction opposite to the direction of a price change. (If hamburger prices increase, the income effect will be a negative one or, in other words, cause the quantity demanded of hamburgers to decline.)

Second, the change in quantity demanded (ΔQ) is also the result of a **substitution effect**—the change in quantity demanded of a good due to a change in its relative price. In this case, as the price of hamburgers falls, the person can substitute the now relatively cheaper hamburgers for fried chicken, pizza, and other foods (we are assuming that the prices of these other foods have not changed). Since there are almost always some substitutes on the market, the substitution effect tends to confirm the law of demand. Taken together, the two effects—income and substitution—ordinarily cause the demand curve to have a negative slope.

Theoretical Exceptions to the Law of Demand

The above market scenario is not, theoretically, the one that always takes place. There are two theoretical exceptions to the law of demand that should be noted.

1. Consumers may value a good just *because* it is relatively expensive, and because only people with high social status consume it. If, for instance, Beluga caviar or imported perfumes sold for a dollar a quart, people might not believe they were worth much. These goods could, after all, be bought by the masses. Such goods, which people buy for the sake of conspicuous consumption and therefore buy more of at higher than at lower prices, are called **Veblen goods**, after Thorstein Veblen (1857-1929), an American economist who wrote a stinging analysis of the motives behind the consumption habits of very rich people. (Veblen's *The Theory of the Leisure Class* caused a sensation when it was published in 1899.)

We see a hypothetical Veblen good demand curve in Figure 4-2. Note that the law of demand is violated; as the price rises (P_0 to P_1), the quantity demanded increases because the conspicuous value of the good is enhanced; as a result, consumers buy more at a higher price than at a lower price. The reverse occurs as price falls and, because of its reduced conspicuous value, the quantity demanded decreases. It is well to remember that the Veblen good is a *theoretical* exception to the law of demand. Veblen offered no systematic

Figure 4-2
A Hypothetical Demand Curve for a Veblen Good

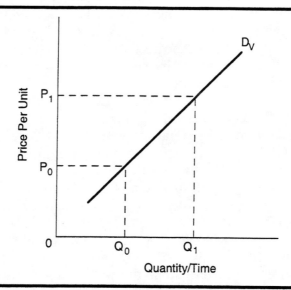

In Figure 4-2, as the price of the Veblen good rises from P_0 to P_1, the quantity demanded of the good rises from Q_0 to Q_1. The reverse (a decrease in quantity demanded) occurs as price falls from P_1 to P_0. The effect is explained by a change in the conspicuous value of the good as price changes.

evidence to support his view that the consumer behavior by the very rich was different from that of others. Although empirical studies have provided little substantiation of Veblen's argument, the Veblen good remains a possible theoretical explanation for an upward sloping demand curve.

2. In terms of the way consumers behave in markets as their real incomes change, most goods are (income) **normal goods**: as real income rises, more is bought; as real income falls, less is bought. There are also (income) **superior goods** (e.g., recreational activities) whose consumption varies in the same direction as real income varies but at a greater rate. In the case of both normal and superior goods, the substitution and income effects from price changes reinforce each other.

As price falls, both income and substitution effects lead to increases in quantity demanded. As price rises, both lead to decreases in quantity demanded. Both effects, in other words, tend to result in downward sloping demand curves. Sometimes though, people may have to spend a large part of their real income on certain inexpensive goods simply because their low incomes permit them few choices. For example, basic food staples such as rice in Asia, or corn or wheat or potatoes in other parts of the world (including poor areas of the U.S.). If the price of one of these staples falls, its consumers have substantially more purchasing power and the income effect becomes potentially more important than the substitution effect. If the price of rice falls in India, the income effect may move in the same direction

Normal Goods
Those that consumers buy more of as their real incomes rise and less of as their real incomes fall.

Superior Goods
Those whose consumption varies in the same direction as but at a greater rate than real income.

Giffen Goods
Those inferior goods with an income effect that moves in the same direction as price and for which the income effect is larger than the substitution effect (an upward sloping demand curve).

Inferior Goods
A general case of goods for which there is a weak income related taste. As price rises, quantity demanded decreases because the substitution of goods outweighs the tendency to buy more with reduced real income (a downward-sloping demand curve).

as price, because people may spend less on rice and spend their newly increased purchasing power on milk, meat, and other high-protein foods. Conversely, when rice goes up in price, because people have less real income to spend, they buy more rice and have to do without the diversified diet. Inferior goods with an income effect that moves in the same direction as price and outweighs the substitution effect—that is, inferior goods that people buy less of as their price falls—are called **Giffen goods**, after Sir Robert Giffen, a 19th century English economist. Such goods constitute a special case of the more general **inferior goods**, in which the income effect moves in the same direction as price, but in which the income effect is outweighed by the substitution effect.

We see in Figure 4-3 a hypothetical demand curve for a Giffen good. Note that D_G, the demand for the Giffen good, is upward sloping, thus violating the law of demand. The explanation for this is that as price rises from P_0 to P_1, the change in quantity demanded for Q_0 to Q_1 is a result of two contradictory effects. The substitution effect of the price increase would be to cause the quantity demanded to be less than Q_0 (to the left of point A). The income effect, however, for this *very* income inferior good causes the quantity demanded to be greater than Q_1 (to the right of point A). Because the income effect is larger and opposite of the substitution effect, the equilibrium quantity demanded increases (to Q_1) as price rises. It is well, as with the Veblen good, to remember that the Giffen good is a *theoretical* exception to the law of demand.

Figure 4-3
A Hypothetical Demand Curve for a Giffen Good

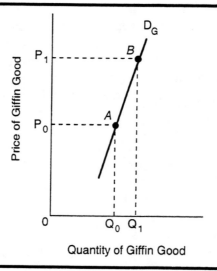

In Figure 4-3, as the price of the Giffen good rises from P_0 to P_1, the quantity demanded in equilibrium rises from Q_0 to Q_1. The substitution effect of the price increase would cause the quantity demanded to be to the left of point A, but the income effect, which would cause quantity demanded to increase, is larger. As a result, the movement is to point B or to a greater quantity demanded.

Utility: Another Way to Explain Demand

Whenever you buy something, you make a choice. In a well-ordered market system, there are many alternative choices. How do you make such choices? Why, for example, do you choose to put part of your paycheck in a savings account rather than spend it all on goods and services? Why do you choose to eat a hamburger rather than a pizza?

The answers lie in the market conditions, in the way the consumer makes choices, and in the consumer's objectives. Let's make the following assumptions about these factors:

1. *Consumers buy competitively.* You, as an individual consumer, have no influence over the market price at which you buy things. There are no quantity discounts, no consumer co-ops. If toothpaste costs a dollar a tube, you pay a dollar. You pay prices as "given."

2. *Consumers have limited money incomes and full information* (at least price information) about the choices available.

3. *Consumers are rational;* they can make choices in a way that moves them toward their objective. They have a set of tastes and preferences which, while they may change over time, are constant at any point in time.

Total Utility
The entire satisfaction from consuming a good.

4. *Consumers seek to maximize their **total utility** or entire satisfaction* within the limits of their money incomes.

These four assumptions are the basis for the study of consumer choice. *Utility theory*, one part of that study, attempts to explain consumer choice on the basis of the *utility*—or the subjectively measured satisfaction—that one may derive from consuming any particular combinations of goods. We shall assume that utility can be measured subjectively in terms of *utils*, or units of satisfaction.

Most consumers in most situations do buy as competitors. You can haggle over the price you pay for a car. You can join a co-op. You can even get a quantity discount (10 percent off on that *case* of beer), but these are the exceptions.

Everyone knows that consumers have limited money incomes; everyone must live within a budget. Also, consumers have easy access to price information via newspapers, television, and other means, even if they do not always understand the technical features of things they buy.

What about rationality? *Rationality*, as we use the word, simply means that what consumers do and how they do it is consistent with achieving the maximum utility (satisfaction) from their choices. The key word *utility* means satisfaction, not usefulness. A new recording by a great new rock group may give you a lot of utility, but have little usefulness, since it will not mow your lawn or cook your food or bring you the evening news.

The Law of Diminishing Marginal Utility

What happens as a consumer (who conforms to our four assumptions) makes choices? There is a certain amount of utility a consumer expects to receive from consuming more of a good. There is always, therefore, a behavioral margin, a tendency for a consumer to buy 1 more (or less) unit of a good or service as its price changes, to the point at which all income is spent. In other words, we make choices at the margin. The additional satisfaction derived from an additional unit of a good purchased is called the **marginal utility** of that good.

What happens to marginal utility as you buy successive units of a certain good (in a given period of time)? Going back to hamburgers: Beyond some point (say a second hamburger at one meal), you get less and less satisfaction from each additional hamburger. The principle that operates here is called the **law of diminishing marginal utility**. The law states that as more of a good is consumed, the added utility of additional units of the good (ultimately) decreases (holding other things constant). Why must price fall to get you to buy more (increase the quantity you demand)? Because additional satisfaction (marginal utility) diminishes as you obtain more units of the same good in a given period of time, holding other things (prices of other goods, income, etc.) constant.

Making Choices that Maximize Utility

In order to maximize utility—in other words, achieve the greatest possible satisfaction—the consumer must make judgments about the marginal utility of each additional dollar spent on the goods. It is well to remember that the marginal utility of a good is subjectively measured. We are not walking computers, yet we are able to compute. Let's take a hypothetical example of consumer choice and see how utility maximization works. Assume that you are a consumer who buys only 2 goods, hot dogs (h) and pizza (p). To get the maximum obtainable utility while living within your income, you will buy a combination of the 2 goods that satisfies the following equilibrium conditions:

1. $MU_h/P_h = MU_p/P_p$

2. $P_h h + P_p z = Y$

The h stands for *number* of hot dogs bought, and the z stands for *number* of pizzas bought. MU represents the marginal utility of a good and P the price of that good. Y stands for income.

Condition 1 tells you that you must make the marginal utility of a hot dog (MU_h) divided by its price (P_h) equal to the marginal utility of a pizza (MU_p) divided by its price (P_p). Roughly, this amounts to making the marginal utility of a dollar spent on pizzas equal to the marginal utility of a dollar spent on hot dogs. Why is this so? Suppose that it was not so. Suppose that you considered the marginal utility of a dollar spent on hot dogs to be greater than the

Marginal Utility
The additional satisfaction from consuming an additional unit of a good.

The Law of Diminishing Marginal Utility
States that as more of a good is consumed in a time period the additional utility of consuming additional units of the good (ultimately) decreases.

marginal utility of a dollar spent on pizza ($MU_h > MU_p$). (The $>$ means "is greater than.") What will you do to maximize utility? You will spend less money on pizza and more on hot dogs. As you give up pizza, you lose their MU (which will increase as you have less of them) and gain the MU of hot dogs (which will decrease as you consume more of them). You will be in equilibrium only when the MU/P, or marginal utility per dollar (price), is the same for both goods.

Condition 2 simply shows that you spend *all* your income (Y) on hot dogs ($P_h h$) (remember that h is the number of hot dogs bought) and on pizzas (z being the number of pizzas bought). In other words, you must make choices that are permitted by your income or live within that income. The second condition is really an income or a **budget restraint**, the set of choices of goods that present income (Y) permits at present prices (P_h, P_p). We see a hypothetical budget constraint for a consumer in Figure 4-4. With income (Y) = $4.50, the price of pizzas (P_p) = $1.00 and the price of hot dogs (P_h) = 50¢, the consumer can choose 4.5 pizzas or 9 hot dogs or any of the combinations that are on the budget restraint. The consumer cannot choose any combinations of the 2 goods that lie above or to the right of the budget restraint because present income and prices do not permit it. Condition 2 of the equilibrium conditions states that the equilibrium quantity demanded of hot dogs as well as that of

Budget Restraint
The set of choices of goods that present income and present prices permit a consumer to make.

Figure 4-4
The Budget Restraint of a Consumer

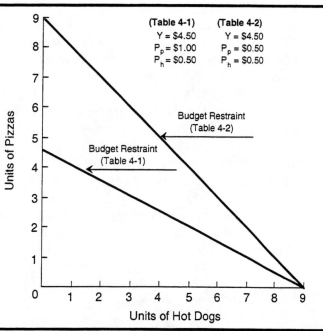

In Figure 4-4, the budget restraint for a consumer is shown from Table 4-1 between 2 goods, hot dogs and pizzas. With income (Y) of $4.50 and with prices, P_p = $1.00 and P_h = 50¢, the consumer can buy 4.5 pizzas or 9 hot dogs and all combinations of the 2 goods that lie on the budget restraint. Also shown is a new budget restraint from Table 4-2 with income (Y) of $4.50 and with prices, P_p = 50¢ and P_h = 50¢.

pizzas will be a combination on the budget restraint. To determine which combination that will be, we will satisfy condition 1, in which the consumer makes MU_h/P_h equal to MU_p/P_p, a process we will illustrate in the next section.

Equilibrium in a World of Many Goods

Of course, this 2-good example is unrealistic. No one lives on just 2 goods; not even Robinson Crusoe did. We are just using this to simplify our model. However, one can readily extend the principle of maximization of utility to any number of goods. The conclusion remains the same: In equilibrium, the consumer will make the MU of a dollar spent on one good equal to the MU of a dollar spent on any other good. Our first equilibrium condition in a world of N goods to choose from becomes $MU_h/P_h = MU_p/P_p = MU_n/P_n$, where n represents the nth or last good.

Utility Maximizing Behavior: an Arithmetic Illustration

Let's assign some numbers to MU and P for an arithmetic illustration.

Joe Bloggs has $4.50 to spend on lunch this week. On Monday he goes to the cafeteria in the student union and finds that this week pizza is $1.00 and hot dogs are 50¢. After griping about prices getting higher, he calculates that the first pizza he eats this week will give him 50 utils (50 utils per dollar), and that his first hot dog will give him 30 utils, or 60 utils per dollar (because he can get 2 for a dollar). Remember, though, that if he bought a second hot dog, its MU would be less than that of the first.

First, he buys a hot dog and then continues to make additional choices every noontime for the rest of this week. But now that he's already had a hot dog for lunch this week, a second hot dog lunch (on Tuesday) doesn't taste quite as good. Its MU falls to 25 (or its MU/P to 50). But that's what the MU/P of a first pizza is! So now he's indifferent; that is, at this point, he'd just as soon buy one as the other. Remember, though, that his income permits him to buy both: he has not reached his budget restraint. But on Wednesday and Thursday (his third and fourth choice days this week), he'll buy a pizza one day and a hot dog the other, in some order (maybe he'll toss a coin).

Table 4-1 shows how Bloggs maximized utility in his choice of luncheon menus. By Friday, not only are Bloggs's taste buds dulled, but he has also reached his budget restraint ($4.50). In equilibrium, then, he will buy 3 hot dogs and 3 pizzas this week.

1. $MU_h/P_h = MU_p/P_p$ (MU per dollar of hot dogs [40] = MU per dollar of pizzas [40])

2. $P_h h + P_p z = Y$ (Expenditures on hot dogs [$1.50] + expenditure on pizzas [$3.00] = income [$4.50])

Table 4-1
Maximizing Utility: Hot Dogs Versus Pizzas Per Week

Hot Dogs ($P_h = 50$¢)				
A	**B**	**C**	**D**	**E**
Number Bought	**Money Spent**	**Marginal Utility**	**MU_h/P_h**	**Choice**
1	.50	30	60	1
2	1.00	25	50	2
3	3.50	20	40	4
4	2.50	15	30	6
5	3.00	10	20	7

Pizzas ($P_p = \$1.00$)				
A	**B**	**C**	**D**	**E**
Number Bought	**Money Spent**	**Marginal Utility**	**MU_p/P_p**	**Choice**
1	2.00	50	50	2
2	3.00	45	45	3
3	4.50	40	40	4
4	4.00	35	35	5
5	5.00	30	30	6

Column A = number of hot dogs or pizzas bought.
Column B = dollars spent on hot dogs or pizza (cumulatively).
Column C = MU per dollar spent on hot dogs or pizzas (MU_h or MU_p).
Column D = order in which consumer makes choices (MU_h/P_h or MU_p/P_p).
Column E = choice.

Deriving a Demand Curve

Now let's examine the demand curve, the essential topic in this section. Suppose we want to know what Joe Bloggs' demand curve for pizzas looks like (Figure 4-5). We know one point on that curve (hypothetical point *A*). When pizzas are selling for $1.00 apiece, Joe will buy 3 per week. Drawing a demand curve, of course, requires at least *two* points (prices, quantities). But the manager of the cafeteria, in an effort to pull in more business, runs a big sale on pizzas and drops the price to 50¢ apiece. The price of hot dogs stays the same (50¢). In Table 4-2, we recalculate the MU per dollar for pizzas at their new, lower price (50¢). Note that Bloggs' budget restraint has been affected by the price reduction. If you go back to Figure 4-4, you see that although he can still buy 9 hot dogs at their (unchanged) price with his (unchanged) money income, he can now buy as many as 9 pizzas as well. The budget restraint, in other words, has rotated upward or to the right from its intercept (9) on the hot dogs axis. When the choices are recalculated with the higher MU_p/P_p values, the first four choices are pizzas. The fifth and sixth choices involve 1 each of the 2 goods. The consumer now has consumed 6 pizzas and 2

Figure 4-5
Joe Bloggs' Demand for Pizzas

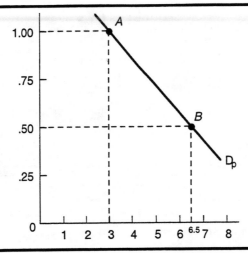

In Figure 4-5, at a price of $1.00 apiece, Bloggs consumes 3 pizzas per week (point *A*). At a price of 50¢ apiece, he consumes 6.5 per week (point *B*).

Table 4-2
Maximizing Utility: Hot Dogs Versus Pizzas Per Week

Hot Dogs (50¢)				
A	**B**	**C**	**D**	**E**
Number Bought	**Money Spent**	**Marginal Utility**	MU_h/P_h	**Choice**
1	3.00	30	60	5
2	4.00	25	50	6
3.5	4.50	20	40	7
4		15	30	
5		10	20	
6		05	10	

Pizzas (50¢)				
A	**B**	**C**	**D**	**E**
Number Bought	**Money Spent**	**Marginal Utility**	MU_p/P_p	**Choice**
1	.50	50	100	1
2	1.00	45	90	2
3	1.50	40	80	3
4	2.00	35	70	4
5	2.50	30	60	5
6	3.50	25	50	6
6.5	4.25	20	40	7

Column A = number of hot dogs or pizzas bought.
Column B = dollars spent on hot dogs or pizza (cumulatively).
Column C = MU per dollar spent on hot dogs or pizzas (MU_h or MU_p).
Column D = order in which consumer makes choices (MU_h/P_h or MU_p/P_p).
Column E = choice.

hot dogs and has (cumulatively) spent $4.00 of his income. His seventh choice would be 1 of each good because $MU_h/P_h = MU_p/P_p$. The problem with that choice is that our consumer *cannot* make it because he would be beyond his budget restraint. For the sake of simplification, the theory assumes that goods are divisible; in equilibrium, then we will permit the consumer as a seventh choice to consume ½ hot dog and ½ pizza.

Bloggs, as we see, has bought a lot more pizzas, 6½ to be exact. At this point he will make the new MU_h/P_h equal to MU_p/P_p. (He'll spend all his money and will be in equilibrium.) Thus, 6½ pizzas per week at 50¢ each constitutes another point on Joe's demand curve (hypothetical point *B*). Connecting points such as *A* and *B*, we obtain curve D_p shown in Figure 4-5. This is Bloggs' demand curve for pizzas.

Why does the curve slope the way D_p does? Because of *diminishing MU*. If the MU of pizzas had not fallen as Bloggs ate more of them per week, this curve would not slope downward. This is an important point to remember. It is also important to remember that it is the *marginal* utility of a good rather than its *total* utility that determines the demand for it—the prices people are willing to pay for various quantities of it.

The so-called **paradox of value** pointed out by Adam Smith in *The Wealth of Nations*, is that people are willing to pay a very high price for diamonds, but only a low price for water. Yet the total utility of water is much greater than that of diamonds. People must have water to sustain their lives, and everybody can get along without diamonds. The MU of diamonds, however, is much higher than that of water under most circumstances. So people are willing to pay more for another diamond than they are for the another unit of water consumed.

Paradox of Value
Is that some goods have great total utility in use (e.g., water) but little in exchange while other goods have relatively little value in use (e.g., diamonds) but great value in exchange. The price we are willing to pay for a good is based on its value in exchange.

Independent Utilities: A Simplifying Assumption

Independent Utilities
The utility of one good does not depend on the consumption of another good.

In the preceding illustration of utility theory, we treated the MU of the 2 goods as independent of each other. The MU of a pizza did not depend on the number of hot dogs consumed and vice versa. While this kept the theory and the analysis easy, it is strictly a simplification of the reality in which goods are not only unrelated to each other or substitutes for each other but also may be complements to each other. In the case of complements, goods consumed together (tapes and tape players, shirts and ties, etc.), the utility of the one good clearly may depend on the consumption of the other.

Market Demand

Market Demand
The sum of the demand curves of all consumers in the market.

Market demand is the sum of the demand curves of all consumers in the market. At each possible price, one adds the quantities demanded by all consumers (assuming no interdependence among buyers). When these points are plotted, they form a demand curve for pizzas such as that in Figure 4-6. Although the market demand curve in Figure 4-6 involves summing the quantities demanded by each of 3 consumers at each possible price, the concept can easily be extended to any number of consumers.

Market demand (D_m), in Figure 4-6, slopes down to the right, just as Bloggs' demand curve in Figure 4-5 did. The reason is the same in both cases: *diminishing MU* as people consume more of a particular good in a given period of time.

Elasticity: Estimating Consumer Responses to Price and Other Changes

The answers to many questions about our market system depend on how much or how little consumers respond in their purchases of a good to changes in the price of that product as well as to changes in such things as income and the prices of other goods. Will a tariff on imported oil cause oil companies to cut back sharply on imports of crude oil and gasoline? If toothpaste goes up to $5 a tube, will people still buy it? Will Detroit break out of its sales doldrums by cutting prices or offering lower interest rates on auto financing? If we have rapid growth, which industries will benefit most? If the price of oil goes down, what will happen to automobile sales? The answers to these and many other questions depend on the extent to which consumers respond to changes in the various things that affect their market behavior.

Figure 4-6
Market Demand for Pizzas in a Three-Consumer Market

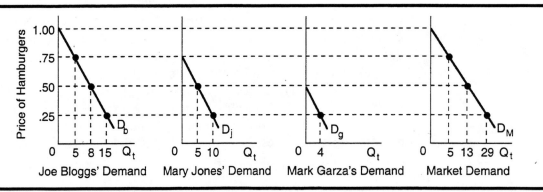

In Figure 4-6, there are 3 consumers of pizzas, Joe Bloggs, Mary Jones and Mark Garza. Each has his or her own demand for pizzas (D_b, D_j, D_g). At each price from zero to $1.00, the market demand (D_M) can be obtained by adding up the quantity demanded by each consumer. At a price of $1.00, none will be demanded (market quantity demanded equals zero). At a price of 75¢, Bloggs will buy 5, the others zero (market demand equals 5). At a price of 50¢, Bloggs buys 8, Jones buys 5, Garza none (market quantity demanded equals 13). At a price of 25¢, Bloggs buys 15, Jones 10, Garza 4 (market quantity demanded equals 29).

Price Elasticity of Demand

Price Elasticity of Demand

$$\left(\frac{\Delta Q/Q}{\Delta P/P}\right)$$

An estimate of the rate at which the quantity demanded of a good changes in response to small changes in its price.

Prices are the key information generate[d] price, as we have seen, are central to the [ ] discussed in terms of substitution and inc[ome] estimate of the rate at which consumers will price of a good is an important tool to p[ ] officials. The estimate, called the **price elas**[ticity] pares the rate of change in the quantity deman[d] rate at which its price changes.

Symbolically, then, the price elasticity [E_d] is the rate of change in the quantity demanded of a go[od ($\Delta Q/Q$) divided by the rate of change in the price of that good ($\Delta P/P$), or

$$\frac{\Delta Q/Q}{\Delta P/P}$$

where Q is quantity demanded and P is price. There are three possible relationships between these two rates of change:

1. **Price elastic demand.** Quantity demanded varies at a greater rate than price. Since $\Delta Q/Q > \Delta P/P$, the elasticity estimate is greater than 1. When $E_d > 1$, we say that demand is *price elastic*.

Price Elastic Demand
A condition in which quantity demanded varies at a greater rate than price.

2. **Price inelastic demand.** Quantity demanded varies at a lesser rate than price. Since $\Delta Q/Q < \Delta P/P$, the elasticity estimate is less than 1. When $E_d < 1$, we say that demand is *price inelastic*.

Price Inelastic Demand
A condition in which quantity demanded varies at a lesser rate than price.

3. **Unit elastic demand.** Quantity demanded varies at the same rate as price. Since $\Delta Q/Q = \Delta P/P$, the elasticity estimate is equal to 1. When $E_d = 1$, we say that demand is *unit elastic*.

Unit Elastic Demand
A condition in which quantity demanded varies at the same rate as price.

Elasticity of Demand and the Slope of a Demand Curve

Elasticity of demand (E_d) is not the same as the slope of the demand curve. The latter measures the absolute change in quantity associated with an absolute change in price. If slopes were used, one could not compare one market with another with respect to the way quantity demanded responds to changes in price, since the units of measurement of quantity and price are very different in different markets. Consider, for example, the differences when one is discussing weekly demand for cars and weekly demand for hamburgers. Therefore, when we divide a percent by a percent, we get a **pure number**—one that is independent of the units of measurement of price and quantity. We define elasticity, thus, as

Pure Number
One that is independent of the units in which it is measured.

$$E_d = \frac{\Delta Q/Q}{\Delta P/P} = \frac{\text{percentage change in quantity demanded/quantity}}{\text{percentage change in price/price}}$$

The Δ (Greek delta) represents a finite change; Q is the quantity demanded; and P is the price.

Computing Price Elasticities of Demand

How do you calculate a price elasticity of demand? Suppose you want to know the *market* price elasticity of demand for hot dogs when the price drops from $1.25 to $1.00 in Figure 4-7. As we have noted, you cannot rely on the slope of D_m because it would not give a number to compare with the price elasticity of demand for other goods.

To get a pure number—one that does not depend on absolute prices and quantities—you need to compare rates of change in quantity demanded and price. We see also an additional problem in Figure 4-7, since we get two elasticities (different coefficients) depending on whether we move from C to D (down the curve) or from D to C (up the curve.) The usual way to solve this problem of differing results is to take the *average rate of change* of quantity demanded divided by the average rate of change of the prices in question. For example, let's calculate the average rate at which quantity demanded (Q) changes as price (P) changes when the price of hot dogs goes from $1.25 to $1.00 (Figure 4-7).

The formula for calculating the average elasticity of demand (E_d), called the **midpoint formula**, is as follows, where Q_1 equals the old quantity, Q_2 equals the new quantity, P_1 equals the old price, and P_2 equals the new price:

Midpoint Formula
A device for calculating the price elasticity of demand by dividing the average rate of change in quantity demanded by the average rate of change in price.

$$E_d = \frac{\Delta Q/Q}{\Delta P/P} = \frac{[Q_2 - Q_1]/[(Q_1 + Q_2)/2]}{[P_2 - P_1]/[(P_1 + P_2)/2]} =$$

$$\frac{\text{change in quantity/average quantity}}{\text{change in price/average price}}$$

Figure 4-7
Market Demand for Hot Dogs

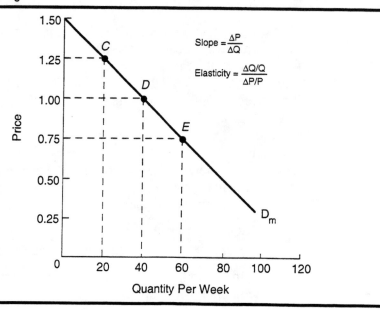

Since you divide both quantities and prices by 2, you are left with the average change in quantity demanded and the average change in price over the arc.

You can now take the data in Figure 4-7 and calculate the E_d for hot dogs that are priced between $1.25 and $1.00.

1. $\dfrac{Q_2 - Q_1}{(Q_2 + Q_1)/2} = \dfrac{40 - 20}{(40 + 20)/2} = \dfrac{20}{30} = \dfrac{2}{3} = .66$

2. $\dfrac{P_2 - P_1}{(P_2 + P_1)/2} = \dfrac{1.00 - 1.25}{(1.00 + 1.25)/2} = \dfrac{-.25}{1.125} = -0.222$

3. $E_d = \dfrac{.66}{-.222} = -3.0$

Note that elasticity comes out as a negative number, since you are dividing a positive ratio by a negative ratio. Since the negative sign has no economic significance, however, you can ignore it.

The price elasticity of demand between $1.25 and $1.00 is 3. In other words, demand is very price elastic; $\Delta Q/Q$, the rate at which the *quantity* of hot dogs sold changed, was 3 times as great as $\Delta P/P$, the rate at which the *price* of hot dogs changed.

If you calculate the elasticity of demand between $1.00 and 75¢, you will discover that it is different from that between $1.25 and $1.00, even though the price drops by the same amount. Although there are constant elasticity of demand curves, they are rare. Normally the price elasticity of demand changes continuously, even along straight-line demand curves (which have constant slopes).

Differing Elasticities of Demand

The best way to understand this is graphically (see Figure 4-8). In our example, demand was price elastic ($E_d > 1$), which is shown in Figure 4-8(*d*). *Price elastic* means that quantity demanded changes more rapidly than price. There are two other possibilities for demand/price elasticity.

1. Demand may be *price inelastic* ($E_d < 1$) as shown in Figure 4-8(*b*). *Price inelastic* means that quantity demanded changes less rapidly than price. In our example, a 10 percent decrease in hot dog prices might have resulted in only a 5 percent increase in quantity demanded. Keep in mind a special qualification about Figures 4-8(*b*) and (*d*). Almost any straight-line demand curve has varying elasticities throughout its length. Some parts of Figure 4-8(*b*), therefore, exhibit greater elasticity than some parts of Figure 4-8(*d*). The 2 curves are shown here merely to illustrate the general configuration of elasticity and inelasticity, not to reflect particular points on either curve.

Figure 4-8
Differing Elasticities of Demand

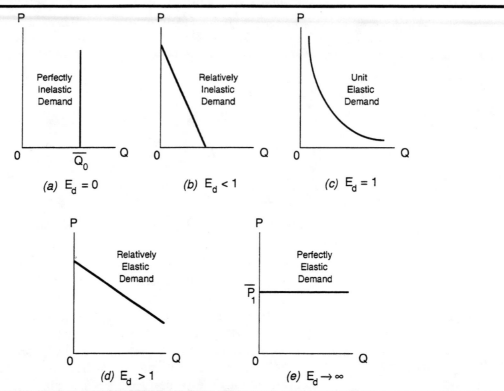

(a) $E_d = 0$

(b) $E_d < 1$

(c) $E_d = 1$

(d) $E_d > 1$

(e) $E_d \rightarrow \infty$

2. Demand may be *unit elastic* ($E_d = 1$) as shown in Figure 4-8(c), with respect to price. This means that quantity demanded changes at the same rate as price. In the example, if a 10 percent reduction in the price of hot dogs brought about a 10 percent increase in the quantity demanded, demand elasticity would have been unitary.

In addition to these ranges of price elasticity, there are two unusual straight-line cases that represent elasticity limits.

Perfect Inelasticity
A condition in which the price elasticity of demand is zero.

1. **Perfect inelasticity**, Figure 4-8(a), is the demand condition in which $E_d = 0$. In other words, for the given range of prices, quantity demanded does not change at all as price changes. (If eyeglasses go up substantially in price, a myopic person will still keep buying them. If insulin goes up in price, the diabetic will continue to buy it.) Remember, though, that elasticity estimates are valid only for a well defined range of observed prices. We cannot be confident that such estimates of consumer responses could be extended to unobserved prices.

Perfect Elasticity
A condition in which the price elasticity of demand approaches infinity.

2. **Perfect elasticity**, Figure 4-8(e), is the demand condition in which $E_d \rightarrow \infty$. (The ∞ symbol means "infinity.") For the given range of quantities, price of the good is constant and the public will buy any quantity of it at the going price.

The demand curve in Figure 4-8(a) is perfectly inelastic; E_d is zero. This means that consumers will buy Q_0 of this product, no matter what the price (at least for the given range of prices). The demand curve in Figure 4-8(e) is perfectly elastic; E_d approaches infinity. This means that consumers will buy any quantity as long as its price remains P_1, and presumably nothing at any higher price.

Demand curves ordinarily do not look like either Figures 4-8(a) or (e). Each is a limit: one (Figure 4-8(a)) the lower, the other (Figure 4-8(e)) the upper. To explain why, we will present the factors that determine price elasticity of demand.

Determinants of the Elasticity of Demand

1. *Substitutability.* The demand curve in Figure 4-8(a) implies that there may be no substitutes for the item (for example, the insulin referred to above). Consumers are willing to buy a certain quantity at any observed price. On the other hand, Figure 4-8(e) implies virtually perfect substitution; any price above P_1 will eliminate demand. Consumers apparently have perfect alternatives to buying this product at any price above P.

Real world elasticities are ordinarily between the two extremes of Figures 4-8(a) and (e). For example, as a general rule, there are good substitutes for toothpaste. There are, on the other hand, no good substitutes for some medicines such as insulin.

2. *Proportion of income spent on the good (budget restraint).* If the price of cars goes up 10 percent, people *must* cut back on the number of cars they buy because their purchasing power (assuming everything else remains constant) compels them to. Thus, the E_d tends to be high for cars and other goods on which people spend a large part of their income. If the price of hamburgers goes up 10 percent, people *need not* drastically cut down the number they buy, because their purchasing power is not greatly reduced.

3. *Postponability (luxuries vs necessities).* Consumers buy some goods now because they cannot postpone buying them. Food and medical care fall in this category; their price elasticity of demand is thus low. But people can postpone purchases of other goods, such as consumer durables (cars, TVs, refrigerators, washing machines, and so forth). Demand for them is quite price elastic. As prices of new cars rise, many people chose to repair older cars, so the E_d for new cars is relatively high. It is tempting to say that goods that have low price elasticities of demand are necessities while goods that have high price elasticities are luxuries. Indeed, a functional way to define a necessity is a good whose consumption cannot be postponed; a luxury, on the other hand, is a good whose consumption can be postponed.

4. *Time*. How consumers react to price changes and how much they react depends on their knowledge of alternatives. While you may say that this is a question of substitution, it takes time to determine and act on alternatives. Notice in the list of selected elasticities in Table 4-3 that some elasticities vary between the short-run and the long-run estimates (airline travel, local public transport). Usually, where time is a factor in E_d, the elasticity is much smaller in the short run than in the long run. If, for example, you must attend a meeting several thousand miles away the day after tomorrow, you have no alternative but to buy an airline ticket at the going price. A small increase in that price would alter your alternatives and behavior very little. On the other hand, if you must attend that same meeting 6 months from now, you may have better alternatives (train, bus, private automobile, buying special fare air tickets); a small increase in airline prices would, in the long run, induce a larger change in quantity demanded than it would in the short run.

Some Selected Price Elasticities of Demand

You can see in Table 4-3 some actual estimates of price elasticities of demand ranging from goods that have almost perfectly inelastic demands (local newspapers, potatoes, electric light bulbs) to those with very elastic demands (airline travel in the long run, furniture, and fresh tomatoes). These are meant to be merely illustrative. Can you explain each of these elasticities? If not, look back at the determinants of elasticities and ask in each case (1) are there substitutes?, (2) do

Table 4-3
Selected Price Elasticities of Demand for Goods and Services

Good or Service	Elasticity Estimate	Elastic/Inelastic
Local newspaper	-0.1	Very inelastic
Potatoes	-0.3	Very inelastic
Electric light bulb	-0.33	Very inelastic
Tobacco products	-0.46	Very inelastic
Airline travel (short run)	-0.6	Inelastic
Local public transport (short run)	-0.6	Inelastic
Physicians services	-0.6	Inelastic
Housing	-1.0	Unit elastic
Refrigerators	-1.1	Slightly elastic
Washing machines	-1.1	Slightly elastic
Sewing machines	-1.1	Slightly elastic
Sporting goods and equipment	-1.2	Slightly elastic
Local public transport (long run)	-1.2	Slightly elastic
Automobiles	-1.5	Elastic
Airline travel (long run)	-2.4	Very elastic
Furniture	-3.04	Very elastic
Fresh tomatoes	-4.6	Very elastic

Source: D. M. Shuffett, The Demand and Price Structure for Selected Vegetables Washington, D.C. U.S. Department of Agriculture, 1954., H.S. Houthakker and L.D. Taylor, Consumer Demand in the United States: Analyses and Projections Cambridge, Mass: Harvard University Press. 1970., Ragnar Frisch. "A Complete Scheme for Computing Direct Demand Elasticities in a Model with Many Sectors" Econometrica, XXVII, 1959.

consumers spend much of their income on the good?, (3) can the consumption of the good be postponed?, and finally, (4) what is the influence of time on the consumers' behavior?

Why Do Elasticities Matter?

Many public agencies as well as private firms and individuals have undertaken to estimate price elasticities of demand. As such empirical estimation is costly, you may well ask why such market studies are important. There are two dimensions to the answer.

Elasticities and Total Revenue

To any firm or industry, total revenue is obtained by multiplying price times quantity sold. Note, as in Figure 4-9, that this is the area under the demand curve at any point (such as A). Whether total revenue will rise or fall as price changes depends on which changes more, price or quantity demanded. We see in Figure 4-9 that as price falls from P_0 to P_1, there is a loss of total revenue equal to the difference in prices times the original quantity, or to the area P_1P_0AB. At the lower price,

Figure 4-9
The Demand Curve and Total Revenue of a Firm

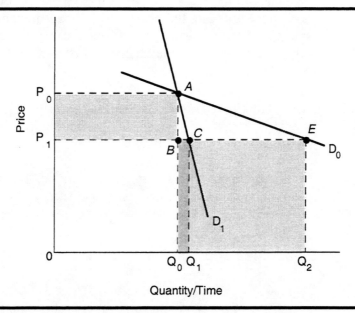

In Figure 4-9, if the firm sells Q_0 at P_0, its total revenue is $0P_0AQ_0$. If it lowers price to P_1, its change in total revenue depends on whether it faces (relatively inelastic) D_1 or (relatively elastic) D_0. In either case it loses revenue P_1P_0AB. If it faces D_1, its gain (Q_0BCQ_1) is less than its loss. If D_0, its gain (Q_0BEQ_2) is greater than its loss. With demand curve D_1, a reduction in price results in a decrease in total revenue. With demand curve D_0, a reduction in price results in an increase in total revenue.

the addition to revenue depends on whether demand below P_0 is D_0 or D_1. D_1 is relatively inelastic and the gain (Q_0BCQ_1) is less than the loss. D_0 is relatively elastic and the gain (Q_0BEQ_2) is greater than the loss. With relatively inelastic demand, total revenue falls as price falls; with relatively elastic demand, total revenue rises as price falls. Notice that this conclusion works in reverse for price increases. As price rises from P_1 to P_0, if demand is relatively inelastic (D_1), the gain (P_1P_0AB) is greater than the loss (Q_0BCQ_1). If demand is relatively elastic, the gain (P_1P_0AD) is less than the loss (Q_0BEQ_2).

Prices Go Up, Some Industries Prosper, Some Suffer

As prices rise, if you observe that producers in the industry prosper or have more revenue, the price elasticity of demand for that industry's product must be less than 1 (inelastic, $\Delta Q/Q < \Delta P/P$). The diamond industry, whose prices are administered by one firm, DeBeers, is an example. If, as prices rise, producers have less revenue, the price elasticity of demand for that industry's product must be greater than 1 (elastic, $\Delta Q/Q > \Delta P/P$). From Table 4-3, you can see that the furniture industry ($E_d = 3.04$) is a likely example.

Prices Go Down, Some Industries Suffer, Some Prosper

If, as prices fall, you observe that producers in the industry suffer or have less revenue, it must be that the price elasticity of demand for that industry's product is less than 1 (inelastic, $\Delta Q/Q < \Delta P/P$). Most basic agricultural industries (wheat, corn, soybeans, etc.) are examples. If, as prices fall, your observe that producers in the industry have more revenue, the price elasticity of demand for the industry's product must be greater than 1 (elastic $\Delta Q/Q > \Delta P/P$). From Table 4-3, you can see that the airline industry in the long run is a likely example.

Prices Go Up or Down, Revenues Remain the Same

If, as prices go up or down, you observe that producers in the industry have unchanged total revenue, it must be that the demand for the industry's product is 1 (unit elastic, $\Delta Q/Q = \Delta P/P$). Note from Table 4-3 that the housing industry is an example. Though not in the table, local telephone calls are another ($E_d = 1.0$).

Elasticities and Total Revenue: A Summation

Table 4-4 contains a summary of the relationships between price elasticities of demand and total revenue for changes in price. Both 5 percent price increase and 5 percent price decrease are considered. Should you lose your bearings in understanding what happens to total revenue of firms and industries when their prices change, this table is a handy and easy reference.

Table 4-4
Elasticity of Demand and Effects on Total Revenue of Price Changes

Elasticity	Elastic or Inelastic	What Happens With a 5 Percent Price Increase?	
		To Quantity	To Total Revenue
$E_d = 0$	Perfectly Inelastic	No Change	Increases by 5%
$0 < E_d < 1$	Inelastic	Decreases by <5%	Increases by <5%
$E_d = 1$	Unit Elastic	Decreases by 5%	No Change
$1 < E_d < \infty$	Elastic	Decreases by >5%	Decreases
$E_d \rightarrow \infty$	Elastic	Decreases to zero	Decreases to zero
		What Happens With a 5 Percent Price Decrease?	
$E_d = 0$	Perfectly Inelastic	No Change	Decreases by 5%
$0 < E_d < 1$	Inelastic	Increases by <5%	Decreases by >5%
$E_d = 1$	Unit Elastic	Increases by 5%	No Change
$1 < E_d < \infty$	Elastic	Increases by >5%	Increases by >5%
$E_d \rightarrow \infty$	Elastic	Indeterminate	Indeterminate

Why Do Elasticities Matter?
An Automobile Industry Example

Some years ago, the automobile industry, under presidential pressure to lower prices, was negotiating a wage contract with the union representing its employees. The union presented a proposal that called for lowering auto prices and increasing wages while arguing that shareholders in the industry would not suffer as a result. The argument of the union was based on the conclusion that the price elasticity of demand for automobiles was 4 (very elastic). A 5 percent reduction in auto prices, it was projected, would result in a 20 percent increase in the quantity demanded of automobiles. The industry's representatives, on the other hand, argued that the price elasticity of demand for automobiles was 0.5 (inelastic). A 5 percent reduction in automobile prices would result in a 2½ percent increase in the quantity demanded of autos. If one accepted the union estimate, reduced prices would increase industry revenues; if the industry estimate was accepted, lowering automobile prices would lead to reduced industry revenues. With the union estimate, the revenue "pie" would grow and everybody (employees, shareholders, consumers) could be made better off; with the industry estimate, the revenue "pie" would shrink and anybody's gain would be the loss of some one else.

Elasticities and Excise Tax Incidence

An excise tax is a tax on a domestically produced (non-imported) good. When such a tax is levied, it raises the cost and, *ceteris paribus*, reduces the supply of that good. Where will the burden of the tax lie, on the producer or the consumer? The answer depends crucially on the price elasticity of demand for the good as we see in Figure 4-10.

In Figure 4-10 we observe in *(a)* a good with relatively inelastic demand (D_i) and in *(b)* a good with relatively elastic demand (D_e). When an excise tax is levied on a good, its payment raises the cost of production (such taxes are paid by the producer directly to the government) and reduces supply from S_0 to S_1. With inelastic demand in *(a)*, the burden to producers in the form of reduced sales $(0Q_0 - 0Q_1)$ is small, while the burden to consumers in the form of higher prices $(0P_1 - 0P_0)$ is large. Most of the burden of the tax falls on consumers. With relatively elastic demand in *(b)*, the burden on producers in reduced sales $(0Q_0 - 0Q_1)$ is large whereas the burden on consumers in the form of higher prices $(0P_1 - 0P_0)$ is small.

A major implication of the above is that governments seeking revenue producing excise taxes should tax goods that have relatively price inelastic demands. A famous Chief Justice of the U.S., John Marshall, remarked that "anything that can be taxed can be

Figure 4-10
The Incidence or Burden of an Excise Tax: Elastic Versus Inelastic Demand

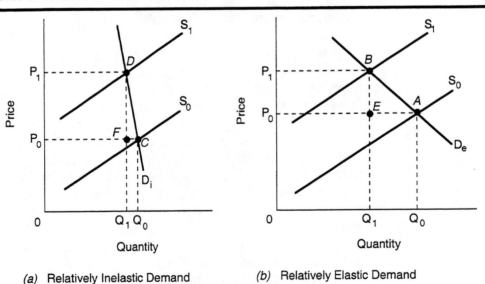

(a) Relatively Inelastic Demand   *(b)* Relatively Elastic Demand

In Figure 4-10, two markets, *(a)* and *(b)*, are portrayed. In both markets, the levying of an excise tax causes supply costs to rise and the supply curve to shift from S_0 to S_1. In *(a)*, demand is relatively inelastic and the decrease in supply leads to a large increase in the equilibrium price (P_0 to P_1), and a relatively small decrease in quantity demanded. The burden of the tax falls heavily on consumers. In *(b)*, demand is relatively elastic and the decrease in supply leads to a relatively small increase in price (P_0 to P_1), and a relatively large decrease in the quantity demanded. The burden of the tax falls heavily on producers.

destroyed." If the purpose of the tax is to "destroy" or reduce the consumption of a good rather than to raise revenue, what should be the price elasticity of demand for that good in order that the tax accomplish its purpose?

Price Elasticity and Straight-Line Demand Curves: A Final Note

Earlier, in Figure 4-8, we looked at two straight-line demand curves that have constant elasticities. One, the perfectly inelastic demand curve of Figure 4-8(a), had a constant elasticity of zero. The other, the perfectly elastic demand curve of Figure 4-8(e), had a constant elasticity that approached infinity. In various places in this chapter, including the section above on price elasticity and the incidence of taxes (Figure 4-10), we have referred to relatively elastic and relatively inelastic straight-line demand curves. Fittingly, we conclude this section on the price elasticity of demand with a relationship between elasticity and usual straight-line demand curves. Since the statistical demand curves we encounter in reality *are* straight lines, the concept is important.

All straight-line demand curves (other than those that are perfectly inelastic or perfectly elastic) have continuously changing elasticities. They contain price elastic portions as well as price inelastic portions and, at their midpoints, are unit elastic.

Let us take as an example; the (hypothetical) linear demand schedule in Table 4-5. The price elasticity of demand is calculated (using the midpoint formula) for the various segments of the schedule from $10 to $1. Notice that the elasticity declines continually from a high of 6.35 (the $10–$9 segment) to a low of 0.157 (the $2–$1 segment). Although the absolute changes in price (ΔP) are constant,

Table 4-5
A Hypothetical Demand and Total Revenue Schedule

Price	Quantity	E_d	Total Revenue
$10	10		$100
		6.35	
9	20		180
		3.39	
8	30		240
		2.15	
7	40		280
		1.44	
6	50		300
		1.00	
5	60		300
		0.69	
4	70		280
		0.47	
3	80		240
		0.30	
2	90		180
		0.157	
1	·100		100

the *rate* of change in price ($\Delta P/P$) is continually changing and getting larger. Notice that the absolute changes in quantity (ΔQ) are constant but that the *rate* of change in quantity ($\Delta Q/Q$) is continually changing and getting smaller. Thus, as we move down the demand curve, E_d becomes smaller for each price decrease. At some point, $5 (or arc $6–$5) on the demand schedule ($\Delta Q/Q = \Delta P/P$) and the price elasticity of demand equals 1. Below this point, demand is price inelastic ($E_d < 1$) and approaches zero as price approaches zero.

In Figure 4-11, the hypothetical demand data from Table 4-5 are plotted in *(a)*. The *AB* segment of the demand curve represents the $10–$9 range or arc. Notice that as price falls and demand is elastic ($E_d = 6.35$) total revenue in *(b)* increases. At point *D*, representing the $6–$5 arc of the demand curve, demand is unit elastic ($E_d = 1$) and total revenue is at a maximum ($300) below point *D*, demand is price inelastic ($E_d < 1$) and as price falls toward *E* and *F*, total revenue decreases.

The basic point deserves to be restated. Straight-line demand curves have constant slopes but continually changing elasticities.

An Implication: Where to Set Price

Suppose that you were the person charged with deciding the range of prices within which to set the price of the firm facing the demand curve in Figure 4-11. An interesting question to ask yourself is: what prices should you rule out? Economists would expect that the firm would set price somewhere between *A* and *D* ($10–$5). Why? The answer is that we should not expect the firm to knowingly operate in the *DF* portion of the demand curve because its revenues would fall as it increases output beyond 60 units; as its costs surely will continue to rise, it would have lower profit or larger losses as it expands output.

Other Demand Elasticities

While price changes are key to the operation of markets, other factors change as well including consumer incomes and prices of other related goods. We held such factors constant in calculating price elasticities of demand; now we shall hold the price of the good in question constant and identify elasticities associated with income changes as well as elasticities associated with changes in the prices of other goods.

Income Elasticity of Demand

Earlier in this chapter, we talked about a (real) income effect from a change in the price of a good. Consumer incomes and spending are

Figure 4-11
Price Elasticity of Demand and Total Revenue on a Linear Demand Curve (from Table 4-5)

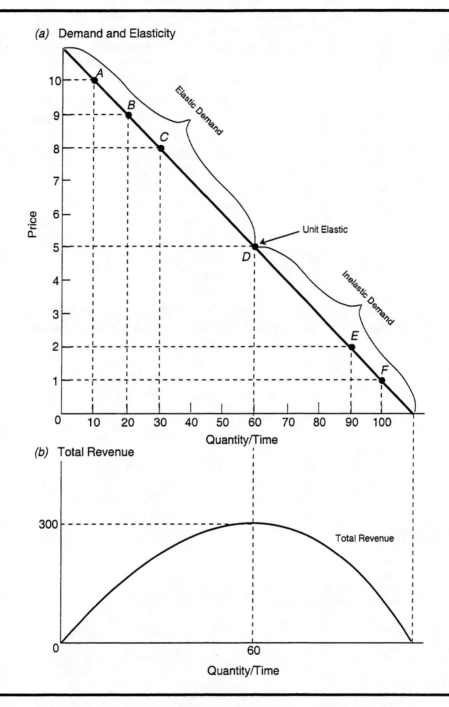

When price is reduced over the range from $10 to $5, demand is elastic ($\Delta Q/Q > \Delta P/P$) and, as a result, total revenue increases to a maximum of $300 at the price (actually 2 prices, $6, $5 since these are arc elasticities) at which demand is unit elastic. As prices below point C in the range from $4 to $1, demand is inelastic ($\Delta Q/Q < \Delta P/P$) and total revenue decreases to $100 and approaches zero as price approaches zero.

also importantly affected by economic growth or decline and resulting changes in money incomes. An indicator of the effect of changes in money income on the demand (size of the market) for a good is the **income elasticity of demand**—the rate at which the demand for a good varies as consumers' incomes vary. As we noted earlier, the demand for most goods varies in the same direction and at about the same rate as the variation in income. Such goods we called *normal goods*. For some goods, however, demand varies inversely with income changes—as incomes rise, demand falls; as incomes fall, demand rises. These goods we called *inferior goods*. Finally, there are *superior goods*—those whose demand varies in the same direction as income varies, but at a greater rate.

In Table 4-6, we see some actual estimates of income elasticities of demand. Note that the income elasticities for some goods are greater than 1 (automobiles, restaurant meals, etc.). These (income) superior goods are sometimes referred to as "luxuries." Other normal goods have income elasticities that are greater than zero but less than 1 (rental housing, fruits and berries, etc.) and are referred to as "necessities." Two goods on the list, margarine and flour, have negative elasticities of demand and are called inferior goods.

Like price elasticities of demand, income elasticities are strongly affected by time. The longer the time dimension, that is, the longer consumers have to react to income changes, the greater tends to be the elasticity. Longer term forecasts of market size by private firms and government agencies are, therefore, heavily conditioned on forecasts of income changes in the economy.

Cross Price Elasticities of Demand

Often, one of the most difficult tasks in analyzing a market is to define the scope or extent of that market. A tool of some usefulness

Table 4-6
Selected Income Elasticities of Demand

Good	Classification	Elasticity
Automobile	Superior	2.45
(Owner occupied) housing	Superior	1.49
Restaurant meals	Superior	1.40
Clothing	Superior	1.02
Tobacco	Superior	1.02
Fruits and berries	Normal	0.70
Rental Housing	Normal	0.43
Butter	Normal	0.42
Margarine	Inferior	-0.20
Flour	Inferior	-0.36

Source: H.S. Houthakker and L.D. Taylor, *Consumer Demand in the United States: Analyses and Projections,* 2nd ed. Cambridge, Mass. Harvard University Press, 1970. Herman Wald, *Demand Analysis,* New York. John Wiley and Sons, Inc. 1953, H. Wald and C.E. Leser, "Commodity Group Expenditure Functions for the United Kingdom, 1948–1957," *Econometrica,* January, 1961.

Cross Price Elasticity of Demand
The percentage change in the demand for one good divided by the percentage change in the price of another good.

in identifying the boundaries of a market is the **cross price elasticity of demand** or the percentage change in the demand for one good divided by the percentage change in the price of another good. In estimating such an elasticity we ask the following question: "If the price of good A goes up (or down) what will happen to the sales of good B?" The answer permits us to identify whether the goods are (1) substitutes, or (2) complements, or (3) whether the 2 goods are unrelated to each other. The three possibilities are:

1. *Substitutes.* As the price of good A rises, there is an increase in the demand for good B. The implication is that a decrease in the quantity demanded of A leads to an increase in the size of the market for B. The 2 goods, therefore, are considered substitutes.

2. *Complements.* As the price of good A rises, there is a decrease in the demand for good B. The implication is that a decrease in the quantity demanded of A leads to a decrease in the size of the market for B. The 2 goods are considered complements, or goods consumed together.

3. *Unrelated.* As the price of good A rises, there is no change in the demand for good B. A decrease in the quantity demanded of A leads to no change in the size of the market for B. The 2 goods are unrelated and are not appropriately looked at as part of the same market.

Cross Price Elasticity Signs

If goods are *substitutes* for each other, we find a positive cross price elasticity of demand (an increase in price of A leads to an increase in the demand for B). If goods are complements we find a negative cross price elasticity between them (an increase in the price of A leads to a decrease in the demand for B). If goods are *unrelated*, we find a cross price elasticity of demand equal to zero (an increase in the price of A will have no effect on the size of the market for B).

Why Do Cross Price Elasticities Matter? An Illustration

Apart from simply identifying the boundaries of a market being studied, the nature and competitiveness of that market may be indicated by cross price elasticities of demand. If goods have high positive cross price elasticities, they may be part of the same industry. An example may help to illustrate this point. After World War II, the U.S. Government sued the DuPont company, arguing that it had monopolized the cellophane market. DuPont responded that the market should be defined not as cellophane but as that of flexible packaging materials. Because there were significant and positive cross price elasticities of demand between cellophane and other packaging materials (waxed paper, etc.), the firm was successful in court showing that it controlled not 75 percent of the (cellophane) market but only about 20 percent of the (flexible packaging materials) market.

APPLICATION:
Will Redistributing Income Make People Happier?

What distinguishes men from pigs is not that they are more happy, but that they can control their environment.

W.A. Lewis

The above title is somewhat deceiving. It may make you think that we are going to deal with the relation between the distribution of income and the happiness of human beings. Actually, economists do not know any more than other people do about what makes people happy. Does having more money make people happier? Or was Groucho Marx right in his cynical comment, "Money can't buy friends, but it sure can buy a better class of enemies."?

The Distribution of Satisfaction
What economists can do is talk about utility or satisfaction, and make assumptions about whether (and at what rate) it changes as people have more income. Two things are self-evident: (1) The utility or satisfaction derived from having more income to spend (or save) is not necessarily the same as the happiness derived from that income. (2) Economists have no "utilmeters" on which to record people's satisfaction. Therefore, the law of diminishing marginal utility of income is only an *assumed* (unproved) relationship. (For example, Elvira Snodgrass is earning $500 a week and gets a $10-a-week raise. Randolph Hertz is earning $100 a week and also gets a $10-a-week raise. According to the principle of diminishing marginal utility of income, Snodgrass' satisfaction is increased less than that of Hertz.)

The little deception in the wording of the title was not designed to mislead you, but to draw your attention to this limitation of economics. We also wanted to lead into a discussion of the important relationship between the distribution of income and the total utility (or satisfaction) of various income groups.

The Distribution of Income
What has happened, in the last 30 or so years, to the distribution of income in the U.S.? Table 4-7 shows that there was relatively little change in the 1960s and 1970s. There has actually been little change since 1947. Other data collected by the federal government (as published in the *Statistical Abstract of the United States*) show that between 1935 and 1947 the distribution of income became less unequal in the U.S. You know that if you assume a *diminishing marginal utility of income*, then redistributing income so that less of it goes to upper-income groups and more to middle- and lower-income groups *increases* the total utility of a nation's people. (The loss in utility by those at the top is more than offset by the gain in utility by those at the bottom, assuming that all people have the same total utility of income functions.)

Table 4-7
Percentage Share of Aggregate Income Received by Each One-fifth of Families and
Unrelated Individuals (selected years)

Income Rank	1950	1960	1970	1980	1985
Total families, percentage	100.00	100.00	100.00	100.00	100.00
Lowest one-fifth	4.5	4.8	5.4	5.1	4.6
Second one-fifth	11.9	12.2	12.2	11.8	10.9
Third one-fifth	17.4	17.8	17.8	17.5	16.9
Fourth one-fifth	23.6	24.0	23.8	24.2	24.2
Highest one-fifth	42.7	41.3	40.9	41.5	43.5
Highest 5 percent	17.3	15.9	15.6	15.7	16.7

Source: U.S. Department of Commerce.

Now what if you do *not* accept the idea of diminishing marginal utility of income? Suppose you believe that the *marginal utility of income is constant*, that each bit added to your income adds the same amount to your satisfaction no matter what your income is. In that case, you could not use utility as an argument in favor of redistributing income. However, you could cite utility to "justify" the fact that the percentage shares of income did not change very much from 1947 to 1971.

Suppose you assumed *increasing marginal utility of income*—people get more and more satisfaction from each increment in their incomes. You could then use utility as an argument for redistributing income in favor of *upper*-income groups. The percentage of income belonging to upper-income groups decreased between 1935 and 1947. In addition, the percentage belonging to the wealthiest 5 percent decreased in the 1960s and slightly in the 1970s (as shown in Table 4-7). The share of income received by the highest 5 percent increased between 1980 and 1985 to 16.7 percent, about the same as in 1950. This redistribution of income must have led to an overall decrease in utility, if you assume an increasing marginal utility of income.

Governments and Income Distribution
Governments have an enormous effect on the distribution of income and thus on total satisfaction or utility of the populace. The strength of this effect depends not only on what governments extract from people in the way of taxes, but also on what people receive in the form of transfer payments (unemployment compensation, subsidies to farmers, social security, and the like), as well as services they receive from governments (police and fire protection, job training, public schooling, food stamps, and the like). Indeed, we should note that the data in Table 4-7 are based on census information and measure only cash incomes. If you add all three elements, you can see that in the past 40 years, government in the U.S. *has* redistributed income. For example, in 1950 households earning more than $7,500 per year received 26 percent of total U.S. income *before* taxes, transfer payments, and government services were considered, but only 19

percent of income *after* these three items were included. At the same time, those earning less than $1,000 received 1.4 percent of income before one took into account the three adjustment factors, but 4 percent after. You can see that some government programs take from the rich and give to the poor.

So whether you believe that government redistribution of income has increased Americans' utility, or welfare depends on whether you believe in increasing or in decreasing marginal utility of income. Many economists assume a decreasing marginal utility of income. Therefore, they feel that the government's redistribution of income has indeed increased total utility.

Note: Although people have used arguments based on diminishing marginal utility to support many government revenue-collecting devices, such as the progressive income tax, this is only one of several reasons given for redistributing income. Other arguments have ranged from moral reasons (a highly unequal distribution of income is "wrong") to the multiplier effect. (More people spend more money when the poor get a larger percentage of national income because the poor spend a larger proportion of their incomes than the rich do.) Arguments against income redistribution have also not rested solely on grounds of utility, but have included the argument that people need income incentives to save (or accumulate capital) and, if the government steps in and redistributes income, it reduces these incentives.

The models and assumptions gained from a study of economics do not lead to any final truths about the "best" distribution of income. The distribution of income in a society affects many aspects of both economic and noneconomic performance. What we have pointed out here is that the utility or welfare of the people is one aspect—and an important one.

SUMMING UP

1. *Demand* is a schedule representing the quantities of a good (a commodity or service) that consumers are able and willing to buy over a given range of prices in a specific period of time.

2. The assumptions on which demand theory rests are (a) that consumers know about, and can choose freely among, alternatives; (b) that consumers seek the maximum satisfaction from the goods they can buy with their limited incomes; (c) that consumers are rational; and (d) that factors other than prices, which might affect demand, do not vary (the *ceteris paribus* assumption).

3. One can explain the *law of demand*, that demand curves slope downward, or that price and quantity are inversely related in two ways: (a) in terms of income and substitution effects, and (b) in terms of *utility theory*.

4. The *income effect* is the change in quantity demanded of a good caused by a change in the consumer's purchasing power resulting from a variation in the price of that good. A decrease in price increases the consumer's purchasing power and an increase in price decreases it. In either case, *for desirable goods*, (normal and superior goods), the income effect causes price and quantity to be inversely related.

5. The *substitution effect* is the consumer's tendency (when the relative price of a good changes) to buy more of a cheaper good and substitute it for a more expensive good. The substitution effect also causes price and quantity to be inversely related. The combination of the two effects—income and substitution—almost always causes the demand curve to slope downward.

6. Goods that are theoretical exceptions to the law of demand and do not have a downward-sloping demand curve are (a) *Veblen goods* (goods for which people prefer to pay higher prices in order to enjoy conspicuous consumption) and (b) very income inferior goods called *Giffen goods*—goods that people buy less of as their prices fall because they can now afford other, more desirable goods.

7. *Normal goods* are those consumers buy more of as their income grows and less of as their income falls. Superior goods are those whose consumption varies in the same direction as that of income changes but at a faster rate. Inferior goods are those whose consumption declines as incomes rise and rises as incomes fall.

8. A *Giffen good* is one with an upward sloping demand. The peculiarly sloped demand curve is explained by a weak substitution effect and a very strong income effect for a very income inferior good. As price falls, consumers tend to buy more as they substitute the good for others that are now more expensive. Consumers have a large income effect from the price decrease and use the increased income to buy other goods instead of the one whose price has fallen. The two effects contradict each other and the net effect is for quantity demanded to fall as price decreases

9. *Utility theory* holds that people choose certain goods and combinations of goods because those choices give them more satisfaction than any other combination. The key assumption of utility theory is that people not only evaluate the utility (satisfaction) of different goods, but whenever they spend their incomes, they rationally choose the combinations that maximize their utility or satisfaction.

10. In utility theory, one assumes that the satisfaction the consumer gets from the last unit consumed—the *marginal utility*—of the good will ultimately diminish. This is called the *law of diminishing marginal utility*.

11. For a consumer to be in equilibrium (that is, to maximize her or his utility), two conditions are necessary (for 2 goods, a and b):

$$MU_a/P_a = MU_b/P_b$$ (MU per dollar must be equal for all goods bought to achieve maximum total utility).

$$P_aA + P_bB = Y$$ (all income must be spent [the budget restraint]).

12. One can extend the conditions for maximization of utility to any number of goods. Downward-sloping demand curves, no matter what number of goods are involved, depend directly on the assumption of diminishing marginal utility.

13. The *paradox of value* is that the price people are willing to pay for a good is determined by its *marginal* utility rather than its *total* utility. Thus, people pay much higher prices for diamonds than for water.

14. The sum of all the individual demand curves is the market demand curve. Since individual curves slope downward (because of diminishing MU), so does the market demand curve.

15. A measure of consumer responses to changes in the price of a good is called the *price elasticity of demand*. One may calculate price elasticities of demand (E_d) by means of the *midpoint formula:*

$$E_d = \frac{\Delta Q/Q}{\Delta P/P} = \frac{[Q_2 - Q_1]/[(Q_2 + Q_1)/2]}{[P_2 - P_1]/[(P_2 + P_1)/2]}$$

16. The *price elasticity of demand* (E_d), the measure of the response of consumers to a change in price of a good is not the slope of a demand curve. It is obtained by measuring the *rate* of change in the quantity of the good that consumers demand in relation to the *rate* of change in its price. The result is a *pure number* one independent of the units of measurement of price and quantity demanded. Demand may be *price elastic; price inelastic or unit elastic.*

price elastic :	$E_d > 1$	$\Delta Q/Q > \Delta P/P$
price inelastic:	$E_d < 1$	$\Delta Q/Q < \Delta P/P$
unit elastic:	$E_d = 1$	$\Delta Q/Q = \Delta P/P$

17. Demand may also be at the extreme limits of demand elasticity: (a) *perfect inelasticity* ($E_d = 0$), in which quantity demanded does not change at all as price changes, and (b) *perfect elasticity* ($E_d \to \infty$), in which the public buys any quantity at the going price.

18. The factors that determine price elasticity of demand are (a) substitutability, (b) proportion of income spent on the good, (c) postponability, and (d) time.

19. Price elasticities of demand are very important when it comes to analyzing many economic problems. Farmers' incomes, monopolistically priced oil imports, taxation, regulation and deregulation of industries are all examples. Elasticities are also very important to firms in setting prices and in labor management relationships.

20. *Price elasticity of demand* is directly related to changes in total revenue. These relationship may be summarized as the following:

    a. Price Increases

        If $E_d > 1$, total revenue falls
        If $E_d = 1$, total revenue is unchanged
        If $E_d < 1$, total revenue rises

    b. Price Decreases

        If $E_d > 1$, total revenue rises
        If $E_d = 1$, total revenue is unchanged
        If $E_d < 1$, total Revenue falls

21. The incidence or burden of a tax is related to the price elasticity of demand. When an excise tax is levied on a good, its supply decreases. If the demand for the good is price inelastic, there will be a relatively small decrease in quantity demanded and a relatively large increase in price. Most of the burden of the tax will fall on consumers of the good. Conversely, if the demand for the good is relatively price elastic, there will be a large decrease in quantity demanded and a relatively small increase in price. Most of the burden of the tax will fall on producers.

22. All straight line demand curves (except those that are either perfectly elastic or perfectly inelastic) have continuously changing price elasticities of demand. Such curves necessarily have an elastic portion and an inelastic portion as well as a point (price, quantity) at which demand is unit elastic. Total revenue is at a maximum at that point. Firms setting price would be expected to operate in the elastic rather than in the inelastic portion of the demand curve.

23. Income elasticities of demand measure the rate at which the demand for a good varies as the incomes of consumers of that good vary. Goods may be (a) *income normal*, goods whose demand varies in the same direction and at about the same rate as income, (b) *income superior*, goods whose demand varies in the same direction but at a greater rate than income, (c) *income inferior*, goods whose demand varies inversely with income.

24. *Cross price elasticities of demand* measure the rate at which the demand for one good varies as the price of another good changes. These measures are sometimes used to (a) identify the scope or extent of a market and (b) define the demand relationship between goods. Goods may be complements, substitutes, or unrelated to each other.

25. (a) If cross price elasticities of demand are positive, the 2 goods are substitutes for each other and firms producing them may be part of the same industry or market, (b) If cross price elasticities of demand are negative, the 2 goods are complements and projections of the demand for the one good may depend in part on changes in the price of the other. (c) If cross price elasticities of demand are zero, the 2 goods are unrelated and firms producing them are effectively independent of each other.

KEY TERMS

Budget restraint
Cross price elasticity of demand
Demand
Giffen goods
Income effect
Income elasticity of demand
Independent utilities
Law of demand
Law of diminishing marginal utility
Marginal utility
Market demand
Midpoint formula
Normal goods, superior goods, inferior goods
Paradox of value
Perfect inelasticity, perfect elasticity
Price elastic, price inelastic, unit elastic
Price elasticity of demand
Pure number
Substitution effect
Total utility
Utility theory
Veblen goods

QUESTIONS

1. What factors do you think are most important in determining your demand for (a) cars, (b) toothpaste, (c) soft drinks, (d) trips to Europe? Do you suppose that these same factors are also most important for consumers in general with regard to these goods? What

factors do you think are most influential in determining the price elasticity of your demand for these goods?

2. What are income and substitution effects? Which of these effects usually has the greater influence on the shape of the demand curve? Why?

3. What is the law of demand? This law is not universal. Under what conditions do you think it does *not* hold true? Would you expect the law to be violated very often? Why or why not?

4. What are the assumptions of the utility theory of demand? Are they realistic? If not, why make such assumptions?

5. Consider the following demand schedule:

Price	Quantity Demanded
$1.00	100
1.50	75
2.00	50
2.50	30

   a. Calculate the price elasticity of demand for price increases from $1.00 to $1.50; $1.50 to $2.00; $2.00 to $2.50.
   b. Indicate for which prices (if any) demand is price elastic; price inelastic; unit elastic.

6. Why is the slope of a demand curve not a good measure of its elasticity? What is a pure number?

7. What seem likely to you to be (a) Veblen goods, (b) Giffen goods? What is the difference between an inferior good and a Giffen good?

8. What are some likely examples of (a) normal goods, (b) superior goods (c) inferior goods?

9. What are the two equilibrium conditions for utility maximization in utility theory? What does each mean? How do they help to explain why demand curves slope downward?

10. How is market demand related to individual demand?

11. Why would we expect firms that set price to do so in the elastic portion of their demand curves?

12. What determines the price elasticity of demand for a good?

13. What is the relationship between the price elasticity of demand and changes in total revenue for (a) price increases? (b) price decreases?

14. If a government wished to levy an excise tax on a good and wanted to collect a great deal of revenue as a result, what kind of a good should it tax in terms of the good's price elasticity of demand? What if it wanted, instead, to reduce the consumption of the good?

15. What would be the sign of the cross price elasticity of demand between 2 goods if they are complements? Substitutes? Unrelated? What are some likely examples of goods that have each of these relationships?

16. What assumption would you make about the marginal utility of income? Why?

17. For what reasons other than the marginal utility of income could you argue for or against redistributing income?

18. Considering both the utilitarian and nonutilitarian aspects of the question, do you believe that income in the U.S. should be redistributed? Why? What effects would such a redistribution be likely to have on American welfare, growth, price stability, and employment?

5 Supply Side of Markets—Production Costs

Capital cities/ABC said earnings jumped 63 percent in the second quarter, due to cost-control measures.

OBJECTIVES

After studying this chapter you will be able to:

- Explain why normal profit is necessary if a market system is to operate efficiently.
- List the reasons why the law of diminishing returns or variable proportions is likely to take effect in the short run in the operations of a business.
- Explain why marginal cost has such a strong influence on the supply response of a firm.
- Have a working knowledge of the following terms and concepts:

Accounting profit	Long-run period
Diseconomics of scale	Marginal cost
Economics of scale	Opportunity costs
Elasticity of supply	Short-run period
Explicit costs	Variable costs
Implicit costs	

Supply Side of Markets - Production Costs

We have examined in detail the theory behind the behavior of consumers and demand. Now we will do the same for the behavior of firms and supply.

What is Supply?

Supply
A schedule relating various prices for a firm's product and the quantity the firm will offer for sale at each of those prices.

Quantity Adjuster
A firm that has no control over the price at which it sells its product. It decides only how much to produce.

To an economist, **supply** is a schedule relating various prices for a firm's product and the quantity that the firm will offer for sale at each of those prices in a specific time period.

We shall concentrate on one firm, the Better Burger Co., and to simplify our analysis we shall assume that it is a **quantity adjuster** or that it has no control over the price at which it can sell its product. It takes price as given and sells as much as it finds profitable at the given price. What determines how much it will produce? Basically, the *costs* of production. Underlying any firm's supply schedule is a schedule of costs.

What Determines a Firm's Costs?

Two factors will determine the cost to the Better Burger Co. of making and selling hamburgers: (1) The *prices* it pays for resources (cooks, waiters and waitresses, buildings, land, finance capital, beef and buns, and the like), and (2) The *productivity* of those resources. For the time being, let's assume that prices of both product and resources are competitively determined and therefore lie outside the control of the Better Burger Co. We will present the technological conditions of supply to show how the productivity of resources determines costs and, through costs, supply.

Opportunity Costs
A measure to a firm of what it must give up in order to produce a particular good.

To society, costs mean **opportunity costs**, or what firms have to give up in order to produce a particular good. These costs include both money costs and nonmoney costs. Nonmoney costs, often called *psychic costs,* are important in determining how people behave economically. Suppose the Better Burger Co. takes great pride in, and derives great satisfaction from, producing a superior hamburger. The entrepreneur who heads Better Burger Co., Bertha Berson, likes making top-notch hamburgers so much that any other job, to induce her to leave the hamburger industry, would have to offer an income great enough to make her overcome her distaste for other businesses.

You saw the effects of opportunity costs when you studied the production-possibilities curve. Since there are alternative uses of resources, Better Burger Co. (or any other firm) must compete for the use of resources. It must bid resources away from other uses, and the prices it pays to do so, times the amounts used, are its *economic costs*. Whether the Better Burger Co. can obtain these resources depends on their productivity when used by the Better Burger Co. compared with their productivity when used by another firm (to produce the same product or a different one).

Explicit and Implicit Costs

Explicit Costs
Those costs for resources directly bought or contracted for in the marketplace.

Implicit Costs
Those costs associated with using self-owned resources.

Firms must buy or contract in the marketplace for most of the resources they use. The costs of these resources are **explicit costs**. The costs of resources a firm already owns are **implicit costs**.

For example, Bertha Berson, the owner of Better Burger Co., has to hire a lot of resources: a manager, cooks, people to wait on tables, a building, and so forth. She hires most of these in the market; she pays wages, rent, and interest to get them. These are her *explicit costs*.

Suppose, though, that she happens to already own a choice commercial lot and that she also has good managerial skills. She decides to build the hamburger stand on her own lot and manage it herself. Is there a cost? Yes, because both the land she owns and the labor she puts into the venture could have been used to produce something else. She might have leased the lot to another firm; she might have found a job elsewhere. To determine Bertha Berson's economic costs, one has to add these implicit costs to the explicit costs.

In order for her to stay in business very long, she must use resources at least as efficiently (productively) as they could be used elsewhere. In order for society in general to conduct its economic affairs most efficiently, *all* firms must use resources as productively as the resources would be used in alternative ways. Thus, firms must cover their opportunity costs, including the implicit costs of using self-owned resources.

Profit

Normal Profit
A payment to entre-
preneurs that just
covers their
opportunity cost.

Economic Profit
A payment to entre-
preneurs that is
greater than their
opportunity cost.

Profit is a part of costs. *Profit* is a return or payment to the entrepreneur, the person who organizes a business venture, who pulls the necessary resources together, takes risks and attempts to make it a going business. Any market system requires people with this skill in order to operate and do so efficiently, and firms must bid for such skills. Therefore Better Burger Co., in order to succeed, must be able to pay for organizational talent and risk taking. Profit is thus an implicit cost to the business. A payment to the entrepreneur just equal to the cost of hiring her or him away from other employment is a **normal profit**. Profits in excess of this (profits larger than necessary to bid for an entrepreneur's services) are called **economic profits**.

Better Burger Company:
An Illustration of Accounting Profit and Normal Profit vs. Economic Profit and Economic Loss

Let's put some hypothetical numbers on the operation of Better Burger Co. and use them to illustrate more concretely the meaning of profits and its alternative measures. In doing this, you can see the importance of opportunity costs in identifying rational supply decisions by this firm and, by extension, all firms.

Bertha Berson is the sole entrepreneur of Better Burger. The firm, in identifying its monthly costs, has both implicit and explicit costs. First, let's look at the implicit costs. Bertha has invested $50,000 of her savings in the business. Although she need pay no interest to obtain this financial capital, its use is an implicit cost to the firm. Suppose that, given her taste for risk, she could have earned $1,000 per month if she had put this money into financial markets (savings accounts, money market funds, etc.). There is an implicit (opportunity) cost to the firm of $1,000 per month. Suppose, also, that Bertha is a graduate dietitian who could have earned $3,000 per month if she had been hired by a food manufacturing firm. The opportunity cost of her labor, even though she pays herself no salary, is an implicit cost to Better Burger of $3,000 per month. Total implicit cost, then, is

A. *Total implicit cost* per month = $1,000 (invested capital) + $3,000 (labor of entrepreneur) = $4,000. The explicit costs of Better Burger will consist of all direct monthly payments for resources. As such, they will include wages and salaries to cooks and other personnel, business taxes, payments to suppliers and the like. Let us suppose that, in an average month, these payments amount to $15,000, then,

B. *Total explicit cost* per month = $15,000. The firm's total costs are the sum of its total implicit costs plus its total explicit costs or

C. *Total costs* of Better Burger = A + B = $4,000 + $15,000 = $19,000 per month.

Is Better Burger Profitable?

Economic profit (Π) is the difference between total revenue (TR) and total costs (TC) or:

$$\Pi = TR - TC.$$

Suppose we take some different possible levels of TR and compare them with the firm's TC to assess its profitability:

Case 1 (Normal Profit, TR = $19,000). Better Burger's TR for the month is $19,000. Since we know its TC are also $19,000 and include both explicit and implicit costs, its revenue, when allocated, covers its entire costs. Note, though, that TC includes the monthly opportunity costs of the entrepreneur ($4,000). Since the firm covers its opportunity costs, it earns a *normal profit* of $4,000 per month. The firm's **accounting profit**, the difference between TR and total explicit costs is also $4,000.

Accounting Profit
The difference between total revenue and total explicit cost.

Case 2 (Economic Profit, TR = $22,000). Better Burger has a TR for the month of $22,000. TR in other words is greater than TC ($19,000) and the difference is *economic profit*:

Economic Profit (Π) = Total Revenue (TR) ($22,000) – Total Cost (TC) ($19,000) = $3,000

Since the firm would earn a normal profit if its revenues were $19,000, the $3,000 value for Π must represent economic profit or a payment to entrepreneurship greater than its opportunity cost. A point to remember is that any firm that earns economic profit will necessarily also earn a normal profit.

In case 2, the firm's accounting profits (TR minus total explicit cost) are $7,000 or the sum of normal profit plus economic profit.

Economic Loss
The excess of total costs over total revenues.

Case 3 (Economic Loss, TR = $18,000). Better Burger has a TR for the month of $18,000. Since TR is less than TC ($19,000), Π has a negative value. The excess of total (opportunity) costs over TR is called an **economic loss**. This economic loss represents a failure to cover the opportunity costs of the firm and means that the firm's self-owned resources, if used elsewhere, would have had a higher value placed on them.

Note, though, that even with an economic loss, there can be an accounting profit. In Case 3, TR ($18,000) is greater than total explicit cost ($15,000). The difference ($3,000) is an accounting profit. Accounting profits can exist in the face of economic losses, in other words, only when some implicit costs of the firm are not accounted for.

Summing Up Profits and Losses

The cases above illustrate the relationship for a firm between TR and economic profit, normal profit, and economic loss. Those relationships may be summarized as follows:

1. *TR = TC.* Opportunity costs are covered, a normal profit is earned.

2. *TR > TC.* Revenues exceed opportunity costs, an economic profit is earned.

3. *TR < TC.* Opportunity costs exceed revenues, an economic loss is incurred.

Now let's see what will happen to productivity and cost as a firm adjusts its rate of output. What will happen to Better Burger Co.'s productivity (hamburgers per hour of labor) as its output changes?

The Influence of Time on Supply: Four Periods

When firms decide to produce more or less of a product, they run into problems of flexibility and constraints on their choices. If the Soviet Union wants to buy 2 million bushels of American wheat after U.S. farmers have already harvested their wheat crop, the farmers cannot make any adjustment in output. The Better Burger Co., however, has greater flexibility. If there is a rush on the Company's burgers on Wednesday, because of a convention in town, by Thursday morning the company can triple output to meet the increased demand.

Economists distinguish between different production (supply) time periods on the basis of this flexibility—this freedom (or lack of it) which a firm and industry have in adjusting output.

Market Period

Market Period
The period in which output is already produced (also called the very short run).

A firm's **market period** or very short-run period is the period *during which output is already produced.* By definition, the firm can no longer adjust the level of production; supply is fixed. For the Better Burger Co., the market period is very brief and no great problem, since it takes only minutes to grind additional meat and produce more hamburgers. For wheat farmers, however, the market period is a matter of months; for tree farmers it may be several years. Economists are more interested in periods in which changes in output can take place than they are in the market period, the least flexible of firms' production periods. After all, once production takes place, resources cannot be reallocated, and questions of efficiency for that period are meaningless to society since opportunity costs are zero.

Ignoring the costs of marketing, a firm's TC in the market period are entirely fixed costs. Such costs, those outlays on resources that have already been made, are also called **sunk costs**. Once the wheat crop, for example, is harvested, all of its costs are sunk costs. Once the fishing fleet has returned to port, all the costs of supplying fresh fish are sunk costs. Since there are no opportunity costs associated with decisions already made and paid for, there is little interest among economists in this period. To firms, on the other hand, whose success depends importantly on successful marketing strategies, the market period may be critical.

We see in Figure 5-1, that a firm's supply curve in the entire market period is a vertical line from the output axis (parallel to the price axis) and located at the level of already realized output ($\overline{Q_o}$). The **elasticity of supply**, E_s, the rate of change in quantity supplied, $\Delta Q/Q$, divided by the rate of change in price, $\Delta P/P$, is zero.

Short-Run Period

The **short-run period** is a period in which the firm has enough flexibility to vary its use of some resources (variable inputs) but during which the firm also has certain *fixed* inputs (for example, plant capacity) that it cannot add to or take away from. The short run is the period in which all output is actually produced.

For example, Better Burger Co. starts with 1 hamburger shop, certain machinery and equipment, a given number of tables and employees, and neon signs in the shape of steers. If hamburger sales boom in the short run, Better Burger Co. can hire more cooks and order more beef and buns, and another carload of ketchup. But what

Figure 5-1
Supply in the Market Period

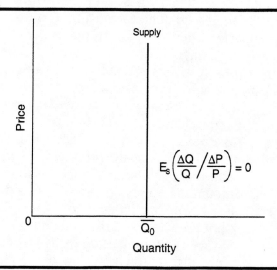

Total costs during the market period are fixed or sunk costs.

happens to costs and supply as more of these variable inputs are used with that same fixed plant?

Long-Run Period

Long-Run Period
A planning period in which firms can choose to vary all inputs and make any choice that present technology permits.

If entrepreneur Berson believes that hamburger sales will continue to rise in the foreseeable future, she may plan to expand her shop or build more shops herself or perhaps start a franchising operation. This leads into the **long-run period**. The *long-run* is a planning period, one in which a firm can vary *all* the resources it uses, including size of plant and amount of equipment. This is not a process of actual production. Rather, it is a process through which the firm can examine all the alternatives that modern technology makes available and choose which way to produce products in the future. Once the firm makes its choice and carries out its plans, it is in the short-run period; it has its plant and equipment set up and can produce things. The only limitation on the firm's choice in the long run is technological availability. For example, Better Burger Co. hires technicians, architects, and engineers who tell Bertha Berson that, given the present technology, there are twenty choices as to size of plant and ways to produce and sell hamburgers. Berson can decide within these limits about plant capacity and amount of automation. ("Microwave ovens, yes. Disposable plates, no.")

Historical Period

Historical Period
The period is one in which technology changes and the effects of such changes on supply are observed.

In the **historical period**, one drops even the limitations of technology. Although no firm can utilize the historical period, from society's standpoint studying the historical period, being able to see the effects of changing technology on productivity, is very important. For example, visualize the hamburger business 50 years ago. Think what has happened since then to the technology of production and distribution. From small mom-and-pop hamburger stands, the hamburger industry has advanced to massive franchise operations, with single franchises selling thousands of dollars' worth of hamburgers per week. Automation of food preparation and even cooking has been developed. Then visualize complex industries such as steel and automobiles. Think of the technological changes that have affected their productivity and supply.

A caution about supply and calendar time: Do not try to sort out these production periods in terms of clock or calendar time. That is not the point. A firm is in three periods—market, short-run, and long-run—simultaneously. It markets its products, varies the output of its present plant, and makes plans for the future all at the same time. The amount of calendar time involved in these periods differs enormously from one industry to another. The short-run, for example, is very brief for hamburger stands but very long for General Motors or other very capital intensive firms and industries. The point here is the supply distinction between the periods. Now let's see what happens to costs and productivity in each period.

Costs and Supply in the Market Period

Variable Costs
Costs that are associated with variations in output.

Since a firm cannot vary the resources it uses in production during the market period, there are no **variable costs** (costs associated with changes in output) at that time. As we have noted before, all costs during the market period fall into the category of *fixed* or *sunk costs* (costs that do not vary with output). Of course, there are costs associated with marketing itself, but these are not production costs (costs incurred in producing the product).

During the market period, just as all costs are fixed, so is total output fixed. The die is already cast, and the firm has a limited amount of product to sell. Supply, therefore, is a vertical line from the output axis (Figure 5-1). Q_o represents the total output already produced. During the market period, there may be variations in demand, and the firm may decide to market more or less of the product, and it can vary the price it charges. Resources, however, cannot be bid into or away from this industry during the market period.

Costs and Supply in the Short-Run Period

As we mentioned before, this is a very important period. In the short-run period, firms produce all their goods and services, and employ all production workers and other resources. What happens to output as firms employ more variable resources along with those that are fixed? In answering this question, we must rely on an important assumption, the law of diminishing returns or variable proportions.

The Law of Diminishing Returns or Variable Proportions

Law of Diminishing Returns (or Variable Proportions)
As a firm uses successive equal increments of a variable resource in conjunction with a fixed resource, additions to output ultimately diminish.

The **law of variable proportions** (often called the **law of diminishing returns**) states that as a firm uses successive equal units of a variable input in conjunction with a fixed input, additions to output (marginal output) attributable to the variable input, ultimately diminish.

Marginal Physical Product
The additional output attributable to added or variable resources.

Let's translate that into hamburgers: The Better Burger Co. circulates an advertisement saying that if you come into the restaurant, you will be served a hamburger within 5 minutes after you sit down, or you'll be given a hamburger free of charge. Business picks up. But the company has only 10 grills, 100 cubic feet of refrigerator space, 100 booths, and various other limitations on plant and equipment. Now suppose that the firm hires more cooks to handle the growing trade. Initially, **marginal physical product**—the additional hamburgers turned out per hour by the additional cooks—may rise, as the firm employs the grills and other equipment more efficiently and fully, and reaps the advantages of specialization. Beyond some point, though, the cooks begin getting in each other's way. This causes the number of additional hamburgers they turn out per hour to decline. Table 5-1 gives a numerical illustration.

Table 5-1
The Law of Variable Proportions or Diminishing Returns (numbers are hypothetical)

Inputs, The Variable Resource (Extra Cooks)	Total Physical Product (Hamburgers Per Hour)	Additional or Marginal Physical Product (Hamburgers Per Hour)	Average Physical Product
0	0		0
		12	
1st	12		12
		18	
2nd	30		15
		20	
3rd	50		16.67
		15	
4th	65		16.25
		10	
5th	75		15
		5	
6th	80		13.5

At first, marginal product rises, as the second and third cooks add more to output than the first. The fourth cook, however, adds less to output than the second and third, though more than the first. Diminishing marginal productivity has set in. The diminished productivity continues as the firm adds the fifth and sixth cooks. At this point, marginal product is approaching zero (the sixth cook only adds 5 hamburgers per hour).

Examples of diminishing returns to the variable input abound. Agriculture provides a particularly clear one. Suppose an Iowa corn farmer has a certain amount of land, 500 acres. The corn has been planted. Land is the fixed input (along with the other resources already employed to plant the crop). Now, the farmer can decide how many times to cultivate the field. Let's suppose that if the farmer does not cultivate at all, the yield will be 30 bushels per acre. If the farmer cultivates once, the yield may rise to 40 bushels. Twice, and the yield rises to 48 bushels per acre. Three times, to 53 bushels per acre. A fourth cultivation may add nothing to the yield per acre.

Although the law of diminishing returns is difficult to demonstrate in practice, its logic is perhaps clearest in agriculture. If there were never diminishing returns, each additional use of a variable resource on a given piece of land would yield either equal or greater increases in output. Therefore, all the world's food (corn or wheat or rice or whatever) could be raised on one plot of land. Thus, one can demonstrate the validity of the law by means of a logical absurdity.

Short-Run Supply

The law of diminishing returns has a great effect on short-run supply for a firm that buys its inputs competitively (that is, at market-given prices).

We have assumed that the firm's variable costs (VC)—costs resulting from increasing output—will not change because of higher prices for wages and other inputs, but *will* change with the changing average and marginal productivity of the variable inputs. Also, the firm's total fixed costs (TFC) do not change as output changes.

Figure 5-2 gives the picture of the firm's TC. As output grows up to Q_0, VC grows, but at a decreasing rate (the slope of TC decreases or gets flatter). This corresponds to increasing marginal productivity (hiring the third cook in Table 5-1). Beyond Q_0, the slope of TC increases, reflecting diminishing returns or diminishing marginal productivity (the fourth, fifth, and sixth cooks). Note that at every rate of output (such as Q_1) the distance between VC and TC is constant and equal to the (constant) fixed cost. Thus, TC equals total variable cost (TVC) plus TFC.

One can derive a firm's unit or average costs from its TC. There are three average costs (Q stands for quantity produced):

$$\text{Average fixed cost} = \text{AFC} = \text{TFC}/Q$$
$$\text{Average variable cost} = \text{AVC} = \text{TVC}/Q$$
$$\text{Average total cost} = \text{ATC} = \text{AFC} + \text{AVC} = \text{TC}/Q$$

Figure 5-3 shows what happens to these costs as output increases. AFC gets smaller and smaller as output increases. (TFC gets divided by larger and larger numbers.)

AVC declines as long as the average productivity of the variable input is growing. In Table 5-1, AVC went down to the point at which the firm hired the third cook, where average physical product

Figure 5-2
Short-Run Total Costs

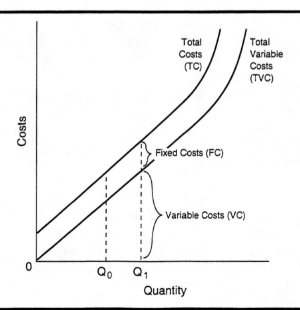

Figure 5-3
The Average and Marginal Costs Per Week of Better Burger Company
(based on hypothetical numbers for Table 5-2)

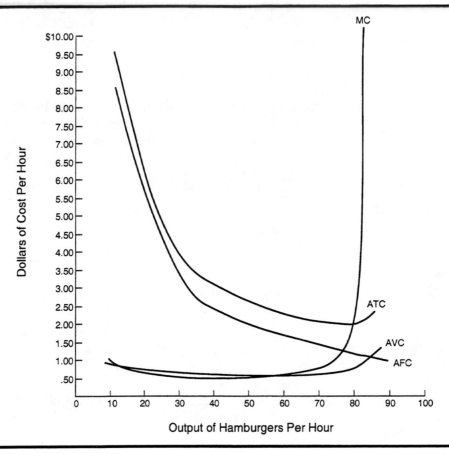

Marginal Cost
The cost of producing
an additional unit of
output.

reached its maximum of 16.67. When average physical product is at its greatest, AVC is at a minimum (see Figure 5-3). ATC naturally depends on both kinds of costs: fixed and variable. As output grows, AFC gets smaller and smaller, and ATC therefore becomes more and more determined by AVC (AVC approaches ATC).

Marginal cost (MC), which is the cost of producing an additional unit of output, is critically important in analyzing the supply of a firm. MC (given constant resource prices) depends entirely on marginal physical product. That is, it depends on the productivity of the input hired to produce an additional unit of output.

The supply curve—what the firm will produce in response to various possible prices—depends on marginal cost, which, as we saw above, depends on marginal productivity. If you examine Figure 5-4, you will see that the short-run supply curve slopes up to the right. The cause of this (given constant resource prices) is rising MC, which, in turn, depends on diminishing returns or diminishing marginal physical

Figure 5-4
Short-Run Supply Curve

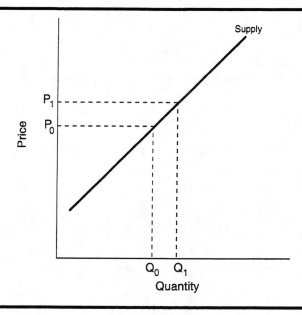

productivity. As marginal productivity decreases (as each additional unit of variable resource produces less and less additional output), MC rises. As MC rises, the firm must receive higher prices for its products in order to make it profitable to produce a greater quantity to sell. Consider the increase in output from Q_0 to Q_1 in Figure 5-4. When the firm runs into diminishing returns (diminishing marginal productivity), its MC (the cost of supplying, $Q_1 - Q_0$) rise, and it must obtain a higher price to induce it to produce additional output.

An Example:
Some Average and Marginal Costs for Better Burger
From Table 5-1, we see that marginal physical product (MPP) rises as the first and second cooks are hired and reaches its maximum (20) with the employment of the third cook. As long as MPP is increasing, MC (column 7) will fall. MC, thus, reaches its lowest level where MPP is greatest. As the fourth, fifth, and sixth cooks are employed, MPP falls; when this happens, MC will rise.

Let us now take the (hypothetical) physical productivity figures of Table 5-2 and translate them into cost figures for Better Burger Co. at various rates of output per hour. We see the numbers in Table 5-2. Columns (1) and (3) repeat the data from Table 5-1. Column (2) is the firm's TVC and is computed by multiplying the units of variable resource input (1) x the price of the competitively employed resource ($10). Column (4) is APP of the variable resource or the number of hamburgers per cook at all levels of resource usage. Notice that as APP rises, the AVC falls and that as APP diminishes,

Table 5-2
Average and Marginal Costs Per Hour for Better Burger Company (based on productivity data in Table 5-1)

(1) Inputs of Variable Resource (Cooks)	(2) Total Variable Cost (TVC)	(3) Total Output of Hamburgers (Q)	(4) Average Physical Product (APP) (3)/(1)	(5) Average Variable Cost (AVC) (2)/(3)
0	$ 0	0		
1	10	12	12.0	$0.83
2	20	30	15.0	0.67
3	30	50	16.7	0.60
4	40	65	16.3	0.62
5	50	75	15.0	0.67
6	60	80	13.3	0.75
7	70	82	11.7	0.85
8	80	83	10.4	0.96

(6) Marginal Physical Product (MPP) $(\Delta 3)/(\Delta 1)$	(7) Marginal Cost (MC) $(\Delta 2)/(\Delta 3)$	(8) Total Fixed Cost (TFC) (100)	(9) Average Fixed Cost (AFC) (8)/(3)	(10) Average Total Cost (ATC) (5) + (9)
		$100		
12	$ 0.83			
		100	$8.33	$9.16
18	0.55			
		100	3.33	4.00
20	0.50			
		100	2.00	2.60
15	0.67			
		100	1.54	2.16
10	1.00			
		100	1.33	2.00
5	2.00			
		100	1.25	1.99
2	5.00			
		100	1.22	2.00
1	10.00			
		100	1.20	2.16

AVC rises. Column (5), AVC is TVC divided by units of output or (2)/(3). Column (6) measures MPP or the number of additional hamburgers associated with each additional cook employed. Column (7) measures MC or the additional cost associated with each additional unit of output. Two things about MC are important to note at this point.

1. MC is a measure of the additional cost of producing more of a product. Since that additional cost can only be the result of hiring more of the variable resource, it can only be an addition to TVC. In other words, MC has nothing to do with fixed cost.

2. As MPP rises (hiring the first, second, and third cooks), MC falls (from 83¢ to 50¢). As MPP falls (hiring all cooks beyond 3), MC rises. In other words, MC is driven by MPP. Once diminishing MPP occurs (the effect of diminishing returns to the variable input), MC rises.

The Role of Fixed Cost

In Table 5-2, column (8) is TFC which is here assumed to be $100. By definition, TFC does not vary with output (Q). Column (9), though, measures AFC or TFC/Q. Note that as output increases, AFC always decreases or, in other words, approaches zero. Column (10) is ATC which is, for each rate of output, the sum of AVC plus AFC (ATC = AVC + AFC).

In Figure 5-3, the cost data from Table 5-2 are plotted graphically. AFC declines continuously as output increases. AVC declines at first as Q increases and then increases. ATC is obtained by vertically summing AVC and AFC at each output rate. Note that ATC is a "U" shaped curve declining at first as both AVC and AFC decrease. Beyond the minimum point of ATC (at 80 hamburgers, ATC = $1.99), ATC rises because the decrease from a falling AFC is more than offset by a rising AVC. MC declines as MPP rises, has its minimum where MPP is greatest (between output 30 and 50 it falls to 50¢) and then rises as MPP diminishes. Note that MC is equal to or cuts AVC and ATC at their minimum points or where both are constant.

Costs and Supply in the Long-Run Period

In the long run, when all inputs are variable and the only limitation is the available technology, what will the firm's cost curves look like? Since supply depends on costs, let's look at long-run costs and then move on to the supply curve itself.

In the long run, all costs are variable ones (TC = TVC). Figure 5-5 shows what these costs look like (still assuming constant resource

Figure 5-5
Long-Run Total Costs

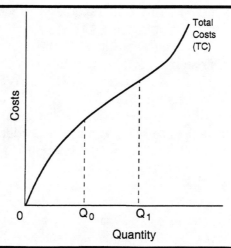

In Figure 5-5, total costs (TC) are shown as rising with output or quantity. Initially, TC rises at a diminishing rate and up to Q_0, there are economies of scale. Between Q_0 and Q_1, TC rises at a constant rate to reflect constant returns to scale. Beyond output Q_1, TC rises at an increasing rate to reflect diseconomies of scale.

prices). Total cost increases in the long-run period as output, *and plant size*, grows. There are three possible rates of such increase.

Economies of Scale
Occur when the cost of each unit produced falls as plant sizes increase. Long-run average costs fall.

1. The rate of growth of TC may slow down so that the slope of TC gradually becomes less steep. This means that the cost of each unit produced gradually becomes smaller as the firm expands and increases its output. (In Figure 5-5, this happens as far as output rate Q_0) When a firm does this, it is achieving what economists call **economies of scale** (when the cost of each unit produced falls as output increases with larger plant size). Economies of scale are usually thought to be caused by the greater efficiency in larger plant sizes associated with increased specialization and division of labor and capital.

Constant Returns to Scale
Exist when TC increase at a constant rate and long-run average costs are constant.

2. TC may just keep on rising at a constant rate; the slope of TC is then constant. (In Figure 5-5, the part of TC from Q_0 to Q_1 reflects this.) In this situation there are **constant returns to scale** and long-run ATC are constant. Larger plants are no more efficient than smaller ones.

Diseconomies of Scale
Exist when long-run TC increase at an increasing rate and long-run average costs are rising.

3. The rate of growth of TC may speed up, so that the slope of TC gradually gets steeper. This means that the cost of each unit produced increases. (In Figure 5-5, this is true for output rates greater than Q_1.) When a firm has this to contend with, it is facing what economists call **diseconomies of scale**.

These three concepts—economies of scale, constant returns to scale, and diseconomies of scale—affect everyone through prices and have a heavy impact on long-run supply. Figure 5-6 gives the general picture. Long-run ATC is a U-shaped curve, an envelope, which encloses all short-run choices about plant size that are possible with present technology. These short-run choices are reflected in the SATCs from 1 to 11. Each of the SATCs represents a particular size of plant and equipment capable of producing various rates of output. The larger plants from $SATC_1$ through $SATC_4$ reflect more efficient technological choices (the economies of mass production). Finally, the SATCs rise from $SATC_8$ through $SATC_{11}$ and reflect inefficiency and the problems of management. From $SATC_5$ through $SATC_7$, there are constant returns to scale; $SATC_6$ is larger than either $SATC_5$ or $SATC_4$, but its unit costs are the same. Suppose you are trying to decide what size plant to build to produce a particular good. You hire engineers, who tell you that there are 11 possible sizes of plant that you could choose: SATCs from 1 to 11. For simplicity's sake, long-run ATC is drawn as a smooth curve.

Again, economies of scale take place until the firm is producing quantity Q_0. Economists say that these economies derive from (1) specialization and division of labor, (2) improvements in management, (3) complete utilization of the productive process and its by-products, and (4) more efficient machines and equipment. For a

Figure 5-6
Long-Run Average and Marginal Costs

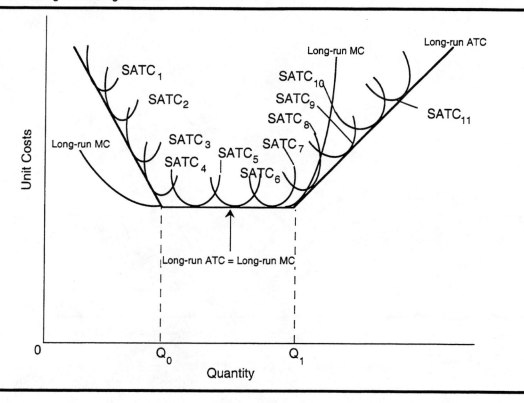

combination of these reasons, the firm's average cost continues to fall, up to Q_0.

Between Q_0 and Q_1, there are neither economies nor diseconomies of scale. One size of plant is as efficient as another. Average cost is constant, and there are constant returns to scale.

After output gets beyond Q_1, diseconomies of scale begin to be evident. The main one concerns management. Consider the problem of communication, which is the key to management. As a firm grows, its channels of communication multiply. Suppose the firm has 2 managerial people; it needs 2 channels of communication. Then, if it adds a third managerial person or department, the number of communications channels rises to 6. This non-linear rise leads to the problem of **discommunication**, or, in other words, the problems and costs that a large organization encounters in achieving effective decision making.

Discommunication
In supply, the problems and costs associated with effective decision making as the scale of production increases.

Thus, a firm's long-run supply may reflect any or all three of these scale conditions: economies, constant returns, or diseconomies of scale. Figure 5-7 compares the supply curves of these scale conditions.

Because the average costs of a firm that is experiencing *economies of scale* are decreasing, the firm will supply more output

Figure 5-7
Long-Run Supply Curves

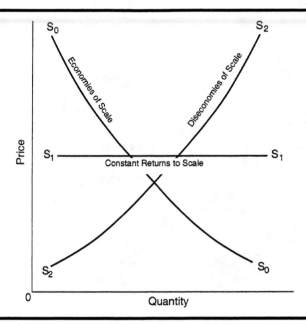

at lower prices than at higher prices. At the same time, its rates of output are greater than before, and so is its plant size. Supply curve S_0 shows this. When the firm experiences *constant returns to scale,* (curve S_1), it has constant average cost and will supply varying amounts of output at a constant price. When the firm has *diseconomies of scale,* its average (and marginal) costs rise, and it will supply more only if it can get higher prices for its output. The upward-sloping supply curve S_2 in Figure 5-7 illustrates this.

Supply Curves for a Whole Industry

To find out what the supply curve for a whole industry (other than an industry with one firm) looks like, one adds the supply curves of individual firms in the industry for a given period.

In the real world, cost conditions for an entire industry may differ from those of the firms that make up the industry. Here we have assumed that all costs relating to economies (or diseconomies) of scale reflect **internal economies of scale**, or those connected with the output decisions of individual firms. There may also be **external economies of scale**, or those brought about by variations in the output of the whole industry or by actions that cannot be controlled by individual firms.

For example, in the hamburger industry, Better Burger Co. can increase its output by hiring more workers at the going wage. If

Internal Economies of Scale
Scale economies connected with the output decisions of a firm.

External Economies of Scale
Scale economies brought about by variations of industry output.

all hamburger firms in the same area hire more people, though, the wages they all must pay their workers will probably rise. The higher wage will increase the MC of all firms and shift the industry's supply curve to the left.

For the present, let's say that a supply curve for an industry derives its shape from the technological conditions of firms (economies or diseconomies of scale) as they expand or contract their output.

Elasticity of Supply

Price Elasticity of Supply (also Elasticity of (Product) Supply) The rate at which the quantity supplied of a good changes as its price changes.

Elasticity of supply, like elasticity of demand, is important when analyzing markets. For example, when the U.S. government lifted all controls from the price of domestically produced crude oil, by how much did oil companies increase the quantities of oil they supplied? And if local government were to remove controls on rental housing prices, what effect would this have on our supply of housing? These questions involve the **price elasticity of supply**, or the rate at which quantity supplied changes as price changes.

Elasticity of supply can be estimated by the same midpoint formula used to estimate elasticity of demand. If Q equals quantity supplied and P equals price, the formula for elasticity of supply, E_s, is:

$$E_s = \frac{\Delta Q/Q}{\Delta P/P} = \frac{\text{change in quantity/average quantity}}{\text{change in price/average price}} = \frac{[Q_2 - Q_1]/[(Q_1 + Q_2)/2]}{[P_2 - P_1]/[(P_1 + P_2)/2]}.$$

We will have to go into further detail later about elasticity of supply. But for now, let's apply it to the production periods we have just discussed. E_s may be (1) elastic, (2) unit elastic, or (3) inelastic.

If firms make no change in the quantity they supply as the price of the product changes, supply is perfectly inelastic (this represents supply in the market period or very short-run period).

If firms increase the quantity they supply at a slower rate than the price of the product increases, supply is price inelastic (as in the case of diminishing returns in the short-run period).

If firms increase the quantity they supply more rapidly than the price of the product increases, supply is price elastic (up to the point of infinite elasticity).

As we have shown, time is a very important factor in determining the elasticity of supply. Elasticity of supply usually increases as the time increases that is available for producers to make adjustments, by bringing in more resources, or by selling off plant and equipment. If you think of the very long-run or historical period, you see that *technological change* is a factor that has greatly increased the elasticity of supply of the economy as a whole, as well as of firms and industries.

Some Final Words About Supply

There are complications in identifying supply in particular markets that differ on the basis of their competitiveness. Under conditions of pure competition, we can readily identify a firm's supply curve. In other kinds of markets, those between pure competition and pure monopoly, this is not the case. For that reason, it is difficult to talk precisely about supply in many market situations. Instead, economists concentrate on cost.

APPLICATION:
Markets for Illegal Goods

There is an old adage, *What the public demands, the market will provide.* In other words, if people know about a good, have a taste for it, and have the income to indulge that taste, entrepreneurs will supply it. They will do so at any price equal to or above their cost of producing and distributing it. This applies not only to goods that are legal, such as cars, groceries, and shoes, but also to those that are illegal, such as cocaine, gambling, and prostitution.

Let's examine the sale of illegal goods. How are the prices of illegal goods determined? What would happen to their prices if they were legalized? We shall examine only the *economic* aspects of illegal market operations. There are, of course, other aspects—moral, political, and medical.

Each time an illegal good is sold, an economic crime is committed. Table 5-3 shows that so-called economic crimes include crimes against the person and against property. They also include arson and vandalism, driving under the influence of alcohol, and tax frauds. But the biggest category of economic crimes is illegal goods and services. According to these estimates, sales of illegal goods and services amounted to about $8.1 billion in 1965, or approximately 54 percent of the total economic impact of crime. More than 85 percent of this involved gambling (illegal gambling, not the legalized gambling of Las Vegas or Atlantic City).

Now remember that data on the GDP do not include sales of illegal goods and services. Therefore, the sales of these illegal things caused the GDP to be understated by about $8 billion. We say about $8 billion, because if these transactions had been legal, their prices would probably have been very different. (We will discuss that in a moment.)

We have not used such old data from choice. Surprisingly, the U.S. has not made figures available on the economic impact of crime since the publication of these data from 1965. These data do give us some idea of the economic cost of crime. However, the data for the early-1990s, if there were any available, would undoubtedly show much higher totals, because the frequency and costs of most kinds

Table 5-3
Economic Impact of Crime, 1965

		Millions of Dollars
Crime against the person		815
Homicide*	750	
Rape*	65	
Crimes against property		3,932
Robbery, burglary, larceny, auto theft*	600	
Unreported commercial theft	1,400	
Embezzlement	200	
Fraud	1,350	
Forgery	82	
Arson and vandalism	300	
Other crimes		2,036
Driving under the influence	1,816	
Tax fraud	100	
Abortion	120	
Illegal goods and services		8,075
Narcotics	350	
Loan sharking	350	
Prostitution	225	
Alcohol	150	
Gambling	7,000	
Total		14,858

* FBI index crimes.

Source: The Presidents Commission on Law Enforcement. *Task Force Report*, Chapter 3.

of economic crimes has increased since 1965. This increase, plus the inflation of the last decade, would make the totals much larger.

The composition of crime has almost certainly changed as well. Abortion during the early stages of pregnancy, while controversial, is no longer illegal. Other factors, however, have increased. White-collar crime, for example, or theft by employees, has risen dramatically since 1970. So has vandalism. Clearly, there has been a massive increase in illegal sales of narcotics. And the percentage of crimes against property as part of the total economic cost of crime has surely increased, since the number of property crimes has increased more rapidly than the number of other kinds of crime.

Pricing Illegal Goods: Alcohol and Narcotics

Whether or not to legalize marijuana, cocaine and other illegal drugs has become a widely discussed issue in the U.S. and there is a great deal of precedent for this kind of national discussion. During World War I, prohibitionists agitated to make the production, distribution, sale, and even the possession of intoxicating liquors illegal, and they succeeded. The nation adopted a constitutional amendment, and Congress passed supporting legislation—the Volstead Act—which became law in 1921. Prohibition has been called "the noble experiment." The people who voted it into law genuinely believed it would do away with alcoholism and other tragic and violent situations caused by the abuse of alcohol. (It took another constitutional amendment, in the early-1930s, to repeal Prohibition.)

An amusing sidelight to Prohibition is that it made an exception of wine that was manufactured for sacramental purposes. After the act became law, the consumption of sacramental wine rose dramatically, which led economists Douglass C. North and Roger Leroy Miller, with tongue in cheek, to wonder whether Prohibition induced Americans to become more religious.

Prohibition led to (1) reduced supplies of liquor, (2) higher prices for alcoholic beverages, and (3) illegal markets (speakeasies, bathtub gin, and so on) to cater to the tastes of people for the product they could no longer buy legally.

What causes results like these? Since Prohibition is no longer a burning issue, let's examine a more contemporary example, illegal sale of cocaine, and reverse the process. Suppose the manufacture, distribution, consumption, and possession of cocaine were legalized. What would be the *economic* effects? Look at Figure 5-8, in which D_i is the demand for illegal cocaine and S_i its illegal supply. The illegal price is P_i, and Q_i ounces of cocaine are sold. Supply S_i for the illicit dealer is determined by the costs of production, including the risks of arrest and imprisonment. In a legal business one can buy insurance against risks, but the cocaine dealer cannot, unless the police can be bribed to look the other way. In any case, risk is an added cost of business.

Information costs, too, are higher. The dealer cannot advertise in newspapers or on TV, and so is denied an efficient mechanism to transmit information to potential consumers.

Effect of Illegality on Demand

What about illegal demand? Presumably some would-be consumers are scared off by the risks of arrest and punishment. On the other hand, there may be some for whom the thrills of furtive purchases and consumption offer positive utility. It is difficult to say precisely what effect illegality has on demand.

It is also hard to say what the effect on demand would be if cocaine were to be legalized. Some evidence regarding a related drug, marijuana, may be instructive, however. In 1975, a study among 23-year-olds at the Institute for Social Research in Ann Arbor, Michigan, concluded that if marijuana were legalized, 15 percent of the subjects would use it more often, 11 percent were uncertain, and 74 percent would be unaffected. The study concluded, "Ironically, the older age groups may be most affected by any changes in the marijuana

Figure 5-8
Pricing of Cocaine

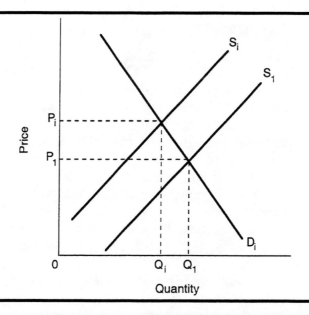

laws, since most young people already seem to have made their choice."

For these reasons, let's suppose that legalization per se would not cause people to substitute cocaine for other drugs, such as alcohol, and thus legalization would not change demand. We do not know what the income elasticity of demand for cocaine is. However, based on the ISR study of marijuana, we shall assume that the price elasticity of demand for cocaine is fairly small (as reflected in the overall shape of D_i, which has varying elasticities along its entire length).

Effect of Legalization on Supply

Supply would almost certainly be increased by legalization, because (1) costs of risks would be lowered (no payoffs), (2) average information costs would fall (there could be advertising, brand names, fda inspection, and so on), (3) larger, more efficient "firms" (the legitimate drug industry) would appear on the market and take advantage of the economies of scale available at all stages of production, from harvesting to retailing. For these reasons, supply in Figure 5-8 shifts from S_i, to S_l. The quantity of cocaine consumed increases from Q_i to Q_l (a relatively small increase, if our assumptions are right). The lower price would probably mainly benefit the relatively low-income customer who may have been excluded from the market at P_i or who had less reliable information about quality than that available to more affluent consumers (who probably had a large number of alternative suppliers).

Reverse Price Discrimination Plus Strict Enforcement: An Alternative?

In Figure 5-8, the demand for cocaine is drawn as a single (relatively inelastic) straight line, D_i. There is reason to believe, however, that D_i may apply to some consumers of the drug but not to others. Let us suppose, as Robert Thomas[1] has argued, that there are two groups of drug consumers, those who are addicted (addicts) and those who consume the drug intermittently or socially (dabblers). Since the elasticity of demand for a good is largely determined by substitutability, percent of income spent on the good and postponability, we would not expect addicts and dabblers to have the same reactions to changes in the price of the drug. They would not, in other words, have the same elasticity of demand for cocaine.

In Figure 5-9, we see the (illegal) market for cocaine drawn as two submarkets to reflect the different price-related behavior of addicts and dabblers. In *(a)*, the demand for cocaine by addicts is drawn as price inelastic, mainly to reflect poor substitutes and an inability to postpone consumption. In *(b)*, the demand for cocaine by dabblers is drawn as relatively elastic to reflect better substitutes and greater ability to postpone consumption. Notice that with supply S_a

Figure 5-9
The Illegal Market for Cocaine as Seen by *(a)* Addicts and *(b)* Dabblers

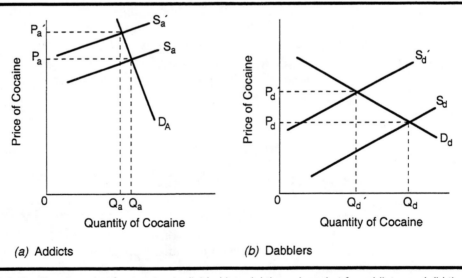

(a) Addicts   *(b)* Dabblers

In Figure 5-9, the illegal market for cocaine is divided into *(a)* the submarket for addicts, and *(b)* the submarket for dabblers. In *(a)* demand is relatively inelastic and in *(b)* demand is relatively elastic. Practicing price discrimination, the dealer charges higher prices in *(a)* to addicts and lower prices in *(b)* to dabblers (P_a, P_d). With strict drug enforcement, supply decreases in *(a)* from S_a to S_a' and in *(b)* from S_d to S_d'. Price rises sharply in *(a)* from P_a to P_a' and quantity declines only from Q_a to Q_a'. With strict drug enforcement in *(b)*, price rises only from P_d to P_d' but quantity decreases sharply from Q_d to Q_d'.

[1]Thomas, Robert, Microeconomic Applications, Belmont, CA. Wadsworth Publishing Company, 1981

Price Discrimination
The charging of different prices to consumers for the same product.

to addicts and S_d to dabblers, dealers charge a higher price to addicts and a lower price to dabblers. The latter may be an effort to induce consumers at the margin to buy the drug, become addicted and join consumers in *(a)*. At any rate, the charging of different prices to consumers for the same product is known as **price discrimination**. It is not surprising that the higher price in a market is paid by those with a less elastic demand since they presumably have less good alternatives than consumers with a more elastic demand.

Effects of Strict Law Enforcement

There is no doubt that drug use and the problems associated with it are considered a major problem by Americans. Increasing concerns about the effects of drugs have led to greater efforts to enforce laws against their illegal use. Many of the resources used in these efforts have been devoted to interdiction of the drugs or reducing their supply. How successful should we expect such actions to be? Figure 5-9 helps us to understand the likely results of reducing the supply of cocaine. A decrease in the supply to addicts in *(a)* (given the inelastic demand) results in a large increase in price (P_a to P_a') and a relatively small decrease in quantity demanded (Q_a to Q_a'). On the other hand, a proportional decrease in supply to dabblers in *(b)* results in a small increase in price (P_d to P_d') but a relatively large decrease in quantity demanded (Q_d to Q_d'). Interdiction would seem to work fairly well in reducing drug usage by dabblers but have a limited effect on usage by addicts.

A second important effect of the reduced supply of cocaine in market *(a)* is the income effect on addicts. Because of the significant increase in the drug's price, addicts must increase their incomes to pay for the maintenance of their habit. Since it is reasonable to suppose that few hold steady jobs and can finance their illegal purchases through increased market incomes, they must turn to increased crimes against property and persons to maintain drug purchases. Society, thus, must bear not only the direct costs of drug consumption (lost output, medical treatment, drug research and the like) but also the indirect costs of increased crime (such as theft, robbery, muggings).

Reverse Price Discrimination: An Alternative?

Dealers, as we have seen, have an incentive to offer lower prices to dabblers than to addicts. Society's interests, however, might be better served by reversing that pattern of price discrimination. By offering lower prices to addicts, crimes committed to finance drug purchases would be reduced while offering higher prices to dabblers would reduce drug usage and deter increases in the number of addicts. An alternative suggested by some is to strictly enforce the drug laws which will reduce drug supplies and raise drug prices, thus reducing the number of dabblers. At the same time, we might lower prices to addicts to prevent an increase in crimes. One way to reduce prices is to provide the drug to registered addicts as was done for several years in the United Kingdom. This policy would involve various degrees of subsidization of the drug to those certifiably addicted. Opposition to the policy has been voiced by many, including "drug czar" William Bennett, who fear a rapid increase in the number of addicts.

Illegal Drug Markets: A Summing Up

Any change in governmental policy concerning illegal drug markets will be controversial. Only strict enforcement of drug laws appears to be non-controversial. Legalization of highly addictive drugs would be very controversial. Decriminalization and subsidized consumption by certified addicts would not necessarily be less so. The point here is not to argue for any particular change but to observe that solutions cannot be identified and assessments of their costs and benefits made unless we recognize that drug usage is a market-related problem and one in which elasticities of demand and supply play a crucial role.

SUMMING UP

1. *Supply* is a schedule relating various prices for a firm's product and the quantity that firm will supply to the market at each price within a given period of time.

2. Supply, which is based on cost, depends on two factors: (a) the prices a firm pays for resources, and (b) the productivity of those resources. Assuming that a firm has no control over the prices of its resources, its supply depends entirely on productivity.

3. To society, costs mean *opportunity costs*, or what it must give up in order to produce X rather than Y. A single firm must therefore use resources productively in order to hire them to its own uses rather than have other industries bid higher and employ them in other ways. In using resources, a firm may incur either *explicit costs* (the direct expense of using resources it buys), or *implicit costs* (the alternative costs of using self-owned resources). The total costs of production include both kinds of costs.

4. *Profit* is a payment to the entrepreneur who assembles resources takes risks, and creates a going firm. A *normal profit* is a payment just large enough to hire the entrepreneur away from other employment.

An *economic* or *pure profit* is any profit in excess of normal profit. If a firm's total revenues are greater than its total costs (including a normal profit), the firm earns an economic profit. If the firm's total revenues are equal to its total costs, the firm earns a normal profit. If the firm's total revenues are less than its total costs, the firm incurs an economic loss, or fails to cover all its opportunity costs.

5. There are time dimensions to supply: a market period, a short-run period, a long-run period, and a historical period. In the *market period*, supply is given, because output has already been produced, so there can be no change in use of resources at this stage. In the *short-run period,* firms can make changes in output by varying some inputs while others remain fixed. The *long-run period* is a planning period, in which the firm can vary all inputs, within the limits of a given set of technological choices. The *historical period* is useful in that one can see how technology has changed and analyze the effects of these changes on supply.

6. In the short-run period, the *law of variable proportions* or *diminishing returns* comes into play. Economists state it this way: As a firm uses successive equal units of a variable input in conjunction with a fixed input, additions to output (marginal physical product) begin to diminish, beyond some point. The effect of this law is that costs ultimately rise in the short run and that the short-run supply curve of a firm slopes upward. This is true in spite of any initial increase in marginal productivity as output expands.

7. Total short-run cost is the sum of total fixed or sunk costs and total variable costs. Average total cost is the sum of average fixed and average variable cost. *Marginal cost* is the cost of producing one additional unit of output. Marginal cost determines the shape of the firm's short-run supply curve.

8. In the long-run period, all costs are variable. As output grows and total cost increases, there are three possibilities: (a) If cost rises more slowly than output, there are *economies of scale.* (b) If cost rises at the same rate as output, there are *constant returns to scale.* (c) If cost rises more rapidly than output, there are *diseconomies of scale.* Economies of scale result from (a) specialization of labor, (b) improved management, (c) improved utilization of productive processes, and (d) improved efficiency of machines and equipment. Diseconomies of scale arise primarily from *discommunication,* or problems that managements of large firms face in trying to communicate.

9. A long-run average-total-cost curve includes all short-run cost curves. So that it will take in all cost possibilities, it is drawn as a U-shaped curve. When there are economies of scale, the long-run supply curve slopes downward, which indicates that as a firm increases its

output, it can lower its prices. Where there are constant returns to scale, long-run supply is a straight line at a given price. Where there are diseconomies of scale, the long-run supply curve slopes upward, which indicates that the firm will supply more output only if prices rise.

10. One can obtain the supply curve for a whole industry (other than a single firm industry) by adding the supply curves of all the individual firms in the industry. This industry supply curve takes its shape from the technological conditions that the firms in the industry must deal with.

11. *Price elasticity of supply* measures the rate at which quantity supplied changes as price changes. Supply may be (a) price elastic, (b) unit elastic, or (c) price inelastic.

12. Time is a critically important factor affecting the elasticity of supply of firms. As the time that firms have to make adjustments in input and output lengthens, elasticity tends to increase.

13. For a purely competitive firm, the supply curve may readily be identified. This is only true of competitive markets. Economists in analyzing noncompetitive markets, therefore, concentrate on the costs of firms.

14. Illegal markets supply commodities and services as long as consumers have the knowledge, tastes, and incomes to demand them, and as long as "firms" can cover their costs (including normal profit).

15. Each sale of illegal goods involves an economic crime. More than half of all the economic impact of crime involves illegal goods and services. The largest percentage of earnings from illegal transactions is from gambling although the data on which this is based are quite old.

16. Making goods and services illegal (if income is spent on them) reduces the GDP because illegal transactions are not included in calculations of national product.

17. Prohibition of alcoholic beverages in the early twenties was the first national experiment in banning "undesirable" goods. It resulted in (a) reduced supplies of liquor, (b) higher prices for alcoholic beverages, and (c) illegal markets.

18. In the case of cocaine, illegality causes higher risks and information costs, and thus smaller supply. For any given level of demand, the price of illegal cocaine tends to be higher than would be that of legal cocaine.

19. If the results of a recent study of Marijuana can be extended to cocaine, legalizing the drug would probably increase very little the

quantity demanded. Any increase would probably derive from use by people in older age groups.

20. Legalization would probably cause the supply of cocaine to increase significantly. Risks and information costs would probably fall, as legitimate drug firms entered the market to take advantage of economies of scale in production and distribution.

21. Legalization of cocaine would probably result in a significant reduction in its price. But whether it (or other illegal goods) should be legalized is not only an economic question; it is also an ethical, moral, and medical question.

22. Illegal drug prices often involve price discrimination, the charging of different prices to consumers for the same good. Buyers with a smaller elasticity of demand are charged higher prices and those with a larger elasticity of demand are charged lower prices.

23. Stricter enforcement of drug laws will reduce drug supplies and increase their prices. Dabblers, those with elastic demands, will reduce consumption as price rises. Addicts, those with inelastic demands, will reduce consumption very little but pay the higher prices. To finance their continued purchases, however, they tend to resort to increased crimes against property and persons.

24. An alternative to simply stricter drug law enforcement is to create reverse price discrimination in drug prices. As prices to dabblers rise, consumption will decrease and society reaps the benefits of that reduction. To prevent increased crime by addicts, society could provide drugs at subsidized prices to those certifiably addicted.

25. Any changes in present day policy are likely to be controversial. All, to be rationally considered, must be viewed as market-related problems involving elasticities of demand and supply.

KEY TERMS

Accounting profit
Averaged fixed cost, average variable cost
Constant returns to scale
Discommunication
Diseconomies of scale
Economic loss
Economies of scale
Elasticity of supply
Explicit costs, implicit costs
External economies of scale

Historical period
Internal economies of scale
Long-run period
Marginal cost
Marginal physical product
Market period
Normal profit, economic profit
Opportunity costs
Price discrimination
Price elasticity of supply
Quantity adjuster
Reverse price discrimination
Short-run period
Sunk cost
Supply
Variable costs

QUESTIONS

1. If you were running a business, what would the *supply* of your firm mean to you?

2. It is necessary, for the sake of social efficiency, that firms bid for resources and pay them their opportunity cost. Why is this so?

3. It's quite possible that there are many people in business who do not consider their *implicit* costs. If so, what effect do you think this is likely to have on the nation's economic efficiency?

4. Why is *normal profit* necessary if a market system is to operate efficiently? What about *economic profits*? Are they necessary too? (Give a thoughtful answer here.)

5. Why would one be unable to associate particular amounts of calendar time with the concepts of market period, short-run period, long-run period, and historical period?

6. List as many reasons as you can why the *law of diminishing returns* or *variable proportions* is likely to take effect in the short run in the operation of a business.

7. Suppose that a firm that is expanding its output has a very large total fixed or sunk cost. What will happen to its average total cost as it expands output? Can you think of any firms or industries in which this is likely to happen?

8. Why does marginal cost have such a strong influence on the supply response of a firm?

9. Can you think of any firms (or industries) in which long-run average cost is likely to (a) fall? (b) remain constant? (c) rise as output increases?

10. Why is elasticity of supply important when it comes to analyzing the operation of a market system? Think back over the last half century: What factor do you suppose has most influenced the elasticity of supply of the aluminum, automobile, and petroleum industries?

11. Alpha Lumber Co. has the following short-run total costs:

Total explicit cost = $40,000
Total implicit cost = $20,000

How profitable (Economic profit, normal profit or economic loss) is the company in each of the following cases:
   a. Total revenue = $65,000
   b. Total revenue = $60,000
   c. Total revenue = $55,000

12. What is the firm's accounting profit in each of the three cases above?

13. What things determine the price elasticity of demand for an illegal good such as cocaine?

14. Why do you suppose the major change in demand for legalized cocaine might come from older people?

15. Evaluate the following statement: "The way to eliminate economic crime is to allow people to buy legally anything they have the income and taste for."

16. What things determine the price elasticity of supply of an illegal good?

17. What is price discrimination? What is meant by reverse price discrimination?

18. Would you favor legalizing some illegal drugs? Why or why not?

19. Would you favor combining strict drug law enforcement with subsidized drug prices to addicts? Why or why not?

SUGGESTED READINGS

Bennett, William J. "A Response to Milton Friedman." *Wall Street Journal*. September 19, 1989.

Dolan, Edwin G., and John C. Goodman. "Illegal Drugs: The Unintended Effects of Prohibition." *Economics of Public Policy*. 4th ed. St. Paul, MN: West Publishing Co., 1989.
Friedman, Milton. "An Open Letter to Bill Bennett." *Wall Street Journal*. September 7, 1989.

Moore, Mark H. *Buy or Bust: The Effective Regulation of an Illegal Market in Heroin*. Lexington, MA: D.C. Heath, 1977.

Raspberry, William. "Would Drugs Be So Dangerous if they were Legal?" *Washington Post*. 11. July 1, 1988.

Reed, Lawrence W. "Would Legalization Increase Drug Use?" *The Free Market*. Vol. 8, Number 2. February, 1990.

Thomas, Robert Paul. "The Price Elasticity of Demand: Social Control of Heroin." *Microeconomic Applications*. Belmont, CA: Wadsworth Publishing Co., 1981.

"White Lines, Bottom Lines. Profile of a Mature Industry." *Dollars and Sense*. December, 1986. Reprinted in *Economics 88/89*. Annual ed. Guilford, CT: Dushkin Publishing Group, 1988.

CHAPTER 6

Market Equilibrium: Do Private Markets Always Produce What is Socially Desirable

"Is privatization the medicine to social illness?"

The Rertreat from Riches - Peter Passesl and Leonard Ross

OBJECTIVES

After studying this chapter you will be able to:

- Define marginal private benefit, marginal social benefit, marginal private cost and marginal cost.
- Describe how prices are established in competitive markets and the difference private (markets) costs and benefits and social costs (nonmarkets) costs and benefits..
- Explain the free rider problem
- Discuss the effects of externalities
- Have a working knowledge of the following terms and concepts:
    Commom property resources
    Equilibrium price
    Internalizing of benefits and costs
    Materials balance approach
    Private equilibrium and social equilibrium
    Public goods

Market Equilibrium: Do Private Markets Always Produce What is Socially Desirable?

We have taken a close look at the theoretical foundations of demand and supply. By putting supply and demand together in a theory that explains how prices are determined in competitive private markets, we will be able to explain the quantities of output a competitive society tends to produce under varying conditions. We will also explore the relationship between the *private* costs and benefits of using resources to produce and exchange goods (the relations established in the market system) and the *public* or social costs and benefits (the costs and benefits to society).

As we have seen, private supply and demand decisions are the result of (profit seeking) cost calculations by firms and (utility seeking) benefit calculations by consumers. Demand calculations are possible only when buyers can estimate subjectively the benefits of choosing various combinations of goods and services. Supply calculations are possible only when firms can identify production choices that will ultimately result in revenues that at least cover opportunity costs or generate normal profits. Both sets of calculations, though, are based on private benefits and costs. As we shall see in this chapter, there may be instances when the social benefits of consuming a good differ from the private benefits of its consumption. Also, there may be instances in which the social costs of producing a good differ from the private costs of its production.

The application in this chapter will explore a case in which private and social costs and benefits might differ, the problem of cleaning up the air.

Equilibrium Price

There is an old saying that you can make an economist out of a parrot by teaching it to say: "Prices are determined by supply and demand." This statement is true of prices under *competitive market conditions*, that is, when buyers and sellers act independently of each other and no buyer or seller has any influence over market price. At the same time, the statement leaves much to be explained, so the parrot would still have a lot to learn.

We shall now review the interrelation of supply and demand. If this material is not fresh in your mind, give it close attention, for it will provide you with a foundation for what follows.

Figure 6-1 shows how supply and demand, in a competitive market, interact to establish prices. Let's say the product is kitchen clocks. Demand slopes down to the right. What price tends to result?

At first glance, it appears that there are many possible prices, any one of which may prevail. Suppliers, looking at their own (private) costs, offer more and more clocks for sale, as the price rises above P_4. Below that price, it does not pay them to supply *any* clocks. Likewise, consumers, examining their own (private) benefits, demand more and more clocks at prices below P_3. The price that tends to be established is an **equilibrium price**.

An equilibrium price is a price that the independent influences of supply and demand tend to create, and that makes quantity supplied and quantity demanded equal.

The equilibrium condition is that quantity demanded and quantity supplied be equal. In Figure 6-1, this happens when clocks

Equilibrium Price
A price created by the independent influences of supply and demand and that makes quantity supplied and quantity demanded equal.

Figure 6-1
Equilibrium Pricing Under Competitive Market Conditions

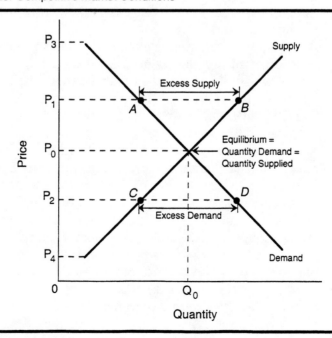

are at price P_0, where demand and supply intersect. So P_0 is the equilibrium price, because at prices above P_0, there is excess supply; firms offer more clocks for sale than consumers are willing and able to buy. For example, at price P_1, firms supply P_1B, whereas consumers buy only P_1A. The difference, AB, is excess supply. In order to clear this market, firms (assuming that they do not want to keep AB), must offer their clocks for sale at lower prices. First, one firm offer clocks at a lower price, then another. The bidding of price downward continues until the price of clocks reaches P_0, at which price firms are supplying precisely the number of clocks consumers will buy.

At prices below P_0, the reverse process (bidding upward of price) occurs. At price P_2, for example, there is excess demand for clocks. Consumers offer to buy P_2D, while firms offer to sell only P_2C. The difference, CD, represents excess demand; in order to satisfy their demand, some consumers offer to pay higher prices. The upward pressure on price stops at P_0, for here there is no excess demand. At this (unique) price, there are as many clocks available as consumers are willing and able to buy.

Private Equilibrium

Private Equilibrium
One which equates the plans of buyers and sellers. It clears markets and makes quantity demanded equal to quantity supplied.

Output rate Q_0 in Figure 6-1 is **private equilibrium**. It establishes a relation between buyers' privately determined benefits and sellers' privately determined costs (including the profit necessary for entrepreneurship).

It is true that this equilibrium depends on the assumption of pure competition and that in the real world a lot of *non*competitive situations exist. (The local gas and electric utilities companies are examples.) And when noncompetitive forces do determine supply or demand, private equilibrium usually leads to less efficiency and less consumer utility than would be the case in a competitive market situation. In the noncompetitive situation, market forces do not work to create prices that result in as much output as consumers want to buy, given their incomes and tastes, nor do market forces compel companies to operate as efficiently as technology permits.

As you will see in the next four chapters, where there are monopolistic market forces, either firms produce less or consumers pay higher prices (or both). Although the absence of pure competition has caused many people to prod the government to change the results of market decisions, even in noncompetitive private markets decisions do get made, resources do get allocated, and the market system does, in essence, ration what is produced. Even in noncompetitive markets, in other words, the plans of buyers and sellers are equated and private equilibria are established.

The question is, in terms of price and output, are the private equilibrium results of the market system consistent with the social or public costs and benefits of using resources?

Cartoon by Joe Mirachi, from *The American Cartoon Album,* edited by Bob Abel, New York: Dodd, Mead, 1974.

"Up another twenty cents a fifth! How do you expect people to survive?"

Social Equilibrium

Decisions made in private markets, even legal ones, are not always socially desirable. For example, the price of gasoline, though higher than it used to be, is still too low to reflect the social costs of using gasoline: pollution, car-strangled cities, the high rate of traffic deaths, and other public problems that private cars create. Similarly, the prices of cigarettes and liquor are too low to reflect the public costs of medical care, research on lung cancer and liver disease, alcoholism, and public protection associated with the private use (or misuse) of these goods. In effect, then, since the prices of cigarettes and liquor do not reflect their full social costs, the public consumes too much of them.

Similarly, there may be instances in which the privately determined price of a good understates the social benefits of its consumption. Education, as we shall see in the application in this chapter, is an example. Since the higher price discourages the consumption of the good, society, in order to have the socially desirable amount consumed, may choose to subsidize its production, reduce its price, and increase the quantity demanded of the good.

We must distinguish between a private cost or benefit and a public one. Just as there is a **marginal private cost** or **benefit** from producing and consuming more or less of a good, there is a

Marginal Private Cost
The cost to a private producer of producing another unit of a good.

Marginal Private Benefit
The benefit to a consumer of consuming another unit of a good.

marginal social cost or **benefit**, which is the added cost or benefit to society of producing and consuming more or less of a good. The *differences* between privately expressed (market) costs and benefits and publicly expressed (nonmarket) costs and benefits are called **externalities**, or *spillover costs* and *benefits* (**spillovers** for short). When you add private costs and cost externalities, you get *social costs*. If there are no cost externalities, private and social costs are the same, and public costs are simply the sum of all private costs.

Effects of Externalities

Figure 6-2 illustrates these externality or spillover effects. Let's use good X as an example. It could be an urban freeway that enables trucks to haul goods to market, or it could be a conveniently located river into which manufacturers dump their plant wastes. In Figure 6-2 demand is the marginal private benefit (or utility) of consuming various amounts of good X, and MC_1 is the marginal private cost to the producer (for simplicity, we shall assume that MC_1 is constant). Equating the marginal private cost with the marginal private benefit, the consumer demands B of good X. However, MC_2 shows the "true" or social costs of producing and using X; we will assume that MC_2 is also constant. At the actual rate of private consumption B, there is a spillover (externality) measured by the vertical distance CD. This spillover represents a social disequilibrium that society must bear (cleaning up the polluted river, adding another lane to the freeway, and so on).

Figure 6-2
Externalities or Spillover Effects

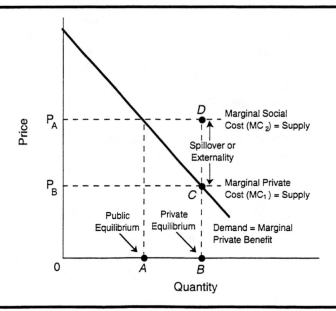

A Tax to Create Public Equilibrium

The public equilibrium in Figure 6-2 is at output A where marginal social costs = marginal private benefit. The private equilibrium is at output B where marginal private benefit = marginal private cost The difference (AB) represents a public disequilibrium. Suppose that the public takes action to correct the disequilibrium (for example, to reduce the number of private cars driven by a single occupant). One way to do this is through a tax, a high enough tax to make private and social cost equal (CD in Figure 6-2). At the higher cost, reflecting the tax, consumption will be reduced to the socially optimal level of A.

The social equilibrium in Figure 6-2 is, as we have said, the point at which the public demands A, for here the marginal social cost equals the marginal private (and assumed public) benefit. For simplicity, we have assumed here that there is no difference between the two benefits. Suppose that the marginal social benefit (MSB) were greater than the marginal private benefit (MPB); this would be a positive benefit externality. In such a case, public demand would be to the right of private demand in the diagram, and social equilibrium would be the point at which $MSB = MC_2$. The new equilibrium point for consumption of the good would be greater than A (or the point at which $MSB = MPB = MC_2$).

If the benefit externality were negative (that is, if the public as a whole demanded less of the good at all prices than private individuals acting singly), then public demand would be to the left of the demand curve in Figure 6-1, and the social equilibrium point would be at a consumption rate less than A.

Internalizing of Benefits
Refers to recognizing and acting on the expected benefits of consumption by individual consumers.

For example, planting trees in a parkway along a suburban street may yield externalities in terms of shade, beauty, and a pleasant play area for children. Here, however, benefits may or may not be **internalized**, recognized and acted on privately in the form of demand by individual homeowners for trees; some people are so thoughtless of their surroundings or so lacking in appreciation of beauty that they could not be persuaded to spend money on trees to beautify their street. If so, society, that is the city government, must provide these trees.

On the other hand, suppose that a single urban homeowner decides to raise chickens and coyotes to sell. Although this homeowners' benefit from doing this may be great, the noise, smell, and the commercial traffic caused by these activities create a negative externality to the neighbors. The neighbors may have these activities banned legally; or they may get together and buy off their peculiar neighbor. That is, they may give the homeowner enough money to compensate for the loss of private benefit—up to the point at which the neighborhood's social benefit is equal to the animal keeper's private loss.

Can Externality be Internalized?

In many cases, government intervention is needed to make individuals recognize and act on spillovers. A person driving home at five o'clock in bumper-to-bumper traffic on the freeway says, "Why don't they put a toll on this road from 4 to 6 so people who *could* drive at off-peak hours would do so?" What the driver is saying is that at rush hour the marginal private cost of driving is less than the marginal social cost (the higher cost being due to noise, air pollution, time lost in traffic, and so forth). "They" refers, of course, to government.

Someone drives by a factory that is belching black smoke or an oil refinery that is dumping effluents into a river, and says, "Why don't they make them filter those exhaust gases or clean up that stuff before they dump it into the river?" Again, what the person is saying is that there is a divergence of the marginal private cost of production and the marginal social cost of production. There is a cost externality that the government should impose on private business as a cost of operating. Other examples of these spillovers abound: Conservation of forest areas, reshaping of the land from which coal has been stripmined are examples. The feature common to most of these externalities is that they affect more than just a small group, and getting them internalized frequently requires government action.

Common Property Resources

Common Property Resources (Common Access Resources) Those that are open to use by everyone. They have, thus, no individual owners.

In a market economy, it would be desirable, even ideal, for all entrepreneurs to bid freely against each other for the use of resources. It is that bidding, of course, that establishes their most value productive uses. A qualification of this, however, lies in the use of those resources that are held and used communally or "in common." Such resources, those that are open to use by everyone and, thereby, have no individual owners, are called **common property resources** (or common access resources).

The principal problem with common property resources as opposed to individual property resources is that they tend to be overused or used in ways that create heavy social costs, since private users fail to fully cost their use. For this overusage not to occur, two conditions must be met: (1) the resource must be a free good; there must be such a large supply relative to the demand that there is no cost to the resources' use, or (2) private users of the resource must fully cost their use in terms of external effects on others. The first condition, while met with some resources applies in fewer and fewer cases in the late-twentieth century. Population growth, increasing population densities in urban areas and development of modern technology have made such resources as air and water less and less often a free good.

The second condition, while sometimes met, is also often violated. Sometimes the violation is deliberate and done with disregard for effects on others; the poaching of the wild game of Africa and Asia and the consequent increasing numbers of animals on the endangered species list is an illustration. Sometimes, however, the condition simply is violated because private resource users have little incentive to fully cost or may even lack adequate information to fully cost their use of common property resources. Examples here include the uses of natural waterways such as rivers, lakes and harbors. Freighters and oil tankers use these waterways as an input in producing their services. Because the marginal private cost of using these resources is small, private users often pay very little for their use. Marginal social costs, however, may be much higher as the 1989 oil spill in Prince William Sound in Alaska demonstrates. The spill imposed large costs on private individuals such as fishermen but even larger social costs in terms of ecological damage and the clean up of the area. In this case, social intervention has taken the form of imposing unlimited liability on resource users. While this internalizes the externality, it deals with its costs ex post or only after they are imposed. Some have argued for social intervention, ex ante; or before the externality occurs as an effort to minimize the likelihood of its occurrence; a legal requirement for double hulling of oil tankers is one remedy that has been suggested.

Government and Property Rights

You can see that the market system sometimes produces wrong signals which both consumers and producers act on. When you take into account the social costs and benefits of using resources, you can see that our market system sometimes encourages people to consume too much of some things and not enough of others. Still, these wrong signals are among the mishaps, the accidental side effects, of a free society in which individuals make choices. People are free to use their private property as they please. If they happen to allocate private resources inefficiently, others must bear it. After all, isn't private property sacrosanct? A look at our legal-economic system suggests that the answer is no.

A private property right—the right to use property according to the tastes of its owner—is not an unrestricted right. For example, if you own a piece of land, you have much freedom of choice as to how to use it. You can leave it vacant, or build something on it, or grow vegetables on it; you can sell it or lease it. The police will remove trespassers from it for you. Still, there are restrictions on your use of your property, though they differ greatly from one community to another. You may not arbitrarily shoot someone who ventures onto your property. Some cities prohibit the burning of trash because of air-pollution and fire-control laws. If the area is zoned for residential uses only, you cannot build a store on your lot.

The important point is that each society must establish, by political means, a balance between private rights and social rights in the use of property. This is true even of a society like that in the U.S., in which individuals control the use of most resources, and the benefits from using them also flow mainly to individuals. Assignment of property rights in any society affects economic activity and the allocation of resources.

In our society, it is pointless to think only of private *or* social rights in property. There are both, of course, and where spillovers exist, where there are large cost or benefit externalities that cannot be internalized, people may ask the government to intervene to correct them. This does not mean, of course, that government ought to step in in each case. A well-kept lawn and garden are an external benefit to nonowners who walk by on the sidewalk. However, no one argues that government should subsidize lawns and gardens because they are a greater social than private benefit.

How Much Government Intervention is Enough?

If governments should not intervene in every spillover, when *should* they intervene? Economic theory does not suggest a rule of thumb, except that where intervention takes place, marginal social benefit should equal marginal social cost. Certainly a spillover should be large enough to warrant using government resources to accomplish that social objective rather than another, both in terms of cost or benefit. Admittedly, this is a very general principle, and leaves much to be desired as a precise means for choosing courses of public action.

The point is that once government intervenes in a spillover situation, it should allocate its own resources efficiently. It should try to make the marginal social benefit of reducing the externality equal to the marginal social cost of doing so. For example, if local governments set out to clean up the air, should they try to get rid of pollution? Economists would say that they should not, at least not as a matter of principle. In New York, the air-conscious city government, pressured by environmental groups, passed a regulation saying that landlords of buildings with oil heat had to use a more expensive higher-grade fuel oil because burning the cheap grades of oil created such a great amount of pollutants. When the landlords complied, they had to raise the tenants' rents to cover the increased costs of fuel. Then along came the fuel shortage in 1973, and the government relaxed the restriction because of the energy crisis. So landlords went back to using the old sludge-filled oil, polluting the air once again. In 1989, a governmental study recommended governmental intervention in greater Los Angeles that would produce an essentially "smog-free" area by 2020. The drastic measures (for example, only electrically powered cars would be allowed) would impose large costs on private individuals and firms. Whatever the outcome of that study and its recommendations, the objective of government in that air shed should not be to produce *completely* clean air but rather to make the marginal social benefit of cleaning up the air equal to the marginal social cost of doing so.

As a government makes an effort to clean up the air, the effort runs into diminishing returns (rising cost) as well as diminishing marginal benefit. Since there are many competing uses of public, as well as private, resources, beyond some point it becomes inefficient (uneconomic) to continue trying to clean up the air. The resources, in other words, would have other, more valued, uses. The same argument applies to reconstructing the terrain surrounding strip mines, protecting endangered species of wild life, and so forth.

Spillovers and Government Intervention

Public Goods
Those whose consumption by one individual does not diminish the amount of them available for consumption by others.

Free Rider Problem
Refers to the fact that once public goods are produced, they are available for consumption by individuals who may have contributed nothing to the cost of producing them.

When there are significant spillovers, should the government take over and start creating the demand for such goods? As a rule, it should not in a private market economy. There is, however, a class of goods that economists call **public goods**. The use of these goods by one person does not reduce the amount other persons may use, *once the good has been produced*. Another characteristic of public goods, in contrast to private goods, is that no one can prevent individuals from using them. This is referred to as the **free rider problem** in that once produced, the good is available for consumption by individuals even though they contribute nothing to the cost of producing it. For example, military goods provide a service we call defense. Once a nation produces an aircraft carrier, the benefits of defense are not transferable from one person to another. Each person "consumes" defense but, in doing so, does not reduce the amount of defense available to other citizens.

Even public goods, however, can become private, with the exception of goods like defense goods with costs and benefits that are *indivisible* (you cannot divide an aircraft carrier into 245 million pieces and give each citizen a piece of it).

A good example of how public goods become private goods is a television signal. Once the signal is broadcast, anybody with a television set in the viewing area can see the picture. The marginal cost is zero. One can assign the benefits to individuals, however, by (1) selling advertising time, the rates for which are based on the number of viewers; or (2) instituting pay television, in which subscribers pay for the programs they watch; or (3) by requiring that everyone must have an annual license for a TV set, and charging a sum of money for the license. (The British and other Europeans do this. With this system, there are no commercials.)

The lesson here is clear. Spillovers tend to generate arguments and cause people to agitate for government intervention. When the government does intervene, however, it does not necessarily supply the goods itself. Government has no more ability to produce steel with nonpolluting furnaces than private industry does. The role of government, therefore, should not necessarily be to produce steel, but rather to force private steel producers to internalize the full social costs of producing the steel. (We shall say more about this in the application that follows).

APPLICATION:
How Much Clean Air Do We Want to Buy?

Those who have read some of the horror stories and doomsday forecasts stacked on the shelves of bookstores are likely to feel that there should be no restrictions on cleaning up air (and water). Paul Ehrlich, author of several of these books, concluded in the 1970s that "Western society is in the process of completing the rape and murder of the planet for economic gain... The days of plunder are drawing inexorably to a close."

A decade or more later, the Ehrlich conclusion seems extreme in many respects. At the same time, severe environmental problems such as acid rain and the controversial "hot-house effect" of global warming remain. Are we, as globally interdependent societies, moving toward crisis levels of environmental pollution?

Dire Predictions and How to Live with Them

In the face of questions like these, how can people ask "How much clean air do we want to buy?" They can for these reasons: (1) Dire predictions (the Club of Rome study, books by Ehrlich and others with the same views) are based on extrapolation—usually linear—of recent statistics on use of resources and growth of population. Economists are wary of such extrapolations because they are based on the view that resources are static, that changes in prices will not affect quantities supplied and demanded of resources, and that rates of population growth will remain the same. (2) Such views imply that private industries, in league with governments, are responsible for what Ehrlich calls "eco-catastrophe." Ehrlich referred to the proinsecticide campaign of the American petrochemical industry, implying that the oil industry operated in collusion with its "subsidiary," the Department of Agriculture.

Economists are not inclined to see environmental pollution as the result of actions by culprits; rather such results are more likely to stem from failure on the part of producers, consumers and governments to internalize the external costs of using resources. As we have seen then, externalities can be internalized so that solutions to environmental problems are available. Indeed, much progress has been made in the 1970s and 1980s in reducing air pollution in metropolitan areas of much of the world.

While economists are not optimistic enough to believe that solutions to environmental problems are quick and easy, they can be found. This relative optimism is based on the following views:

Materials-Balance Approach
The materials-balance approach explains environmental pollution as the result of transforming resources through production and consumption into new (waste) forms.

1. Environmental problems are basically economic in origin. Each year the U.S. uses a certain amount of input (raw materials, fuel, and so on) in producing our national product. In consuming these goods and services, people dispose of waste products (throwaway bottles, factory wastes, worn-out cars, soaps, human excreta, plastic articles, paper, and so forth). This approach to explaining environmental problems as the result of transferring resources into new forms is called the **materials-balance approach**.

2. So long as the earth's ecological systems were able to absorb these wastes and recycle them, clean air and water were free goods, those that no scarce resources had to be used to produce. They did not become scarce commodities, goods with a price, at the same time everywhere. The great industrial cities, such as Pittsburgh and Birmingham, England, were the first places to experience a scarcity of these goods. Then scarcity spread throughout the world, depending on factors such as wind patterns, water tables, rate of growth, density of population, and amount of industry.

3. Today, because of (a) population growth, (b) technological change (new powerful pesticides and fertilizers, leaded gasoline, detergents), (c) economic growth (more industrial output), and (d) lack of incentives to avoid pollution, these blessings of nature, clean air and water, have become scarce commodities, ones which must be priced. They must be rationed and allocated like other goods. But this rationing will most likely not happen without government intervention.

The Price of Breathing

Clean air can be priced. St. Louis is an example. Economist Robert E. Kohn estimated the price (cost) of attaining statutory goals of air quality in the St. Louis airshed. One can draw a diagram of the situation, letting S represent the supply of clean air. This supply curve slopes upward because of rising marginal cost. That is because it becomes more and more difficult, with existing technology, to further reduce the amount of polluting particles in the air.

What about demand for clean air? Since clean air is a public good (its benefits are indivisible and apply to all), the demand for it must be "public." It must be a community demand. In Philadelphia, for example, economist Robert Ridker estimated Philadelphians' willingness to pay for clean air. He offered a sample group a choice of pure air (no pollutant), clean air in and around their own houses, and a community solution that would give the entire neighborhood clean air. Ridker found a downward-sloping demand curve. People would be willing to "buy" more clean air as the price of it fell.

How much clean air is a community likely to buy? Look at Figure 6-3. People's preferences are reflected in D_c, community

Figure 6-3
Community Pricing of Clean Air

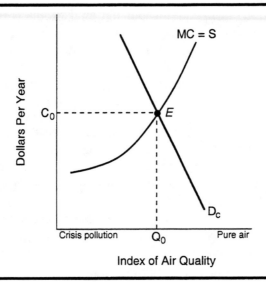

demand (which might be established by sampling or by voting). The supply of clean air is given by MC = S. (Supply differs from community to community because of varying economic and physical conditions.) The equilibrium amount (or degree) of clean air is E (midway between the "Pure air" and "Crisis pollution" points). Q_0, in other words, represents the optimal level of air cleanliness.

The cost of meeting this market-determined standard is C_0. Since clean air is a common or public good, it is indivisible so far as individuals are concerned. Therefore, the public would have to pay the costs, by (1) special taxes on polluters (that is, on businesses, automobile owners, trucking firms, and so on), or (2) selling "rights" to pollute at a fixed amount that would preserve Q_0, clean air. Presumably, a profit-maximizing business would not buy more rights to pollute than would be profitable. Ultimately, as the price of a fixed supply of pollution rights rose, it would become more profitable for the business to install antipollution equipment than to buy rights to pollute.

Enforcing Limits on Air Pollution: Hard Choices

This market approach does not satisfy everyone. For example, there are those who argue for laws that set limits on air pollution (such as the mandatory automobile emission standards set by the Environmental Protection Agency) or prohibit it entirely. These people feel that persuasive articles setting forth standards of pollution are too technical for consumers to appreciate. Informing consumers fully would cost too much and take too long. The government should therefore impose a set of public standards. People who espouse such legislation agree that the added costs of cleaning the air should be largely (or entirely) passed on to consumers, perhaps in the form of a special tax.

Some people maintain that neither of these approaches (consumer determined or legislation determined) are adequate. These people are not necessarily members of the doomsday groups. They simply believe that clean air has an esthetic value that the other groups overlook or undervalue. However, who is to determine esthetic standards if not the consuming public or its elected representatives?

SUMMING UP

1. This chapter deals with two related subjects: (a) a review of how prices are established in competitive markets, and (b) the difference between private (market) costs and benefits and social (nonmarket) costs and benefits.

2. There is only one *equilibrium price* in a competitive market. It is the price that clears the market or makes quantity supplied and quantity demanded equal. In a competitive market, supply and demand forces are independent of each other.

3. Any price above equilibrium results in *excess supply*. Any price below equilibrium results in *excess demand*. Competitive (independent) bidding by consumers and producers eliminates either excess supply or demand and moves price toward the equilibrium point.

4. A *private* (market) *equilibrium* establishes a relation between private benefits to buyers and private costs (including normal or entrepreneurial profit) to sellers.

5. Even where noncompetitive markets exist, the market achieves private equilibrium and rations output on the basis of price, incomes and tastes of buyers, and so on. There is no assurance, however, that private competitive or noncompetitive results are socially desirable.

6. In some cases the privately established prices of goods (and rates of production and consumption) do not reflect the "true" social costs and benefits of using resources. (For example, gasoline prices are not high enough to reflect the social costs of cleaning up the air pollution caused by automobile exhaust emissions.) There is a *marginal private cost* or *benefit* and a *marginal social cost* or *benefit* for each good supplied. Where these two costs or benefits differ, there is an *externality* or *spillover* effect that measures the difference.

7. If the marginal private cost of supplying a good is lower than the marginal social cost of supplying it, the difference is a cost spillover or externality, and consumers act on prices that do not reflect the true social costs of supply. Consumers, therefore, use "too much" of the good. If there is a non-internalized social benefit associated with the production and consumption of a good, private citizens produce and consume "too little" of it.

8. Externalities *can* often be internalized, but frequently the government must intervene to bring this about, since private individuals cannot always get together and internalize large differences between private and social costs and benefits. One way the government can intervene is by taxing private activities by an amount that makes their private cost equal to their public cost.

9. Government's role in the internalization of spillover is to ensure that producers of a good or service incorporate the full social costs and benefits in the price of the product. This does not mean that government should necessarily step in and produce the goods whenever spillovers exist, or that in order to ensure internalization, it should do away with private property rights.

10. In a market economy it is desirable to have all would-be users of resources compete freely for their use. There is a problem though, with common property (or common access) resources, those that are open to use by everyone. As they tend to be undervalued by private users, they are typically overused. Such resources include air, water, fishing grounds, etc.

11. In order that excessive use of common property resources not occur, one of two conditions must exist: (a) the supply of the resource is so great relative to the demand for it that no scarce resources need be employed to produce it, or (b) private users of the resource fully cost the effect of their use on others. The problem is how to effectuate the second condition.

12. Costs of overuse of common property resources are sometimes imposed deliberately and with disregard for others as in the poaching of endangered animals. Sometimes, the costs are imposed because private users have little incentive or inadequate information to act upon. Oil spills are often an example. Here, unlimited liability requirements or a mandating of the technology of production may be necessary.

13. Each society must establish, by political processes, a balance between private and social rights with regard to the use of property. However, government does not have to become involved in all divergences between the two sets of rights, only in those in which the differences are great and in which large numbers of people are affected.

14. When government *does* intervene in spillover cases, it should do so to the point at which the marginal social benefit is equal to the marginal social cost.

15. There are certain goods that are public goods, those whose consumption by one person does not reduce the amount available for consumption by others. Consumption of these goods involves a free rider problem since they are available for consumption even by those who do not pay for them. To have these goods produced, therefore, requires a publicly (governmentally) determined demand decision. Defense goods are the classic examples of public goods.

16. Some people (the Club of Rome, writers such as Paul Ehrlich) believe that unrestricted economic growth and population increase are causing the destruction of the world's natural ecosystems and that our present-day industrial economies have a disastrous effect on the world environment.

17. Doomsday forecasts appear to be based on (a) linear extrapolations of statistics on use of resources and growth of population, and (b) the idea that private (market) and government action are responsible for "eco-catastrophes."

18. Economists, in general, hold the following views: (a) Environmental problems are economic in origin. They depend on nature's ability to absorb and recycle wastes created in production and consumption. (b) So long as the earth's ecological systems were able to absorb these wastes and recycle them, clean air and water were free goods. (c) Because of population growth, technological change, and lack of incentives to refrain from polluting, so many wastes have been created that the earth can no longer absorb and recycle them without the public's having to pay certain costs.

19. Economists maintain that one can put a price on environmental repair, including the cost of obtaining clean air. Experiments in St. Louis indicate that one can establish the prices of supplying certain levels of clean air and that the supply curves slope upward. In Philadelphia, economists found that they could determine community preferences of "demand" for clean air and that the equilibrium point for clean air is between pure air and crisis pollution.

20. Government could meet the costs of achieving the equilibrium amount of clean air by (a) putting special taxes on vehicles and industries that emit pollutants, or (b) selling a fixed (equilibrium) amount of "rights" to pollute (the rising price of these rights would ultimately induce firms to pay for air-cleaning equipment).

21. Another solution is for government to legislate standards for clean air and use taxes or special levies to pay the costs. This solution bypasses consumer tastes for clean air, but causes us to rely on the

technical knowledge of experts and the collective decisions of elected officials.

22. Neither market nor government mechanisms for obtaining clean air satisfy the purists, who argue for pure air on esthetic grounds.

KEY TERMS

Common property resources
Equilibrium price
Externalities (spillovers)
Free rider problem
Internalizing of benefits and costs
Marginal private benefit, marginal social benefit
Marginal private cost, marginal social cost
Materials balance approach
Private equilibrium, social equilibrium
Public goods

QUESTIONS

1. What would happen to the full public equilibrium in Figure 6-2 if there were a negative benefit externality (if marginal social benefit were less than marginal private benefit)?

2. Think of some markets in which competitive conditions exist; then think of some in which *non*competitive conditions exist. Are equilibrium prices established in both?

3. Should economists advise the government to intervene in each situation in which spillovers exist? Why or why not?

4. Is there an air pollution problem in your area? How does it reflect spillovers? What kind of action (and how much) do you think the government should take toward reducing this pollution?

5. Are you, your family, your neighbors, or your friends involved in projects that involve external benefits? What are they, and how do they reflect spillovers?

6. What are some examples of public goods that would not be produced unless governments decided to demand them?

7. Economists and biologists come to very different conclusions regarding doomsday forecasts about the future environment of the earth. Can you give reasons for these differences?

8. How much clean air would you be willing to pay for (either through taxes or in other ways) in your community?

9. Would you be willing to pay for more clean air as the price of it fell? Why?

10. When a community chooses to buy more clean air, what does it have to give up in return?

11. Which method (market or government) do you prefer for obtaining cleaner air and for determining how much of it to "buy"? Why?

12. Suppose that you live and work in a city located on a lake. Around the lake are located many industrial plants that provide thousands of jobs to local residents. Because the lake is treated as a common property resource, the plants surrounding it, through dumping effluents into it, have turned it into an eyesore as well as one in which fish no longer live. The Environmental Protection Agency (EPA), in response, proposes a plan under which all firms would be required to install expensive new equipment to treat the effluents and restore the lake's purity. Local representatives concluding that the EPA plan will cause the loss of many jobs, order a referendum on whether the plan should be instituted.

How would you vote in the referendum?

SUGGESTED READINGS

Annual Report. Washington, D.C.: Council in Environmental Quality, Annual.

Crocker, Thomas D. *Economic Perspectives on Acid Disposition Control.* Boston, MA: Buttersworth Publishers, 1984.

Dolan, Edwin G., and John C. Goodman. "Acid Rain: The Economics of Opportunity Cost." Ch. 2. *Economics of Public Policy.* 4th ed. St. Paul, MN: West Publishing Co., 1989.

"George Bush Proposes a Market for Cleaner Air." *The Margin.* (Pp 13-15). September/October, 1989.

Hailstones, Thomas J., and Frank V. Mastrianna. "Clean Air—Are We Willing to Pay the Price?" Ch. 10. *Contemporary Economic Problems and Issues.* Cincinnati, OH: Southwestern Publishing Co., 1988.

Thomas, Robert P. "Environmental Problems: A Novel Way to Control Pollution." Ch. 28. *Microeconomic Applications.* Belmont, CA: Wadsworth Publishing Co., 1981.

Thomas, Robert P. "Altering Property Rights: Dealing With Oil Spills." Ch. 29. *Microeconomic Applications*. Belmont, CA: Wadsworth Publishing Co., 1981.

Tietenberg, T. H. *Emission Trading: An Exercise in Reforming Pollution Policy*. Washington, D.C.: Resources for the Future, Inc., 1985.

Tregarthen, Timothy. "The Warming of the Earth." *The Margin*. November/December, 1988.

Yanarella, Ernest J., and Randall H. Ihara. *The Acid Rain Debate*. Boulder, CO: Westview Press, 1985.

CHAPTER
7

Pure Competition

There are 14 million firms in the U.S., one firm for every 10 adults. Seventy-five percent of these firms operate as sole proprietors, 13 percent as partnerships, and 12 percent are organized as corporations. However, the corporate form of business, which accounts for 12 percent, is our most important form of business organization. Ninety-five percent of all manufacturing, for example, is done by firms which are organized as corporations. Three hundred thousand new corporations are organized in a typical year. It is estimated that 40 million Americans are direct stockholders in corporations and that another 50 million own shares indirectly through pension funds.

OBJECTIVES

After studying this chapter you will be able to:

- Define the four basic market structures.
- Describe the five characteristics of perfect competition.
- Use a firm's cost-and-revenue data to analyze how much to produce, and determine profitability of production and shut-down point if losses are being incurred.
- Explain the benefits and disadvantages to society from production occurring in perfectly competitive industries.
- Discuss the role of government in agriculture.
- Explain how New Zealand benefited from the elimination of government in their agriculture industry.
- Have a working knowledge of the following terms and concepts:

Marginal revenue	Role of MC, MR, ATC, AVC
Perfect competition	Short-run break-even point
Price taker	Short-run shut-down point
Profits	Supply curve

Pure Competition

The individual family farm and General Motors—both are firms but do they act the same way with respect to pricing their products and to deciding how much to produce, that is, their supply? Are the market conditions facing them both the same? Must the farm and GM compete with the same number and kinds of firms? Is the farm's ability to make profits the same as that of GM? After all, a family farm, with say 600 acres of farmland, and the board of directors of GM, with their billions of dollars of investment and receipts and hundreds of thousands of employees, both operate enterprises for the purpose of earning profits.

Anyone would admit that the market conditions facing the two firms above differ considerably. In this chapter we will examine the different market conditions that confront individual farm enterprises, or a local public utility, or the corner drugstore, or even GM. When one understands these differing market conditions, one can analyze how these various firms behave with respect to pricing, production, profit, and loss. We can then compare how firms and industries with differing market conditions affect general economic activity and how well they allocate a market economy's resources.

In this chapter we will discuss the market classification known as pure competition. As you read through the chapter, you may get the impression that economists feel that pure competition is a good thing. But what about the agricultural industry? Farmers produce in a competitive industry, in which the government continually interferes, trying to alter the effects of competition. Does the government really want competition? Do farmers really want it? The problem is that due to all that interference, consumers, as we shall see in the application in this chapter, must pay higher prices for food. A situation that is often called the "farming mess."

Market Classifications

Obviously, firms in different industries encounter different market situations. Market conditions for GM are, as we have already suggested, quite different from those of individual farmers. By this, we mean that the number of firms ease of entry and exit, and economies of scale, among other things, differ from one industry to another. Economists have grouped these differing market characteristics into four main types or models:

1. *Pure* or *perfect competition* concerns the highest degree of competition. (Theoretically, *perfect* competition is even more competitive than *pure* competition, because it embodies the condition of perfect knowledge. That is, "perfect competition," to economists, is a situation in which every firm and every consumer is perfectly informed about the economic situation in the market. However, here we shall restrict our discussion to the more realistic situation of pure competition.)

2. *Monopolistic,* or *imperfect competition* encompasses both competitive and monopolistic elements, but proportionally more competitive elements.

3. *Oligopoly* exhibits the elements of monopoly more strongly than monopolistic competition does.

4. *Pure monopoly* has minimal competitive elements.

The diagram below shows the four types as a continuum, ranging from the most competitive to the least competitive.

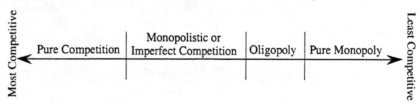

In this chapter we will analyze purely competitive industries.

Characteristics of Pure Competition

1. *Pure competition* assumes that no one firm or group of firms can affect market price by making this or that decision about production. No one firm can perceptibly affect price. In other words, no single firm—regardless of how much it may produce—has a share of supply big enough to affect price in the market by varying its output. Furthermore, there are no groupings of firms that can make collusive decisions about output. In effect, then, each firm is independent of every other firm and is influenced only by factors that affect the entire market.

2. In a purely competitive industry all firms produce a **homogeneous product**, one that is so standardized that buyers do not differentiate between the output of the various producers. It is immaterial to the buyer *whose* product he or she buys. For example, to a buyer purchasing wheat, the grade-A red winter wheat of Farmer Nielson is the same as the grade-A red winter wheat of Farmer Gomez in the next county.

3. When industries are purely competitive, there is freedom of entry for new firms into the industry and freedom of exit for old firms from the industry. This ease of entry and exit ensures the highest degree of mobility of resources. This means that there are no restrictions (such as licensing requirements, for example) that prevent firms from producing those commodities that yield the largest anticipated rate of profit.

4. A basic assumption of the purely competitive model is that both buyers and sellers know enough about price and quantity to be able to make intelligent decisions. Buyers' or sellers' lack of knowledge cannot give any individual or group an advantage.

Since its product is homogeneous, the purely competitive firm does not advertise. As the consumer does not distinguish between the output of the various firms it would be foolish for Farmer Nielson to increase his cost by advertising. Claiming that *his* grade-A red winter wheat is better than anyone else's would only increase cost for the firm that is advertising in a market in which it must sell at the same price as all other firms. If advertising *does* succeed in convincing buyers that one firm's product is better than another firm's, the product is no longer homogeneous, and the firm is no longer a purely competitive one. Firms in a competitive industry may form an association, which may advertise the industry's product but not the product of any one firm. Ads telling us to drink milk, wear woolen clothes, or drink Florida orange juice are examples of this form of industry-wide advertising.

Pricing Decisions

Because of the above characteristics, the purely competitive firm cannot influence price by varying its output. It can sell all it wants to produce at the going market price, since its output is a negligible part of total supply. Each firm, in other words, is a **price taker**, one which acts on a price that is beyond its control. The firm, therefore, will not reduce its price below market price because that causes it to forgo revenue unnecessarily. And of course the firm will not raise its price above the market price, for that would mean that it would not sell any of its product. Conversely, since the product is homogeneous, the consumer's only consideration in buying it is price. In effect, the individual firm that is purely competitive has no pricing policy. The firm's product price is a given, a price determined by the market as a whole. No matter how much the firm produces, it receives the same price. A purely competitive firm is, in effect, independent of other firms; it is not affected by other individual firms, but by the entire industry.

Output Decisions

The basic decision that all competitive firms must make is how much to produce. This decision is affected by the period of time under consideration. Let's analyze the firm's behavior, first in the short run and then in the long run.

We assume that, in a capitalistic system, any firm wants to produce at that rate at which its profits are the highest or its losses the lowest. In other words, in a purely competitive industry (as in any industry), the firm makes supply decisions—relating its costs to its revenues—so as to produce the amount that will maximize its profits or minimize its losses.

PURE COMPETITION IN THE SHORT RUN

Short run is defined as a period of time long enough to allow variations of some factor inputs, and therefore variations of production, but not long enough to allow variations in the size of the plant or in technology. (In some industries, the limiting factor is human capital. For example, in the field of medical care in the short run, the number of doctors is fixed.) In the short run, the firm has both variable and fixed costs. Also, in the short run, new firms cannot enter the industry because the time is not long enough to enable newcomers to build plants. In addition, there's not enough time for existing firms to expand or liquidate their existing plants. So plant size is fixed, but the rate of utilization of the plant is not.

One can approach the analysis of the firm in pure competition in two ways: (1) by comparing total cost and total revenue, and (2) by comparing average and marginal revenue and average and marginal cost. (These two approaches, of course can be used for all the market classifications.) The more useful approach is the one emphasizing the relationships between average and marginal revenues and costs. In this chapter, which deals with pure competition, we will also include an analysis of total cost and revenues to give an indication of how one can use such an analysis.

Total Revenue and Total Cost

Economic profit is one that is above a normal profit. Table 7-1 contains data on total revenues and costs for a purely competitive firm which can sell any of its product it produces for $10 each.

Table 7-1
Pure Competition: Revenues and Costs

1	2	3	4	5	6	7	8	9	10	11	12
Output	Price	Total Revenue	Marginal Revenue	Fixed Cost	Total Variable Cost	Total Cost	Average Fixed Cost	Average Variable Cost	Average Total Cost	Marginal Cost	Profit
1	$10	$ 10		$5	$10	$ 15	$5.00	$10.00	$15.00		$–5
2	10	20	$10	5	19	24	2.50	9.50	12.00	$ 9	–4
3	10	30	10	5	27	32	1.60	9.00	10.60	8	–2
4	10	40	10	5	34	39	1.20	8.70	9.90	7	1
5	10	50	10	5	40	45	1.00	8.00	9.00	6	5
6	10	60	10	5	45	50	.83	7.50	8.33	5	10
7	10	70	10	5	51	56	.71	7.30	8.00	6	14
8	10	80	10	5	58	63	.62	7.20	7.82	7	17
9	10	90	10	5	66	71	.55	7.30	7.85	8	19
10	10	100	10	5	75	80	.50	7.50	8.00	9	20
11	10	110	10	5	85	90	.45	7.70	8.15	10	20
12	10	120	10	5	96	101	.41	8.00	8.41	11	19

Note: Short-run costs and revenues for a purely competitive firm.

(Note that profits are shown in column 12.) Figure 7-1(*a*) shows a total-revenue curve and a total-cost curve derived from Table 7-1. Beginning at output 4 on the curve, total cost lies below the curve for total revenue, and the firm makes an economic profit. Output will be at the level at which profits are at a maximum, at outputs 10 and 11. At those outputs, the distance between the total-cost curve and the total-revenue curve is the greatest. The firm earns an economic profit of $20.

Normal profit is a return that is just large enough to keep the entrepreneur producing. In other words, normal profit covers the opportunity cost of the entrepreneur. That is, normal profit must at least equal what the entrepreneur could obtain from producing some other commodity or working for some other firm. Another possible situation would be one in which the firm obtains only a normal profit. This occurs at price $7.82. In Figure 7-1(*b*), price is $7.82 and total revenue is equal to total cost at output level 8. Remember that *a normal profit is included in total cost* so that when total costs and revenues are equal, the firm receives a normal profit.

Economic loss with production. Whenever a firm cannot cover all of its opportunity costs, it sustains an economic loss. In Figure 7-1(*c*), at a price of $7.50, the total-revenue curve lies below the total-cost curve and so the firm sustains an *economic loss with production.* Total revenue is equal to total variable cost. The firm has enough revenue to cover its out-of-pocket or variable costs so it will continue to produce until it can *liquidate.* (By liquidate, we mean sell out entirely or convert all plant capacity to making some other product.) The firm, in other words, will produce where the difference between total cost and total revenue is least in order to minimize its loss.

Figure 7-1

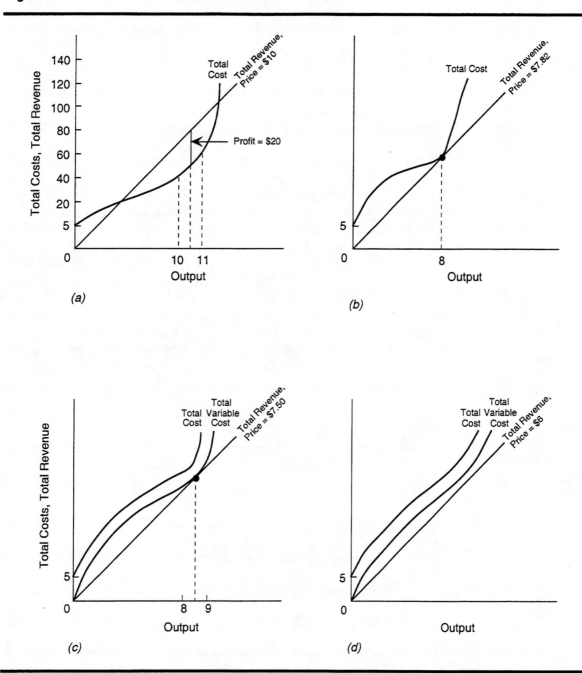

(a) Maximum economic profit is at outputs 10 and 11. The vertical distance from total cost to total revenue is greatest at those outputs. *(b)* Firms obtain only a normal profit at output 8 (when price is $7.82). At output 8, the total-revenue curve is tangent to the total-cost curve. *(c)* At price $7.50, total revenue does not cover total cost. The least loss (the vertical distance from total revenue to total cost) occurs when output is between 8 and 9. Total revenue covers total variable cost, and the firm continues to produce in the short run. However, in the long run, it will leave the industry. *(d)* At price $6, total revenue is less than both total cost and total variable cost. The firm has a greater economic loss when it produces than when it shuts down, and in the long run it leaves the industry.

Economic loss resulting in shut down. In Figure 7-1(*d*), at a price of $6, the total-revenue curve lies below the total-cost and the total-variable-cost curves. The *economic loss* is so great it exceeds total fixed cost. The firm thus decides to shut down and minimize its loss by paying only its fixed cost.

Profit Maximization: Marginal Cost Equals Marginal Revenue

Economists conclude that *profit maximization* or *loss minimization* occurs at the level of production where marginal costs (MC) and marginal revenue (MR) are equal or MC = MR. For an explanation of how this profit maximizing rule is obtained, see the box below. This is only logical. Economic profit (Π) as we see in the box below is the difference between total revenue (TR) and total cost (TC). When the cost (the addition to TC of producing one more unit) is less than the MR (the addition to TR that the firm derives from selling that one additional unit), it stands to reason that total profits increase. The firm is adding more to its revenue than to its cost. Thus, it will increase production as long as its MC is less than its MR.

Now suppose the scale tips and MC becomes greater than MR when the firm produces that one additional unit. Then total profits go down; more is added to cost than to revenue. A firm will not produce at any level at which MC is greater than MR.

The Rule for Profit Maximization

Profit (Π) = Total Revenue (TR) – Total Cost (TC), or

    a. $\Pi = TR - TC$

For profit to be at a maximum, a firm must produce the quantity (q) at which any added output (ΔQ) will add nothing to profit, or (from the definition of profit in (a) above),

    b. $\Delta\Pi/\Delta Q = \Delta TR/\Delta Q - \Delta TC/\Delta Q = 0$

The firm will produce additional output up to the output rate at which $\Delta\Pi/\Delta Q = 0$. Rearranging the terms in (b) above by moving $\Delta TC/\Delta Q$ to the right of the equality sign (which changes its sign) yields

    c. $\Delta\Pi/\Delta Q = \Delta TR/\Delta Q = \Delta TC/\Delta Q$

Since $\Delta TR/\Delta Q) = MR$ and $\Delta TC/\Delta Q = MC$, the necessary condition for a profit maximum is

    d. $\Delta TR/\Delta Q = \Delta TC/\Delta Q$, or MR = MC

In summary, the firm continues to increase its output as long as the addition to output adds less to cost than to revenue (that is, as long as profit increases). But the firm does not produce when MC becomes greater than MR (that is, when profit decreases). The point of maximum profits is the point at which the 2, MC and MR are equal. This applies whether the firm is incurring losses or making a profit.

Now let's illustrate this with numbers. We will use the data from Table 7-1 for a purely competitive firm with a price of $10 for its product (the firm takes this price as given). At output 8 (column 1) MR is $10 (column 4) and MC (column 11) is $7. If the firm produces that 1 extra unit, profits (column 12) will increase by $3, to $17. For outputs 9 and 10, MR is still higher than MC, and profit is increasing.

But now look at output 11. MC is equal to MR ($10 each). Here profit is at its highest: $20. (At output 10, profit is also equal to $20. Remember that normal profit is included in costs. The firm would produce output 11 because even though that output does not add to economic profit, it does add to normal profit.) Above output 11, MC is greater than MR, and profit declines. Only at output 11—where MC is equal to MR—is profit at its maximum.

Therefore, to maximize profits or minimize losses, the rate of output should be the rate at which MC equals MR.

Remember that a *normal profit* is the return to the entrepreneur that is just large enough to induce him or her to continue producing that commodity, instead of engaging in some other economic activity.

There are four possible situations for the firm in the short run: (1) The price per unit is high enough for the firm to make an economic profit. (2) The price per unit is just high enough to enable the firm to cover all costs, including a normal profit. (3) The firm does not receive a price high enough to cover all costs, but it is to its advantage to continue to produce in the short run. (4) The price per unit is too low to cause the firm to produce in the short run.

Stated briefly, the four situations are *economic profit, normal profit, economic loss with production*, and *economic loss with shut down*.

The Competitive Firm's Market Situation

A purely competitive firm, as we saw earlier, is a *price taker*, one whose selling price is determined independently of it and its own output decisions. If the firm were a **price seeker**, it would have to set the price of its product(s) as well as determine its most profitable output rate. Put in a slightly different way, the purely competitive firm is a **quantity adjuster**, a firm that can have no effect on price but can choose the quantity it wishes to produce. Because there are many firms in a competitive industry, variations in output by one

Price Seeker
A firm that must set the price of its product(s) as well as determine its most profitable output rate.

Quantity Adjuster
A firm that can have no effect on price but can choose the quantity it wishes to produce.

firm have no effect on the industry-wide price at which each firm sells.

To illustrate the role of the individual competitive firm, we have reproduced in Table 7-2 the hypothetical price and quantity data from Table 7-1.

The central fact in Table 7-2 is that the competitive firm expects to sell any of its output rates (1 through 12) at the industry-wide price of $10. As a result, its conjecture is that price, average revenue (AR), is constant. Importantly, each additional unit of output produced adds the same amount to the firm's TR, an amount of $10. If follows, then, that price equals AR and MR (columns 2, 4, and 5) = $10. *For the price taking firm, P = AR = MR.*

The Competitive Firm's Conjectural Demand Curve

Faced with a market in which P = AR = MR, the individual price taker must establish a basis for its profit maximizing output decision. To do so, it must decide what its own demand and supply condition is. Let's first see how it establishes a conjecture about its own demand curve. This is illustrated in Figure 7-2 in which the industry market *(a)* is represented as well as that of the individual firm *(b)*. While price is the same in *(a)* and *(b)*, the quantity measures are obviously much larger in *(a)* than in *(b)*. At any *(a)* established industry price, the price-taking firm in *(b)* expects to sell any output it produces at that price so that its conjectural demand, D_c, is horizontal to the quantity axis at each price. At an industry price of $10, for example, the individual firm's conjectural demand curve is D_c and at that price, price equals AR and MR. At any other price, a new conjectural demand curve is formed such as D_c' at an industry price of $7.

Situation 1: Economic Profit

Now look at Figure 7-3. The line for average fixed cost per unit is not drawn, since it is the vertical distance from the average variable cost

Table 7-2
Pure Competition: Price, Quantity, Total Revenue, Average Revenue, and Marginal Revenue

(1)	(2)	(3)	(4)	(5)
(Quantity) Q = Output	P = Price	(1 x 2) TR = Total Revenue	($\Delta 3/\Delta 1$) MR = Marginal Revenue	(3/1) AR = Average Revenue
1	$10	$ 10		$10
2	10	20	$10	10
3	10	30	10	10
4	10	40	10	10
5	10	50	10	10
6	10	60	10	10
7	10	70	10	10
8	10	80	10	10
9	10	90	10	10
10	10	100	10	10
11	10	110	10	10
12	10	120	10	10

Figure 7-2
The Conjectural Demand Curve of an Individual Competitive Firm

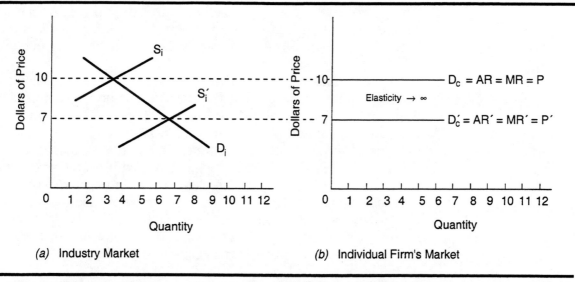

(a) Industry Market   (b) Individual Firm's Market

In Figure 7-2, diagram *(a)* represents the overall competitive industry market of which the individual competitive firm is a member. With industry demand, D_i, and industry supply, S_i, an equilibrium price is established at $10 where quantity demanded equals quantity supplied. The individual firm, expecting to sell any of its output rates at the industry-wide price, conjectures that its demand curve, D_c, is perfectly elastic at a price of $10. D_c, thus, is horizontal to the price taker at any industry price. Since price is a given to such a firm, demand equals price equals AR equals MR (D = AR = MR = P). Should a new price occur in the industry's market, a new perfectly elastic demand conjecture is formed such as D_c', which results from an industry price of $7 caused by supply S_i'.

Figure 7-3
Situation 1: Economic Profit for a Purely Competitive Firm (plotted from data in Table 7-1)

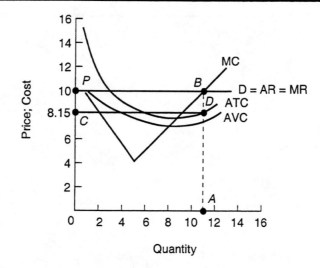

Economic profits exist because price (P = 10) is greater than cost per unit (C = 8.15).

(AVC) curve to the average total cost (ATC) curve. The demand, AR, and MR curves are the same, and are perfectly elastic for this reason: The purely competitive firm lacks control over price. As we have said, price per unit is taken as given and is the same regardless of the output of the firm. Since each unit produced sells for the same price, AR and MR are synonymous.

We assume that any firm's production goal is to maximize profits or minimize losses. The firm reaches this point when its output is such that MC is equal to MR. Figure 7-3 shows that, at price $10, this profit maximum is at output 11. TR is price ($10) times output (11), or $110. TC is output 11 times cost per unit ($8.15), or $90. Total profit (TR – TC) is $20. Technically, profit is at a maximum at either output 10 or 11. We are here assuming that the firm will produce output 11 rather than 10 because its profit does not diminish. Now we know that a normal profit—that is, a profit large enough to keep the firm producing—is included in TC. Therefore, that profit of $20 is a profit above normal, or an economic profit.

Situation 2: Normal Profit
We can also analyze economic profit and normal profit visually and in more general terms without using numbers. Figure 7-4 shows that price per unit is *P* (from the origin, along the vertical axis to point *P*). At that price one sees the curve for perfectly elastic conjectural demand, AR, and MR. To repeat, the quantity the firm produces is the amount that maximizes profits or minimizes losses. This quantity is the amount at which MC equals MR. Figure 7-4 shows this rate at point *B*. Since quantity is measured on the horizontal axis, point *B* corresponds to quantity *A*.

Figure 7-4
Situation 2: Normal Profit for a Purely Competitive Firm

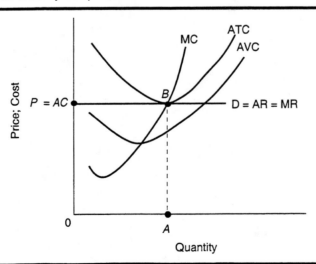

The profit is only a normal one because price per unit is only just high enough to cover cost per unit (also *P*). Demand is tangent to the lowest point on the ATC curve.

TR is price per unit times quantity, or the area of the rectangle 0PBA. At quantity A, TC per unit is measured by a perpendicular from A to the ATC curve at point B. Since cost is measured on the vertical axis, cost per unit is AC. TC is cost per unit AC times quantity produced A, which is represented by the area of the rectangle 0$ACDA$. TR, the area of 0PBA, is equal to TC, the area 0$ACDA$. Since a normal profit is included in TC, the excess of revenues over cost, is zero. The competitive firm earns a normal profit. For an economic profit to exist; thus, would require that price (P) be greater than average cost (AC) as was shown in Figure 7-3, short-run economic profit or a price above AC in a competitive industry must result from resource immobility or the inability of competitive firms to expand the size of its plant, that is, to build new plants or expand existing ones. In the short run, in a purely competitive industry, a firm can make an economic profit because other, newer firms cannot enter the industry and, by competing, reduce that profit. Again, Figure 7-4 illustrates this price, AC, and normal profit situation and, because of its importance, bears repeating.

The D = AR = MR curve in Figure 7-4 is perfectly elastic and tangent to the ATC curve at its lowest point. The MC curve cuts the ATC curve at its lowest point. Therefore, TR (price per unit P times quantity produced A, or the area of rectangle 0PBA), is equal to TC (AC times output A, or the area of rectangle 0$ACBA$). Since, as we said before, normal profit is included in cost, it can be seen that the firm receives a normal profit.

The firm we are discussing is typical of the industry, and is at a stable position. The firm has reached its optimal level of output by producing at a level that maximizes profit. Remember that this is the short run, so firms cannot enter or leave the industry, because they do not have time. This same constraint applies to all the other firms in the industry.

Situation 3: Economic Loss with Production

Situations 3 and 4 involve the possibility of economic losses in the short run. When a firm's in that kind of spot, the question is not just how much it should produce, but whether it should produce at all.

Remember that in the short-run firms do not have enough time to liquidate their plants, so they incur certain fixed costs whether they produce or not. Since they have to pay these fixed costs regardless of output, revenues must be at least high enough to cover any additional or variable costs caused by production. Therefore, in the short run, the firm will produce as long as its variable costs are covered.

Figure 7-5 shows the relationship between revenue and cost for situation 3, in which the firm experiences economic losses. The price per unit exceeds variable costs per unit, but not TC per unit. The firm thus produces in the short run, despite its economic loss.

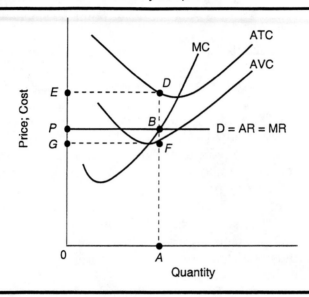

In spite of its economic losses, the firm continues to produce, because price per unit (*P*) is less than cost per unit (*E*), but higher than variable cost per unit (*G*). If the firm produces, it loses area *PEDB.* If it shuts down, it must pay all fixed costs (area *GEDF*). So it loses less by keeping on producing. It reduces its loss by *GPBF.*

To minimize losses, the firm produces the number of units at which MC equals MR (output *A*). Price per unit is *P* and TR is the area of the rectangle 0*PBA*. ATC per unit at output *A* is *E*, and TC is the area of rectangle 0*EDA*. TC (area 0*EDA*) is larger than TR (area 0*PBA*). Total economic loss is equal to the excess of TC over TR, or area *PEDB*. Loss per unit at output *A* is equal to *PE*.

Recall that this firm in the short run cannot liquidate and do away with all losses. All it can do is keep on producing, and incur its losses of *PEDB*. Or it can shut down. If it shuts down, it must still pay its fixed costs. Average fixed cost per unit at output *A* is the distance between average total and AVC, or *F D*. Total fixed cost is represented by the area of the rectangle *GEDF*. In this situation, the firm takes less of a beating if it goes ahead and produces. In other words, the firm earns more revenue by producing its product than it spends on the variable costs of producing it. Revenue covers all variable cost, plus some fixed cost (it covers *GPBF* of fixed cost). In the long run, however, this firm will have to either liquidate or vary the size of its plant.

Situation 4: Economic Loss with Shut Down
In situation 4, the firm's losses are greater than its fixed costs, so it minimizes its losses by shutting down and paying only its fixed costs. Figure 7-6 illustrates this situation.

With a conjectural demand curve that lies below the AVC curve, the firm receives price per unit *P*. At this price, there is *no* level

Figure 7-6
Situation 4: Economic Loss with Shut Down for a Purely Competitive Firm

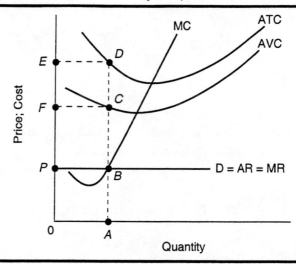

The firm loses more if it produces than if it shuts down, because price per unit (*P*) is less than both ATC per unit (*E*) and AVC per unit (*F*). If the firm produced, it would lose area *PEDB*. This is greater than the fixed cost area (area *FEDC*) that the firm has to pay if it shuts down. By shutting down, the firm reduces its loss by *PFCB*.

of output at which AVC per unit is less than or equal to price. No matter what the level at which the firm might produce, its variable costs—that is, the additions to cost due to production—would always be higher than the revenues the firm would get by selling its output. If the firm were to produce anything, it would produce at the level of output at which MC would equal MR at output *A*. Price per unit is *P* and revenue is area 0*PBA*. At output *A*, the AVC per unit is *F* and the variable cost is area 0*FCA*. Variable cost is greater than revenue.

At output *A*, average total cost per unit is *E* and TC is area 0*EDA*. Since revenue is area 0*PBA* and TC is area 0*EDA*, if the firm produces, it incurs economic losses equal to area *PEDB*. If the firm shuts down, it will have to pay all fixed costs (*FEDC*). Figure 7-6 shows that average fixed cost at output a is the vertical distance from the AVC to the ATC, or *FE*. If the firm produces, its economic losses are area *PEDB*. But if it shuts down, its losses are only area *FEDC*. So the firm will shut down in the short run rather than produce its product and reduce its loss by *PFCB*. Of course, we are assuming that the firm ignores any long-run start-up costs in making this decision.

Pure Competition, Short Run: A Summary

In the short run the purely competitive firm may encounter any one of four possible profit or loss situations. These situations that we looked at before are summarized in Figure 7-7.

Figure 7-7
Summary of the Short Run for a Purely Competitive Firm

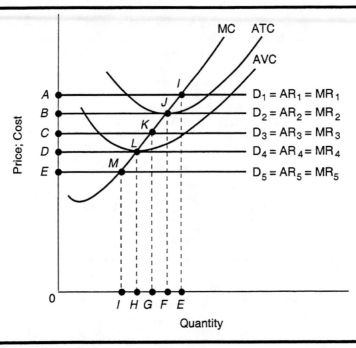

The four possible situations the firm encounters in the short run. At price *A*, the firm obtains an economic profit. At price *B*, it obtains only a normal profit and point *J* is the firms break-even point. At price *C*, it incurs an economic loss, but continues to produce. At price *D*, the firm just covers its variable costs and point *L* represents the firm's shut-down point or price below which it will shut down to minimize loss. At price *E*, the economic loss exceeds fixed cost so the firm shuts down and the quantity supplied is zero.

Break-Even Point or Price
Occurs when a firm just covers its opportunity costs. A price that equals average cost and MC is a break-even price.

Shut-Down Point or Price
The rate of output that corresponds to a price equaling AVC. TR equals TVC.

Situation 1. Price is higher than ATC, and the firm earns an economic profit. Figure 7-7 shows that if price is *A* and output (MC = MR$_1$) is *E*, revenue is 0*AIE*. Since price is greater than average cost, the firm earns an economic profit.

Situation 2. In Figure 7-7, price, which is just equal to average cost, is *B*, and quantity (MC = MR$_2$) is *F*. TR is equal to TC, and since a normal profit is included in cost, the firm earns only a normal profit. Point *J*, where Price = ATC = MC is called the **break-even point** or **price** since the firm's TR equals TC. The firm, earning a normal profit, covers all of its opportunity costs.

Situation 3. Price is less than ATC but greater than AVC. Figure 7-7 shows this situation where price is *C* and output is *G* (MC = MR$_3$). TR is less than TC, so the firm sustains a loss. However, revenues cover all variable costs plus some fixed costs. The firm loses less if it keeps on producing than it does if it shuts down.

Situation 4. Price is equal to AVC. Figure 7-7 shows that price is *D*. This firm's output is *H* where MC = MR$_4$. Point *L*, where price equals AVC is referred to as the **shut-down point** or **price** of the firm. In other words, at any price below *D*, the firm will have TR less than the TVC.

Situation 5. Price does not even cover AVC. Figure 7-7 shows this situation where price is *D*. If the firm were to produce at that price, its output would be *H* (MC = MR$_4$). However, revenue does not cover all of variable cost, and thus, obviously, it does not cover the firm's fixed costs. The firm will be able to minimize its losses only if it shuts its doors and pays just its fixed costs.

In situations 3, 4, and 5 the firm will in the long run either liquidate or adjust the size of its plant.

Marginal Cost: The Competitive Firm's Short-Run Supply Curve

A supply curve shows the quantities a firm is willing to offer for sale at various prices. In Figure 7-7, one sees that the MC curve above the minimum of the AVC curve is in fact the short-run supply curve for the purely competitive firm. At price *A* one can find the quantity the firm is willing and able to supply by following the perfectly elastic conjectural demand curve at price *A* to the MC curve at *I*, or quantity *E*. The same applies to prices *B* and *C* and all other possible prices above the AVC curve. At prices below that curve, production will be zero, as the firm shuts down to limit its losses to only its fixed costs. Therefore, for the purely competitive firm in the short run, the MC curve above the AVC curve is equivalent to the supply curve. In Figure 7-8 we see a competitive firm's short-run supply curve. Note that the supply curve originates at point *A* or the shut-down point (a price, P$_0$, equal to AVC). Below point *A*, although there is a MC

Figure 7-8
The Marginal Cost Curve as the Competitive Firm's Short-Run Supply Curve

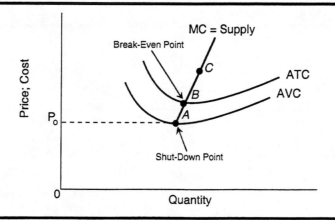

In Figure 7-8, the short-run supply curve of a competitive firm originates at point *A* where price (P$_0$) equals AVC. At any price below P$_0$, the firm will shut down and the quantity supplied is zero. At all prices above P$_0$, the firm will equate that price (= MR) with MC to determine the profitable quantity to supply. Points *B* (break-even point) and *C* are on the firm's supply curve. *A*, *B*, and *C*, together with all other points on the rising MC curve above *A*, constitute the firm's supply curve.

curve, quantities supplied are zero. To maximize profit or minimize loss, the firm takes any price above P_0 and responds by equalizing that price (and MR) with MC to determine quantity supplied. Points A (shut-down point), B (break-even point) and C $(P > AC)$ are all on the firm's short-run supply curve (MC = Supply). One can draw the supply curve for the whole industry in the short run by combining the relevant sections of all the competitive firms' short-run MC curves. A qualification will be made to this conclusion later when we talk about industry cost conditions.

PURE COMPETITION IN THE LONG RUN

Long run is defined as a period of time long enough to enable firms to vary all factor inputs, including plant capacity, but not long enough for technology to change. In the long run, new firms can enter the industry and build new plants, and existing firms can expand plants and build new ones. In the same period of time, existing firms can do the opposite, that is, liquidate plants and leave the industry.

Figure 7-9(*a*) embodies the assumption that in the short run the firm reaps economic profits at price A and quantity C. In the long run, new firms, anxious to take advantage of the economic profits, enter the industry, and existing firms (if they are not at their long-run optimal scale) expand their plants. Naturally, this increases industry supply from S_1 at price A. See Figure 7-9(*b*). This expansion continues until supply increases to S_2 at price B. At price B with $D_2 = AR_2 = MR_2$, the typical firm makes only normal profits. At that point there are no incentives for additional firms to enter the industry.

Figure 7-9
Pure Competition

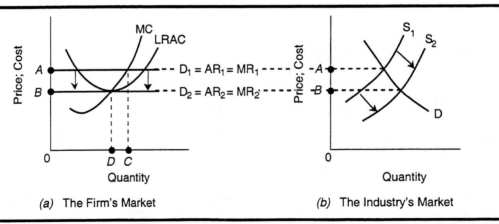

(a) The Firm's Market   (b) The Industry's Market

(a) The Typical Firm. The long-run adjustment to a short-run economic profit occurs when $D_1 = AR_1 = MR_1$ is shifted down as firms enter the industry and increase supply, part *(b)*, from S_1 to S_2. *(b)* The Industry. Price decreases to B. In part *(a)*, $D_2 = AR_2 = MR_2$ at price B results in only a normal profit.

Figure 7-10(a) shows that the firm incurs economic losses in the short run at price A. In the long run, such a firm may liquidate its plant and leave the industry. In Figure 7-10(b), supply (S_3) for the industry decreases (shifts up to the left) and price increases. In Figure 7-10(a), as price increases $D_3 = AR_3 = MR_3$ rises to $D_4 = AR_4 = MR_4$. This cuts out economic losses and the typical firm makes only normal profits.

The important point is this. *In long-run competitive equilibrium, typical firms receive normal profits.* As they enter or leave the industry, these firms change supply and thereby price, which eliminates economic profits or losses. Remember, though, that the long run is a *planning period*, not a period of actual production. Therefore, although each firm expects to reap economic profits, all firms tend to implement plans that result in a level of supply and a price that eventually make possible only normal profits.

Increasing-Cost, Constant-Cost, and Decreasing-Cost Industries

The above analyses of long-run equilibrium at normal profits were based on the assumption that the cost curves of the firms we are discussing do not change as the output of the industry changes. As you already know, and as the various cost curves show, costs within the firm do change as the firm varies output. Costs of all firms may also change when the output of the industry changes. These cost changes, which affect all the firms in the industry and which shift the cost curves up or down, are examples of what economists call

Figure 7-10
Pure Competition

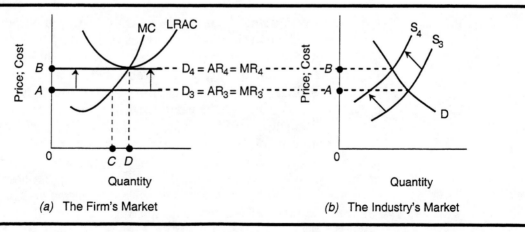

(a) The Firm's Market   (b) The Industry's Market

(a) The Firm. The long-run adjustment to economic losses occurs when $D_3 = AR_3 = MR_3$ is shifted up as firms leave the industry and decrease supply (part (b)) from S_3 to S_4. (b) The Industry. Price increases to B, and $D_4 = AR_4 = MR_4$ at price B results in only a normal profit.

External Economy
A cost decrease originating outside of the individual firm.

External Diseconomy
A cost increase originating outside of the individual firm.

externalities. They are a result of changes in factors external to the firms themselves. An **external economy** is a cost decrease originating outside the firm, caused by changes in output by the industry that reduce costs to the individual firm. A decrease in prices of materials or wages that results from variations in industry output is an external economy. An **external diseconomy** is a cost increase originating outside the firm, caused by changes in output by the industry, which increase costs of the individual firm. An example is the need to use less well-trained labor because the better-qualified laborers have already been hired. This situation, as the industry's output increases, reduces the firm's efficiency and increases its costs.

One can define an industry in terms of how variations in output affect the costs of the individual firms within the industry. In an industry with increasing costs, the cost curves of individual firms shift upward as output increases in the industry as a whole. In an industry with decreasing costs, the cost curves of individual firms shift downward as output increases in the industry as a whole. In a constant-cost industry, the cost curves of individual firms remain stable as the output of the industry as a whole changes.

Increasing-Cost Industry
A multi-firm industry in which cost curves of individual firms shift upward as industry output increases.

Increasing-Cost Industries

In an **increasing-cost industry**, as the output of the industry increases, external diseconomies (factors outside the firm) create increasing costs (shifting the cost curves of the individual firm upward). One common form of external diseconomy occurs when the industry has a significant share of the demand for its resource input. When the industry as a whole increases its output, demand for resources or raw materials increases, which has the effect of increasing the prices of the resources. This increase in prices of inputs increases costs to the firm at each level of output; that is, it shifts the cost curves of the firm upward. For example, Farmer Brown in Kansas demands such a small part of the total supply of fertilizer that any increase in demand for fertilizer to increase his output does not affect price. However, if all the farmers in the Midwest increase output, thus increasing demand for fertilizer, then the demand curve for fertilizer shifts to the right, thereby increasing the equilibrium price of fertilizer. Then the higher cost of fertilizer causes a shift upward of the cost curve of Farmer Brown.

In the short run, for an increasing-cost industry, when there are economic profits, supply increases as new firms enter to take advantage of the economic profits. The addition of new firms has two effects both of which lead toward the elimination of economic profits. The first you are already familiar with. Increased industry supply reduces the price of the product, shifting the $D = AR = MR$ curve down, to eliminate economic profits. Figure 7-11 shows that the curve $D_1 = AR_1 = MR_1$ shifts to $D_2 = AR_2 = MR_2$. At the same time, increased industry supply increases the demand for inputs of various factors, and the prices of these factors increase. Increased prices of

Figure 7-11
Long-Run Equilibrium, Increasing-Cost Industry

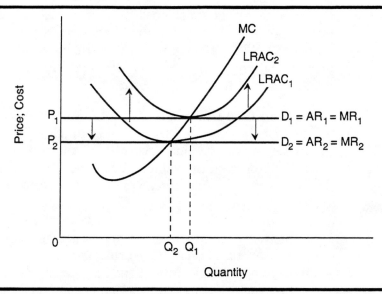

Two forces produce long-run equilibrium for a firm in an increasing-cost industry when the firm incurs an economic profit in the short run. The entry of new firms increases supply and reduces product price. $D_1 = AR_1 = MR_1$ falls to $D_2 = AR_2 = MR_2$. Also, increased industry supply increases the price of factor inputs, increasing the cost to the individual firm. $LRAC_1$ shifts up to $LRAC_2$.

factors in turn shift the cost curves of the individual firm upward, eliminating economic profits. In Figure 7-11, $LRAC_1$ shifts up to $LRAC_2$. In the long run, the reverse occurs if the firm has incurred an economic loss in the short run.

Constant-Cost Industries

In a **constant-cost industry**, the individual firm's cost curves remain stable as the output of the industry varies. External economies and diseconomies offset each other, or they are absent. A main explanation for a constant-cost situation is that the industry demands such a small part of the total supply of its factor inputs that variations in industry output do not affect their price. This leaves costs to the individual firm unaffected. For example, in any city, neighborhood dry-cleaning outlets use labor that is primarily low skilled, and use only a small part of the total supply of the low-skilled labor in the city. Any increases or decreases in the size of the dry-cleaning industry as a whole will not affect demand for such labor, and thus the wage rate for low skilled labor is unaffected. If there is no increase in wage rates, there is no increase in costs to the firm.

In the analysis of the long-run elimination of an economic profit depicted in Figures 7-9(a) and (b), we were assuming a constant-cost industry. The economic profit was eliminated in the long run by new firms entering the industry, thereby increasing the

Constant-Cost Industry
A multi-firm industry in which the cost curves of individual firms remain unchanged as industry output increases.

supply and reducing the price of the product. Falling $D_1 = AR_1 = MR_1$ in Figure 7-9(a) squeezes out the economic profit. The reverse occurs with an economic loss. In an increasing-cost industry, both falling product price and rising firm cost curves work toward the elimination of the economic profit in the long run. In a constant-cost industry, falling product price is the only factor that moves the firm to long-run equilibrium at only normal profit.

Decreasing-Cost Industries

Decreasing-Cost Industry
A multi-firm industry in which the cost curves of individual firms shift downward as industry output increases.

In a **decreasing-cost industry**, as the output of the industry increases, external economies reduce costs to all the individual firms. These external economies may include an increased supply of required skilled labor that reduces wage rates, and reduced need for premiums to induce labor to come to underdeveloped areas as these areas begin to grow. Also, with increased pressure from the growing industry, government may take action to improve transportation. For example, radar was developed during World War II, and after the war, was adapted to nonmilitary uses. At first, technicians skilled in radar were very scarce and wages paid to them were relatively high. As the industry expanded, this labor supply increased considerably and relative wages paid to technicians decreased.

Also, in a decreasing-cost industry, there are two factors at work: *changing product prices* and *changing costs*. In an increasing-cost industry, these two factors work together to eliminate profit. But in a decreasing-cost industry, these two factors work against each other to prolong the making of an economic profit. You can see this in Figure 7-12. As new firms enter an industry and make an economic profit, the supply of an article increases and price P_1 falls. Thus, also $D_1 = AR_1 = MR_1$ falls. This fall itself tends to eliminate profits. However, as the industry expands, external economies appear and the LRAC for each firm, $LRAC_1$, tends to fall. This fall by itself tends to increase economic profits. If costs fall more rapidly than product price, then economic profits increase. However, the long-run equilibrium in Figure 7-12 occurs because a decreasing-cost situation is only a temporary one. Eventually all decreasing-cost industries become either constant-cost or increasing-cost industries. For example, in a developing country, when the premium to bring workers to the newly opened areas need no longer be paid, the cost premium ends. When the government builds a road or railroad in the area of industrial activity, thus reducing costs to the firm, it is again a one-time occurrence. But the shift of an industry to a constant-cost or increasing-cost status must come about from the following: The industry grows to a level at which its share of total demand for its resources is so large that further growth increases demand and price of its input. This, in turn, increases costs.

In summary, then, firms operating in a constant-cost industry can achieve long-run equilibrium with only normal profits by shifting price, and thereby shifting demand, average revenue, and MR. For

Figure 7-12
Long-Run Equilibrium, Decreasing-Cost Industry

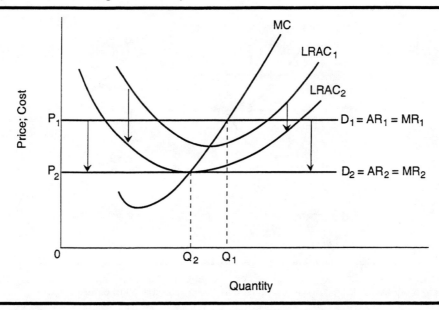

In a decreasing-cost industry with an economic profit in the short run, firms enter the industry and increase supply of the product while decreasing price. $D_1 = AR_1 = MR_1$ and P_1 shift down. At the same time external economies occur, decreasing the cost curves $LRAC_1$. Eventually the equilibrium situation of $D_2 = AR_2 = MR_2$ and $LRAC_2$ produces price P_2 and quantity Q_2.

those operating in an increasing-cost industry, two factors eliminate economic profits or losses in the long run: changing product prices and changing costs. However, it may take a very long time for firms operating in a decreasing-cost industry to achieve long-run equilibrium, because decreasing prices tend to be offset by decreasing costs. Eventually, these industries become either constant-cost or increasing-cost industries, which assures them long-run equilibrium at normal profits.

THE ADVANTAGES OF PURE COMPETITION

In conditions of long-run equilibrium, the typical purely competitive firm earns only a normal profit. When it reaches this point of normal profit, price (MR) is equal to MC at the lowest point on the average cost curve (see Figure 7-13).

This equality (P = MR = MC = AC) is important, because it is the basis for the analysis of the advantages of pure competition. Such an analysis sets forth the welfare conditions that many economists consider optimal. We are not using *welfare* in the usual sense here. In economic discussions, one can in large measure substitute *welfare conditions* for the term *advantages of competition*. These advantages are grouped under two main headings: (1) The purely competitive firm

Figure 7-13
Long-Run Equilibrium, Purely Competitive Industry

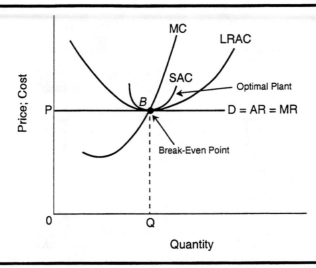

In the long run only a normal profit is possible. Price, demand, and MR are equal to MC and average cost at *B*, which is the low point on the long-run average cost curve. It is also the point of full capacity.

(and industry) produces at the most efficient level. (2) Competition forces industries to produce an array of products at prices just covering alternative or opportunity costs of production.

Most Technically Efficient Level of Cost

Competition forces the typical purely competitive firm to produce in the long run at the most efficient (lowest) level of unit cost. There are three main reasons for this:

1. The purely competitive firm has no control over price, so its MR curve is perfectly (or infinitely) elastic. Competition forces price in the long run to the point at which the typical firm can make only normal profits. Figure 7-13 shows that at that price the low point of the average cost curve is tangent to the D = AR = MR curve. This low point on the LRAC curve is also considered the level of **economic capacity**, which is the level of production that can be achieved at the lowest per-unit cost with the optimal plant.

Economic Capacity
The level of long-run production that is achieved with the lowest per-unit cost of the optimal plant.

If the firm in the long run chooses to produce less than this, excess capacity will accrue. If it produces more than this, it operates above capacity. Excess capacity will also accrue if the firm fails to produce at the lowest average cost with the optimal size of plant. Competition forces a firm to strive for both optimal scale and optimal level of production on that scale. In other words, competition forces the firm to produce at the lowest level of cost, at the lowest point on the LRAC curve.

2. A related point is that the typical purely competitive firm has to use the most up-to-date methods of production. If it does not, then its costs will be higher than those of other firms in the industry, and since all firms sell at the same price, the normal-profit prices received by the typical firm will cause the old-fashioned, technologically backward firm to have higher costs and fewer profits. Eventually it will incur losses. If Farmer Nielson is relatively slow to adopt a new improved strain of corn, his yield per acre falls below that of the rest of the industry (that is, the other farmers who are not slow). His cost per unit of corn produced is higher than the cost per unit to Smith, Brown, and Robinson. Competition will force the price of his corn down to the point of normal profits for typical firms, who *are* using the improved strain of corn. The high cost to Farmer Nielson then results in an economic loss and exit from the industry. So pure competition leads to up-to-dateness.

3. In pure competition the product is homogeneous: One product is like another. So an individual firm is not spending any money on advertising. Therefore, selling or advertising costs do not have to be added in to the costs of production. The industry, unlike the individual firm may, however, find it rational to spend on advertising. It may do so because it is in competition with the products of other industries. The highly competitive beef industry, for example, advertises its products widely through an industry-wide association.

Most Allocatively Efficient Combination of Products

The fact that an industry produces its output with the greatest efficiency does not necessarily mean that the output is composed of the kinds of products consumers most prefer. In a purely competitive market, however, competition forces an industry to produce an output consumers most prefer. Here again, the equality between price (P), marginal cost (MC), and marginal revenue (MR) at the point of production is the signal that these results are occurring.

Price measures the worth of the product to the consumer at the margin, and *MC* is what measures the opportunity cost to society of producing the last unit of the product. In other words, price measures the benefit to the consumer of the last unit to be produced, while MC measures the sacrifices of other products that have to be made for that last unit to be produced.

Now let's see what happens when price, MC, and MR are not equal. When price is greater than MC, consumers are sacrificing more at the margin to buy the good than the value of other products they might buy. The industry is not producing as much of the product at consumers prefer. Where price is less than MC, the opposite occurs. The industry is producing more of the product than consumers prefer, in terms of the sacrifice of alternative goods.

Because of (1) competition, especially by firms entering and leaving the industry, and (2) the desire to maximize profit, the purely competitive firm produces its product at the point at which MC = MR = P. This leads to equality between the degree to which the consumer values the product and the degree to which the consumer values alternative products. In other words, the composition of output is that which consumers most prefer (given their incomes, tastes, and so on).

Welfare of Buyers and Sellers: Consumers' and Producers' Surplus

The advantages of a market economy lie, at heart, in meshing the interests of consumers and producers, a meshing that results from voluntary exchanges. It is in the interests of both groups to minimize the opportunity costs of making their choices. Consumers will benefit if their utility maximizing choices involve minimum opportunity cost; producers will benefit if the profit maximizing choices likewise involve minimum opportunity cost. Society benefits if output of a good expands to the point at which the additional benefits to consumers and the additional costs to producers are made equal. It can be shown that pure competition tends to produce these results. Let's see, in stages, how this happens.

Benefits to Consumers: Consumers' Surplus

Consumers' Surplus The difference between what consumers would be willing to pay for a good and what they actually pay for it.

Consider that in most instances in which we make choices as consumers, we are able to buy all we choose of a good at a single going price. Yet, were it necessary for us to do so, we would doubtlessly pay higher prices for some of the units bought. The difference between what we would be willing to pay for the quantity of a good we buy and what we actually pay is called a **consumers' surplus**. We see this surplus illustrated in Figure 7-14.

In Figure 7-14, D is a downward sloping demand curve whose unusual look is based on a step function, one in which demand is segmented rather than continuous. Nonetheless, D is like other demand curves seen in text in that it is based on the assumption of diminishing marginal utility or benefit to the consumer. With its relatively high marginal benefit to the consumer, a price of P_4 would willingly be paid by the consumer for the first unit. P_G, the going (competitive) price is paid instead and the difference $P_4 - P_G$ or the shaded area A is the consumers' surplus on the first unit consumed. Similarly, the consumer would willingly pay (lower) price P_3 for unit 2 but actually pays P_G and the difference $P_4 - P_G$ or area B is the benefit surplus on the second unit. The benefit surpluses on the third and fourth units are C and D and represent diminishing additional consumers' surpluses as the individual's demand curve approaches the going price. If the consumer's equilibrium quantity demanded is 4 units, the total consumers' surplus on this good is the sum of the shaded areas $ABCD$.

Figure 7-14
Consumers' Surplus

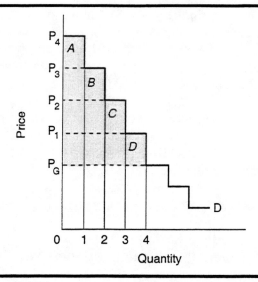

In Figure 7-14, D represents a discontinuous (step) demand curve for an individual. Based on that demand, the consumer would be willing to pay P_4 for the first unit of the good. The consumer, instead, pays the single competitive price P_G; the difference $P_4 - P_G$ or the shaded area A is the consumers' surplus on unit 1 of the good. For the second unit of the good, the consumer would pay P3 but reaps the surplus ($P_3 - P_G$). The surplus on the third unit is $P_2 - P_G$ and on the fourth unit is $P_1 - P_G$. A, B, C, and D are the total consumers' surplus.

Can we then add up these private individual benefits at the going (competitive) price and obtain the *social* benefits or surplus of competitive prices. The answer is yes, but only on a special assumption that needs to be explicit. To equate private and social benefits requires the assumption that the distribution of income upon which individual demand curves are based is optimal. Markets treat dollars spent equally; the rich and the poor alike spend income and, in doing so, determine how resources are used and what is produced. The rich, however, get more votes. Were the distribution of income to change, the structure of demand would also change and consumers' surpluses would be altered. The assumption that the current distribution of income is optimal is necessarily controversial. Nonetheless, we shall make it at this point and interpret the summation across all consumers of areas such as *ABCD* in Figure 7-14 as both added personal benefits and added social benefits.

Benefits to Producers: Producers' Surplus

Benefits accrue not only on the demand side but also on the supply side of markets. Whenever a firm sells its products at a price above marginal cost, it is receiving a benefit (not necessarily a profit) because it is more than covering its opportunity costs at the margin. The differences between the actual selling price of a good and the marginal cost of producing it are called **producers' surplus**. We see this surplus on the supply side in Figure 7-15.

In Figure 7-15, MC is represented as step function rather than as the smooth function we have seen before. P_G is the going price and the firm can sell all it produces at that price. MC which is rising with each additional unit produced, is the lowest price at which the firm would be willing to sell any of the units produced. If the firm produces and sells four units, it accumulates a surplus on each one. On unit 1, it receives the difference between price and the MC of that unit $(P_G - MC_0)$ or the shaded area A. On unit 2, it receives the difference between the selling price and that unit's MC $(P_G - MC_1)$ or the shaded area B. Similarly, it receives the shaded area C on unit 3 and D on unit 4. The total producers' surplus on the 4 units produced then equals $ABCD$ or is the entire shaded area above MC and below P_G.

Competitive Equilibrium:
Maximum Benefits to Consumers and Producers

We have seen that consumers receive a surplus when they pay a price less than what they would be willing to pay for the quantity they purchase of a good. Likewise, producers receive a surplus when they receive a selling price above the MC of the quantity of a good they offer for sale. As we see in Figure 7-16, the combined consumers' and producers' surplus is maximized by competitive equilibrium pricing.

Figure 7-15
Producers' Surplus

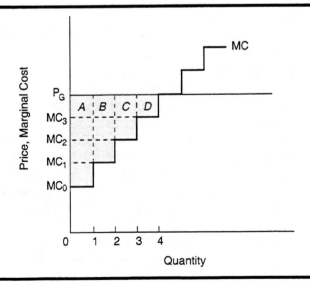

In Figure 7-15, P_G is the going price and the individual producer can sell any of its output at that price. Unit 1 is produced with a MC of MC_0 but sells at P_G; the excess of price over MC $(P_G - MC_0)$ or A is the producers' surplus on that unit. Similarly, unit 2 has a MC of MC_1 and the difference between selling price and MC $(P_0 - MC_1)$ or B is the surplus on unit 2. If the firm produces and sells 4 units, its surplus will be $ABCD$.

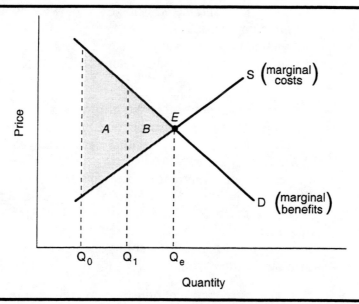

In Figure 7-16, the benefits of increasing output so long as there is a combined consumer and producer surplus are shown. If output increases from Q_0 to Q_1, there is a combined surplus equal to the shaded area A. Increasing output from Q_1 to Q_e results in a combined surplus equal to the shaded area B. The surplus to both consumers and producers is maximized at the competitive equilibrium output, Q_e.

The downward sloping demand curve, D, may be thought of as representing a set of benefits to consumers that diminish at the margin as more of the good is consumed. The upward sloping supply curve, S, may be thought of as representing a set of opportunity costs to producers that increase at the margin as more of the good is produced. In competitive equilibrium as we already know, price will be established at a level that equates quantity demanded with quantity supplied. The social benefits of expanding output to this point (point E in Figure 7-16) can readily be seen. If we begin at a lesser output rate of Q_0 in Figure 7-16, the combined consumers and producers surplus of expanding out to Q_1 is the shaded area A. Further expansion of output from Q_1 to Q_E creates a combined surplus of B. In competitive equilibrium this combined surplus or set of benefits to consumers and producers is maximized. In other words, the marginal benefit to consumers is made equal to the MC to producers.

Markets other than pure competition do not guarantee that output will be expanded to the rate that maximizes consumers' and producers' surplus. Indeed, as we shall see, where monopoly or imperfectly competitive markets exist, output is restricted to levels less than Q_e in Figure 7-16 and there are significant efficiency losses to society.

THE DISADVANTAGES OF PURE COMPETITION

We have discussed the advantages; now what about the *dis*advantages of pure competition?

Compared with markets of other kinds, the purely competitive market has a number of disadvantages. Let's look at three of the most important ones.

1. For pure competition to exist, products must be homogeneous. In many instances such as in commodity markets, technical homogeneity exists and is merely a fact, not a disadvantage. With other products, however, particularly consumer goods, buyers may have preferences for product differentiation. In a society in which consumers desire differences in style, homogeneity becomes a significant limitation. You cannot, for instance, get 245 million Americans voluntarily to wear identical blue jeans. Differences based on varying styles provide the basis for product differentiation, and this will lead to a departure from pure competition.

2. A purely competitive industry may not be able to adopt the existing technology in many industries and still remain purely competitive. The best of modern technology—based on assembly-line production, automation, and various feedback systems requires such a large output in order to reach economies of scale that, given the sizes of markets, only a few firms can exist in each industry. If some agency (for example, the government) forces a purely competitive situation, industries may have to sacrifice economies of scale or the opportunities to use modern technology. It is hard to imagine that enough firms can keep afloat in industries such as automobiles, steel, aluminum, oil refining, and so on, to make possible purely competitive pricing behavior. On the other hand, we do not know how many firms are required to create this situation.

3. Purely competitive firms are usually quick to adopt known improvements in technology. However, given today's financial climate for science and technology, it is unlikely that firms in a purely competitive industry will have the resources to engage in extensive research and development. To achieve positive results, research and development in science and technology require very large amounts of money and often have long-term payouts. Only fairly large firms can afford to spend that much. However, public agencies and nonprofit institutions do carry on much research and development. Imposing purely competitive conditions would surely shift more research and development activity to such agencies. Indeed, big technological strides in highly competitive industries generally do originate outside the industry, as in agriculture and the garment industry, for example. Impressive improvements in agricultural productivity have originated from research by government agencies, as well as by manufacturers of agricultural equipment, fertilizer, chemicals, and seed. In the garment

industry, improvements in sewing machinery have come from the equipment makers, not from the garment firms themselves.

An industry, therefore, that appeals to consumers on the basis of style or quality, or that gains significant efficiency from economies of large scale, or that needs large research facilities to develop technology, may move from a purely competitive market to a market with elements of monopoly. As long as the industry gains such advantages, the loss of the advantages of pure competition may possibly be offset. However, the intensity of monopoly may become so great that its costs outweigh the efficiency advantages.

One final note about the disadvantages of pure competition: The conclusion that a purely competitive system produces that combination of goods that consumers prefer takes into account only activities carried on in a market environment. However, in both competitive and noncompetitive markets, the process of production itself generates costs and benefits that we have not considered in our look at markets. There are many social costs of production. Perhaps the most important and most pressing have to do with pollution as well as with the consumption of noxious products such as illegal drugs.

THE RELEVANCE OF PURE COMPETITION

One may well ask: Why study the purely competitive model? Isn't our economy dominated by big business? *Is* there such a thing as a purely competitive industry?

One can defend the relevance of the purely competitive model on various grounds:

1. Certain industries do closely resemble the model. The contracting aspect of the garment industry is a good example. The contractor only produces the garments and does not design or sell them. The number of these contracting firms is large, their size small, and their capital requirements low, especially when compared with those of other manufacturing industries. We can most easily understand this industry's behavior in terms of the purely competitive model. Stock and commodity exchanges are other examples

2. The purely competitive model provides an insight into how an industry can be affected by outside forces that distort its purely competitive structure. For instance, agriculture should, except for government intervention, be considered a purely competitive industry. To understand the agricultural situation fully, one must have some understanding of the purely competitive model.

3. In order to understand *im*perfectly competitive market structures, one must have some understanding of purely competitive ones, because they provide the ideal to use as a yardstick for other market classifications. From the 19th century to the present, economists have used conclusions drawn from the purely competitive model to analyze capitalism. And one can understand certain elements of monopolistic markets best in terms of their departures from pure competition.

4. Essentially, the purely competitive model assumes an economic situation devoid of interference. It is a situation in a vacuum. But the physicist also makes similar assumptions and considers models in a vacuum. For example, the first step in understanding ballistics is the assumption that the projectile is traveling in a vacuum. Afterward, the physicist can make adjustments for real-world factors such as friction from the air, and direction and velocity of wind.

5. When you understand the purely competitive model, you can recognize the beneficial impact of increased competition. You can see how competition leads to lowered prices, costs, and profit margins, and how it increases the efficiency of allocation of resources. You need to understand the purely competitive model in order to grasp the arguments regarding antitrust actions, reduction of tariffs and import quotas, and the arguments about freer trade in general.

APPLICATION:
Do We Really Want Competition?

We have just concluded that a big advantage of competitive markets is that they allocate an economy's resources in the most efficient manner (1) to produce goods at the lowest possible cost and (2) to produce that combination of products the consumer most prefers. As we have seen, they create incentives to expand output to the point at which marginal benefits of consumers and producers are made equal. In view of these results, it might seem that where the conditions for such competition exist, as in much of agriculture, we would work to preserve them. However, throughout history, both in the U.S. and in other countries, governments have used many devices to interfere in agricultural markets.

Agriculture in the U.S. seems to fit the characteristics of the purely competitive model. There are more than 2 million farms, and none—even the largest—is big enough to affect supply noticeably. On the whole, farms produce homogeneous products. These products are graded; but any farms' wheat is much like other wheat of the same grade, and this is also true of eggs, milk, and meat. It makes little difference which farm produced the product ultimately bought in a store.

Yet the government, since 1929, has actively attempted to influence the prices of farmers' products. It has done so by manipulating supply, and to some extent demand.

Not only does the government interfere in competitive agricultural markets, but its agricultural policy seems to satisfy no one. As we move into the 1990s, everyone criticizes it—consumers, economists, politicians, even many farmers. It is like the other welfare programs; they please practically nobody, but we cannot seem to find an alternative to them.

Origins of the Government Intervention

For more than 20 years prior to the depression of 1921, U.S. agriculture bloomed as never before. Before World War I, there was great foreign demand for U.S. agricultural products. The high immigration rate produced high domestic demand as well. During the war, foreign agricultural production decreased as Europe shifted its resources to producing war materials. This had the effect of further increasing foreign demand for U.S. farm produce. Agricultural prices increased faster than general prices, and farmers' real incomes rose. The mechanization of agriculture accelerated. Farmers who tried to increase their individual outputs by buying more land caused land values to rise rapidly.

After the war, the picture began to change. Foreign agriculture slowly recovered, and so the overseas demand for U.S. agricultural products fell. Also, immigration halted because of new restrictions. The depression of 1921 was very severe, although it was short; and agriculture suffered greatly. Prices of agricultural products fell drastically—much further than prices in general. Farm incomes naturally fell too and remained below nonfarm incomes. This fact, coupled with high mortgage levels, put the U.S. farmer in a tight squeeze. Thus, one can see that U.S. agriculture was already depressed by the 1920s. The general depression of the 1930s only made things worse.

Farmers pressured the government for help, so in 1929 the government set up the Federal Farm Board, whose aim was to stabilize supply by storing over supplies of farm products until they were needed. But this program did not counter falling prices and incomes, so Congress replaced it with the Agricultural Adjustment Act of 1933, which aimed at increasing prices by bringing about a forced—and artificial—reduction in supply. Ever since 1933, there has been a series of programs designed to do the same thing, in other words (1) to decrease the supply of farm produce by limiting acreage and withdrawing some land from production and (2) to increase the incomes of farmers relative to the incomes of nonfarmers. Therefore, the U.S. government, for the last 60 years, has persisted in interfering directly in competitive agricultural markets. What are the reasons for this policy?

No Bed of Roses: Agricultural Economic Problems

Demand

Agriculture, by its very nature, engenders fluctuating prices and unstable incomes. And both prices and incomes have to do with demand and supply. First, let's look at demand.

The demand for any particular food is highly price inelastic. This means that when the price of a food product goes down, the quantity of it demanded increases by a smaller percentage than the percentage of decrease in price. Therefore, when the price of apples falls, the farmer's revenue from the apple crop also falls. Thus, farm prices and farm income are very sensitive to changes in quantities supplied. Food *in general* (1) has no substitutes, (2) is a necessity, and (3) is perishable—all factors causing inelasticity.

The demand for food also has a low income elasticity. (Remember that income elasticity measures the degree to which people's demand for an item increases or decreases with changes in their incomes.) For example, if income elasticity were equal to 1, a 1-percent increase in income would produce a 1-percent increase in demand for food. In the U.S. today, the income elasticity for food is around .2, which is very low. A person's income must increase by $5 before her or his demand for food increases by $1. As a person's income goes up, the percentage of it spent for food goes down. (This is understandable, since the *percentage* of income a low-paid worker spends on food is much greater than the percentage of income that a bank president spends on food.) In effect, the higher a person's income, the lower his or her income elasticity of demand for agricultural products. One can then say that the more highly developed an economy, the lower the income elasticity of demand for foods. Therefore, there is little stimulus to growth in the demand for food in the U.S. economy even when there is economic growth and a general increase in income.

Thus, the demand for food is both price and income inelastic. Small variations in supply have large effects on price. Figure 7-17 depicts a demand curve for food that is generally price inelastic, although it has different elasticities at each price. An increase of supply from S_1 to S_2 has a much greater impact on prices than on quantity.

Demand, as we have said, also tends to grow slowly. In the long run, the only factor that may increase demand for food (in other words, that may shift the demand curve up to the right) is an increase in the number of buyers because of population growth. In the U.S., at least, the 1970s and 1980s have seen a continuing decline in the net rate of population growth. Economic growth and increasing individual income have a minimal effect on demand for food because of low income elasticity. There is little likelihood that people will start demanding greater amounts of food. With all the articles stating that obesity is unhealthy, it is even possible that people's demand for food

Figure 7-17

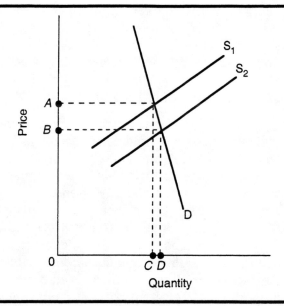

With a given shift in supply, the highly inelastic demand for food results in significant changes in price, with very little change in quantity.

may lessen (though not our exports to other countries, including those with low per capita incomes). Variations in price expectations can have only a short-term effect. In brief, analyses of those factors affecting demand for food (or affecting the position of the demand curve) seem to indicate that the demand for food is relatively stable. Demand growth, where possible, seems tied to increasing international competitiveness of agricultural exports.

Supply: Short Run

Supply is the dominant force in determining variations in the agricultural marketplace. The factors affecting supply can be divided into long-run and short-run factors. In the short run, there are three main points to consider:

1. Agriculture is a highly competitive industry that encompasses a very large number of firms. No one firm (or group of firms) has any perceptible control over supply. Therefore, firms cannot artificially restrict supply in order to influence price, though some farm organizations try from time to time. The individual firm must sell at the prevailing market price. When increases in supply reduce prices—and in agriculture, farmers' income—farmers although permitted by law to behave collusively, cannot band together and artificially restrict supply by concerted action to stop the falling trend of their incomes. It just won't work out.

The actions of the National Farmers' Organization (NFO) during the 1960s are a case in point. In an effort to restrict supply and increase price, the NFO persuaded its member farmers to hold back from the market supplies of beef, milk, and various other products. Needless to say, the effort failed. So one must conclude that if supply is to be reduced artificially in order to stimulate income, the government must do the manipulating, and its strategies must apply to all of agriculture. Another possibility to reduce supply is a more rapid exit of farmers from agriculture.

2. Farmers' fixed costs run uncomfortably close to their TC. There are high fixed costs of interest on land investment—either explicit in terms of interest charges on mortgages, or implicit in terms of imputed interest on owner-invested capital. The cost of maintenance and depreciation on equipment and buildings (these are fixed costs) are also high. Because there are not many jobs available for farm families as an alternative to farm work (at least in the short run), the farm family's labor must also be considered a fixed cost. Remember that firms that are losing money continue to produce in the short run if their losses are less than their fixed costs. Farmers with such a high proportion of their total costs fixed have less tendency to give up in the short run because they are losing money. Supply of food in the short run, then, tends to remain high despite farmers' economic losses. So supply of food, like demand for it, tends to be price inelastic.

3. Farmers can influence the total amount of certain foods available by controlling the amount of land and other resources they devote to production. Weather, however, can produce great variations in the expected levels of production, since a flash flood or a freak hailstorm can wipe out many square miles of ripe grain. And because weather varies so enormously from year to year, the supplies of foodstuffs also vary from year to year. Good weather can greatly increase supply, which can reduce both price and farm incomes. Bad weather, such as the drought of the late-1980s, may reduce supply and increase price and overall farm incomes. But this does not necessarily benefit the agricultural population as a whole. In fact, the only farmers who benefit from reduced supply because of bad weather are those who have escaped the bad weather; those who have endured the bad weather usually do not have enough product left to take advantage of these higher prices. For example, the severe drought in the Southeastern U.S. during 1986 wreaked havoc in a variety of agricultural markets in spite of the fact that large crops had been planted. A farmer can take out crop insurance. But in the long run, crop insurance is not an adequate solution to the age-old problem of the weather.

Supply: Long Run
According to the purely competitive model, in the long run firms enter an industry to compete for economic profits. When losses prevail, firms leave the industry. This means that in the long run, in a given industry, only a normal profit will exist for the typical (farm) firm. This assumption of normal profits is based on the mobility of

resources; that is, resources move into and out of a competitive industry quite readily.

In agriculture, however, resources are notoriously immobile, especially when it comes to leaving the industry. In other words, farmers tend to stick it out on the farm, come what may. There are two main reasons for this immobility, one economic, and the other social:

1. *The economic cause.* The uses of agricultural resources are highly specialized. There are few alternative uses, especially for such machines as grain combines, balers, and corn planters, or for such farm buildings as silos and barns. There are also few alternative uses for agricultural products. (What use are chickens for anything but food?) Even farm labor is fairly specialized. Although the level of skills demanded of a farm worker is relatively high, many of these skills are not needed once the worker steps outside the farm world. Many farm laborers in order to make a living elsewhere, as other than common labor, would need considerable retraining. In other words, alternative opportunities opportunity costs) of resources now employed in agriculture are relatively small. In fact, many of these resources may be trapped in agriculture and have no significant alternative uses.

2. *The social cause.* Farmers may be reluctant to leave their rural environment. People find it hard to leave their friends and homes. And the different cultural and social conditions in urban areas may discourage farmers from leaving rural areas.

We do not mean to imply, though, that there is no outward mobility of resources from American agriculture. Quite the contrary. Over the longer term, Americans in the twentieth century have left farms in very large numbers. In 1920, almost 32 million of us or almost 30 percent of the population lived on farms. By 1987 about 5 million people or 2 percent of the population lived on farms. That percentage is expected to continue to decline. The number of farms has similarly declined from about 3 million in the mid-1970s to about 2.2 million in the late-1980s.

Continuity of Production

Agricultural industry has limited control over its own supply situation. In an assembly-line industry, management can plan output precisely, for each week, day, or even hour, because this kind of operation means continuous production. In agriculture, production is not continuous. The time needed to increase your output may vary from 6 months for raising pigs to 3 years or more for raising a fruit crop. In September, farmers must make decisions about the production of wheat that cannot be harvested until the following August. Decisions about how much land to plant with wheat are based on prices and projection of prices a year before the harvest. Not only can weather conditions change output drastically, but by the time the harvesting of the crop takes place, the projected output may be too little or too much to fit the situation and the prices on which those projections were based may be quite wrong.

Technological Change

Agriculture in the U.S. has seen rapid technological development over the last century, especially since World War II. Productivity has increased even more rapidly in agriculture than in manufacturing. However, this new technology developed in large measure independently of individual farmers. The federal government, through the Department of Agriculture (established in 1861) and its encouragement of land-grant colleges (1864) and experiment stations (1888), was the most important contributor to these innovations. Suppliers of farm machinery, fertilizer and chemicals, and bug and weed killers also contributed significantly, and many of these businesses took advantage of technology first developed at the agricultural experimental stations.

This technological revolution tremendously increased farm laborers' productivity. In 1820, one farm worker produced enough to feed 4 people. By 1930, this had increased to 10. This increase was largely due to the shift from horses to tractors, which released millions of acres of farmland formerly used to raise food for the horses. By 1950, 1 farm worker's output could feed 15 people. However, from 1950 to 1970, only 20 years, the number of people that 1 farmer could feed jumped from 15 to 46, an amazing increase in labor productivity. Indeed, in the last 40 years, agricultural productivity has grown by 130 percent, a growth that substantially exceeds that of any other industry. Furthermore, many of the productivity-increasing innovations—especially plant breeding and the use of chemicals—enormously increased the yields of the land itself (though chemical use has, itself created environmental problems).

This dramatic development naturally increased the supply of farm products many times over. However, the benefits of this increased productivity have not been evenly distributed. Many farmers have neither the training nor the knowledge to utilize the new technology adequately, and their farms are too small to benefit from the scale economies of new machines and techniques. Thus, the difference in productivity between a farm of adequate size, with a proper complement of machinery, run by a farmer with modern skills and knowledge, and the small-scale farm with inadequate machinery, run by a farmer without up-to-date knowledge, is striking.

The Agricultural Support Program

Prior to the 1973 Agricultural Act, the government's farm-support program functioned primarily in three directions: (1) efforts to

"It's time he had a chemistry set if he's going to be a farmer."

increase prices of farm products by reducing the supply, (2) efforts to remove land from production, and (3) efforts to stimulate demand for farm products.

Parity
In agriculture, a set of agricultural prices that creates equality of purchasing power between farm and non-farm incomes.

The effort to stimulate prices followed the concept of **parity**. Parity, in agriculture, meant manipulating agricultural prices so that the purchasing power of the money that farmers receive for their products in 1 year is equal to the purchasing power of the money they received for their products in some acceptable base year. The period from 1910 to 1914 is usually considered the golden age for U.S. farmers, so let's take this period as the base years.

Now, suppose that in 1910-1914 shirts were $2 apiece and wheat $1 a bushel. A farmer would have had to sell 2 bushels of wheat to buy 1 shirt. Now, say that in 1977 the same shirt cost $6. If 100 percent parity exists, wheat should be selling at $3 a bushel, so that the farmer would, as in 1910-1914, be able to sell 2 bushels of wheat and have enough money to buy 1 shirt. In other words, one compares an index of prices of farm products with an index of prices of products farmers bought in the base year, then seeks the same relationship for prices for, say, 1989 (or whatever year we're concerned about). Until the early-1970s, the trend was for the prices of farm products to rise more slowly than the prices of goods bought by farmers. The government tried to support farm prices on the basis of parity; but it did not have to support them at 100 percent of parity.

To support farm prices, the government had to keep them above an equilibrium level. In Figure 7-18, the equilibrium farm price is *A*, but this is too low for the government's goal of parity prices for farmers; the government wants price *B*. However, if the government just supports prices at *B* and lets it go at that, there is disequilibrium in the market. An excess supply, *EG*, is created, which the government must eliminate, or else it cannot maintain the price of *B*. To do this, it must either reduce supply to intersect demand at point *C*, or increase demand to intersect supply at point *D*, or a combination of both.

When you look at Figure 7-18, you can see that it is not enough for a government just to support prices. At the same time it has to restrict supply—which it has done by limiting the number of acres of certain products that farmers can plant. The government itself increased demand by buying up and storing millions of tons of agricultural products. Simultaneously, it set up programs to stimulate *non*government demand for these products.

Other government programs—the soil conservation program and the soil bank program—were aimed at lessening the number of acres involved in the production of field crops. The government's soil conservation program, initiated in 1936, encouraged farmers to stop planting certain field crops on land threatened by soil erosion. At government expense, farmers planted the acres in grass, put in terraces, and began to follow the scientific methods of contour plowing. Quite literally, this program has conserved soil. The soil bank program, begun in the 1950s and phased out in the late-1960s, paid farmers to remove land from production.

Figure 7-18
Price Supports

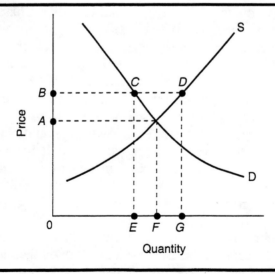

Government efforts to support prices of farm products so that they are at *B*, above the equilibrium price *A*, generate an excess supply, *EG*. If the price *B* is to be maintained, either demand must increase or supply decrease.

Efforts to Reduce Direct Government Intervention

The Agriculture and Consumer Protection Act of 1973 sought to reduce direct government intervention and to at least nudge agricultural markets back toward the freely competitive conditions of earlier decades. Instead of clearly defined parity price supports, "target" prices were created. These prices, although a modified form of parity prices, had little effect because farm prices remained high through 1975.

Back to Government Intervention: 1976 through 1989

As bumper crops sharply reduced farm prices in 1976 and 1977, farmers lobbied heavily for a return to direct intervention to support farm incomes. The immediate outcome was the Food and Agriculture Act of 1977 which created flexible price supports and farm income maintenance targets. A return to freer agricultural markets seemed to have been shelved. The Reagan Administration, in an effort to reduce the cost of these programs, instituted the Payment-in-kind (PIK) program in 1983. Under PIK, the government sought to restrict supply by giving farmers the right to government held crops in return for restricting acreage. Although the goal was to reduce costs, the PIK program alone exploded in cost to over $19 billion by 1985.

The Food Security Act of 1985 not only provided direct income support to the farm sector but required acreage restrictions in an effort to reduce growth in supply. By 1986, its costs had risen to $26 billion a year.

Government Intervention on the Demand Side

A well-known government program aimed at directly stimulating demand for agricultural products is the food-stamp program. Low-income families can get stamps from the welfare department, take these to their local supermarket, and buy food with them. A second program calls for direct distribution of food to needy families. And, third, there is the free school lunch program, which also stimulates domestic demand. It has the additional effect of providing many children in deprived areas with the only hot, balanced meal they get during the day.

Still another program stimulates foreign demand for American agricultural products. Under the foreign-aid program, famine-struck countries apply to the U.S. government for food. In recent years, the U.S. has sent billions of dollars' worth of wheat and other grains to countries such as Ethiopia.

Agricultural products with domestically supported prices are too expensive for many foreign countries to buy, however. So in order to keep agricultural exports competitive, the U.S. government pays the difference between domestic and foreign prices. For example, when the U.S. shipped mammoth amounts of wheat to the Soviet Union in 1972, the government subsidized the sale, so that the Soviets bought the wheat at cheaper prices than American consumers could buy it! In 1973, the 9 countries in the European Economic Community (EEC), especially Great Britain, had a massive surplus of butter; in order to support butter prices and keep dairy farmers from going broke, the EEC bought up 400,000 tons of butter and stored it, meanwhile looking desperately for customers. Along came the Soviets, happy to take it off their hands, if the price was right. So the EEC sold 200,000 tons of butter to the Soviets at rock-bottom subsidized prices, which created the politically awkward situation of Soviet consumers being able to buy British butter at a cheaper price than the British could. In the 1980s, subsidizing U.S. agricultural prices has created problems with allies such as Australia.

Has Intervention Worked?

As you have probably gathered, the federal agricultural support program has a lot of flaws since we are selling wheat at prices below its average cost to the Soviet Union and others. It cannot seem to solve the problems of small operators, who comprise a majority of U.S. farmers. Indeed, most of the benefits of government programs have gone to large commercial farms that need no such support. It places a heavy burden on consumers, in the form of high prices, at the same time that it penalizes consumers with the cost of taxes for running the program.

Thus, a policy leading to direct support of prices instead of direct support of farmers' incomes, puts a double burden on the general public, which has to pay higher-than-equilibrium prices for food and at the same time pay taxes to support the farm program. Figure 7-18 shows that, in order to achieve the target prices the Department of Agriculture considers desirable for agricultural products, the government must force prices higher than they would be under conditions of competition. In addition, these high, artificially supported prices generate surpluses that the government must deal with, at a cost that is, of course, borne by the taxpayer.

Government efforts to restrict supply by ordering farmers to limit acreage planted and to reduce land under cultivation have been ineffective, for several reasons: (1) Farmers, reasonably enough, take their *least*-productive land out of production. This reduces the impact of acreage restrictions, since the land farmers stop planting has a low yield anyway. (2) Farmers apply more fertilizer and use more pest-control measures on the higher-yield land, which is still under cultivation. Substantial increases in yields per acre result, which of course again thwarts the effort to reduce supply. In effect, under this acreage-reduction program, supply tends to increase, not decrease!

The programs designed to stimulate demand for farm products also do not do well. The school lunch program, the food stamp program, and the program for direct distribution of food to the poor have not been well funded and have suffered from too much local political interference. And they have not significantly affected demand for farm products, either.

Did the Agricultural Support Program Help All Agriculture?

Not only did the federal farm support program put severe burdens on the consumer and taxpayer, but it did not solve the problem of low and unstable incomes for many farmers in the U.S.

Small farm enterprises just do not have enough resources—land, machinery, and skills—to be able to earn a living comparable to that of non-farm families. Because the volume of their output and the size of their land holdings are inadequate, small farms are helped only minimally by the farm-support program. Getting higher prices for their produce is not enough to bring their incomes to target levels.

Low-income farmers are, in essence, welfare cases. In most areas, though, the fact that they own a farm keeps them from qualifying for welfare programs. Now suppose these farmers left agriculture entirely and that their land was retired from production. Then the amount of farm products would drop off sharply and the farmers that remained would undoubtedly get higher incomes, perhaps high enough to make farming a profitable business for them. It has been estimated that current and projected future demands for farm products could be met with a decline of one third in the farm population of the U.S.

Owners of relatively large farms can take full advantage of support programs. This shift from small, inefficient-size units to larger-size farms decidedly increases the efficiency of allocation of total resources. Technological change has made the small farm comparatively inefficient, and one should not bemoan its passing, at least on economic grounds. But on both ethical and economic grounds, it is hard to justify government subsidies to farmers who already have incomes considerably higher than the average American. It is worth noting that in the 1980s, the Crown Prince of Lichtenstein, who is part owner of a large agricultural enterprise in the U.S. received an agricultural support payment of $2 million!

So farmers with too little income cannot get more; and farmers with big incomes get even bigger ones. As Alice would say, the situation gets "curiouser and curiouser."

Exports

It appeared to many in the late-1980s that rising exports of American agricultural products represented the only means through which restoration of a competitive farm sector could occur without a massive exodus of resources from that industry. Export growth was difficult in the early to mid-1980s because of the high exchange rates of the dollar against major trading currencies. In the late-1980s, a weakening dollar stimulated demand for American wheat and other agricultural staples. Still, there are perils ahead. Two examples are especially worth mentioning. The U.S. has sought in recent years to open access to Japanese markets and has achieved some success. Likewise, the U.S. is negotiating with the European nations who in 1992 will create a unified system of markets within the European Community. It is important to the future of American agriculture that access to European markets be maintained after 1992.

U.S. Agricultural Policy: A Reprise

Almost no one is satisfied with the results of 60 years of agricultural market intervention. As an income maintenance program designed to preserve the culture and values of rural America, its results have been perverse; small farms have received few of the benefits. Efforts to restrict supply in a technologically dynamic industry have simply not worked. Efforts to increase demand have had very modest successes. Costs to consumers, both direct and indirect have been high. In an era of large federal budget deficits, the programs seem to many to be inordinately expensive. In view of all this, where do we go from here? Sad to say as we enter the 1990s, there appear to be no real efforts to identify the alternatives and debate their relative merits. Although economists would advance the merits of restoring competition and its rational allocation of resources, there appears to be almost no political initiative in that direction in spite of political rhetoric.

SUMMING UP

1. In the theory of the firm, the four major market classifications are pure competition, monopolistic competition, oligopoly, and pure monopoly.

2. *Pure competition* has the following characteristics: (a) There are so many firms that no one firm or group of firms has any control over price. (b) There is a *homogeneous product*. (c) There is freedom of entry into and exit from the industry. (d) There is full information for buyers and sellers.

3. In the short run, two approaches can be used to analyze the behavior of the purely competitive firm as to output, price, and profit or loss: the comparison of TC and TR, and the comparison of AR and MR and average costs and MC.

4. By assumption, the level of output that the firm seeks is the one at which profits are at a maximum or losses at a minimum; that is, the output at which the vertical distance between the TC and TR curves is at a maximum (for a profit) or at a minimum (for a loss).

5. An *economic profit* exists when the TR curve lies above the TC curve. A *normal profit* exists when the TR curve is tangent to (just touches) the TC curve. An *economic loss with production* exists when the TR curve lies between the TC and TVC curves. An *economic loss with shutdown* exists when the TC and TVC curves lie above the TR curve.

6. Economists assume that all firms will produce at that level of output that maximizes profits or minimizes losses, which is the level at which MC equals MR.

7. In pure competition, since the individual firm cannot influence price, no matter how much it produces, price does not vary with output. This means that the firm's conjectual demand, AR, and MR curves are the same and are perfectly elastic for the firm.

8. A competitive firm is a *price taker*, one whose output decisions have no influence on industry price. Non-competitive firms are *price seekers*, ones that not only make output decisions but also must set price. A competitive firm, thus, is a *quantity adjuster* who chooses output rates but not price.

9. As a conjecture about its market, the competitive firm believes that at the prevailing industry-wide product price, it can produce and sell all it chooses at that price. Since all units sell at the same price or AR, MR equals AR and price (P = AR = MR). The price taking competitive firm's conjectural demand curve is perfectly elastic at the industry established price.

10. In the short run, purely competitive firms face four possible profit-loss situations. (a) When price is greater than ATC, the firm makes an economic profit. (b) When price is equal to ATC, the firm makes a normal profit. (c) When price is less than ATC, but greater than AVC, the firm incurs losses, but, to minimize loss, keeps on producing the product. (d) When price is less than AVC, the firm, to minimize losses, shuts down and just pays its fixed costs. The reason these situations exist is that, in the short run, firms can neither enter nor leave the industry.

11. In a *purely competitive industry,* in the long run, only normal profit for the typical firm can exist. Entry and exit of firms assures this result.

12. In the long run, in an increasing-cost industry with economic profit, resources are bid into the industry. As this happens, industry supply grows and industry price moves toward a new higher level of average cost at which the typical firm earns a normal profit.

13. In the long run, in a constant-cost industry with economic profit, resources are bid into the industry as firms seek increased total profit. As this happens, industry supply grows and industry price moves back

toward the old level of average cost at which the typical firm earns a normal profit.

14. In a decreasing-cost industry with economic profit, resources are bid into the industry as firms seek increased total profit. As this happens, industry supply grows and industry price moves to a new lower level of average cost for the typical firm. At this price, the firm earns a normal profit.

15. If an economy were composed wholly of purely competitive industries, resources would be allocated most efficiently to produce that combination of products consumers preferred most, given consumers' incomes, tastes, and so on. Price, in other words, would be equal to MC.

16. Consumers acquire a benefit whenever their actual payments for a good are less than what they would be willing to pay for it. That benefit is called a *consumers' surplus*. This surplus graphically can be represented as the area under the downward sloping demand curve at the competitive price.

17. Producers acquire a benefit whenever their revenues more than cover their opportunity costs. That benefit is called a *producers' surplus*. This surplus can be represented graphically by the area above the upward sloping supply curve at the competitive price.

18. In competitive equilibrium, where quantity demanded equals quantity supplied, output is expanded to the point at which the marginal benefit of consumers equals the MC of producers. At any output rate less than that, marginal benefit exceeds MC and, as output grows, there is an added consumers' surplus as well as an added producers' surplus. The combined surpluses, thus, are maximized in competitive equilibrium.

19. We can translate the combined consumers' and producers' private surpluses into social benefits if we assume that the distribution of income is optimal. A change in the distribution of income would clearly change the structure of demand and the marginal benefits on which it is based. Although the assumption about income being distributed optimally is restrictive, it is often made.

20. Although pure competition is advantageous, governments throughout the world—including that of the U.S.—have interfered in the workings of market forces in agriculture, the industry that comes closest to fitting the description of pure competition.

21. Since the depression of 1921, U.S. farmers, except in brief periods, have had unstable and relatively low incomes, compared with nonagricultural workers.

22. From the standpoint of demand, the reasons for agriculture's relatively shaky position are (a) price inelasticity of demand and (b) low income elasticity of demand. Therefore, as the supply of agricultural products increases, prices fall relatively more than quantity demanded rises, and farm incomes fall. Factors that tend to increase demand (changes in tastes, money income, population, expectations of future prices) are not strong enough to compensate for price inelasticity.

23. Among the factors determining agricultural income, supply tends to be dominant. Supply, however, tends to be highly variable; it resists decreases, and has a strong tendency to increase.

24. Agricultural supply tends to be highly variable because (a) no one farmer or group of farmers can control supply, since conditions are purely competitive, (b) weather has an enormous and unpredictable effect, and (c) production of farm products is discontinuous.

25. The supply of agricultural products resists decreases for the following reasons: (a) In the short run, farmers have large fixed costs, so they have to incur large losses before they admit defeat and shut down. (b) In the long run, the farmer's resources are immobile, so the farmer stays on the farm, aware that job chances for a farmer in the nonfarm world are scant (opportunity costs are low) and that the personal and social costs of adjusting to a new environment would be great.

26. The great improvements in agricultural technology, stimulated by the Department of Agriculture and by industries that provide materials such as machinery, fertilizer, chemicals, and animal feed, have led in the long run to increases in the supply of farm products.

27. Before mid-1973, U.S. farm policy was based on a program of price supports, coupled with acreage restrictions and government purchases and storage of surpluses. The Department of Agriculture determined the price to be supported by using the concept of *parity* as a rule of thumb.

28. To increase demand and decrease supply of agricultural products, the government (a) reduced supply by means of soil conservation, soil bank programs, and acreage restrictions, and (b) stimulated demand by means of food stamp and school lunch programs and by direct distribution of surplus foods to needy families.

29. A price-support program forces on consumers prices that are higher than equilibrium. When the government buys and stores surpluses, it has to tax consumers to pay for the program. The government's programs to remove land from production are ineffective, because the land that farmers remove from production is mostly less productive land. Restrictions on the number of acres a farmer can cultivate may not cut back supply if farmers concentrate

on their more productive land and use more fertilizer and chemicals to increase its yield.

30. The government's demand-stimulating food programs are ineffective although efforts to stimulate exports and subsidize their prices, though costly, have sometimes succeeded.

31. In the mid-1970s, there was a movement away from direct government price and income intervention. Falling agricultural prices after 1976, however, lead to various legislative efforts to restore price supports and restrict agricultural supply. The Payment-In-Kind program of 1983 is among the recent such efforts. Costs of these programs have mushroomed.

32. The millions of farmers who operate on a small scale have relatively low incomes, mainly because they do not have enough resources—land, machinery, and skills—to invest in their farms and achieve scale economies. Most of the benefits of government intervention have gone, instead, to large successful farm enterprises.

33. As we enter the 1990s, almost all are in agreement that after 60 years of government intervention (a) it has been very costly and (b) it has not accomplished its objectives. Even so, there appear to be no serious efforts to identify and evaluate alternative approaches including the restoration of free competitive agricultural markets.

KEY TERMS

Allocative efficiency, technical efficiency
Break-even point
Constant cost industry
Consumers' surplus
Decreasing cost industry
Economic capacity
External economy, external diseconomy
Homogeneous products
Imperfect competition
Increasing-cost industry
Normal profit
Parity
Price seeker
Price taker
Producers' surplus
Profit maximization rule
Pure competition
Pure monopoly
Quantity adjuster
Shut-down point

QUESTIONS

1. Why would you classify general agriculture as a purely competitive industry? What characteristics of modern agricultural industry do not seem to conform to the concept of pure competition?

2. Explain how the equality of marginal cost and marginal revenue maximizes profits or minimizes losses.

3. Explain the origin of the purely competitive firm's *conjectural demand curve*. How does this lend to P = AR = MR and a perfectly elastic demand condition for the individual firm?

4. The following figure represents a purely competitive firm in the short run with average total, average variable, and marginal costs as shown. Answer the following questions related to the firm's profitability:

   a. If the firm takes a price of $5 as given, what is its most profitable rate of output? Will the firm earn a profit?

   b. If the firm takes a price of $6 as given, what is its most profitable rate of output? If there is a profit, what type is it, accounting profit or normal profit?

   c. If the firm takes a price of $7 as given, what is its most profitable rate of output? What type of profit does it earn, accounting, normal, or economic?

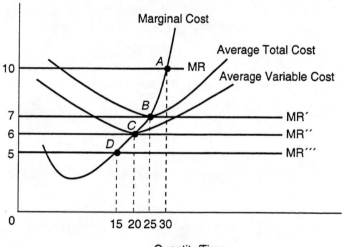

   d. If the firm takes a price of $10 as given, what is its most profitable rate of output? What type of profit does it earn, accounting, normal, or economic?

   e. What point in the figure above represents the firms breakeven point? Its shut-down point?

5. Using diagrams wherever possible, explain the long-run equilibrium of a purely competitive firm in a constant-cost industry. Show what would happen to price, output, and costs if market demand were to (a) decrease, (b) increase.

6. Work out the long-run equilibrium (question 4) for a firm in (a) an increasing-cost industry, (b) a decreasing-cost industry.

7. In long-run equilibrium, what does P = MR = MC = AC mean? What is economic capacity?

8. Explain why each of the following industries is or is not purely competitive: coal mining, production of high-fashion garments, wheat farming, automobile manufacturing. For those industries that you did not classify as purely competitive, what factors caused you to exclude them from the classification? (Hint: consider carefully whether individual firms in each of these industries are *price takers* or *price seekers*.)

9. Explain the concept of *consumers' surplus*. Do the same for *producers' surplus*. Why does competitive equilibrium pricing and output lead to a maximization of these surpluses?

10. Under what condition are the maximized benefits to consumers and producers in question 9 transformed into benefits to society?

11. Using the theory of demand, explain the shape and degree of stability of the demand curve for food.

12. Using the theory of the firm in a purely competitive market, explain why low farm incomes have little effect on the output of an agricultural firm in (a) the short run, (b) the long run.

13. We maintain that the supply of agricultural products is highly variable in the short run and shows a long-run tendency toward increases. What creates these results?

14. Explain why small farm enterprises have received few of the benefits of government intervention.

15. What has been the agricultural policy of the U.S. government since 1977? Has that policy been successful? Why or why not?

16. Upon what does the future growth of demand for U.S. agricultural products seem mainly to depend? What are the problems in this?

17. What changes, if any, in U.S. agricultural policy would you favor? Why?

SUGGESTED READINGS

Adkins, Lynn. "Farm Crisis: The Worst is Yet To Come." *Duns Business Month*. September, 1986. Reprinted in *Economics 88/89*. Annual ed. Guilford, CT: Dushkin Publishing Group, 1988.

Boechge, Michael D. "Policy Options for Agriculture." *Economic Perspectives*. Federal Reserve Bank of Chicago. November/December, 1985.

Dolan, Edwin G., and John C. Goodman. "Farm Policy: Welfare for the Rich?" Ch. 7. *Economics of Public Policy*. 4th Ed. St. Paul, MN: West Publishing Co., 1989.

Duncan, Marvin R. "U.S. Agriculture: Hard Realities and New Opportunities." *Economic Review*. Federal Reserve Bank of Kansas City. February, 1989.

Hailstones, Thomas J., and Frank V. Mastrianna. "Agriculture—Why the Crisis." Ch 4. *Contemporary Economic Problems and Issues*. 8th ed. Cincinnatti, OH: Southwestern Publishing Co., 1988.

Nazario, Sonia L. "Federal Farm Programs are Criticized for Discouraging Alternative Practices." *The Wall Street Journal*. September 8, 1989.

Tregarthen, Timothy. "Drought Sends Farm Prices Soaring." *The Margin*. January/February, 1989.

_____. "American Consumers Get Milked Again." *The Margin*. January/February, 1989.

CHAPTER 8

Monopoly

The U.S. Post Office was organized in 1789 and immediately began losing money. One of the reasons that it lost money was competition. To fight off the competition, the post office turned to Congress. In 1845, Congress strengthened the restrictions on private first-class mail service. This saved the post office from extinction and allowed it to continue its policy of uniform rates regardless of the cost of service.

J. C. Goodman and E. G. Dolan

OBJECTIVES

After studying this chapter you will be able to:

- Explain the term monopoly and some of the common barriers to entry.
- Analyze the cost and revenue data, and determine what the optimal level of production is, determine if profits are being made and if losses are occurring whether to shut down or keep operating.
- Explain the concept of natural monopoly.
- Discuss the cost to society when production occurs in a monopoly industry.
- Have a working knowledge of the following terms and concepts:

Barriers to entry	Natural monopoly	Price searcher
Monopoly	Near monopolies	

Monopoly

Monopoly is a dirty word in the English language. Both U.S. history and English history are filled with condemnations of monopoly. English Common Law, the basis of most U.S. law, treats monopolistic acts as restraints of trade and, therefore, as illegal. In 1886 the federal government created the Interstate Commerce Commission to regulate abusive actions of railroads. The Sherman Antitrust Act of 1890 was the first of a series of laws, including the Clayton Act of 1914 and the Robinson-Patman Act of 1936, that aimed at controlling monopoly and unfair competition. The Federal Trade Commission and the antitrust division of the Justice Department in Washington, D.C., are the federal "watchdogs" against monopoly. Whether such efforts successfully fight monopoly is not now the question, but they do testify to the low social esteem in which monopoly is held.

Books condemning monopoly abound: Loyd's *Standard Oil Trust* and Ignatseo Donnelly's *Caesar's Column* are examples from the beginning of this century. Baran and Sweezy's *Monopoly Capitalism* and The Friedmans' *Free To Choose* are more recent examples worthy of mention.

But what is monopoly? How does one define it? What are its characteristics? What is monopoly power? And, most of all, what does monopoly do in contrast with competition that generates such disapproval as well as arguments to regulate its behavior?

Pure competition is at one end of a scale measuring degrees of competitiveness. At the other end is pure monopoly, whose behavior and performance we will examine in this chapter.

Pure Monopoly
A market in which there is one seller of a product for which there is no good substitute.

Pure Monopoly: A Definition

In a **pure monopoly** there is only one firm in the industry. Indeed the word monopoly means "single seller." Also the monopoly must be

Monopoly Power
The ability of a firm to set and maintain its price above competitive (marginal cost) levels.

able to maintain its position by producing a product for which there is no good substitute. (Some economists say that the term *pure monopoly* applies only where there are no substitutes. By this definition, pure monopoly is very rare. We shall use a less rigid definition for our purposes here.) Finally, there must be major barriers to entry. That is, it must be impossible for other firms to break into the field. (Although firms in other industries may produce substitute products.)

It is important that you be able to distinguish between *monopoly* and **monopoly power**. *Monopoly* means there is only one firm in the industry. *Monopoly power* means that the one firm can set and maintain its price above competitive (marginal cost) levels. A pure monopolist has monopoly power. But monopoly power may also be possessed by more than one firm in an industry. In this chapter, and also in later chapters, we shall explore the subject of monopoly power more fully.

Even though the pure monopolist is the only firm in the industry, there are still certain restraints on its ability to manipulate price and profits.

1. The monopolist, although not getting direct competition from other firms producing the same product, does, as we noted above, run into competition from firms in industries that produce products with some degree of substitutability. For example, Polaroid has a monopoly on instant-copy cameras, but still has competition from firms making other *kinds* of cameras. (In a case like this, you must be careful how you define an industry. In the camera industry in general, Polaroid is one of a number of firms. In the field of instant-copy cameras, Polaroid, as its successful suit against Eastman Kodak in the 1980s demonstrated, is the monopoly firm as long as its patent is valid.) And Alcoa, before World War II, had a virtual monopoly on aluminum; yet the firm still had to worry about materials that afforded close competition, such as steel and tin. Alcoa thus used self-discipline; it set its prices low enough to prevent firms in other industries from being tempted to devise better substitutes for aluminum. In other words, the degree of monopoly is usually proportional to the substitutability of the monopoly's product.

The monopolist fully appreciates this form of competition. The merger between Hazel-Atlas Glass Company and Continental Can Company was a good example of efforts to reduce competition induced by inter-industry product substitution.

2. Monopolists must avoid making enemies because they run the risk of political repercussions. They are not usually protected by anonymity. Both government and consuming public usually know what firms are monopolies. So the monopolistic firm must be careful in pricing, since both public and government know more about its policies than they do about the pricing of firms in less concentrated industries.

3. A monopoly is constrained by the demand for its product. Since it is the only firm in a given industry, it has complete control over supply it can restrict or expand supply to obtain a target price. However, it does not control *demand*, because all the buyers in the market determine demand. (It may, however, try to influence demand through advertising.) So although the monopoly influences price by controlling supply, it cannot determine the quantities that consumers will demand. As a result, monopolies, contrary to the myths surrounding them, do *not* always make profits. This inability to control demand limits the ability of the monopoly to set prices. A second myth about monopolies is that they set the highest possible price. As we shall see in this chapter, monopolies, like other firms, set profit maximizing prices.

4. When it comes to profits, the monopolistic firm is restrained by current demand and cost conditions. Although by controlling supply, it can influence price, its lack of control over the quantity of product demanded limits its ability to earn profits as indicated above.

Barriers to Entry

Barriers to Entry
Factors that prevent other firms from entering a monopolist's market.

Let us repeat that the monopoly has complete control over supply, since it is the only firm in the industry. If it is to hang onto its monopoly position, however, there must be some mechanism that prevents other firms from breaking into the field. In other words, there must be effective **barriers to entry**. The most important barriers to entry are:

1. *The entrenched firm's control of patents and secret processes.* U.S. patent laws give a firm exclusive rights to produce a product or use a process for 17 years. Thus, a patent is a monopoly right to control production of a product. Polaroid, to repeat, is the only firm that can produce the instant-picture camera. The United Shoe Machinery Company is another example. For many years it was the only firm producing shoemaking machinery, because it owned hundreds of patents on various machines that made shoes. And then there is Alcoa, whose original monopoly position in the aluminum industry was built on a patent right. (For an informative discussion of Alcoa's behavior, see Chapter 5 of Leonard Weiss's *Economics and American Industry*.)

2. *Economic warfare.* There are various kinds of economic warfare that can prevent firms from establishing themselves in an industry, or even eliminate firms that are already there. For example, it was alleged that the Standard Oil group, before 1900, eliminated competition by setting different prices in different regions. Critics said that if they had a local competitor they wanted to get rid of, they cut prices in the competitor's region, while keeping their prices

higher in the rest of the country. Eventually, these localized low prices, unjustified by cost differentials, drove local competitors into bankruptcy, after which the Standard Oil group raised its prices again. Other economists have concluded that Standard did not behave this way and that it would have been unprofitable to do so.

3. *The entrenched firm's control of sources of supply.* A firm that has established itself strongly in a given field can create an effective barrier to entry into the field by other firms by gaining control of the supplies of raw materials. For example, U.S. Steel, when it was founded in 1903, controlled large amounts of soft coal and most of the coking facilities around Pittsburgh; furthermore, it controlled the Mesabi iron ore deposits. And prior to World War II, Alcoa was able in large measure to control the aluminum industry because it controlled the bauxite deposits in North America.

4. *Obstacles due to economies of scale.* In a number of industries, the technology required to produce the goods is such that a firm has to produce large rates of output in order to reach optimum scale (lowest cost per unit). For example, in the auto industry, optimum scale and lowest per-unit cost occurs around 500,000 units. This means that a new firm trying to break into the field would have to start production on a huge scale, and have enough demand to sell those cars; otherwise, cost per unit would be too high to be competitive. Furthermore, in any such large-scale industry, a new firm would need, from the beginning, a nationwide system of sales outlets, repair centers, and warehouses containing spare parts. These things may be hard for a firm to achieve when it is just entering an industry.

5. *The problem of product differentiation.* To enter an industry, a firm may have to be able to differentiate its product from those of its competitors and obtain strong customer loyalties. This may be a major barrier to entry. Established firms have the advantage here, since it may cost less per unit of sales to maintain customer loyalty than to create it (though evidence on this is mixed). Advertising is a crucial— and expensive—element in product differentiation. The substantially higher advertising costs for a new firm may be a formidable barrier to entry. The cosmetic industry is an example. Some cosmetic firms spend more than 30 percent of the value of their annual sales on advertising. (Until the federal government restricted cigarette advertising, the cigarette industry was an often-cited example of this sort of barrier-protected field.) The soap industry spends more on advertising its products than it does on producing them.

The automobile industry is another big advertiser. Its advertising campaigns must be national in scope to match the national market for cars. Consumer acceptance may be created only gradually, over a number of years, the resulting high levels of expenditures for advertising, thus, may be a deterrent to entry.

It is important to note that the effects of advertising in competition are in dispute among economists. Some studies have concluded that it is often a barrier to entry while others have concluded that it enhances entry of new firms. Whether advertising is less effective for new firms and, thus, more costly, is also in dispute.

6. *Government-created barriers.* Government policies in many areas—such as licenses, zoning, franchises, and import quotas (plus the patent right, already mentioned)—create barriers to entry. Government-created restrictions on entry into taxicab services, bus transportation, local telephone services, electricity, gas, and water production, to name but a few, have led some economists to conclude that government has done more to create monopoly than to destroy it.

Governments, having created monopolies, often take the responsibility for regulating them as to prices and other policies. This is done supposedly to protect the consumer from those who exercise monopoly power. Such government-created and government-regulated monopolies are called **regulated monopolies**. They include such industries as telephone, gas (for homes), electricity, and urban mass transit.

Note two things: (1) A monopoly is not the same thing as a large-scale firm. For one thing, there may be more than one large-scale firm in a given industry. Thus, they are not pure monopolies. For example, U.S. Steel and Bethlehem Steel are both large-scale firms, but both are in the same industry. They are not monopolies. (2) A pure monopoly may be a relatively small firm. Suppose that there's only one druggist, or one dentist, or one lumberyard in a small town. That drugstore and dentist and lumber yard are monopolies, because they are the only firms in their respective categories in town. So it is not size that makes a monopoly. It is the *size of the relevant market* that determines the size of the pure monopoly.

Regulated Monopolies
Usually industries in which government franchises create monopoly and in which regulatory agencies govern firm behavior.

Pure Monopoly: MR, AR, and D

Since the monopoly is the only firm in the industry, it can control supply and can influence equilibrium price. Remember, however, that the monopoly cannot control the quantity the public demands. Indeed, since there are some substitutes for the monopoly's product, if the firm wishes to increase the quantity demanded, it has to reduce the price, to induce consumers to buy more. Therefore, in a monopolistic market, price must decline as output increases. This is unlike the case of a purely competitive market (in which price for the individual firm does not vary with output).

Let's look at a set of hypothetical demand data for a monopoly (Table 8-1). Note that as output increases, price decreases. (Remember that columns 1 and 2 represent the demand schedule.)

Table 8-1
Output, Price, and Revenue for a Monopoly

1	2	3	4	5
Quantity	Price	Total Revenue = (1 x 2)	Marginal Revenue = (Δ3/Δ1)	Average Revenue = (3 / 1)
1	10	10		10
			8	
2	9	18		9
			6	
3	8	24		8
			4	
4	7	28		7
			2	
5	6	30		6
			0	
6	5	30		5
			-2	
7	4	28		4

Note: Since the monopolistic firm's demand is the same as the industry's, in order to sell more, the monopolistic firm must lower price. In column 2, per-unit price declines as output increases. AR (column 5) also declines, but MR (column 4) declines more rapidly. MR is the change in TR for each unit increase in output. The reason it falls more rapidly is that the price decline applies to all units sold at that level, not just the extra unit.

Total revenue (TR) (column 3) at first increases sharply as price falls. The increase becomes less rapid as output increases further. *TR* (column 3) reaches a maximum at outputs 5 and 6, and then begins to fall at output 7. *Average revenue* (AR) (column 4) is simply TR (column 3) divided by output (column 1) and is the same result as the price or demand column. *Marginal revenue* (MR) is the change in TR due to a small, or one-unit, change in output. (We are assuming here that the monopolistic firm sets only one price for its product at each level of output.) Because the lowered price applies not only to the last unit sold, but to all units sold at that price and quantity, MR falls more rapidly than price (AR). As long as TR is increasing, MR is positive. This is true at rates of output from 1 to 5, inclusive.

When TR reaches a maximum (is greatest), MR is zero (at outputs 5 and 6). When TR is decreasing, MR is negative (at output 7).

By plotting the data in Table 8-1, one gets curves for demand (columns 1 and 2), AR (column 5), and MR (column 4) as in Figure 8-1. The demand and AR curves are equal and slope downward to the right, reflecting the fact that the monopolistic firm—in order to increase the quantity demanded by the consumer—must lower the price of the product. The MR curve of the monopolistic firm—unlike that of the firm in pure competition, is not the same as the demand (AR) curve, but slopes downward more steeply, and is below it.

Figure 8-1

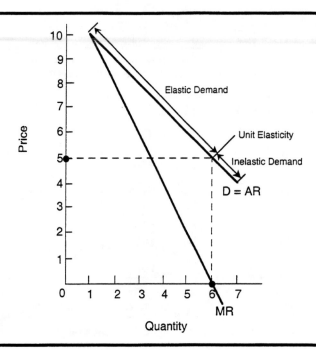

When MR is zero, demand is unit elastic. When MR is positive, demand is elastic. When MR is negative, demand is inelastic.

Elasticity of Demand

Table 8-1 and Figure 8-1 can be used to show the various ranges of elasticity on the monopoly's demand curve. Recall that if price declines and TR increases, demand must be elastic. When MR is positive (up to output 6), TR increases as price declines. Therefore, the portion of the demand curve vertically above the rates of output at which MR is positive is elastic, as Figure 8-1 indicates. Keep in mind the fact that when price falls and TR is unchanged (at a maximum), elasticity is unitary. Table 8-1 shows that when price falls and total revenue is unchanged, MR is zero (output 6 or actually 5 and 6). Figure 8-1 shows that demand is of unitary elasticity at that output rate at which MR is zero. Again, remember that when TR decreases as price falls, demand is inelastic. Table 8-1 shows that at output 7, TR falls; as price declines, MR is therefore negative. You can see in Figure 8-1 that the part of the demand curve above the output rate at which MR is negative is inelastic.

Now, let's summarize price elasticity on the demand curve (E_d).

1. Above output levels at which marginal revenue is zero, E_d is equal to 1 or is unitary.

2. Above output levels at which marginal revenue is positive, E_d is elastic (above the point or range of unitary elasticity on D = AR).

3. Above output levels at which marginal revenue is negative, E_d is inelastic (below the point or range of unitary elasticity on D = AR).

Pure Monopoly: Short Run

Now that we have examined the pure monopoly's demand and revenue curves, we can include its cost curves and examine its behavior with respect to output, price, and profits. Let's first analyze the behavior of the pure monopolist just *in the short run*. (We will deal with the long run later on.)

Remember that, in the short run, firms can neither enter nor leave the industry. Therefore the monopoly encounters the same four possibilities that face the purely competitive firm:

1. When price exceeds average total cost (ATC), the monopoly will make an economic profit.

2. When price is just equal to ATC, the monopoly will make only a normal profit.

3. When price exceeds average variable cost (AVC), but falls short of ATC the monopoly will sustain a loss, but in the short run continue to produce.

4. When price is not high enough to cover AVC, the (unregulated) monopoly will sustain such a loss (more than its fixed costs) that it will choose to shut down.

Figure 8-2 shows the way the situation looks for the pure monopoly that makes an economic profit. As in the case of pure competition, the monopolistic firm has maximum profits (or minimum losses) at the output at which marginal cost (MC) is equal to MR, at output A. The monopolistic firm determines the price, however, at the demand curve, not the MR curve. To find out what price the monopolist would set in order to sell output A, one draws a perpendicular from A to point B on the demand curve. To measure price, one draws a horizontal line toward the left, from B to the vertical axis, which hits the axis at P. So the monopoly's price is P. TR (P x Q) is measured by the area $0PBA$. At output A, the monopolistic firm's average cost (cost per unit) is represented by a perpendicular from A to the ATC curve at point E, or the distance $0C$. TC is represented by the area $0CEA$. So, since TR are larger than TC, the monopoly makes a profit (TR – TC), which is represented by area $CPBE$.

Now we can see that in the short run economic profits can exist under both pure competition and pure monopoly. The reason is that firms cannot enter the industry in the short run.

Figure 8-2
Situation 1: Economic Profit for a Monopolistic Firm

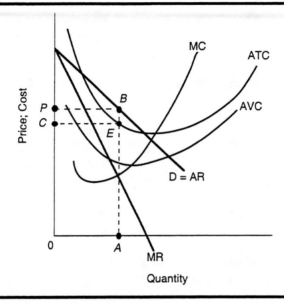

Price *P* is higher than ATC, *AE*. TR, 0*PBA*, is larger than TC, 0*CEA*. The monopolistic firm makes an economic profit, in the short run, of *CPBE*.

Figure 8-3 shows the way the situation looks for the pure monopoly that is making only a normal profit. Once again, equilibrium output is the output at which MC is equal to MR (output *A*). The monopolistic firm determines the best price by drawing a perpendicular from a to the demand curve at point *B*; in other words, price *P*. TR is area 0*PBA*. Cost per unit is also the perpendicular from *A* to the ATC curve, or again *AB*. And so TC is also area 0*PBA*. Since revenue is equal to TC and a normal profit is included in TC, the monopolistic firm, in this situation, makes only a normal profit.

Figure 8-4 shows the third situation that the pure monopoly may encounter in the short run: the monopoly incurs an economic loss, but keeps on producing anyway. Profit-maximizing output is still at the level at which MC is equal to MR. One determines the monopolistic firm's price again by drawing a perpendicular from the equilibrium rate of output *A* to the demand curve at point *B*; price is *P* (that is, the equivalent horizontal distance along the vertical axis, or *AB* = 0*P*). Revenue (price x quantity) is then area 0*PBA*. Cost per unit at output *A* is the perpendicular from *A* to ATC, measured on the vertical axis; in other words, ATC is 0*C* (or *AE*). Cost is then area 0*CEA*. It is plain that TC exceeds TR. The monopolistic firm's loss is the difference, or area *PCEB*.

In the short run, the monopolistic firm, just like the firm in pure competition, must decide whether to keep on producing or shut down. If the monopolistic firm gives up, shuts down, and stops

Figure 8-3
Situation 2: Normal Profits for a Monopolistic Firm

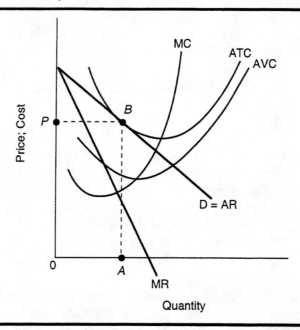

Price P is equal to ATC, *AB*. TR, 0*PBA* is equal to TC, 0*PBA*. The monopolistic firm, in the short run, makes only a normal profit.

Figure 8-4
Situation 3: Economic Loss with Production for a Monopolistic Firm

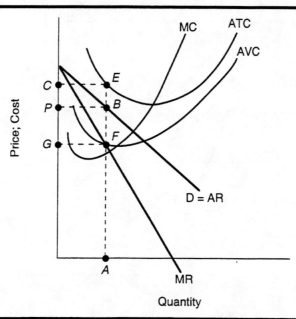

Price P is less than ATC, 0*C*. TR is area 0*PBA*; TC is area 0*CEA*. The loss, or area *PCEB*, is less than fixed costs, *GCEF*. *Moral:* In the short run, if price is between ATC and AVC, the monopolistic firm loses less if it keeps on producing than if it shuts down.

production, it will still have to pay all fixed costs (*GCEF*) in the short run. If it keeps on producing and its losses are less than its fixed costs, it loses less by producing or reduces its loss by *GPBF*.

Figure 8-4 shows that fixed cost per unit is the vertical distance from the AVC curve to the ATC curve at output *A*. Note that this can be measured on the vertical axis by *GC*. Fixed cost is then area *GCEF*. The amount of money the monopoly loses is less than total fixed cost, being only area *PCEB*. The monopoly, in other words, is able to cover part of its fixed costs out of its TR. The part covered is the area *GPBF*. Should the firm shut down, it would lose its entire fixed cost, *GCEF*. In this situation, in the short run, the monopolistic firm would continue production, but in the long run it would either liquidate or adjust its scale of production.

For example, if total fixed costs are 25, then 25 must be paid whether the firm produces or not. If the firm loses 15 by producing, it will be better off producing and losing 15 than shutting down and paying 25 in fixed costs. If the firm produces, it loses 15; if it shuts down, it loses 25.

Figure 8-5 shows situation 4, in which the monopolistic firm loses more money than the amount of its fixed costs by continuing to produce and so must shut down. At output *A*, the firm can get only price *P* for its product, which is less than AVC. If the firm keeps on producing, its losses will be area *PGFB*. If the firm shuts down,

Figure 8-5
Situation 4: Economic Loss Without Production for a Monopolistic Firm

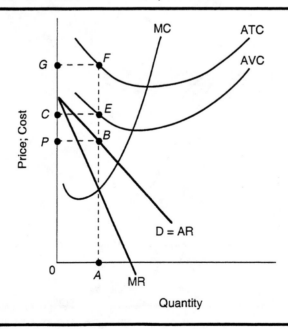

Price *P* is less than both ATC, *AF*, and AVC, *AE*. If the firm kept on producing, it would lose money (area *PGFB*). If it shut down, it would also lose (area *CGFE*). So in the short run, the monopolistic firm loses less by shutting down than by keeping on producing.

it will have to pay only the amount of its fixed costs (area *CGFE*). The monopolistic firm therefore loses less money (area *PCEB*) if it shuts down.

Pure Monopoly: Long Run

Remember, in the long run, in a purely competitive market, a typical firm can make only normal profit (profit just large enough to keep it producing). So many firms enter the market that firms cannot typically earn an economic profit (profit above normal), while the exit of firms from the market tends to eliminate economic losses. In pure monopoly, in the long run, firms do not enter the industry, because of barriers to entry. Although a monopolistic firm may liquidate and avoid economic losses, economic profits cannot be eliminated by the entry of firms. If firms could enter, they would increase supply, reduce price, and reduce the economic profit.

In the case of a pure monopoly, in the long run, two possible situations can exist: (1) Because there is no mechanism to prevent firms from making an economic profit, they probably will make one. (2) Price may be so low that the monopoly cannot make an economic profit, and therefore, makes only a normal profit. Economic losses cannot exist, because in the long run, a firm that expects to incur economic losses liquidates or leaves the industry.

In the long run, the pure monopolistic firm will probably make an economic profit. Figure 8-6 shows that the output that would maximize the monopoly's profits would be the output at which marginal cost equaled marginal revenue at *A*. When that output corresponds to the demand curve, the monopoly's best price is at *P*. Revenue is area 0*PBA*. Average cost (AC) at output *A* is *C*; cost is then area 0*CEA*. Since cost is less than revenue, the economic profit is area *CPBE*.

However, in the long run, the monopolistic firm may possibly earn only a normal profit. Figure 8-7 shows that the long-run average-cost curve (LRAC) is tangent to the demand curve at point *B*. The demand curve shows that the monopolistic firm could sell output *A* for price *P*. Revenue and cost are equal at 0*PBA*, so the monopolist earns only a normal profit. If the monopolistic firm—perhaps by advertising—can shift its demand curve to the right, it can increase its profits.

Pure Competition Versus Pure Monopoly

Let's assume for the moment that cost curves are the same for both a purely competitive industry and a purely monopolistic firm. Figure 8-8 compares their relative performances. In this figure, MC and AC curves apply to both market classifications. For pure competition, the D = AR = MR curve is horizontal to the quantity axis at P_c. For pure monopoly, these curves slope downward.

Figure 8-6
Economic Profit in the Long Run for a Monopolistic Firm

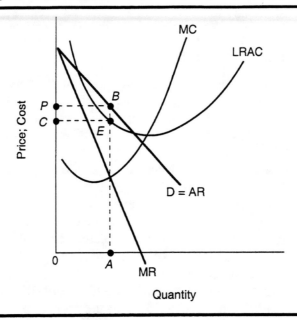

In the long run, the firm can make an economic profit, provided that price (*P*) is greater than LRAC (0*C*). TR (area 0*PBA*) exceeds cost (area 0*CEA*). There is thus an economic profit (area *CPBE*).

Figure 8-7
Normal Profit in the Long Run for a Monopolistic Firm

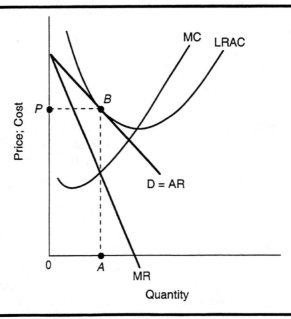

In the long run, the firm may make only a normal profit, provided that price *P* equaled AC. Revenue and cost are both equal to area 0*PBA*. Thus the firm would make only a normal profit.

Figure 8-8

Demand, Revenue, and Cost Curves for Both the Purely Monopolistic and Purely Competitive Industries. Pure competition is indicated by the subscript c, pure monopoly by the subscript m.

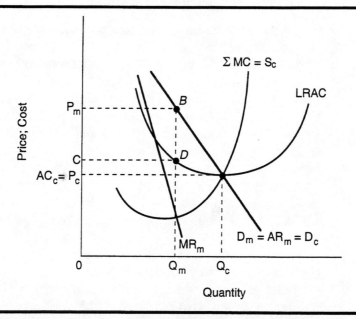

In Figure 8-8, with demand curve, D_c and supply curve, $\Sigma MC = S_c$, a purely competitive industry will produce Q_c and price, P_c, will equal minimum AC, AC_c. The industry will earn a normal profit. The purely monopolistic industry, with demand curve, D_m, and MC curve, ΣMC, will produce Q_m (where $MR_m = MC$), will set price P_m, operate with average cost C and earn economic profit, $BDCP_m$.

Under the above conditions, pure competition has the following advantages over monopoly:

1. Purely competitive industries produce a larger output (Q_c) than firms that are pure monopolies (Q_m) and sell it at a lower price, P_c, as compared to the monopolies' price of P_m.

2. Two facts apply to long run circumstances of pure monopoly and pure competition: (a) Because a purely monopolistic firm is likely to earn an economic profit and purely competitive firms are likely to earn only normal profits, profit is usually a smaller part of market incomes under pure competition. (b) In pure competition each factor of production receives its competitive opportunity cost. We see this result in Figure 8-8. The competitive industry produces Q_c and sells at a price equal to AC. TR equals TC and a normal profit is earned. The monopoly producing Q_m sets price P_m which is above AC (C) and TR exceeds TC. An economic profit is earned. But the pure monopoly's profit is only partly a payment of opportunity cost. Part of the monopoly's profit (its economic profit) is due to the control over prices of the product through the control over supply, which it exercises because of barriers to entry. Under pure competition, then, market earned incomes are based entirely on productivity. Under pure

monopoly there may be economic profits that are not based on productivity, but rather on the ability of monopolists to block entry and prevent reallocation of resources.

3. A purely competitive industry produces at the most efficient level of production, that is, at minimum AC; in other words, at the low point on the LRAC curve. The purely monopolistic firm is not likely to keep on producing until it reaches the low point on the LRAC curve because its demand curve is not horizontal, but slopes downward. So the purely monopolistic firm usually produces a smaller rate of output than the competitive industry which produces at Q_c. (Figure 8-8 shows this level at output Q_m.) Therefore the purely monopolistic firm's costs per unit are higher than the purely competitive firm's costs per unit. Even if the monopolistic firm produces at minimum AC (if its MR cuts the minimum point of LRAC), it will set a price above AC and MC and receive an economic profit.

Remember that the LRAC curve encloses a series of short-run cost curves, each at a successively larger scale or size of operation. In the long run, the typical purely competitive firm uses the most efficient scale and also produces at the most efficient point (minimum AC) on that short-run average-cost curve. Assuming that the monopolistic firm's cost curves are identical with those of the competitive industry, one finds that the monopolistic firm tends to use a scale smaller than the most efficient one and produces on that scale above minimum AC. Thus, for the purely monopolistic firm, cost per unit is usually higher in the long run than for the purely competitive firm.

4. When there is pure competition, in long-run equilibrium, price equals not only AC but also marginal cost. Under these conditions, competitive firms allocate their resources most efficiently to produce that combination of goods that consumers most prefer. But when there is pure monopoly, price is not only above AC but also higher than MC. From the point of view of the whole economy, this means that the monopolistic firm has fewer resources allocated to producing its product than its consumers prefer. So the monopolistic firm does not produce as much as consumers are willing to buy at the marginal cost of production or operates with **allocative inefficiency**. When price exceeds marginal cost, consumers place a higher value on additional units of the product than on other products that can be produced with the same resources.

Allocative Inefficiency
The tendency for monopoly firms to set prices above MC and to allocate fewer resources to producing their products than consumers prefer.

Monopolies and Supply Decisions

Competitive firms have a supply curve that is based on their MC of production. The reason for that is that such firms are price takers; they react to a given price by deciding what should be the most profitable quantity to supply. Monopoly firms, on the other hand, do not have a supply curve. Monopolies, looking at their MC and at the various quantities of their product demanded at different prices must set price. Monopolies are necessarily price seekers.

There are, as we indicated earlier, various myths or fallacies about monopoly, some of which have been around for a long time. One is that monopolies, because they "control" their markets, always earn monopoly (economic) profits. As we have seen, monopolies cannot control the demand for their product and, at least in the short run, may even sustain economic losses. In the long run, though, there is a tendency for monopolies that remain in business to earn economic profit and that tendency is due to the restricted entry that sets monopoly and competitive markets apart.

Utilizing Technology Effectively: Natural Monopoly

Natural Monopoly
Exists in an industry if there are economies of scale up to the output rate that fills the market. A single firm is more efficient than any larger number of firms.

Technology affects purely monopolistic and purely competitive market situations in two ways: (1) It creates differences in economies of scale, and (2) it raises the question of which type of market most encourages technological development. Let us look at each situation in turn. In many cases, our assumption that cost curves are similar for both competitive industries and monopolistic industries may not be valid. In industries characterized by pure monopoly, modern technology often dictates a high level of output before a producer can realize all available economies of scale. Indeed, there may be economies of scale that exist up to point at which industry output fills the market. Such an industry is called a **natural monopoly**. If an industry with these characteristics were to be subdivided into enough firms to establish pure competition, the volume of output per firm would not be great enough for all those small firms to realize the economies of scale possible to users of that technology. In such a situation, pure competition would likely result in high costs, high prices, and low output.

Figure 8-9 shows a LRAC curve for a natural monopoly. Recall that the LRAC curve is a planning curve that encompasses a series of short-run average cost curves, each representing a larger scale of operation. If there were only one firm in a given industry, it could produce 20,000 units of the product with an AC of $10. But if that industry's output were split up among two firms, each would produce 10,000 units with an AC of $20. So if enough firms existed to create pure competition, each firm would operate with higher AC than would a (single firm) monopoly.

Monopoly and the Creation of Technology

Some economists (including John Kenneth Galbraith, in his book *Economics and the Public Purpose*) imply that large-scale firms are necessary to ensure technological development. The big research and

Figure 8-9
The Long-Run Average Cost of a Natural Monopoly

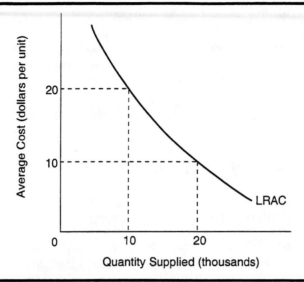

In Figure 8-9, the LRAC curve of a natural monopoly is presented as negatively sloped throughout all quantities supplied. The most likely organization of this market is that of a single firm supplier. If, for example, the quantity demanded were 20,000, it could be supplied by one firm with unit costs of $10 or by two firms with unit costs of $20. The likely result is that one (cost minimizing) firm would exist.

development facilities necessary to develop new techniques cost a lot of money. And money in such large amounts just is not in the budgets of smaller purely competitive firms. One could conclude that the larger the firm, the more it could spend on research and development and the greater the technological innovation would be.

Technology: Dynamics Versus Statics

A famous economist, Joseph Schumpeter, argued that monopoly and the expectations of higher returns on investment in an industry protected against entry, are an important inducement to innovation. This controversial argument suggests that static (at a point in time) comparisons of competition and monopoly are not really as useful as dynamic (over time) comparisons. As monopoly industries that have high costs invest in developing new products or new ways of producing existing products, their costs fall over time and society benefits from these innovative activities. This is particularly true if, as Schumpeter argued, there is a tendency for other entrepreneurs to imitate the activities of the successful monopolist and reduce or eliminate its monopoly profits. The empirical studies of this argument have led to mixed results and economists are not in general agreement about the validity of Schumpeter's argument.

But is it true that only the larger firms spend a great deal of money on research, or use their money to ensure technological development? Purely competitive firms often adopt technological innovations at a faster rate than monopolistic firms in order to keep ahead of their competitors. Such firms must be up to date in order to survive. The monopolistic firm does not have pressure from competitors to force it to adopt improved techniques. In fact, if the firm has plant and equipment that innovations would render obsolete, this factor alone slows the process of adopting innovations. For example, after World War II, the West Germans (who had lost most of their steel capacity during the war) had to develop new machinery, which included many innovative techniques in steel manufacturing. In the U.S. in the mid-1950s, steel companies began to borrow these techniques. But it was the *smaller* steel companies—not U.S. Steel (USX)—that did so first.

Some economists disagree with the theory that the larger the firm the more likely it is to make rapid technological advances. One study concludes that small and medium-size firms produce more innovations per dollar of research funds than larger ones do. Many of the "high-tech" firms in computers and related industries such as bio-medical research began as small scale activities seeking to develop and implement new technology. In addition, large firms have little access to ideas from people actually working on the production line. The study claims that many creative discoveries come from individuals working alone or in small research facilities. Creative researchers are often nonconformists, and even first-rate discoveries may seem at first glance to lack any immediate practical application. In addition, bureaucratic inefficiency seems to blunt the impact of the inventions of large research organizations. The study concludes that for firms beyond a certain size technological productivity tends to decline. However, the "small" firms in this study were much larger than the typical purely competitive firm.

The relation between technological productivity and size of firms is even more complex. The smaller firms usually seem to pioneer in the early, low-cost, high-risk stages of an innovation. In the final development stage, when costs get higher but risks get lower, the larger firms come along and take over. We should also remember that much research and development work is undertaken or sponsored by government. To the extent that the results of this research (new processes, techniques) are made available to the public, they are as readily used by small firms as by large firms.

It is apparent that not only big firms sponsor research and development or adopt new ideas and put them into effect quickly. Competition makes the little firm run to keep up; the absence of competition enables the big firm to go slowly, and this factor slows the adoption of new ideas. Much research remains to be done before a fair and generalized comparison of competition and monopoly can be made in terms of technological change.

Regulated Monopoly

As you recall, one barrier to entry into an industry is the existence of government induced monopoly. In some industries the consumer would not gain anything in terms of either lower costs or convenience if more than one firm produced the product or service in the same area. This is because there are tremendous economies of scale. Examples of these natural monopolies are the public utilities, such as gas, electricity, water, local telephone services, and bus service. Governments (local, state, and federal) have recognized this and granted individual firms exclusive rights to produce in certain geographic areas. When it grants a monopoly, the government usually also promises to prevent the firm from exploiting its legally established monopoly position. (That is why these franchised companies are called regulated monopolies.) So the government establishes a commission to regulate these firms. The commission must assure the firms a normal profit, or "fair rate of return," or else they would not produce. At the same time, theoretically, the commission is supposed to set prices to prevent the monopoly from making economic profits while generating for the firm a "fair rate of return."

Figure 8-10 shows that the unregulated monopoly maximizes profits at quantity A, that it charges price P_m, and that it makes an economic profit equal to area CP_mBD. Now suppose that the government declares this monopoly to be a public utility, and sets up

Figure 8-10
Regulated Monopoly

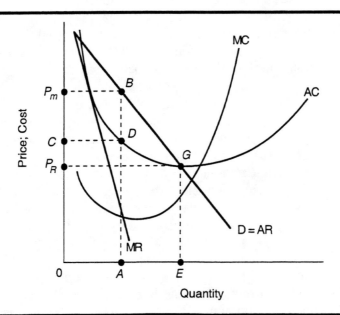

The pure monopoly produces at the point at which MC equals MR, at A; price is at P_m. The regulating commission sets the output and price of the regulated monopolist at the point at which AR equals AC, at output E and price P_R. Its revenue and also its cost equal $0P_RGE$; it earns only a normal profit.

a commission to ride herd on it. The utility commission, mindful of its duty to the public, sets a price that will ensure only a normal profit. (Recall that a normal profit exists when AR is equal to AC.) A normal profit occurs at 2 points on AC in Figure 8-10—points D and G. Because it produces a normal profit at a much lower price and larger output than D the commission chooses point G, and sets the price at P_R. Output is then going to be E. Cost will equal revenue, so this regulated monopoly will earn only a normal profit. Note that the regulated monopoly produces more (E instead of A) and sells it at a lower price (P_R instead of P_m) than the unregulated one.

Although prices are theoretically lower and output higher for the regulated than the unregulated monopoly, price is still greater than MC. The purely competitive result that price equals MC (the value consumers place on the last unit is equal to the sacrifices of other goods that are made to produce it) is still not duplicated by the regulated monopolist. The problem is to curtail monopoly profits by regulation.

Seems simple, doesn't it? The commission sets a price for the utility at which AR equals AC, and the monopoly makes only a normal profit. The commission periodically revises prices to adjust for changes in costs and demand.

However, when one tries to put this theoretical model into practice, there are problems. How does one compute "normal" profit? Is it the traditional profit for that industry? Or is it the profit a given firm makes in industries that contain other firms of comparable size? But an economic profit may already be built in. Should the commission compute depreciation at original cost or replacement cost? What about the value of good will? In all of this, there is an inherent problem. The cost data on which regulation is based are derived from the statements of regulated firms. Such firms, thus, have an incentive to overstate their costs which constitute the base against which the "fair rate of return" is allowed.

Cost Overstatement Under Regulation: An Example

An example of this incentive to overstate costs under regulation was reported in *The Wall Street Journal* in January, 1990. Nynex Corporation, the parent company of both New York Telephone and New England Telephone created a subsidiary unit for the purpose of buying supplies. The idea was to accrue quantity discounts which could lower costs that could be reflected in lower (regulated) telephone rates. The problem was that Nynex had an incentive to inflate the prices of this equipment to its two regulated subsidiary companies. The Federal Communications Commission (FCC) estimated that about $120 million of extra cost was tacked on by Nynex. Why did the firm apparently behave this way? Because the extra costs, once accepted by the regulatory commission, became a part of each subsidiary's (New York Telephone and New England Telephone) cost base against which "fair rate of return" was allowed.

Under regulation, then, even when regulators allow AC prices, consumers may end up "overpaying" for telephone services.

Politics is another important problem. Naturally, everyone assumes that commissions will regulate with impartiality. But the people on these commissions are political appointees. So there are always complaints that various regulatory commissions, federal and state, decide cases on the basis of favoritism, not facts, and that they do not pay attention to consumers or their interests.

Regulation of (Multi-firm) Monopolistic Industries: An Airline Example

Although this chapter deals with pure monopoly, regulation is often applied, as well, to multi-firm monopolistic industries. It is worth noting that the questions addressed above about public regulation apply equally to single-firm and multi-firm industries. Consider the case of the airline industry which was regulated by the Civil Aeronautics Board (CAB) from the 1930s to the early-1980s.

When airline price and route regulation was originally considered, some argued that the industry was a natural monopoly. Whatever was the case in the 1930s, changing technology and growing market sizes soon dispelled that notion. Nonetheless, from the mid-1930s on, airline fares and routes were directly established by the CAB (the Federal Aviation Administration (FAA) still regulates airline safety). This publicly administered cartel or group of firms acting as a monopoly, was widely thought to be the beneficiary of monopoly prices and monopoly returns. Evidence suggests, though, that industry regulation in this case produced unintended results so far as rates of return for airlines were concerned. While the CAB set cartel prices for the industry, the costs of firms rose substantially. Deprived of the ability to compete with each other in price, airlines turned instead to costly non-price competition (meals, in-flight movies, etc.) to bid customers away from each other. Consumers, however, were not able to choose whether to buy such services since they could not buy from a "no frills" airline whose costs and prices would be lower. As a result of all of this, even at the non-competitive cartel prices, costs rose until any monopoly return tended to disappear.

The problem with airline price regulation was that it (1) caused more resources to be used to produce airline services than otherwise would have been the case, and (2) consumers were deprived of the opportunity to decide how many of those resources should be used in the industry in terms of the prices they were willing to pay for air fares.

Price Discrimination

Thus far, we have assumed that monopoly firms charge all customers the same price for their goods or services. But we have not discussed

Price Discrimination
The practice of charging different prices for units of a product that are physically homogeneous.

Perfect Price Discrimination
The practice of charging consumers the highest price anyone will pay for each unit of a good sold.

Second Degree Price Discrimination
The practice of charging different prices to different groups of buyers.

price discrimination. **Price discrimination** occurs when a firm charges different prices for a given commodity, despite the fact that the units of this commodity are physically homogeneous.

In its technical economic sense, price discrimination also occurs when prices are the same but the MC of supplying each product is different. One product may have a larger profit margin than another. This form of discrimination, however, is often legal; a firm may take widely different profits on 2 different products and be within the law. To be technically correct, price discrimination exists when the price to consumer A divided by the MC of that unit of product is not equal to the price to consumer B divided by the MC of that unit. However, for our purposes, we shall consider price discrimination to exist when different prices are charged for different units of the same product. Price discrimination cannot take place under pure competition; it requires some form of monopoly power. But a firm that has monopoly power will not *necessarily* discriminate in pricing. There are two main categories of price discrimination:

1. A firm charges consumers a different price for each unit sold and it is always the maximum price that any consumer will pay. This is called **perfect price discrimination**, and it is rare.

2. A firm charges different prices to different groups of buyers. This, more usual case is called **second degree price discrimination**.

Conditions Necessary for Price Discrimination

1. A consumer who buys something for a low price must not be able to resell it to somebody else who would have to pay more. For example, 2 buyers, A and B, each buy 1 good; A pays 10¢ and B pays 20¢. The firm must prevent A from reselling the good to B for *less* than 20¢. Otherwise, reselling would create only 1 price for the good.

2. The price elasticity of demand for each consumer or for each submarket must be different. Only if these elasticities of demand are different can the price-discriminating firm increase its profits by charging different prices.

There are four conditions under which resale will not take place, and price discrimination is possible:

1. B doesn't know that A paid less.

2. B *knows* that A paid less, but doesn't care, because B feels that her or his good is better than the one that A bought (the goods are not homogeneous).

3. The good is a service (such as medical care). If the same doctor operates on 2 patients, A cannot resell his or her $100 appendectomy to B, who must pay $500.

4. The 2 buyers are separated by distance or by legal restrictions. (In the case of distance, the difference in price may be only as large as the cost of transportation. In the case of legal restrictions, when the 2 buyers live in 2 countries, the difference in price may be only as large as the tariff.)

Graphic Analysis of Price Discrimination

You know by now that a firm will maximize profits by producing at the level at which MR equals MC. When a monopolistic firm has the power to discriminate between buyers when it comes to pricing, it is operating in more than one market. So it will maximize profits by producing in each market that output at which MC is equal to MR. If demand is equally elastic in the different markets, MC and MR will also be equal at the same price. Therefore, in order for price discrimination to add to the profits of the firm, the elasticities of demand of the different markets or buyers must differ. When elasticities of demand differ, prices also may differ.

If the firm can separate its market into two markets—one with an elastic demand, D_2, the other with a less elastic demand, D_1—the monopolist will discriminate in price between the two. Figure 8-11 assumes that MC is horizontal for both markets. The monopolistic firm maximizes profits by equating MC and MR in each market. The result is price discrimination, with a higher price, P_1, in the market *(a)* with the less elastic demand curve and a lower price, P_2, in the market *(b)* with the more elastic demand. The consumer with few alternatives has a less elastic demand curve and pays a higher price than the consumer with many alternatives.

Figure 8-11
When two markets have different elasticities of demand, price discrimination increases profits.

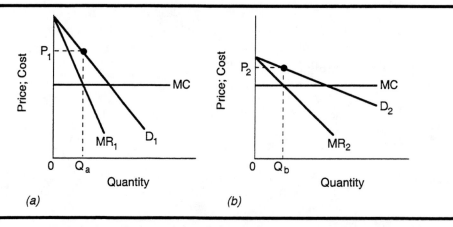

(a)   *(b)*

In Figure 8-11, the monopoly looks at its market as two submarkets. By assumption, its MC of supply are the same to both markets. Submarket *(a)* is one in which demand is relatively inelastic. The monopoly produces Q_a in that market (MC = MR_1) and sets profit maximizing price P_1. Submarket *(b)* is one in which demand is relatively elastic. The monopoly produces Q_b in that market and sets profit maximizing price P_2. Consumers with a less elastic demand are charged a higher price (P_1) than those with a more elastic demand (P_2).

Price discrimination is not profitable when elasticities are the same in both markets. For example, if price discrimination were applied to left-handed people at a bookstore, profits would not be increased. The price elasticity of demand for books is presumably the same for both lefties and righties. With different prices, MC and MR would not be equal and, therefore, profits would not be maximized.

An example of the use of price discrimination is the field of electric utilities, where price discrimination is common. Households have the most inelastic demand since there are no effective substitutes for electricity for home lighting. For homes with low rates of consumption, price per unit of electricity is high. Demand for appliances such as electric ranges and driers is made more elastic because of this rate schedule. As a household uses more electricity, the unit price it must pay for electricity decreases, which encourages consumers to use more electric appliances. Because of regulation, much of the gain from price discrimination in the electric-utility industry is passed on to the consumer in the form of a generally lower level of prices. A reversal of this form of price discrimination began in the late-1970s. For instance, California, in 1976, approved a rate schedule for electricity and gas under which those households that use less of these energy sources will pay lower rates than those that use more. This move to reduce energy consumption in the interest of conservation may change the whole pattern of price discrimination in the energy industry and result in reverse price discrimination.

Another example of price discrimination is in theaters. Differing areas of the theater have different elasticities because of more or less favorable positions. People's demand for *good* seats is inelastic and seats in those locations cost more. Through price discrimination, theaters maximize their total profits.

Welfare Effects:
A Comparison of Monopoly and Competition

So far, we have seen that where monopoly exists, product output tends to be reduced and price tends to be higher than would be the case if the industry producing the product was purely competitive. We see these results summarized in terms of their welfare effects in Figure 8-12. To make the comparison fair and meaningful, the supply of the industry $(S = \Sigma MC)$ is assumed to be the same whether produced by a single firm or by a collection of competitive firms. We are *not*, in other words, comparing a natural monopoly with a competitive industry.

The competitive industry result in Figure 8-12 may be summarized as follows: (1) industry output would be Q_c where quantity supplied equals quantity demanded, (2) industry price would be P_c which will "clear" this market. At price P_c, consumers' surplus

Figure 8-12
A Welfare Comparison of Monopoly and Competition

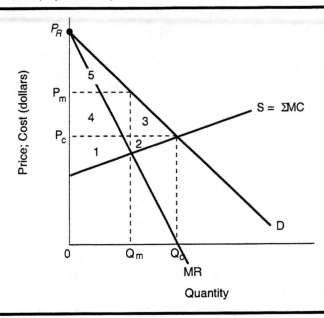

In Figure 8-12, a competitive industry will produce output Q_c and sell its product at price P_c. Consumers' surplus will equal 5 + 4 + 3 and producers' surplus will equal 1 + 2. A monopoly industry will produce output Q_m and sell its product at price P_m. Consumers' surplus under monopoly will equal 5. Producers' surplus will equal 1 + 4. The "deadweight" loss (a loss to everyone) is 3 + 2. Part of consumers' surplus under competition (4) becomes a producers' surplus.

is represented by the area under the demand curve above P_c or the combined areas 5 + 4 + 3. Producers' surplus is the area above the MC curve but below P_c or the combined areas 1 + 2. Under conditions of competition output expands to the point at which the marginal benefit of this product to consumers is made equal to the MC of producing it. These private consumer-producer benefits are also benefits to society on the assumption that the distribution of income is optimal.

The monopoly industry result can be summarized similarly: (1) the monopoly facing downward sloping MR will produce Q_m and (2) acting as a price seeker, will set price P_m. Monopoly, in sum, results in reduced output ($0Q_c - 0Q_m$) and a price, P_m, that is above MC. Note that there is, at the reduced output, a welfare loss to both consumers (triangular area 3) and to producers (triangular area 2). The combined loss to consumers and producers (3 + 2) is referred to as the **deadweight loss of monopoly** since it is a loss that does not become the gain of the other party. At monopoly output Q_m and with price P_m, there is a gain to producers that represents a loss to consumers. The producers' surplus at that output is no longer simply area 1 but also area 4. Area 4, though, represents a reduction in consumers' surplus.

Deadweight Loss of Monopoly
A welfare loss to society of consumers' and producers' surplus that results from monopoly. It is a loss not captured by someone else.

The Welfare Effects of Price Discriminating Monopoly

If we conclude that monopoly output results in a reduction in consumers' surplus (3 + 4 in Figure 8-12) and an increase in producers' surplus (4 − 2), at the monopoly established price, what will be the welfare effects of monopoly if price discrimination is practiced? The answer may be seen in Figure 8-12. What would happen to the consumers' surplus remaining under monopoly (area 5) if, instead of setting one price (P_m) for its product, the monopoly engaged in perfect price discrimination or charged the highest price any buyer would pay for each of the $0Q_m$ units produced? The highest price anyone will pay for any unit of the good is represented by P_R or the reservation price. If the $0Q_m$ units of the product were completely divisible and the monopoly sold each such unit for the highest price any buyer would voluntarily pay, area 5 would be additional revenue to the firm from price discrimination. As a consumers' surplus, it would disappear (be equal to zero) and would become a part of the producers' surplus. That surplus, in perfect price discriminating monopoly would equal the combined areas 1 + 4 + 5.

Since perfect price discrimination is rarely if ever practiced, there is a more basic lesson here. As the degree of price discrimination increases, the monopoly's revenues increase and the consumers' surplus diminishes.

APPLICATION:
Regulation Versus Deregulation—When are Airline Markets Contestable?

We have seen that it is theoretically possible for well-intentioned and well informed public regulation of a monopolistic industry to produce results that approximate those of a competitive industry. Regulated prices can be set at MC and/or AC levels. While setting MC prices for natural monopolies will necessitate public subsidies, allocative efficiency can, theoretically, be achieved through enlightened public regulation.

In view of the above, why has the U.S. in the 1970s and 1980s embarked upon an era of deregulation of several major industries? Has disillusionment with over a century of public price regulation set in? If so, it may be because the experience of regulation, at least in some instances has differed substantially from its theoretical expectations. Though it is too early to write a clear answer to the future of public regulation in this country, we can evaluate some of the recent experience with deregulation and, by comparison, put it in perspective with the longer history of the costs and benefits of regulation that extend back into the 19th century.

Transportation Regulation: Public Interest or Industry Captured?

Apart from local public utilities that are generally considered natural monopolies, the (interstate) transportation industry has been one of the most prominent examples of monopoly regulation in the U.S. This process began at the federal level in the 1880s with the creation of the Interstate Commerce Commission (ICC). The ICC regulated railway transport and, from the 1920s, also the trucking industry. In the 1930s, the CAB was created to regulate the airline industry.

Contestable Market
One in which there are no significant losses from entry or exit due to sunk costs.

Perfectly Contestable Market
One in which there are no losses from entry or exit due to sunk costs.

It is particularly instructive to focus this look at regulation versus deregulation on the airline industry because it provides more clear evidence of the effects of both than any other transportation case. The Industry also provides some interesting insights into the question of when markets are contestable. A **contestable market** is one in which new firms can enter or exit without significant losses from sunk costs. Economists William Baumol, John Panzar, and Robert Willig have established a limiting concept of **perfectly contestable markets** in which there are no losses from entry or exit due to sunk costs. The importance of contestability is that it provides a measure of how readily and rapidly new firms can enter in response to the expectation of economic profit and how readily they can leave in the face of expected economic losses.

The Industry Under Regulation

Capture Hypothesis
The view that regulatory agencies are often captured by the industries they regulate and serve industry interests rather than those of the public.

While regulated by the CAB, the airline industry market was clearly one with little or no contestability. The Board determined not only prices firms could charge but also which firms could operate as well as the routes they could fly. For almost 40 years, no major new firms appeared. Some have argued that this publicly controlled cartel was administered not in the public's interest but instead by an agency that was "captured" by the industry. This view of regulation, advanced by Nobel Laureate George Stigler, holds that regulatory agencies, when captured, serve the interests of regulated firms rather than those of the public.

CAB regulation kept airline prices high but these high prices did not necessarily translate into economic profits for firms in the industry. As we noted earlier, airlines deprived of the freedom to engage in price competition, turned instead to non-price competition which raised their costs. This increase in costs accompanied by the costly CAB requirement that firms fly unprofitable routes simply led to more resources being used to provide airline services but (high) airline prices that resulted in only normal profits. In other words, regulation created a serious distortive problem with regard to the use of resources employed in the industry. By the mid-1970s, there was increasing pressure to ease entry into the industry and, ultimately, to deregulate the non-safety aspects of its operation.

What to Expect from Deregulation: A Brief Review

In 1978, legislation was enacted that would phase out the CAB and effectively deregulate all non-safety aspects of the airline industry. We see in Figure 8-13 what economic principles suggest the results of that deregulation would be. A cartelized industry would produce where MR equals MC while a competitive industry will produce where price equals MC. The competitive price, P_c, will equal MC; the monopoly price, P_m, will exceed MC. Competitive output will expand to the point at which the marginal benefit of airline consumers equals the MC of airline firms. The cross-hatched area in Figure 8-13 represents the combined gain in consumers' and producers' surplus that results from deregulation and decartelization of the industry.

Deregulation: The Short Run

Many of the expected benefits of deregulation seem to have been created between the demise of the CAB in 1981 and the mid-1980s. Whereas there had been 28 airlines licensed to fly in 1976, there were 61 operating in 1982. Timothy Tregarthen has shown that fares (revenue per passenger-mile) fell continually from 1981 to 1986. While rates rose at times, these increases were due to inflation especially to the dramatic jump in jet fuel prices in the early-1980s.

Figure 8-13
A Comparison of the Results of a Competitive Airline Industry and those of a Monopoly (Cartel) Industry

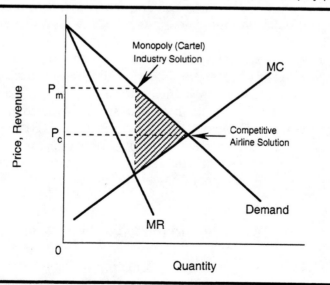

In Figure 8-13, a competitive airline will equate MC (quantity supplied) and quantity demanded and airline price will be P_c, a price equal to MC. A monopoly (cartel) industry solution will be where MC equals MR and price will exceed MC. The cross-hatched area is the deadweight loss of monopoly or the area of gain in consumers' and producers' surplus that is created by competition.

Though it is unlikely that all of the gain in consumers' and producers' surplus in Figure 8-13 was obtained, a Brookings Institution study estimates the gain per year between 1976 and 1986 at $6 billion.

Deregulation: The Long Run and Reconcentration

We know by now that firms in a competitive industry sell like products at like prices. That does not necessarily mean, however, that competitive firms have the same costs. The airline industry produces clear evidence in these regards. Faced with recession and rising fuel costs in the early-1980s, some well managed firms sought to contain costs by (1) raising the rate of utilization of aircraft on long distance flights and (2) reducing labor costs. American Airlines, for example, created a soon copied "hub and spoke" system under which it funnels passengers on shorter flights into a hub city and combines them onto its longer flights, thus raising its capacity utilization and lowering its costs per passenger mile on the longer ones. Other airlines sought concessions from labor unions or, through bankruptcy, voided costly labor agreements. Still other firms such as Braniff ultimately faced bankruptcy.

Airline Mergers

High cost, less profitable firms in any industry are tempting targets for takeovers and mergers. By the mid-1980s, entry of new firms was replaced by a wave of mergers. Under the CAB, mergers had been rare; the Department of Transportation, to whom merger approval had passed, was more approving. Northwest merged with Republic, TWA with Ozark, and Texas Air acquired Eastern, to name a few. These mergers, combined with the hub and spoke system and the limited number of gates and landing rights (slots) at airports, seemed to have introduced a new element of monopoly into the industry. As a result, some economists have questioned whether the industry is still contestable enough to be competitive. Before deregulation the 5 largest airlines flew 63 percent of passenger miles. By mid-1989, the 5 largest (American, Delta, Continental, Northwest, United) were flying 70 percent of passenger miles.

Contestability and the Number of Firms

Can the airline industry remain "workably" contestable in the face of growing concentration and a decline in the number of (long-haul) firms? Evidence clearly suggests that the market is not *perfectably* contestable. Still, that would not matter greatly if firms could, as Tregarthen observes, make "hit and run" attacks on monopoly profits. A study in *The Journal of Law and Economics* in 1987 suggests that this may be difficult and that the number of firms does matter in making the market more toward the competitive solution in Figure 8-13. Potential competition as well as actual competition, as the 1987 study shows, restrain monopoly practices and move the market toward the competitive (P = MC) efficient solution.

Barriers to Entry

Studies show that the hub and spoke system limits entry because new firms find it difficult to obtain landing rights at already crowded airports dominated by firms with already established hubs. One economist has also argued that frequent flyer programs increase "firm loyalty" of consumers and restrict entry. Clearly, though, the major barrier to entry is the existing capacity of airports. Some airports such as LaGuardia and Kennedy in New York have already been declared full and others are approaching that point. Airlines are now allowed to sell their "slots" at these sites and their rising prices reflect the monopoly problem and the barriers to entry.

Continued contestability in the airline industry seems to depend importantly on easing entry, and growth of airport facilities seems an important complementary ingredient in doing that. Tregarthen reports that the federal excise tax on passenger fares and jet fuel had accumulated over $5 billion by late-1987. Its lack of disbursement has been attributed to an effort to make the federal deficit look less severe. A more rational pricing system for airport facilities, together with the expansion of those facilities should at least increase the number of *potential* competitors and restore the movement toward the competitive solution begun in the period from 1976 to 1986. A first sign of this appeared in mid-1989 with the approval of plans to build a new airport in Denver costing more than $3 billion; the airport would be the first major new facility since the Dallas-Fort Worth Airport in 1974.

Reregulation?

The late-1980s have witnessed a number of calls for the restoration of airline regulation. While there may be merit in increased safety regulation (though studies show that safety has increased since deregulation), few economists would likely argue for a return of the CAB. There is no evidence that the industry is a natural monopoly and to recreate the earlier cartel would reimpose the deadweight losses of earlier times. Economist Steven Morrison, one of the authors of the 1987 study in the *Journal of Law and Economics* says that the airlines' "problems can be solved with better pricing of airports. Going back to the old days of regulation would be a great mistake."

SUMMING UP

1. The following are the characteristics of a *pure unregulated monopoly*: (a) There is only one firm in the industry. (b) It produces a product for which there are no good substitutes. (c) There are barriers to entry of other firms. The pure monopolist is constrained by (a) competition from firms in other industries that produce substitutes, (b) fear of antagonizing the public and the government, (c) inability to control the quantity consumers demand (although the pure monopoly can control price), and (d) current cost conditions.

2. Some of the barriers that may keep new firms from entering a monopolistic industry are (a) entrenched firm's control of patents and secret processes, (b) economic warfare, (c) the entrenched firm's control of sources of supply, (d) obstacles due to the necessity for large-scale production in order to achieve economies of scale, (e) higher cost of initiating consumer acceptance than of maintaining it, (f) government-created barriers to entry.

3. In pure monopoly, the monopolistic firm's demand is the same as demand for the industry as a whole. To increase the quantity consumers demand, the monopolistic firm must therefore lower price. As a result, the MR curve lies below the demand AR curve, and falls more steeply.

4. In the short run, because plant capacity is fixed, the pure monopoly has the same four profit-loss possibilities as the purely competitive firm: (a) Price is higher than ATC, and the monopoly earns an economic profit. (b) Price is equal to ATC, and the monopolist earns only a normal profit. (c) Price is less than ATC, but higher than AVC, and the monopoly incurs an economic loss, although it continues to produce in the short run. (d) Price is less than AVC, and the firm shuts down to reduce loss.

5. A business firm—whether monopolistic or competitive—produces at the level of output at which MC is equal to MR. Since MR lies below the demand curve, the monopolistic firm's price (which is established on the demand curve) is higher than MC.

6. In the long run, there are two possible monopoly solutions: (a) Firms cannot enter the industry because of barriers to entry; thus, in a pure monopoly, the monopolistic firm will probably make an economic profit in the long run. (b) Sometimes prices are only high enough to cover AC; in that case the monopolistic firm will make

only a normal profit. The firm will not plan to take losses in the long run, because if losses are expected, the firm will liquidate.

7. When one compares the long-run equilibrium positions of the purely-competitive industry and the purely-monopolistic industry, assuming that their cost curves are the same, one finds the following: (a) The purely-competitive industry produces a larger output than the purely-monopolistic industry, at a lower AC. The competitive industry will produce at a price equal to AC and MC. The purely-monopolistic industry will set a price that is above MC and likely above AC. (b) If the monopolistic industry and the purely-competitive firm should produce the same output, the monopolist charges a higher price. (c) Under pure competition, only normal profits are earned, while under pure monopoly there probably will be economic profits. (d) Pure monopolists tend to produce at less than economic capacity. (e) Since, under pure monopoly, price is higher than MC, the amount of output produced by a monopoly is not the amount consumers most prefer (*allocative inefficiency*).

8. In some industries (natural monopolies), the consumer would be at a disadvantage in terms of cost if more than one firm were to produce in a given area. So the government awards a franchise to one monopolistic firm. Such firms are regulated by the government, and are called *regulated monopolies*. These firms produce with economies of scale up to the output rate at which the market is filled.

9. The regulatory commission theoretically tries to set a price at which the monopolistic firm earns only a normal profit. This price level is that amount of output at which AR (or demand) equals AC, and leads to a lower price and higher output than that obtained under unregulated pure monopoly. In practice, regulation may or may not produce this result.

10. A monopoly, because it must act as a price seeker, does not have a supply curve in the sense that a purely competitive firm does. A common myth about monopolies is that they always earn economic profits. In fact, monopolies in the short run may incur losses, earn normal profits or earn economic profits.

11. When a monopolist charges different prices for different units of a commodity, it is practicing *price discrimination*. (a) The main condition necessary for price discrimination is that a buyer of a commodity be unable to sell it to someone else who has been charged a higher price for the same commodity. (b) Price discrimination can be profitable only if the elasticities of demand differ among different buyers or groups of buyers.

12. A monopolistic firm—like any other business firm—when it wants to practice price discrimination, maximizes profit by producing

products at a rate at which MC equals MR in each market. If elasticities of demand differ in each market, the monopoly will charge different prices in each, equating MR to MC in each market. The lower the elasticity of demand, the higher the resulting price.

13. Purely competitive industries will produce a rate of output at a MC price that maximizes the combined consumers' plus producers' surplus. Output is expanded to the point at which the marginal benefit of the product to consumers is made equal to the MC of producers.

14. A monopoly industry, equating MR and MC, will produce less than a competitive industry and set a price above MC. There is under monopoly a loss of consumers' surplus as well as producers' surplus. This combined loss, a loss to all in society, is referred to as the *deadweight loss of monopoly*. Because the price set by the monopoly exceeds MC, part of consumers' surplus is transferred to producers as a producers' surplus. The gain in producers' surplus is larger than the loss of producers' surplus from reduced monopoly output.

15. If monopolies practice price discrimination, there is a further loss of consumers' surplus. In the limit, perfect price discrimination results in the complete loss of consumers' surplus which becomes an addition to producers' surplus.

16. Enlightened public regulation, theoretically, can accomplish many of the functions of competition in monopolistic markets. However, experience with regulation, especially in transportation industries, has differed substantially from such theoretical expectations. By the 1970s, there were calls to ease or eliminate non-safety regulation of such industries. This application focuses on regulation and deregulation in the airline industry. Price regulation, undertaken by the CAB, began in the 1930s and effectively ended in the early-1980s.

17. An examination of the airline industry permits us to focus on the *contestability* of markets in which we ask if new firms can enter or leave the industry without incurring large sunk costs. A market is *perfectly contestable* if there are no losses from sunk costs as a result of entry or exit. Contestability is a measure of how readily economic profits or losses can induce entry into or exit from an industry.

18. Under the CAB, the airline industry was a publicly administered cartel. Some conclude that the CAB was *captured* by the industry. Airline prices were high and costs were increased as airlines engaged in non-price competition and flew unprofitable routes as required. Because of high costs, however, it is likely that the industry earned only normal profits but misallocated resources to produce airline services.

19. Deregulation would be expected to increase output (passenger miles flown) and to result in lower prices. Theoretically, it would be expected to approximate a more nearly competitive industry solution with the allocative efficiency of MC prices. Following deregulation, the number of firms in the industry increased substantially and airline prices, adjusted for inflation, fell. By one estimate the consumer and producer benefit amounted to $6 billion per year between 1976 and 1986.

20. By the mid-1980s, there was a movement toward merger in the deregulated airline industry. A number of firms created hub and spoke systems that lowered their long haul costs but also made it more difficult for potential competitors to break into the market at hub cities. This has led some to conclude that the industry market is no longer contestable. The primary barrier to entry appears to be the lack of a complementary input, airport capacity and landing slots at existing airports, some of which already have been declared full.

21. Although cancelled flights, delays and the like have led some to argue for reregulation of airlines, few economists would see that as the preferred solution. Consumer as well as producer interests are probably better served by restoring the contestability of airline markets. A major expansion of airport facilities seems to be an important ingredient in doing that.

KEY TERMS

Allocative inefficiency
Barriers to entry
Capture hypothesis
Contestable market
Monopoly power
Natural monopoly
Perfect price discrimination
Perfectly contestable market
Price discrimination
Pure monopoly
Regulated monopoly
Second degree price discrimination

QUESTIONS

1. In a pure monopoly, the monopolistic firm is the only one selling the product; therefore there are no constraints on what the firm can charge or on the profit it can make. Do you agree? Why?

2. "Monopolies always earn economic profits because of their privileged market positions." How would you evaluate this statement?

3. Discuss various barriers to entry into an industry, explaining how they can engender a monopoly situation. Are any of these barriers socially desirable? Why?

4. Assuming that the same cost curves apply to both purely competitive and monopolistic industries, compare their relative performance in terms of price, output, and profit. Use diagrams. Since industries of both kinds produce at a level at which marginal cost equals marginal revenue, to what do you attribute the differences between their performances?

5. What is a natural monopoly? Discuss the relative degree and timing of utilization and development of technology in (a) a purely monopolistic and (b) a purely competitive system. What is an example of a natural monopoly in your area?

6. An alternative to pure unregulated monopoly is regulated monopoly. Compare the ways price and output are determined under unregulated monopoly and under regulated monopoly. Do you think regulated monopoly is a practical alternative to pure private monopoly or near monopoly? Why?

7. The hypothetical figure that follows is that of a monopoly firm operating in the short run. Based on this figure, answer the questions below.

a. If the monopoly firm is unregulated and seeks to maximize profit, what will be its (1) output rate, and (2) price?

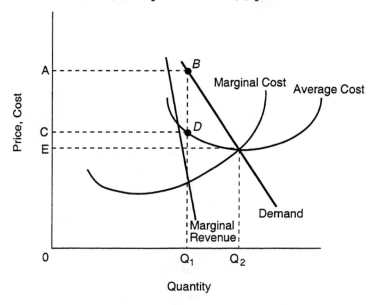

b. If you were a regulator charged with setting this firm's price and your objective was to produce a market result as close as possible to that of pure competition while creating for the firm a "fair rate of return," what price would you set? What would be the regulated firm's rate of output at that price?

8. Under what conditions is it profitable for a monopolistic firm to practice price discrimination?

9. Draw diagrams for two submarkets and show at what levels a monopolistic firm would produce and what prices it would charge to consumers, if it were given the chance to practice second degree price discrimination.

10. What are the deadweight losses of monopoly? Does anyone benefit from these losses?

11. What happens to consumers' surplus if monopolies practice perfect price discrimination?

12. Under what conditions may monopolies foster productivity growth?

13. Why do monopolies, in contrast with purely competitive firms, not have a supply curve?

14. What were the functions of the CAB when it regulated the airline industry?

15. What is a *contestable* market? A *perfectly contestable* market?

16. Was the airline industry market, while regulated, contestable?

17. What is the *capture hypothesis*? In what sense was the airline industry under CAB regulation a cartel?

18. What does economic theory suggest about the results of deregulating and decartelizing an industry?

19. What were the short-run results (1976-1986) of airline deregulation?

20. What factors since the mid-1980s appear to have made airline markets less contestable?

21. If the two solutions to the problems of contestability in (7) above are (a) regulation or (b) restoring contestability, which would you support? Why?

22. What seem to be some of the measures necessary to increase contestability in airline markets?

SUGGESTED READINGS

"Airline Deregulation: Is Flying the Cheaper Skies Safe?" *The Margin*. September/October, 1988.

Bailey, Elizabeth E., David R. Graham, and Daniel P. Kaplan. *Deregulating the Airlines*. Cambridge, MA: MIT Press, 1985.

Castro, Janice. "The Sky Kings Rule the Routes." *Time*. May 15, 1989.

Dolan, Edwin G., and John C. Goodman. "Flying the Deregulated Skies: Competition, Price Discrimination, Congestion." *Economics of Public Policy*. 4th ed. Ch. 9. St. Paul, MN: West Publishing Co., 1989.

McGinley, Laurie. "Federal Regulation Rises Anew in Matters that Worry the Public." *The Wall Street Journal*. April 21, 1987.

"The Railroads: Back on Track?" *The Margin*. September, 1987.

Tregarthen, Timothy. "Airline Deregulation: Turbulant Skies Ahead." *The Margin*. December, 1987.

CHAPTER 9

Monopolistic Competition

"These days, I need all the friends I can get. This is a tough business I'm in. You really have to hustle to make a buck. And right now I need the bucks. I'm due for a new wrecker. A new car. And my wife's screaming for an avocado refrigerator. That's why, when you drive into my station, I'm going to come out smiling. I'm going to wash your front window. Your back window. Now, to be honest, I'm not really crazy about having to work this hard, but I need that new wrecker, the new car and like my wife says, what's an avocado kitchen without an avocado refrigerator? Try me, I can be very friendly."

Sunoco Oil Company Advertisement

OBJECTIVES

After studying this chapter you will be able to:

- Define the characteristics of a monopolistic and oligopolistic industry.
- Explain the three general phases of the monopolistic industries' maturation process.
- Explain marginal analysis as it applies to monopolistic and oligopolistic businesses.
- Describe how monopolistic and oligopolistic competition affects society.
- Explain why price leadership is common in an oligopolistic industry.
- Explain the significance of a kinked demand curve.
- Have a working knowledge of the following terms and concepts:

Conglomerate mergers	Oligopoly
Horizontal mergers	Price leadership
Kinked demand curve	Product differentiation
Maturation process	Rate of return regulation
Monopolistic	Sherman Antitrust Act
Natural monopoly	Vertical mergers

Monopolistic Competition

A man reminisces:

> When I was a lad in the 1930s I used to go food shopping with my mother. In those days there weren't supermarkets all over. We, my mother and I, would walk around the corner and down the block to a small collection of stores at the farthest corner. First we would go to the grocery and buy canned goods, paper products, and dairy products. Then we would walk next door to the fruit and vegetable store, and afterward to the meat store. We never went to the fish market on the block. (Mother was sure their fish wasn't fresh.) Once a week she took the bus to a fish market about ten blocks away.
>
> Each store was so small that customers had to stand outside if more than ten came at the same time. There were thousands of these small retail mom-and-pop stores in the city. Each had a special advantage in its own neighborhood, because my mother would go to strange stores only with reluctance, both on account of the inconvenience of going greater distances and also because she knew, trusted, and liked the local owners.

For many decades, economists employed the working assumption that market performance could be understood by employing the theories of pure (or perfect) competition and pure monopoly. Markets were characterized either by free entry, many firms and homogeneous products or by a single firm, absolute barriers to entry and the irrelevance of product homogeneity. By the 1930s, some economists began to question whether these two polar extremes were sufficient to understand the workings of modern market economies. Two especially contributed to this debate and to our further understanding of such economies. One, Edward Chamberlain of Harvard University, developed a theory that fit neither of the two extremes; he entitled his model *Monopolistic Competition*. The second, a British economist, Joan Robinson of Cambridge University, working at the same time but independently of Chamberlain, developed a very similar model and entitled it *Imperfect Competition*. For all practical purposes, the two terms are interchangeable and their meanings are the subject of this chapter. After we have examined the theory of monopolistic or imperfect competition, we will ask an important related question: In many industries is monopolistic competition as close as we can or would want to come to pure competition? Is it, in other words, an acceptable substitute for pure competition?

What is Monopolistic Competition?

Monopolistic Competition
A market in which there are (1) many firms, (2) differentiated products, and (3) relatively easy conditions of entry and exit.

Monopolistic competition includes strong elements of competition, but at the same time also has elements of monopoly. The three main characteristics of monopolistic competition are (1) a large number of firms, (2) relative ease of entry into the market (and exit from it), and (3) a differentiated product.

At one extreme of monopolistic competition, each firm in the industry acts independently of the others, so that the action of any one firm does not affect the actions of the others. This was the assumption of Chamberlain. A view that may be more appropriate to many examples of monopolistic competition is that any one firm may be in close competition with another one or with a few firms that are nearby, and it has to react when the others change prices. There is unrecognized interdependency between competitors that are in close interaction. They must react to each other's changes, especially changes in price. But a given firm is influenced only incidentally by firms that are farther away. For example, a Laundromat is influenced by other Laundromats that draw customers from its neighborhood, but not by Laundromats far enough away to be inconvenient to its customers. This has led some economists to argue that such markets are really localized oligopolies.

The fact that there are many firms in a monopolistically competitive situation is a competitive element that restricts the ability of firms to control price through product differentiation. Significant differences in price between firms quickly lead customers to abandon the loyalties engendered by product differentiation and to buy from the firm that offers lower prices. ("Never mind that brand X comes in a prettier box than brand Y. Can I get brand Y a dollar cheaper?")

A second and arguably more important competitive element is the *relative ease of entry* into monopolistically competitive industries. This factor reinforces and maintains the competitive element of many firms in the industry, and also restricts a firm's ability in the long run to exploit product differentiation.

In purely competitive situations, there is complete freedom of entry. But in monopolistic competition, product differentiation which often takes the form of brand name or firm loyalty can act as a barrier to entry, in that it can keep a monopolistically competitive firm from duplicating the product of another firm. Therefore, one cannot say that there is "complete" freedom of entry as in pure competition; one must qualify this and say there is "reasonable" freedom of entry.

Finally, we should note in comparing pure and monopolistic competition that the products produced in monopolistically competitive industries are differentiated. **Product differentiation** means that consumers do see differences between the output of different firms. In other words, they have a preference for the products of one firm over those of another. This is an element of monopoly, for it enables the individual firm to charge different prices from those of its competitors, because customers are loyal to the firm's product. Usually, the greater the differentiation, the greater the firm's ability to charge a higher price than its competitors. In other words, the greater the differentiation, the greater the monopoly power of a given firm. The basis for product differentiation varies: It may be a brand name, a trademark, a store name, a difference in quality or services or timing of services, or a difference in location. Monopolistically competitive firms, like other firms with some degree of monopoly authority, are price seekers, not price takers.

Product Differentiation
The preference of consumers for the products of one firm over those of other firms.

Sources of Product Differentiation

The example at the beginning of this chapter of the mom-and-pop retail store embodies several forms of differentiation. The owners' personalities cause customers to either like or dislike them. The services they offer (such as delivery or credit) help draw customers also. But the most important form of differentiation is location. The grocery store around the corner is more convenient than the one ten blocks away. Locational differentiation, though it is not the only form of differentiation, is the most important form in a number of industries. This is true of laundromats, gasoline service stations, dry-cleaning shops, and restaurants.

The individual firm in a monopolistically competitive situation knows that it can best reduce the intensity of the competition by accentuating differences in its product. When a firm puts a lot of effort and money into differentiating its product from everyone else's, strong product rivalry can develop.

Product variation should not be confused with selling efforts. Differences in location and in efforts to change the quality of the product are clear examples of variations in the product. When a pizza parlor not only has a good location but also takes special care and uses extra ingredients to make a good pizza, it is differentiating its product. If the pizza parlor advertises its pizza, it incurs selling costs. So in monopolistic competition one has to count in two more forms of costs that are added to production costs: (1) cost of creating product differentiation, and (2) costs of selling that differentiated product to customers.

Advertising

Another factor that affects a monopolistically competitive industry is advertising. In pure competition, an individual firm's advertising is ineffective because of product homogeneity. It is for this reason that purely competitive firms will not find it profitable to advertise. In pure monopoly, advertising merely creates public good will or stimulates general demand for the product at the expense of another industry's product; there is no interfirm advertising. In monopolistic competition, however, advertising that emphasizes the firm and its product may create or intensify existing differentiation. The greater the consumer acceptance created through advertising, the greater the firm's ability to differentiate its product, and the stronger the firm's monopoly power. The greater its monopoly power, the more it can vary its prices above those of others in the industry.

Advertising may affect the firm's demand curve in two ways: (1) It may increase demand for the firm's output, shifting the demand curve up or to the right, as customers want more of the product. (2) It may cause consumers to have a stronger attachment to the product, which reduces the firm's price elasticity of demand.

Product Differentiation and the Price Elasticity of Demand

As we noted above, the firm seeks to differentiate its product because that increases its ability to set prices above marginal costs. We see the various degrees of product differentiation in Figure 9-1. Note also that these degrees of product differentiation translate into differences in the price elasticity of demand facing the firm. In one limit, if the firm was completely unsuccessful in differentiating its product, that product would be homogeneous, a perfect substitute for that of other firms in the industry (or product group to use Chamberlain's term). At price P_0, its demand would be D, a perfectly elastic demand.

If the firm in Figure 9-1 is partially successful in differentiating its product, it will face D′ reflecting a slightly differentiated product and a demand condition that is less elastic than D. At prices above P_0, demand will be *relatively* less elastic than D. If the firm is even more successful in differentiating its product, it will face a demand curve such as D″, reflecting a highly differentiated product

Figure 9-1
Product Homogeneity, Product Differentiation, and the Elasticity of Demand for a Firm

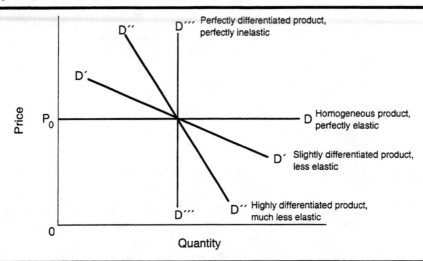

In Figure 9-1, D is the (limiting) perfectly elastic demand curve facing a firm if its product is homogeneous or undifferentiated from that of other firms in the industry. D′ is the less elastic demand curve of the firm if it has slightly differentiated. D″ s the highly inelastic demand curve of the firm if it sells a highly differentiated product D‴ is the (limiting) perfectly inelastic demand curve facing the firm if it sells a product that is perfectly differentiated.

and a *much* less elastic demand than D at prices above P_0. In the limit, if a firm is completely successful in differentiating its product, it will face D‴, reflecting a perfectly differentiated product (no other firms' products are regarded as substitutes) and will face a perfectly inelastic demand at all prices.

The *central points* to remember in this are the following: (1) The less differentiated is a firm's product, the greater is the price elasticity of demand for its product, (2) the more differentiated is a firm's product, the smaller is the price elasticity of demand for its product, and (3) other things equal, a price seeking firm prefers a less elastic (more differentiated) demand to a more elastic (less differentiated) demand.

When a firm increases its monopoly power by stepping up differentiation of its product, it increases its costs at the same time, even though it gains greater control over price. The firm must add to its ordinary production costs the costs of maintaining and intensifying product differentiation. These additional costs fall into two classes: (1) selling costs, often the biggest, which consist mostly of advertising costs, and (2) costs of changing the shape, color, package, and so on, of the product itself; for example, the cost of designing a new soft drink container.

Figure 9-2 shows selling costs and costs due to product differentiation added to production cost for a monopolistically competitive firm. Both kinds of costs (undertaken in order to intensify differentiation) eventually suffer from diminishing marginal returns.

Figure 9-2
Costs of Selling and Product Differentiation Added to Costs of Production for a
Monopolistically Competitive Firm

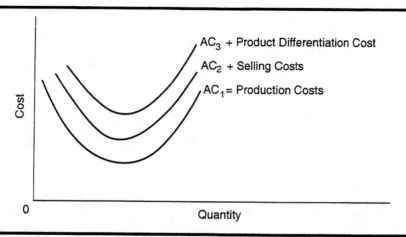

Average cost (AC_1) equals production costs; AC_2 adds selling costs to AC_1; and AC_3 adds cost of product differentiation to the other two costs.

The reason is that a firm must make larger and larger expenditures to bring about an equal increase in differentiation. However, in monopolistic competition, firms are small, and each one services a limited local market. Advertising in monopolistically competitive industries is therefore primarily local in coverage. It is worth noting, though, that there are exceptions to this as in the clothing industry in which larger firms engage in national advertising.

Two points about advertising should be emphasized: First, many industries characterized as monopolistically competitive may do little if any advertising; for example laundromats, drugstores, dental services, and medical services. Second, some monopolistically competitive industries as noted above buy national advertising. Big brand-name oil companies advertise nationally, and local service stations benefit from this advertising. Many franchised businesses—such as Kentucky Fried Chicken and McDonald's—have national advertising campaigns that help the individual local firms.

Monopolistic Competition: The Short Run

Figure 9-3 permits us to compare purely competitive, purely monopolistic, and monopolistically competitive firms in terms of their demand and revenue conditions. Recall that in pure competition the individual firm has no control over price. Therefore, the curves depicting its demand, average revenue (AR), and marginal revenue (MR) are perfectly elastic at the market price. (See Figure 9-3(a)). In pure monopoly there is no competition. Demand and AR curves slope downward.

Figure 9-3
Demand, Average Revenue, and Marginal Revenue for the Typical Firm in *(a)* Pure Competition,
(b) Pure Monopoly, and *(c)* Monopolistic Competition

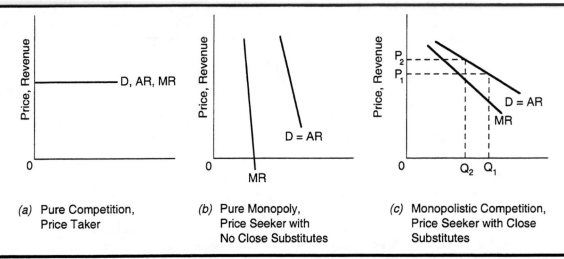

(a) Pure Competition,
   Price Taker

(b) Pure Monopoly,
   Price Seeker with
   No Close Substitutes

(c) Monopolistic Competition,
   Price Seeker with Close
   Substitutes

In Figure 9-3, the demand curve (D, AR, MR) of the typical purely competitive price taking firm in *(a)* is perfectly elastic. The relatively inelastic demand curve of the price seeking pure monopoly in *(b)* is downward sloping (D = AR) and MR is less than AR or price. The demand curve of the typical monopolistically competitive price seeking firm in *(c)* is downward sloping and relatively more elastic than that of the pure monopoly but less elastic than that of the pure competitor because of product differentiation; MR is less than AR or price.

MR curves fall still more sharply, and lie below the demand and AR curves. (See Figure 9-3(*b*)). The pure monopoly must lower price to increase quantity demanded. In monopolistic competition, on the other hand, the individual firm has some control over price, in the sense that it can raise its price and not lose all its customers. This control is due to product differentiation. Thus, the firm's demand (AR) curve is not perfectly elastic, but slopes downward. However, since there are many firms in the industry and entry is easy, competition is strong and the individual firm's ability to vary price is restricted. (See Figure 9-3(*c*)).

Figure 9-3(*c*) shows however, that the monopolistically competitive firm's demand curve is not perfectly elastic. Price can increase from P_1 to P_2 and quantity sold may decrease only from Q_1 to Q_2. The firm does not lose all its customers. However, because of the competitive elements in a monopolistically competitive industry—large number of firms and ease of entry—this small rise in price results in a large fall in quantity demanded.

Competition: A Reprise

Now let's sum up the three market classifications discussed so far. In pure competition, the demand curve is perfectly elastic, and is represented by a horizontal line. In a monopolistic competition, product differentiation gives the firm some control over price, so the demand and AR curve slopes downward. And, since price varies with quantity demanded, MR decreases more rapidly and lies below the demand, AR curve. In pure monopoly, the demand curve is not as elastic as in pure competition or monopolistic competition.

The monopolistically competitive firm, like the purely competitive and purely monopolistic firms, maximizes profits (or minimizes losses) by producing at the level at which marginal cost (MC) equals MR. In the short run, monopolistically competitive firms, like those in the other market classifications, cannot enter the industry by building new plants, and cannot expand existing facilities, and cannot liquidate their plants. In the short run, then, the entry of firms and the expansion of facilities cannot cause a firm's economic profits to disappear. Thus, firms faced with economic losses must either produce or shut down and pay fixed costs. In the short run, the monopolistically competitive firm with a given set of supply (cost) conditions faces the same four possible profit or loss situations as firms in the other two market classifications.

The Four Short-Run Profit and Loss Positions of a Typical Monopolistically Competitive Firm

In Figure 9-4, we see illustrated graphically the four possible short-run profit or loss positions of the typical monopolistically competitive firm:

1. Situation *(a)*. *Demand is great enough to generate an economic profit.* In the range in which the firm sets price, the demand AR curve lies above the short-run average cost (SRAC) curve. Since price (P_{MC}) is greater than average cost (AC), the firm earns an economic profit.

2. Situation *(b)*. *Demand is high enough to generate only a normal profit.* Price is at the point at which the demand AR curve is tangent to average total cost ($P_{MC} = AC$). Total revenue (TR) and total cost (TC) are equal when the firm produces Q_{MC}. (Remember that a normal profit is already included in TC.)

3. Situation *(c)*. *Demand may be high enough to cover at least variable cost and the firm incurs an economic loss.* But the firm will continue to produce in the short run, because price is greater than average variable cost (AVC < P_{MC} < AC). The economic loss the firm incurs by producing is less than the firm will incur if it shuts down and experiences a loss equal to total fixed cost. It produces Q_{MC} to minimize loss.

4. Situation *(d)*. *Demand may not be high enough to cover variable costs.* With such large economic losses, the firm shuts down in the short run. In the range in which price is set, price is less that AVC. The demand curve lies below the AVC curve (AR < AVC). By

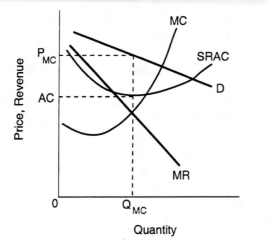

(a) The firm earns an economic profit.

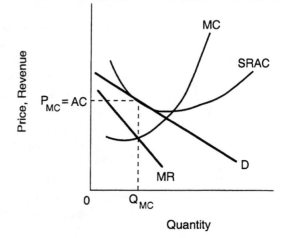

(b) The firm earns a normal profit.

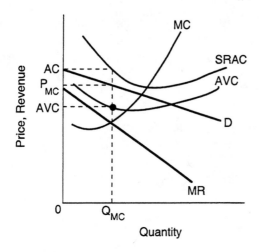

(c) The firm incurs an economic loss but produces.

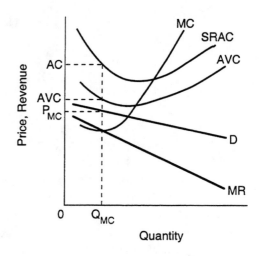

(d) The firm would incur an economic loss greater than fixed cost and shuts down.

In Figure 9-4, situation (a) is one in which the firm is able to set a price above AC ($P_{MC} > AC$) and earns a short-run economic profit. In situation (b), the firm is able to set a price equal to AC ($P_{MC} = AC$) and earns a normal profit. In situation (c), the firm is able to set a price less than AC but greater than AVC ($AVC < P < AC$) and incurs a loss less than its fixed cost so it produces Q_{MC} to minimize its loss. In situation (d), the firm is only able to set a price that is less than AC and AVC ($P < AVC < AC$) and would incur a loss greater than its fixed costs; to minimize the loss it produces zero rather than Q_{MC} (shuts down).

shutting down, the firm loses only an amount equal to its fixed cost, while if it continues to produce, it will lose more than its fixed costs. It shuts down and produces zero rather than Q_{MC}.

The only difference in the diagrammatic presentation of these four situations is that in monopolistic competition the demand (AR) curve is more elastic than it is in pure monopoly, but, as we saw earlier in Figure 9-3, is not perfectly elastic, as it is in pure competition.

Monopolistic Competition: The Long Run

In the long run, in monopolistic competition, firms can enter the industry with reasonable freedom. If there are economic profits to be made in the industry in the short run (short-run situation *(a)* in Figure 9-4), firms enter in the long run to attempt to earn profits for themselves. But the fact that more firms are dividing up the market reduces the public's demand for the product of each individual firm. This has the effect of squeezing out the economic profit by shifting the demand curve of the typical firm downward or to the left until all economic profit is eliminated for the firm. The economic profit is also squeezed out when firms engage in price cutting to gain customers. Economic profits are further drained away when firms intensify their efforts to differentiate their product, and in doing so increase their selling costs and costs of differentiation. In the long run, therefore, the result is usually only a normal profit.

So it is no surprise that Figure 9-5 shows the typical monopolistically competitive firm, in the long run, earning only a normal profit. Let's see why. The firm has very limited control over price, in spite of product differentiation, because there are many firms in the industry and there is ease of entry. In Figure 9-5, D_1 shows the firm's economic profits in the short run. In the long run D_1 falls to D_2, as firms enter the industry and subdivide demand. With D_2, profit-maximizing output will be at the level at which marginal cost (MC) equals MR. Output will then be A. To find the price that will be charged at output A, one draws a perpendicular to the demand curve and a horizontal to the vertical axis. Price is then P_{MC}. Since the demand curve is *tangent* to the AC curve, AC equals price. TC equals TR, and the typical firm receives only a *normal profit*.

An Exception to Normal Profit
However, in long-run equilibrium, there is an exception to this presumption of only normal profit. In a monopolistically competitive situation, there are different degrees of product differentiation. And an atypical firm may differentiate its product from that of its competitors so greatly that other firms do not provide enough competition to take

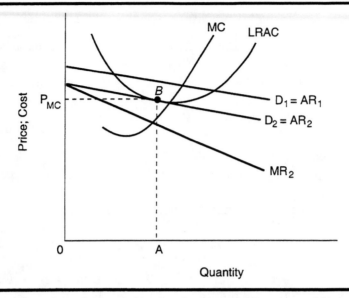

In Figure 9-5, a typical monopolistically competitive firm faces a declining demand for its product as new firms enter the industry. Demand decreases from $D_1 = AR_1$ until demand is tangent to long-run average cost (LRAC) with $D_2 = AR_2$. When price (P_{mc}), equals AC (LRAC), normal profits are earned and there is no further incentive to enter the industry.

away its economic profit. Thus, in the long run, it is possible for a non-typical monopolistically competitive firm to earn an economic profit. For example, a long-run economic profit may be earned by a service station in an exceptionally good location, a restaurant with an outstanding chef, or a brand-name product that consumers prefer to other products, as the result of a successful advertising campaign.

Figure 9-6 shows what this looks like. Output is A (where MC = MR), and price is given by a perpendicular to the demand curve (AB), with price P_{MC}. Cost per unit is a perpendicular to the LRAC curve, or E. TR, area $0P_{MC}BA$, is greater than TC, area $0ECA$. The difference, area $EP_{MC}BC$, is economic profit.

Note, however, that the situation to be expected for the *typical* firm is one of tangency between D = AR, and LRAC. In this case there is only a normal profit. Some economists say that the economic-profit situation is really a case of oligopoly. It is oligopoly in the sense that insufficient competition exists because there are few competing sellers located near the firm. The problem is too complex for us to draw any conclusions here.

In the long run, there are no economic losses, because firms that take a loss or cannot cover their opportunity costs leave the industry. Each of the firms that remain has a larger share of the market, because there are fewer of them. This shifts their demand curves upward and squeezes out the economic loss.

Figure 9-6
Long-Run Economic Profit for an Atypical Firm Under Monopolistic Competition

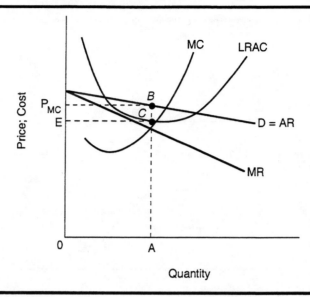

In Figure 9-6, an atypical firm has succeeded in maintaining sufficient differentiation of this product in the long run that demand (D = AR) lies above the AC (LRAC) in the output range in which price (P_{mc}) is set. The firm produces output A and its price is above its AC (P_m > E); as a result the firm earns an economic profit.

Monopolistic Competition: The Excess Capacity Argument

When you compare monopolistic competition with pure competition (Figure 9-7), bear in mind that many of the conclusions drawn from the comparison of pure monopoly and pure competition also apply here. Figure 9-7 is based on the assumption that the cost curves in the two classifications are the same.

When there is just normal profit (the most probable long-run situation in both monopolistic and pure competition), the price is lower (P_C) and the output higher (Q_{MC}) under pure competition than under monopolistic competition (P_{MC}, Q_{MC}). Also, the monopolistically competitive firm produces at less than capacity (it has output less than that which corresponds to the low point on the LRAC curve), and with higher levels of unit cost, than the purely competitive firm.

Since the typical firm in both market classifications is small, it is reasonable to assume similar cost curves. When we discussed pure monopoly, we had to consider the economic effects of differences in economies of scale and encouragement to technological innovation. These considerations generally are not relevant to monopolistic competition.

In monopolistic competition, there are higher unit costs than in pure competition, and production is at less than capacity. Many economists have characterized this failure to produce at capacity as

Figure 9-7
Long Run Comparison of Monopolistically Competitive Firms and Purely Competitive Firms:
The Excess Capacity Argument

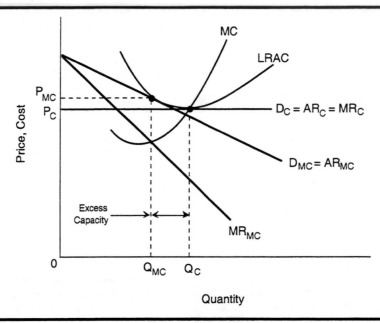

In Figure 9-7, subscript MC refers to monopolistic competition and subscript C refers to pure competition. With demand curve $D_C = AR_C = MR_C$ and given competitive price P_C, the typical purely competitive firm will produce Q_C at minimum AC and economic capacity (P = MC). With downward sloping demand curve $D_{MC} = AR_{MC}$ and with $MR_{MC} < AR_{MC}$, the typical monopolistically competitive firm will produce where $MR_{MC} = MC$ or Q_{MC} and set price P_{MC} ($P_{MC} > MC$). As compared with competitive firms, monopolistically competitive firms will produce with excess capacity ($Q_C - Q_{MC}$).

Waste of Monopolistic Competition
The failure of monopolistically competitive firms to produce at minimum LRAC or, in other words, the tendency to produce with excess capacity.

the **waste of monopolistic competition**. For example, the facilities of most gas stations are hardly ever used to capacity for any length of time, even when there is plenty of gasoline. This is also true of laundromats, restaurants, and grocery stores.

Note in Figure 9-7 that in monopolistic competition, the MR curve lies below the demand curve. Since in order to maximize profits or minimize losses a firm must see that its MR equals its MC, price is always higher than MC. Therefore, in monopolistic competition, as in pure monopoly, firms do not use resources in a way that is socially efficient. Indeed, it is fair to say that this tendency for price to exceed MC (P > MC) is the cost that consumers bear for product differentiation.

Remember that the condition that makes pure competition most attractive is that it ensures that resources are most efficiently allocated to produce that combination of goods consumers prefer. This is so because under pure competition (1) price equals MC, (2) AR equals AC, and (3) quantity produced is at the minimum point on the LRAC curve. These conditions do not exist for the monopolistically competitive firm, because under monopolistic competition (1) price is higher than MC and (2) quantity produced is at a point less than the minimum AC. Therefore, one concludes that under monopolistic competition resources are not as efficiently allocated as they are under pure competition. The tendency to expand output to the rate that equates marginal benefits to consumers and MC to producers is absent under monopolistic competition. As a result, there is some of the welfare loss of monopoly associated with this type of market.

Monopolistic Competition: A Caveat

In spite of the statement above, we need to keep in mind that the demand curve for a monopolistically competitive firm is typically highly elastic. One economist, Leonard Weiss, says the price elasticity of demand is typically 5.0! The results—in terms of the relations between price, cost, and output—often approach those of pure competition. In many monopolistically competitive industries, these differences or wastes may not be large enough to be significant. Furthermore, whatever inefficiencies do result from monopolistic competition may be interpreted, as we noted earlier, as the cost society must pay to obtain the variety of choices (benefits) that product differentiation gives the consumer. But more about that in the final section of this chapter.

A Policy Question:
Is Monopolistic Competition Often as Close as We *Can* Get and *Want* to Get to Pure Competition?

We have examined the kind of market known as pure competition and discovered that its biggest advantage is the efficient allocation of resources that occurs when MC (what it costs the firm to produce one more unit of product) becomes equal to price (what the consumer is willing to pay for that last unit produced). But outside of agriculture and commodity and stock markets, pure competition is rare. And even inside agriculture, government interference blurs the distinctions. As a fitting conclusion to our look at markets that are "not quite" purely competitive, let's reiterate how product differentiation arises and assess its costs and benefits.

Forms of Differentiation: A Reminder
Location. There's an old saying that if you want opportunity to knock, you must put your door where opportunity is likely to be. This is particularly true for the millions of small-scale businesses in a monopolistically competitive industry. For them, *location* is a prime element in product differentiation. For example, for a laundromat, location is the main form of differentiation. It also helps if the place is clean, if the machines work, and if the attendant is courteous. But these are small factors compared to location. If people must choose between 2 laundromats in 2 different locations, charging the same

price, they generally go to the one that is closer. Customers who live an equal distance from the 2 are indifferent. But if Laundromat A charges more than B, they go to Laundromat B. Laundromat B also gains the favor of all those who find the inconvenience of going to B less onerous than the extra price charged by A.

When location is what makes one firm's product differ from another's, competition reduces price differentials between the 2 firms, so that the only difference that remains is the inconvenience of travel. But to utilize their plant and equipment efficiently, both firms need a certain volume of business. Thus, they must draw customers from outside the immediate neighborhood. However, they cannot price discriminate by charging customers who live nearby a higher fee than customers who live far away. If they could, they could attract clients from a considerable distance. ("I can wash everything in the house for a buck and a half if I'm willing to drive all the way over to U-Save Washeteria.") But laundromats must offer one price to all comers. This competitive element is what we mean when we say that a *firm's ability to exploit the advantages of location is limited.*

Quality of service is a second major form of product differentiation. A good cook can put a restaurant on the map, even if it's a little hole in the wall. On the other hand, even the dining room at the Ritz will eventually lose customers if the waiters have dirty fingernails and the waitresses are uppity or the food is poorly prepared. For a corner grocery store, differentiation may depend on how helpful the clerks are or on the days and hours of services. In a barber shop or a hairdresser's, trade may pick up if there is an operator who, customers think, performs miracles with hopeless hair.

One cannot easily estimate the value people place on these forms of differentiation. Their impact varies, depending on people's utility functions—in other words, on what it takes to satisfy them. People's feelings about these forms of product differentiation may be strong, weak, or indifferent.

Suppose Hungry Joe's Steak House raises its prices. People who are indifferent (or who make no particular identification with Hungry Joe's) take their business to the Steak Pit, across the way, where prices are a bit lower. No matter that the Steak Pit has a waitress who snarls when you ask for a spoon. These customers regard the two firm's products as good substitutes.

So when it comes to quality of service, here too a *firm's ability to exploit product differentiation is limited.* The reason is that those people with weak feelings about quality of service switch to cheaper products when price differentials widen. But to achieve efficient production, all firms must have a certain minimum volume of business. So competition, coupled with the fickleness of the public, limits a firm's ability to exploit these nonconcrete forms of differentiation.

Fads and fashions seem to come and go, often with bewildering speed. When hula hoops were introduced in 1958, the manufacturer enjoyed the economic success (and profit) associated with selling 110 million of the toys at $3.50 each. The highly differentiated product was an enormous success although it could just as easily have been an enormous flop. After all, no firm has an accurate devise for gauging the tastes and preferences of consumers *before the fact*. The public's tastes can change quickly, though, and 27 months after their introduction, demand dropped until it finally stabilized at about 1 million per year. As the demand declined, the economic profit associated with hula hoops was likely bid out of the industry. This is a very important point to remember about successful monopolistically competitive firms. Economic profits in an industry with free entry, especially one that depends on highly variable consumer tastes, are likely to be short lived. It is interesting to note, as does Suzanne Tregarthen, that hula hoops are coming back into growing demand in the late-1980s, as the original consumers introduce them to their children. How long will the economic profits and prices above MC last this time?

There are many other means of product differentiation, including advertising. Once a firm differentiates its product from that of its competitors, it can use advertising to intensify the difference by implanting it more strongly in the public's mind. This applies both to informational advertising, which lowers the information costs of consumers ("Our shop is right next to Grand Central Station"; "Our cleanser contains no abrasives") and non-informational advertising known as "puffery" ("Love that green box!"; "Don't squeeze the Charmin"). Advertising—if it is informational—does not create differentiation. It only magnifies it.

Because monopolistically competitive firms are typically small and operate in small market areas, their advertising must be local in scope. Therefore, their ads are relatively low cost and do not offer much of a barrier to entry of new firms. Indeed, advertising may enhance entry in many instances. And because of the large number of monopolistically competitive firms and the similarity of their products, advertising is not likely to be a great factor in reducing price competition among them.

Conclusions About Monopolistic Competition

Purely competitive markets and monopolistically competitive markets are very similar. Generally speaking, both consist of many small-scale firms. Both markets are easy for newcomers to break into and leave. Purely competitive industries turn out a homogeneous product; monopolistically competitive industries turn out a differentiated one. The *nature* of the product is what makes the difference. It does not matter whether the differentiation is technical. What matters is how consumers regard the products of different firms. So a monopolistically competitive firm cannot become a purely competitive one. A monopolistic competitor cannot overcome problems caused by differences in location (a gas station on a busy turnpike versus one on a lonely country road). Nor can people who offer personal services—such as barbers or clothes designers—make their services homogeneous. Nobody would even want them to.

As we have seen, it is possible for a firm to so differentiate its product that it can make an economic profit. It may take a great deal of advertising to achieve this differentiation. Or perhaps the product has considerable differentiation built into it (for example, a gas station at the intersection of 2 turnpikes or a restaurant with a top-notch chef). At any rate, the degree to which products can be differentiated is limited. The competition brought about by the large *number* of firms forces price to the point at which most firms can make only normal profits. Free entry into the industry virtually guarantees this result in the long run.

In brief, in many industries, for those products that can be differentiated, monopolistic competition *is* as close as we can get to competition. What is perhaps more important in an economy in which consumer tastes are "sovereign," it may well be as close as we *want* to get. We humans are very diverse and prices slightly above MC may well be a cost we are willing to bear for the benefit of expressing our differences in taste and preference.

SUMMING UP

1. By the 1930s, some economists questioned whether pure competition and pure monopoly alone could explain a modern market economy. Edward Chamberlain developed a theory of monopolistic competition and Joan Robinson a very similar theory of imperfect competition to fill this seeming void.

2. The three main characteristics of *monopolistic competition* or *imperfect competition* are that (a) the number of firms in the industry is large enough that the actions of one firm do not affect the actions of other firms, (b) the product is differentiated, so that the firm gains some control over price, and (c) there is reasonable ease of entry into the industry. In addition, a monopolistically competitive firm unlike a purely competitive firm may gain advantages from advertising.

3. Because a given firm can vary its price without losing all its customers, the demand (AR) curve is highly, but not perfectly, elastic, and the MR curve lies below it.

4. Product differentiation or preferences by consumers for the product of one firm over those of another firm derive from many things including (a) location, (b) personal services, (c) advertising.

5. Product differentiation is related to the price elasticity of demand for a firm's product. The less differentiated the product, the smaller is the price elasticity. A firm prefers a more differentiated (less elastic)

demand to a less differentiated (more elastic) demand because of greater ability to set price above that of other firms in the industry.

6. In the short run, the monopolistically competitive firm faces the same four possible profit or loss situations as a firm in a purely competitive or a purely monopolistic situation: economic profit, normal profit, economic loss with production, and economic loss with shutdown.

7. In the long run, because of easy entry and the large number of firms in a monopolistically competitive industry, the probability is that a firm will earn only a normal profit. However, because of relative product differentiation, a firm may make an economic profit. Economic losses do not occur, because any firms that might incur losses in the long run would instead leave an industry with free exit.

8. In the long run, competitive firms produce at minimum AC (economic capacity) and sell at a price equal to MC. Monopolistically competitive firms, however, operate with excess capacity and, while setting a price equal to AC, sell at prices greater than MC. The failure to utilize plant and equipment to capacity levels is referred to as the "wastes of monopolistic competition."

9. In comparison to a typical firm in pure competition, a typical firm in monopolistic competition has higher prices, lower output, and higher AC. Resources are not allocated efficiently because price is greater than MC, and output is at a point that is less than the minimum point on the AC curve. The excess of price over MC is the price consumers pay for differentiated products and a wider variety of choices. However, because of the relatively high degree of competition, these differences may not be significant.

KEY TERMS

Monopolistic competition
Product differentiation
Waste of monopolistic competition

QUESTIONS

1. Define monopolistic competition, and discuss the importance of product differentiation. Give a number of examples of monopolistically competitive industries. In each case, what is the basis of its product differentiation?

2. Compare the curves for average and marginal revenue for firms in monopolistic competition to the average and marginal revenue curves for firms in pure competition and pure monopoly. Why are they different?

3. What are the possible long-run situations with respect to profits or losses for firms in monopolistic competition? Draw the appropriate diagrams.

4. Assuming identical cost curves, compare the economic performance of a firm in monopolistic competition and a firm in pure competition in terms of output, profit or loss, and efficiency. Is the assumption of identical cost curves realistic? Why?

5. In the hypothetical figure below, we see a typical monopolistically competitive firm in long-run equilibrium. Answer the following questions about its market position.

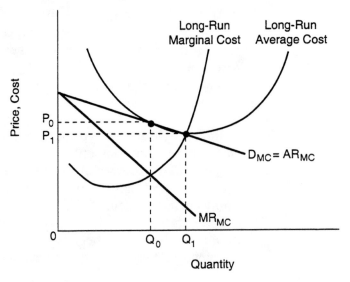

a. What price will the monopolistic competitor set in the long-run? What will be its output rate?

b. What profit will the firm earn, a normal profit or an economic profit?

c. If the firm were a pure competitor, at what price would it sell its product? What would be its output rate?

d. What distance in the figure above represents the firm's excess capacity or the "waste of monopolistic competition"? What determines how great this waste is?

e. Where would the demand curve of the firm ($D_{MC} = AR_{MC}$) have to lie in order for the firm to be an atypical monopolistic competitor earning an economic profit?

6. How are the price elasticity of demand and product differentiation related? Why does a price seeking firm prefer a more differentiated to a less differentiated product?

7. Evaluate the following statement: "Since costs are higher in monopolistic competition, society would clearly be better off in such industries with pure competition."

8. What are the differences between pure competition and monopolistic competition?

9. Describe the different ways firms achieve product differentiation in various industries that may be called monopolistically competitive.

10. Name three monopolistically competitive industries, and identify their chief form of product differentiation. What would be required in order that these industries become purely competitive?

11. Is monopolistic competition as close in many retailing industries as we can usually get to pure competition in the U.S.? Why or why not?

12. If you balance the "wastes of monopolistic competition" against the freedom to express individual tastes and preferences, would you be willing to try to do away with product differentiation to obtain more efficiency in the allocation of resources?

SUGGESTED READINGS

Dobson, John M. "American Enterprise in the Modern World." *A History of American Enterprise*. Especially Ch. 11. Englewood Cliffs, NJ: Prentice Hall, 1988.

McKenzie, Richard B. "Free to Lose: The Bright Side of Economic Failure." *The Entrepreneur*. Summer, 1986. Reprinted in *Economics 88/89*. Annual ed. Guilford, CT: The Dushkin Publishing Group, Inc., 1988.

Thomas, Robert P. "Monopolistic Competition: The Rag Trade." *Microeconomic Applications*. Especially Ch. 17. Belmont, CA: Wadsworth Publishing Co., 1981.

Tregarthen, Suzanne. "The Hula Hoop Comes Around—Again!" *The Margin*. September/October, 1987.

Tregarthen, Timothy and Suzanne. "Hard Times for Fast Food." *The Margin*. November/December, 1988.

CHAPTER 10

Oligopoly

"What's good for the country is good for General Motors, and vice versa."

Charles E. Wilson

OBJECTIVES

After studying this chapter you will be able to:

- Compare the role of advertising in oligopolies with the role of advertising in other market structures.
- Explain the difference between a trust and a cartel.
- Explain the assumptions of the Edgeworth model
- Describe what is conscious parallelism.
- Have a working knowledge of the following terms and concepts:

Cartel	Kinked demand
Conscious parallelism	Oligopoly
Duopoly	Sales maximization hypothesis
Interdependency	Trust

Imperfect Competition Among the Few

Definition of Oligopoly

Back in 1953, President Eisenhower appointed Charles E. Wilson, then president of General Motors, as Secretary of Defense. When the appointment came before the Senate for confirmation, Wilson promised that he would sever all ties with GM before he took office. Senator Richard Russell, then chairman of the Senate Armed Services Committee, asked, "Would you make a decision adverse to General Motors?"

Wilson answered, in what has been one of the most quoted remarks made by a businessman in the past century: "What's good for the country is good for General Motors. And vice versa."

Wilson's statement contained a great deal of truth, because one-sixth of the nations jobs depend to some extent on motor vehicle production and use, and GM although declining in its dominance of the automobile industry, remains the largest firm in that industry.

The American automotive industry employs almost a million workers. The 6 top firms in the automotive industry make 92 percent of all cars and trucks and car bodies produced in the U.S.

This same top-heaviness or concentration also occurs in other industries, aluminum, for instance. The 4 largest firms in the aluminum industry produce 96 percent of the aluminum made in the U.S. Steel is another example. The 4 largest steel companies in the U.S. manufacture more than 50 percent of the steel produced in the U.S.

These examples are in sharp contrast with the apparel industry which is monopolistically competitive and in which the top 4 firms producing women's and misses' dresses produce only 6 percent of industry output.

Oligopoly
An industry with a few sellers. Products may be homogeneous or differentiated and there are substantial barriers to entry.

So you can see that many basic industries in the U.S. economy are characterized not by pure competition, not by monopolistic competition, not even by monopoly, but by the dominance of a small number of firms. This market situation is called **oligopoly** (literally, a "few sellers"). Its other characteristics are that it may have homogeneous or differentiated products and that it has substantial barriers to entry of other firms into the industry.

Oligopoly is an important market model in this study because it fits much of the basic manufacturing activity of the U.S. economy. Indeed oligopoly and "big business" are nearly synonymous in modern economies. Oligopoly encompasses the bulk of manufacturing and food processing. The automobile and steel industries, oil refineries, aluminum-producing industries, and many other industries are oligopolistic. To understand a large part of the American economy, one must understand oligopolistic markets.

Following this chapter, we will present an application dealing with oligopoly: case studies of the behavior of oligopolistic industries.

Number of Firms: Small

In an oligopolistic industry, there are only a few firms that dominate the market. By few, we mean that the number of dominating firms is so small *that the actions of one affect the actions of all other firms in the industry.* This interaction is called **interdependency** and is recognized by the interdependent firms. That is, firms in oligopolistic industries know that they are interdependent as to policies of price and output.

Interdependency
The condition that exists in an industry when the actions of one firm affect the actions of all other firms in the industry.

Let's consider automobiles again. Four firms turn out 92 percent of the cars and trucks produced in the U.S. Ford Motor Company, to protect its own markets, must try to foresee what GM, Chrysler, and other firms are likely to do with regard to pricing, styling, and other sensitive aspects of production. And how will these firms react to changes in pricing, styling and other aspects by Ford? In other words, automobile companies are interdependent, and each reacts to the economic decisions of the others in the industry.

Of the 22 firms in the steel industry, as we said, the top 4 produce 50 percent of the output and tend to dominate the smaller firms. In the computer field, the number of firms is larger, but IBM is the dominant firm by far.

Product: Both Homogeneous and Differentiated

Some oligopolistic industries produce a homogeneous product and others differentiated products. Examples of homogeneous products include steel and electrical equipment. Most steel items are produced according to specifications. The buyer specifies the desired strength, composition, weight, and shape of the steel product, and most steel companies can meet these specifications. The same can be said of electrical equipment. Although different companies may offer their customers variations in the way of credit terms, delivery, or servicing, both sets of products are essentially homogeneous.

The automotive industry is an example of differentiated oligopoly. In that industry companies go to great lengths to turn out differentiated products. They want consumers to be able to distinguish one car from another on the basis of name, car model, styling, and quality. Intensive advertising magnifies these real and not so real differences.

However, firms in oligopolistic industries that produce homogeneous products do not have much chance to compete with each other, except by pricing. Oligopolistic industries that produce differentiated products (such as cars, washing machines, cigarettes, and computers) can always introduce variations in their products and call attention to the difference by advertising. This lessens the necessity to compete with other firms' prices. Nonprice competition may replace price competition.

Barriers to Entry: Substantial

Since there are only a few firms in an oligopolistic industry, there must be substantial barriers to entry of new firms. We have talked at some length about the various barriers to entry. In an oligopolistic industry, of the many barriers to entry, the following are most likely to keep out newcomers: (1) patents and copyrights; (2) technology that requires such high levels of output for the firm to reach economies of scale that new firms must start producing in enormous quantities; (3) the size of the market in relation to the economies of scale; (4) various forms of economic warfare that can prevent new firms from entering the industry or force small, weak ones out; (5) costs of product differentiation (new firms *may* have to spend much more to get consumers to accept their product than existing firms spend to maintain consumer acceptance); (6) control of sources of raw materials by existing firms; and (7) various activities of government that restrict entry, either deliberately or incidentally (for example, patents, licensing, government contracting, and marketing quotas).

Behavior of the Oligopolistic Firm

Oligopoly is the only kind of market that encompasses recognized interdependence between firms. How do rival firms react to decisions of other firms in an oligopoly?

Unfortunately for the sake of simplicity, there is no single set of reactions. Theorists have argued about and empiricists have observed a variety of ways interdependent firms react. Oligopoly, thus, does not lend itself to a single model of a market as do pure competition, pure monopoly, and monopolistic competition. In an oligopolistic industry, there are as many ways theoretically that an individual firm can behave as there are assumptions about reaction patterns.

How May Interdependent Firms React? Organization and Collusion

Uncertainty about the reactions of rival firms, coupled with the recognition of interdependency, often create in oligopolistic industries a search for a means of "stabilizing" industry markets. Stability may have many dimensions but predictable prices and predictable market shares are surely among the most important ones. Broadly speaking, the search for a stable reaction pattern involves two key dimensions: (1) interdependent firms may seek to organize the industry market, and (2) such firms may create a pattern of explicit or implicit collusive behavior.

To identify the spectrum of oligopolistic markets as well as to assess the economic effects in different industries, economists traditionally divide oligopolies into three classes. These divisions are based on differences in reaction patterns:

Oligopoly Class	Reaction Pattern
I	Organized, collusive
II	Unorganized, collusive
III	Unorganized, non-collusive

We will examine each of these oligopoly reaction patterns in turn. Our purpose is to understand the reasons for these differences in behavior and, more importantly, to weigh their effects on society and its uses of resources.

Class I Oligopolies: Organization and Collusion

Trust
An organization that controls the voting shares of an industry and thus can set output rates and prices like a multi-plant monopoly.

Cartel
An organization made up of independent firms who join together to set output rates and prices in a way that will give them the benefits of monopoly.

If the industry's market is unstable, perhaps with market shares changing widely, price wars developing from time to time and, in general with conditions that make short-run output and long-run planning decisions difficult to execute, firms may turn to monopolization as a way to create stability. As with multi-plant monopoly, rivals may create an explicit organization to enforce predictable prices and market shares. While there are many forms of business organization that might be employed, we will mention two of the most prominent: (1) trusts, and (2) cartels. A **trust** is an organization that controls the voting shares of the nominally independent firms in the industry. Because it can assign output rates, divide markets and set prices, the trust has total control of the industry as would a multi-plant monopoly. A **cartel**, unlike a trust, is made up of independent firms who join together to set output rates and prices in a way that will give them the benefits of a monopoly.

We see in Figure 10-1 how a cartel (c) or trust (t) would likely set price and determine output for the group. Examining the market, industry demand is identified as D and marginal revenue as MR. Summing the marginal costs (MC) of individual firms in the group yields $\Sigma MC_{c,t}$. Cartel or trust decision makers, seeking to maximize

Figure 10-1
Price and Output Decisions by a Trust or Cartel: Organized, Collusive Oligopoly

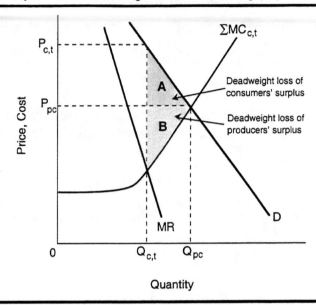

In Figure 10-1, the cartel (c) or trust (t), acting for the industry examines the industry demand (D) and marginal revenue (MR). Summing the marginal costs (MC) of its member firms ($\Sigma MC_{c,t}$), it sets a price ($P_{c,t}$) that will maximize industry profits and produces $Q_{c,t}$. It assigns output rate (shares of the market) that will minimize the total cost of producing $Q_{c,t}$. The purely competitive solution in Figure 10-1 is where ΣMC cuts demand with output Q_{pc} and price P_{pc}.

group profits, equate marginal cost and MR, and decide that the group will produce $Q_{c,t}$ and set price at $P_{c,t}$. In assigning output rates among member firms, units of output will be produced by the firm with the lowest MC. As costs rise at one plant, other plants will be brought into production and, in equilibrium, MC will be equated throughout the industry.

Efficiency Effects of Class I Oligopolies

An examination of Figure 10-1 will show that class I oligopolies tend to produce the same efficiency losses as pure monopolies. Note that the same loss of consumers' and producers' surplus (deadweight loss = A + B) occurs in both cases. Output ($Q_{c,t}$) is reduced below that of pure competition (Q_{pc}) rather than expanded to the rate that equates the marginal benefit of consumers with the MC of producers. Allocative inefficiency, in other words, tends to be the same in class I oligopoly as in pure monopoly.

Social Reaction to Class I Oligopolies: The Antitrust Laws

In view of the above conclusions, it is not surprising that a nation whose economic traditions and rules are founded in the anti-monopoly provisions of English common law rarely sanctions class I behavior. Probably prohibited in that common law, the behavior was explicitly banned in the Sherman (anti-trust) Act of 1890. Section I of that Act declares that:

Every contract, combination in the form of trust or otherwise, or conspiracy, in restraint of trade or commerce among the several states or with foreign nations, is hereby declared illegal.

Although weakly enforced in its early years, the Sherman Act was strengthened by the Clayton Act of 1914 which banned the use of price discrimination to restrain trade. The Act also restricted or banned other anti-competitive behavior such as **interlocking directorates** where individuals serve on the boards of directors of more than one firm within the same industry. Other legislation followed including the Federal Trade Commission Act which created a Federal Agency (FTC) to police deceptive advertising and "unfair methods of competition." Along with these acts came the Robinson-Patman Act of 1936 which banned selling products at "unreasonably low prices" to reduce competition. Finally, the Celler-Kefauver Act of 1950 prohibited firms from acquiring the assets of other firms if the effect would be to reduce competition.

Although these laws were intended to deal with much more than class I oligopoly behavior, their interpretation by the courts has created guidelines, though not always clear ones, for evaluating oligopoly behavior. One such guideline is known as the **per se rule** under which certain types of business behavior are deemed to be illegal, per se. The behavior itself, in other words, is presumed illegal. Conduct or proved behavior rather than intent is the test under this rule. Presumably, most if not all class I behavior which leads to organizing markets, falls under this *per se* rule. The government need merely prove the occurrence of the behavior to show its illegality.

In the application in this chapter, we will examine some actual cases of oligopoly behavior including some that fall within class I. A famous such case occurred in the 1960s with the conviction of various individuals who sought to "stabilize" the electrical equipment industry market by rigging its bid prices.

It is worth reminding ourselves that governments sometimes sanction the kind of covert collusion seen in class I oligopolies. Recall that the CAB administered a cartel in the airline industry for decades. The federal government establishes sugar import quotas for countries in order to keep U.S. sugar prices at non-competitive levels. The key point to remember though is that covert, collusive (class I) behavior is generally deemed to be illegal *per se* unless it is *specifically* sanctioned by government.

Class II Oligopolies: Unorganized But Collusive

It is organizing markets, practices such as "rigging" prices and getting together to divide up markets that incur the wrath of public disapproval and the severe penalties including jail terms that may be

Interlocking Directorates
A practice in which individuals serve on the boards of directors of more than one firm in the same industry.

Per se Rule
A rule in law that certain acts are illegal in and of themselves, no matter what their intent.

meted out under the antitrust laws. Although such behavior continues (about a dozen cases per year are prosecuted under the federal antitrust laws), its opportunity costs for oligopolistic firms are high.

To avoid the clear illegality of covert collusion as well as the uncertainties and inflexibility of non-collusive oligopoly, many industries have turned to various forms of implicit collusion that do not involve organization. Once such form is called **price leadership**, a practice under which a dominant firm in an industry establishes prices that are then followed by other firms in the industry. The leader-follower agreement, while almost always tacit rather than explicit, tends to be widely observed throughout the industry. The steel and automobile industries have been cited by those who have studied them as examples of price leadership by dominant firms. In the case of steel, the dominant firm (at least in the twentieth century) has been U.S. Steel (now USX). In the automobile industry, the dominant firm (at least since the 1930s) has been GM. Price leadership does not mean that no other firm ever sets prices or that other firms necessarily wait for the dominant firm to announce new prices; rather, it means that at most points in time other so called "fringe" firms *adjust* their prices to those of the leader. Notice, however, that this is not a market sharing agreement as such; indeed, market shares may change.

Figure 10-2 depicts graphically how prices and output rates might be determined in a dominant firm—fringe firm class II oligopoly. The dominant firm observes industry demand D and also estimates the demand for its own output ($d_{price\ leader}$) and MR ($mr_{price\ leader}$). Acting exclusively on its own market situation, the price leader equates its own MC ($MC_{price\ leader}$) with mr, produces Q_d and sets price P_d. Note that in Figure 10-2, the dominant firm is shown with higher MC than those of the fringe firm ($MC_{fringe\ firms}$). The dominant firm is prepared to let the fringe firms fill any share of the market they find profitable so these firms, in the aggregate, equate their (lower) MC with MR_f. Why is the price of the dominant firm equal to MR for the fringe firms? Because, they are now price takers and can sell all the steel they wish to produce at that price; i.e., $P_d = MR_f$. The fringe firms equate mr_f with MC_f and produce Q_f or in other words fill the remainder of the market ($Q_l - Q_d$) at P_d. The total quantity supplied and demanded at price P_d is Q_l of which the dominant firm fills Q_d and fringe firms fill Q_f.

Efficiency Implications of Class II Oligopoly
It is easy to see why the interdependent private firms represented in Figure 10-2 would regard the leader-follower relationship as mutually beneficial. The price leader, faced with (relatively high) costs would be able to set a price that at least covers its opportunity costs. The fringe firms, acting on that price and producing with lower costs could produce as much steel as they wish (up to the point at which industry quantity supplied = quantity demanded). The fringe firms

Price Leadership
A form of implicit collusion in which a leader firm sets prices that are observed and followed by other firms in the industry.

Figure 10-2
Price Leadership by a Dominant Firm (Class II Oligopoly)

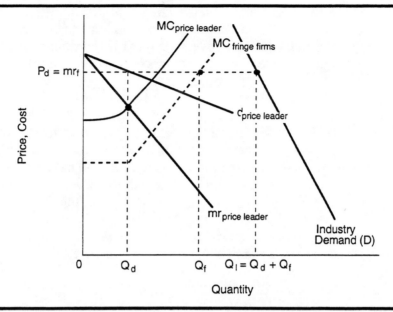

In Figure 10-2, a dominant firm exercises price leadership in a class II oligopolistic industry. The dominant firm is shown as having higher MC ($MC_{price\ leader}$) than the fringe firms ($MC_{fringe\ firms}$). Estimating the demand for its own output ($d_{price\ leader}$) and its MR ($mr_{price\ leader}$) the firm sets a price (P_d) that will maximize its own profit and produces Q_d. Fringe firms, acting on P_d find that they are price takers, thus ($P_d = mr_f$. Fringe firms equating mr_f with their MC produce Q_f. The price leader and the fringe firms together fill the market at P_d; i.e., industry output (Q_l) equals output of the dominant firm (Q_d) plus output of the fringe firms (Q_f).

would presumably have higher rates of return than the dominant firm. No one, privately, would clearly benefit more from the alternative of price competition.

What, though, of *society's* interests from such an arrangement? Remember that in a competitive industry, price tends in the long run toward the average and the marginal cost of the *typical* firm. Competitive firms have an insistent pressure to innovate in order to keep costs down and to achieve rates of return equal to opportunity costs. In the hypothetical case in Figure 10-2, price will clearly tend to exceed MC (allocative inefficiency) and there will be at least some of the deadweight losses of monopoly. Perhaps as importantly, the dominant firm has little incentive to innovate, at least until its high cost plants are liquidated. While the fringe firms have an incentive to innovate and produce more low cost steel at the leader's price, the entire industry may be one with a relatively slow rate of innovation.

Some students of the American steel industry believe that the model in Figure 10-2 explains much of that industry's slow rate of innovation and, in the post World War II period, at least part of its relatively non-competitive position in international steel markets. By comparison with a more competitive industry, the industry might well deserve a grade of "D" for innovation.

Can all of the conclusions above about the class II oligopoly of Figure 10-2 be extended to other class II industries? We warned you at the outset of the chapter that oligopolies are not simple to analyze. The answer is *no*. Imagine that the cost conditions of firms in the industry were reversed. What if the dominant firm were also the one with the lowest marginal costs. While the price leader under those circumstances would set a price above its MC and allocative inefficiency would result, the firm, in order to maintain its dominance would have an incentive to innovate. The "typical" firm would tend to behave more like a competitive firm in terms of innovation. Fringe firms would have little choice but to follow both the leaders' prices and its pattern of innovation. Those who have studied the automobile industry believe that it has exhibited a pattern of this sort and might deserve a "B+" for innovation as compared with the "A" of a competitive industry. Again, it is important to remember that oligopolistic industries must be studied almost case by case to understand their conduct and performance.

Class III Oligopolies: Unorganized, Non-Collusive

You might suppose that interdependent firms searching for market stability and predictability and ruling out organization as an acceptable response, would create some pattern of tacit collusion such as price leadership. Not necessarily so. What if no firm succeeds in establishing its dominance? What happens, in other words, if an oligopolistic industry has neither organization (no "smoke-filled" rooms and price rigging) nor collusion (no leader-follower relationship)?

This question about a third pattern of oligopoly behavior arose in the mid-20th century because some economists[1] thought they observed a new and puzzling phenomenon in oligopoly markets; that of price rigidity. Prices in competitive markets as well as in monopoly and monopolistically competitive markets may adjust rapidly to changing cost or demand conditions. Even OPEC's administered price for oil to say nothing of highly competitive prices such as shares on the New York Stock Exchange move up or down in response to such changes. Why then, thought some, do we observe that some oligopoly prices (especially consumer durables such as washing machines, refrigerators, TV sets, and computers) seem to change only infrequently and often only by large amounts. One explanation offered was based upon a peculiar assumption about how class III oligopolists react to each other. That assumption gave rise to the kinked demand curve model.

---

[1] Especially Paul Sweezy in the United States and R. L. Hall and C. J. Hitch in the United Kingdom

The Kinked Demand Assumptions

We see in Figure 10-3 how the assumptions of the kinked demand model create the kink or discontinuity in the demand curve. The initial equilibrium or going price for the oligopolistic firm is $20. This is where demand curve D and demand curve d intersect. The relatively inelastic curve (D) above the price of $20 is based on the presumption that rivals will ignore any price increase by this firm. The relatively elastic demand curve (d), on the other hand, is based on the presumption that rivals will follow any decrease in price below $20 by the firm. The key assumption in this model is the following:

Rivals are expected to follow price decreases but to ignore price increases.

Based on this assumption, it is unprofitable for the oligopolistic firm either to raise price or lower price. If it raises price in Figure 10-3 to $22, quantity demanded falls to 1,400 rather than the 1,900 that would result if rivals followed its price initiative. TR would decrease (from $40,000 to $30,800). If the firm lowers price to $18, quantity demanded increases to 2,200 rather than the 2,800 that would

Figure 10-3
The Kinked (Conjectural) Demand Curve of a Class III Oligopoly Firm

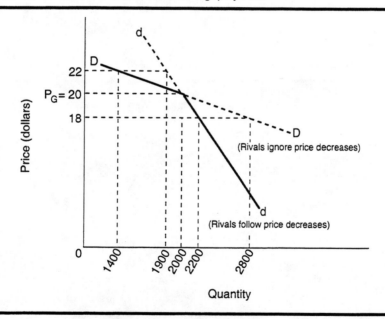

The kinked demand model assumes rivals will ignore price increases but follow price decreases. In Figure 10-3, the going price for the oligopolistic firms' product is P_G = $20. At that price, if it changes price (for example, lowering it to $18), the effect on the quantity demanded, its product depends on the reaction of rival firms. If rivals ignore the price decrease quantity demanded is 2,800 and TR rises (from $40,000 to $50,400). If rivals follow the decrease, TR falls ($40,000 to $39,600). If the firm raises price and rivals ignore the price increase, quantity demanded decreases to 1,400 and TR falls (from $40,000 to $30,800). If the firm raises price and others follow the price increase, quantity demanded falls to 1,900 and TR increases ($40,000 to $41,800). The firm's conjectural demand curve, therefore, is the solid portion of D above $20 and the solid portion of d below $20. The demand curve is discontinuous or has a kink at the going price.

result if rivals ignored its price decrease. TR would fall as a result of a price decrease (from $40,000 to $39,600). The net result of the assumption above is that the firm (and all such firms in class III oligopolies) would not change price; prices would be sticky or rigid both upward and downward.

Kinked Demands, Sticky Prices, and Sluggish Output: Is This the Worst of Oligopoly?

In Figure 10-4, we can see more clearly what the allocative implications of kinked demand oligopoly are D_K, the kinked demand curve is derived from the solid portions of the two demand curves (D, d) in Figure 10-3. Since demand is relatively elastic for prices above $20, there is one MR curve for those prices (MR [P > $20]). Since demand is relatively inelastic for prices below $20, there is a different MR curve for those prices (MR [P < $20]). At the kink ($P_G = $20), there is a *gap* between these two MR curves within which the firm operates. It produces 2,000 units at the going price of $20.

The firm, according to this model would not undertake to change price and output because it would be unprofitable to do so. Prices could be sticky for long periods of time even if there were mild inflation or if demand changes occurred. Only if MC shifted upward or downward by enough to cut either MR for price increases or price decreases would the firm change price and output. The key implication of this model then is:

Figure 10-4
The Kinked Demand Curve and Price and Output Rigidity in Class III Oligopoly

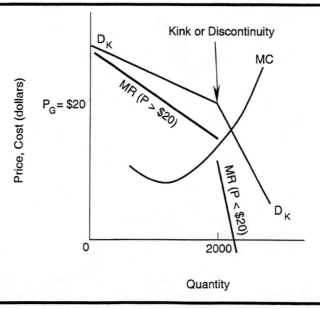

In Figure 10-4 the MC of the class III oligopoly are added to the kinked demand curve of Figure 10-3. The firm will continue to sell at the going price ($20) and produce the equilibrium output (2,000) so long as the MC curve cuts the discontinuous portion of the MR curves for price increases (MR [P > $20]) and price decreases (MR [P < $20]).

Prices are rigid in class III oligopolies. Changes in price and output occur infrequently and then only as a result of major variations in cost or demand that cause all firms in the industry to adjust price.

Relevancy of Kinked Demand Oligopoly

It is worth reminding ourselves that the kinked demand model applies only to oligopoly cases in which there is neither organization nor collusion. Some economists have been highly critical of the model for they regard it as having little or no public policy implication. It would certainly be a mistake to conclude that oligopolies in general are unresponsive to changes in cost (that they neither undertake nor implement changes in technology) as well as unresponsive to changes in demand (that they do not respond to or seek to cause changes in consumer tastes and the like). We observe the opposite in many oligopolistic industries. Indeed, it may be that technological innovation and the research and development activities that precede it are at least as prevalent in oligopolistic industries as in others. We clearly observe that advertising and other activities intended to change firm demand curves and to create brand loyalty are higher in such industries than in others. If oligopoly firms (in all three classes) choose not to engage in price competition, they seem often to turn instead to various forms of nonprice competition.

Nonprice Competition Among the Few

It is somewhat ironic that one observes either very intense price rivalry, including warfare, in oligopolistic industries or virtually none at all. It may seem, in other words, that either all firms want (unsuccessfully) to be the leader or firms create stability through collusion or organization. However, firms in oligopolistic industries do compete aggressively for larger shares of the market. And since they use price competition infrequently in their struggle, they substitute various forms of nonprice competition, such as styling, services, quality, and advertising. Let's look at each of these briefly.

Styling

One common form of nonprice competition is variation in the styling of the commodity. One company differentiates its product from that of the others by changes in color and shape—that is, in style. For example, washing-machine manufacturers offer a selection of colors rather than only white, and build in an array of buttons, dials, and levers to attract buyers. Automobile manufacturers, of course, use styling as a tool of competition to such a degree that they spend billions to retool every few years, just so their cars will look different.

Services

Variations in services rendered are another well-known form of nonprice competition in oligopolistic industries. For example, in the computer industry, software services vary, both in extent and quality. These services, which include items such as the training of staff and the offering of a number of standard programs, go along with the hardware and are important factors in determining sales. (IBM has a strong competitive advantage in these services.) Retail chains of stores use delivery service and various kinds of credit terms to attract customers. All these are forms of nonprice competition.

Quality

Quality is one form of nonprice competition that definitely benefits the consumer: firms compete with each other by improving the quality of their products. For example, in the automobile industry, innovations such as fuel injectors, power brakes, power steering, better gasoline mileage, and many other improvements have given their initiators competitive advantages. (Some representatives of the Chicago school of economics, a group of economists whose thinking has been influenced by the work of Milton Friedman, say that if true differences in quality exist, there are really two different products. For our purposes here, it makes little difference whether the products are considered differentiated or close substitutes.)

Nonprice competition in the form of variations in styling, services, and quality may definitely benefit the consumer. Or, some argue, they may be useless to the consumer and a waste of resources. The garment industry is well known for introducing new styles to make people feel that their present clothes are out of date. Is this a waste of resources? Or do consumers derive utility from a continuously changing set of choices? Economists, unable to measure consumer tastes, find it difficult to agree on the answer. The automobile industry is another example. The social (or even economic) rationale behind the auto makers' compulsion to change body styles every few years escapes many observers. Yet, an argument can be made again that consumers derive utility from these opportunities to express individual tastes and preferences.

Advertising

An important form of nonprice competition in the consumer-goods markets is advertising. Rather than compete by lowering their prices, oligopolistic firms often try to influence demand by advertising. Let us now take a hard look at advertising. What are the pros and what are the cons?

The Case for Advertising. Five main arguments have been used to justify advertising on the grounds that it is beneficial to the consumer and improves the allocation of resources:

1. Advertising increases the demand for the firm's output, and as a result the price to the consumer decreases. Because of increased

demand, the firm makes more of the product, which means that this increased demand has the effect of raising the level of output, and thus lowering the cost per unit (on the assumption that initially average cost falls as output rises; in other words, that there are economies of scale). This decrease in production cost per unit may outweigh the increase in selling cost caused by advertising. Then the price to the consumer may decrease and resources may be used with increased efficiency.

Figure 10-5 shows the situation graphically. Suppose a company does not advertise. With demand d, it may set price *BA*. Then the company starts advertising, and the demand for its product increases (curve shifts to the right) to d′. So it increases output to *C*. "Cost" now includes both production and selling costs. However, the improved efficiency, due to economies of scale as output increases, more than compensates for the higher cost of selling the product. The AC of making the product is therefore less (*CD*) *with* advertising than without (*BA*). Thus, there is a possibility that the company may cut its prices as from *BA* to *CD*.

2. Advertising lowers the information costs of consumers. It provides information that consumers need in order to make intelligent choices among competing products. There is such a large number of commodities and they have so many variations, that the consumer benefits from lower cost choices. Who (and where) are the sellers? What does the product do? What are the differences between it and similar products? Advertising can provide this information; in some cases, advertising is the only source of it. Imagine if there were no newspapers or other means to convey retail prices to buyers at low

Figure 10-5

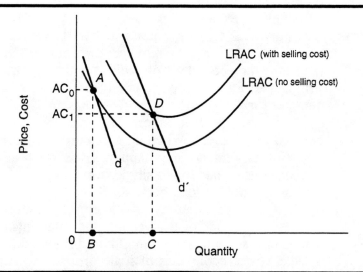

In Figure 10-5, AC is lowered from AC_0 to AC_1. An increase in demand for a product from d to d′, brought about by advertising, can decrease the unit cost of it enough to offset the increased cost of selling it, and may make it possible for the company to sell the product for less.

cost. How much greater would the opportunity costs to consumers be if they had to obtain this information by other more costly means?

3. Advertising produces the money to support, partly or completely, the media for mass communication. Television is almost wholly supported by advertising, and this is "free" to viewers. (Of course, American viewers must put up with the commercials. But in England and in other countries in Europe, although there are no commercials, TV owners must pay a high annual license fee for each set they own.) Newspapers and magazines would cost a lot more if they did not carry advertising. In other words, advertising provides "free" TV and makes possible newspapers and magazines that the public can afford to buy. By now, we hope that you will recognize that this is a specious argument since resources with opportunity costs must be used to produce these media, no matter how the resource funding is obtained. In other words, here, as in all cases, there is no "free lunch."

4. Advertising, as a side benefit, often conveys to the public helpful messages incidental to advertising the product. For example, toothpaste ads have stimulated better dental-care habits.

5. Advertising enables firms to differentiate their products. Consumers seem to have a taste for product differentiation. In other words, they like variety, and advertising enables firms to give them variety. Additionally, this ability to differentiate may facilitate entry of new firms and enhance market competitiveness.

The Case Against Advertising. Now let's look at the opposite side of the coin, the arguments against advertising.

1. Advertising may increase an individual firm's demand and cause its output to increase, achieving economies of scale, so that production costs fall more than selling costs. In this way, advertising may enable the individual firm to cut its costs. However, advertising has a beneficial effect on the entire economy only if the increased demand (and thus the economies of scale) for the product of the individual firm that advertises is not diverted from rival firms, thus reducing the demand for *their* products, and increasing *their* costs. There is no evidence, though, that advertising does increase aggregate or total demand in a society. When an economy is at full employment, this diversion of demand may happen. Even when advertising does not stimulate the demand for a single firm's product, it causes changes in the composition of total demand. Since the public has only so much income, and the economy at full employment so many resources, increased demand for a given product must mean a decline in the demand for some other commodity (or commodities) and a reduction in other firms' economies of scale. In other words, the benefits one firm gains from advertising may at the same time worsen the cost situation for some other firms. Society thus may not gain a *net* increase in technical efficiency (reduction in cost).

Even if production costs for an individual firm did fall more than selling costs increased, this decrease would benefit the consumer only if prices were to fall as a result. And companies lower their prices only if it is profitable to do so. So a new company that enters a monopolistically competitive industry can use advertising to stimulate demand and to gain economies of scale. When the monopolistic competitor runs into this competition, it cuts prices. But in an oligopolistic industry, since price competition is unlikely, the benefits of cost reductions may not be passed along in the form of lower prices. Furthermore, some argue that advertising increases the strength of product differentiation, and that this reduces, rather than increases, competition.

A substantial part of the money spent on advertising does not lead to overall improved economies of scale. A lot of advertising is retaliatory; it is just a company's way of competing with others and retaliating against the advertising of other firms.

Firms use competitive-retaliatory advertising as a substitute for price competition. It may surprise you to know that the various firms in a given industry work out a balance as to the relative intensity with which they will advertise. Periodically, however, an advertising war breaks out. For example, in the soap industry in the mid-1960s, an advertising war broke out between Procter and Gamble and Lever Brothers. Procter and Gamble wanted to take some share of the market away from the industry leader, Lever Brothers, and therefore launched a vigorous advertising campaign for their product, Dash. There were detergent ads everywhere, with washing machines ten feet tall. Lever Brothers fought back for their detergent All by showing a man messing up clean clothes and saying, "All out cleans them all." The net results were no improvement in economies of scale, a somewhat larger share of the market for Procter and Gamble, and tens of millions of dollars of advertising costs added to the cost of soap to the consumer.

2. To the extent that an advertisement gives information the consumer needs in order to make rational choices, that advertisement is economically justified. On the other hand, the advertising may be simply "puffery" or non-informational. Since costs to consumers include not only the prices paid for goods but the information cost to make rational choices, informational advertising may actually lower costs. Puffery consists of an ad showing a beautiful woman squeezing out of a tube of shaving cream or a football player yelling, "I've come back." Some advertising may even be false and misleading. It is the job of the Federal Trade Commission to restrain or prevent such practices that seem to be confined primarily to firms that do not depend on repeat business.

3. The argument that advertising provides "free" TV and cheap newspapers and magazines is not, as we indicated before, valid. The huge sums of money that companies pay out in advertising fees to the

various media must come from somewhere; they are included in the prices of the products. (Some thoughtful observers have pointed out that when advertising "pays" for TV, it merely redistributes the cost of TV to many people who do not watch TV but use the products advertised.) The consumer pays for TV, newspapers, and magazines, not directly, but indirectly, when she or he buys the product advertised. The indirectness of this payment blurs the consumer's understanding of the link between costs and services. Furthermore, the consumer who pays, albeit indirectly, for the media does not have any control over the media. The advertisers not only do not really pay for the media, but they can, and often do, unduly influence what appears in the media.

(The question of who really pays advertising costs, like the question of who really pays excise or sales taxes, is more complex than this brief rundown would lead you to expect. Who does the actual paying depends to a great extent on the elasticities of demand and supply. However, if we assume that manufacturers have long-run costs that are constant, the conclusion that the costs of advertising by oligopolistic industries are passed on to the consumer is substantially correct.)

4. The argument that toothpaste ads have encouraged the public to form better dental habits may hold water, but advertising in other areas is not so beneficial. For example, television ads can encourage the public to form harmful habits: For years, until the ban on cigarette advertising on TV, the cigarette companies sold cancer along with their cigarettes. TV advertising also exercises subtle influences on

"The commercials will be on in a minute—we can say grace then."

the public's attitude toward women. The Comet cleanser and Folger coffee ads demeaned women by depicting them as being incapable of making a good cup of coffee or of cleaning a sink. Car advertisements feature beautiful women in scanty clothes along with the cars; this is one of the most blatant examples of the use of sex to sell a product. While the effort may be successful, its social consequences may impose other kinds of costs. In the 1980s, such sexual stereotyping was extended to men who were portrayed as ineffective, even buffoons.

Hardly anyone wants to ban advertising altogether, if only because advertising's information-giving function is a vital one in this complex economic world. However, there are a number of problems: (1) advertisers circulating misinformation, (2) nonsense ads and economic warfare through advertisements, and (3) high levels of retaliatory advertising.

Profit Maximization: Fact or Fancy?

In our analysis of the four market classifications we assumed that any firm produces at the level of output, and charges the price, that will maximize its profits. In both purely competitive and monopolistically competitive situations, this assumption of profit maximization is probably valid. The pressures of competition and the fact that the individual firm has very little or no control over prices mean that most firms must seek profit maximization. (In monopolistic competition, the individual firm does have some ability to affect price, but very little.) However, some economic theorists doubt that in monopoly and oligopoly each firm aims at output and price that result in profit maximization. These theorists have summed up their doubts in the following six ways:

1. The individual firm, whether it wishes to maximize profits or has some other priority, does not have enough data accurately to compute demand, AR, MR, and MC. Without this information, the firm will not know the level of output and price that will cause MR to equal MC.

2. A firm may be afraid that the government will bring an antitrust action against it if it tries to maximize its profits. A firm that succeeds usually wants to expand, and presently it may be the firm that dominates a given industry, which may trigger an investigation or an antitrust suit. For example, during the mid-1960s, to avoid a possible antitrust suit, GM deliberately restricted sales in order to keep from increasing its percentage of the market.

3. A firm may want to avoid adverse public reaction, which is why monopolistic and oligopolistic firms may elect not to push their prices up to the point of profit maximization. In 1989, a manufacturer of an anti-AIDS drug lowered price and offered the drug free to some consumers in response to public outcry. Since oligopolistic firms are

larger and fewer in number than others, they are more visible to the public. (Points 2 and 3 do not refute the assumption of profit maximization; they only point out that at times profit maximization is limited by nonmarket factors.)

4. Firms may decide not to try to maximize profits in the short run in order to keep profits low, and thus discourage potential rivals from entering the industry. This is so because, despite the difficulties of entering monopoly and oligopoly industries, if the profits are high enough, some firms will try. (Not attempting to maximize profits in order to deter entry of new firms is sometimes called **entry limit pricing**.) Here again, the assumption of profit maximization is not violated. The fact that some companies do not try to make maximum profits out of fear of potential competition only points up the complexity of estimating profit maximization as well as the time frame in which it occurs.

> For example, before World War II, Alcoa's long-run pricing policy was predicated partly on the idea of low prices, with the aim of discouraging potential competition. Also, in the funeral industry there is evidence that morticians used less than maximum prices to discourage new people from entering the funeral business.

5. *Sales Maximization*: For firms whose decision makers are not the owners of the firm, a condition that is true of many if not most oligopolies, other considerations than profit maximization may determine price and output. Profit maximization is a process of optimizing whereas the firm's managers may be more concerned with **satisficing** or seeking an acceptable or satisfactory level of profit. This argument is especially associated with Nobel laureate Herbert Simon.

> One important specification of the arguments about satisficing versus maximizing profit is contained in the hypothesis that firms maximize sales rather than profit. This idea, advanced initially by economist William Baumol of Princeton University, is particularly interesting because of its possible applicability to non-owner managed firms. There is some evidence that the salaries and other benefits of such corporate executives are more closely related to the size of the firm than to the firm's rate of return. Managers might, then, have an interest in a larger firm with a larger share of the market than with a more profitable firm. We can see in Figure 10-6 how the two approaches (optimization versus satisficing) work.

> In Figure 10-6, the oligopoly firm seeking to maximize profit will equate MR and MC, produce Q_{PM} (PM for profit maximizing) and set price P_{SM} (SM for sales maximizing). The economic profit it earns is the lighter shaded area or $(P_{PM} - P_{SM}) \times Q_{PM}$. This is the same short-run possible result that we have seen with competitive firms, monopoly firms, and monopolistically competitive firms. If the firms' managers seek to satisfice by achieving a profit that is consistent with maximizing sales or the size of the firm, they will

Entry Limit Pricing
The practice by monopoly and oligopoly firms of setting prices below profit maximizing levels in order to deter entry of new firms.

Sales Maximization Hypothesis
The argument that firms seek to maximize sales or the size of the firm rather than the firm's profit.

Satisficing
A decision to seek an acceptable or satisfactory level of profit as opposed to a maximum level of profit.

Figure 10-6
Profit Maximization Versus Sales Maximization for the Oligopolistic Firm

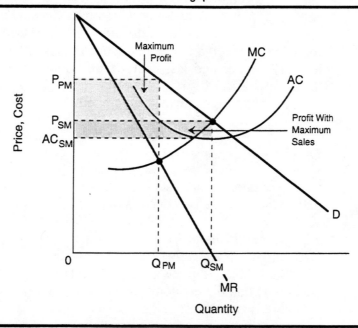

Maximizing profit requires that the firm produce the rate of output at which MC = MR. The profit maximizing firm above will produce Q_{PM} and set price P_{PM}; it will earn economic profit ($P_{PM} - P_{SM}$) x Q_{PM} or the lighter shaded area shown. Maximizing sales requires that the firm produce the output rate at which MR = 0 or Q_{SM}. The sales maximizing firm will set price P_{SM} and earn economic profit ($P_S - AC_{SM}$) x Q_{SM} or the darker shaded area shown above.

produce where MR is zero (MR cuts the quantity axis) and will produce Q_{SM}. With sales maximization, the firm set price P_{SM} and earns "satisfactory" profit ($P_{SM} - AC_{SM}$) x Q_{SM} or the darker shaded area shown in Figure 10-6.

The important conclusion of the sales maximization argument is:

Firms maximizing sales will produce a greater rate of output and set a lower price than will firms that seek to maximize profits (given the same demand and cost conditions).

Profit Maximization: Summing Up

In spite of the various qualifications we have looked at, most economists continue to regard the profit maximization hypothesis about firms (including oligopolistic ones) as extremely useful. They do not believe that it provides an exact fit to the behavior of any particular firm. Firms may indeed satisfice, they may try to grow by maximizing sales or they may set prices low enough to limit the entry of rivals. They may, in other words, engage in many and complex forms of behavior. Yet the profit maximizing (optimizing) argument is alive and well. Only if we wish to study a particular firm, akin to studying a tree in a forest, do we need to examine its exact pattern of behavior. If instead, we seek to compare the conduct and behavior of many firms in the same or different industries, akin to studying the forest, the profit maximization approach has great merit. In particular it is (1) simpler and less costly than a more complex approach and (2) it appears to give a better approximation to explaining *comparative* firm behavior than any other.

Oligopoly: Summing Up

On the whole, economists criticize oligopolies for the same reasons they criticize pure monopolies and monopolistic competitors. In an oligopoly, MR is less than AR (see Figures 10-1 and 10-2). Therefore, oligopolistic firms other than sales maximizing oligopolies set their prices higher than, rather than equal to, MC. As we have said, it is only when MC and price are equal (as they are in purely competitive situations) that the economy is producing at optimum efficiency, that is, that resources are efficiently allocated to produce the combinations of output consumers prefer, given their tastes and incomes.

We have seen that oligopolies are not simple to analyze and understand because of the wide variation of reaction patterns among interdependent firms. Some may react by organizing and explicitly colluding as if they are one firm (trusts, and in modern times, cartel). Here, the result is the same as pure monopoly, at least as long as the "players" all abide by the rules agreed upon. From the standpoint of society, the result is less output, higher prices and a distortion in the allocation of resources.

In other (class II) oligopolistic industries, patterns of implicit collusion arise such as price leadership by a dominant firm. As we have seen, by comparison with competitive industries, there are welfare losses (P > MC) and distortions in resource allocation. How great these losses and distortions are can vary from industry to industry depending upon the incentives of the dominant firm, particularly its incentives to innovate.

In still other (class III) oligopolistic industries, no dominant firm emerges and, in addition to the distortive (P > MC) effect of oligopoly, there may also be a sluggish industry, one in which prices are inflexible, output unresponsive to changes in demand and in which there is little incentive to innovate.

In sum, then, oligopolies suffer by comparison with competitive industries no matter what their reactions to interdependence. The extent of the unfavorable comparison, though, depends on (1) whether and how oligopolistic firms react by organizing and colluding, and (2) whether oligopolies or competitive industries do a better job of innovating (new products and processes, new ways of producing old products, etc.).

But are Costs Lower in Competitive Industries?

Are costs really higher in oligopolistic industries than in purely competitive ones? No one knows for sure but some have argued that this is not so. In many industries, technology is such that it takes a large operation to achieve economies of scale. In such industries, if enough firms entered the field to duplicate purely competitive conditions, each would be so small that it would not stand a chance of achieving most economies of scale and would produce with higher AC.

Some people argue that the present state of technology is such that it requires large research facilities and huge amounts of money to bring about innovations. John Galbraith is one who takes this position as an argument in favor of large scale oligopolistic firms. Galbraith feels that oligopolies, in spite of their faults, foster improved technology because the larger the firm, the larger the amount spent for research, and thus the faster the development of technology.

Two other economists, J. D. Jewkes and Edwin Mansfield, take an opposing viewpoint. They argue as follows: (1) Medium-size and smaller firms (the smallest discussed is a thousand employees) have the highest proficiency in technological development. (2) During its early high-risk, low-cost phase, an invention is usually developed by smaller firms; then during the finishing, or low-risk, high-cost stage, it is taken over by larger firms. So the more competition there is between firms in an oligopolistic industry, the lower the economic profit and the more urgent the drive toward technological innovation. The more firms, the greater the tendency toward price competition and away from nonproductive, nonprice competition.

APPLICATION:
Some Cases of Oligopoly Behavior

Class I Oligopoly:
Organization and Covert Collusion in the Electrical Equipment Industry

As we noted earlier, some oligopolistic industries produce homogeneous or standardized products. Buyers of these products, seeking to minimize their acquisition costs, have no preference for the product of one firm over another. Price, in other words, is the only thing that determines whether a firm gets the business. Some oligopolistic industries that find themselves in this situation include steel, basic aluminum and the industry whose collusive behavior we are going to examine in this application, electrical equipment.

To set the stage, let us note that electrical equipment, bought almost entirely by other industries, and by governments, is largely standardized (though some is customized), is sold through suppliers who respond to offers to bid that contain its technical specifications and has a highly cyclical (variable and discontinuous) demand.

In 1961 a major scandal rocked the business world, especially the electrical equipment industry. Executives from all the firms in the industry were convicted of violating the Sherman Antitrust Act by conspiring to fix prices and shares of the market. These executives, the *Wall Street Journal* pointed out, were not criminals; they were respected members of their communities. But white-collar criminals often have these characteristics. Why did they commit such a knowing violation of the law? And how did they do it?

The stimulus of World War II and the Korean War caused the electrical equipment industry to build up a lot of excess capacity. At the same time, price competition was fierce, degenerating at times into price wars. This was especially true in 1955, the year of the so-called "white sale," when prices were cut by up to 50 percent. This happened again to a lesser extent in 1957. Profits dropped; some firms even suffered losses.

Since orders for electrical equipment, when they came along, were mostly large, the industry suffered from a feast-or-famine market. Individual orders were crucial to small firms struggling for survival, and there was great instability in market shares of the industry as a whole. The threat of bankruptcy hung constantly over the smaller firms.

The result of the white sale of 1955 was that General Electric (GE) and Westinghouse—the two biggest firms—gained an even larger share of the market. Some of the smaller firms complained to the antitrust division of the Justice Department, and there was talk of a possible antitrust suit by the government against GE and Westinghouse. Ironically, this very threat of antitrust action caused GE and Westinghouse to try to stabilize the markets to protect the smaller firms and to protect themselves against government action.

Executives are always under pressure to produce more and more; that is, to make profits for their corporations. In the highly interdependent world of electrical equipment, the executives realized they could do this by reducing the intensity of competition. With the firms' excess capacities and large fixed costs, and with the complexity of the industry and the prevalence of the custom of making firms submit sealed bids, price leadership was simply not practical. The only alternative seemed to be express or covert collusion: the under-the-table agreement.

The motives behind this secret agreement to fix prices included the following:

1. To stabilize the market by reducing the competition that was causing losses.

2. To fix prices so as to raise the overall level of profits to all companies and provide predictable market shares.

3. To avoid antitrust action by guaranteeing shares of the market to all firms at prices profitable to the smaller firms. This would prevent an increase in concentration.

The *Wall Street Journal*, in January of 1962, said that the social environment of the executives involved in the conspiracy helped explain why the conspiracy came into being. The executives of all these companies came out of the same kinds of colleges and had the same work experience. They were all engineers who, at some point on their way up the corporate ladder, left practical engineering for sales. All had worked in more than one firm in the industry, and the larger corporations (especially GE and Westinghouse) provided executives for the smaller ones. They all thought alike, knew each other, and were typical organization men. During their professional meetings, they began to discuss their problems: How to stabilize the market by eliminating competition?

Thus was the conspiracy born. These men undoubtedly knew that what they were doing was illegal, but they also undoubtedly did not consider it immoral. Their problem was not simply to meet and fix prices; it was more complicated. They had to set up shares of the market, and make up a system of rotation on sealed bids, so that one company would be the low bidder at one time, another at another time, and so forth. The complexities of the market required that they construct a regular bureaucracy to carry out the conspiracy in the various kinds of equipment markets. All this meant frequent meetings, consultations, and memos. No wonder the Justice Department uncovered the conspiracy! And, no wonder the *per se* rule applied to this kind of behavior.

There is evidence that the bureaucracy had a hard time keeping the conspirators in line as to prices. Collusive (cartel) agreements are inherently unstable because of the attractiveness of cheating. Some firms seemed to have joined the conspiracy more for the purpose of snooping and finding out what the others' prices were going to be than of cooperating. Since covert collusion is illegal, violation of the collusive agreements could not be enforced and any company could defy the illegal organization.

Violations of the ground rules about shares of markets were less of a problem. However, the bosses had to work out complex systems of sharing the market, dividing the market as to different kinds of equipment and also as to different sections of the country. Sometimes firms balked at the system, and so the executives had to work out new methods of dividing the market. At one point, they had to rework their figures on shares entirely in order to account for the entry of a new firm into the conspiracy.

All in all, the problems of setting up and operating the collusive conspiracy were difficult, complex, and cumbersome. The need for secrecy and the clear illegality of the conspiracy obviously added difficulties, both administrative and psychological. However, the fact that the conspiracy was formed and did function for more than four years, even in the face of all these difficulties, shows just how great may be the temptations of oligopolists who cannot substantially differentiate their products to engage in clearly illegal acts to "stabilize" their markets.

In the electrical equipment case, the efficiency losses to society from an effective cartel could have been large. Cheating, though, probably reduced losses. As one of the defendants noted: "No one was living up to the agreements and we...were being made suckers." One must wonder what, other than desperation would lead executives to react in this manner. The penalties are potentially high: (1) current law provides up to three year prison terms (a far tougher provision than in 1961), (2) fines (almost $2 million in the electrical case), and (3) heavy repayments to those overcharged as a result of the conspiracy. Douglas Greer reports that these repayments amounted to more than $500 million in the electrical case because awards were trebled. The antitrust laws permit courts to multiply the damage (overpayment) estimates by a factor of 3.

Have we seen the last of price fixing conspiracies? Almost certainly not! With over 600 federal prosecutions of price fixing cases in this century, we will likely continue to see not only foreign cartels (OPEC, etc.), but also to witness oligopolists in the U.S. turning to such measures.

Class II Oligopoly:
Unorganized But Tacit Collusion in the Steel Industry

Conscious Parallelism
A practice in which a dominant firm sets its prices and other firms set theirs in a way that parallels those of the price leader.

If unsanctioned covert (explicit) collusion is clearly illegal, oligopolists may, turn to patterns of collusion that are less clearly violations of antitrust laws. These patterns involve tacit collusion, also called **conscious parallelism**, a practice in which a dominant firm establishes its prices and other firms set theirs in a way that parallels those of the price leader.

If you were the chairman of a non-dominant firm in an oligopoly (called a "fringe" firm), why would you consciously tailor your prices to those of a dominant firm? The answer seems to vary widely from one industry to another. Basically, though, it must lie in the expectation that being a follower of the dominant firm would be more profitable than an alternative pricing strategy (ignoring the dominant firm, seeking to become the price leader, engaging in price warfare, etc.). The dominant firm may be the lowest cost firm in the industry in which case competition could ultimately drive industry price below the AC of the fringe firms. We see such a hypothetical case in Figure 10-7. The dominant firm with LRAC, AC_d, could survive and earn a normal profit even if price competition were active in the industry. Fringe firms 1 and 2, on the other hand, would be operating with economic losses at that price and ultimately would leave the industry. Such firms not unexpectedly choose to "follow the (price) leader."

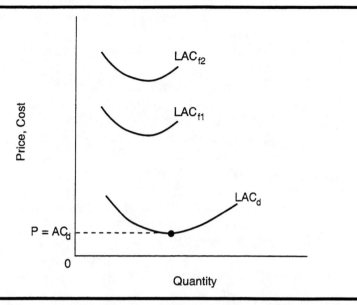

In Figure 10-7, the AC of the low-cost dominant firm are shown as LAC_d. Those of the two higher cost fringe firms are shown as LAC_{f1} and LAC_{f2}. If the dominant firm sets its prices above AC (and MC) to achieve its own maximum profit, those prices will be higher and more satisfactory to fringe firms than if price competition drove industry price toward the AC of the dominant firm ($P = AC_d$).

Not all dominant firms are low-cost firms as we saw earlier. Let's look at an actual case of high-cost firm dominance, the steel industry of the U.S. through much of the 20th century. Until recent years, the dominant firm in the industry was U.S. Steel (U.S.S.) a product of the merger movement of the early-1900s. A firm created by J. P. Morgan and other financiers, it represented a financial consolidation of existing steel firms (Carnegie Steel, Mellon, and others). To acquire these firms, the financiers paid prices far above market values. Nonetheless, the world's first "billion dollar firm" began life as a potentially dominant figure in an industry in which it controlled about 65 percent of capacity.

From an industry that had both price competition and incentives to reduce cost (for which Andrew Carnegie was famous), the American steel industry soon became one in which conscious parallelism was deeply embedded. U.S.S. and its chairman Elbert Gary wanted to set steel prices so that they would permit a profitable payout on the old (costly) facilities combined in the new firm. No other firm in the industry came close to "big steel's" size or resources so there was a tendency to follow its leadership. For some years, price leadership took the form of the "Gary Dinners" in which steel executives were "wined and dined" at the Gary home after which steel prices changed throughout the industry. Dangerously close to organized collusion, the "Dinners" were discontinued as shown in the antitrust suit against U.S.S. shortly after its formation (a suit won by

U.S.S.). Following the end of the "Dinners," a pattern of tacit collusion developed in which other firms in the industry simply adjusted their prices to those announced by U.S.S.

The patterns of conscious parallelism in the steel industry seemed for many years to suit the interests of all the private parties. From the standpoint of the dominant firm, price leadership permitted it to (1) achieve its target rate of return while (2) gradually reducing its share of industry output and its exposure to antitrust suits. If you look again at Figure 10-2, you can see that fringe firms selling at U.S.S.'s price and with lower costs would have rates of return above that of the dominant firm. Because of their relative profitability and because U.S.S. would not contest a growing share of the market for them, fringe firms had both the ability and the incentive to expand and to adopt new technology as a means to contain costs. The supply curve of the fringe firms would shift rightward over time relative to that of "big steel."

Today, the American steel industry looks very different from its 1901 appearance. U.S.X., as it is now named, produces only about 20 percent of domestic output and has not been a clear price leader since the late-1960s. Other big steel producers (Bethlehem, etc.) announce changes in steel prices about as often as U.S.X. "Big steel" has modernized much of its plant and the American steel industry is now cost competitive with those of other countries. What, then, were the *social costs* of conscious parallelism?

To begin with, all oligopolies impose some if not all of the deadweight losses of monopoly. Output tends to be lower and prices tend to exceed MC, no matter what type of oligopoly behavior we compare with that of pure competition. Still, critics of these static comparisons argue that oligopolies involve large firms that both undertake research and development activities more readily than competitive firms and also implement (invest in) the technology. If we grant this counter argument to the unfavorable comparison of oligopoly, how would the steel industry in the U.S. stack up in terms of technological change during the dominance of U.S.S.? Many students of the industry think the answer is *not very well*. While smaller (sometimes new) firms adopted new technology, the industry leader did so only slowly. This was not because of a lack of alternative production methods. The basic oxygen furnace (BOF) was available shortly after World War II and was rapidly adopted by European and Japanese firms. Only in the 1960s and 1970s was the BOF adapted by U.S.S. along with the continuous casting process that has dramatically reduced costs of production.

While acknowledging that (basic) steel production is biased toward large scale plants, could we have had more competition in the American industry? Clearly, the answer seems to be *yes*. What if the Attorney General had won the original antitrust suit against U.S.S.? Price competitiveness would surely have driven steel prices toward the unit costs of a *typical firm* rather than those of (high cost) U.S.S.

Technological innovation might have been accelerated because there would have been no "price umbrella" for an inefficient firm to hide under.

Caveat: There has been substantial criticism of antitrust enforcement on the ground that often it has been targeted against firms whose market position (dominance) has been achieved by greater efficiency and greater sensitivity to the tastes of consumers while ignoring other oligopoly firms that are inefficient, less responsive and less visible. While there is substantial merit in this criticism, it surely has little applicability to the steel industry. U.S.S. as we have seen, did not achieve or maintain its 5-decade long dominance by either means.

Class III Oligopoly:
No Dominant Firm in the Soft Drink Industry

Duopoly
An industry with two interdependent major sellers, although there may be a number of fringe firms as well.

As we know, neither organization nor collusion may exist in an oligopolistic industry. Evidence suggests that this is the case in the soft drink industry. Essentially a **duopoly**, an industry with two interdependent major sellers, the industry has several fringe firms in the national market and a much larger number of minor players in local and regional markets.

For much of the period since World War II, the two major firms have been Pepsico, the producers of Pepsi Cola (Pepsi) and The Coca Cola Co., producers of Coca Cola (Coke). Other players with significant but non-dominant market shares are Seven-Up, Royal Crown, and Dr. Pepper. While market shares differ from one area of the country to another, Pepsi and Coke are the duopolists of our essay. Both firms not only produce the syrup that is the key ingredient to their popular products but also operate some of the bottling plants (45 percent for Coke, 40 percent for Pepsi) that produce and distribute the final product. Neither Coke nor Pepsi will cede dominance of the industry to the other. In a market with output of over $40 billion annually, there is a strong incentive to enlarge market share, even marginally. Price cutting is one way to do this; advertising and bad judgment on the part of the other firm are alternatives. Since advertising invites retaliation and bad judgment cannot be counted on, price cutting is frequent in the retail soft drink market. Sometimes, price cutting leads to all-out price warfare, at least in local markets. How can we explain this duopolistic result and what are its consequences?

The Edgeworth Model of Duopoly
English economist Francis Edgeworth long ago proposed a model of *duopoly* (two interdependent firms) that seems to go a long way toward explaining the recurrent price cutting and price warfare observed in the soft drink industry. Edgeworth's model is based on the following assumptions:

1. Two firms dominate the market.

2. The product(s) produced is regarded as virtually identical by buyers.

3. Neither firm in the short run can fill the entire market (a capacity constraint).

4. Each firm believes that its rival will ignore a price decrease (a reversal of the kinked demand model shown earlier).

Our analysis here draws heavily on a very instructive article by Timothy Tregarthen in *The Margin* of March/April, 1989.

Assumption 1, that there is no appreciable product differentiation in the soft drink market may be somewhat unrealistic. Nonetheless, variable market shares and sales suggest that Coke and Pepsi are *reasonably* good substitutes for each other. Examination of Figure 10-8 leads to some interesting duopoly results. Both Coke and Pepsi have the same MC (MC_{pepsi}, MC_{coke}) that are constant until they reach their (plant) capacity and then increase sharply. In the model shown, each faces a demand (D_{coke}, D_{pepsi}) that represents half the market. Each acting monopolistically would produce the same profit maximizing output Q_m and sell at the monopoly price > MC.

Figure 10-8
The Edgeworth Model and the Soft Drink Market

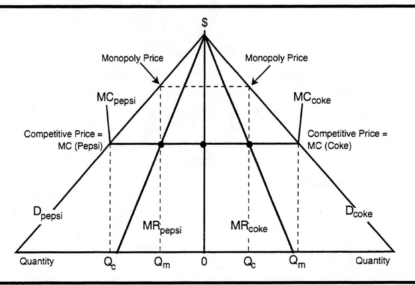

In Figure 10-8, the duopolists have the same MC (MC_{coke}, MC_{pepsi}) and each faces a demand curve (D_{coke}, D_{pepsi}) that represents ½ of the market D_{coke}, D_{pepsi}. If each behaved monopolistically, they would share the market, produce like amounts (Q_m, Q_m) and set a like price above MC (monopoly price > MC). With excess capacity at that price, either would be tempted to cut price and increase sales if it anticipated the other would not follow. As one reduces price and the other follows, warfare drives price toward the competitive level, price = MC. One of the firms is then likely to raise price back to the monopoly price in the anticipation (hope) that its rival will also do so. If that happens, the monopoly result is recreated but one or the other may yield again to the incentive to cut price. Price, thus, alternates between monopoly and competitive levels with recurrent price wars in between.

Each firm though has excess capacity at that price and faces a temptation to reduce price and expand its capacity utilization of plant. Either one may do so if, as the model assumes, it believes that its rival will not follow suit. As Coke (or Pepsi) does so, however, the rival firm also cuts price and a price war may develop until price falls to the competitive level, competitive price = MC. Consumers are benefitted by this cutting of price since a price equal to MC implies that allocative efficiency results.

Ultimately, one of the firms will, as Tregarthen notes, "look longingly at the monopoly solution" and raise price back to the monopoly price in the anticipation that the other will (sensibly) go along with the price hike. If this happens, the (shared) monopoly solution is restored. But does monopoly restoration mean *the* end to price wars? Probably not, says Tregarthen. Soft drinks are sold as "loss leaders" by retailers and bottlers offer negotiated discounts to retailers to get them to advertise the product. The advertising, however, is a signal to the other firm to lower price in the local market; both firms may be off again on the path of price warfare. As Tregarthen comments: "But it's easy to imagine Edgeworth chuckling to himself as he hears talk of an end to price wars. The fuel for another price war is there..."

An interesting feature of this particular price warfare model of oligopoly is that it suggests that the social result is to create prices that bounce back and forth in an almost ping-pong fashion between monopoly distortion (P > MC) and competitive efficiency (P = MC). This should not be taken to mean that price warfare eliminates the inefficiency of monopoly or shared monopoly (duopoly) markets. Remember that monopoly prices tend to be *restored* in the Edgeworth model.

SUMMING UP

1. Oligopolies are industries in which there are a few sellers. The following are the characteristics of *oligopoly*: (a) The actions of one firm affect the actions of all the others. (b) The product may be either homogeneous or differentiated. (c) There are substantial barriers to entry of new firms into the field.

2. *Interdependency* means that the actions of one firm affect the actions of other firms in the industry. Because of this interdependence, there are as many models of oligopoly behavior as there are theories about how firms react to the actions of others.

3. Oligopolistic industries vary according to reaction patterns of interdependent firms. Economists divide oligopolies, therefore, into three groups based on these reaction patterns:

Class I: Reaction Pattern = Organized, collusive

Class II: Reaction Pattern = Unorganized, collusive
Class III: Reaction Pattern = Unorganized, non-collusive

4. In class I oligopolies, interdependent firms get together (organize) and engage in explicit collusion (trusts, cartel). Some group acts for the industry as would be the case with a multi-plant pure monopoly. Trusts exercise complete control of the industry and cartel depend on enforceable agreements among firms.

5. With class I oligopolies, where they succeed in acting for the industry, the results are the same as those of pure monopoly. Output is reduced below that of competitive industries and price exceeds MC. The welfare losses (deadweight losses) are the same as in pure monopoly.

6. Historically, reactions to trusts led to the enactment in the U.S. of a series of laws called the "antitrust" laws. The Sherman Act (1890), the Clayton Act (1914), the Federal Trade Commission Act (1914), the Robinson-Patman Act (1936), and the Celler-Kefauver Act (1950) are the major such federal laws.

7. Under the above laws, all acts by firms that "restrain trade" are considered illegal (unless specifically sanctioned by governments). The *per se rule* of courts in interpreting the Sherman Act holds that certain acts are illegal, *per se*, or merely because they take place. The conduct, rather than intent, is judged unlawful. Presumably, all unsanctioned class I (private) oligopoly reactions are illegal under this per se rule because they have exactly the same effects as unregulated pure monopoly.

8. In class II oligopolies, there is an effort to avoid the illegal acts of organization and to create stable (legal?) patterns of implicit collusion. While there are many such possible patterns that can and have been tried, *price leadership* is one of the most prominent.

9. Price leadership involves a dominant firm in an industry setting prices that are observed and followed by other "fringe" firms in the oligopolistic industry. This leader-follower relation tends, where established, to be relatively stable and widely observed.

10. The results of price leadership appear to differ from industry to industry. While all involve allocative inefficiency (prices > MC), the leader may be a firm with few incentives to innovate or one with strong incentives to do so. The long-run social effects in terms of technological innovation may differ substantially from one case to another.

11. In class III oligopolies, there is no organization; i.e., there is no cartel or dominant firm. One hypothesis about how such inter-dependent firms may react is found in the kinked demand model of

oligopoly which seeks to explain why some oligopoly prices are rigid or inflexible.

12. The kinked demand model is based on the assumption that rival firms will ignore price increases but will follow price decreases. As a result, the class III firm conjectures that if it raises price and others ignore it, the firm will face a relatively elastic demand for its product; an increase in price will decrease the firms TR. If the firm, on the other hand, lowers prices and rivals follow, it faces a relatively inelastic demand; i.e., a decrease in price will also decrease the firm's TR.

13. The kink in the class III firm's demand at the going price produces two MR curves, one for price increases, the other for price decreases. There is a gap between these two MR conditions in which the firm operates and it finds, as a result, that it cannot profitably raise or lower prices.

14. Those who regard the kinked demand model as applicable to many oligopolies conclude that such firms are unresponsive to changes in costs or to changes in demand (consumer tastes, etc.). Other economists conclude that the assumption on which the model is based are unwarranted in most oligopoly markets.

15. Since in an oligopoly price competition is infrequent, *nonprice competition*—including variations in styling, services, quality, and amounts of advertising of a given product—are widely practiced.

16. The following are arguments made in favor of advertising: (a) Advertising can lead to increased demand for a product so that companies produce more of it, achieving economies of scale, so that the firm's production costs decrease more than its selling costs increase. This enables the firm to cut its prices. (b) Advertising lowers information costs, it conveys information consumers need in order to make rational choices. (c) Advertising pays for the media, either in whole or in part. (d) Advertising may convey messages beneficial to the public. (e) Advertising furthers product differentiation, thus giving the public greater variety from which consumers derive utility. Advertising also may make entry into markets easier and thus add to their competitiveness.

17. The arguments against advertising are: (a) Much of advertising is nonproductive, competitive-retaliatory advertising that does *not* create economies of scale. (b) A great deal of advertising does not impart information; in fact, sometimes it is either puffery or even disseminates misleading information. (c) The media's revenues from advertising are passed on to the consumer in the form of higher prices which the consumer must pay for the product advertised; advertising also gives advertisers undue influence over the content of the media. (d) Advertisements have social costs; for example, they may encourage

unhealthful activities, such as consumption of tobacco and alcohol, and present a demeaning, exploitative or stereo-typical view of women and men. Some argue that advertising costs are a barrier to entry into an industry.

18. Some theorists argue that not all firms strive to maximize their profits; these theorists give the following reasons for their contention: (a) Firms generally do not have enough data to compute their MR and MC. (b) Firms may curb their drives for profit because they fear possible antitrust action. (c) Firms may elect not to maximize profits because they want to avoid adverse public opinion. (d) Firms may engage in *entry limit pricing*, that is they keep their profits lower than necessary to discourage new firms that might try to enter the industry. (e) Firms may give higher priorities to considerations such as increasing their shares of the market and volume of sales than to profit maximization. The sales maximization argument is a variant of *satisficing* that firms have "target" levels of satisfactory profits rather than maximum profits as their goal. However, all these criticisms, rather than refuting the profit-maximization assumption, point up the difficulties of estimating and achieving it.

19. The sales maximization argument leads to the conclusion that firms seeking to expand and maximize sales produce more and charge lower prices than those that seek to maximize profits.

20. The profit maximizing hypothesis is simpler than others, gives a basis for comparison of different firms and is still widely employed by economists.

21. Oligopoly behavior and its results are as varied as are the reaction patterns of interdependent firms. All such reactions, however, when compared with the results of pure competition, are unfavorable to oligopoly. Oligopolies (except for sales maximizing ones) invariable set prices above MC which result in allocative inefficiency. Class I oligopolies have all the deadweight losses of pure monopoly. Class II oligopolies have varying results depending on the implicit collusion and the incentives of dominant firms. Class III oligopolies, it is argued, result not only in output restrictions and allocative inefficiency but also in rigid prices and slow adaptation to technological change and changes in demand.

22. The application considers cases of oligopoly behavior in each of the three classes identified earlier. The first section deals with covert collusion in the 1960s in the electrical equipment industry. A second section concerns tacit collusion in the steel industry during much of its modern history. A final essay deals with non-collusive behavior between duopolistic firms in the soft drink industry.

23. The 1961 case of price fixing by the manufacturers of electrical equipment is an example of covert collusion regarding prices and

market shares. The electrical equipment manufacturers needed covertly collusive agreements because the sealed bid system of pricing made price leadership impossible.

24. The chief motives for price fixing were (a) to stabilize the market by eliminating the competition that was causing losses, (b) to fix prices so as to raise the overall level of profits, and (c) to avoid possible antitrust action by guaranteeing shares of the market to all firms at prices profitable to the smaller firms.

25. The executives involved were all organization men from similar backgrounds. They knew that what they were doing was illegal, but they apparently did not consider it immoral.

26. Cheating on the electrical price fixing agreements may have reduced somewhat the potentially large monopoly (deadweight) losses. Such continuing reactions to interdependence are understandable but surprising in view of the large penalties (3-year prison terms, fines, treble damage awards) that may now result.

27. In view of the total number of oligopoly firms, price fixing conspiracies are relatively rare. Nonetheless, with over 600 federal prosecutions since 1900, we have almost certainly not seen the last of them.

28. *Conscious parallelism* (tacit collusion) is a practice in which a dominant firm sets its prices and other (fringe) firms adjust to those of the price leader. This was a long standing practice in the steel industry after 1901.

29. U.S.S., the steel price leader, set prices to achieve its own target rate of return while permitting fringe (lower cost) firms to fill the remainder of the steel market. Since U.S.S. began as a (consolidation induced) high cost producer, steel prices were relatively high. Smaller firms with lower costs had higher rates of return than U.S.S.

30. Conscious parallelism in steel served the interests of all private parties. Small firms were profitable and grew larger over time. U.S.S. achieved its desired profitability and saw its (highly visible) share of the market decline.

31. The American steel industry now is very different from its earlier structure. It has no clearly dominant firm. Over its history from 1901 to the 1960s, it not only showed the deadweight losses of monopoly pricing and output but also was slow in terms of innovation (particularly on the part of the dominant firm).

32. The steel industry probably could have been more competitive. If U.S.S. had lost its first antitrust case, there probably would have been more firms and more competitive pricing. This not only would have

reduced the deadweight losses but would have intensified pressure for the typical firm to innovate.

33. While antitrust prosecution may often have penalized dominant firms that were efficient and responsive to consumers, that would not have been the case in the steel industry.

34. Two major firms may share a market, a market structure known as *duopoly*. The soft drink industry appears to be such a case.

35. Coca Cola and Pepsico dominate the soft drink industry in the U.S. and also own a significant number of local bottler-distributors. Each has an incentive to cut price and expand output.

36. In the Edgeworth (duopoly) model, (a) two firms dominate the market, (b) the products of each are virtually identical, (c) neither has enough capacity to fill the *entire* market and, (d) each firm believes that its rival will ignore price decreases.

37. Applying the Edgeworth model to non-collusive soft drink duopoly leads to the following results: With a shared monopoly, each firm facing half the market and having the same MC will produce the same rate of output and sell at the same price (both monopoly results). Each firm having excess capacity is tempted to cut price and expand sales. The rival firm, however, follows the price decrease, leading to price warfare. Warfare drives price down to the competitive level, where price = MC.

38. In Edgeworth type oligopoly, duopoly behavior, price tends to bounce between monopoly prices and competitive prices. When MC prices are established, one of the duopolists is tempted to restore monopoly pricing hoping that the rival will follow. When competitive prices are reached, one of the duopolists will try to restore the (shared) monopoly.

39. Restoration of monopoly prices in a duopoly market does not mean the end to price wars. The temptation to cut price is always present.

KEY TERMS

Conscious parallelism
Duopoly
Entry limit pricing
Interdependency
Interlocking directorates
Kinked demand
Oligopoly
Per se rule

Price leadership
Sales maximization hypothesis
Satisficing
Trust, cartel

QUESTIONS

1. Compare the role of advertising in oligopolies with the role of advertising in pure competition and pure monopoly.

2. What are the assumptions on which the kinked-demand oligopoly model is based? Draw a diagram of the model, showing a firm in profit-maximizing equilibrium. Why is there a kink or bend in the demand curve and a discontinuity in the marginal-revenue curve?

3. Why are prices so inflexible in a kinked-demand oligopoly situation? How widespread would you expect such situations to be?

4. Why may the firms in an oligopolistic industry choose to collude on prices? Why will they follow a price leader? Are prices as inflexible in class II as in class III situations? Why or why not?

5. Compare economic performance in an oligopolistic market with that in a purely competitive one. Is oligopoly the best market structure for rapid technological development? Why or why not?

6. Do you think that, on balance, advertising is beneficial to U.S. society as a whole? Give reasons for your opinions.

7. You have just been appointed an economic adviser to the Antitrust Division of the Attorney General's office. Your first task is to present a position paper on the government's role in preventing the use of monopoly power. Write your own position on that question, remembering that (a) you are concerned with *government's* role in monopoly power, and (b) there are advantages and disadvantages that must be weighed. Which kinds of oligopoly behavior, if any, would you seek to restrain or prevent? Why?

8. In the figure that follows, we see a hypothetical oligopoly firm choosing between maximizing profit and maximizing sales. Answer the questions below about that firm.
   a. If the oligopoly seeks to maximize *profits*, what will be its (1) price, (2) output, and (3) total (economic) profit?
   b. If the oligopoly seeks to maximize *sales*, what will be its (1) price, (2) output, and (3) total (economic) profit?

9. What are some of the major market-determined barriers to entry into oligopolistic industries? Government-determined barriers?

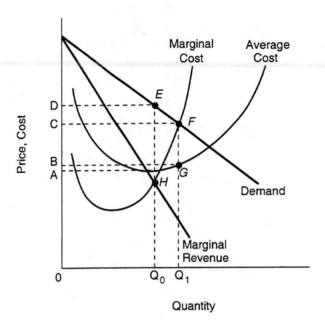

10. Why might oligopolistic firms engage in class I (cartel) behavior? Why is such behavior illegal, *per se*, unless explicitly sanctioned by government?

11. What is the difference between a trust and a cartel? Which is more stable? Why?

12. In an overall evaluation of pure competition and oligopoly, which will come closer to (a) allocative efficiency and (b) which is more likely to foster technological change?

13. In which of the three oligopoly cases discussed, was society's (consumers and producers) loss clearly the greatest? Why?

14. In view of the severe penalties that may be applied against price fixing conspiracies, why do we continue to observe behavior similar to that in the electrical equipment industry?

15. What specific conditions gave rise to the electrical price fixing conspiracy? Why was it less than completely successful?

16. What are the present penalties under the law for price fixing conspirators?

17. Why did U.S.S. want to be the industry price leader? Why did other (fringe firms) go along?

18. What were the efficiency effects of price leadership in the steel industry? Was innovation retarded? Why?

19. Why did U.S.S. want to see its share of the market decline over time?

20. What is *conscious parallelism*? Is this explicit or tacit collusion?

21. Would the U.S. have benefitted from having a more competitive steel industry from 1901 to 1960? Could it have had a more competitive industry?

22. What is *duopoly*? Does this characterize the soft drink industry?

23. What are the assumptions of the Edgeworth model of duopoly? Are they completely appropriate to the soft drink industry?

24. How does price warfare in an Edgeworth type duopoly lead to a fluctuation of prices between monopoly and competitive levels?

25. Although prices may stabilize at monopolistic levels in a duopoly, price warfare always seems a possibility. Why?

SUGGESTED READINGS

Alsop, Ronald. "Brand Loyalty is Rarely Blind Loyalty." *Wall Street Journal*. October 15, 1989.

Greer, Douglas. "Price and Production Behavior: Cartel Practice and Policy." Ch. 12. *Industrial Organization and Public Policy*. 2nd ed. NY: Macmillian, 1984.

Thomas, Robert P. "Antitrust Loss: The Electrical Conspiracy." Ch. 18. *Microeconomic Applications*. Belmont, CA: Wadsworth Publishing Co., 1981.

Tregarthen, Timothy. "Coke vs. Pepsi: A Truce in the Cola Wars?" *The Margin*. March/April, 1989.

Weiss, Leonard. *Case Studies in American Industry*. NY: John Wiley and Sons, Inc., 1967.

Government and the Modern American Economy

Coca-Cola made its controversial bid to acquire Dr. Pepper primarily to scuttle PepsiCo's proposed takeover of Seven-Up, documents show. The government thwarted both acquisitions on antitrust grounds.

OBJECTIVES

After studying this chapter you will be able to:

- Explain the difference between a horizontal and a vertical merger.
- Describe zero sum, negative sum and positive sum games.
- Explain why economists re skeptical of the argument that rent seeking leads to increased efficiency.
- Have a working knowledge of the following terms and concepts:

  Concentration ratios   Pareto optimal rule change
  Herfindahl index   Rent seeking activities
  Logrolling

Government and the Modern American Economy

What should be the role of government in America's economy? From the federalist debates of our earliest national history through the "Reagan Revolution" of the 1980s, few questions have been more persistently or vociferously addressed. There are many possible answers: Government as the facilitator. Government as the arbiter of ground rules. Government as the regulator. Government as the guardian against monopoly. Government as the promoter of full employment. These are only a few such possible roles and each can be played in combination with others as well as with different emphases.

A significant part of the pressure for government to become a more active player in the economy grew in the past century from an apprehension by various groups that "big business" had become dominant. The "public's" interest, said many, needed to be represented and who better than its elected representatives to fulfill that role? Antitrust legislation, public regulation, and progressive income taxes were a few of government's responses. In this chapter, we will look at some of these governmental activities and the rationales upon which they are based. We will also consider some of the recent evidence regarding the competitiveness of the American economy. Is it becoming more monopolistic and in need of an increasingly "visible hand" by government or is it becoming more competitive with an increasing role for the "invisible hand" of self-regulating markets?

In the second part of this chapter we will examine how government decisions affecting the economy are made. Can economic principles explain such public decisions as well as assess their impact? An increasing number of economists believe that the answer is *yes*. Their studies, called *public choice*, seek to apply the economic principles we have applied to private decision making and to public decision making as well. While controversial, public choice economists have provided some insightful views of both the origins and effects of governmental economic policies.

Government and Antitrust: The Rule of Reason

Rule of Reason
Involves a broad judicial determination of the reasons for a firm's conduct and the effects of that conduct on restraint of trade.

Enforcement of antitrust laws involves government in a joint role of arbiter of ground rules (what kinds of business behavior are (1) illegal on their face, (2) questionable and *may* involve restraint of trade, or (3) clearly lawful.) and guardian against monopoly. Some practices (e.g., conspiring to fix prices) are illegal, *per se*. Other practices (e.g., price leadership), however, involve tacit rather than explicit Collusion and may or may not restrain trade. Judicial determination in such matters involves applying the **rule of reason** rather than the *per se rule*. Recall that the per se rule involves consideration of the conduct of firms. Under the rule of reason, courts engage in a broad examination of the reasons for a firm's behavior and determine whether or not that behavior has lead to a restraint of trade.

At times, applying the rule of reason has lead to a firm being found guilty of restraint of trade. In the earliest such case in 1911, the Standard Oil Co., which controlled 90 percent of the industry market was found to have behaved unreasonably and to have used business practices (mergers, etc.) as a part of a deliberate effort to dominate the oil industry. The firm was forced to break up into various independent firms (Standard of New York [Mobil], Standard of New Jersey [Exxon], Standard of California [Chevron] and so forth).

The rule of reason, though, does not clearly identify, *ex ante*, what behavior is acceptable and what is not. That rule, when applied to U.S. Steel (U.S.S.) in 1920 resulted in a finding of not guilty. "Big steel," the court said, may have tried to monopolize the steel industry but had failed. Mere size, said the Supreme Court, does not restrain trade. The government had not shown that the firm had used its size or specific business practices (the "Gary Dinners" had been abandoned) to unreasonably restrain trade. Conscious parallelism, in other words, had survived the test of legality in that case.

A rule of reason, unlike a per se rule is subject, in other words, to wide and varying judicial interpretation. In 1945, just 25 years after the U.S.S. decision, the courts held that mere size could indeed be evidence of restraint of trade. The Aluminum Company of America (ALCOA), which controlled 90 percent of the aluminum ingot market, was found guilty of restraining trade even though its conduct was not deemed unreasonable or unlawful. The courts, in other words, had turned to an examination of industry *structure* rather than *conduct* in determining violations of the antitrust laws.

Mergers and Antitrust

Horizontal Mergers
Those between firms in the same industry.

Vertical Mergers
Those between firms in different industries.

A major structural change widely observed in the 1980s was a wave of mergers. Some of the mergers were **horizontal** (mergers of firms in the same industry) and others **vertical** (mergers of firms in different industries). Of greater interest to the Justice Department are (horizontal) mergers within an industry for these are considered more likely to restrain trade.

Unfortunately, the rule of reason gives little or no clear guidance about which mergers are socially acceptable. In 1982, the Justice Department finally issued some guidelines to fill this void, and as a result, market share, long regarded as a guide to acceptable mergers, was more clearly defined.

Concentration Ratios
A measure of the combined market shares of an industry's largest firms.

Many economists consider a measure of concentration within an industry to be a useful guide to merger policy. Until 1982, **concentration ratios**, measures of the market share of an industry's largest firms were employed by Justice as a tool in approving or contesting mergers. If, for example, an industry has 25 firms and the four largest firms have sales shares of 30 percent, 22 percent, 15 percent, and 3 percent, with the remaining 20 firms each having 1 percent of sales, the concentration ratio for the industry is 70 percent (30 + 22 + 15 + 3). This ratio would constitute a likely signal that Justice would not approve further horizontal mergers in the industry.

Concentration ratios, however, pose serious problems of interpretation. In our hypothetical example above, the 4 largest firms are fairly equal in size. What if the concentration ratio of 70 percent was observed in an industry in which the largest firm had 67 percent of the market while the next 3 largest firms each had 1 percent? Likelihood of the exercise of market power seems much higher in the second case than in the first.

Herfindahl Index
Obtained by summing the squared percentage market shares of firms in an industry.

The 1982 Justice Department guidelines sought to correct for the lack of policy clarity in concentration ratios. Substituted for concentration ratio measures of market power were measures based on the **Herfindahl index**. This index is figured by squaring the percentage market share of each firm in the industry and then adding the squares. Note that the Herfindahl index is a more sensitive measure of market power than the concentration ratio because it gives greater emphasis to (dominant) firms with unusually large market shares.

Table 11-1 contains some Herfindahl indices for 3 hypothetical oligopoly industries. All 3 are 4-firm oligopolies with a cluster of 20 fringe firms each of which produces 1 percent of industry output. Industries I, II, and III have a common 4-firm concentration ratio of 80 percent. Antitrust policy based on concentration ratios would presumably treat all 3 industries alike. Herfindahl indices for the 3 industries, however, are not alike. In industry I, market power is only slightly concentrated within the top 4 firms; the Herfindahl index is 1,798. In industry II, the 4 firms have equal (20) shares of output and the concentration ratio, 1,620, is even lower than in industry I.

Table 11-1
Herfindahl Indices in Three Hypothetical Oligopolistic Industries

Firm	Industry I		Industry II		Industry III	
	Market Share (Percent)	Market Share (Squared)	Market Share (Percent)	Market Share (Squared)	Market Share (Percent)	Market Share (Squared)
A	30	900	20	400	77	5,929
B	22	484	20	400	1	1
C	15	225	20	400	1	1
D	13	169	20	400	1	1
Remaining 20 firms at 1% each	1	20	1	20	1	20
4-Firm Concentration Ratio	80		80		80	
Herfindahl Index		1,798		1,620		5,952

In industry III, market shares are very unequally divided; the largest firm produces 77 percent of industry output while the next 3 firms produce 1 percent each (as do the other 20 firms). Industry III has a much larger Herfindahl index of 5,952. If you were the Assistant Attorney General in charge of the antitrust division, which of the 3 would most likely be a candidate for antitrust action, including opposition to mergers between firm A and other firms in the industry?

Are Big Firms Bad for the Economy?

Enthusiasm for antitrust enforcement, especially that involving the rule of reason, waned in the 1980s. Some celebrated cases were even dropped. In 1969, the Justice Department brought suit against IBM under Section II of the Sherman Act. The firm controlled nearly 70 percent of the domestic electronic data processing market and was not completely unlike industry III in Table 11-1. IBM's defense against the suit was based on the argument that its market share had been attained through innovation (newer and better products) as well as through greater efficiency (cost differences due to economies of scale). The trial began in 1975 and lasted for 7 years. In the interim, the structure of the computer industry changed substantially. In the U.S., as well as in Japan and elsewhere, many new firms entered. In 1982, looking at the changed industry and assessing the extent of a monopoly problem, the Attorney General decided that the case was without merit.

How Important is Static Pure Competition?

The IBM case may well illustrate some of the basic problems with antitrust enforcement and may also explain why enforcement has diminished in terms of government priorities. Some of the major concerns as we enter the 1990s are:

1. *Static views of pure competition.* The benefits of competition may not explain very well the sources of the long term dynamic benefits of economic development. Joseph Schumpeter argued that economic development is the result of markets that are changing as a result of innovation or processes that produce new products and eliminate old products. Firms that do a better job of innovation and are more successful in producing what consumers want to buy may end up temporarily with a disproportionate share of the market. To punish these firms for their successful innovation would be counter-productive of society's long-term interest in growing efficiency and in satisfying consumer tastes.

2. *International competition.* IBM lost its dominant position in the computer industry in substantial measure because of competition from foreign firms. Tariff and other trade barriers among industrial nations have declined since World War II and there are freer flows of goods and services today than at any time in this century. A firm may dominate a domestic industry but face intense competition from foreign producers. One of the clearest examples of this lies in the American automobile industry. For many years after 1950, antitrust officials considered bringing suit against GM which produced about 50 percent of U.S. automobiles. Today, it seems very unlikely that GM would be the target of such an action. Why? In part, because when the domestic industry failed to produce the cars Americans wanted to buy, Japanese and other foreign producers easily entered the domestic market and quickly captured a large share. Whatever insulation the domestic industry enjoyed from competition has been eroded if not destroyed. A key lesson in this is that markets open to foreign competition may not be good targets for antitrust activity.

How Competitive is the U.S. Economy? More Antitrust or Less?

Concern has long existed over the growing size of businesses and that concern has been increased by the merger movement of the 1980s. Whereas in 1950, the 100 longest firms controlled about 40 percent of manufacturing assets, by the late 1980s, the share had increased to about 50 percent. Size, though, does not easily equate with market power. As we have seen, a huge firm such as GM may face intense competition. To put arguments about future government policy toward the economy in perspective, let's look at some of the recent evidence on competitive trends in the American economy.

Many students of American industry have sought answers to the question: Has the economy become more or less competitive in recent decades? Most such studies have relied on concentration ratios in one form or another as the basis for their conclusions. A recent study by William Shepherd (*The Review of Economics and Statistics*, 1982) provides some rather conclusive evidence. Shepherd's broadly based study divided American industry into four general classifications:

1. Pure monopolies: One firm controls the market and has succeeded in blocking entry.

2. Dominant firms: One firm controls more than 50 percent of the market and has no close rivals.

3. Tight oligopolies: Four top firms control more than 60 percent of the market and have relatively stable market relations (shares) based on cooperation.

4. Effectively competitive industries: No firm is dominant, there is little concentration, few barriers to entry and little evidence of collusion.

Table 11-2 permits us an overview of Shepherd's conclusions regarding competitive trends. Note that there was a slight trend toward effective competition from 1939 to 1980 (from 52.4 to 56.3 percent of national income). In the 22 years from 1958 to 1980, however, there was a major trend toward creation of national income in effectively competitive industries (from 56.3 to 76.7 percent).

Table 11-3 shows a more detailed view of each of the 8 sectors in Shepherd's study (from agriculture, forestry, and fishing to services). Although there were some clear gains from 1939 to 1958 (mining, transportation and public utilities), there were some clear losses (agricultural, forestry, and fishing). There are, though, across-the-board gains between 1958 and 1980. In only one (agriculture, forestry, and fishing) is the gain modest; all other sectors show substantial if not spectacular in increases in competitiveness.

Table 11-2
Competitive Trends in the American Economy, 1939-1980

Percentage of National Income from Each Industry Type			
Market Classification	**1939**	**1958**	**1980**
Pure Monopoly	6.2	3.1	2.5
Dominant Firm	5.0	5.0	2.8
Tight Oligopoly	36.4	35.6	18.0
Effectively Competitive	52.4	56.3	76.7
	100.0	100.0	100.0

Source: William G. Shepherd, "Causes of Increased Competition in the U.S. Economy, 1939-1950." *Review of Economics and Statistics*, 64. (November, 1982), 618, Table 2.

Table 11-3
Competitive Trends in the U.S. Economy by Industry Sector, 1939-1988

Sectors of the Economy	National Income from Each Sector in 1978	Percentage of Each Sector Rated as Effectively Competitive		
	Billions of Dollars	1939	1958	1980
1. Agriculture, Forestry, Fishing	54.7	91.6	85.0	86.4
2. Mining	24.5	87.1	92.2	95.8
3. Construction	87.6	29.9	55.9	80.2
4. Manufacturing	459.5	51.5	55.9	69.0
5. Transportation, Public Utilities	162.3	8.7	26.1	39.1
6. Wholesale, Retail	261.8	57.8	60.5	93.4
7. Finance, Insurance, Real Estate	210.7	61.5	63.8	94.1
8. Services	245.3	53.9	54.3	77.9
9. Totals	1512.4	52.4	56.4	76.7

Source: William G. Shepherd, OpCit., 618, Table 2

Why the Increased Competition from 1958 to 1987?

Shepherd concludes that there are three major reasons for increased competition in the American economy from 1958 to 1980:

1. *Foreign Competition*. Many tightly-knit domestic oligopolies (autos, steel, etc.) found themselves facing intense competition from abroad. Though there was pressure to create trade barriers (tariffs, quotas), most such pressure was successfully resisted. Shepherd believes that about ⅙ of growing competitiveness was due to foreign competition.

2. *Deregulation*. Airlines, trucking, and banking were all industries subject to major deregulation between 1958 and 1980. Reducing barriers to entry, broadening market opportunities and creating price competition all aided in this effect. Shepherd's conclusion is that deregulation accounted for about ⅕ of the growth in competition.

3. *Antitrust Activity*. Individual antitrust actions are almost impossible to pin point in terms of their overall effect on competition. Nonetheless, Shepherd believes that these effects in the aggregate accounted for about ⅔ of the trend toward effective competition. The "climate" of antitrust may send important long-term signals to firms and have more lasting effects than either deregulation or changes in foreign competition.

The Shepherd study suggests that antitrust activity can have a positive and significant effect on the competitiveness of the American economy. This does not necessarily mean, though, that *increased* antitrust activity is called for. When applied to firms that dominate industries through mere size or collusion, it can enhance competition. When applied to firms that have become big through innovation and sensitivity to consumer tastes, antitrust could have the opposite effect.

Antitrust Laws: Changes in the Future?

Concern about a possible loss of competitive edge by American firms in such high-tech fields as computers, superconductors, and high definition TV has led some economists and legislators to propose changes in antitrust laws. Say critics of current laws, "American firms must undertake risky research and development activities on such huge scales that no single firm, however large, can afford it." Such firms, it is argued, must be given explicit permission to undertake the expensive joint ventures required in such areas without fear of antitrust suits. Firms in other countries such as Japan freely join together for such activities. Several bills pending in Congress in 1989 would permit U.S. firms not only to undertake joint R & D activities, but also to engage in joint marketing activities of resulting products. The most controversial aspect of this is how to accomplish the objective of "industrial competitiveness," in the world economy without diminishing competitiveness between firms or even giving rise to price fixing conspiracies at home. Still, it seems likely that some changes in the antitrust laws (that already permit joint research activities) are likely.

Public Choice: Can Economic Principles Explain Government Decisions?

Governments, as we have seen, play many microeconomic as well as acroeconomic roles. In an economy such as that of the U.S., where private individuals act as buyers and sellers, government activities are designed to (1) assist in the establishment and enforcement of private property rights, (2) create a demand for public goods not otherwise arising from private markets, (3) create legal ground rules that enhance competition and, where necessary, regulate natural monopolies, (4) address shortfalls of private markets through deterring negative externalities while stimulating positive externalities, (5) promote maximum employment and stable price levels, and (6) act to define an equitable distribution of income while undertaking programs to achieve it.

One may assume, as we have done to this point, that the choices made by governments in carrying out the above activities are both correct and correctly timed. Such optimal government decisions depend upon public decision makers who, like "philosopher kings," have perfect information and authority as well as a perspective that depends solely on the welfare of the society rather than their own. We would *not* expect that perspective or those socially optimal decisions to be made in the private sector. Indeed, we have assumed that producers, try to maximize their self-interest positions (profit), while consumers seek to maximize their self-interest positions (utility). Is it appropriate, then, to assume that these same individuals when they seek to influence or make public choices are "angels" rather than people pursuing their self-interest? An increasing number of economists, those pursuing a study of *public choice* economics, think not. Public choice students, in fact, think that the same principles that are applied to private economic decisions can be applied to those that are public.

It is to the explanation of public choices that we now turn. Among the questions to be addressed are: (1) to what groups do public decision makers seek to appeal?; (2) does the process of public decision making permit coalitions of interest groups to exercise undue influence in public choices?; (3) how representative is U.S. democracy?; 4) how are the costs and benefits of public choices distributed?; (5) what are the effects on efficiency from public choices that create benefits for particular groups?; and (6) can the financing of public choices distort resource usage by driving resources into the underground economy?

The Economy: The Name of the Game and the Rules

All of us are familiar with playing games, sometimes directly as participants, other times as observers. The economy itself can be viewed as a game, one in which we are all players. The players in the economic game are consumers and producers. As with any game, the economic game must have rules and the rules must be enforceable. There are rights and obligations that arise in any game (each of us must have ownership rights in our "chips," and there must be a means to enforce agreements among us to exchange "chips"). In many games, private parties seeking their self interests hire third parties (referees, umpires, etc.) to arbitrate disputes. In the case of market economy disputes, it often falls to government to provide the basic rules under which the game is played and also the means for resolving disputes between the players (e.g., the courts).

What is a Fair Game?
Fairness is an important aspect of any game, including the economic one. Fairness has two dimensions: (1) Is the *process* fair, or are the rules unbiased?, and (2) Is the *outcome* or result fair? The process is fair if there is no cheating; for example, if one player bribes the referee, the process becomes unfair. The fairness of outcome is more difficult to define. If a few players end up with most of the gains, is the result fair? Some would say it is not unless the players start off on an equal footing (same number of chips, knowledge of the game, skill, etc.).

Can All Players Be Made Better Off?

Zero-Sum Game
Winnings = losses in a game.

Negative-Sum Game
Winnings < losses.

Positive-Sum Game
Winnings > losses.

All games have a value; there are winners and losers and the value of the game is determined by subtracting losses from winnings. All games, though, do not have the same value. If winnings = losses, the game is **zero sum**. If winnings < losses, the game is **negative sum**. If winnings > losses, the game is **positive sum**.

In reality, there are all 3 games for us to play. A game in which there is a fixed amount in the "pot," such as poker, is a zero-sum game because all winnings by one individual are the losses of someone else. Playing the slot machines at Las Vegas or Atlantic City is a negative-sum game because the winnings are less than what a player puts into the "pot" (the house cut and tax payments on winnings being the difference).

What about the economic game, the gains and losses from voluntary exchanges between buyers and sellers in a market economy? While it is common for people to consider it a zero-sum game, in fact, since typically both sets of players are made better off, a positive-sum game. Consumers accrue consumers' surplus and producers ultimately accrue a producers' surplus at least equal to a normal profit.

Rules and Rule Changes

Pareto Optimal
A rule change that makes at least one person better off while making no one else worse off.

Just as games may have various outcomes, they also may have different rules. As rules change, the distribution of winnings and losses may be affected. Economists refer to a rule change that creates a net benefit to someone as **Pareto optimal**[1]. Specifically, such a rule change makes at least one player better off while making no other player worse off.

Changes in rules may (1) affect the outcome of the game while it is being played, or (2) may alter the result after the game has been played. Changes in tariff laws, minimum wage laws, environmental protection requirements, and health and safety requirements are examples of the first. They change the ways we produce products, their costs and prices and, in general, producer and consumer decisions. Changes in the tax laws and income transfer programs are examples of the second. Of course, how we play the game is partly a function of what we expect the rules to be. Thus, if government is expected to change tax laws to raise marginal tax rates, individuals may choose not to play the game or to play it differently. This was seen vividly some years ago when Sweden raised its marginal income tax rates to over 100 percent! Not surprisingly, some Swedes who would have been in that tax bracket chose not to play at all and left the game (Sweden's economy). Similarly, if one community offers welfare benefits significantly higher than those of another, players likely will move to the one with the greater expected winnings.

---

[1]After a distinguished Italian economist, Vilfredo Pareto

Where rules may be changed it becomes both possible and profitable for special interest groups to seek changes. I can use my resources to play under the existing rules or devote some of them to seeking changes that would increase my expected winnings. Such changes, then, become a potentially rich "vein" for players to "mine" as they seek assistance from government in their pursuit of self-interest. As rules change, they may produce positive-sum results (more benefits than losses), negative-sum results (more losses than benefits) on more zero-sum results (additional benefits = additional losses). In view of this it is important to assay whose interests are served by public choice making in a governmental system such as that of the U.S.

Public Choices in American Democracy: Whose Tastes Count Most?

Direct Democracy
A governmental system in which citizens directly choose the rules under which they will be governed.

In **direct democracies** such as New England town meetings and state-wide referenda, citizens choose the rules under which they will be governed. Majority rule determines the outcome of such processes, so it is the preferences of the typical or median voter that prevail. To understand why this is so, let's look at a model of median voter choice making.

The Median-Voter Model
Why do the tastes and preferences of median voters often dominate choices in directly democratic societies? Let's consider a hypothetical example to answer the question. Suppose that you (Z) and two good friends (X and Y), have gone off to college and, instead of living in the dormitories, choose to rent an unfurnished apartment. To furnish the apartment, you must agree on what type of furniture to rent. We will assume the rental prices do not vary with style or, in other words, all three choices, early American, transitional or baroque are available to you for the same price. Let us suppose also that each of you has a different preference; you (Z) have a strong preference for transitional furniture, one of your roommates (X) has a strong preference for baroque and least prefers early-American while the other roommate (Y) has a strong preference for early-American and least prefers baroque. Whose preferences will prevail; which choice of furniture styles will result?

We see the three sets of preferences displayed in Figure 11-1. Strength of preference ranging from most preferred to least preferred is shown on the vertical axis. Types of furniture are shown on the horizontal axis. Y's tastes decline from least preferred (early-American) to baroque; X's tastes rise from least preferred (early-American) to baroque. Your (Z's) tastes rise from least preferred (transitional) and then decline toward a median taste for baroque.

Figure 11-1
Preferences for Furniture to Furnish an Apartment

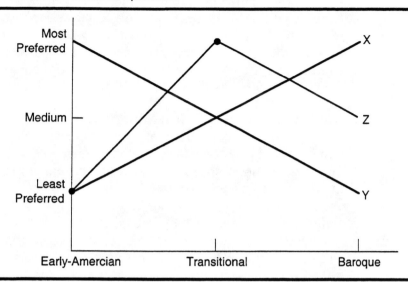

A vote on each paired alternative is now taken among the three of you with the understanding that a majority will prevail. A vote on early-American against either transitional or baroque will fail because it gets only one vote. A vote on baroque against either transitional or early-American will fail for the same reason. When, however, transitional is paired against either of the other styles it wins because it is most preferred by the median-voter and least opposed by the others.

Translating this into public choices, the median-voter's tastes will win out. Note, however, that it is only his or her tastes that are *strongly* served by the resulting choice. Others in the society will end up with more or less of the goods than they prefer. This contrasts sharply with private choices, those made in private markets and involving voluntary exchanges, where each voter (consumer) can purchase not only those goods most preferred, but also the "market basket" of such goods that maximizes the individual's utility.

Denying the Median Voter: Logrolling

Logrolling
The practice of trading votes or trading support for one issue in order to obtain support for another.

In the previous example, you and your roommate were confronted with making one choice. In reality, there are often many choices to be made and voters may form coalitions or trade support among themselves. This practice of trading support for one decision in return for support for another is called **logrolling**. Suppose that a second choice to be made in our hypothetical apartment furnishing example was what type of rug to put on the floor. You (Z), the median voter, prefer no rugs on the floor, X prefers oriental-style rugs, and Y prefers solid-color rugs without design. Normally, of course, you as the median voter would get your way. But suppose your roommates, X and Y, who realize that none of their preferences are fully satisfied, form a coalition. Y agrees to support X's taste for baroque furniture in return for Y's support for solid-color rugs. Each then has one of his first choices satisfied and as a result, more baroque furniture and solid-color rugs are demanded than would be the case if the tastes of the median voter had dominated.

No Clear Winners: Cyclical Majorities

If logrolling does not occur, you might suppose that the clear majority winner would reflect the tastes of the median voter. Not so. Majorities may arise, that are not stable and which depend entirely on the order in which choices are presented (thus, the power of controlling the agenda!). Let's go back to our example of furnishing the apartment and of choices to be made by individuals X, Y, and Z. Remember that we suppose individual choices to be based on a consistent set of tastes and preferences. We see 3 such sets below in which the voters are offered 3 choices in succession regarding furniture styles:

Individual	Order of Preference
Y	A, B, C
Z	B, C, A
X	C, A, B

A = early-American furniture
B = transitional furniture
C = baroque furniture

If these 3 people vote on successive pairings of the choices, what will happen? Offered a choice between A and B (early-American or transitional), which will win? Early-American (A) because both Y and Z prefer it to B. If the choice is between A and C, the decision will be in favor of C because Z and X prefer it to A. The lack of symmetry between individual and group decisions can be seen here. Since A is preferred to B, and C is preferred to A, a rational individual would choose C over B. If the group choice, though, is between C and B, B will win because individuals Y and Z prefer B to C. There are two important points that this illustrates:

1. Outcomes of group voting on choices depend on the order in which the choices are presented.

2. Unlike individual choices, group voting may produce unstable or cyclical majorities which, although based on individual tastes and preferences, result in inconsistent collective choices.

Fortunately, when the number of voters is large, the chance of cyclical majorities or unstable outcomes is fairly small.

Representative Versus Direct Democracies

Representative Democracies
Systems of government in which voters choose elected representatives to make public choices.

Public choices are rarely made directly by the people (the voters) in late-20th century democracies. Of the myriad of such choices, relatively few (though often some important ones) are submitted to referenda. Instead, we observe **representative democracies**, ones in which voters in local, state, and federal elections choose representatives who are supposed to make choices that reflect their constituents' tastes and preferences.

As we saw in the preceding section, public choices in direct democracies often reflect the preferences of median voters. While we would expect this to occur also with choices in representative democracies, such choices are removed from direct expression of voter's preferences and raise a set of issues that we will now explore.

What are the Objectives of Public Choice Makers?

Recall our earlier assumptions that consumers seek to maximize utility and producers seek to maximize profit. Although these assumptions do not give an exact fit to individual economic behavior, they provide us with a clear cut perspective in which to view and predict market decisions by both groups. What may we assume is the objective of government, the third major player in a market economy? Governments as institutions and processes have neither utility nor profit. Yet, people who make public choices do have identifiable self-interests. One workable hypothesis is that political representatives, seeking their self-interest and making public choices, attempt to *maximize their public support*. Choices that accomplish this objective presumably result in re-election as well as political advancement.

Once we introduce the self-interest assumption about public decision makers, it becomes possible for private groups (producers as well as consumers) to try to influence public choices in a way that reflects their own narrow self-interest positions. The electorate at large, the median voter and majority opinions, in other words, may matter less in these circumstances.

An example of how public choices may be "distorted" or non-representative of the preferences of a majority of voters will illustrate this important difference between direct and representative democracies. One of the many commodities bought by American consumers is sugar, a good produced in many countries of the world. Ordinarily, we should expect the price of sugar in the U.S. to be very close to the price in other countries with any difference over time being attributable to costs of international shipment. Were the price to be higher in America than in other world markets, sugar supplies would increase in the U.S. and domestic prices would move toward a common level in all markets in which the good is traded. Note, though, that such commodity movements are based on free entry into U.S. markets or on free trade. In fact, sugar prices in U.S. markets are not the same as those in other parts of the world. Consumers in

America pay prices that are about 100 percent higher than those in international markets. The reason why this does not attract a larger sugar supply is because free entry into U.S. markets does not exist. A non-market barrier to entry into U.S. markets was created long ago in a public choice decision to create a quota system for foreign producers who wish to export sugar to America. This welfare loss to consumers and producers amounts to several billion dollars per year. Clearly, however, if a referendum were held on whether consumers prefer present public policy on free trade, the utility maximizing median-voter's preference would be for the latter. Why, then, has representative democracy resulted in a public choice that serves the purposes of a relatively small special interest group? Public choice economists believe that **rational ignorance** is at the heart of the answer.

Rational Ignorance
The argument that when the benefits of a public choice are highly concentrated and its costs highly diffused, it is rational for those who bear its costs to ignore them.

Rational Ignorance

Public choices affecting the price and availability of goods and services are made by the thousands. In view of this, you and I, as individual consumers, are affected only slightly by *each* of those choices although significantly by all of them taken together. We have almost no incentive to react, therefore, to any particular choice. The quotas on sugar imports help to illustrate this important point. Benefits of the program (the monopoly returns to those who sell sugar at the higher protected price) are concentrated among a relatively small group of individuals and firms. Costs of this public choice, on the other hand, are spread over millions of individuals and households primarily in the form of higher sugar prices. It is easy, then, to understand why you or I as voters, though aware of the costs, would find it rational to ignore them rather than to expend our time trying to change the public choice. This is especially true since the likelihood of our vote changing the outcome is extremely small.

Sugar import quotas are merely intended to be illustrative. The same principle of rational ignorance can be extended to many other public choices. Quotas on automobile imports and tariff surcharges on steel and motorcycles are other recent examples of public choices raising prices to consumers, but in which benefits are concentrated and costs are diffused. In the application in this chapter, we will look in more detail at a long standing public choice to support milk prices and see how rational ignorance helps explain a price-increasing public program that has existed for decades.

Public Choices:
How are Costs and Benefits Distributed?

In all of the above examples, benefits of public choices were concentrated while costs were diffused. Clearly, this is not charac-teristic of *all* public choices. In general, costs may be borne by many as well as by few voters and benefits may be spread over many voters or concentrated among a few. Benefits and cost, therefore, may be distributed in four ways: (1) both benefits and costs are diffused, (2) costs are diffused and benefits are concentrated, (3) both benefits and costs are concentrated, and (4) benefits are diffused and costs are concentrated. This array of possibilities is shown in Figure 11-2.

These distributions are important to understanding public choices in a representative democracy in which, as we noted earlier, special interest groups may seek to influence decisions to their own (narrow) benefit. Let's look at each of these cases in turn:

Case 1: Costs and benefits are diffused or spread over many voters. Classic examples here include the system of civil and criminal justice (e.g., anti-drug programs) and pure public goods such as defense systems (e.g., Trident missiles, B2 bombers, etc.). While special interests may seek advantage from the provision of particular goods and services in this category, the constituency for the goods themselves is quite broad and payments for them are similarly broad.

Case 2: Costs are diffused and benefits concentrated. The examples we noted earlier (sugar quotas, automobile quotas, etc.) are all case 2 types of public choices in which concentrated benefits provide the potential for large payments to special interest groups while diffusion of costs minimizes the outcry or resistance to such

Figure 11-2
Ways in Which Costs and Benefits of Public Choices May Be Distributed

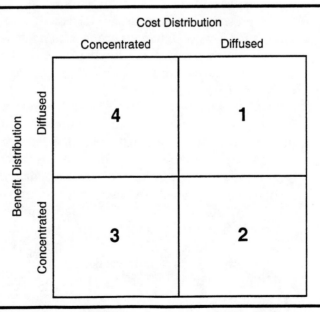

In Figure 11-2, distribution (1) is a case in which both costs and benefits are diffused, (2) is a case in which costs are diffused and benefits are concentrated, (3) is a case in which the costs and benefits are concentrated, and (4) is a case in which benefits are diffused and costs are concentrated.

Special Interest Laws
Those that confer concentrated benefits but impose diffused costs on voters.

Competing Interest Laws
Those in which special interest groups on both sides of a legislative issue vie for favor in order to obtain concentrated benefits.

choices. These choices tend to give rise to **special interest laws** with concentrated benefits and diffused costs.

Case 3: Costs and benefits both are concentrated. Here, special interest groups on both sides of a legislative issue seek large benefits from influencing legislation. This gives rise to **competing interest laws** or those in which one special interest group vies with another for legislative favor in order to obtain concentrated benefits. An example of this is to be found in legislation regarding tariffs or quotas on imported automobiles. Domestic manufacturers may support such bills while those who import automobiles for sale in this country are likely to oppose them.

Case 4: Costs are concentrated and benefits are diffused. Sometimes, a public choice will impose heavy costs on a small group but confer widely diffused benefits. How likely, though, is such legislation to be enacted? The few whose special interests would be harmed have an incentive to mount a strong campaign of resistance to the bill and may besiege their elected representatives with calls, letters, and telegrams of opposition, (to say nothing of contributions to reelection campaigns). The many who would benefit (each only slightly) however, are likely to remain rationally ignorant of the legislation and do little or nothing to support it. An example of this type of legislation would be a tax that is to be borne by only one industry. Particularly if the industry is well organized and vocal in its opposition while beneficiaries are unorganized or even rationally ignorant, the chances for passage seem slight.

When Special Interests Seek Rents

In a representative democracy, there is, as we have seen, a potential benefit for a special interest group which can secure from government a privilege that would not be available to it in market places. Such privileges may take the form of direct government expenditure programs (purchases or subsidies), monopoly-like grants (tariffs and quotas, for example) or, in general, any government activity that increases the return from using resources in a particular use above that just necessary to induce that use of the resource. As we saw earlier in this book, owners will continue to employ resources in a particular use only if they can cover the resource's opportunity cost. A return to the resource owner above this (minimum) return is called a **rent**.

Rent
A payment to resource owners above that which would just induce them to employ resources in a particular use.

Rent Seeking Activities
Those undertaken by special interest groups to obtain privileges from governments that will raise their return above opportunity cost.

Efforts on the part of resource-owning special interest groups to obtain from government privileges resulting in payments above opportunity cost are called **rent seeking activities**.

Economists are increasingly concerned with rent seeking activities. The main reason is that they add to the serious distortions in resource usage that are common to monopolistic activities. In other words, rent seeking further reduces the benefits of a competitive economy. There are two reasons why this is so: (1) rents created by government favoritism are another form of monopoly privilege, and

(2) special interest groups divert resources from directly productive uses to rent seeking (lobbying and the like). It is even possible that firms that are productively efficient but inefficient at rent seeking will fail while other less productive firms that are adept at rent seeking will prosper. The net result for society is a loss of productivity, and real income.

It is worth reminding ourselves of the welfare losses of monopoly. These can be seen again in Figure 11-3 which represents an industry market that is initially competitive but changed (perhaps by government decision) into one that is monopolistic. Initially, competitive equilibrium is at B where industry demand (D) and industry supply (LRAC) intersect. Output is Q_c and price is P_c, consumers receive a surplus equal to the area ABP_c (what they would have voluntarily spent to obtain Q_m but are not required to because of competition and its essential condition of free entry). Now, suppose that government confers a monopoly privilege (tariff, quota, licensing and the like) on this firm so that free entry no longer exists. Monopoly output will decline to point C with Q_m produced and price set at P_m. The monopoly privilege results in a reduction in consumer's surplus from ABP_c to ADP_m. Profits attributable to monopoly, however, amount to DCP_cP_m which is a transfer from consumers to producers. The welfare loss of monopoly is DBC or the loss in consumer's surplus that is a deadweight loss, one to society that is not transferred from one group to another.

Figure 11-3
Competitive Industry Equilibrium, the Welfare Loss of Monopoly, and Rent Seeking

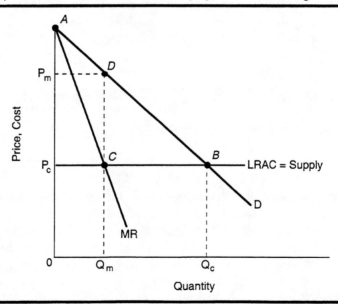

In Figure 11-3, the long-run supply curve of a constant cost industry is represented by LRAC. If the industry is competitive, industry equilibrium will occur at B with output, Q_e and price, P_c. Consumer surplus will equal the area ABP_c. If the industry is monopolistic, equilibrium will occur at C with output, Q_m and price, P_m. Consumer surplus will diminish to ADP_m. The welfare loss to society of monopoly privilege is $ABP_c - ADP_m$. Additionally, the resources used in rent seeking will represent a loss.

There is, ironically, a kind of competition that the monopoly profit or rent sets in motion. Since there are numerous contenders for the privilege that creates the rent, firms will devote resources to seeking the privilege and the rents. These resources, however, do not result in output but are rather a distortion that results from rent seeking.

How To Seek Rents: Political Action Committees

To engage in successful rent seeking, special interest groups must have a means to influence the process by which legislation is enacted. At the national level, all legislation originates with Congress and it is to that body that such groups must devote a large part of their activities. Public choice economists argue that a major objective of members of Congress (and other legislators) is reelection. As political campaigns are (increasingly) expensive, one potential means to influence Congressman is by contributing to their campaign funds. In the last 25 years, the U.S. has witnessed a dramatic growth in the number and size of special interest organizations designed to do this. Such organizations often are called **political action committees** or **PACs**. In the 10 years from 1974 to 1984, the number of PACs increased from about 600 to about 4,000 and in the latter year, these groups contributed over $100 million to congressional candidates alone. In the Federal elections of 1984, PACs contributed almost 45 percent of the funding for the campaigns of members of the house of representatives and 75 percent of the PACs' candidates won! Amounts contributed by individual PACs vary with the particular issues being considered in the Congress. A bill to eliminate mortgage interest deductions from income taxes for example, is almost certain to generate large contributions and extensive lobbying by groups such as the National Association of Home Builders. A bill to limit fees to doctors who treat medicare patients, on the other hand, is almost certain to energize the efforts of the American Medical Association and related groups. It is not surprising that these two PACs were the largest in terms of contributions to Congressional Campaigns in the 1984 elections. Since 1984, other special interest groups have emerged; perhaps the largest today is the American Association of Retired Persons (AARP) which is very active in contributing to the campaigns of Congressional Candidates who favor expansion or at least maintenance of Social Security and medical programs as well as the provision of catastrophic illness benefit programs. PACs may represent industries (Association of Milk Producers), Unions (Letter Carriers Union), professional groups (American Medical Association) or virtually any group whose self-interests are significantly affected by governmental decisions.

PACs or Political Action Committees Organizations that channel funds from special interest groups to the election campaigns of politicians.

How Does Rent Seeking Affect Efficiency?

Successful rent seeking clearly transfers income from one group to another. To the extent that such efforts do not affect the size of the national income, one group's gain is simply another group's loss and, while an equity issue may arise from the transfer, society *as a whole* is no worse off as a result.

To the extent , though, that rent seeking takes resources away from more productive uses and causes them to be used solely for the sake of getting income via government decisions, overall production and income fall and the national income pie shrinks.

In a noted book published in the 1980s, Mancur Olson[2] argues that the actions of special interest groups are unlikely to cause economic efficiency to increase. Indeed, a special interest group is likely to benefit from government activities even though those activities reduce social efficiency. If farmers, for example, succeed in transferring income to themselves through tariffs, price supports and the like and this increases prices for farm products, farmers will pay some of the costs. Since these costs, however, will be spread over a much larger (250 million) group, farm incomes will increase more than farm costs. On balance, then, farmers are made better off while society is made worse off. Farm special interests, which we will examine more closely in the upcoming application, are but one of many competing interest groups (lawyers, teachers, unions, barbers, beauticians, etc.) who, while rationally pursuing self-serving income transfers from government, decrease an economic society's real income.

Resources Going Underground: The Role of Government

Not all people in a epresentative democracy join together as special interest groups, form PACs and go rent seeking in the halls of congress. Indeed, many times citizens want governments to stay as far away as possible from them as a result of government decisions. A prime example of the reason for this is found in tax laws and their enforcement.

Tax Avoidance
The process by which tax obligations are minimized by lawful use of the provisions of tax laws.

Tax Evasion
The illegal process by which tax obligations are either not reported or incorrectly reported in order to evade payment.

When you and I pay taxes that are based on the result of our economic activities (sales taxes on goods bought, excise taxes on goods produced, income taxes on personal incomes and business earnings), our net incomes or returns are diminished. We may well **avoid** as many tax payments as possible through understanding and use of the provisions of the law. If our economics activities are illegal (e.g., drug trafficking) or if we simply think taxes are too high and seek (illegally) not to pay them, we may engage in **tax evasion**, or non-payment of taxes.

Tax evasion is more common than one might suppose. Millions of Americans may make incomes from tips and the like that are not reported. Even more significantly, many resources undoubtedly are devoted to uses in the *underground economy*, ones in

---

[2] *The Rise and Decline of Nations* (New Haven, Conn., Yale University Press, 1982)

which transactions take place that would otherwise give rise to tax obligations if the transactions were reported. Have you or someone you know ever been offered a lower price on some commodity or service if payment is made in cash? If so, one possible explanation is that the seller plans not to report the income for tax purposes; the seller has, in other words, joined the underground economy.

The higher the tax rates, the greater is the incentive to evade taxes including engaging in underground economic activities. As you would expect, there are no exact data on the value of underground activities, but a 1981 estimate of the Census Bureau put the value of non-reported economic activities at well over $200 billion or 7.5 percent of the GDP. Estimates for that same year by the Internal Revenue Service put the loss in tax revenues from evasion at over $90 billion. One of the major arguments for lowering marginal tax rates in 1986 was that more economic activities would occur legally and as a result, government revenues would rise as tax evasion diminished. It is still too early to know if this is happening.

Is Public Choice Anti-Government?

Some economists have argued that public choice perspectives on government activities are ideologically biased and that public choice economists are anti-government. Defenders of public choice respond that neither of these allegations is correct and that students of public choice assign a critical role to government in the operation of a private enterprise economy. Nobel Laureate James Buchanan, a founder of public choice, argues that government alone can create the "rules of the game" that clearly permit property rights to be established and enforced. In turn, this system of rights is key to the complex exchanges that make modern economies more productive and better able to serve the tastes and preferences of their citizens.

As we have seen in this chapter, public choice arguments center on the fear that self-interested public decision makers will be "captured" by special interest groups whose objectives will be furthered at the expense of the general public. Say public choice advocates, such as Dwight Lee and Robert Sexton, "Transcending social objectives do not motivate and direct political action." Self-interested politicians follow policies that are just as narrow as those in the private sector. In the case of income redistribution for example, public choice scholars are doubtful that government programs help the poor and point to the fact that even after the correction of social welfare programs, the poor are perhaps worse off now than before. In addition, say proponents of public choice, such programs create disincentives that reduce productivity.

Public choice economists would deny that they are anti-government. As Lee and Sexton put it: "Public choice economists lean toward less government not because they want less from government but because they believe it is important to get more from it."

APPLICATION:
The Dairy Lobby—Are Both Consumers and Cows Milked?

Agricultural interests are a very powerful special interest group and milk producers are one of its most powerful members. Although farmers began organizing in the 19th century (to support railway regulation), they began to lobby heavily for government protection from market determination of their prices and incomes in the 1920s. Their efforts were capped with success in the 1930s with the passage of the Agricultural Marketing Agreement Acts of 1933 and 1934 which were designed to prevent "ruinous competition". In the more than a half century since, both State and Federal government programs have expanded into almost every aspect of farm output and marketing.

From the farmer's point of view, government intervention is necessary to maintain an equitable relationship between the prices for their products and those farmers pay for resources as well as consumer goods. The farmers plight derives in part from low price and income elasticities of demand. When prices fall in the face of rapidly growing supplies, farm incomes also fall. To get incomes up, thus, requires increasing demand or reducing supplies to raise farm prices, a result that markets in recent decades have not consistently produced.

Price Floors
Target prices below which government does not allow market prices to move.

The Association of Milk Producers is, as already noted, one of the most active lobbies in Washington and one of the largest contributors to congressional election campaigns (almost $1,200,000 in 1984 alone). As a result of its lobbying efforts, the Federal Government has adopted a two-prong approach to supporting dairy prices: (1) the government directly purchases products made from milk (dry milk, butter, cheese); and (2) **price floors**, target prices below which milk prices are not permitted to move, are imposed on milk prices. In this application, we will examine these programs in order to understand who bears their costs and who receives their benefits.

A Model of the Milk Market

Figure 11-4 represents a hypothetical milk market. Left to its own equilibrating forces, the market would establish a price of $2.00 per gallon where quantity demanded equals quantity supplied (50 million gallons). Now, the Congress, responding to the special interest groups representing dairy farmers decides that the price of milk is "too low" and sets a floor price for milk at $3.00 per gallon. Consumers respond by reducing the quantity demanded of milk to 40 million gallons per week. Producers, seeing the high price as an added incentive, increase the quantity supplied to 55 million gallons per week. The difference between quantity demanded and quantity supplied, 15 million gallons

Figure 11-4
The Milk Market Before and After Price Intervention

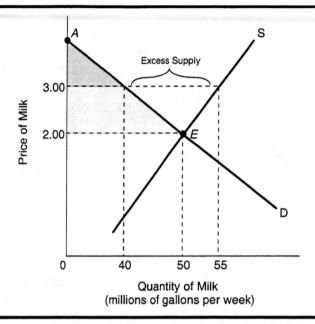

Quantity of Milk
(millions of gallons per week)

In Figure 11-4, a competitive market with demand, D, and supply, S, will establish an equilibrium (*E*) with price = $2.00 per gallon and quantity = 50 million gallons. Congress, deciding that $2.00 is too low, orders a milk price floor of $3.00 per gallon. As a result, the quantity demanded of milk declines to 40 million gallons per week but the quantity supplied increases to 55 million gallons with a surplus or excess supply of 15 million gallons at the floor price. To maintain the floor price, the government must buy the excess 15 million gallons.

per week is a surplus or excess supply in the market. Were the surplus to continue, price would tend to be driven downward below the floor price. To prevent this from happening, the government must buy up the excess supply in the form of manufactured milk products.

The Experience of Milk Price Supports

Does the experience of milk price supports correspond to the result of the hypothetical model in Figure 11-4? In early-1989, the Commodity Credit Corporation, the agency of the Agriculture Department charged by Congress with accomplishing its price support goals, had bought and stored 5.7 *billion* pounds of cheese, butter and non-fat dry milk. This is the equivalent of about 9 billion pounds of milk. The Commodity Credit Corporation, in other words, has become the buyer of last resort in the milk market, spending several billion dollars a year purchasing whatever is not sold (at the floor price) in the market. The Department of Agriculture, through a complex system of establishing classes of milk (grades A, B, or C), sets minimum prices in 41 regions for each grade and buys from farmers at the average of 3 prices. According to James Bovard, the regulations alone to accomplish this take up 3 volumes and require 600 government employees to administer. Milk is also effectively prevented from being moved from one region to another to be reconstituted. By one estimate, permitting these inter-regional shipments could save tax payers and consumers almost $1.5 billion per year.

Apparently, the dairy industry thinks it needs *more* protection. Although support prices had been scheduled in the Agricultural Reform Act of 1986 to be reduced, Congress mandated an increase in 1989 as a part of its drought relief program.

How Much Does the Program Cost?

There are both direct costs and indirect costs in the milk price support program. The former includes the administrative costs referred to above plus the costs of buying and storing manufactured milk products. In 1983, the latter costs amounted to $2.6 billion dollars when the government bought 10 percent of total dairy industry output. Since 1980, these direct costs have amounted to more than $15 billion. Such costs became so large that the Reagan Administration started a "Whole Herd Elimination Program" in which farmers bid for a price at which they would slaughter their herd and get out of the dairy business for at least 5 years. Ironically, at the same time, production quotas were being granted to new producers who wanted to enter the industry to secure all the (government guaranteed) monopoly returns! Because of enforcement problems (incentives to cheat) as well as unfavorable publicity, the program to kill dairy cattle was shelved.

Indirect costs of dairy price supports are even greater than those that are direct. These are primarily in the form of (1) higher prices to consumers ($2.00 to $3.00 in Figure 11-4), (2) reduced consumption of dairy products (50 to 40 in Figure 11-4), and (3) the loss in consumer's surplus (the darker shaded area in Figure 11-4). According to Bruce Gardner, the support program raises the price of manufactured milk by about 30 percent over the (equilibrium) price. Timothy Tregarthen reports that in 1985 dairy products valued at $67 billion were produced in the U.S. If this was 30 percent higher then it would have been without price supports, Tregarthen calculates that the "cost of dairy products was increased by more than $15 billion that year or $172 per household."

Further indirect costs are to be found in the decline in consumption of dairy products. Based on demand elasticity estimates for fresh milk (-63), butter (-73), cheese (-52), and cottage cheese (-11), and on the assumption that dairy product prices would have been 23 percent lower without price supports, one study concludes Americans would have consumed 17 percent more butter, 12 percent more cheese, and 25 percent more cottage cheese. This is in addition to the 16 gallons of milk per year that weren't consumed. As Tregarthen says of the price support program, it "not only cost the average family money, it deprived it of milk as well!"

Why Not a Competitive Milk Industry?

Could America have a competitive dairy industry? Unquestionably, the answer is *yes*. As far back as 1914, however, public choice has been in the opposite direction. The Clayton Act exempted farmer coops from the antitrust laws and instead, in the case of dairy farmers, permitted them to join collusively to set monopoly prices for milk. Monopolists that practice price discrimination can add to their profits. In the case of milk products, price discrimination is against fresh milk (Class 1) (an inelastic demand) and in favor of Class 2 milk (an elastic demand). Most economists today see no reason not to allow markets to establish milk prices. Conditions for competition (free entry, price flexibility, number of producers, etc.) exist. The monopoly that exists is not only permitted by public policy but actively enforced by it. Modern refrigeration and transportation technology has broken down the barriers to inter-regional milk shipments. A competitive national dairy product market is a real option for the nation.

Why Don't Consumers Resist?

By now you no doubt anticipate the answer to the above question. Dairy product laws and regulations are special interest in nature. Public choice theory predicts that such "rules of the game" are likely to be found in cases where costs are diffused and benefits are concentrated. The dairy lobby works very hard, spending $1 to $2 million dollars a year protecting its special interests. The costs as we have seen, are substantial. Bovard says direct and indirect costs since 1980 exceed $1,000 per family. Nonetheless these costs ($100 to $200 per year per family), are relatively insignificant when spread over 250 million people. They are apparently not enough to create a letter writing campaign to congressmen, much less a consumer revolt. Congressmen therefore, facing costly reelection campaigns, have strong incentives to seek PAC contributions from the dairy industry with little fear of facing the wrath of their rationally ignorant constituents as they vote for dairy subsidies.

What kind of game is the dairy game? A *negative sum* game in that the losses exceed the gains. Even though overall productivity suffers, dairy farmers receive *net* benefits (benefits > costs). Is the game likely to change to a competitive (positive sum) game in the foreseeable future? Economists, especially public choice economists, are doubtful. Proposals to limit congressional terms or to restrict special interest contributions to congressional campaigns seem to go nowhere or to be ineffective. In the meantime, America has a much less allocatively and technically efficient dairy industry and consumers bear high costs.

SUMMING UP

1. The role of government in the American economy has been controversial from the nation's earliest history. Part of the pressure for a larger government role came from concerns about "big business" and economic concentration.

2. Antitrust legislation and its enforcement have been major government activities in the last century. Antitrust enforcement may be based on either (a) the *per se rule* (activities that are illegal on their face) or (b) the *rule of reason* in which reasons for business conduct as well as its effects must be assessed.

3. The rule of reason does not clearly identify in any broad sense what business behavior does or does not restrain trade. After the 1940s, courts turned to industry *structure* rather than *conduct* to determine if trade had been restrained.

4. Mergers, both *horizontal* (between firms in the same industry) and *vertical* (between firms in different industries) have increased in recent years. For long, the results of such mergers were looked at in terms of their effects on *concentration ratios* (combined market shares of an industrys' largest firms) to assess whether trade would likely be restrained.

5. Because of problems with concentration ratios, the 1982 Justice Department guidelines turned to *Herfindahl Indices* (sums of the squared percentage market shares of an industrys' firms) to determine restraint of trade. Such indexes are much more sensitive to concentration of economic power than simple concentration ratios.

6. In recent years, market changes including growing international competition, have diminished the market power of many large firms in the U.S. industries. Because of these structural changes, Antitrust prosecution has become much more selective and a more dynamic rather than static view of competition has been adopted.

7. Firm size does not easily equate with firm power. According to a 1982 study by William Shepherd, the American economy became significantly more competitive between 1939 and 1980, especially in the period from 1959 to 1980.

8. Shepherd concludes that increasing competition in the American economy has been caused by, (a) foreign competition, (b) deregulation, (c) antitrust activity.

9. Changes in antitrust laws are being considered that would permit American firms to engage in joint research, product development, and

marketing activities to enable them to compete more effectively with firms abroad that are not constrained by American-style antitrust laws.

10. Governments play many economic rules. The basis for government decision may be assumed to be, (a) optimal decisions correctly timed and in the overall interests of society, or (b) self-interest orientated decisions made by public officials who are concerned with reelection.

11. Public choice begins with the assumption that it is self interest that dictates governmental decisions.

12. Governments must establish the rules of the economic game and the means for resolving disputes among the players. A fair game is one with, (a) a fair process and (b) a fair outcome.

13. Economic games, like all games, can (a) *zero sum* (winnings equal losses), (b) *negative sum* (losses greater than winnings), and (c) *positive sum* (winnings greater than losses). The economic game may be a positive sum game if it is played properly; all can be made better off.

14. The rules of the economic game can change. A change that makes one person better off while making no one else worse off is considered *Pareto optimal*. Once rules can be changed, it may benefit players to seek rule changes in their own self-interest.

15. In direct democracies in which voters make the choices directly, majority rule usually determines the outcome and it is the preferences of the typical or median-voter that prevail. This is so because other preferences cannot normally prevail.

16. Median-voter tastes can be denied through *logrolling* or trading of support for one issue in order to obtain support for another. Coalitions, in other words, may be formed.

17. *Cyclical majorities* may exist in democratic choice making. The choices that are adopted may depend on the order in which choices are presented. Such problems though are not likely to be major when the number of voters is large.

18. In direct democracies most public choices are not made directly by voters but by their elected representatives. Public choice theorists assume that such representatives try to maximize their self-interests in casting their votes. The assumption is that these representatives attempt to maximize their political support.

19. Public choices that serve the self interest of elected representatives may not reflect the preference of the majority of voters. Sugar quotas

and other government actions that raise prices to a (large) group of consumers to benefit a (small) group of producers illustrate this.

20. The large group of voters may not react to government actions that serve narrow special interest groups because of *rational ignorance* (the benefits of the action are concentrated while the costs of the action are widely diffused).

21. The possible ways in which costs and benefits of public choice may be related are (a) benefits and costs are diffused, (b) costs are diffused and benefits are concentrated, (c) both benefits and costs are concentrated, and (d) benefits are diffused and costs are concentrated.

22. With case (a), the constituency for the goods is broad since many pay and many benefit. With case (b), there is a tendency for *special interest laws* to emerge. With case (c), there is a tendency for *competing interest laws* to emerge. With case (d), legislation is unlikely to succeed.

23. Special interest groups in a representative democracy may seek rents, payments to their resources above that necessary to induce their employment. These rents are analogous to and add to monopoly profits and the losses in consumer welfare. *Rent seeking activities* lead to an erosion of the benefits of competition and a loss of productivity and real income.

24. Rent seeking frequently is pursued through the activities of political action committees (PACs) which channel funds from special interest groups to political election campaigns. These contributions have grown greatly in recent years and tend to influence heavily legislative outcomes that favor special interest groups.

25. Economists are skeptical that rent seeking leads to increased economic efficiency. Such activities take resources from directly productive activities and cause them to be used in a search for monopoly-like returns.

26. Special interest groups are likely to benefit even if society and its efficiency are harmed by special interest legislation.

27. Tax laws lead people to seek *tax avoidance* (minimize their legal tax obligations). They also led to *tax evasion* (the non-payment of taxes from illegal activities plus the non-reporting of otherwise taxable economic transactions). In the latter case, many exchanges occur in the *underground economy*. As tax rates rise, the incentive to engage in underground transactions increases.

28. Some argue that public choice is anti-government. Public choice students respond that more government does not necessarily mean better or a more representative government, since public choices may simply serve narrow special interests, not the public at large. Public choice proponents argue that they want to get more from government, not have more of it.

29. Agricultural interests have sought parity prices and government protection and price supports.

30. The Association of Milk Producers is a very active special interest lobby, spending $1 – 2 million per year on congressional campaigns. The federal government supports dairy industry prices by (a) direct purchases, and (b) *price floors*.

31. Price floors, those below which market prices are not allowed to move, result in (a) reductions in quantity consumed, and (b) production surpluses. To support prices, government must buy and store the surpluses.

32. In the case of dairy price supports, the government buys large (and growing) surpluses, with inventories of billions of pounds of cheese, butter and non-fat dry milk. Enforcing the price support regulations has large administrative costs. Price support levels have actually risen in recent years.

33. There are direct as well as indirect costs to dairy price supports. Direct costs are the cost of purchasing and storing surpluses plus the cost of administering the program. Indirect costs consist of (a) higher prices to consumers and (b) reduced consumption of products with price floors.

34. Dairy prices are set collusively by Dairy Coops with the consent and enforcement authority of government. In addition, prices are set to discriminate against buyers of fresh milk. Most economists see no reason why markets should not establish dairy product prices; a national competitive dairy market could be created.

35. The dairy game is a negative sum game and is a Case 2 instance where costs are diffused and benefits concentrated. Congressional candidates have an incentive to accept large contributions from the industry PAC (which seeks the rents or concentrated benefits) while worrying little about the revolt from rationally ignorant constituents who see the diffused costs as relatively insignificant.

36. A more competitive dairy industry seems unlikely. Foreign competition is discouraged and no change in the distribution of costs and benefits from present protection of the industry seems likely.

KEY TERMS

Competing interest laws
Concentration ratios
Direct democracy
Herfindahl index
Horizontal mergers, vertical mergers
Logrolling
Pareto optimal rule change
Political action committees (PACs)
Price floors
Rational ignorance
Rent
Rent seeking activities
Representative democracy
Rule of reason
Special interest laws
Tax avoidance
Tax evasion
Zero sum, positive sum, negative sum games

QUESTIONS

1. What are some of the economic roles that governments may play?

2. What is the difference in terms of antitrust enforcement between the *per se* rule and the rule of reason? Which is more difficult to interpret?

3. What is the difference between a horizontal merger and a vertical merger?

4. In what ways do concentration ratios and Herfindahl indexes differ? Why is a Herfindahl index a more sensitive measure of concentration and potential restraint of trade?

5. In his study of the American economy from 1939 to 1980, William Shepherd concluded that competition has increased. What caused the economy to become more competitive?

6. Firms in Japan and Europe are often permitted to join together to develop new products. What changes in antitrust laws are being considered in the U.S. in order to facilitate American firms doing likewise?

7. What assumptions can one make about the nature of government decisions (public choices)? What assumption do public choice theorists make?

8. How may one measure the fairness of a game?

9. What are some examples of games that are (a) zero sum, (b) negative sum, and (c) positive sum?

10. Why are the preferences of the median voter usually satisfied in a direct democracy? How does logrolling affect the outcome?

11. Why is the problem of cyclical majorities less important when there are many voters?

12. Do you agree that public choices in an indirect democracy may not reflect the preferences of the typical voter?

13. Why is it rational for voters to ignore many government activities that impose costs on them?

14. In what situation are special interests laws likely to emerge? Competing interest laws?

15. What are some examples of rent seeking activities? What do PACs have to do with these activities?

16. Why are economists skeptical of the argument that rent seeking leads to increased efficiency?

17. In the figure below, we see a hypothetical comparison of competitive and monopoly equilibrium in a constant cost industry. Answer the following questions that compare the two results.

   a. If the industry above is competitive, what will industry output and price be?

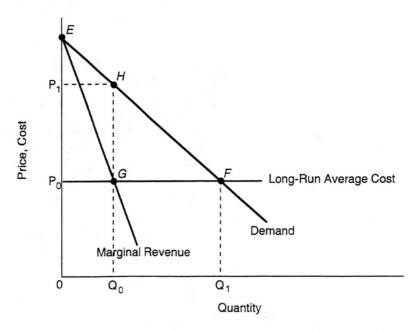

b. If the industry price and output are competitively determined, what will be the area of the consumers' surplus?

c. If the industry above is made monopolistic, what will be industry price and output?

d. What is the loss in consumers' surplus if price and output are monopolistically determined? What is the welfare loss to society from monopoly privilege?

e. Is there a further loss to society from rent seeking activities? If so, what?

18. Which is lawful, *tax avoidance* or *tax evasion*? Which tends to cause resources to be diverted to the underground economy.

19. Do public choice economists want diminished responsibility for government?

SUGGESTED READINGS

Anderson, Terry, and P. J. Hill. *The Birth of a Transfer Society.* Stanford, CA: Hoover Institution Press, 1980.

Bovard, James. "A Subsidy Both Wooly-Headed and Mammoth." *The Wall Street Journal.* 17. April, 1985.

_____. "The Sacred Cows that Keep Milk Prices High." *The Wall Street Journal.* May 5, 1989.

Dolan, Edwin G., and John C. Goodman. "Farm Policy, Welfare for the Rich?" *Economics of Public Policy.* 4th ed. St. Paul, MN: West Publishing Co., 1989.

Food and Agriculture Policies for the 1980s. Washington, D.C.: American Enterprise Institute, 1981.

Hailstones, Thomas J., and Frank V. Mastriana. *Contemporary Economic Problems and Issues.* 8th ed. Ch. 4. Cincinnati, OH: Southwestern Publishing Co., 1988.

Hailstones, Thomas J., and Frank V. Mastriana. "Government Regulation—Why the Controversy." Especially Ch. 6. *Contemporary Economic Problems and Issues.* 8th ed. Cincinnati, OH: Southwestern Publishing Co., 1988.

Jackson, Brooks. "PAC Money Talks Louder Now." *The Wall Street Journal.* 24. December, 1984.

Learn, Elmer W. "Agriculture Price and Income Policy: A Need for Change." *Contemporary Policy Issues*. January, 1986.

Lee, Dwight, and Robert Sexton. "Public Choice is Not Anti-Government." *The Margin*. November/December, 1988.

McKenzie, Richard B. "Political Ignorance: An Empirical Assessment of Educational Remedies." Blacksburg, VA: University Publications, 1977.

Olson, Mancur. "What We Lose When the Rich Go on the Dole." *The Washington Monthly*. 49. January, 1984.

_____. *The Rise and Decline of Nations*. New Haven, CT: Yale University Press, 1982.

Tregarthen, Timothy. "American Consumers Get Milked Again." *The Margin*. January/February, 1989.

_____. "Sugar Restrictions: A Sweet Deal Gone Sour." *The Margin*. September, 1987. (A satirical view of sugar quotas).

Tullock, Gordon. "Toward A Mathematics of Politics." Ann Arbor, MI: University of Michigan Press, 1972.

CHAPTER
12

Factor Markets— Capital and Natural Resources

A society should invest in education, as in anything else, up to the point at which the marginal social cost is equal to the marginal social benefit.

OBJECTIVES

After studying this chapter you will be able to:

- Differentiate between a closed market economy and an open market economy
- Explain how supply and demand work to determine the amount of factor of production a firm in a competitive market employs.
- Explain the marginal revenue product.
- Have a working knowledge of the following terms and concepts:

Derived demand	Resource externalities
Human capital	Signaling
Marginal physical product	

The Factor Market - Capital and Natural Resources

Closed Market Economy
One that does not engage in trading products, services, or resources with other economics.

Open Market Economy
One that trades products, services or resources with other economies.

Factor Markets
Those in which the prices of resources are established and in which resources are allocated.

In this chapter, we will show how *factor* markets work, how the prices of factors, that is, prices such as wages for labor and interest payments on capital, are established. You should then have a complete picture of the operation of the market system in a **closed market economy**, one that does not engage in trading products, services or resources with other economies. Later, we shall add in these international flows to complete the picture of **open market economies**.

What are Factor Markets?

Consider the many boards of directors of companies across the length and breadth of the U.S. Imagine them sitting in boardrooms, making decisions about how much to invest and about how much steel, how many refrigerators, how many tons of bananas or vats of wine or thousands of shoes they will produce next year. These people—few in number, relatively speaking—determine the U.S. output of goods and services. They govern the supply side of *product markets*. Each adult, on the other hand, participates in the **factor markets**, those markets in which the prices of resources—labor, capital, land, and entrepreneurship—are established and in which resources are allocated. Indeed, all market incomes are derived from these factor markets.

Most people get "income" from wages or salaries. Others—a growing number—get income from interest, rents, or profits. The entire market incomes of a society are made up of these four kinds of payments. Of course, market incomes are not the only income sources in a society. Government transfer payments (unemployment compensation, food stamps, and so on) supplement these market incomes.

Factors: Supply and Demand

The prices of factors of production, like the prices of products, are determined by supply and demand. If you have a firm grasp of these concepts from earlier chapters, this section will be easier for you. We are not going to simply repeat the analysis, however, because there are important differences between supply and demand in product markets and supply and demand in factor markets. In this chapter, we are going to concentrate on the *demand* for factors of production. Later, we will examine the *supply* and pricing of factors.

What Determines the Demand for Factors?

Derived Demand
A demand for a factor of production, one that is derived from the expected demand for the product that the factor produces.

Demand for a product depends on the utility or satisfaction people expect to get from it. Demand for a factor, however, is an indirect or **derived demand**. That is, it is derived from the expected demand for a given product that the factor produces. You buy a new car because of the satisfaction you will get from it. The Ford Motor Company builds a new assembly plant, not because its officers derive satisfaction from looking at it, but because they have certain expectations about the demand for new cars that this plant can help to satisfy.

Three things determine the demand for any factor of production and can shift the demand curve for it. Only a change in the *price* of a factor can cause a change in the *quantity demanded*. However, a change in any of four determinants will change or shift the demand for the factor.

1. *Changes in the amount of product demanded.* Suppose that Americans' demand for cars increases. Then the demand for steel, aluminum, rubber, and labor time of automobile workers will increase. So will the demand for many other things that are used in automobile production. This also works in reverse. For example, some years ago, the Roman Catholic Church in the U.S. relaxed its ban on eating meat on Friday. The result was a decrease in the demand for fish (with a corresponding increased demand for meat). This meant a decreased derived demand for the labor of fishermen, for fishing boats and equipment, and for all factors used to harvest and process fish.

2. *Changes in the productivity of resources.* People who are running businesses hire the most productive resources (factors) they can and combine them in the most productive ways they can. The most productive resources are the "first hired and the last fired." And as a resource's productivity increases, so does the demand for it. Many things influence the productivity of a resource: (a) the productivity of other resources ("This machine makes it possible for me to turn out twenty times what I used to by hand"); (b) technology ("This *new* machine is a lot faster than the old one"); (c) managerial ability ("Our

new boss sure knows how to get the work out"); and (d) the skills and innate abilities of labor.

3. *Changes in the prices of other factors of production.* Let's continue to assume that firms seek to maximize profits. To do this, they try to produce their product at the least possible cost and at the most profitable rate. Therefore, in combining resources, they must consider not only relative productivity of factors but also relative prices of factors. Much of the amazing development of technology in the U.S. is due to the efforts of American businesses to find new machines and capital-intensive processes that will reduce the unit costs of production. A lot of what is called *technological unemployment* (the displacement of labor by capital) can be blamed on the relatively faster increase in the cost of wages (because of pressure by unions and minimum wage laws) than in the cost of capital which has led to a tendency to substitute capital for labor.

4. *Changes in the quantities of other factors employed.* There are important complementarities that exist between factors of production. Thus, if more and better capital is employed in a productive process, the labor employed along with that capital will experience rising productivity. As a result, there will be an increase in the demand for those labor skills. As specialized equipment such as computers and word processors have been employed by many firms in recent decades, the productivity of labor to those firms has risen.

An Example of Factor Demand

Let's look at a hypothetical firm to see how its derived demand for resources is determined. The Universal Study Guide Company is a profit-maximizing firm. For simplicity, let's say that it is a pure competitor in both its product market and its factor market. This means that it is unable to influence either the price of study guides (those all-purpose study aids for college students) or of labor (the variable factor used in producing the guides).

How many workers will Universal Study Guide hire? Recall that it will maximize its profits by producing a study guide up to the point at which marginal revenue (MR) equals marginal cost (MC). Since we have assumed that labor is the firm's only variable cost, it will hire workers up to the point at which laborers will no longer add to its profits. (In other words, at some point more workers will begin to add more to the firm's cost than to its revenue.) To establish this point, we must introduce a new concept: **marginal revenue product (MRP)**, which is the change in total revenue (TR) associated with a change in the use of the variable input. Table 12-1 gives numbers to show the importance of MRP to the Universal Study Guide.

Marginal Revenue Product (MRP) The change in a firm's TR associated with a change in the use of a variable input.

Table 12-1
Demand for a Resource (Labor) by Universal Study Guide Company in a Purely Competitive Market

1	2	3	4	5	6
Units of Variable Resource	Total Product	Marginal Physical Product	Product Price	Total Revenue	Marginal Revenue Product
(L = labor)	(TP = output per day in thousands)	($MPP_L = \Delta TP/\Delta L$) = ($\Delta 2/\Delta 1$)	(P)	(TR = TP x Q) = (2) x (4)	(MRP = VMP = MPP_L x P) = (3) x (4)
0	0		$2	0	
		30			$60
1	30		2	60	
		27			54
2	57		2	114	
		24			48
3	81		2	162	
		20			40
4	101		2	202	
		18			36
5	119		2	238	
		15			30
6	134		2	268	
		12			24
7	146		2	292	
		10			20
8	156		2	312	
		8			16
9	164		2	328	
		5			10
10	169		2	338	
		0			0
11	169		2	338	

Law of Variable Proportions
The assumption that as a firm adds successive equal increments of a variable input in conjunction with a fixed input, beyond some point the additions to output from the variable input will diminish.

Marginal Physical Product
The addition to output of each additional unit of the variable input.

Column 1 of Table 12-1 shows units of labor (L) hired to produce study guides as the price of the resource changes. These workers represent successive equal units of labor. Thus, they enable us to observe the operation of the **law of variable proportions** (or diminishing marginal productivity)[1]. As a firm uses successive equal increments of a variable input in conjunction with a fixed input (or inputs), beyond some point the additions to output attributable to the variable input will diminish. Column 2 shows total product (TP, *or output of study guides*). It shows the way output increases through the tenth unit. Up to that point, each additional unit of labor produces some added product. The eleventh unit of labor, however, does not produce anything. Perhaps, the worker must wait to use a machine.

Column 3 represents the **marginal physical product** (MPP_L). This is the addition to the output of study guides on the part of each additional of labor. You can see that MPP_L, keeps decreasing until, finally, when Universal Study Guide hires the eleventh unit of labor, MPP_L reaches zero. Perhaps this result was not immediate. Initially, the MPP might have increased, or at least remained constant. But finally, it goes toward zero.

---

[1]A law that is familiarly known as the *law of diminishing returns*.

Column 4 shows that Universal Study Guide takes as given a competitive study guide price of $2. This is the price at which the firm can sell all the guides it produces with the labor it hires. TR (column 5) is the product of price (column 4) times output (column 2). TR rises along with output. It also reaches a maximum when total product does. This happens when the tenth unit of labor is hired. *MRP* is the addition that each extra unit of a resource (labor, in this case) makes to TR. You can see that MRP keeps getting less and less for Universal Study Guide, as it hires more and more workers. It follows that if the firm faces a price of its product that is constant due to competition and has a constantly decreasing MPP it is bound to have a diminishing MRP.

How much labor will Universal Study Guide hire? Table 12-1 does not give this information. One can assume that the firm will hire whatever amount of labor is most profitable. The profitability of labor is determined by the relation between what labor adds to the firm's *cost* and what it adds to the firm's revenues. To figure profit on the use of labor, therefore, cost (price paid to labor times amount hired) is subtracted from revenue (price of product times output produced). Remember that we are assuming a simple marketplace in which Universal Study Guide both hires labor competitively and sells its product competitively. So not only is there a constant price ($2) for study guides, but there is also a constant wage for labor (not determined by Universal Study Guide).

Suppose that Universal Study Guide can hire all the workers it wants to—all that it can profitably employ—at the going wage. (We will not yet take into account unions, minimum wage laws, company towns, and such considerations.) We will first examine a simple, purely competitive market process, and then add real-world complications.

Figure 12-1 shows the market process with the MRP of labor (MRP_L) plotted from the data in Table 12-1. Remember that every time Universal Study Guide hires an additional laborer, MRP_L declines because of diminishing marginal physical productivity. Since the firm sells study guides competitively, this is a special case of MRP.

Value of Marginal Product
The product of MPP times product price (MPP x P).
Note: When MR = P for a firm (the competitive case), VMP = MRP since P = MR.

In the special competitive product market case, MRP (MPP x MR) is the same as **value of marginal product** (VMP = MPP x P): what each additional unit of the resource (labor) contributes to the output of the firm as valued by consumers. This is true because under competitive market conditions, P = MR. In other words, study guides sell for $2 apiece no matter how many of them the firm makes and each sold adds the same amount to the firm's TR. Later on, we will make Universal Study Guide a noncompetitive firm to see what happens when price is greater than MR. To review the changes that occur in a firm's product market when there is no pure competition.

For Universal Study Guide, its demand for labor is MRP_L = VMP_L of Figure 12-1. Again, this demand for labor slopes downward

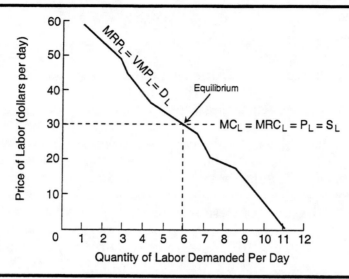

In Figure 12-1, the firm's demand curve for labor ($MRP_L = VMP_L = D_L$) slopes downward because of diminishing marginal physical productivity as more labor is employed. Since the firm sells study guides competitively, their MR and price are equal and $MRP_L = VMP_L$. The firm hires labor competitively and can employ any quantity at a price of $30 per day. The MRC of labor is thus, constant and represents the firm's supply of labor ($MC_L = MRC_L = P_L = S_L$). The equilibrium quantity of labor to employ is that which makes labor's contribution to additional revenue (MRP_L) equal to labor's contribution to additional cost (MRC_L). In Figure 12-1, quantity demanded of labor equals quantity supplied of labor at an employment rate of 6 units per day.

Marginal Resource Cost (MRC)
The additional cost of one more unit of a resource.

because of diminishing marginal physical productivity. How much labor will it hire? Well, that depends on the price of labor (P_L). Let's suppose that the going wage for study guide workers is $30 per day. This constant wage is also the MC of labor (MC_L), or the **marginal resource cost** of labor (MRC_L), which is what it costs to hire one more unit of the resource, labor, shown by the dashed line $MC_L = MRC_L = P_L = S_L$ (MC of labor equals MRC of labor equals price of labor equals supply of labor).

The most profitable number of workers to hire is 6, because the sixth worker hired adds the same to revenue as to cost, $30 to each ($MRP_L = MRC_L$). Universal Study Guide will hire the sixth unit of labor and no more. If it hired fewer workers than this, it would be giving up some profits; if it hired more than this, its profits would begin to decrease.

Again, you have encountered the familiar concept of market equilibrium, that markets clear where quantity supplied equals quantity demanded. MRP_L or VMP_L, once the marginal physical productivity of labor declines, is the competitive firm's demand curve for labor. And MC_L (MRC_L) is the competitive firm's perfectly elastic supply curve for labor. Quantity supplied and quantity demanded are equal at the equilibrium point—where there is neither excess demand nor excess supply.

To Maximize Profit, Minimize Cost

We have examined business firms' average—and marginal—cost curves. Yet how do we know that those are the firm's costs? We assume that Universal Study Guide will make every effort to maximize profits. Therefore, it combines its resources in such a way that *cost is minimized*, for any rate of output. Since profit is TR minus total cost (TC), the firm, to maximize profit, will wish to produce any output with the least cost.

Note: A general rule for minimizing the cost of using resources: Combine resources in such a way that a dollar spent on one input yields the same output as a dollar spent on any other input.

Here's a general rule about minimizing cost: Resources are combined at least cost when a dollar spent on one input yields the same amount of output as a dollar spent on any other input.

Suppose that Universal Study Guide, for example, has two variable inputs—labor (L) and capital (K). The firm decides to juggle the ratios of these two inputs and see what happens. So it spends a dollar less on capital, which means that it has to give up 10 guides ($MPP_K = 10$). It takes that extra dollar and spends it on labor. This leads to a gain of 12 guides ($MPP_L = 12$). So its net gain is 2 study guides. In this trial-and-error way, the firm keeps on juggling, until it establishes the following equilibrium (least-cost) relationship:

$$\frac{MPP_K}{P_K} = \frac{MPP_L}{P_L}$$

This equation says that the MRP of capital divided by the *price* of capital is equal to the MPP of labor divided by the *price* of labor. This is just a restatement of the general rule about minimizing cost, and it applies to points on the curves that show a firm's average cost (AC) and MC. (Remember that the rate of output that is profit maximizing also requires that MRC = MRP.)

Demand for a Resource by the Market as a Whole

You have seen that the competitive firm's demand for an input is the same as the MRP of that input, or the VMP You can find out the demand for the whole industry by adding the demand of each firm at each likely resource price. But you can do this only so long as there are no **resource externalities**, changes in *costs* of resources that are not attributable to the employment decisions of a single firm.

Resource Externalities Those changes in costs of resources that are not attributable to the employment decisions of a single firm.

Suppose that the wage rate of labor used in producing study guides falls from $30 to $26 a day (a whole class graduates with study-guide-making skills and depresses the wage). Table 12-1 suggests that Universal Study Guide will take advantage of cheaper labor and hire 1 more laborer at the new wage rate (to make MRP = MRC = $26). Now suppose, however, that *every* study guide manufacturer acts on the new wage rate, and starts to hire more labor. The *entire* guide industry may employ enough of the labor skill so that it does not hire labor competitively. If so, the industry's wage rate is bid up (an increasing-cost industry). The higher wage causes guide makers' MRC to rise. This reduces the equilibrium quantity of labor each firm demands. So to find out how much labor the industry demands, we add the equilibrium quantities of labor demanded by all these firms after the externalities are incorporated. The economy is not a simple place even for a firm operating in a purely competitive market.

Elasticity of Demand for a Resource

Elasticity of Resource Demand
The rate at which the quantity demanded of a resource changes as the price of the resource changes.

The **elasticity of resource demand** is the rate at which the quantity of a resource demanded changes as the price of the resource changes. (You can remember this definition if you connect *elasticity* to the amount of *stretch*, or change.)

Imagine that you are president of Universal Study Guide, and you must watch the prices of all the factors closely, so you can juggle your production schedule to maximize profits. The elasticity of your demand for one of these factors—labor—as the wage rate changes is determined, basically, by four things:

1. *The rate at which the MPP of the factor (labor) declines.* The amount of this MPP depends on the technology of the production process. The less rapidly labor's MPP decreases as Universal Study Guide adds labor, the less elastic the firm's demand for labor.

2. *The price elasticity of demand for the final product (guides).* Since the demand for this resource is a derived demand, if a small change in product price causes a large change in quantity demanded (if the price elasticity of demand for the final product is large), there will be a large change in the quantity of labor hired to produce study guides. In general, then the greater the price elasticity of demand for the final product produced by the input, the greater its resource elasticity of demand (the two elasticities are directly related).

3. *The proportion of the TC of production represented by the factor.* Suppose labor costs make up 70 percent of the cost of producing guides. And say the guide makers' union demands a 5-percent wage increase. If Universal Study Guide grants this increase, it will significantly increase the firm's AC and MC. So the firm will reduce the quantity it produces, which will cut down on the supply of guides available. The market price will go up, and the public will buy fewer guides. If this happens, there will be a significant decrease in the quantity of labor Universal Study Guide demands. In other words, the greater the proportion of total production cost accounted for by the factor, the greater its resource elasticity of demand. (The two factors —percentage of resource cost and factor elasticity of demand—are directly related.)

4. *The degree of substitutability for the factor.* Suppose that the Bleep Company (unlike Universal Study Guide) employs a large number of

Chapter 12: Factor Markets - Capital and Natural Resources   371 variable factors. The elasticity of demand of the Bleep Company for any *one* factor will be greater. Universal Study Guide, on the other hand, uses only one variable factor (at least in the short run) and only two, even in the long run. This causes the firm's $MRPL_1$ (see Figure 12-1) to be relatively steep. That is, there is no substitutability, because Universal Study Guide cannot substitute something else for labor. Thus, the less substitutability there is of one factor for another, the smaller its price elasticity of demand. (Substitutability and elasticity of resource demand are directly related.)

Income Distribution: "Fair" or "Unfair?"

According to the theory of marginal productivity, resources under competitive market conditions will be paid an amount of money equal to their MRP (or their VMP). In other words, in the case of labor, people will be paid what they contribute in value to the output of the firm or employer. This conclusion has led some advocates of competitive capitalism to argue that competitive markets lead to a "fair" or "just" distribution of income. Justice, in these cases, has different meanings. Other critics say that the market distribution is unjust.

Most economists would say that there are problems in identifying a just distribution of income for reasons that include the following:

1. *It is difficult (if not impossible) to separate the productivities of resources or to measure their contribution to output.* The theory of marginal productivity has a built-in assumption that one can identify and quantify the changes in output attributable to hiring more or less of a single input. But when you get down to cases, the productivity of one unit of labor (or other kind of factor) depends not only on its own productivity, but the productivity of the capital (and other resources) with which it works. We noted this in connection with the discussion of the elasticity of resource demands. Even if paying resources their value of marginal productivity were regarded as equitable, it would be difficult to establish how *much* they should be paid.

2. *Economists shy away from talking about a "just" or "fair" distribution of income.* Who is to say unambiguously that one income distribution is fairer than another? Words like *just* and *fair* are value-laden. What is fair in the 1990s in the U.S. may well be unfair at another time or to other people. So economists concentrate on efficiency, price stability, growth, and other implications of income distribution.

The theory of marginal productivity is useful as a guide to the firm's profit-maximizing demand for resources, but you should not read more into it than that.

Demand for Resources Among Monopolistic Firms

Industries in which products are sold noncompetitively demand resources too, of course, though, as we shall see, not the same amounts. Suppose that Universal Study Guide, by a combination of circumstances, becomes the only producer of guides. Universal Study Guide, in other words, becomes monopolistic. (We will also assume that the Justice Department does not intervene to invoke the antitrust laws against guide makers, and that study guides cannot be imported.)

Since demand for resources is derived from demand for products, Universal Study Guide's change to a monopoly demand for products determines what happens to its resource demand. For the time being, for convenience, we shall continue to assume that the firm's supply of resources is competitive. (That is, its MRC is equal to the competitively determined resource price.)

Now that Universal Study Guide is noncompetitive, it has a substantial percentage of the market demand for study guides. Remember the discussion of diminishing marginal utility and of income and substitution effects? If so, you will also recall that the curve depicting market demand shows an inverse relationship between price and quantity demanded. When price goes up, quantity demanded goes down. If a firm wants to sell more of a product, it must lower the price. When Universal Study Guide was in a purely competitive market, the demand curve for its product was perfectly elastic. However, as a monopolist, it must deal with a demand curve *less* than perfectly elastic. In fact, the demand curve of any monopolist slopes downward.

Accordingly, for these new demand conditions, let's recalculate Universal Study Guide's demand for labor. Table 12-2 gives the overall picture. Note two things: (1) We are assuming that the marginal physical productivity of labor is the same to Universal Study Guide whether the firm is competitive or noncompetitive. (2) We are assuming, to simplify the market picture, that Universal Study Guide, now that it is a monopolist, is not really a bigger firm than it was as a competitive firm (its cost curves are the same). It is simply the only seller in the study guide market.

Now let's see what happens to Universal Study Guide's hiring practices when it moves from a competitive to a noncompetitive situation. Its choices about hiring labor (column 1) are the same in a noncompetitive situation as they were in a competitive one. Actually, this is unrealistic. Because if the whole study guide industry were to become monopolistic, and if market demand stayed at the same level as before, the firm that is still in the running would probably be larger. So it would hire more labor and produce more guides than it would if it were a smaller, competitive producer.

The simplified picture here, however, enables us to observe what happens to a firm's demand for labor solely as a result of having no competition in the product market. Columns 2 and 3 remain the

Table 12-2
Demand for Resources by Universal Study Guide Company in a Pure Monopoly

1	2	3	4	5	6
Units of Variable Resource	Total Product (TP = output per day in thousands)	Marginal Physical Product $(MPP_L = \Delta TP/\Delta L) = (\Delta 2/\Delta 1)$	Product Price (P)	Total Revenue (TR = TP x P)	Marginal Revenue Product $(MRP = \Delta TR/\Delta L = MPP_L \times MR)$
0	0		$2.00	0	
		30			$57.00
1	30		1.90	57.00	
		27			45.60
2	57		1.80	102.60	
		24			35.10
3	81		1.70	137.70	
		20			23.90
4	101		1.60	161.60	
		18			16.90
5	119		1.50	178.50	
		15			9.10
6	134		1.40	187.60	
		12			2.20
7	146		1.30	189.80	
		10			-2.60
8	156		1.20	187.20	
		8			-6.80
9	164		1.10	180.40	
		5			-10.40
10	169		1.00	169.00	
		0			0
11	169		1.00	169.00	

same (by assumption) when Universal Study Guide becomes a monopolistic firm. However, column 4, product price, is different. As Universal Study Guide produces and sells more and more guides, their price falls. Because the price goes down (because the firm does not take price as given), the *MRP* (MPP_L x MR) is no longer the same as the *VMP* (MPP_L x P). The reason is that MR is less than P. Note that monopolistic Universal Study Guide's MRP is now less for *each* amount of labor hired (up to the point at which MPP = 0) than it was under competition.

In other words, for a monopolist, hiring more labor does not produce as much additional revenue as it would for a competitive firm.

Figure 12-2 compares the two situations. The $MRP_L = VMP_L$ curve for competition is the same as it was for the competitive situation in Figure 12-1. The former equilibrium rate of employment was 6 workers per day. At this level, Universal Study Guide's marginal revenue product for labor was equal to its MRC, or the daily wage paid to those extra workers (shown by E_c, or the equilibrium point in a situation of competition, in Figure 12-2).

Now Figure 12-2 shows the new (noncompetitive) MRP of labor (column 6 in Table 12-2) plotted to the left of the competitive one. Labeled MRP_L, it reflects the fact that labor's MRP declines

Figure 12-2
The Universal Study Guide Company's Equilibrium Demand for Labor Under Conditions of Competition (E_c),
and its Demand for Labor Under Conditions of Monopoly (E_m)

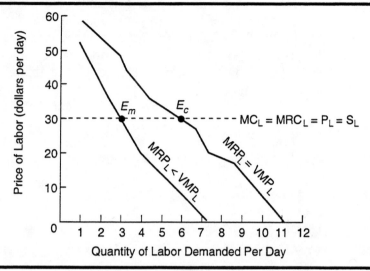

Figure 12-2 depicts the labor market for a firm when that firm hires labor competitively but (1) sells its products competitively and (2) sells its products monopolistically. The competitive equilibrium in (1) occurs where MRC equals MRP equals VMP ($MRC_L = MRP_L = VMP_L$) at E_c with 6 units of the resource employed per day (the result from Figure 12-1). In situation (2), the firm as a monopolist faces a downward sloping product demand and, as a result, MR is less than price (MR < P). MRP becomes less than VMP and the firm's demand for labor shifts to the left ($MRP_L < VMP_L$). The firm, producing fewer study guides profitably. Equating ($MRP_L < VMP_L$) with MRC_L, the monopolistic producer hires 3 units of the resource at E_m.

with a falling product price, as the firm sells more and more study guides. Remember that labor's competitive wage ($30 per day) is still the same. Now E_m shows the new employment equilibrium in a monopolistic product market situation: between 3 and 4 units of labor per day. Remember that we are assuming here that the output of study guides and units of resource are completely divisible. If they are not divisible, the firm will hire the third worker, but not the fourth, since the fourth will add less to revenue than to cost.

Remember that the demand for labor is derived from the demand for products. A noncompetitive seller finds it profitable to produce less of the product and hire less labor than a competitor would. Equilibrium output of study guides decreases and, as a result, Universal Study Guide hires fewer workers than it would if it were operating in a purely competitive market.

Product Monopoly: Is it a Problem in Factor Markets?

An important point from the discussion above is the following:

Introducing monopoly (of whatever degree) into product markets results in a decrease in the demand for resources employed to produce those products.

We see this leftward shift in the demand for labor by universal study guide in Figure 12-2. This could well be viewed as a social problem since not enough of this labor skill is being employed to create competitive levels of output in the study guide market. Does this mean, though, that the *labor* market is allocatively inefficient? Put another way, is there a labor market action society could take that would make this market more efficient? The answer is no, because the problem, while a demand problem is external to the labor market.

The decline in employment in Figure 12-2 is simply the labor market reaction to the problem of product monopoly. If considered a problem, a solution (such as antitrust enforcement) would have to be found in the study guide market rather than in the labor market.

APPLICATION:
How Much Education Should We Buy?

An educated person is one who voluntarily does more thinking than is necessary for his own survival.

Anonymous

Ever since the days of the early settlers in the U.S., people have believed in the power of widespread education to guide everyone to create a better way of life, as well as greater productivity. Education has many advantages other than economic ones. It transmits the national culture to the next generation. It creates a more informed electorate. (Frederick the Great said, "An educated people is easily governed.") Nonetheless, education raises economic issues, governments have set up and financed public education at all levels, from the elementary school through the university. After all, producing education, like all other things, requires resources. That education and those resources can be produced and employed publicly or privately. In the U.S. over 80 percent of total expenditures on education are public. At the same time, private institutions also deliver systems of education.

There are many issues related to education that America faces in the 1990s. Included are performance levels of students, whether students and their families should be treated as consumers and allowed to choose schools and whether we as individuals and as a society are putting the proper amount of resources into the production of education. It is to the last of these three that we turn in this application. Thus, the title, *How Much Education Should We Buy?*

Are we investing in either sense, the correct amounts in educating people? Economists in recent years have come to identify a fifth factor of production to add to land, labor, capital, and

Human Capital
Term used to identify the resources consisting of the productivity of individuals due to innate ability, education and acquired skills.

entrepreneurship. The fifth factor, **human capital**, refers to the improvements in labor skills (increase in marginal physical productivity) that are attributable to innate ability, education or other training. Economist Burton A. Weisbrod says that since 1900, total U.S. expenditures on education have increased four times as rapidly as expenditures on physical plant and equipment. It is possible, therefore, that the U.S. is investing too much in human capital, as opposed to other resources.

What is the "correct" amount of investment in education (or human capital)? Douglass C. North and Roger Leroy Miller point out in their book *The Economics of Public Issues* that the "correct" amount is the one at which "the return on investment in human capital is equal at the margin to other types of investment" (that is, the opportunity costs of capital are equated at the margin). In other words, one must compare the costs and benefits of investment in education with the costs and benefits of other types of investments.

The costs of education are (1) costs borne by students (such as room, board, books, and tuition); (2) costs borne by the public in the form of subsidies (collected through property taxes, appropriations by state legislatures, and so on); and (3) the opportunity costs to students, or what they could have earned if they had held full-time jobs during the time they were in school (research has shown this to be about half of total educational cost).

"Amazing when you think of it. $11,365.42 worth of knowledge in you and you don't look a bit different."

The benefits of education are (1) that people with education have higher lifetime earnings than they would have without their education; (2) that education has value as a consumer good (it makes possible greater enjoyment of books, music, paintings, and so on); and (3) that society gains external benefits by having better educated citizens (there is less crime, voters are better informed, taxpayers are able to make out their own tax returns, and so on).

However, to determine the present value of these costs or benefits, you must discount back to the present both the *stream of costs* (the flow of costs over the educational lifetime of students) and the *stream of benefits* (the flow of benefits over the expected lifetimes of students). Think of it this way: A dollar in hand today is worth more than a dollar promised to you a year (or 5 or 10 years) from now because of the interest you can earn over the future period on the dollar held now. The same is true for society as a whole. It, too, can enjoy the power of compound interest. It therefore must discount future dollars in favor of present dollars.

The difficulty with ensuring that the costs and benefits are equal at the margin—that is, that individuals as well as the nation, are buying the "correct" amount of education lies in the fact that there are three potentially different assessments of costs and benefits. Students make one assessment, their parents make another, and government makes a third. Rates of return are likely to look different to each, because students often pay very little of even the direct costs of their education. Therefore, the benefits, in terms of added lifetime income (plus psychic benefits), almost always exceed the costs. (Students, of course, rarely make these decisions until they are of college age.) Parents usually bear most of the direct costs of pre-collegiate education, and such costs are often large for private elementary and high schools. Thus, parents derive mainly psychic returns, such as seeing their children graduate, or knowing that their children are more secure economically. Since these psychic returns are mental and emotional, the rates of return for parents are difficult to estimate.

Therefore, there is a possible divergence between private rates of return on investment in education to students and to parents. However, the *private rates of return*—those that do not take into account indirect social costs and external benefits—are impressive. In a paper entitled, *"Human Capital: Policy Issues and Research Opportunities,"* T. W. Schultz estimated percentages of return per dollar of investment in education as follows:

Type of Education	Rate of Return
All U.S. education	10-15%
Primary education	35%
Secondary education	25%
College education	15%
Graduate education	15%

These rates depend on the rate at which one discounts future income. Nonetheless, these rates are greater than the average rate of return on capital investment in the U.S. The increase that education seems to bring to lifetime income alone ($350,000 for a high school graduate versus $586,000 for a college graduate) appears to warrant a high rate of private investment.

One must not, however, assume that *all* the increased earnings are due to education. It may well be that those with higher levels of education have greater abilities to begin with (higher marginal productivity). Even in the absence of the educational difference, there might still be some differences in income. The very high rate of estimated return on investment in primary education suggests that money invested in U.S. education should be reallocated so that a greater percentage of it goes to primary schools. Remember, though, that these rates are based on a given stock of capital. The figures do not suggest that such rates would hold true for all levels or all flows of capital into education.

Age-Earnings Profile Shows the relationship between annual incomes and age for groups with various levels of education.

We see in Figure 12-3 the relationship for private individuals between annual incomes and age for groups with levels of education ranging from elementary school through post-graduate education. This relationship is known as an **age-earnings profile**.

Confirming the relationship between education and income shown in the Schultz data, this Census Bureau study, indicates that (1) earnings of groups of individuals rise with education, and

Figure 12-3
Age-Earnings Profiles of Males by Education, 1984

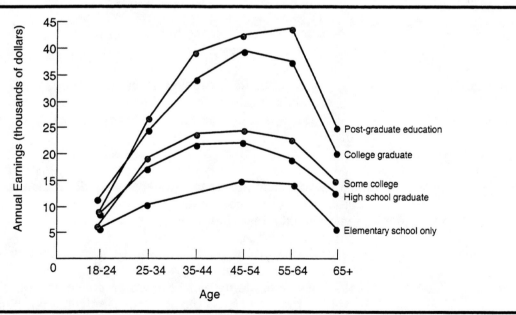

Figure 12-3 shows average earnings in the U.S. for different ages and levels of education. Each level is represented by a different curve. Earnings increase with education and, up to a maximum, with age.

Source: U.S. Bureau of the Census, Current Population Reports, Series P-60, *Money Incomes of Household, Families, and Persons in the United States: 1984*, Table 34.

(2) incomes rise with age and then flatten out or decline (while this applies to people in different age groups, earnings rise with age for an individual to the age of 70).

Does this interpretation of these data mean that added education leads to higher marginal productivity? Perhaps. Studies of individuals with the same IQ show that additional education leads to higher income. The problem, though, is with what IQ measures: clearly it does not measure *intensity* of effort on the part of individuals. Some of us simply work harder than others. Some economists, based on the work of Michael Spence, conclude that employers pay higher wages to more educated workers because education is a signal to employers about productivity influencing aspects of behavior (time orientation, acceptance of directions, meeting of targets, and the like) that are difficult to directly assess. This idea that education is a **signaling** device is thought not only to explain why employers pay higher wages and salaries to those with more education even though such education may not directly increase their productivity.

Signaling
The idea that employers pay higher wages to more educated workers because the education is a signal of other aspects of productivity increasing behavior.

Society's "Purchase" of Education

What about the return to society at large on investment in education? The public, by paying taxes, puts up a considerable part of the costs of both private and public education about ⅓ of private education revenues and over 80 percent of those in public education. To what extent should the public subsidize the education of individuals? The economist's answer is that the public should subsidize to an extent sufficient to exhaust the *externalities* of education, so that the supply of education is increased and the price of it is reduced to the point at which the *socially* desirable amount of education is "produced and consumed."

According to economist Donald Winkler, the arguments in favor of public subsidization of education are based on the following considerations. All but the first two have some externalities attached to them.

1. *Imperfections in the capital market.* Some argue that education must be subsidized because low-income students cannot go into the capital market and borrow the money to "buy" an education (what collateral could they offer?)

2. *Income redistribution.* Those who believe that income should be distributed more "equitably" feel that educational subsidies are a useful means of doing this. Subsidies can both transfer income directly to low-income people and broaden the base of human capital (raise the productivity of low-income people). This causes future income to be distributed in a more nearly equal manner. (A study of

higher education in California during the 1960s suggests, however, that educational subsidies redistributed income in favor of middle- and upper-income groups.)

These two arguments are not very convincing to most economists. After all, even if capital markets were perfect (that is, even if each individual had equal access to them), and even if income were redistributed to fit some particular notion of what is right, people might still underinvest in education because they could not take advantage of the *social* benefits of education. (They could not appreciate the value of education to the public.) The remaining arguments for subsidizing education rest, therefore, on externalities.

3. *Economic growth.* A well-known study by Edward Denison concluded that 12 percent of the economic growth of the U.S. between 1927 and 1957 was attributable to increased human capital. Other, more recent studies generally confirm this. Here we are mainly concerned with the net benefit of subsidizing education and the effect of this subsidy on economic growth.

4. *Reduced crime rates.* The opportunity cost of committing a crime is higher to better educated people than to less well-educated people. Thus, the better educated are much less likely to commit crimes. (Over 10 percent of the American population had completed 4 years of college, but less than 1 percent of the criminal population has that much education.)

5. *Improved learning environment.* The greater the degree of education of parents, the more readily their children, and their children's peers, learn. This is a benefit to society.

6. *Better citizenship.* There is evidence that educated people participate more actively in politics and, in this sense, are better citizens. One cannot place monetary value on good citizenship, but surely it benefits society significantly.

7. *Certification.* A degree certifies to society that a student has satisfactorily carried out certain programs of study. If it were not for this system, businesses and government agencies would have to pay the costs of this certification, of finding out what career the student was best suited for.

8. *Higher tax returns and lower transfer payments.* A study in the 1970s showed that college-educated people paid higher taxes on their (same) incomes than people who were not college educated. Educated people are also probably more able to prepare their own tax returns than noneducated people.

To summarize, parents and students have their own estimates of the costs and benefits (rates of return) that they derive from investment in education. Because the divergence between these estimates may be large, it is unlikely that private U.S. investment in education is the "correct" amount. Nonetheless, income growth, whether from productivity increase or from signaling, appears to warrant large private expenditures on education. Public subsidization of the consumption of education is based primarily on internalizing external benefits that private individuals cannot.

SUMMING UP

1. This chapter deals with the operation of *factor markets*, especially the way the *demand* for factors, or resources, of production (labor, land, capital, and entrepreneurship) is established. It is as important to understand factor markets as it is product markets, since factor markets are the source of our entire market incomes and allocate all inputs used to create products and services.

2. Combining product and factor markets and showing their interdependencies will permit an examination of the operation of a *closed economy,* one in which goods and resources flows occur without international trade.

3. Factor prices, like product prices, are determined by supply and demand. However, there are important differences between the pricing of factors and the pricing of products.

4. Demand for factors, unlike demand for products, is a *derived demand*. That is, a firm bases its demand for factors on the anticipated demand for its products.

5. Four things that determine the demand for a factor of production are (a) changes in the amount of demand for the end product, (b) changes in the *marginal physical product* (MPP) (which is influenced by the productivity of other resources, technology, managerial ability, and labor skills), (c) changes in the (relative) prices of other factors of production (for example, much technological unemployment is due to the fact that labor's wages have risen faster than the cost of capital), and (d) changes in the quantities and types of other resources employed since the productivity of a factor depends on the other factors with which it is employed.

6. A profit-maximizing firm hires a factor of production (such as labor) up to the point at which that factor adds as much to revenue as it adds to cost.

7. *Marginal revenue product* (MRP) is the addition to TR associated with a change in the use of a variable input. The *law of variable proportions* (or diminishing returns) says that when a firm uses successive increments of a variable input in conjunction with a fixed input, increases in output diminish beyond some point. Thus, the law

of variable proportions affects MRP. Even when factor prices are competitive (constant to the individual firm), MRP ultimately diminishes because of diminishing MPP.

8. For a competitive firm, the MRP of a factor of production equals the firm's demand for that factor. The competitive firms' supply schedule of that factor is the same as the *marginal resource cost* (MRC), or price of the factor. The profit-maximizing competitive firm hires enough of the factor to make the MRP of the factor equal to its MRC.

9. A profit-maximizing firm tries to produce any rate of output (including its most profitable one) with the least TC. To minimize cost, it employs resources until the point at which the MPP per dollar spent on each resource is equal:

$$\frac{MPP_K}{P_K} = \frac{MPP_L}{P_L}$$

10. One obtains the total demand for a resource by adding the individual firms' demands at each price. This method works so long as there are no *resource externalities,* or changes in costs of resources that are not attributable to the employment decisions of the individual firm. If resource externalities exist, one must incorporate changes in costs of firms from industry demand changes in order to determine the change in each firm's demand for a factor.

11. The *elasticity of resource demand* is the rate at which the demand for a factor of production changes as its price changes. This elasticity of demand depends on four factors: (a) The rate at which the MPP of the factor declines as a firm uses more of it. (b) The price elasticity of demand for the final product the factor is used to produce. (c) The proportion of the TC of the product that is represented by the factor in question. (d) The degree of substitutability for the factor.

12. Some people say that private competitive markets produce the "best" distribution of income because, according to the theory of marginal productivity, each factor of production is paid what it is "worth," its MRP or *value of marginal product* (VMP) (or what it contributes to the revenue of the firm). Economists discount this argument for the following reasons: (a) It is difficult to separate the productivity of one input from the productivity of another. (b) Economists do not like value-laden normative terms like *best distribution,* since no one really has an objective measure of what the best distribution is.

13. If a firm that has been selling its products in a competitive market becomes a *non*competitive seller, it gains control of a significant part of the market demand. It obtains monopoly power. Then, in order to sell more of its product, it must lower the price. Even if the noncompetitive firm uses resources with the same productivity as the

resources used by the competitor, marginal revenue productivity (marginal physical productivity times MR) for the monopolist is less than value of marginal product (MPP times product price). The reason is that when a firm has to lower the price at which it sells its product, the price of the product is more than the firm's MR.

14. Even if the supply of a given resource remains competitive, firms that sell their products on a noncompetitive basis hire less of the resource, since they find that it produces less revenue for them than it does for a competitive seller. This means that monopolistic firms do not employ enough of the resource to produce the product with allocative efficiency or the amount of it that will yield the maximum satisfaction to consumers.

15. Introducing monopoly into product markets results in reduced demand for resources. If this effect is seen as a problem, it must be "attacked" in the product rather than the factor market.

16. The effects of education are both economic and noneconomic. But the "correct" amount of education that individuals and society should buy is a matter subject to economic analysis.

17. Producing education requires using resources that have opportunity costs. In the U.S. about ⅓ of private education is publicly subsidized and over 80 percent of public education is subsidized. In recent years, there have been discussions of whether the U.S. is investing the "correct" amounts in education.

18. Economists view expenditures on education as investment in *human capital*, which refers to the improvement in labor skills (increase in marginal physical productivity) attributable to innate ability, acquired skills, and education. A society should invest in education, as in anything else, up to the point at which the marginal social cost is equal to the marginal social benefit.

19. The social costs of education are (a) direct costs borne by students; (b) costs borne by the public in the form of subsidies; and (c) the opportunity costs to students, the income given up by students who do not work because they are in school. The social benefits are (a) the higher lifetime earnings attributable to education, (b) the value of education as a consumer good, and (c) the external benefits to society of having an educated populace.

20. The costs and benefits of education can be viewed as *streams*, or flows over time. To establish the present value of each cost and benefit, one must discount it back to the present time. This is because of the opportunity cost (foregone interest income) of investing in the future.

21. Students, parents, and governments see costs and benefits differently. More education may be highly beneficial to a student who pays little of its cost. But it may or may not be beneficial to parents or to the government. The government alone can incorporate the external benefits of education.

22. Data suggest that the *private rates of return* on education—those that leave out the social costs and benefits—are high for all levels of education (at least as high as for other forms of capital investment). An *age-earnings profile* for different age groups shows that groups of individuals with more education have higher incomes though they may decline for groups in later years.

23. The arguments that education brings social benefits that warrant public subsidization are based on the following considerations: (a) Imperfections in the capital market make borrowing to buy an education impossible for low-income students. (b) Educational subsidies lead indirectly to income redistribution. (c) Increased human capital leads to economic growth. (d) Education reduces crime rates. (e) Education improves learning environment. (f) Education leads to better citizenship. (g) Education provides career orientation. (h) Education eventually produces higher tax returns and lower transfer payments. (The last six of these benefits represent external benefits to society.)

24. Because of the divergences between the estimated costs and benefits to students, parents, and government resulting from investment in education, it is unlikely that U.S. investment in human capital, for either private individuals or the society, is the "correct" amount.

25. Age-earnings profiles clearly show that annual earnings increase for groups with various levels of education. Individual earnings increase to about age 70.

26. Some economists conclude that while education may not directly increase an individual's productivity, the habits associated with that education (time orientation, etc.) are a *signal* to employers to pay wages to those with larger amounts of education.

KEY TERMS

Age-earnings profile
Closed market economy
Derived demand
Elasticity of resource demand
Factor markets

Human capital
Law of variable proportions or diminishing returns
Marginal physical product
Marginal resource cost
Marginal revenue product
Open market economy
Resource externalities
Signaling
Value of marginal product

QUESTIONS

1. What is a closed economy? An open economy?

2. What do *factor markets* mean to you? If you have participated in these markets, which one(s)? If not, which do you expect will be most important to you during your economically active life?

3. How do supply and demand work to determine the amount of a factor of production a firm in a competitive market employs? What does *marginal revenue productivity* have to do with competitive demand for a resource?

4. What is the difference between *value of marginal product* and *marginal revenue product*? Under what conditions are they the same? Under what market conditions are these two not the same in value?

5. Represented below is a labor market in which a firm hires labor competitively and (a) sells its products competitively or (b) sells its products as a monopolist. Answer the following questions about this market.

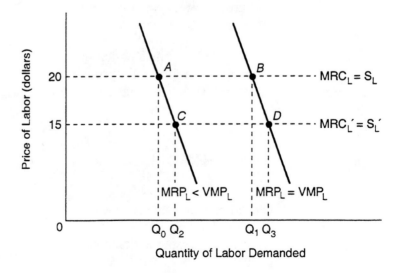

a. If the competitive wage is $20, how many units of labor will be hired by the firm if it sells its product(s) competitively?

b. What is the amount of labor employed by the firm at a wage of $20 if it sells its products monopolistically?

c. If the competitive wage falls to $15, how much labor will be hired by the firm if it sells its products monopolistically?

d. At a competitive wage of $15, how many units of labor will be employed by the firm if it sells its products competitively?

e. In general: what causes $MRP_L = VMP_L$ as well as $MRP_L < VMP_L$ to slope downward?

f. In general: what does monopoly in a firm's product market do to its demand for a resource such as the labor in the figure above?

6. Would the problem of technological unemployment be eased if we allowed the competitive market system to function more completely? Why, or why not?

7. What would happen to the demand for factors of production if we enforced the antitrust laws more vigorously against noncompetitive firms? Would this be true for noncompetitive firms that are, for technological reasons, more efficient than competitive ones?

8. In the argument that competitive private markets lead to the "most desirable" distribution of income, what considerations are left out?

9. Suppose that you are a professional football player. Would you want to see abolished the reserve clause binding you indefinitely to the team with which you have a contract? Why?

10. Do you, as a *consumer* of higher education, consider it a desirable good? Why or why not?

11. Since you are an *investor* in higher education (at least you are paying some of its direct costs), what do you think will be your rate of return when you get a B.A. degree? What about an M.A. or a Ph.D.?

12. Do you think that the rate of return on investment in your education is the same to your parents or to your state government as it is to you? Why or why not?

13. What do you think will happen to the rate of return on educational investment as the U.S. approaches zero population growth?

14. Do you think it is legitimate to view people as human capital? Why or why not?

15. Given the rates of return on investment in education that you have seen, would you (or society) be better off investing in education, in corporate bonds, in a new highway system or in an income-maintenance plan?

SUGGESTED READINGS

Becker, Gary S. *Human Capital: A Theoretical and Empirical Analysis With Special Reference to Education*. 2nd ed. NY: National Bureau of Economic Research, 1975.

Kendrick, John W. "Happiness is Personal Productivity Growth." *Challenge*. May/June, 1987. Reprinted in *Economics 88/89*. Annual ed. Don Cole (ed). Guilford, CT: Dushkin Publishing Group, 1988.

Medoff, James L., and Katherine G. Abraham. "Experience, Performance, and Earnings." *Quarterly Journal of Economics*. December, 1980.

Mincer, Jacob. *Schooling Experience and Earning*. NY: National Bureau of Economic Research, 1974.

Spence, Michael. *Market Signaling: Informational Transfer in Hiring and Related Screening Processes*. Cambridge, MA: Harvard University Press, 1974.

Willis, R. J. "Wage Determinants: A Survey and Reinterpretation of Human Capital Earning Functions." O. C. Ashenfelter and R. Layird (eds). *Handbook of Labor Economics*. Amsterdam: North Holland Press, 1985.

Windham, Douglas. *The Economics of Education: A Survey in Contemporary Economic Issues*. Neil W. Chamberlain (ed). Homewood, IL: Irwin, 1973.

How Wage Rates and Other Factor Prices are Set

Labor is an input just like capital or land. All are used to produce goods and manufacturers must contract each of them.

OBJECTIVES

After studying this chapter you will be able to:

- Describe your own Labor Supply Curve.
- Explain factors that determine the wide range of wage rates you see in the world around you.
- Answer the question "How much is pay equity worth?"
- Explain a closed shop and union shop.
- Have a working knowledge of the following terms and concepts:

Backward bending	Quasi rents
Crowding theory	Technical factor exploitation
Featherbedding	Unions
Job discrimination	Wage discrimination
Labor supply curve	

How Wage Rates and
Other Factor Prices are Set

Supply of Resources
The quantities of a resource offered to a firm at various prices.

We have focused on the *demand* for resources, or factors of production. Importantly, we built on the fact that demand for resources is a derived demand and that it decreases as competition in the product markets becomes less. This happens because noncompetitive, profit-maximizing industries produce less and hire fewer resources than competitive industries. However, we assumed, in order to simplify, that even for noncompetitive producers, a firm's **supply of resources** (the quantities offered to it at various prices) is competitively determined. Actually, as everyone knows, that is often not the real situation. Imagine GM, for instance, being unable to influence the wage rate of automobile workers.

So we will drop the assumption of pure competition in the factor markets, and discuss noncompetitive supply and pricing of labor to see how it differs from competitively determined results. Finally, we will discuss other factor prices, specifically rents, interest, and profits in the same way.

Wages: Competitive Versus Noncompetitive

Labor is an input just like capital or land. All are used to produce goods and manufacturers must contract for each of them. Now, to analyze the supply of labor, we are going to make an assumption about the relation between wage rate and the quantity of a labor skill supplied. Our assumption is that *the quantity of a labor skill supplied increases as the wage rate rises* (a law of supply applied to labor markets). The labor supply curve in Figure 13-1 reflects this assumption. It shows that at any higher wage, more labor time will be available than at any lower one. For example, if the wage paid to skilled operators of certain machines is $6 per hour, laborers are willing to work approximately 30 hours per week. But if the wage

Figure 13-1
Supply Curve for One Kind of Labor Skill

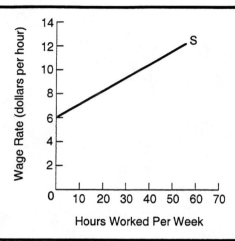

In Figure 13-1, the *total* supply (S) of a particular kind of labor skill is drawn as upward sloping. As the wage rate rises, the quantity supplied of labor time increases.

Backward-Bending Labor Supply Curve
A labor supply curve of an individual in which quantity supplied of labor rises with the wage rate but in which the quantity supplied declines beyond a certain wage.

goes to $10 per hour, they will work 50 hours per week. The reason is that most people want more money income (the marginal utility of income is positive to almost all of us), at least in a developed economy in which desirable goods and services are everywhere available. With a higher wage, they can get more of these goods and services (at a given level of retail prices). We arrived at this hypothetical labor supply curve by adding the quantities of labor time offered at each wage rate for all individuals possessing this given skill. Now one may draw the conclusion that the labor supply curve for each individual is also an upward-sloping line. But that is not necessarily so as we see in Figure 13-2.

The curve in Figure 13-2 is one which economists call a **backward-bending labor supply curve.** Here the individual is willing to work more hours as the wage rate rises, but only up to a certain point (in this case, the point at which the wage rate reaches $8 per hour). Above $8, the amount of labor time offered declines (the curve bends backward). The reason is that there is a tradeoff between the *marginal utility of income and the marginal utility of leisure.*

Imagine your own labor supply curve. If your wage rate were to rise, you would be willing to work more hours per week (the *income effect* of the wage increase). To do so, you would have to sacrifice an equal amount of leisure, such as going to the beach, reading, visiting friends, or whatever (the *substitution effect* of the wage increase). You would continue to give up the leisure (whose marginal utility increases as you have less of it) and acquire more income (whose marginal utility diminishes as you have more of it) up to the point at which the marginal utilities of the two are equal (at a wage of $8). At a wage above $8, if you were like the person in Figure 13-2, you would begin to substitute leisure for income.

Figure 13-2
Backward-Bending Individual Labor Supply Curve

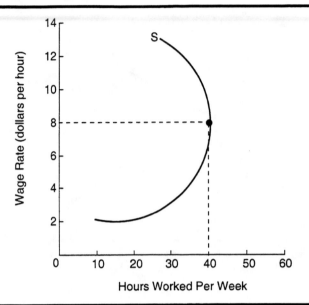

In Figure 13-2, the labor supply curve of an *individual* is drawn as backward bending. As the wage rate rises, the quantity supplied of labor increases. As this happens, the marginal utility of income diminishes while that of leisure increases. At some wage ($8 in Figure 13-2), the marginal utility of income equals the marginal utility of leisure. Above the wage of $8, the marginal utility of leisure exceeds that of income and the quantity of labor decreases.

Perhaps you are not used to thinking of leisure as being a good. Nonetheless, you *can* treat it as such. Indeed, if you are to understand the supply of labor, you *must* treat leisure as a good. If the opportunity cost of leisure (the amount of income you give up to get it) rises, you will substitute money income for leisure (the substitution effect). But as your income grows, you demand more leisure, since most people have a strong taste for it (the income effect). The steady growth of productivity in the U.S. in the twentieth century has raised U.S. incomes. Today Americans often choose to trade off a significant part of potential income for additional leisure. The declining average workweek in the U.S. through much of the twentieth century is evidence of the trend toward more leisure.

Even though there is a *backward-bending labor supply* curve for individual member of the labor force, there is an *upward-sloping labor supply* curve for the entire supply of a particular labor skill (Figure 13-1). The reason is that the labor market is made up of many people, each having different tradeoffs between income and leisure. That is why the individual curves do not all bend backward at the same wage. There are always some individuals who abide by the "Protestant ethic" and who always prefer work and income to leisure. It is also true that labor can move from one skill market to another. Thus, as the wage rises, the quantity supplied of the skill whose (relative) price has increased will grow. Because of these influences, the labor supply curve is most likely to be upward sloping, and we will use that shape in our analysis of labor markets. It is a convenient assumption at this point and also reflects the reality of labor markets which are studied statistically.

Why Not a Single Wage Rate?

We have been talking about the labor market as if there were just *one* going wage rate. We know this is not realistic. The principles of labor pricing we are going to discuss here are valid in any labor market. But we must account for the fact that, in reality, there are many different wage rates. Laborers with different skills are paid at different rates. (The mechanic does not earn the same rate of pay as the chairman of the board of GM.) Even laborers with the same skills are often paid differently. The difference may be due to differences in productivity, differences in location (wages are higher in New York than in Mississippi) or to discrimination (Jane Mechanic may not earn as much as Jack Mechanic). Let's examine some reasons why.

Different Skills and Different Supplies of Skills

The innate abilities of each human being differ from those of every other human being. Add to these differences the variations in training, experience, and education. All these factors account for the variations in wages and salaries earned by people in different occupations and professions. These factors also account for differences in the labor payments to people within the same labor market. For example, it does not take as long or cost as much to acquire the skills of a mechanic as it does to acquire the skills of a physician (even though the skills of a mechanic are often substantial). It takes even longer—and costs even more—to become a neurosurgeon than to become a general practitioner.

The Elasticity of Supply of Labor The rate of change in quantity supplied divided by the rate of change in the wage rate:

$$\frac{\Delta Q_s}{Q_s} \bigg/ \frac{\Delta W}{W}$$

where W equals the wage rate.

Part of the difference in wage levels derives from the **elasticity of supply of the labor** involved, the rate of change in quantity supplied as the wage rate changes. For example, in the U.S., physicians are the highest paid of all professional groups for the following reasons: (1) Their education and training cost a great deal. Their high salaries are a "payout" to the private and public investment in human capital. (2) The supply of physicians is very inelastic.

Figure 13-3 illustrates this point. Here D stands for people's demand for the services of physicians. S and S_1 stand for two different supply conditions of medical services, S_1 being less price-elastic that S. (The quantity of physicians' services rises less rapidly with their price along S_1.) The American Medical Association, by its power to certify hospitals and medical schools and by its control of state licensing of physicians, can reduce the elasticity of supply of physicians. It can thereby cause physicians' salaries to be

Figure 13-3
Hypothetical Supply and Demand for Physicians

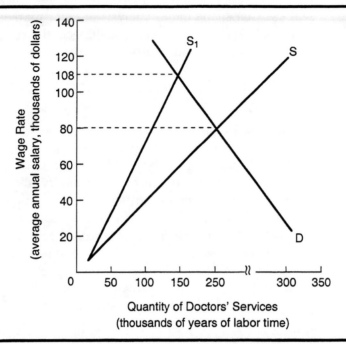

In Figure 13-3, D represents the demand for the services of physicians. S and S_1, represent two different supplies of those services with S, being less elastic than S_1. With the more elastic supply, S, the equilibrium wage (salary) of physicians is $80.000 per year. With the less elastic supply, S_1, the equilibrium wage is $108,000 per year.

$108,000 per year (where S_1 = D) rather than $80,000 per year (where S = D).

The medical profession is not unique, of course, in its ability to restrict the elasticity of supply of its members. Trade unions exert the same kind of control. The key point is that:

The less elastic the supply of a resource, the higher is its wage (or other payment), for a given demand condition.

Different Wages and Same Skills

Sometimes people with very similar skills (for example, workers in the construction and home-repair industries) receive very different wages. The reasons are as follows:

1. *Short-term increases in the demand for one skill as opposed to another.* Sometimes there is not freedom of entry into a field of labor (as when a bricklayers' union will not admit new members). However, if there is freedom of entry, movement from one area of skill into the other should reduce these differentials.

Wage Discrimination
Consists of paying
labor on some basis
other than produc-
tivity.

Job Discrimination
Consists of hiring
labor on some basis
other than produc-
tivity.

2. *Wage and job discrimination.* In **wage discrimination**, employers *pay* employees on some basis other than their productivity, such as age or sex. Thus, the difference in wages derives not from a difference in productivity but from difference in non-market-induced demand. In **job discrimination**, employers *hire* employees on some basis other than their productivity. (For example, whites are hired, but blacks are not, or men are hired, but women are not. Sometimes only a token number of a minority group are hired.) We shall have more to say about this important subject later in this chapter.

3. *Nonmonetary considerations in job decisions.* For example, if you get a Ph.D. in economics, you may decide to take a lower salary as a college professor than you could earn by getting a job in government or business. Presumably, the difference in wage is not as important to you as your enjoyment of teaching or the prestige attached to a professorship. These "psychic" considerations also work in reverse. To induce individuals to untertake jobs that are risky and unpleasant may require higher wages to compensate for the disutility. Miners going into deep and dangerous mines to produce coal and other minerals may require such inducements.

4. *Immobility of labor.* There are reasons (often self-imposed) why people will not move to better-paying jobs. ("Nobody's going to make me move away from good ol' River City. I'd die of homesickness in 6 weeks.") This attitude can cause an oversupply of a skill in a given area, and depress the wage rate below what it is in other areas. This kind of immobility often hampers the efficient working of markets. But since it results from people exercising their right to choose location, a free society must regard it as a necessary cost of economic and social freedom.

How Wages are Set: Competitively Priced Labor

Wages are the price one must pay for that necessary commodity, labor. Let's look at the way a wage is set competitively and the way both competitive and noncompetitive firms respond to it.

Figure 13-4 sets forth the facts in readily understandable form. For convenience, we will continue to use the study guide industry as the source of the derived demand for labor skills.

Figure 13-4(a) shows what happens when the competitive factor market sets the wage scale. The independent influences of supply and demand determine the equilibrium wage rate. The supply curve of labor, S_M (or market supply) slopes upward, for reasons we have already discussed (income versus leisure). We are assuming for simplicity that there is no union and no minimum-wage law. There are only laborers, independently seeking jobs in the study guide industry. Each has her or his own tradeoff values between income and leisure. To figure out the overall demand for labor (D_M or market

Figure 13-4
Competitive Wages and Responses of Firms to Such Wages

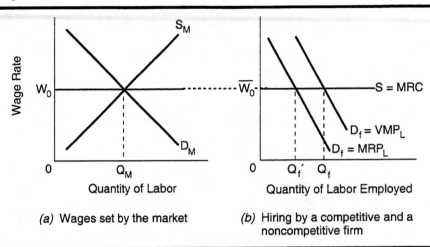

(a) Wages set by the market

(b) Hiring by a competitive and a noncompetitive firm

In Figure 13-4(a), the competitive labor market in which labor skills used to produce study guides is pictured. With industry demand, D_M, and industry supply, S_M, an equilibrium wage of W_0 is established and Q_M of labor skills are hired. In Figure 13-4(b), a single firm hiring of this labor skill is represented. As a price taker, the firm decides how many jobs to offer at the competitive wage and, thus, at W_0 the firm's supply of labor is perfectly elastic and $\overline{W_0} = MRC$. If the firm sells its products competitively it makes $MRC = VMP_L$, and hires Q_f of the resource. On the other hand, if the firm sells its products monopolistically, it makes $MRC = MRP_L$ and hires Q_f' of the resource.

demand), we add the demands of all the single firms across the range of possible wage rates. Figure 13-4(b)'s curve showing these demands slopes downward because of the (ultimately) diminishing marginal physical productivity of labor. No single firm, by varying the amount of labor it hires, can influence wages in the market as a whole. The equilibrium (market-clearing wage is W_0. At W_0, there is neither excess supply nor excess demand, and the industry employs Q_M of labor.

Figure 13-4(b) shows that each firm that hires this kind of labor takes $\overline{W_0}$ as given. Since it can't influence the wage rate, the firm's supply of labor is perfectly elastic, and is represented by the straight line $S = MRC$ (supply equals marginal resource cost). Each time the firm hires one more laborer, it adds the same amount to its total costs (TC).

Universal Study Guide, as you remember, is a profit-maximizing competitive firm. The value of its marginal revenue product (MRP) (its marginal physical product (MPP) times its product price) is equal to its demand for labor. Therefore, it will hire one worker, then another—up to the point at which *MRC*, the amount that one additional laborer adds to TC, is equal to *value of marginal product* (VMP), the amount that the one additional laborer adds to total revenue (TR).

When both product and factor markets are competitive, Universal Study Guide will hire Q_f of labor. (Q stands for "quantity" and f stands for "factor.") Labor is paid its VMP and consumers get the number of study guides they want. That is, they get all they are willing and able to buy at a price that just covers Universal Study Guide's opportunity cost at the margin of using labor (and all other resources, as well).

Suppose now that the study guide industry goes through an upheaval. There are mergers and consolidations. As a result, each study guide manufacturer ends up with a certain amount of monopoly power. Each firm now has the ability to influence the price of study guides through its own decisions about production. Look at Figure 13-4(b). See those downward-sloping demand curves, D_f (D for "demand" and f for "factor")? That is Universal Study Guide's factor demand curve. You can see how its situation has changed. In order to sell more guides, it must lower the price of each one (the marginal revenue (MR) from study guides will be less that their price). And, as a result, MRP will be less than VMP.

In the real world, the downward-sloping demand curve is a fact of life for most producers of goods and services. In other words, as a firm hires another worker, and then another, and then another, the advantage becomes less each time. Each additional worker ultimately adds less to the firm's revenue than the one before. The reason is not only diminishing marginal productivity but also that the price of the product goes down each time the firm produces additional units of it.

Labor's contribution to revenue becomes MRP_L (MRP x MR). This is less than VMP_L (MRP_L curve lies to the left of the VMP_L curve). The Universal Study Guide hires labor competitively, so it makes the given $\overline{W_0}$ (its MRC) equal to MRP_L and hires Q_f' laborers, fewer than it used to hire. Its decrease in laborers does not significantly affect the total employment picture, however, since Universal Study Guide, by assumption, hires an insignificant number of workers. Consumers, however, now get fewer guides than they would prefer, and the price will rise above marginal cost (MC).

How Wages are Set: Noncompetitively Priced Labor

How can a situation with a *lack* of competition develop in the labor market? Noncompetitiveness enters into the labor market in three main ways:

1. A company may grow so big that it hires a significant part of the supply of a specialized type of labor. It will then no longer accept the wage rate as given. Instead, it will bid for labor and affect the wage rate because it is a monopsonistic firm. A *monopsony* is a market situation in which there is *only* one buyer of a given resource. Types of buying power can range from monopsony, to oligopsony (a *few* buyers), to monopsonistic competition (*many* buyers), to perfect competition. For simplicity, we will treat here only the case of a **pure monopsony**, a single employer that sets wage rates.

Pure Monopsony
A labor market situation in which there is one employer that sets wage rates.

2. Laborers may organize a union (a labor monopoly) and bargain for their wage (with either competitive or noncompetitive producers, often in response to monopsony power).

3. Government may intervene in the labor market to create or reinforce noncompetitive conditions. For example, the government may set minimum wage levels.

In an effort to formulate a set of principles to explain modern noncompetitive labor conditions, we will examine these influences. We will also examine some of them in combination with others. We will look at the situations (A, B, and C) involving combinations of product markets and factor markets.

Situation A: Monopsony in the Labor Market, Competition in the Product Market

Suppose that Universal Study Guide Company becomes a monopsonistic firm. This puts the company in a class with the owners of professional sports teams, some of which have reserve (or option) clauses in their contracts with players, requiring them to bargain exclusively with that one club. This has a major effect on the supply of labor, the equilibrium quantity of labor it will demand, and the wage rate it will pay. Table 13-1 and Figure 13-5 will help you to visualize all this.

Remember from our discussion of the Universal Study Guide Company, that the *MRP of labor (MRP$_L$)* is equal to the Universal Study Guide's *demand for labor*. The amount of labor the company will employ varies *inversely* with the wage rate. (The lower the wage, the more hired.) Suppose that Universal Study Guide is the *only* firm in the area that hires workers with this kind of skill. Since the study

Table 13-1
Demand for Labor by a Monopsonistic Employer that Sells Products Competitively (hypothetical data)

A				B					
Resource Cost				Revenue Product					
1	2	3	4	5	6	7	8	9	10
(Average Cost of Labor) = Wage	Units of Labor	Total Resource Cost	Marginal Resource Cost of Labor	Units of Labor	Total Product	Marginal Physical Product	Product Price	Total Revenue Product	Marginal Revenue Product (MRP$_L$ = VMP$_L$)
$5	10	$50		10	20		$2.00	$40	
6	15	90	$8.00	15	30	10	2.00	60	$20
7	20	140	10.00	20	38	8	2.00	76	16
8	25	200	12.00 ← Equilibrium	25	44	6	2.00	88	12 ← Equilibrium
9	30	270	14.00	30	49	5	2.00	98	10
10	35	350	16.00	35	52	4	2.00	104	6

Figure 13-5
The Supply of a Resource and the Marginal Resource Cost of Labor to a Monopsonist

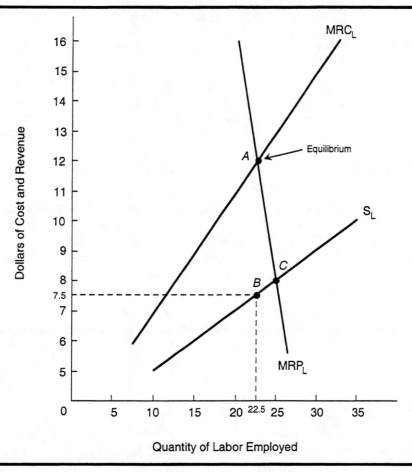

In Figure 13-5, the supply of labor to a monopsonist, S_L, is upward sloping. Because the monopsonist must increase the wage offer to obtain an increase in the quantity supplied of the resource, the MRC_L will be higher than the wage and MRC_L will lie above S_L (from Table 13-1).

guide factory is the only place for local workers to get a job, Universal Study Guide is the only bidder for labor and faces the entire (upward sloping) supply of that labor. In order to hire more workers or get the staff to work a longer week, it must be willing to pay a higher wage. Therefore, S_L is Universal Study Guide's supply of labor.

In Table 13-1, Universal Study Guide's MRC_L shows what happens. Since Universal Study Guide can hire more labor only if it pays a higher wage than before, MRC_L is greater than the wage at any level of employment. Table 13-1 shows a supply schedule for labor by a monopsony employer. Thus, MRC_L is drawn above S_L in Figure 13-5. (In other words, for each Q, level of employment, the *added* resource cost (RC) is greater than the wage associated with that amount of employment.)

We see in Table 13-1, the supply schedule (columns 1 and 2) when plotted as a supply curve is upward sloping. In order to hire more labor, the monopsonist must raise the wage (e.g., to increase employment from 10 to 15 units of labor, the wage must be increased from $5 to $6 for laborers employed. Total resource cost (TRC) (column 3) is the product of wage times units of labor (columns 1 x 2). MRC (column 4) the addition to TRC *per additional unit* of resource is $\Delta3/\Delta2$ (e.g., TC rises from $50 to $90 only $40 when employment rises from 10 to 15 units of labor. Dividing the $40 of added cost by the 5 additional units of labor input yields a MRC of $8.00).

In Figure 13-5, we see the labor supply schedule, S_L, plotted from Table 13-1. MRC (column 4) is plotted above the labor supply curve to reflect the fact that the monopsonist must pay a higher (single) wage to employ increasing amounts of labor.

In part B of Table 13-1, we see the monopsonist's revenue product data. Column 8 shows that the firm sells its products at a constant price of $2 each or, in other words, that it is a competitive firm. TR product (column 9) is the product of output (total product, column 6, times product price, column 8). MRP, or VMP, (column 10) is obtained by multiplying the MPP_L (column 7) by MR. Since for our competitive seller, product price (column 8) is equal to MR, MRP is obtained by multiplying column 7 by column 8, which results in the MRP data appearing in column 10.

How Many Jobs to Offer: MRP = MRC

The rule for the profitable amount of a factor to employ is analogous to the firms' rule for the profitable amount of its product to produce. Recall that the latter rule was to make MR = MC. In a factor market, including a labor market, it is profitable for a firm to continue hiring a resource so long as its employment adds more to revenue (MRP) than it adds to cost (MRC). Thus, as long as $MRP_L > MRC_L$, the firm, including Universal Study Guide, will continue profitably to offer more jobs. In contrast, the firm would never find it profitable to offer employment to a resource if that decision added more to cost than to revenue ($MRC_L > MRP_L$). The equilibrium (profit maximizing) number of jobs to offer thus, is the quantity at which $MRP_L = MRC_L$.

In Figure 13-5, we see that equilibrium employment, where MRP is equal to MRC, occurs when Universal Study Guide employs 22.5 units of labor. The wage it must pay (indicated by a vertical line from 22.5 to the supply curve) is 7.5. Note though that at that level of employment the wage is less than the MRP, which is 12. In a purely competitive factor market, labor is paid a wage equal to its MRP or VMP. If you look at Figure 13-5, you will see that if this labor market were competitive, employment would expand to the rate at which the supply of labor (S_L) cuts the demand for labor (D_L) or to point *C*. At that equilibrium, labor would be paid a wage equal to its VMP and MRP and the total payment to labor would equal its contribution to the revenues of the firm.

The monopsony equilibrium in Figure 13-5 is at *A*, where labor's MRP_L and VMP_L is equal to the factor's MRC. Note that this equilibrium is to the left of the competitive equilibrium at point *C*. A key point to remember is:

Introduction of monopsony into a factor market leads to a reduction in the employment of the resource.

Technical Factor Exploitation
The failure of a monopsonist to pay a factor of production its MRP or VMP (also called monopsony profit).

At the (reduced) monopsony level of employment, the employer will pay a wage necessary to employ that amount of the factor. In Figure 13-6, if a vertical is extended from the equilibrium amount of the factor (22.5) to the supply curve (S_L), the monopsonist must pay $7.50 to obtain the most profitable amount of labor. This wage, though, is less than the MRP or VMP which is $12. The difference, the failure of a monopsony to pay a wage equal to MRP or VMP is called **technical factor exploitation** or *monopsony profit*. The shaded area in Figure 13-6 ($12 – $7.50 x 22.5 units of labor) is the total factor exploitation attributable to monopsony.

Figure 13-6
Employment of Labor by a Monopsony Employer that Sells its Products as a Pure Competitor (hypothetical data from Table 13-1)

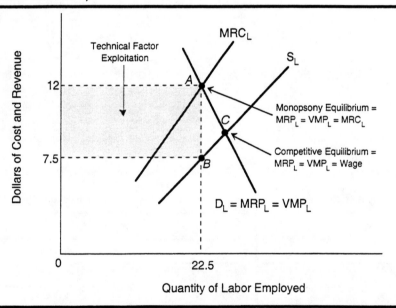

In Figure 13-6, the data from Table 13-1 are plotted to represent the employment of labor by a monopsony employer that sells its products competitively. Supply, S_L, is represented as upward sloping. MRC_L lies above the supply or average cost of labor curve because to hire more labor the firm must raise the wage to all workers hired. The demand for labor is downward sloping and equal to labor's MRP_L or VMP_L. The most profitable amount of labor to employ is the quantity at which MRP = MRC or at the midpoint of 20 and 25 units or 22.5. The average wage to obtain that quantity of labor is $7.50 whereas, at that level of employment, labor's MRP is $12. The difference ($4.50) is the per-unit technical factor exploitation of the resource by a monopsonist. That average difference times the quantity of labor employed represents the total factor exploitation and is shown in the shaded area.

Situation B: Monopsony in the Labor Market, Monopoly in the Product Market

A monopsony labor market is further affected when the sole employer also sells its products monopolistically rather than competitively. We saw in situation A that monopsony in a labor market that is otherwise purely competitive (labor-supply competitive, product-sales competitive) leads to a reduction in employment, a lower wage, and to technical factor exploitation (wage less than the VMP_L). These results are shown in Table 13-2 and Figure 13-6.

In Table 13-2, we have taken the resource cost data (A) from Table 13-1 and columns 5, 6, and 7 of the revenue product data (B) from that table. The change in situation B is found in column 8 dealing with product price of the employer. The firm is now a monopolist and, as such, faces a downward sloping demand for its product which shows up as a falling price associated with larger rates of output. For the firm, MR is now less than product price. As a result, the MRP_L (MRP_L x MR) diminishes not only because of diminishing MPP (column 7) but also because the firm must lower price to sell more of its product (column 8). In column 9, we see TR product (column 6 x column 8). MRP (column 10) is obtained by multiplying MPP by MR or the change in TR product per unit change in labor employed ($\Delta 9/\Delta 5$).

Note that MRP (MPP x MR) is now less than VMP (MPP x product price). This is so because MR to the monopolistic firm is less than product price. (Column 10 in Table 13-2, in other words, is less than column 10 in Table 13-1.) Firms in both situation A and situation B will hire labor up to the employment rate at which MRP equals MRC. We saw in Table 13-2 (and Figure 13-6) that the monopsonist—monopolist will offer fewer jobs. The equilibrium employment of labor in situation B is 15 units as opposed to the 22.5 units employed in situation A. The drop in employment is the labor

Table 13-2
Demand For Labor by a Monopsonistic Employer that Sells Products Monopolistically (Hypothetical Data)

A				B					
Resource Cost				Revenue Product					
1	2	3	4	5	6	7	8	9	10
(Average Cost of Labor) = Wage	Units of Labor	Total Resource Cost	Marginal Resource Cost of Labor	Units of Labor	Total Product	Marginal Physical Product	Product Price	Total Revenue Product	Marginal Revenue Product ($MRP_L = VMP_L$)
$ 5	10	$ 50		10	20		$2.00	$ 40.00	
6	15	90	$ 8.00 (Equilibrium)	15	30	10	1.90	57.00	$17.00 (Equilibrium)
7	20	140	10.00 ← Equilibrium	20	38	8	1.80	68.40	11.40 ← Equilibrium
8	25	200	12.00	25	44	6	1.70	74.80	6.40
9	30	270	14.00	30	49	5	1.60	78.40	1.60
10	35	350	16.00	35	52	3	1.50	78.00	-0.40

market is the effect of product market monopoly. Monopoly industries in other words produce less than competitive ones, ceteris paribus).

We see these results from Table 13-2 plotted in Figure 13-7. The monopsony firm selling products as a monopoly faces downward sloping demand curve $D_L = MRP_L < VMP_L$. With an upward sloping supply of labor, S_L, the MRC_L lies above the S_L curve. Equilibrium is at point D where $MRC_L = MRP_L$. The firm hires 15 units of labor and pays the wage ($6) necessary to employ that amount of the factor. Again, as in Figure 13-6, the monopsonistic employer, unlike one that hires competitively, hires fewer units of labor and pays a wage that is less than the MRP_L. As in the earlier case, there is technical factor exploitation or monopsony profit as shown in the shaded area (DF) or $(11.40 - 6.00) \times 15$.

Monopsony and Competition Compared in Labor Markets

Now look at Figure 13-8 in which we can compare and contrast the various combinations of labor markets and product markets so far

Figure 13-7
Employment of Labor by a Monopsony Employer that Sells its Products as a Monopoly (hypothetical data from Table 13-2)

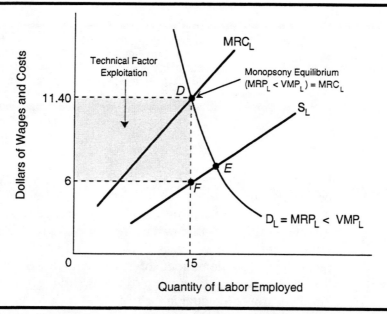

In Figure 13-7, the data from Table 13-2 are plotted to represent the employment of labor by a monopsony employer that sells its products monopolistically. Supply, S_L, is represented as upward sloping. MRC_L lies above S_L because, like all monopsonists, the firm must raise the wage to hire more labor. The demand for labor, $D_L = MRP_L < VMP_L$, is downward sloping for two reasons: (1) MPP declines, and (2) the firm as a monopolist must lower price to sell increased output of its product. Equilibrium for the firm is at D where $MRP_L = MRC_L$. The firm hires 15 units of labor and pays a wage of $6. Since the $MRP_L > Wage_L$, there is again technical factor exploitation of ($11.40 - $6) \times 15$ or the shaded area. Again, had this been a purely competitive *labor* market, equilibrium would have been at E where S_L, cuts D_L and labor would have been paid its MRP and more labor would have been employed.

Figure 13-8
A Comparison of Labor Hiring in Fully Competitive Labor Markets, Labor Markets with Monopsony and Product Competition, and Labor Markets with Monopsony and Product Monopoly

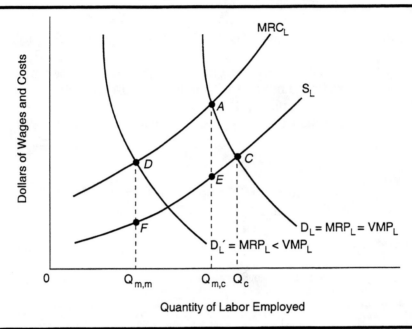

Quantity of Labor Employed

In Figure 13-8, employment of labor is compared among (1) competitive labor markets (both supply and demand are competitive) where equilibrium is at C and the wage equals VMP, (2) competitive supply of labor to a monopsony selling products competitively where equilibrium is at A and the wage is less than VMP ($E < A$) (with a reduced quantity demanded of labor) and (3) competitive supply of labor to a monopsony selling products monopolistically where the wage is less than MRP ($F < D$) (with a further reduction in the quantity demanded of labor. Both A and D equilibria lead to technical factor exploitation (wage less than VMP or less than MRP).

examined. For simplicity, we will do so without numbers in order to concentrate on conceptual differences. If the labor market were completely competitive (no monopsony, competitive supply of labor and competitive demand for the firm's products), equilibrium employment would occur at C where the quantity supplied of labor and the quantity demanded of it are equal. The market would be cleared (no involuntary unemployment) and the wage at that level of employment would equal labor's VMP.

(Competitive) equilibrium employment is affected by monopsony through a change from point C to point A where MRP = $VMP_L = MRC_L$. Monopsony results in a decline in the profitable quantity demanded of labor. The wage falls also since the firm will pay a wage less than MRP and VMP_L (at point E). The difference, $A - E$ times the quantity of labor employed ($Q_{m,c}$, or quantity with monopsony and product competition) again represents *technical factor exploitation* or *monopsony profit*.

The introduction of monopoly in product markets (situation C) causes MRP to be less than VMP (the shift of labor demand from D_L to $D_L´$ in Figure 13-8). In equilibrium at point D, $MRP < VMP_L = MRC_L$. The decline in employment from A to D, however, is due to an imperfect (noncompetitive) product market rather than to monopsony. In both cases of monopsony, labor is paid less than its MRP ($A - E$ in situation 2) and ($D - F$ in situation 3) where employment declines to $Q_{m,m}$ or quantity hired with monopsony and product monopoly. Summarizing these labor market effects in Figure 13-8, we find that:

1. (Situation 1) The fully competitive equilibrium is at point C where the quantity demanded of labor equal the quantity supplied at a wage that is equal to the VMP (MPP x product price).

2. (Situation 2) Monopsony employment of labor causes MRC to be greater than the wage at all levels of employment. The equilibrium shifts from C to A; and there is a decline in employment and the wage is less than the VMP_L. The difference (VMP – wage of labor, or $A - E$ in Figure 13-8) is called technical factor exploitation, the failure of monopsonistic employers to pay labor its contribution to the revenue of the firm.

3. (Situation 3) A combination of monopsony in a labor market with monopoly in the employer's product market results in a shift of equilibrium from A to D onto a further decline in employment. Again there is technical factor exploitation ($D - F$ in Figure 13-8).

Monopsony: A Summary Point
There are, in summary, two major factor market effects of monopsony:

1. Fewer units of resources are employed

2. Resources are paid less than their VMP or MRP (there is technical factor exploitation)

Professional Sports and Monopsony
An interesting illustration of this monopsony "exploitation" is to be found in professional sports. For decades, professional athletes, including baseball players were subject to the reserve clause, a provision under which, once drafted by a team, they could bargain for salary and other benefits only with that team. This was clearly a case of monopsony with a single employer confronting many individual athletes. A player's MRP consists of the money value of the additional tickets to games that the player will generate. (As George Steinbrenner of the New York Yankees once put it, "how many fannies they can put in the seats.") With an upward sloping supply of labor, the MRC is greater than the wage since hiring more players means raising salaries for all players (MRC > wage). The monopsony

team will pay a wage less than the MRP of the player. Economist Gerald Scully estimated that, prior to the abolition of the reserve clause in baseball in 1976, players were paid only about ⅕ of their net MRP! Since 1976, baseball players can become free agents after 6 years and, in the competitive labor market that has ensued, player salaries have soared. Presumably, salaries today tend to be equal to net MRP, with differences in salaries explained by differences in revenue productivity ("super stars" earn more than average players).[1]

Situation C: Bilateral Monopoly (One Employer, One Union)

Unions
Monopolistic suppliers of labor or collective bargaining agents.

Closed Shop
A labor market in which individuals must become members of the union in order to obtain employment.

Union Shop
A labor market in which individuals who are employed by a firm must then join the union.

Bilateral Monopoly
A situation in which a monopsony employer confronts or bargains with a monopoly union.

In the past, there have been two main reactions to monopsony power. One has been the organization of laborers into **unions** that is, monopolistic suppliers of labor or collective bargaining units. The other has been government intervention to counteract monopsony power. To be effective, a union must exert some degree of monopoly power. Where there is a **closed shop**, the contract requires that people join the union before they can work for the firm. In the case of a **union shop**, workers must join the union once they are employed by the firm. In such cases, the union itself may be a pure monopoly. In other words, it is the only seller of labor services to a firm or industry.

Let's introduce a union with a monopoly supply of labor into our company town. Amalgamated Study Guide Workers has a monopoly on labor. The Universal Study Guide Company has a monopsonistic position with regard to hiring the union's members. So one monopoly is face to face with another—a **bilateral monopoly**.

Figure 13-9 shows the range of wages and employment. The supply and demand relations are conceptually the same as in Figure 13-7 but the numbers are again omitted for simplicity. Universal Study Guide wants to hire Q_1 guide workers and pay them a wage of W_1. What wage will the workers' union try to get? Presumably, W_2 (at which $MRC_L = MRP_L$). At that wage level, labor would be paid its MRP, or the value of what it contributes to the revenues of the firm.

The bilateral monopoly model shows that wages will fall in the range between W_1 and W_2. That is, the wage will be between the MRP_L (the highest wage the firm will pay for Q_1 labor) and the wage that will just bring forth the equilibrium (profit-maximizing) number of laborers (where a vertical from Q_1 cuts the S_L curve). This model does not show precisely what the wage will be. The actual wage will depend on the relative bargaining strength of labor and management.

One *possible* result of this bargaining process is a wage of W_3. Look at Figure 13-9 now, and follow this closely. If W_3 is the wage settled on, the Universal Study Guide Company's MRC becomes

---

[1]For a fascinating discussion of monopsony in professional sports, see Timothy Tregarthen's "Players Head for the Courts" in *The Margin*, November, 1987.

W_3CDMRC_L. The wage W_3 is what the company pays to all labor

Figure 13-9
Bilateral Monopoly in the Study-Guide Industry

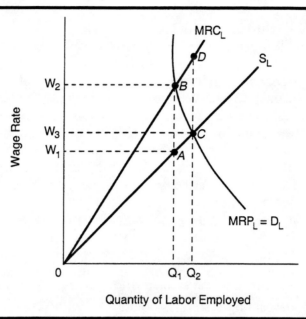

Quantity of Labor Employed

In Figure 13-9, a monopsonist faces a supply of labor, S_L, and a MRC greater than the wage at all levels of employment. The firm's demand for labor is $MRP_L = D_L$. The monopsonist would normally equate MRP and MRC_L and at point B, hire Q_1 of labor, pay wage W_1 and accrue monopsony profit (factor exploitation) of $(W_2 - W_1) \times Q_1$. A union representing the individual laborers might take Q_1 as given and bargain for a wage as high as W_2 (exclusive union). Alternatively, the union might seek to expand jobs and membership by bargaining for W_3 at which wage the monopsonist will hire Q_2 of labor and pay a wage equal to MRP_L.

hired, out to point C on the supply curve. At this wage of W_3, the union will not supply any more than Q_2 of labor. If Universal Study Guide decides to hire more labor, it must pay overtime (look at S_L and MRC_L). A wage of W_3 will cause Universal Study Guide to behave like a competitive employer. It will hire more workers up to the point at which the wage (now MRC_L) equals MRP (point C).

An Important Point About Bilateral Monopoly
From this model, one learns an important fact. When monopsonistic firms bargain with monopolistic unions, the wages that result may eliminate some (theoretically, even all) of the monopsony profit or factor exploitation the firms have. However, even monopolistic unions cannot, by bargaining, get a wage that will eliminate the product-market monopoly position of firms. That is, the unions cannot *induce* firms to produce enough to make wages equal the VMP_L. There is one exception: When a union bargains about wages with a firm that *is* a competitive product seller, it can make the wage equal to the VMP_L. Even in this case, though, the union has not changed the market for the firm's product, nor has it eliminated monopoly power.

It has simply eliminated any monopsony power that the firm might have had and, as a result, the market reacts competitively. Examples of this are the construction industry unions that deal with independent competitive contractors.

Exclusive and Inclusive Unions

All unions do not necessarily have the same objectives. Clearly, one of the major ways in which they may differ is with respect to priorities concerning number of jobs and levels of wages. A union whose primary objective is through bargaining to maximize the wages of its members may settle for fewer jobs (a smaller union) and relatively well paid members. Such bargaining agents are called **exclusive unions**. Many of the craft unions, (plumbers, electricians, brick masons, etc.) seem to fall into this category. Other unions may have as a primary objective expanding the numbers of jobs (size of the union) and be willing to trade off some potentially bargainable wage gains to accomplish this goal. Such bargaining agents are referred to as **inclusive unions**. A number of unions that represent various skills throughout an industry (industrial unions) such as the automobile and steelworkers unions seem to fit this description.

If we refer back to Figure 13-9 we can see how the different bargaining strategies could lead to different results in terms of jobs and wages. The employer in Figure 13-9 as we have seen would wish to hire Q_1 of labor (where MRC = MRP) to maximize its profitable employment. If an *exclusive* union were formed to bargain with Amalgamated Study Guide, it might take Q_1 jobs as a given and seek the maximum wage the company would be willing to pay to employ that number of study guide workers. Presumably, that wage, as we saw earlier, would be W_2, where the wage would equal the MRP_L. Should this bargaining strategy succeed, the technical factor exploitation by a monopsonist would disappear and labor would be paid its marginal revenue product and, in total, all it contributes to the firm's revenues.

Suppose, though, that the union bargaining with Amalgamated Study Guide is an *inclusive* union, one that seeks to expand jobs beyond Q_1 and maximize its membership. What wage above W_1 could the union seek that would result in more than Q_1 job offers? The answer is W_3. At this wage, as we have seen, the MRC_L is constant to the firm at W_3 and it hires all the labor that is profitable, which is where MRC = W_3 = MRP or at point *C*. The union will have expanded employment from Q_1 to Q_2. The inclusive union too will have eliminated the technical factor exploitation since the wage will equal the MRP_L and labor will be paid what it contributes to the revenue of the firm.

Other Strategies: Ways to Increase Jobs and Wages

Where unions have expansion of jobs or maintenance of jobs as a prime objective, they may adopt various devices to restrict employer choices about how to produce goods or where to obtain resources

Exclusive Unions
Bargaining agents that agree to restrict union size and maximize the wage gains of their members.

Inclusive Unions
Bargaining agents that seek to expand the number of jobs offered and, thus, the size of the union.

to produce those goods. An example will help to illustrate these practices.

Economists assume that firms will try to minimize the cost of producing goods. This is, in fact, a part of profit maximization since profit represents the difference between TR and TC. Keeping costs down, however, may be difficult in the face of practices such as **featherbedding**, the practice of requiring that a certain number of employees be used to produce a product or service. For many years, railroads were required by union contract to have firemen (who shoveled coal) on trains even though coal burning locomotives had been abandoned in favor of diesel powered locomotives. Union rules still require that unnecessary musicians be employed where bands and orchestras perform under union contract. While such practices expand union employment, they raise costs and create distortions in resource usage.

Another way to enhance jobs of union members is to restrict choices of firms about where to buy resources. Union support for tariffs and quotas on internationally traded goods is an example of this activity. Such practices not only distort the uses of resources through changing the relative prices of inputs but also enhance the monopoly power of domestic unions as well as producers.

Featherbedding
A practice in which unions require a certain number of jobs for the production of goods or services.

The Government Steps In: Minimum-Wage Laws

The third player that can influence wages is the government. Among other ways, governments may wield this influence by enacting minimum-wage legislation or setting floors under wages. Unions are among the foremost proponents of minimum-wage laws and, among the arguments advanced in their favor, two are especially noteworthy:

1. Minimum-wage laws counteract the monopsony power of business firms by setting wages at a level that more nearly equals the MRP_L.

2. Minimum-wage laws force employers to pay laborers socially acceptable and "equitable" wages, particularly in industries in which laborers are not organized. One problem with this argument is that it represents a value judgment about what is "equitable." As you have seen before, there is no unique distribution of income that is equitable. There is also no uniquely "equitable" wage. Another, and perhaps more significant problem is that employers can not easily be forced to do that which is unprofitable.

Let's examine Figure 13-10, which deals with the first point. Suppose that the study-guide industry had not been unionized. Instead, suppose that Congress sets a minimum wage at W_m. The senator who wrote the bill says that the purpose of the law is to ensure a "decent" income for any worker whose output is shipped across state lines. (This includes the workers in the study-guide industry.)

Figure 13-10
Effect of Minimum-Wage Legislation in Competitive Labor Markets

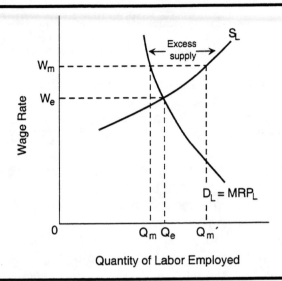

In Figure 13-10, the demand for labor ($D_L = MRP_L$) and the supply of labor (S_L) produce equilibrium employment of Q_e and a wage rate of W_e. If a minimum wage of W_M is imposed, W_M becomes the MRC of the employer. MRP = MRC = W_m at Q_m and employment is reduced. There is excess S_L equal to ($Q_m' - Q_e$).

Before the minimum-wage law was enacted, the equilibrium wage paid to guide workers would have been W_e. At that wage level, demand (MRP_L) would have intersected supply (S_L). Now the senator pushes the bill through Congress, setting W_m as the minimum wage. This means that laborers who are willing to work below the minimum wage (W_m) no longer have any bearing on the level of employment, since no one can work legally for less than W_m. Thus, W_m becomes MRC, up to the point at which W_m cuts S_L.

What happens to employment? It falls from Q_e (where S_L cuts MRP_L) to Q_m (where W_m cuts MRP_L). Now you will notice an unpleasant side effect of such laws. At the minimum wage there is *involuntary unemployment*. At wage W_m, firms employ only Q_m of labor, even though workers are willing to supply Q_m'. So the passing of the minimum-wage law means that the actual rate of employment falls below the level that prevailed before the law was enacted. The government has raised the wage above the MRP of some workers. This is the most important drawback to minimum-wage legislation.

You can see that, in a market economy (as opposed to a command economy), the government can legislate wage rates by passing laws, but it cannot legislate the number of jobs available. This means that it cannot legislate the market incomes of the populace.

The Past and Future of Minimum-Wage Laws

The first federal minimum-wage law was enacted in 1938 with the wage floor set at 25¢ per hour. Because coverage by the law was relatively restricted and the wage below the revenue productivity of most workers, its effects on employment were negligible. By the 1970s, however, minimum wage rates began to rise rapidly and were extended to most of the members of the labor force. What were the effects? In large measure, the answer turns on the kinds of labor markets in which individuals effectively covered by the law (those whose market wages would have been below the minimum wage) seek jobs. As we have seen in this chapter, those markets may be competitive or they may be monopsonistic.

Figure 13-10 dealt with the case of a competitive labor market. Clearly, a minimum wage such as W_m results in losses of jobs for some $(Q_e - Q_m)$ and wage gains for others $(W_m - W_e)$. Those who find jobs at the higher wage and obtain all the hours of employment they seek are better off; those who find less employment or who are unable to find jobs at all are worse off. The excess supply of labor that results in such markets depends on the elasticities of demand and supply for such skills. These skills are heavily concentrated among the young (16-20 years), minorities, and other groups with relatively little work experience.

The case of monopsony is potentially different as we see in Figure 13-11. In the monopsony labor market represented, the

Figure 13-11
Effects of Minimum-Wage Laws in Monopsony Labor Markets

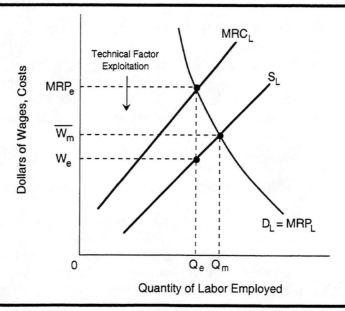

In Figure 13-11, the supply of labor to a monopsonist is S_L and the MRC of labor is MRC_L. With labor demand ($D_L = MRP_L$), the monopsony will hire Q_e and pay a wage of W_e. If a minimum wage of $\overline{W_m}$ is imposed, $\overline{W_m} =$ MRC and a new equilibrium employment is established at Q_m. Employment is increased to the competitive level (where S_L and D_L intersect) and the wage equals labor's MRP.

monopsonist would hire Q_e labor (MRP = MRC) pay a wage of W_e and that wage would be less than the MRP_e of labor. The difference, $(MRP_e - W_e)$, represents technical factor exploitation. Now suppose a "correct" minimum wage of $\overline{W_m}$ is imposed and that, at this floor wage ($\overline{W_m}$ = MRC), employers can hire all they wish at that wage that is voluntarily supplied. With MRC = $\overline{W_m}$, employers will make $MRC_L = W_m = MRP_L$, and will hire Q_m of labor and pay a wage equal to the MRP_L. The "correct" wage will clear the labor market (quantity demanded = quantity supplied) eliminate monopsony exploitation and increase employment.

The Evidence:
Monopsony Versus Competitive Labor Markets

In a study appearing in the *Journal of Political Economy* in June, 1982, Peter Linneman assessed the effects (gains and losses) from sharp increases in minimum wages in the mid-1970s (1974 [$1.60 to $1.90], 1975 [$1.90 to $2.10]). If labor markets for such skills were primarily monopsonistic, we would expect to see primarily winners (more jobs, higher wages); if labor markets were competitive, we would expect to see many losers as well as gainers. Linneman's conclusions can be summarized as follows:

Minimum Wage Increases

Losers	Gainers
Women (70% lost)	White Males (75% gained)
Unskilled Workers (70% lost)	Black Males (60% gained)
	Union Members (90% gained)

The conclusion of the Linneman study puts in serious doubt the monopsony argument for minimum-wage laws. It appears that there were many losers as well as gainers and that their labor markets (at least for such skills) are substantially competitive. A second important conclusion, says Donald Bumpass[2] is that the losses were often among those (women and unskilled workers) who at least arguably were among the laws' intended beneficiaries.

A new minimum-wage law is in effect in 1990, after no increases since 1981. It will be instructive to see if the experience of the 1970s is repeated at this point. Many economists would conclude that minimum-wage laws are a clumsy device for increasing the incomes of (relatively) low wage earning groups and may have perverse effects on many within those groups. An interesting feature of the new law is the "training wage" which will permit employers to pay a lower wage to new hires for a limited period of time. Will this two-tier minimum wage mitigate the employment effects of the legislated wage increases?

---

[2]Donald Bumpass, "George Bush, Congress and the Minimum Wage," *The Margin*, September/October, 1989.

More About Wage Discrimination

When we look at job and wage structures in the world around us today, two things stand out: (1) The differences between the wages paid to one worker and the wages paid to another are sometimes greater than one can explain in terms of differences in their productivity (MRP). (2) All people in the labor force do not have equal opportunities for jobs. How can we explain this market behavior? Increasingly, economists have turned to *economic discrimination* as the clue.

What is Economic Discrimination?

Economic discrimination, as noted earlier, exists in markets when firms deal with people (consumers and producers of goods, or buyers and sellers of resources), on the basis of something *other* than market considerations. We have already mentioned one form of economic discrimination—the kind firms may practice in the pricing of goods and services. Earlier in this chapter we mentioned two different forms of economic discrimination: job discrimination and wage discrimination. *Job discrimination*, recall, is the situation in which firms hire (or do not hire) workers on the basis of some consideration other than their productivity (their race, sex, age, religion, or whatever). *Wage discrimination* is the situation in which firms pay people wages that are lower than the wages would be if the firms were considering only people's productivity. (This form of discrimination is also based on such factors as race, sex, age, and religion.)

Present Discriminatory Activity Basing jobs and wages on criteria other than productivity.

Results of Historical Discrimination Effects on present jobs and wages of past discrimination.

It is hard to identify these forms of economic discrimination, and even harder to measure them or determine how much discrimination is still being practiced. There are two aspects of discrimination to look for: **present discriminatory activity** (PDA), or current practice of basing jobs and wages on criteria other than productivity, and the **results of historical discrimination**, or the effects on today's jobs and wages of economic discrimination in the past. We will illustrate both.

Suppose that Thelma Smith, a black woman, is job hunting. (We are assuming that she is qualified by intelligence and other job characteristics.) If firms will not hire her because of her race and/or sex, she is the victim of *job discrimination*.

But suppose that she does get a job. However, the firm pays her less than they pay her white, male co-workers. Then she is a victim of *wage discrimination*. In both cases, the results are due to *PDA*.

Now suppose that she is not a victim of PDA. Suppose she gets a job that uses all her skills, and that the firm pays her the same wage as her white, male co-workers. Is it possible for there still to be discrimination, even though there is no PDA? Yes. Because if Thelma Smith has in the past been denied access to good education on account of her race or sex, her skills may be less than they otherwise would have been. This *result of historical discrimination* represents an underinvestment in human capital. The discrimination she suffers from is not her employer's fault or even necessarily the fault of present social practices. It results from a body of social preferences and prejudices gradually built up over centuries past. Around these preferences and prejudices grew a whole lore of snobbish and unfounded convictions. ("Women's place is in the home. She shouldn't be out driving a truck or managing a company." "Women don't need to be paid the same as men. After all, they have husbands to support them. They only work to supplement the family income." "Black people have natural musical and athletic ability, but they don't have the drive to become entrepreneurs." And so forth.)

Understanding Discrimination

Crowding Theory
A theory that explains wage and job discrimination as the result of groups being crowded into and out of certain occupations.

You can see the direct economic effects of job discrimination in the supply-and-demand conditions of labor markets. It will help you to understand discrimination, therefore, if we use some supply-and-demand tools of analysis. One of these is called **crowding theory**. This is the theory that economic discrimination leads to groups of people (women, blacks, Chicanos, and so on) being crowded *into* certain occupations, and *out of* others. For example, in the United States, the great majority of elementary-school teachers are female. The majority of physicians are male.

Figure 13-12 shows how crowding affects wages. In Figure 13-12(a), D_t represents demand for teachers, S_m represents the supply of male teachers, and S_{m+f}, the supply of male plus female teachers. Since most elementary-school teachers are female, the result is that women are crowded into this field. The wage is W_1. If there were no crowding—if women were able to get jobs in all fields on the basis of their abilities and preferences—the supply of female teachers would be reduced. The total supply might fall to some level such as S_{m+f}' and the wage might rise to W_2.

Figure 13-12(b) shows what happens to wages to those labor markets from which women (or blacks or Chicanos) are partly excluded. The supply of male physicians is S_m and total supply is S_{m+f} (which reflects the fact that most doctors are male). Demand for the services of doctors is D_d and the wage if W_1. If crowding did not exist, more women would become MDs. The supply would increase to some level such as S_{m+f}' and the wage would move to some level such as W_2.

What are the Consequences of Crowding?

1. Wages in those occupations into which people are crowded are lower than they would be if productivity and personal preferences were the factors that dictated people's choices of jobs.

Figure 13-12
Effects of Crowding on Wages

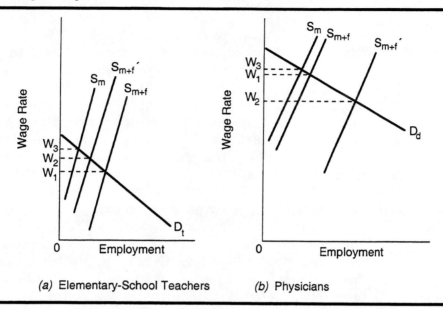

(a) Elementary-School Teachers   (b) Physicians

In Figure 13-12(a), the demand and supply of elementary-school teachers is represented. S_m is the supply of male teachers, S_{m+f}, is the supply of male plus female teachers. Without crowding, the wage would be W_2 (S = S_{m+f}') for there would be fewer females in that profession. With crowding and increased supply S_{m+f}, the wage is W_1 instead

In Figure 13-12(b), the demand for physicians is represented. S_m is the supply of male physicians and, with crowding out, S_{m+f} is the supply of male plus female physicians which results in a wage of W_1. Without crowding, the supply of male plus female physicians would be larger, S_{m+f}' and the wage would be W_2 instead of W_1.

2. The result of item 1 is that the relative incomes of certain groups are strongly affected. Groups crowded into low-paying occupations have much lower average incomes. (For example, in 1986, the median income of non-white families in the U.S. was $19,832. The median income of white families was $30,809.)

3. Both society and the individuals subject to discrimination lose as a result of these factors. PDA causes people to be shunted into jobs that do not fully utilize their skills. For example, a woman who is a trained chemist and is forced to take a job as a typist because of crowding has a lower MRP as a result. Society is, thus, misallocating its resources. (This is one source of underemployment.) The results of historical discrimination mean that society loses because it underinvests in human capital. It fails to educate groups of people that are crowded or to most productively utilize its human resources. Thus, society must forgo the higher productivity and full-employment GDP that it could employ if there were no results of historical discrimination. (For example, in 1986, only about 10 percent of blacks were college graduates while about 20 percent of whites were college graduates.)

Unequal Wages for Equal Jobs

Crowding does explain why some people are excluded from some jobs, or have slight chance of entering some fields of endeavor. But it does not explain why people who work at the same jobs, and have the same skills, do not all receive the same pay. Figure 13-13 will help you understand this. There S_{m+f} represents the supply of male plus female labor with a given skill. D_m, in Figure 13-13(b) represents employers' demand for male workers with these skills, and D_f, in Figure 13-13(a) represents the demand for female workers with the same skills. (Note that we are assuming that the skills of the two sexes are the same. If they were not, we could not consider them as part of the same labor market.)

The demand for a factor of production depends directly on that factor's MPP and on the price of the product it is hired to produce. Since there is no difference between these factors for men and for women in the same labor market, the difference between the two demand curves in Figure 13-13 must be attributed to a "taste for discrimination" on the part of employers. In this case, both males and females will be employed, but males will be paid W_m and females W_f. (Here we are assuming, for the sake of simplicity, a supply of labor that is perfectly inelastic.)

What are the consequences of the wage discrimination shown in Figure 13-13?

1. The distribution of income is skewed in favor of men and against women, even when discriminating firms employ women on a supposedly equal-opportunity basis.

Figure 13-13
Taste for Discrimination and their Effects on Wages

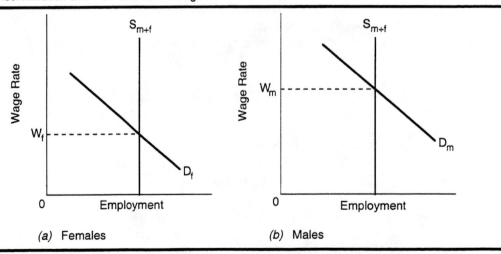

(a) Females   (b) Males

In Figure 13-13, the supply by males and females of a certain skill is represented by S_{m+f}. The demand of employers for males with that skill is D_m in Figure 13-13(b) and the demand for females with that skill is D_f in Figure 13-13(a). Although the skills (MRP) are the same, a different wage is paid to males (W_m) and females (W_f). The difference ($W_m - W_f$) is not based on a productivity difference and is attributable to a "taste for discrimination."

2. Figure 13-13 shows no underemployment (loss of productivity). However, there is a new form of economic exploitation. It is the exploitation that exists when labor is paid less than its value of marginal product or marginal revenue product. This new form is due to wage discrimination. It is reflected in $W_m - W_f$, which is the difference between the wage paid to men and that paid to women. (For example, in 1986, the median income of male managers and proprietors was $36,380. The median income of females in the same jobs was $26,400.)

A Note of Caution

Customer Discrimination Job and wage discrimination that results from the tastes of a firm's customers.

Our analysis of discrimination in jobs and wages between men and women is based on the assumption that both groups are equally productive. But if women appear to be more prone to absenteeism or to have a faster rate of job turnover (due to pregnancies, necessity of caring for children, and so forth), then they are presumed to be less productive than men as employees. Also, women in many occupations presently tend to work fewer hours than men; this accounts for part of the difference in their incomes. Finally, our analysis has implied that it is only employers who practice job and wage discrimination. But research indicates that **customer discrimination**—job and wage discrimination resulting from the tastes of buyers, such as a preference for being waited on in restaurants by men or by whites—may be just as influential in explaining employers' discrimination. However, there is evidence that, even after all the above factors are taken into consideration, about ¼ of the 40-percent wage differential between men and women is indeed attributable to discrimination.

Cartoon Feature Syndicate

"It seems to me the majority of people in this country belong to some minority group!"

What Can Be Done About Discrimination?

A long held but increasingly disputed view is that American society is a melting pot, that minority groups ultimately become absorbed into the mainstream of the economy. This idea may have been valid for males in the earlier minority groups (for example, Irish immigrants in the 19th and early-20th centuries). But many argue whether it is working as well for other groups: blacks, Chicanos, Puerto Ricans, women, older Americans. If time will not solve the problems of economic discrimination, what other remedies are there?

Public Action

Laws against economic discrimination go back to the early history of the U.S. The Fourteenth Amendment to the Constitution prohibits some forms of discrimination. The controversial Equal Rights Amendment would have done away with others. Civil rights legislation of the 1960s (especially the Civil Rights Act of 1964) outlawed discrimination in employment on the basis of race or sex. The Equal Opportunity Commission in 1972 gained the power to sue employers for noncompliance. Today, all employers with more than 50 workers who hold federal contracts of $50,000 or more are required by law to have affirmative-action employment plans. However, there is no way of knowing as yet how successful these legal efforts have been—or may be in the future or whether they will give rise to reverse discrimination.

Movement in recent years toward the goal of full employment has been another way to help reduce wage and job discrimination. In all likelihood, it has created more opportunities for minority groups and women than for whites and males. The reason is that when times get hard, it is minorities and women that are the "last hired, first fired." This is true, at least, of private employers. Public employers (government at the federal, state, and local levels), however, when they create jobs to help ease an employment gap, tend to hire both minorities and women to a disproportionate extent.

Private Action

Many economists (including, Milton Friedman) argue that *competitive pressures* on profit-maximizing employers do a lot to reduce job and wage discrimination. Competitive firms that exhibit a "taste for discrimination" find that their workers' productivity is lower and their costs higher. Ultimately, since they sell at the same prices as non-discriminating employers, they must either abandon discrimination or be driven out of the marketplace. (These economists concede, however, that monopolistic employers do not necessarily succumb as readily to these pressures.)

Unions

Unions may hold out hope for some minority and female workers. Some blacks and women, however, have found it hard to join unions. Examples are trade unions, such as plumbers, electricians, and the construction trades. The industrial unions (automobile workers, steelworkers, and so on) have, on the other hand, racked up a good record of admitting, minorities and women.

Creating Entrepreneurs

The picture looks brighter when minorities and women become entrepreneurs. The idea of black capitalism is gaining strength, for example; and black employers will not discriminate against blacks (presumably). Nor will women employers discriminate against women (presumably). Hence, there are an increasing number of such organizations as the Women's Bank of New York, which opened its doors in 1975. Some of these organizations, however, have failed and others have sought a more general market.

Other Factors of Production: Land, Capital, and Entrepreneurship

We have established some general principles of supply and demand as they affect the pricing of labor. Now we will extend those same principles to the pricing of *land* (rents), *capital* (interest), and *entrepreneurship* (profits).

Land and its Rent

Will Rogers said, "Buy land. They ain't makin' any more of it." That, in fact, is a peculiar feature of land. Unlike other resources, land is nonreproducible. There is only so much of it. Of course, you can clear land that is covered with trees or boulders. Or you can wall off parts of the sea, and thus reclaim land from the water. By such methods, you may in the long run slightly increase the amount of usable land. But from all practical standpoints, one can assume that the supply of land is fixed, or perfectly inelastic.

Pure Economic Rent
The payment to a resource whose supply is perfectly inelastic.

Economists refer to the payment made for *any* resource whose supply is perfectly inelastic as **pure economic rent**. Calling it "*economic* rent" keeps people from getting it mixed up with the popular use of the word *rent* (as in "I paid the rent on my apartment"). Rent in this popular sense, though, includes the interest on borrowed capital, the profit that accrues to the entrepreneur, the wages paid to the gardener, and so on.

What determines the price of land, or the price of any resource with perfectly inelastic supply? *Demand* does. Figure 13-14 shows how this works. S is the supply of a certain type of land. There is just 1 acre of it in the middle of a big city, so the supply is perfectly inelastic. D_2 is the initial demand for this land, and R_2 is the equilibrium rent. (Let's say that this is a competitive market, and that

Figure 13-14
How Land Rents are Determined

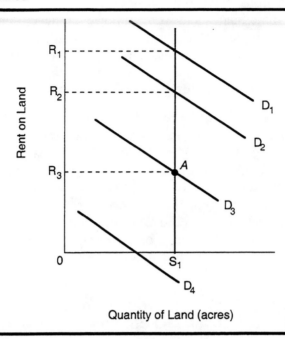

Quantity of Land (acres)

In Figure 13-14, the supply of land, S, is perfectly inelastic. If demand is less than supply (D4 < S) there is no payment to the resource, which is a free good. As demand for the resource increases, its price is demand determined and rises proportionately. Payments to the resource are "pure economic rents."

all this land is equally productive, so there is *one* rent.) Now demand increases to D_1. There can be no increase in quantity, so the rent rises to R_1. Similarly, if demand decreases to D_3, rent declines to R_3. All of the payment to this resource is a pure economic rent.

But now suppose that there's a large supply of this land. The supply is then great relative to the demand. (Look at demand curve D_4 in Figure 13-14.) Since the demand for land is not as great as the supply at any price, the land will not command a price. It is, in fact a **free good**, one whose prize is zero. This condition may actually exist today in some frontier areas. It existed in parts of the U.S. in the 18th and 19th centuries, when families who were willing to endure the hardships of homesteading could take up farming on unused land, including "free" land owned by the federal government. (Even this land was not entirely free, because settlers had to clear it and so forth.) Obviously, this is not common in market economies today.

Free Good
A good whose supply and demand create a zero price.

Rents as Signals: Valid or Not?
Prices established in markets (rather than being arbitrarily set elsewhere) are useful signals to indicate where too many or too few resources are being used. In other words, prices serve to gauge the efficiency of an economy. If wages rise in one area or in one occupation, workers find out about it. To workers, it is a signal to

move to that area or retrain for that job (assuming that there are not any market or government barriers). Interest rates and rates of profit act as signals, too, in much the same way.

Can rents on land serve this same function of fitting supply to demand? The answer has two parts:

1. In the aggregate, the answer is no. No matter how high or how low rents are, landowners cannot rush into the market and supply more or less land. The supply of land is fixed. In this sense, rents on land are a *surplus* (some say *unearned*). They do not act as an incentive to make the market operate more efficiently through causing supply adjustments.

In the aggregate, land is a gift of nature. Rent is certainly not necessary to ensure the supply of it. Therefore, should rents be paid on land? Some have argued that the answer is no. The most famous proponent of doing away with land rents was the American economist Henry George, who, in a book *Progress and Poverty* published in the 1880s, argued that taxing away rents completely would not change the availability of land or impair the working of the economy. George believed that as an economy developed (as it gained more people and as people got higher incomes), the demand for land would grow (as from D_2 to D_1 in Figure 13-14) and rents would rise. George pointed out that these payments would not be the result of productive activity on the part of landowners. Rather they would come about because of the fact that supplies of land were fixed. There could never be increases in supply. Henry George argued that a single tax on land could replace all other forms of taxation, without ill effect on the economy. The burden of the tax would fall entirely on the landowner. Suppose that rents on land rose from 0 to R_3 (Figure 13-14). A tax of $0R_3$ would eliminate the rent increases. And the tax would not affect the supply of land or the price of it. People who agreed with George (and there were many) became known as "single taxers."

The reasoning of the single taxers is subject to criticism, though. For one thing, it is hard to separate rents on land from payments for other factors. How much of the payment to a landowner is for ownership of the land? How much is for improvements on it? Would a single (land) tax really finance governments? Almost certainly it would not—not a modern government, anyway. Finally, how can one say that rent on land is unearned, while at the same time saying that capital gains (which usually result from no productive effort on the part of the gainer) are earned? Let's say that your great grandmother bought 1,000 shares of Coca-Cola stock in 1910 for $5,000, and that it is worth $25 million today. Did your great grandmother *earn* this increase in capital value any more than a person who bought a parcel of land in downtown Boston in the same year earn the increase in value of that land?

2. For particular parcels of land rather than the total supply of land, the answer is less clear. Perhaps you use your land to put up an office

building. Your neighbor uses a similar tract of land to plant an apple orchard. You receive a higher rent on your land than your neighbor receives. This is the concept of **relative rents**. Consumers and producers evaluate the worth of land according to the use to which it is put. Relative land rents thus serve as signals to indicate the most value-productive uses of land. Even so, once the rents exist, they can indeed be taxed away without affecting the supply of land. This fact has been noted by many cities. City councils have historically structured their tax systems in favor of taxes on land instead of taxes on the incomes of individuals or businesses.

It is important to note that relative rents play a crucial role in making decisions about how to use and how intensively to use land. Perhaps the world's highest land rents are to be found in central Tokyo. As a result, the land is used almost exclusively for commercial and industrial uses and buildings reach higher and higher. Prime farm land in Kansas, however, yields its highest relative rents in agricultural uses.

Quasi Rents or Common Rents

While there are resources or goods in *perfectly* inelastic supply (all things such as land, and Picasso and Van Gogh paintings, that cannot be produced), far more resources are in *relatively* inelastic supply. There are, for instance, many singers but few with the ability of Ella Fitzgerald or Michael Jackson, or Luciano Pavarotti. There are many heart surgeons but few with the skills of Drs. Michael DeBakey or Norman Shumway. All of these individuals are in occupations or professions that have opportunity costs associated with them (there are other uses for them). The difference between the actual payment to such a resource and its opportunity cost payment (what it would take to just use it in its most highly valued use) is called a **quasi rent** or a **common rent**.

We see in Figure 13-15, how quasi or common rents are determined. The resource represented is a particular kind of labor skill (baseball pitcher, rock singer, physician, or whatever) and S is the (upward sloping) supply of that skill. The wage that would just induce the skill to be employed in this use (as opposed to next most valued use) is W_0. The actual wage being paid at the margin to units of this resource (the highest wage) is W_a. At any wage above W_0, units of this resource are receiving two kinds of payments. The opportunity cost payment—what it would take to induce their employment in this use—is the area *under* the supply curve at W_0 and at all wages above W_0 out to the quantity of labor actually employed. Thus, if W_a is the actual highest wage, the area $0W_0AQ_a$ (the darker shaded area in Figure 13-15) is the opportunity cost or direct wage payment. Because the units of this resource receive payments greater than the darker shaded area, their payment includes a return above opportunity cost. The total payment to this resource if Q_a is employed is $0W_aAQ_a$ which incorporates both the darker shaded area ($0W_0AQ_a$) plus the

Figure 13-15
Quasi Rents or Common Rents Accruing to a Resource

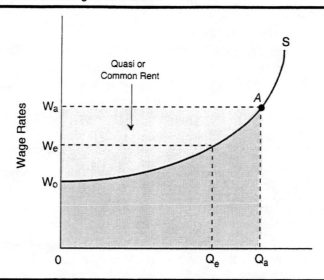

In Figure 13-15, the supply of a resource (S) is represented as upward sloping because it has alternative uses on an opportunity cost greater than zero. W_0 is the value of that most productive alternative use on opportunity cost. The quantity supplied increases as the resource's price rises (e.g.; Q_e to Q_a as wage rises from W_0 to W_a). The difference between an actual wage paid such as W_e and the opportunity cost wage W_0 is a quasi rent. The entire quasi or common rent to the resource is the difference between the highest actual wage, W_a, and the opportunity cost wage times the amount of the resource employed, or $(W_a - W_0) \times Q_a$, the darker shaded area in Figure 13-15.

lighter shaded area (W_0W_aA). The lighter shaded area, the area *above* the supply curve, or the payment above opportunity cost is due to the relatively inelastic supply of the resource. This payment due to relative inelasticity is the quasi or common rent.

Note that most (virtually all) resources receive some quasi or common rents. The sources of these rents (based on relatively inelastic supplies) are threefold:

1. Qualitative differences in resources. Not all units of a resource are equally productive. A baseball pitcher with an earned run average of 1.90 is more revenue productive than an average pitcher. An attorney who has won all of his or her difficult cases is more productive than one who has a "run-of-the-mill" record.

2. Locational differences in resources: parcels of land, for example, are not equally productive. Some agricultural land may be better drained, have easier access to markets or, for various reasons, have greater revenue productivity than others.

3. Innate physical differences in resources: land, for example, may contain few or many sub-soil resources such as oil or other minerals. In addition, these resources may be very expensive or very inexpensive to extract. Among the lowest extraction costs for oil are those of Saudi Arabia. Because petroleum (of a particular grade) sells

at the same international price, the lower cost producers will earn a quasi-rent as part of their revenues.

Capital and Interest Rates

Physical Capital
The tools and instruments of production.

Financial Capital
Savings available to supply to firms for investment in physical capital.

There are two forms of capital: **physical capital**, or the tools and instruments of production (plant, machinery, and the like); and **financial capital** or money that has been saved and that may be supplied to firms that want to invest it in physical capital. Here we will discuss the financial capital market (the capital-goods markets function like other product markets).

The market that deals with financial capital is like other markets in that it is influenced by both supply and demand. The supply of capital is the savings of a society, the private savings of individuals and businesses. Businesses often finance their investments out of their retained (nondistributed) earnings. To the extent that they do this, they do not actually go to the capital markets to obtain financing. Even so, the opportunity cost to them is the interest rate, which is what they *could* have earned if they had supplied these funds to the capital market, rather than retaining them and using them internally.

We shall assume that the quantity of capital supplied does respond to changes in interest rates. Remember that interest rates are the prices that banks and other financial institutions pay to savers. Interest rates are also the prices that firms must pay to borrow funds. This means that as the interest rate increases, the amount of loanable funds available to business firms also increases. When interest rates are very high, savers increase their efforts to save.

A firm's *demand* for funds depends on the relations between the cost (price) of borrowed capital and the return expected by the firm (the MRP of capital). As long as a firm's return on its capital investment is greater than the interest rate, the firm will borrow—presumably up to the point at which the two are equal. That is, it will borrow until its MRP of capital (MRP_K) is equal to the rate of interest on the borrowed capital (R_K).

Figure 13-16 shows how interest rates are determined. In this illustration, the equilibrium interest rate is 8 percent. At this rate, according to the loanable-funds theory, the quantity supplied equals the quantity demanded of capital (the sum of the demands of individual firms). But there is not one interest rate, but many. Why do interest rates vary? Variation may be traced to the following four factors:

1. *Risk.* The greater the chance that a borrower will default on a loan, the higher the interest rate needed to protect the lender against this risk. New York City must pay a higher rate to borrow (that is, to sell its bonds) than the state of New York does (which is still higher than that of some of the other states, such as California).

2. *Liquidity.* The harder it is to dispose of a debt instrument, that is, to convert it into money, the greater the risk of loss and the higher the interest rate.

Figure 13-16
How Interest Rates are Determined in a Capital Market

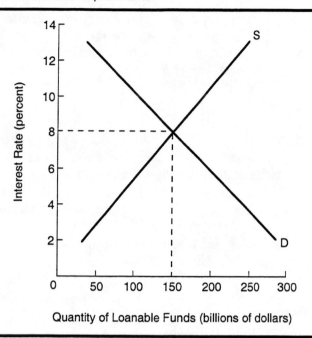

Quantity of Loanable Funds (billions of dollars)

3. *Length of loan.* The longer the period of time of the loan or debt instrument, the higher generally is the interest rate.

4. *Competitiveness.* The more competitive a particular capital market is, the lower the interest rate in that market.

Government and the Capital Market

Governments (especially the federal government) are involved in all the factor markets in the U.S. However, they have a special concern for the capital market and the level of interest rates. The government itself is a major demander of funds in the capital market. The funding and refunding of the federal debt is accomplished primarily in these markets, and the buying and selling of federal debt has a major effect on interest rates. When the government is borrowing heavily, individuals sometimes have difficulty obtaining a mortgage loan. Much of the supply of loanable funds is used up by government.

You can see that interest rates are not only prices that ration the supply of capital, they also have a strong effect on investment, home building, and the economy as a whole. The government, therefore, does not allow interest rates to seek any level that is warranted by supply and demand. The Federal Reserve, by intervening in capital markets, can manipulate the rates of interest everyone must pay. The interest rate is considered too important from a *macroeconomic* point of view to be allowed completely to find its own level in a competitive capital market.

Entrepreneurship and Profit

Entrepreneurship is the function of organizing labor, land, and capital into a firm capable of producing and marketing a commodity or service. Entrepreneurs assume the risks of using resources to produce goods and services, and economists regard this function as a separate factor of production. The payment received by entrepreneurs is called *profit* (a return that is over and above normal profit, which is an opportunity cost payment). The "profit" referred to here is **economic profit**, which is the difference between a firm's TR and its TC (the figure called "TC" includes a normal profit).

Economic Profit
Profit that is above normal profit. When there is economic profit, TR is greater than TC (including the opportunity cost of entrepreneurs).

The pursuit of profit is a principal motivation for entrepreneurs to perform their function. (However, vanity, the pursuit of power, and other less easily measured factors undoubtedly play a role as well.)

Let's consider one entrepreneur, Martin Bloggs, a part-time inventor. After years of work, he has come up with the all purpose study guide. He leaves his dull job with Ajax Publishers and sets out to found the Universal Study Guide Company. He borrows from banks; he hires labor, leases land and a building, buys machinery, and starts producing guides. Will he make an economic profit? If so, what will lie behind it? To answer, let's look at three interrelated theories of economic profit:

Monopoly Power. Economic profit cannot exist in the long run in a competitive market. If a firm has continued or long-term economic profits, therefore, it has some *monopoly power*. Let's say that Martin Bloggs gets a patent on Universal Study Guides. No one else can produce them (with his process) for 17 years. He also trademarks the name of his product. This legal monopoly prevents, or retards, the entry of other firms into the study guide industry. It also causes the output of guides to be lower and the prices of them higher than would be the case if there were competition. For example, instant-copy (Polaroid) cameras were very expensive when Dr. Edwin Land started producing them years ago. When the patents run out and the other camera companies can finally produce their own models, prices will go down.

What can be done about these profits that accrue to a monopolist?

1. Those high rates of profit can be relied on to act as incentives to attract others to produce similar products. This increases the competitiveness of the market. For example, for years before Hoffman-Laroches' patent on valium, one of the nation's most widely prescribed drugs, ran out, other pharmaceutical firms worked feverishly to produce their own generic versions of the drug. As a result of their ultimate introduction the price of "valium" has fallen dramatically in recent years.

2. Antitrust laws, government contracting, and whatever other tools are available can be used to attack the source of monopoly power. For example, after World War II, to weaken the monopoly power of the

Aluminum Company of America (Alcoa), the government sold aluminum plants to 2 new firms, Reynolds Metals and Kaiser Aluminum.

3. Monopoly power (in both product and factor markets) can be recognized as an inevitable consequence of barriers to entry into both product and factor markets and dealt with by directly involving government in the market system. This can be done through controls on wages, prices, and profit (this has been done before, as in World War II). Some economists, notably John Kenneth Galbraith, argue that the U.S. should be doing this today.

Innovation. Joseph Schumpeter, an economist at Harvard, said that *innovation*—introducing new products or new processes—is what causes an economy to *develop*, rather than just grow. So one could view economic profit as a temporary repayment to people who perform this unique function. Martin Bloggs (or Edwin Land, or Henry Ford), thus, earns a high short-term profit *as a result* of throwing the market system off kilter by introducing innovations. As others enter the new industry, or use the new process and increase the supply of the product, these profits will disappear. (For some, there may even be losses.)

Risk and Uncertainty. When Bloggs starts producing guides, he may run into all sorts of problems. His *risks* include industrial accidents, deaths of executives, bad debts, and so forth. Bloggs can, if he wants, buy insurance against these and other risks. But there is no protection against *uncertainty*. For example, no one can sell Bloggs an insurance policy against having the foreman decide to go off and join a commune in the middle of filling an important order.

Once uncertainty enters the picture, both losses and profits become equally possible. "Playing the game" for profits is an important incentive for entrepreneurs.

Is Profit Earned?

It is necessary to pay people back for taking the risks involved in introducing innovations. On the basis of these concepts (and even on the basis of legal rights, such as patents), economists often say that short-term economic profits are earned. They are earned in that they are a necessary incentive. They bring to our society the important, perhaps indispensable, economic functions of entrepreneurship and innovation.

APPLICATION:
Comparable Worth—Market Distortion or Sensible Correction for Discrimination?

Since the 1940s, participation by women in the labor force has risen steadily. From 37 percent in 1960, the rate of those having paid employment reached 56 percent in 1988. In the latter year, however, earnings of women were about 69 percent of those of men. Even where full-time employment earnings are compared (fewer women work full time), earnings of females are about 77 percent of those of males. Many students of labor markets have concluded that some—perhaps a significant part—of the difference in male-female earnings is due to wage and job discrimination.

As early as 1963, the Federal Equal Pay Act made unequal pay for equal work illegal. A controversy continues about whether, in the interim, failure of male-female earnings to reach equality is due primarily to discrimination or to other market related considerations. Although there can be no doubt that "crowding" exists (women comprise about 90 percent of registered nurses and 85 percent of kindergarten teachers and secretaries, for example), is the resulting difference in male-female wages evidence of discrimination or is it the result of voluntary choices about which jobs to take and how many hours to work?

Two Views About the Earning Gap

Two clearly contrasting views exist about the gap in female-male earnings and they lead to directly opposed views about public policy and its desired as well as likely effects on that gap. Let's contrast these two views before looking at some of the evidence and controversies.

View A: "Most of gap between earnings of men and women is due to choices made by both groups about what jobs to accept, how long to work and when to enter and leave the labor force. Women's wages tend to be lower because they make choices that have lower (revenue) productivity but allow them greater latitude about moving into and out of paid employment."

View B: "Because of crowding and other forms of discrimination, women don't have the same job choices as men and, as a result, find themselves in occupations with lower wages even though the skills required of them are fully comparable to those required by men in better paying jobs." Customs, traditions and other more overt forms of discrimination have created an allocation of skills and abilities that, in the case of women, do not reflect productivity differences.

Interestingly, for students of economics, the debate between proponents of these two viewpoints can be seen as over the efficiency of labor markets. Holders of view A believe that labor markets in which the skills of women and men are priced are efficient. Efficient (competitive) markets allocate labor according to its relative productivity and assure factor payments that equal value of marginal product (VMP). Women, thus, having innate skills and abilities equal to those of men, earn lower wages because of choices made about types of jobs to seek and about entry and exit from paid employment.

Holders of this view argue that as women enter the same occupations as men and remain in them for comparable periods of time, the gap between earnings will tend to disappear.

Holders of view B see labor market outcomes quite differently. Inefficiency in allocation occurs because women are crowded into lower paying occupations that result from tradition and customs as well as the tastes for discrimination (job and wage discrimination) on the part of employers and their customers. By this view, markets can be made more efficient and the wage gap eliminated through government intervention in two forms: (1) employers must, through force of law or persuasion, hire women as readily as they would men in occupations from which women have been "crowded out," and (2) wages for jobs involving "comparable" skills must be equalized by law. The latter proposal is referred to as a program of **comparable worth**. Under this plan, panels of experts would evaluate the intellectual and physical demands of various jobs, assigning points to each factor. The total number of points would establish the difficulty (or ease) of the job and jobs with the same number of points would have to receive equal pay.

Comparable Worth
A proposal under which wages would be established based on the intellectual and physical demands of various jobs. A total number of points would be created for each job and jobs with the same numbers of points would receive equal wages.

Discrimination or Voluntary Choice: The Evidence

Before turning to the specifics of comparable worth—a highly controversial proposal—let's look at some of the evidence regarding the sources of the wage gap between men and women. We have posed the disagreements between advocates of view A (labor markets are efficient) and group B (labor markets are inefficient and biased against women) as though they are in polar disagreement. In fact, both groups agree about the source of part of the wage-earnings gap. Studies indicate that approximately half of the gap is attributable to measurable influences that include (1) differences in hours worked, (2) years of experience in an occupation, (3) seniority with a particular employer, and (4) levels of education. Clearly, these factors tend to create productivity differences to employers that, in efficient labor markets, correlate closely with differences in wages and salaries. None of these factors involve discrimination or a breakdown in the workings of markets. In other words, when women work as long, have as much experience, the same seniority with employers, and similar levels of education, this part of the gap tends to disappear. As choices open to women grow and their freedom to accept them improves, their incomes will closely approximate those of men. Such things as improved child care, for example, will permit this process to work. As Catherine England notes, "As long as men and women choose to play different roles in the home, they will necessarily play different roles in the market place. Equal opportunity should not be confused with equality of results."

Some data suggest that this part of the gap that is due to occupational choices may be narrowing if not disappearing. According to Dolan and Goodman, data for 1985 show that young women (ages 20-24) earn almost 86 percent as much as men in that age group while older women (age 45-54) earn 59.6 percent! As the two economists note, an optimistic (group A) view of this result is that the gap is disappearing as a result of decisions voluntarily made in labor markets; a pessimistic (group B) view, though, is that the problem continues since women are not yet able to reach the higher salary levels of top jobs as they grow older. Their career paths, say pessimists, are capped at lower levels than those for men.

The remainder of the wage gap is even more subject to differing interpretation and dispute. The gap is closely correlated statistically with marital status. Unmarried men and women have about the same earnings. Group A sees this as evidence that when women make voluntary choices that are the same as those of men, they earn as much as their male counterparts. Group B sees this result differently; men can have both marriage and family while women must choose.Group B also points to the fact that married men earn more than non-married men which suggests to them that marital status, per se, is not an important explanatory factor in the earnings gap.

Choice of Occupation

As it turns out, the most important additional explanatory variable is choice of occupation. Dolan and Goodman report that 90 percent of the earnings gap can be explained when this factor is included.[3] Occupation for occupation (physicians, typists, attorneys, assembly line workers or whatever), men and women of equal seniority earn about the same. About 40 percent of the difference in male-female earnings, in other words, is explained by the fact that women work more often in low paid jobs than do men. Crowding is so strong that almost two thirds of women would have to change occupations to eliminate crowding!

Group A Versus Group B: A Policy Synopsis

Unfortunately, explaining almost all of the earnings gap does not lead to agreement about what to do about it. Let's look at groups A and B in terms of their recommendations for public policy responses to the earnings gap:

Group A: Policy Recommendation
Leave wage determination to what are basically efficient labor markets. Markets punish employers that discriminate because they have higher costs than those who do not discriminate and who choose employees solely on productivity grounds. Wage differences, thus, reflect productivity differences and are an indispensable guide in a

---

[3]Edwin G. Dolan and John C. Goodman. *Economics of Public Policy*. 4th ed. (p. 130). St. Paul: Nest Publishing Co., 1989.

market economy to the allocation of a nation's labor force, both female and male. The earnings gap is the result of men and women making different but voluntary choices about occupations and full- versus part-time employment. In a free economy and society, there is nothing wrong with both groups looking rationally at their tastes and opportunity costs and making different choices about jobs as well as investments in education. Besides, in view of the laws against job and wage discrimination, if women change their tastes and choose to enter the same labor markets on the same conditions as men, the gap will narrow or be eliminated. If a gap remains, it is simply a reflection of differences in voluntary choices.[4]

Group B: Policy Recommendation

Wage determination cannot be left entirely to labor markets since they reflect the inefficiency and inequity attributable to the segregation (crowding) of women into certain occupations as well as lower limits to rank and salary attributable to tastes for discrimination, Even if women and men start out in the same occupation, women cannot progress on the same terms as men. The choices of women, thus, are not entirely voluntary and simply enforcing the equal opportunity provisions of laws will not eliminate the part of the earnings gap due to discrimination by employers. Eliminating demand-side wage discrimination in labor markets, therefore, requires correcting for pay differences that reflect discrimination rather than productivity differentials. "Pay equity" adjustments or "comparable worth" enforced by law can offset the effects of wage discrimination.[5]

Comparable Worth: More Fairness or Fewer Jobs?

As we noted earlier, having experts compute equivalent jobs and wages rather than letting free markets do so is a very controversial idea. Many economists including Walter Williams of George Mason University argue for resisting this temptation to intervene in labor markets and to substitute the calculations of planners for those of private employers. Many other economists, including Barbara Bergmann of the University of Maryland, conclude that mandated comparable worth wages can be accomplished with few distortions in labor allocation or unemployment and that the program can serve as a healthy corrective to the influences of employers who discriminate on the demand side of the market.

Pay equity or comparable worth advocates began pushing their cause with civil suits under the 1964 Civil Rights Act. The legal theory that employers may violate the law when they pay market

---

[4]This is essentially the view expressed by economist Walter Williams in *Explaining the Economic Gender Gap* (see Suggested Readings).
[5]This view is expressed by economist Barbara Bergmann in *Pay Equity—Surprising Answers to Hard Questions* (see Suggested Readings).

wages remains controversial and the Supreme Court has yet to rule finally on the legal issues. In the meantime, several states, including Washington and California have enacted comparable worth programs for public employees. Only one nationwide program, that of Australia, has been enacted. As it is an instructive laboratory experiment, we will return to the results of Australian experience later.

The Argument Against Comparable Worth

The most general argument advanced against comparable worth is that it will result in fewer jobs and by changing the relative prices of labor and capital, a tendency to substitute capital and eliminate jobs for laborers. We can see this argument in its simplest form in Figure 13-17. With competitive (efficient) labor markets such as that (hypothetically) represented, an increase in wages from the market wage, W_m, to a higher "equitable" or "comparable" wage, $\overline{W}_c$, will result in a decline in employment from Q_m to Q_c. Still, those who find jobs and for as much time as they wish to work, will benefit. The cost or loss in jobs and earnings due to comparable worth is represented by the lighter shaded area $(0Q_m - 0Q_c) \times W_m$. The benefit or gain in earnings is represented by the darker shaded area $(\overline{W}_c - W_m) \times Q_c$.

In the efficient labor market represented in Figure 13-1, an equilibrium wage of W_m will result and Q_m of the labor skills will be employed. If a "pay equity" or comparable worth wage of $\overline{W}_c$ is mandated, marginal resource cost (MRC) increases to that level for

Figure 13-17
The Labor Market for Skills Subject to Crowding: The Effects of Comparable Worth in a Competitive Market

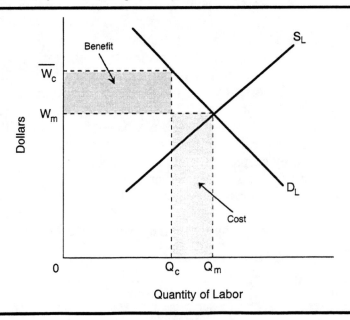

employers and only Q_c of the skills are employed. The difference in jobs, $(Q_m - Q_c)$ x W_m represents the cost of comparable worth while benefits to those employed are represented by $(\overline{W_c} - W_m)$ x Q_c.

Opponents of comparable worth believe that the cost/ benefit ratio of comparable worth is high. Employers will not only hire fewer women but will choose to hire only the most productive female workers. Since productivity depends importantly on length of time on the job and on work continuity, many of those not hired or let go will be married women who might choose not to work full time or to interrupt their careers to have children. Comparable worth, say opponents, would thus have a disproportionately negative effect on upward economic mobility at the very time when many married women are investing more heavily than before in human capital (education) for high productivity careers such as law, medicine, and business management.

The Case for Comparable Worth

Proponents of comparable worth do not deny that there will be displacement effects such as those in Figure 13-17. Barbara Bergmann, however, concludes that these effects will be fairly small. She cites a study by Gregory and Duncan that concluded that employment effects in Australia in the 1970s from an effort to eliminate half of the earnings gap were quite small. Another study, however, concluded that the effort slowed the increase in female employment by ⅓ and increased unemployment of women by 0.5 percentage points.

What are Large or Small Costs and Benefits?

Interestingly, both group A (opponents) and group B (proponents) agree that comparable worth could do much to narrow the earnings gap. In the Australian case, base pay for female workers increased from 65 percent to 90 percent of that of male workers between 1970 and 1980.

At heart, the question of whether the benefit/cost ratio of comparable worth is favorable or unfavorable turns largely on two considerations: are labor markets efficient and are attitudes and practices changing so that women will have an equal set of job choices that they can exercise according to their own tastes and preferences? If so, "pay equity" can be achieved without dislocation or resource distortion caused by *mandating* comparable wages. If not, then closing the earnings gap and eliminating much economic discrimination against women may require the kind of market intervention that is envisioned in a comparable worth program.

What is "equity" in pay and how much is it worth? As Bergmann notes, "Economists have long derided St. Thomas Aquinas' idea of the just price. But what people think is right and decent does influence their economic actions." Others would respond that it is not necessarily equitable to close the earnings gap for those who find jobs and pursue career paths by limiting the jobs and career paths of married women. In all of this, the fact is, of course, that there is no unique or completely agreed upon notion of equity.

Comparable Worth: Its Future

It is difficult at best to assay the future of comparable worth. Even its legality, as we noted earlier, remains finally to be determined as it applies to private employers paying market wages. If finally enacted, what form might it take? Probably not the all encompassing setting of wages that would replace market determination with central planning. Bergmann suggests that this approach would be "expensive, unwieldy, and unnecessarily intrusive." As an alternative, the program might take the form of guidelines for job and wage comparability, which as Bergmann suggests, would have an appreciable effect even without an enforcement mechanism.

What seems likely as America enters the 1990s is that comparable worth and pay equity will remain issues even as labor force participation by women continues to grow. How to deal with the earnings gap and whether to intervene in labor markets to diminish it are questions that the members of the American electorate and their representatives will probably confront in upcoming years.

SUMMING UP

1. In this chapter, we discussed competitive and *non*competitive pricing, not only of labor but of land, capital, and entrepreneurship. These elements are called factors. Payments to factors are *wages, rents, interest,* and *profits.*

2. Wages are determined by the supply of and demand for labor. The quantity of labor supplied rises as the wage rate increases. Therefore, the supply curve of labor slopes upward. The supply of labor also depends on people having a positive marginal utility of income. In other words, it depends on people wanting more income with which to buy goods and services.

3. The labor supply curve of each individual does not always slope upward. The curve may bend backward if people satisfy themselves that they have enough goods and services. They may decide to trade off some income for more leisure. Thus, above a certain wage rate, as wages go up, individual workers may offer to work less rather than more.

4. Leisure can be treated as a good. The demand for leisure as a tradeoff for income results from the *income effect* (our demand for leisure changes with changes in our incomes) and the *substitution effect* (the quantity of leisure demanded changes as its price changes).

5. In spite of *individual backward-bending labor supply curves*, the curve for the *total* supply of labor slopes upward, because all individual labor supply curves do not bend backward or bend backward at the same wage rate.

6. Also, various types of labor may command different wage rates, even for persons with similar skills. The difference in wages may be due to *location* (you can make more money repairing air conditioners in New York City than in Alaska) or to *discrimination* (male mechanics make more money than female mechanics.)

7. Much of the difference in wage rates derives from differing elasticities of supply of different kinds of labor. In the U.S., physicians have the highest incomes of any professional group. Part of this income differential is due to the inelastic supply of physicians.

8. People with very similar skills sometimes receive widely differing wages. The usual reasons are: (a) *Short-term increases in the demand for a given skill.* (b) *Wage and job discrimination.* For example, employers may refuse to hire any, or hire only a few, women workers or members of racial minorities, and after hiring, employers may pay women and minority workers less than the other workers. (c) *Nonmonetary considerations.* The satisfaction of performing some jobs may transcend monetary reward; for example, a college professor may accept a relatively small salary because the personal satisfaction of teaching outweighs a larger salary in the business world. (d) *Immobility of labor.* People may not move to better-paying jobs.

9. In a competitive situation, wages are set by the twin influences of supply and demand. A profit-maximizing firm that is a competitive seller of its products will hire enough labor to make the laborers' *value of marginal product* (MPP times product price) equal to their *marginal resource cost* (the addition to TC attributable to the hiring of additional labor). MRC is also equal to the wage rate, since, to a competitive employer, the wage is a constant or given factor.

10. If firms start to sell their products noncompetitively, the demand curve for their products begins to slope downward. To sell more of their product, they must reduce the price. Therefore, each time they hire an extra laborer in order to produce more of their product, the additional revenue they gain from hiring that extra laborer becomes less and less. Now, noncompetitive monopolistic firms will hire just enough labor to make the competitive wage (MC) equal to the MRP (MPP times MR). Since MR is less than the price of the product, the firm hires fewer laborers and consumers get less of the product than they would buy if markets were competitive.

11. Noncompetitiveness finds its way into the labor market in three main ways: (a) a firm may become *monopsonistic,* the only employer around to hire a particular type of laborer. (b) Laborers may organize a union, which is a monopolistic seller of labor's services. (c) Government may intervene in the labor market, by means of such devices as minimum-wage laws.

12. Monopsonistic firms must hire laborers in a market in which the curve showing the supply of labor is an upward-sloping one. In order to hire more and more workers, the monopsonist must pay a higher and higher wage. Therefore, the monopsonistic firm's MRC is not equal to the wage rate, but is greater than the wage rate. The profit-maximizing monopsonistic firm (which is a competitor in its product market) will hire just enough labor to make the MRC equal the MRP and the VMP. Thus, monopsony, as compared with pure competition in the factor market, means that (a) the number of workers hired by a firm or industry falls off, and (b) the wage rate falls, since the wage rate becomes less than the value of the workers' MRP or VMP.

13. When a monopsonist sells its products monopolistically, it will hire enough labor to make the marginal resource cost of labor equal to labor's MRP that is less than VMP ($MRC_L = MRP_L < VMP_L$).

14. All monopsonies pay labor or other resources less than what they contribute to the firm's revenues (wage less than VMP or wage less than MRP.

15. Monopsony in labor markets results in less employment as well as a wage less than VMP or MRP.

16. When workers organize a union (and thus gain a monopoly on a certain kind of labor skill) and come face to face with a monopsonistic firm, the market becomes a *bilateral monopoly.* When the two bargain and establish a wage, the figure they arrive at will be somewhere between the MRP or VMP of labor and the wage that will just call forth the equilibrium amount of labor demanded (indicated by the supply curve of labor). The exact level of wages depends on the relative bargaining strength of labor and management.

17. Exclusive unions may seek to maximize the wage of their members and restrict the union size. Inclusive unions may trade off wage gains and seek to increase employment and the size of the union. Unions may also seek to expand jobs for members through featherbedding and support for tariffs.

18. One thing that *may* come about as a result of bilateral monopoly is that the wage rate will do away with monopsony power and bring about a wage that is equal to the MRP.

19. Minimum-wage laws create costs as well as benefits. They may lead to a decline in employment and in workers' incomes especially if labor markets are competitive. If the minimum wage is enforced, the higher MRC may cause firms to hire fewer laborers, and even, in the long run, to substitute capital for labor. This leads to an oversupply of labor. If workers cannot find jobs elsewhere, unemployment or underemployment soon becomes a problem. Theoretically, the minimum wage may be set to offset monopsony wages and increase the number of jobs, though recent evidence suggests that there are widespread gains *and* losses from minimum wages and that labor markets are basically competitive.

20. When employers pay employees less than the employees' value of marginal product or MRP, *technical factor exploitation* exists.

21. Economic discrimination consists in dealing with consumers, producers, and buyers or sellers of resources on the basis of considerations *other* than market considerations.

22. *Job discrimination* consists of denying a job on some basis other than productivity considerations (race, sex, age, and the like). *Wage discrimination* consists of paying equally productive individuals different wages or salaries.

23. Economic discrimination arises from two sources; (a) *present discriminatory activity* (jobs and wages not determined by productivity), and (b) *results of historical discrimination* (effects on present economic activity of previous discrimination.

24. *Crowding theory* analyzes the effects of discrimination on the basis of supply and demand effects. Crowding refers to the concentration of women and minority groups into certain occupations and out of others. As a result, wages are lower in "crowded" occupations and higher in "uncrowded" ones.

25. Society loses as a result of crowding because it does not fully utilize the productivity of women and minorities. This loss of productivity reduces the value of goods and services produced.

26. When employers pay unequal wages to persons of equal productivity, it is usually because the employer or the employer's customers have a "taste for discrimination." Such a taste results in two different demand conditions, one for whites or males, or both, the other for women or minority workers, or both. The effect is to cause women and minorities to be paid a lower wage. The difference between the wage of the two groups is a form of wage exploitation based on race or sex.

27. Wage discrimination, unlike job discrimination, does not result in loss of productivity, or in underemployment. It does, however, skew income away from women and minority groups.

28. The idea of the melting pot has not worked rapidly to end job and wage discrimination against women and members of minority groups. Other remedies are public action or private action.

29. Public action against discrimination may take the form of legislation, or it may take the form of moving toward full employment. Private action may take the form of (a) letting competitive pressures eliminate discrimination, (b) encouraging union membership for women and minority-group members to become entrepreneurs, who will not discriminate (presumably) against their own kind.

30. Land—unlike other resources—cannot be increased. It is therefore in perfectly inelastic supply. Economists refer to the payment made to any resource whose supply is perfectly inelastic as *pure economic rent.*

31. The price of land, like the price of any resource with inelastic supply, is determined by the demand for it. If demand increases sharply, rents increase sharply. If demand decreases sharply, rents decrease sharply. If the supply of land is very large relative to the demand for it, the rent will be zero. In this situation, land becomes a *free good* (as it is in some frontier societies).

32. In the aggregate sense, rents on land are not a valid indicator of the efficiency of an economy. No matter how high rents are, no one can add more land to the total supply. This has led some economists to argue in favor of taxing away all land rents. This idea has met with heavy criticism.

33. When it comes to particular parcels of land, *relative rents* (that is, rents that vary according to the use to which the land is put) do indicate which uses of land are the most value productive. Even so, these rents can be taxed away without affecting the supply of land.

34. Payments to resources that are in *relatively* inelastic supply that are above that resource's opportunity costs are called quasi rents or common rents. Such rents are quite common and derive from differences in productivity among units of a resource as well as differences in location and innate physical differences.

35. There are two kinds of capital: *physical capital* and *financial capital.* The markets for financial capital are resource markets, whose *supply* comes from private (household and business) savings. The *demand* for financial capital comes from households, businesses, and government. Businesses will demand capital (that is, borrow money) as long as the marginal revenue product of the capital they borrow exceeds or is equal to its cost (the rate of interest, which is what it costs to borrow money).

36. The loanable-funds theory holds that the interest rate (the price of capital) is the rate that makes supply of funds equal to demand for funds.

37. There are many interest rates. Differences in rates depend on (a) risk, (b) liquidity, (c) length of loan, and (d) competitiveness in the capital markets.

38. One reason that governments intervene in capital markets is that interest rates do more than just ration the supply of capital. They also affect investment and the performance of the economy as a whole.

39. *Entrepreneurship* is the function of organizing labor, land, and capital into a firm capable of producing and marketing a commodity or service. The return to the entrepreneur who does this organizing and operating is called *economic profit*. There are three reasons why economic profit exists: (a) *Monopoly power*. A monopolist's patents, for example, are barriers to entry preventing movement of other firms into the field, which would drive prices down to competitive levels. (b) *Innovation*. The entrepreneur introduces new products or processes. *Profit* is a short-term reward for performing this function. (c) *Risk and uncertainty*. The entrepreneur must assume risks and accept the results of *uncertain* acts. It is just as possible to have losses as profits, and the entrepreneur who runs such a risk in pursuit of profits must be rewarded to insure that the risk taking function is fulfilled.

40. Many economists say that short-term economic profits are a necessary incentive to entrepreneurship and to the introduction of innovations, especially in view of the uncertainty and risks. Radical economists do not agree.

41. Labor force participation by women has grown substantially since the 1960s. An "earnings gap" continues to exist, however, between the earnings of male and female workers. Part of the gap is almost certainly due to crowding and economic discrimination.

42. Two contrasting views on the earnings gap are: group A, the gap exists because women do not choose the same occupations and not work as long or enter and leave the labor force the same as men, and group B, the gap exists because women have different job choices and through discrimination are crowded into jobs with lower wages than men.

43. Those who espouse view A regard labor markets as efficient; women have lower earnings than men because of their voluntary choices about occupations and patterns of working. Those who espouse view B regard labor market efficiency as compromised by tastes for discrimination of employers and their customers. The way to eliminate this inefficiency is by mandating that wages be equal for jobs of comparable skill and difficulty (comparable worth).

44. Groups A and B agree that about half of the earnings gap is due to differences in hours worked, years of experience in occupation, seniority, and levels of education. None of these involve discrimination; as these differences disappear, so does the wage gap. That part of the gap due to differences in occupational choices seems to be narrowing if not disappearing. The fact that younger women earn almost as much as young men may be evidence of that. The continuing gap between earnings of older women and men is, however, interpreted pessimistically by group B.

45. The gap is correlated closely with marital status. Unmarried men and women have about the same earnings. Group A sees this as evidence of efficiency; when men and women make the same job choices, they have the same earnings. Group B, however, argues that marital status, per se, is not very significant since married men earn more than unmarried men.

46. Choice of occupation is the most important factor in explaining the earnings gap not explained by the factors identified in (4) above. When the factors in (4) and occupational choice are included, about 90 percent of the gap can be explained. To eliminate this element of the earnings gap would require a massive change in occupations by women.

47. Policy recommendations by the groups A and B differ greatly. Group A argues for leaving efficient labor markets alone and letting men and women make voluntary choices. According to this view, when the choices are different, the results will be different but different results are not a reason for public intervention. Group B argues that intervention is called for since men and women do not have the same choices open to them because of crowding and discrimination. "Pay equity" advocates argue for a program of comparable worth or wage equivalence calculated and enforced through the law.

48. A final determination remains to be made about whether private employers paying market wages can be guilty of discrimination. Some states have enacted such programs for public employees and Australia has a national program of this type.

49. Comparable worth opponents believe that raising wages in occupations in which women are disproportionately represented will lead to fewer jobs for women as well as particularly adverse results for married women who are less productive to employers since they enter and leave more often than unmarried women. Proponents of comparable worth believe that these effects will be fairly small and cite a study of such effects in Australia in the 1970s as evidence. Evidence of these effects, however, is mixed.

50. Comparable worth can close if not eliminate the earnings gap. Opponents believe that the cost (loss of jobs and earnings)/benefit (higher wages and earnings) ratio of the program is unfavorable particularly since they believe that markets can eliminate the effects of discrimination on male/female earnings. Proponents of comparable worth believe that the ratio is favorable and the equity effects of such a program, even if voluntary in nature, will be significant.

KEY TERMS

Backward Bending labor supply curve
Closed shop, union shop
Crowding theory
Elasticity of resource supply
Featherbedding
Free Good
Inclusive union, exclusive union
Pure economic rent
Pure monopsony
Quasi rents or common rents
Relative rents
Technical factor exploitation
Unions
Wage discrimination, job discrimination

QUESTIONS

1. What does your own labor supply curve look like? As the rate of your wage changes, what factors affect your willingness to work?

2. What is a backward-bending supply curve of labor? Do you think that it probably does exist in the real world? If so, why?

3. Which factors determine the wide range of wage rates you see in the world around you? Which factors do you think are most responsible for differences in wages for individuals with (a) the same skills and (b) different skills?

4. If you were offered a job doing the thing you most enjoy, would you take a lower salary for that job than for a job that was humdrum or unpleasant? If so, what would you call the difference between the amount of money you would earn at the enjoyable job and the amount you would earn at the dull one?

5. Do competitive employers set wages? Why or why not? What are some examples of local competitive employers in your area?

6. What effects do monopsonies have on jobs and wages? If you were running things, what would you do to reduce the monopsony power of certain employers? Have unions done a good job of reducing employers' monopsony power? Have minimum wage laws? What determines the costs and benefits of minimum wage laws?

7. What is a closed shop? A Union Shop?

8. What are the ways unions may create more jobs? What are the differences between exclusive and inclusive unions in these regards?

9. Do you think heavy taxation of land can (a) provide a significant part of government's revenues? (b) be an efficient—and equitable—source of revenue?

10. Think about the incomes of The Rolling Stones and Jose Canseco. Do you consider part of their salaries rent? Why? Is it earned?

11. Consider the following figure which illustrates a hypothetical labor market in which the supply of a certain skill is represented by S_L.

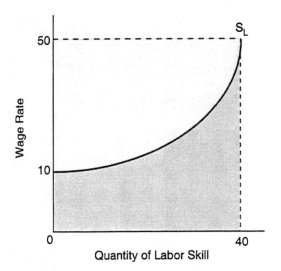

a. What is the opportunity cost payment to this labor skill?
b. If the current employment of this skill is 40 units, which represents the (1) quasi rent and (2) the opportunity cost payment (the lighter shaded area or the darker shaded area)?

12. What accounts for the wide range of interest rates?

13. Do you think that the profits entrepreneurs get are necessary to the successful functioning of the American economy? Why or why not?

14. What is economic discrimination? What is the difference between wage discrimination and job discrimination?

15. What is the relationship between competition in markets and economic discrimination?

16. What factors can explain the earnings gap between women and men that do *not* involve economic discrimination?

17. How do the differences in viewpoint between opponents of comparable worth (group A) and proponents of the program (group B) relate to the efficiency of labor markets?

18. How would wage levels be established for various jobs under comparable worth?

19. Does a difference in market earnings between men and women necessarily reflect economic discrimination? (Consider your answer to this question very carefully).

20. How can occupational choice explain so much (40 percent) of the earnings gap between women and men? What would be required to eliminate this part of the gap?

21. What is the problem with correlating marital status with the earnings gap?

22. What is the labor market policy recommendation of group A? That of group B?

23. If labor markets are efficient, will comparable worth create more or fewer jobs for women? What of earnings for women?

24. What is the major argument against a comparable worth program? The major argument for such a program?

25. How does one address or answer the question: "How much is pay equity worth?"

26. Which do you favor: Letting markets work to establish wage levels or a program of comparable worth? Why?

SUGGESTED READINGS

Aaron, Henry J., and Cameron M. Lougy. *The Comparable Worth Controversy*. Washington, D.C.: The Brookings Institution, 1986.

American Enterprise Institute. *Affirmative Action and the Constitution*. Washington, D.C., 1987.

Associated Press. "Nursing Shortage: Hospitals Feel Effects of Feminism, Low Salaries." *Cape Cod Times*. July 14, 1987. Reprinted in Robert L. Moore and James D. Whitney. *Microeconomic Principles in Action*. Englewood Cliffs, NJ: Prentice Hall, 1990.

Bell, C. Shaw. "Comparable Worth: How Do We Know it Will Work?" *Monthly Labor Review*. December, 1985.

Bergmann, Barbara R. *The Economic Emergence of Women*. NY: Basic Books, 1986.

_____. "Pay Equity—Surprising Answers to Hard Questions." *Challenge*. May/June, 1987. Reprinted in *Economics 88/89*. Annual ed. Gielford, CT: Dushkin Publishing Group, Inc., 1988.

Brown, Clair, and Joseph A. Pechman (eds). *Gender in the Workplace*. Washington, D.C.: Brookings Institution, 1987.

Dolan, Edwin G., and John C. Goodman. "Equal Pay for Comparable Work: Women's Issue of the 80s." *Economics of Public Policy*. 4th ed. Ch. 10. (Pp. 128-142). St. Paul, MN: Net Publishing Co., 1989.

Ferber, Marianne E., Carole E. Green, and Joe L. Spaeth. "Work, Power and Earnings of Women and Men." *American Economic Review*. May, 1986.

Gold, Michael Evans. *A Debate on Comparable Worth*. Ithaca, NY: Industrial and Labor Relations Press, 1983.

Gregory, Robert G., and Ronald C. Duncan. "The Relevance of Segmented Labor Market Theories: The Australian Experience of the Achievement of Equal Pay for Women." *Journal of Post Keynesian Economics*. Spring, 1981.

Remick, Helen. (ed). "Comparable Worth and Wage Discrimination: Technical Possibilities and Political Realities." Philadelphia, PA: Temple University Press, 1984.

Tregarthen, Timothy. "Critical Condition: Supply of Nurses Wearing Thin." *The Margin*. October, 1987.

Williams, Walter E. *Explaining the Economic Gender Gap*. Dallas, TX: National Center for Policy Analysis, 1983.

CHAPTER
14

Patterns of International Trade

The primary objective of a trade policy should be to keep world markets open to international specialization and exchange. The benefits of free international trade far outweigh the advantages that narrow sectors gain through protectionism. Economic change is not to be feared but welcomed as a natural consequence of healthy growth. The U.S. economy is increasingly producing high-value output based on technical advantages and providing valuable services to other countries in such forms as engineering and finance. Economic welfare will be greater if the changes are allowed without government restrictions based on an outmoded view of the economy.

Rising Protectionism and U.S. International Trade Policy

Ruth E. Muskus, Federal Reserve Bank of Kansas City
July/August, 1986, p. 17

OBJECTIVES

After studying this chapter you will be able to:

- Discuss the importance of international trade to the U.S. economy.
- Explain how international trade increases the wealth of a nation.
- Describe the different forms that trade restriction can take.
- Discuss the role of GATT in international trade.
- Have a working knowledge of the following terms and concepts:

Absolute advantage	Imports
Autarky	Infant-industry argument
Cheap–foreign–labor argument	Macroeconomics–employment
Comparative advantage	argument
Embargo	National security argument
Exchange rates	Quotas
Exports	Tariffs
GATT	

Patterns of International Trade

Throughout this book, we have looked at the many facets of a single market economy. For the most part, we treated that economy as *closed* or as one that engages in domestic economic activities only. The purpose of this was part of the larger approach of the text; to begin with simple principles and then gradually to make them more general and more complex until they could shed light on a wide range of economic problems

Now, let us look at the American economy as *open* or as one that engages in both domestic and international economic activities. This means that America not only trades with other nations, but also must finance that trade. As we enter the twenty–first century, international trade by the United States is not only growing, but also becoming a more important part of its economy. Arguments have flared again, as they have any times in our history, over the conditions under which this country should trade with others. One thing is clear, however: with combined exports and imports in 1997 of more than one and one half *trillion* dollars, the U.S. is the world's largest trading nation and a nation for which trade has again become a key sector of its economy.

What Makes Up Trade?

Exports
Commodities and services sold to other nations.

Imports
Commodities and services bought from other nations.

Trade consists of **exports**—commodities and services sold to other nations—and **imports**—commodities and services bought from other nations. Suppose that a dealer in San Francisco imports a Toyota. The price the importer pays (plus any shipping charges paid to foreign shippers) is added to the total of U.S. imports. Similarly, when a Japanese grain dealer imports American wheat, the payments that U.S. wheat sellers receive (plus any payments to our own shippers) are added to the total of our exports.

Visible Items
Those physical commodities that are exported or imported by a nation.

Invisible Items
The services including financial services associated with exports and imports by a nation.

International trade, thus, is made up of both **visible items** and **invisible items**. The visible items are the commodities (cars, wheat, television sets, petroleum, machinery, and so on) that are exported and imported. Invisible items are the services, including financial services (services of exporters and importers, ship rentals, cost of financing, and so on) which are exported and imported.

How Important is Trade to America?

Only a few years ago you might have said: "Look, the U.S. is a big nation; it produces a great variety of goods and services and has vast natural resources. Surely trade with other nations isn't all that important to us. Why devote a whole chapter to it?" Now, hardly a day passes without reference in the media to the importance of foreign trade to our economy and to the jobs of its people. Deficits in trade (imports > exports) are front page news to which stock markets react. Negotiations between the U.S. and Japan over further opening of Japanese markets to American exports are both economically and politically sensitive. Arguments about "free trade" versus "fair trade" are not merely academic issues. International trade and the financing of that trade had, by the mid 1990s, become vital issues and seem likely to increase in importance as the nation progresses into the twenty-first century.

America's Balance of Trade and Net Foreign Trade

Commodity Balance of Trade (X-M)
The value of commodity exports less the value of commodity imports.

It is worthwhile to repeat that both commodities and services are traded internationally. Commodity exports (X) (wheat, computers, and the like) and commodity imports (M) (autos, textiles, and the like) determine the **commodity balance of trade** so that when only commodities are considered:

$$X - M = \text{Commodity Balance of Trade}$$

When the commodity balance of trade is positive (X > M), a nation is selling more of its goods and services abroad than it is purchasing from other nations. This positive balance is commonly referred to as a "favorable" balance of trade. When the commodity balance is negative (X < M), the nation is purchasing more goods and services from abroad than it is selling to other economies; the negative balance is commonly referred to as an "unfavorable" balance of trade. While one should be cautious about reading too much into the terms "favorable" and "unfavorable," it is well to remember that differences between exports and imports (sales and purchases) must be financed each year by every nation.

Net Foreign Trade (NFT)
A measure of the trade balance that includes services. It is measured by taking the commodity balance and adding in net services (service exports – service imports).

When services (transportation, insurance, financial services, and the like) are included in the balance, however, we arrive at a measure of **net foreign trade,** or one which subtracts imports from exports (X – M), but adds in net services (S_N) (service exports – service imports). Thus net foreign trade is:

$$(X - M) + S_N = \text{Net Foreign Trade (NFT)}$$

NFT, thus, is a measure of the balance on both goods and services. Clearly, one way in which a deficit in the commodity balance (X < M) may be financed is through a positive net services (service exports > service imports) balance.

What has been the record of the American economy in recent years regarding the commodity balance and net foreign trade? From Table 16-1, several trends may be seen in both the commodity balance and in net foreign trade. From 1960 to 1975, America had a "favorable" commodity balance (X > M), even though there were typically small deficits in net services (service exports < service imports). Overall, net foreign trade, though typically small, was positive, reaching $12.4 billion in 1975. After 1975, America had consistently "unfavorable" commodity trade balances (X < M) reaching a high of over $130 billion in 1993. At the same time, after 1985, it began experiencing large positive net service balances (service exports > service imports), which partially offset the commodity deficits. Net foreign trade reached a recent year's low of -$28.5 billion in 1991, but grew again to $110.1 billion in 1997. The dramatic growth of the average NFT deficit (after 1980) seems to have come about because of:

1. *Changes in exchange rates.* Between 1980 and mid 1985, U.S. dollar/foreign currency exchange rates soared. Against the currencies

Table 14-1
U.S. Exports, Imports, Net Services, and Net Foreign Trade, 1960-1998 (billions of dollars)

Year	Merchandise Exports (X)	Merchandise Imports (M)	Net Services (S_N)	Net Foreign Trade* (X – M) + S_N
1960	19.7	14.8	-1.4	3.5
1965	26.5	21.5	- .3	4.7
1970	42.5	40.0	- .3	2.2
1975	107.1	98.2	3.5	12.4
1980	224.3	249.8	6.1	-19.4
1985	215.9	338.1	0	-122.1
1990	389.3	498.3	31.0	-78.8
1995	575.8	749.5	73.9	-99.8
1996	612.0	802.6	82.8	-107.8
1997	679.3	877.2	87.8	-110.1
1998**	499.9	684.4	69.7	-114.8

*Merchandise plus Services (may not add because of rounding)   ** First three quarters

Source: *Economic Report of the President*, 1999.

of America's major trading partners, the dollar increased in value almost 70 percent. Goods imported into the U.S. became relatively cheaper while American exports became relatively more expensive. Our rising quantity demanded of imports and the declining quantity demanded of our exports pushed X – M to ever larger negative figures. After mid 1985, the dollar declined against the currencies of our major trading partners, especially against the Japanese yen. Because of this, export growth was strong, more than doubling between 1985 and 1993.

2. In the face of the tax changes and other stimulative actions from 1982 on, the American economy and the real incomes of its citizens grew (except for the recession years of the early 1990s). Since Colonial days, Americans have had a strong (income-related) taste for imported goods. A growing demand for imports, even in the face of rising prices, added fuel to the large deficits, which were only partially offset by commodity positive net service balances.

But is Trade as Important to Us as to Others?

Perhaps you are saying, "All right, granted that foreign trade *can* have an effect on the U.S. economy, and will continue to do so in the twenty-first century; is the effect really important compared to the other factors that influence jobs and the welfare of Americans?" One way to answer the question is to look at how large a part exports or sales abroad are of the GDP or final value of all goods and services produced in America. Table 16-2 shows that for the U.S., exports make up a smaller percentage of GDP than they do for some of the other nations listed. Trade constitutes only 11 percent of U.S. total output, but for the other nations, which account for a large part of the world's trade, the figure ranges up to 185 percent (Singapore).

Do these figures mean that trade is relatively unimportant to the U.S.? The answer is, emphatically, *no*—for the following reasons:

1. The percentage of total output made up of exports has almost doubled since 1970. The 11 percent represents an important part of

Table 14-2
Exports as a Percentage of Total Output for Selected Nations

Nation	1970	1991
Belgium	92	141
Italy	16	0
United Kingdom	14	29
Singapore	102	185
Germany	21	34
Japan	11	10
United States	6	11

Source: World Bank, *World Development Report*, 1993.

the demand for U.S. output and thus the derived demand for labor (jobs) and other resources. If this foreign market for U.S. goods were to disappear, it would mean not just an 11 percent reduction in GDP, but a much larger reduction.

2. The additional demand created by trade enables American firms to operate more efficiently and to achieve economies of scale that might not otherwise be possible. Because of this international trade, manufacturers are able to lower their costs. This means not only potentially lower prices to consumers (both for exported goods and for goods produced in the U.S. from exported inputs), but also more profitable investment opportunities and demand for labor (jobs).

3. The growth of export importance is interesting historically. Early in U.S. history, trade was very important to the economy of the U.S. Then as the U.S. came of age the importance of foreign trade declined. Now there is a clear resurgence of international trade as a mainstay of the U.S. economy.

4. One big reason for the increased importance of trade is the growing dependence of the U.S. on imports of raw materials. The U.S. now imports almost 50 percent of the petroleum it uses (as late as the 1950s it was an exporter of oil). And although the U.S. has huge mineral resources, it must import 100 percent of the chromium and tin it uses, as well as between 90 and 100 percent of such minerals as cobalt, manganese, platinum, and nickel. In other words, the U.S. *needs* foreign trade for the sake of our industrial economy.

Of course the U.S. must, as we noted earlier, pay the countries from which it imports in their own currencies. Japanese business firms want yen, not dollars, so that they can pay their workers and other costs. In turn, to earn these foreign currencies, the U.S. must export its own goods and services as well as import capital.

The Gains from Trade

Earlier in our history there were those who argued for isolationism, both politically and economically. Today, we are seeing a resurgence of such arguments. Today there might be some who would say: "Apart from those needed minerals (and we can probably find substitutes even for many of them in the long run), I fail to see that we are necessarily better off because of trading. After all, we can use macroeconomic policy to achieve full employment, even without trade. Surely if we made the effort, we could produce just about everything we want. Let's keep the jobs at home in the U.S. Where is the advantage to be had from trade?"

The answer to the above question is not obvious. The U.S. is among a few fortunate nations that probably could—from a technical point of view—achieve **autarky**, economic self-sufficiency. Most food can be grown in the U.S.—even tropical fruits. The nation could achieve self-sufficiency in energy too, if it chose to do so. But is complete self-sufficiency necessarily desirable for the U.S. or for any nation? Virtually all economists say no, for reasons we shall now examine.

Trade and Comparative Advantage

In discussing the reasons for trade among nations, one immediately encounters two terms: the **absolute advantage** and the **comparative advantage** that each nation has in producing things. We can best define these terms by example.

Let's say that you are a graduate engineer, and you set up a personal small business of your own. You have an assistant named Pat Bloggs, who does the filing and other routine jobs in your office. You pay Bloggs $30 a day to perform these tasks, while you, as a professional engineer, earn $100 a day. After a particularly hellish week, in which drawings have gone to the wrong firm and correspondence has been mislaid in the wrong folders, you review the operation of the office. You realize that you can do these routine chores much more efficiently than Bloggs. Thus you have an *absolute advantage* over Bloggs. Should you fire Bloggs and do the job yourself? No! The $100 a day you earn as an engineer reflects your marginal revenue productivity (MRP); the $30 reflects Bloggs' *MRP*. Therefore, you should stick to your specialty of engineering, because in this you have a *comparative advantage*. In other words, you are relatively more productive as an engineer than as an office assistant. There is a lesson to be learned here. Even a person with an absolute advantage in doing *every* task should specialize in that field in which her or his comparative advantage lies.

We demonstrated how this principle works when we were discussing the market system of a single country: for efficiency's sake, resources should move to their most productive alternative uses. A city could hire engineers to sweep the streets, and they would probably do a great job. But it would be foolish for a society to employ its engineers in this way, since their comparative efficiency is greater when they are building roads, bridges, and offshore drilling rigs.

Now let's apply this idea of comparative advantage to trade between nations. In the real word, international trade involves many nations and thousands of commodities and services. To keep things simple in this illustration, though, we shall deal with only two nations, the U.S. and Honduras. We will examine the trade in only 2 commodities that each country can produce—tractors and bananas. Discussing additional goods and countries would not change the basic principles; it would just make the relationships more complex.

Table 16-3 shows the production-possibilities (PP) schedules for the U.S. and Honduras. Each country is capable of producing both bananas and tractors. However, note that the rate at which tractors can be traded off for bananas (that is, the rate at which the output of tractors decreases as the output of bananas increases) is very different for the two countries. The reason is that there are different resource endowments in the two countries including climate and human capital.

Figure 16-1 illustrates the PP for the two countries. Unlike the PP curves we saw earlier, these "curves" are straight lines. That is, they reflect a constant rate of exchange of tractors for bananas (we are assuming that the cost of producing each item is constant). Later in this chapter we will discuss PP curves that are concave to the origin and reflect increasing real cost.

Table 14-3
Production-Possibilities Schedules, United States and Honduras
(hypothetical)

United States		Honduras	
Units of Tractors	Units of Bananas	Units of Tractors	Units of Bananas
50	0	0	100
40	5	5	80
30	10	10	60
20	15	15	40
10	20	20	20
0	25	25	0

Figure 14-1
Production Possibilities for the United States and Honduras

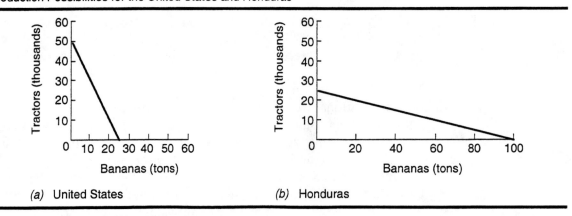

(a) United States

(b) Honduras

The Terms of Trade

Terms of Trade
The rate at which a nation's exports and imports exchange. In real terms, the number of its exports necessary to obtain its imports. In financial terms, the ratio of export prices to import prices x 100.

Now that we have established that the U.S. should specialize in producing tractors, and Honduras should specialize in bananas, the real **terms of trade** (the relation for a nation at which its exports exchange for imports) must be decided. That is, a ratio must be determined at which Honduran bananas will be exchanged for U.S. tractors. There must be an advantage for each country. The Americans must get more than $1/2$ unit of bananas for each unit of their tractors, and the Hondurans more than 1 unit of tractors for 4 units of their bananas.[1]

Each country must get more for its products in the world market than it would if it had sold them domestically. If both countries are to benefit, the actual exchange rate must lie between $1T = 1/2B$ (preferred by Honduras) and $1T = 4B$ (preferred by the U.S.).

The exact terms of trade will depend on the market demand for both products. Market demand depends on the degree to which one can substitute other products for either commodity, and on the relationship of demand to supply. If there are no good substitutes for tractors, and if demand for them is large relative to supply, the exchange rate (terms of trade) will be in favor of the U.S. If conditions are reversed, the terms of trade will be favorable to Honduras.

Gains from Trade

Suppose that the exchange rate moves to $1T = 2B$. Figure 16-2 shows what happens to production and consumption in both countries. Look at the replotted PP curves of both countries. The dark lines (called consumption-possibilities curves), indicating consumption after trade, show what each country can consume if it specializes in

Figure 14-2
Production-Consumption Possibilities for the United States and Honduras (after trade)

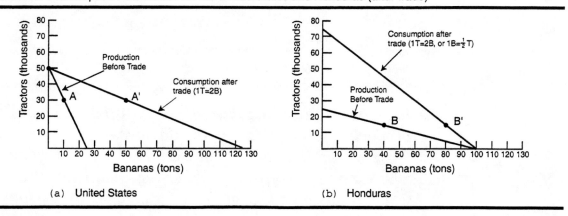

(a) United States

(b) Honduras

---

[1]We are working here with the real terms of trade. In reality, of course, it is the prices of exports and imports that determine a nation's (financial) terms of trade.

the good in which it has a comparative advantage and exports part of its output. We can see first how this process of mutually beneficial exchange occurs through an arithmetic example. Table 16-4 shows what happens when one tractor can be exchanged for two tons of bananas (1T=2B). That exchange rate is the same as one ton of bananas for one half a tractor (1B=1/2T). Each country benefits by taking some of the output of the good in which it has a comparative advantage (tractors for the U.S., bananas for Honduras) and exchanging with the other country for the good in which it does not have a comparative advantage (bananas for the U.S., tractors for Honduras).

If instead of consuming the 50 units of tractors it can produce, the U.S. exports 10 to Honduras, it can consume 40 units of tractors and 25 tons of bananas (instead of the 40 units of tractors and 5 tons of bananas possible without trade). If, at the same time, Honduras, instead of consuming the 100 tons of bananas it can produce, exports 20 tons to the U.S., it can consume 15 units of tractors (instead of the 5 units possible without trade). Let us take one other consumption with and without trade point. If the U.S. consumes 30 units of tractor and exports 20 to Honduras, it can consume 50 tons of bananas (instead of the 10 tons without trade shown in 16-3). Honduras, on the other hand, can export 40 tons of bananas to the U.S. and consume 30 tractors instead of the 15 it could consume without trade.

Table 14-4
(Hypothetical) Consumption Possibilities Schedules after trade, United States and Honduras

United States		Honduras	
Units of Tractors	Units of Bananas with trade	Units of Tractors with trade	Units of Bananas
50	0	0	100
40	25	15	80
30	50	30	60
20	75	45	40
10	100	60	20
0	125	75	0

The important result that Table 16-3 together with Table 16-4 and Figure 16-2 enables us to see is:

As long as a nation has a comparative advantage in producing some things, it should specialize in producing those things. It should then export part of the goods for which it has a comparative advantage and import goods in which it has a comparative disadvantage. By so doing, it will have more to consume.

This is true even if the nation has an absolute advantage in producing everything it consumes.

What Determines Comparative Advantage?

Since we have shown that comparative advantage is a mutually advantageous basis for trade, we need to identify the factors that determine a nation's comparative advantage. Also we want to ask the question: Are nations locked into a particular comparative-advantage position, or do their positions change?

First, *nations have differing comparative advantages,* for the following reasons:

1. Different nations have different endowments of natural resources, both in quantity and quality. For example, nations such as the U.S., Canada, the Soviet Union, and the People's Republic of China have large quantities (although different proportions) of relatively high-grade resources (petroleum, mineral deposits, topsoil, and so on).

2. Different nations have different physical features (mild or extreme climate, many or few natural harbors).

3. Different nations are at different stages of development of markets. For example, the U.S., Japan, and the countries in Western Europe have well-developed capital markets, reflecting large supplies of savings that can be transformed through investment into capital, including human capital (skills and abilities resulting from investment in education). In other countries, markets may be either rudimentary or nonexistent.

4. Different nations have different supplies of factors of production, including labor. For example, China and many other less-developed countries have large supplies of labor relative to capital.

A country tends to specialize in products (or services) that intensively use those resources in which it is relatively rich.

Second, the *comparative advantages of nations change.* Nations are not locked into a position with respect to comparative advantage. For example, the U.S. began as a nation rich in land and short of capital and labor. Today, it is relatively rich in capital and land, and relatively short of labor. (This has nothing to do with our unemployment rate. It means that as the U.S. presently produces things—even at full employment —capital and land are abundant relative to labor.) Up until the Civil War, the U.S. specialized in land-intensive agricultural exports (cotton, tobacco, rice, and so on). Today, it specializes in exports that are capital-intensive and land-intensive. For example, in 1992 more than 30 percent of U.S. exports were comprised of manufactured goods—all fairly capital-intensive. Another 10 percent were grains and cereals, which are land-intensive. Thus, almost half of U.S. exports were derived from processes that were capital- and land-intensive. On the other hand, the U.S. mainly imports things (coffee, cocoa, inexpensive textiles, handicrafts) that are relatively labor-intensive. (Although automobiles, steel, and other such goods are exceptions.)

Demand Considerations

As we have seen, domestic economic trade is based on the benefits of voluntary exchange.

International trade, whether between nations or, as is most often the case, between individuals, is also based on the expected benefits of voluntary exchange. We saw in Figure 16-2 that supply (cost-based) considerations make it possible for nations, through exchange, to consume more with trade. There are also important benefits to trade that derive from demand considerations. The structure of demand differs greatly from one country to another as well as from one part of the world to another. The primary reason for these differences lies in the diversity of tastes and preferences that exists among individuals within countries as well as between different nations. Consider tastes in food and clothing. Americans (both North Americans and Latin Americans) prefer coffee; the English and many Asians prefer tea. The Japanese prefer fish; Americans have a much stronger taste for beef, pork and chicken. Out of these differences arises a willingness to pay prices for goods and services that differs substantially from one area to another and thus gains to be had in exporting.

There are many arguments about changing the comparative advantages of countries, especially about whether comparative-advantage trade tends to help the poor-trading nations to develop. In the application in this chapter, we will examine some of these arguments.

Increasing Costs and Other Cautions

In the case involving the U.S. and Honduras, we concluded that each would produce only its most advantageous good—tractors or bananas. We showed that bilateral exchange between the two nations would make both better off in terms of the quantities of the 2 goods available for consumption. There are some qualifications to the argument, however.

1. As each country reallocates its resources from the disadvantageous good to the advantageous one, it will run into *increasing costs*. For example, as the U.S. produces more tractors, the cost (in bananas not produced) may rise, until it reaches a point at which it would be better off if it produced some bananas of its own rather than always exchanging tractors for Honduran bananas. Honduras, whose costs of producing bananas also rise, may be better off producing some of its own tractors. The point is that increasing costs cause international specialization to be less than complete.

2. When two countries specialize in making things in which they have a comparative advantage and then trade with each other, achieving the greatest possible production, we assume that there is full employment in the trading nations. However, at times this trade means reallocating resources and, when this results in unemployment, the countries' output may fall below the PP curve. So there are some possible undesirable effects for a country from trade. But there are various macroeconomic (fiscal and monetary) tools that a nation can use to achieve its employment goals, and there are microeconomic tools that can be used to reallocate resources in efficient resource markets (job retraining, for example). Thus, many economists feel that the risk of creating temporary unemployment is not a compelling reason to forego trade.

3. The principle of comparative advantage depends heavily on *competition* in international trade. If the tractors are produced by a monopolistic firm but the bananas are exported by competitive firms, Honduras may not fully reap the benefits of trade. If monopolistic export boards (perhaps government ones) negotiate the terms of trade (American wheat for Russian oil, for example), one cannot tell what the outcome will be. This is also true of bilateral monopoly. The end result depends on the relative skills and bargaining strengths of the participants.

4. If there are *externalities*, the terms of trade may not reflect the real costs of production. The countries may produce and exchange either too little or too much. (Suppose that the tractor factories pollute the water and air and that their costs do not reflect the added social costs of cleaning up the environment.)

5. The principle of comparative advantage depends on the fact that relative prices (the American price of tractors and the Honduran price of bananas) reflect relative scarcities of resources in each nation. If the prices do not reflect these scarcities, an international (as well as domestic) misallocation of resources occurs. Suppose that the U.S. subsidizes the tractor industry. Then international prices of tractors (the terms of trade) would not reflect underlying relative scarcity and companies would produce more tractors than is efficient (and trade them). (Americans would, in effect, be producing tractors when they should be producing bananas.)

Protectionism
Efforts by governments to protect domestic firms and industries from the competition of imported goods.

6. The biggest obstacle to trade being conducted according to comparative advantage is **protectionism**—the efforts of governments to protect domestic firms or industries from the competition of imported goods. Consequently, there has been little completely free trade in modern times (or indeed at any time). Let us now look at how nations may protect trade and the arguments surrounding these practices.

The Means of Protection

There are two principal means by which countries usually intervene to protect their own industries from overseas competition: tariffs and quotas.

Tariffs
Taxes levied on imported goods.

Tariffs

The most common means of protection are **tariffs**, which are taxes levied on imported goods. Figure 16-3 shows how a protective tariff works and also shows its effects on trade and prices. Before trade begins, the U.S. demand for bicycles is D_{US} and the supply is S_{US}. Equilibrium price is P_1 ($Q_1 D_{US} = Q_1 S_{US}$). At this price, Q_1 of bicycles are sold. (Presumably, bicycles are goods in which this country has a comparative *dis*advantage.) Now trade opens up. The U.S. begins to import foreign bicycles (from Japan, Italy, and France). The supply of bicycles increases to $S_{US \& foreign}$. Equilibrium price falls to P_2, and Q_1 bicycles are sold. The supply increases until the price of bicycles in the U.S. is equal to the price of bicycles abroad (not including transportation costs). As long as the American price is higher, foreign producers will continue to export bicycles in order to sell in the more profitable American market.

Figure 14-3
How a Protective Tariff Works

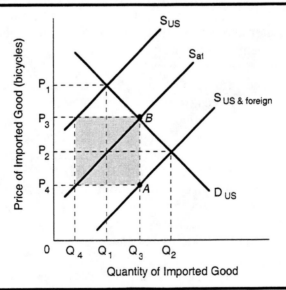

Figure 16-3 illustrates the effects of a protective tariff. The domestic supply of the good is S_{US} and the domestic demand is D_{US}. Without trade equilibrium price is P_1 and Q_1 of the good is sold. If free trade in the good occurs, imports increase the domestic supply to $S_{US \& foreign}$. As a result of trade, price declines to P_2 and Q_2 of the good is sold. Both the decline in price and the increased consumption of the good ($Q_2 - Q_1$) are benefits to consumers attributable to trade. If a protective tariff of AB is imposed, supply declines to S_{at}, with the tariff, price rises to P_3 and quantity sold declines to Q_3. Both the increase in price (P_2 to P_3) and the decrease in consumption of the good ($Q_2 - Q_3$) are costs to consumers attributable to protectionism.

Now suppose that the bicycle manufacturers complain to Congress, as the Bicycle Manufacturers' Association did in the 1970s. They argued as follows:

> A deluge of imported bicycles into the U.S. has increased imports from 19.8 percent of our market in 1964 to 37.1 percent in 1972. We don't feel our business should go down the drain. Standards must be established that would automatically impose restrictions on imports competing with American products.... This is not protectionism.

Let's say that the bicycle lobby convinces Congress that this argument is valid, so that Congress and the President levy a tax—a tariff—on imported bicycles. The tax which is equal to AB in Figure 16-3 increases the cost of importing bicycles and reduces the supply to S_{at} (supply after tariff). The new equilibrium price is P_3, which is higher than the pre-tariff price (by $P_3 - P_2$). The number of bicycles sold goes down (by $Q_2 - Q_3$). Note that part of the gain to consumers from all the foreign bicycles coming into the country is eliminated. If the tariff had been higher, imports might have ceased altogether, and supply might have fallen back to S_{US}. Then price would have gone back up to P_1 (with only Q_1 sold).

"He wasn't even warm—was he, Mom?"

So the tariff hurts consumers, because now they must buy bicycles at a price higher than the international price, and they are getting fewer bicycles. The tariff also hurts foreign bicycle manufacturers, because the net price they receive (after paying the tariff) is P_4. In addition, the tariff hurts U.S. firms that may use the product as an input (messenger services and the like). The total revenue to the U.S. government from the tariff is shown by the shaded area. This is the unit tariff per bicycles ($P_3 - P_4$) times the number of bicycles imported ($Q_3 - Q_4$). (At price P_3, American manufacturers supply Q_4.)

Elasticity and the Burden of the Tariff

You probably recognize that the burden of the tariff (either the higher price to consumers or the lower net price to sellers) is distributed on the basis of the price elasticity of demand for the imported good. We see in Figures 16-4 and 16-5 how the distributive burden of the tariff is related to elasticity. There may be both a *consumer burden*, the portion of a tariff paid by consumers in higher prices, and a *producer burden*, the portion of a tariff paid by importers in a lower net price and reduced sales of the imported good.

Figure 14-4
The Burden of a Tariff with Inelastic Demand

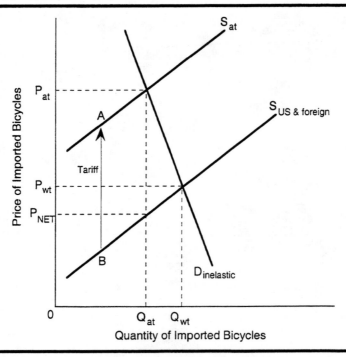

The burden of a tariff is related to the elasticity of demand for the imported good. Figure 16-4 illustrates the relationship for the case in which demand is price *in*elastic. Without a tariff, supply is $S_{US \& foreign}$, price with tariff is P_{wt}, and quantity sold before the tariff is Q_{wt}. A tariff of AB on the imported good decreases supply after tariff to S_{at}. As a result, price rises to P_{at} and quantity sold declines to Q_{at}. There is a large increase in price (P_{wt} to P_{at}) relative to the decline in sales ($Q_{wt} - Q_{at}$). Most of the burden of the tariff is borne by consumers in the form of higher prices, though foreign producers also are burdened by the lower net price (P_{NET} as opposed to P_{wt}).

In Figure 16-4 the demand for the imported good is price inelastic, implying that poor substitutes exist for the good or that consumers spend relatively little of their incomes on it. With unrestricted trade, the bicycle market clears at Q_{wt} (quantity without tariff) and at price, P_{wt} (price without tariff). After tariff AB is levied, supply is reduced from $S_{US \& foreign}$ to S_{at} (supply after tariff). Now the market is cleared at Q_{at} and P_{at} (quantity and price after tariff). Most of the market burden $(P_{at} - P_{wt})$ is borne by consumers in the form of higher prices but part, $Q_w - Q_{at}$ is borne by producers in the form of reduced sales and a lower net price (P_{NET}). Clearly, however, consumers absorb most of the burden.

In Figure 16-5, we see the reverse. The demand for the imported good is price elastic; implying that relatively good substitutes for the imported good exist or that consumers spend a significant part of their income on it. With unrestricted trade, the market clears at Q_{wt} and P_{wt}. After tariff AB is imposed, supply falls from $S_{US \& foreign}$ to S_{at} and the market clears at Q_{at} and price P_{at}. The consumer burden $(P_{at} - P_{wt})$ is relatively small while the

Figure 14-5
The Burden of a Tariff with Elastic Demand

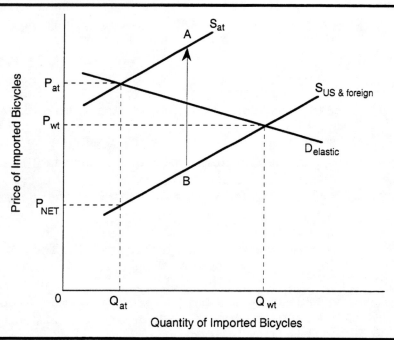

We see in Figure 16-5 how the burden of a tariff is distributed when the demand for the imported good is price elastic. Before the tariff, with elastic demand $D_{elastic}$ and supply $S_{U.S. \& foreign}$, price is P_{wt} and the quantity sold of the good is Q_{wt}. When tariff AB is imposed, costs of importing the good rise, and supply declines to S_{at} resulting in a higher price (P_{wt} to P_{at}) and a decrease in the quantity of the good sold (Q_{wt} to Q_{at}) and a lower net price (P_{NET}) to foreign producers. There is a large decrease in quantity sold relative to the increase in price and most of the burden of the tariff falls on firms importing the good.

producer burden ($Q_{wt} - Q_{at}$) and the lower net price ($P_{wt} - P_{NET}$) is relatively large. Clearly, when demand is elastic, most of the burden falls on producers in the form of reduced sales and lower net prices

Is anyone better off as a result of the tariff? Yes, the American bicycle manufacturers are. They do not have to pay the tariff, so they keep the full price (P_{at}) of their product. This is higher than P_{NET}, which is the price foreign makers have after they pay the tariff. The federal government is better off by the amount of revenue. The tariff, in other words, represents a loss in income by consumers, which is transferred to the government and to protected domestic firms.

Beyond the burden, two points about tariffs should be emphasized: (1) When the government imposes a tariff, it makes a *net addition to domestic monopoly power.* In our example, bicycle manufacturers had been getting a competitively set international price for their product. Now they are getting a more monopolistically established price instead. (Though in this case the government, rather than private business, is the agent that creates the monopoly influence.) Thus, tariffs defeat our objective of having a competitive market system. (2) When the government imposes a general tariff (or other trade restriction), it *reduces the number of good substitutes that consumers have for domestically produced goods.* This, in turn, may make the demand *more price inelastic* and (because it increases monopoly power) may cause prices in the long run to rise by an even greater amount than the amount of the tariff itself.

Import Quotas

Import Quotas
Restrictions imposed by governments on the quantity of a good that may be imported.

The second major means governments use to protect their industries against competition from abroad is **import quotas**, that is, restrictions on the quantity of goods that may be imported. In one way, the effects of quotas are much like those of tariffs. Look again at Figure 16-3. Suppose that Congress, instead of enacting a tariff, had said that only $Q_3 - Q_4$ bicycles could come into the U.S. Supply would still have dropped to S_{at} (or S_{aq} to stand for supply after quota). Total supply (Q_3) would have been domestic supply (Q_4) plus foreign supply ($Q_3 - Q_4$). Consumers would be affected just as adversely and U.S. bicycle makers would still get the higher price, P_3. The difference is that *a quota is not a revenue-producing device* (the shaded area would not exist), so the government would not get any extra tax revenue. Foreign bicycle makers would get the same price as domestic makers, P_3 (less transportation costs, of course), and domestic consumers would carry the burden of the quota.

Import Embargo
A prohibition, imposed by government, against importing certain goods.

The most extreme form of a quota is an **import embargo**, which is an absolute prohibition against importing a good. If Congress had imposed an embargo on foreign bicycles, supply would have reverted to S_{US}. Price would have risen to P_1 (domestic producers would have been restored to whatever monopoly power they originally had).

Embargoes are relatively rare in American history. In 1808, during the Napoleonic wars, President Jefferson imposed one. After 1962, the U.S. government embargoed trade with Cuba (no Cuban cigars, sugar, or rum). Until the 1970s, there was a U.S. embargo on trade with the People's Republic of China. It is worth noting that when embargoes are lifted, they are usually lifted in the interest of political expediency (détente, for example) rather than in the interests of free trade. Embargoes are usually short-term political penalties against antagonistic nations. In 1996, the decades long embargo against Cuba was intensified after tensions rose between the two governments.

Export Quotas: Rational Ignorance by Consumers?

As we have seen, quotas have effects similar to tariffs except that they do not generate revenues for governments. In protecting domestic producers, governments sometimes assign shares of their domestic markets to foreign exporters. Examples of this in the U.S. include imports of textiles, apparel, and sugar. The American government assigns quotas to foreign governments (Dominican Republic, Taiwan, etc.), and those governments, recall, assign the quotas to their own producers. In all cases, of course, American consumers pay prices above the world price (for example, more than twice the world price of sugar). Clearly, American sugar producers have benefited as well as foreign producers who are able to obtain quota shares. By one estimate, the value of these monopoly rights (rents) to foreign producers in 1993 was over $11 billion.

Rational Ignorance
The argument that when the benefits of a public choice are highly concentrated and its costs highly diffused, it is rational for those who bear its costs to ignore them.

Why, you may ask, do such clear and obvious impediments to free trade exist when millions of consumers are harmed and a few thousand (domestic and foreign) producers reap the benefits. Why should consumers ignore these added costs rather than inform themselves fully and attempt to resist efforts by government to impose such costs? Many economists believe that the explanation lies in the concept of **rational ignorance**, the rationality of consumers in ignoring many proposals of government in view of the large costs of informing themselves about such proposals and the small individual benefits of doing so. It is worth reminding ourselves of this idea. Take the case of sugar quotas which were renewed in 1996. Would you, for example, as a consumer of sugar, bother to inform yourself about monopoly sugar prices in the U.S. and lead a campaign to overturn the public decision to impose a quota system? Even if you were successful in eliminating quotas (a very unlikely result for one voter), the benefit/cost ratio of this activity to you would be unfavorable. Notice, though, that the same calculus would not apply to most private consumption decisions. Would you inform yourself about the private choice between a Chevrolet Corvette and a Nissan 300-ZX? In the latter instance, the benefits and costs would be quite different and almost certainly would make it irrational to ignore the information needed to be fully informed.

Many economists would argue that quotas are clearly less preferred to tariffs where governments intend to restrict international trade. Notice that tariffs create tax revenues whereas quotas generate benefits only to private producers. At least with tariffs, the revenues *could* be used to reduce other taxes as well as to fund public expenditure programs. It is for this reason that some economists, faced with the political difficulties of eliminating quotas, have proposed auctioning the rights to export quotas. Presumably, the rights would bring something close to the $11 billion referred to earlier.

Arguments in Favor of Protection

As already noted, the U.S. has rarely if ever practiced completely free trade. (Neither have many other countries.) Americans frequently say they believe in competition. But many, including many of their elected representatives, seem to argue against it when it is to their financial advantage. Economists in general—most U.S. economists, that is—sing the praises of free trade. But apparently, the economists who make public policy cannot completely convince the government. In the mid 1990s, we again see efforts to impose new restrictions on trade between the U.S. and other nations. In view of this continuing push for protectionism, let's examine the arguments most commonly advanced in favor of restricting trade.

The Infant-Industry Argument

The infant-industry argument is as follows: Industries that are just starting cannot meet the pressures of competition by similar, already established industries located in other, more industrially mature countries. Such infant industries deserve the protection of a tariff or other protective device, and they must be sheltered until they have become big enough to take advantage of economies of scale.

This argument may seem reasonable. However, there are opposing arguments: (1) Tariffs and other forms of protection, once enacted, are extremely hard to abolish. For example, the bicycle industry still enjoys tariff protection. So do the automobile and steel industries and many other U.S. industries that are hardly infants. (2) If an industry needs to be protected before it is mature, direct government subsidies are preferable, since they make the costs of such protection explicit. (3) The logic of the infant-industry argument is difficult to apply, since it is hard to know (in either a developed or underdeveloped nation) *which* infant industries will (and should) survive. Short of pursuing a goal of autarky, a nation must choose, without any clear guidelines, *which* infant industries to put into its protective and expensive incubator. The protecting nation runs the risk not only of distorting its uses of resources but even of ending up with an industry that fails anyway, especially if the protection is finally withdrawn.

The National-Security Argument

The national-security argument is as follows: The U.S. can never really be certain of the supply of a good produced in a foreign country. The nation cannot even depend on its present friends to help in a tight spot. This means that, when it comes to defense goods, U.S. security must take precedence over U.S. economic efficiency.

This argument is difficult for economists to judge, since there are no objective criteria by which to evaluate the tradeoff between increased national security and decreased industrial efficiency. Economists can only identify the costs involved in (1) levying tariffs, or (2) directly subsidizing firms that make defense goods. Almost all economists would say that direct subsidies are preferable, because they more clearly identify the costs involved.

The Cheap-Foreign-Labor Argument

The cheap-foreign-labor argument can best be summed up in two examples. The American textile industry, say proponents of protection, must be protected from imported textiles from nations such as Malaysia, Thailand, and the Peoples Republic of China. Wages in Thailand and other such nations are so low that American firms cannot price their textiles low enough to compete. Florida farmers must be protected from the winter produce of Mexican farms where agricultural labor is paid $3 per day. How, say some Florida farmers and their elected representative, can they possibly compete with Mexican farmers whose labor costs are only 3 to 5 percent of their own? Although this argument is persuasive to many people, it is irrelevant to economists because (1) the higher wages of Americans presumably reflect higher marginal productivity; (2) it is socially inefficient to have an American firm that cannot compete with labor-intensive imports try to do so; and (3) it is less costly to retrain labor and reallocate resources to more efficient uses than it is to protect an inefficient industry (however, remember the exception: the national-security argument.); and (4) wage costs are only part of the costs of production. Costs per unit of product produced depend not only on prices paid for labor but on labor's productivity. Much of the seeming advantage of low wage countries seems to be disappearing in the 1990s. Much of this advantage has been in "blue collar" labor cost, which is declining and will continue to decline as a portion of total cost in the upcoming century. Already, as Peter Drucker has observed, this no longer provides a competitive edge to low wage countries, and, as a result, we are witnessing a return of industries to the U.S. to take advantage of lower transport costs.

The Macroeconomic-Employment Argument

The macroeconomic-employment argument is that during hard times the U.S. can "export" some of its unemployment. (This is sometimes called a *beggar-thy-neighbor* argument.) Large segments of the business community (except big importers) and of labor often support this idea. The principle is to create more jobs at home by excluding, or sharply restricting, imports. Such an increase in domestic demand for formerly imported goods causes the U.S. to move toward full employment.

Has the U.S. followed the beggar-thy-neighbor principle? Figure 16-6 shows what has happened to tariffs during our "hard-times" periods. You can see that tariffs have been high during most recession and depression periods, such as the mid-1870s, 1890s, early-1900s (though they were falling then), and 1921. They were especially high in the early years of the Great Depression (the Hawley-Smoot tariffs, in 1930, were the highest in modern American history). The purpose of the so-called Tariff of Abominations (1828) was to protect U.S. infant industries such as textiles and iron. Tariffs have from time to time protected American makers of every sort of commodity. Cheese, watches, cameras, musical instruments, and machinery are some that come to mind.

Economists usually feel that a beggar-thy-neighbor action is not likely to succeed. Even if it does work initially, the cost is great because such actions invite retaliation in the long run by other countries. (If the U.S. raises its tariff on bananas, Honduras will raise *its* tariff on tractors.) A trade war is likely to result and every nation will be hurt. The reason is that as tariff walls go up, governments try

Figure 14-6
History of American Tariffs

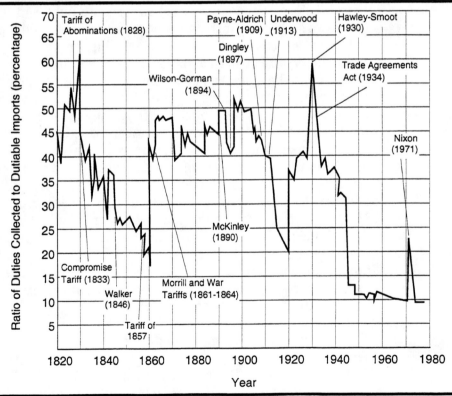

Source: U.S. Department of Commerce, Historical Statistics of the U.S. and Statistical Abstract of the U.S., 1982.

to stimulate domestic demand, through tax cuts, increased government spending, and lowered interest rates. Assuming that previous international trade has reflected a comparative advantage, the U.S. will increase its domestic output, substituting homemade products for imported ones, at the expense of efficiency. Without trade, even if the U.S. reaches full employment, there will be relative inefficiency in the industries producing these products. Thus, the level of U.S. production of goods and services will be lower than if the tariff had not been introduced.

Retaliation for "Unfair" Trade Practices

Proposals to restrict trade are often based on the view that they are necessary to punish unfair trading practices by other nations. Such proposals frequently include the following reasoning: "Since free trade does not, and perhaps cannot exist, trade restrictions can be used as leverage against unfair traders to create a system of fair trade." In part, this rationale is found in the provisions of the Trade Agreement Act of 1979. Among the provisions of the act is one prohibiting foreign firms from dumping or selling products in the U.S. at prices lower than those in their own domestic markets. The act provides that, on a finding of dumping by the International Trade Commission, the President may impose penalties against foreign producers.

Economists are divided on the question of penalizing dumping. Some say that dumping is merely a subsidization of domestic consumers by foreign producers. Why turn down a gift? Others say that dumping may be predatory, an attempt to suppress competition or prevent its development through entry into an industry. The problem with this rationale for trade restrictions is that it supposes that dumping may create monopoly. Many economists would say that if it does, the monopoly profits will serve as a stimulus to entry anyway, and tend to eliminate the benefits of dumping.

The Rustbelt: Protecting Declining Industries

Many of the arguments for trade restriction in the past decade came from elected officials of areas with declining industries or industries containing antiquated plants and equipment. An argument was advanced that is the reverse of the infant-industry argument. Such industries, it is said, need temporary protection while they phase out or cut back production and during the period in which jobs are found for workers in other industries. While plausible, the argument suffers from many of the same problems as the infant-industry argument. Which industries should be protected? How much cost is reasonable? An illustration will suffice. About 75 percent of all shoes sold in the U.S. are imported (mainly from Brazil, Taiwan, and The Republic of Korea). In an effort to protect this declining industry, Congress, in 1985, studied imposing import restrictions that would have saved more than 30,000 jobs in the industry. The cost *per job*, however, in terms of higher prices and other costs, would have been about $68,000! Publicity about the costs led to the demise of the proposal.

An equally serious problem is in choosing the industries that are declining and face ultimate elimination. Only a few years ago, the American steel industry seemed a candidate with the closing of much of its older plants and equipment and the consequent loss of jobs in the Mid-west. With the exchange rate changes of 1987–1988, however, the steel industry again became fully competitive and operating at high levels of capacity. The "rustbelt" now is prospering and has low unemployment rates. Would protection have been either necessary or wise?

International Trade Policy Since World War II

General Agreement on Tariffs and Trade (GATT)
An international organization created in 1947. Its objectives included fostering freer trade throughout the world.

As we have seen, tariff levels have fluctuated greatly throughout American history. After World War II, the U.S. was instrumental in creating the **General Agreement on Tariffs and Trade (GATT)** in 1947. From 23 original members, it has grown to more than 117 nations in 1995 and now includes much of Eastern Europe and even such nations as the People's Republic of China and Russia. Dedicating itself to fostering trade and lowering tariffs, GATT has held a series of meetings, or "rounds." The three most recent rounds— the Kennedy Round (1967), the Tokyo Round (1979), and the Uruguay Round (1994)—have resulted in major tariff reductions. The Uruguay round alone will reduce tariffs by 40 percent.

World Trade Organization (WTO)
A successor organization to GATT whose primary purpose is to further liberalize world trade.

The Uruguay round resulted in the creation of a new international organization, the **World Trade Organization (WTO)**. The WTO is the successor to GATT and has the same basic objective, that of further liberalizing trade. All member states have rights and obligations within this organization. A difference between the WTO and GATT, however, is that developing nations, like the industrial nations, will have an obligation to liberalize trade. Indeed, by 2002, preferential trade policy treatment for the developing nations will be eliminated. A new legal system is also created within the WTO to resolve trade disputes among the member nations.

Regional Trade Agreements

While GATT and WTO grew after 1947 as organizations that are global in scope, a parallel pattern emerged in which nations have joined to form regional agreements also designed to liberalize trade among their members. These agreements have taken three different forms:

Common Markets
Agreements for free trade, common tariffs and free movement of capital and labor.

Customs Unions
Agreements for free trade and common tariffs.

Free Trade Agreements
Agreements for free trade among members.

1. Common markets
2. Customs unions
3. Free trade agreements

The most comprehensive of the three is **common markets**, which provides for (1) free trade among the members, (2) common tariffs for trade with non-member states, and (3) free movement of capital and labor among the members. A **customs union**, on the other hand, is less comprehensive and provides for free trade among members and common tariffs for trade with non-members. Finally, a **free trade agreement** is least comprehensive providing only for free trade among member states.

Current Regional Trade Arrangements

The most successful free trade agreement since World War II is the European Union (EU). Many nations that did not wish to join the EU formed the European Free Trade Association (EFTA) in 1960, and have since negotiated free trade agreements with the EU. The combination of EU-EFTA nations forms a free trade area which encompasses a population of over 300 million and constitutes the largest free trade market today.

Western hemisphere nations are moving to create a free trade market that may be even larger than that in Europe. In 1988, the U.S. and Canada signed a free trade agreement eliminating tariffs on all goods and virtually all services by 1999. The *bilateral* free trade flows are the largest in the world. In 1993, the agreement was expanded with the inclusion of Mexico and an agreement to phase out all tariffs in this trilateral trade over a period of 15 years. The **North American Free Trade Association (NAFTA)** included a provision to ultimately include all western hemisphere nations. This goal may be difficult to achieve, however, in view of the continuing controversies surrounding NAFTA and the narrow margin of its congressional approval in 1993.

North American Free Trade Agreement (NAFTA)
An agreement among the U.S., Canada, and Mexico to create a free trade area among the three nations over a period of 15 years.

Multilateral Free Trade: Its Future

The period since 1947 has seen impressive gains in free trade through much of the world. World trade today is probably freer (though not yet fully free) than it has ever been. Does this mean that the culmination of the trade liberalization of the past half century will be truly global free trade? While most economists would wish the answer to be yes, the answer is not that clear. There are at least two alternatives to free trade that will contend for dominance over the next 10 to 20 years.

1. Growth of regional trading blocs that erect barriers to external trade while furthering free trade among members (for example, a European bloc contending with a western hemisphere bloc.)

2. Growth of state-directed trade. In spite of the seeming demise of central planning (the old Soviet Union, the "old" People's Republic of China, etc.), forces may already be seen urging at least a partial return to state economic direction.

Economists are sure only of this. Although both of the above arrangements may produce some short term gains for some states, both will produce greater real losses in contrast with global free trade. If this conflict of trade policy philosophies or ideas is compared to a prize fight, world trading history since 1947 seems to have free trade ahead on points, but no knock out is in sight!

Free Trade: A Reprise

Before 1947, the U.S. and other trading nations were free to impose or raise tariffs. Tariff increases frequently lead to retaliation and, at times, "trade wars" with major reductions in the volume of trade. The 1930s, as we have seen, were especially characterized by these conditions. Some economic historians conclude that protectionism contributed significantly to the lengthening of the great depression.

APPLICATION:
Does Trade Create Development?

During the 1960s, 1970s, and 1880s, it became apparent that nations such as Mexico, Brazil, Korea, Taiwan and Singapore were developing major manufacturing sectors and that international trade was playing a key role in this process. Indeed, these nations came to be known as the newly industrializing countries (NICs), in contrast with the less-developed countries (LDCs). The emergence of the NICs seemed to reignite a long-standing debate among economists and others, not only about the future course of economic development, but also about the role of international trade in fostering such development.

In the 1980s, the "debt crisis" of some of the NICs and many of the LDCs further complicated efforts to assay the relationship between trade and development. That the issues will continue to be important to all nations, rich, poor and in between, seems nearly certain. Development cannot begin or continue without capital and other imports, and importing cannot occur unless nations have export earnings with which to finance imports. Likewise, debt cannot be serviced, much less repaid except out of export-derived revenues. In an increasingly interdependent international economy, few issues take on more importance than the relationship between trade and development.

The Relation Between Trade and Development

To establish this relationship, we must find a relation between exporting-importing and the increase in productivity that is the key to development. Opinions are divided about whether trade—especially trade based on comparative advantage—enhances economic development. In this application we will examine some of the controversies surrounding this subject.

The Classical View

Early economists, including Adam Smith and David Ricardo, believed that trade was essential to economic development, or to what Smith called "the wealth of nations." Writing about the country's efforts to produce things that it could import more cheaply, Smith said, "The value of its annual produce is certainly more or less diminished, when it is thus turned away from producing commodities evidently of more value than the commodity which it is directed to produce."

This idea of maximizing the wealth of a nation through trade, however, is based on a static situation (*static* meaning timeless). Much of the argument over its validity arises from the distinction between the static economic position of a country at a point in time, and the improvement (or deterioration) in the country's position that occurs over time. Let's illustrate the difference between these two perspectives.

At its beginning, the U.S. started out with a certain endowment of land, labor, capital, and entrepreneurship. For simplicity, assume that all its resources were integrated into the market system. Now ask yourself the following questions: (1) In any given year—for instance, 1940—would the per capita national income be higher if the U.S. followed a policy of free trade? Or would it be higher if it imposed restrictions on trade? (2) Which policy—restricted trade or unrestricted trade—would cause income to grow faster from one date to another (for instance, from 1940 to 1990)?

Figure 16-7 will help you visualize the answer. It shows that in 1940 the U.S. could have two levels of per capita income: $1,400 or $1,450. The $1,400 figure corresponds to the level if the government enforced protective practices (such as tariffs or quotas). It represents many possible levels of income resulting from different combinations of trade restrictions. Each of the combinations causes resources to be used in ways that are *less* productive than would be the case if there were free trade, or if there were comparative-advantage trade. The $1,450 represents the *free*-trade (comparative advantage) case.

Therefore, the answer to question 1 is that at any point, its process of development, a nation will have a higher income if it

Figure 14-7
Growth Paths of the United States: Free Trade and Protectionism

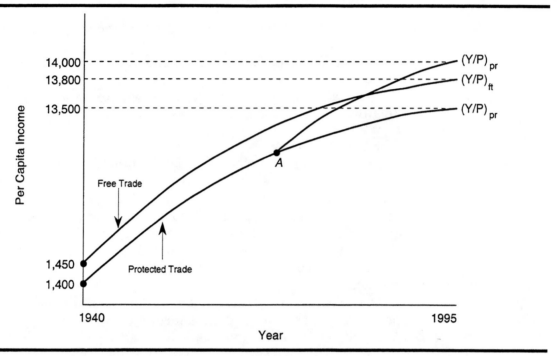

engages in free trade and utilizes all its resources on the basis of comparative advantage.

Now what about *growth* as it relates to international trade? Which policy—comparative-advantage (free) trade or some sort of protective tariffs or quotas—would yield the U.S. the greater growth in income during the period from 1940 to 1995? Adherents of the classical economic view say that comparative-advantage trade would give the greatest growth, because a nation that trades according to the principle of comparative advantage allocates its resources to their most productive uses. Thus, the nation is maximizing its productivity. With free trade, as income grows over time, along $(Y/P)_{ft}$ in Figure 16-7, the size of the nation's market grows. There is specialization and division of labor. Capital increases and productivity increases as well.

The growth path with protected trade $(Y/P)_{pr}$, begins at a lower level ($1,400) in 1940 and in 1995 results in a lower level of per capita income ($13,500) as well. This is because even with full employment of its resources, allocation is less efficient and productive with protection than with (comparative advantage) free trade. This is the traditional view of the relationship between trade and development and the reason why many economists espouse free trade as the desired policy objective of developing nations.

Reservations About the Traditional View

There are objections to the above scenario. Some economists feel that a policy of comparative-advantage trade is not, in the long run, the best policy for developing nations. They feel that one cannot prove an explicit relationship between growth and free international trade. Economist Hollis Chenery has been one of the doubters. Chenery, for a long time an official of the U.S. Agency for International Development (USAID), has argued that there are five reservations that point to the wisdom of modifying comparative advantage as a policy to enhance economic development for NICs and LDCs:

1. *Factor costs.* The benefits of comparative advantage depend on factor markets producing equilibrium prices of resources. This means that the prices reflect "true" relative costs of production. Consider the imperfections in labor or capital markets that one sees in developing countries (for example, the U.S. in the 19th century or in virtually all LDCs today). As development takes place, markets perform more efficiently. There are often dramatic changes in factor costs, and thus in comparative advantage.

2. *Export markets.* Comparative-advantage trade gives rise to specialization. NICs and LDCs frequently come to specialize in producing—and exporting—just one, or a very few, raw materials. Then they must import food and raw materials that they do not produce along with manufactured (and semimanufactured) products. The result is an unstable economy, which is tied to the fluctuating prices of raw materials. (For example, the world price of copper plunged 65 percent in the early 1970s. Chile, which produces one-eighth of the world's copper, suffered acutely.) You can see that following a policy of comparative-advantage trade makes it hard for an underdeveloped nation to keep its economy stable. In addition, price and income elasticities of demand for these countries' raw materials are low, though data are conflicting. (When the price of copper falls on the world market, and a country's chief export is copper, it cannot make up in export earnings for the drop in price by selling a greater quantity to its industrialized neighbors.) So the terms of trade, the ratio of export prices to import prices, may turn against the exporter of the raw material. The reason is that the poor nation—for example, Chile—must continue to import manufactured goods, whose prices (compared to the price of the exported copper) are now relatively much higher.

Many economists fail to see factors 1 and 2 as being necessarily valid arguments against a developing country's specializing in its comparative advantage raw-material exports. In their view, a developing nation's rate of return on investment in its raw material is greater than the rate of return it *would* get if it tried to build up other internal projects, such as factories, even after correcting for factor costs and fluctuating world prices.

3. *Productivity changes.* Manufacturing, by its very nature, may enhance the skills of labor and management more than agriculture does. So some economic advisers urge a developing nation to stress manufacturing, even at the expense of comparative-advantage exports. Some of the NICs appear to have done so. Others disagree, asking whether such an advantage exists. Perhaps, they say, the developing nation could make as much headway by concentrating on agriculture as by concentrating on manufacturing. Some of the LDCs are attempting to reemphasize agriculture. All agree, however, that the nation must make allowances for productivity changes in allocating its resources—even if it does not, in the long run, opt for manufacturing as the area of concentration.

4. *Dynamic external economies.* As an industry grows, its costs fall. Or demand for its output increases. As a result, the costs of other industries may also fall. There may, in fact, be a whole group of investments that are profitable *only if they are undertaken together.* Comparative advantage, manifested in market signals such as equilibrium prices, does not under these conditions indicate to a nation how it should allocate its resources. Suppose, for example, that the underdeveloped nation increases its investment in industry and realizes certain of these external economies. This will reduce the costs of more than one industry. But, some economists say, perhaps it would have realized even more external economies if it had allocated its capital to comparative-advantage agriculture. For example, it could have built fabricating plants, including expanding the production of the raw material.

5. *Uncertainty and flexibility.* Some economists feel that changes in the market can happen so quickly, and are so hard for policy makers to foresee, that a diversified economy—one that can quickly adjust to changes in supply and demand—is better (and certainly more flexible) than one that relies on a single product, or only a few products. Economist C. P. Kindleberger has argued that the terms of trade now discriminate against the raw-material-exporting nations and favor the industrialized nations, because the raw-material-exporting nations lack flexibility. So it seems that a developing nation might be well advised to sacrifice some short-term efficiency in the interests of longer-term flexibility, and a capacity to adjust more rapidly to changes in world supply and demand.

A serious problem with this, though, is that inefficiency often involves creating monopoly privileges and rents that are very difficult to eliminate in the long run. Many examples of this problem can be found in some of the NICs and LDCs. A report in the *Wall Street Journal* in November 1986 indicated that in Indonesia—a country possessed of many exportable natural resources including oil—export revenues have done little to finance broadly based economic development programs. Principal among the reasons for this has been the substitution of bureaucratic import controls and corruption for free trade. A small oligarchy, including the Presidents' family, has received monopoly rights over imports and control over access to import quotas along with (monopoly) distribution rights to products within the country. Such monopoly pricing might ordinarily attract investors into these industries but investment licensing has prevented that. Higher monopoly prices make Indonesian exports less competitive and reduce export earnings, thereby reducing the ability to finance developmental imports. Recently, a proposal has been made in Indonesia to develop an expanded automobile industry. A member of the President's family has again been given monopoly rights and it seems likely that an efficient competitive automobile industry in the country is unlikely. It is not surprising that bureaucratization and corruption have made the export position of many LDCs less competitive. Indeed, their share of world exports has been falling since the 1950s.

Those With Reservations: Modify Free Trade

Those who have reservations about comparative-advantage trade and its ability to insure or accelerate growth argue for modifications in trade policy. Such modifications may involve significant departures from free trade. Some of the measures adopted include (1) rationing of trade (foreign exchange) earnings either direct controls or through multiple pricing (exchange rate) controls, (2) providing direct subsidies or tax incentives to firms that produce import substitute products, and (3) creating import-export monopoly agencies to obtain lower prices for imports and capture revenue from domestic producers for governmentally determined development uses. To the extent that these noncompetitive market interventions are effective, proponents say that the growth path with protection, $(Y/P)_{pr}$ in Figure 16-7, can accelerate at some point (point A in Figure 16-7), utilizing dynamic externalities and other advantages to propel the nation onto a new path that will generate higher real income at the end of the period ($14,000 versus $13,800) than would be the case with free trade.

Debt Problems of the LDCs and NICs

With the dramatic exception of the "Asian Tigers" (South Korea, Taiwan, Hong Kong, Singapore, Malaysia, and, recently, Thailand), the trade positions of the LDCs and NICs deteriorated in the 1970s and 1980s. Most of the LDCs exports continue in the 1990s to consist of primary commodities. For many of them (Indonesia and Venezuela excepted), agricultural primary commodities dominate their exports. Such products have declined in value from more than one-third in 1955 to less than 14 percent in 1986. While those that export fuels benefited (until the mid-1980s) from rising prices, this added, ironically, to the financial problems of others. The dramatic increase in manufactured engineering products has benefited some NICs (especially the "Asian Tigers") while it has had little effect on many LDCs whose manufactured products are not competitive in world markets.

Faced with rising import prices (especially fuels) and softening primary commodity export prices, many NICs and LDCs turned to international capital markets and borrowed heavily in the 1970s. In some instances, the long-term investment credits were wisely invested and resulted in dramatic productivity growth and growth in exports (e.g., South Korea). In other instances, the long-term credits appear to have been less wisely employed, often in the bureaucratic controls and corruption to which we referred earlier. Some countries, especially in Latin America (Brazil, Argentina, Peru) appeared to be on the verge of inability to even service the interest payments on their debts (often 50 percent or more of their GDPs). Liberalization of economic policy in the 1980s and 1990s, especially in Argentina and Chile, has eased some of these concerns.

Implications for Trade Policies

For many years, representatives of the LDCs and, to a lesser extent, the NICs, argued for creating a special system of trading and financial preferences for the "developing nations." At times, especially at the United Nations Conference on Trade and Development (UNCTAD), they lobbied for a system under which there would be guaranteed export prices for primary commodities, easier access to markets in industrial nations and long-term capital flows to LDCs and NICs at preferential interest rates. Those pressures, however, seemed to abate until the debt crisis of the 1980s.

In the 1980s, we heard again arguments for trade preferences. One NIC (Brazil) temporarily suspended interest payment on its debt. An LDC (Peru) announced it would pay no more than 15 percent of its GDP in interest payments on its external debt. Two American Secretaries of the Treasury have argued for more public and private capital flows to LDCs and NICs at below market interest rates. Which shall it be in the future, free trade in commodities services and capital or a "new (non-free trade) order" of trading relationships? As we indicated in the preceding chapter, free trade has gained, but there are real concerns about the future. Economists are not of one mind about which trade policies are consistent with sustained growth and development. Many would agree with Arnold Harberger[2] that free trade, and a minimum of government involvement in domestic and international economic affairs, is preferable. Other economists would

---

[2] *World Economic Growth: Cases of Developed and Developing Nations.* San Francisco: Institute for Contemporary Studies, 1984.

agree with Hollis Chenery that free (comparative-advantage-based) trade may be stacked against the LDCs and NICs. For them, government action is called for to encourage the real and financial trading relationships that will permit more and more LDCs to become NICs and for the NICs to become major industrial countries.

SUMMING UP

1. In this chapter, we look at a market economy as one that is open, or that trades (exports, imports) with the rest of the world. For the U.S., international trade has grown in its importance to its economy.

2. Trade consists of *exports*—commodities and services sold to other nations —and *imports*—commodities and services purchased from other nations. Exports and imports consist of both *visible items* (commodities) and *invisible items* (services).

3. The *commodity balance of trade* measures the difference between commodity exports and commodity imports (X - M).

4. *Net foreign trade (NFT)* is the commodity balance (X – M) difference between exports (X) and imports (M), plus net services (service exports – service imports):

$$NFT = (X - M) + S$$

Foreign trade is important, even to a diversified economy such as that of the U.S.

5. NFT can exert a significant macroeconomic influence on the level of income and employment, the demand for goods, services and the creation of jobs. This is so even in the U.S., in which exports (and NFT) form a smaller percentage of output than they do in many other major trading nations. (However, in dollar volume, the U.S. is by far the largest international trader and the percentage of its output made up of exports has nearly doubled since 1980.)

6. Between 1960 and 1980, the U.S. usually ran a small trade surplus or trade deficit (X < M). After 1983, the U.S. ran up increasingly large trade deficits that seemed to be due to exchange rate changes and the income taste of Americans for imported goods.

7. Trade is important to the U.S. for these reasons: (a) Trade constitutes an important part of demand for U.S. output, and hence demand for labor (that means more jobs) and other resources. (b) Demand that results from trade enables many U.S. industries to operate more efficiently and on a larger scale. (c) The percentage of U.S. GDP represented by trade has grown in recent years. This reflects a greater interdependence with other nations. (d) The U.S.

needs imports of raw materials, such as certain key minerals, in order to operate many industries.

8. *Autarky* (economic self-sufficiency), although it may be technologically possible for the U.S., is economically unwise, because the U.S., by specializing in items in which it has a comparative advantage, can realize gains from trade.

9. *Absolute advantage* refers to a nation's ability to produce all of a good it consumes more efficiently than any other nation. (Some nations may have an absolute advantage in all goods.) *Comparative advantage* refers to a nation's being more efficient in producing some good or goods than in producing others (even though the nation may also be absolutely more efficient than its neighbors in producing everything).

10. At any given time, nations have certain production possibilities. These are reflected in their PP curves (assuming full employment and given technology). So long as any two nations have different internal rates of exchange (tradeoffs) between producing the same 2 goods, it is mutually beneficial for each to specialize in producing the good in which it has a comparative advantage.

11. By specializing in producing those things in which it has a comparative advantage, and by trading what it does not consume to other nations for goods in which *they* have a comparative advantage, a trading nation can have more goods to consume (the consumption-possibilities curves will be above the domestic PP curve). Differences in tastes and preferences of consumers in different countries also create gains from trade.

12. Comparative advantage derives from (a) different endowments of natural resources, (b) different physical features (climate, harbors, and so on), (c) different states of development of markets (for example, some nations have well-developed capital markets), and (d) different supplies of labor.

13. Comparative advantages change, sometimes dramatically. The U.S. began with a comparative advantage in land-intensive commodities, which it exported. Today it has a comparative advantage in capital-intensive as well as land-intensive goods.

14. If nations run into increasing costs as they specialize, the specialization will not be complete. They will produce a wider variety of goods. (For example, Honduras will produce some of its own tractors, the U.S. will produce some of its own bananas.)

15. Some people disapprove of foreign trade because of the unemployment that occurs when resources (especially labor) must be reallocated as a result of that trade. To economists, this is not a compelling argument against an open economy. They point to the

macroeconomic tools that can be used to increase employment, and the microeconomic tools that can be used to reallocate resources (for example, job retraining).

16. Comparative advantage depends on competition. When competition does not exist, or when nations with equal advantage do not trade competitively with each other, some of the benefits of comparative-advantage trade are lost.

17. Trading nations that are burdened by *externalities* may produce and trade too much or too little for comparative advantage to work. Prices for goods exported must accurately reflect relative scarcity of resources.

18. The theory of comparative advantage depends on relative prices reflecting relative scarcities of resources in each nation. If prices do not reflect these scarcities, an international misallocation of resources occurs.

19. The biggest obstacle to free trade is *protectionism,* the effort to protect farmers and industries from the competition from lower-priced goods imported from foreign countries when there is free international trade.

20. The two major means of protectionism are (a) *tariffs,* which are taxes levied on imported goods, and (b) *quotas,* which are limitations on the quantity of imports.

21. Tariffs and other trade restrictions reduce the supply of goods and raise the prices charged consumers. They also add to the monopoly power of domestic producers, and they may reduce the number of good substitutes available to consumers, making domestic demand for a good more inelastic. One thing in their favor is that they produce revenue for governments.

22. The burden of a tariff consists of a *consumer burden,* that part of the tariff paid by consumers in a higher price, and the *producer burden*, that part paid by sellers in a lower net price and reduced sales. The more inelastic is the demand for the imported good, the greater is the consumer burden. The more elastic is the demand for the imported good, the greater is the producer burden.

23. Quotas do not produce revenue for governments. Otherwise the effects of quotas are similar to those of tariffs. They reduce supply, raise prices to consumers, and enhance the monopolistic position of domestic producers. The most extreme form of quota is an *embargo,* an absolute prohibition against importing a certain good or trading with a certain country. Export quotas are sometimes assigned not only to protect domestic firms but to favor foreign countries and firms.

Voters (consumers) may not resist the higher prices of these quotas because of rational ignorance.

24. Arguments in favor of protectionism are as follows: (a) the *infant-industry argument* (firms that are new and small need to be protected until they are large enough to compete with more established firms in foreign industries); (b) the *national-security argument* (uncertainty of foreign supply, plus need for a reliable source of military hardware, means that domestic producers must be protected, even if they are inefficient); (c) the *cheap-foreign-labor argument* (domestic firms that must pay high wages should be protected against imports from countries in which wages are low); (d) the *macroeconomic-employment argument* (recessions and depressions can be "exported" if a nation puts up barriers to trade that reduce imports without reducing exports); (e) retaliation for "unfair" trading practices (make them trade fairly) and; (f) protection of declining industries (help such industries temporarily) during phasing out.

25. Economists generally reject these arguments that favor protectionism, with the exception of the national-security argument, for which there is no objective basis for evaluation. However, even in the case of protection given to industries producing goods needed for national security, economists feel that there should be direct subsidies instead of tariffs, so that the costs of protection are clearly identified.

26. Beggar-thy-neighbor tariffs are likely to be ineffective, even counterproductive. When one nation sets up high tariffs, other nations retaliate. As a result, without specialized trade, nations have fewer goods and services to consume, even when they have full employment.

27. In 1947, the world's major trading nations created GATT, the *General Agreement on Tariffs and Trade*. By 1995, it had grown to over 117 nations dedicated to liberalizing trade.

28. The Uruguay round of GATT talks (1994) created a new trade organization, the *World Trade Organization (WTO)* which will seek to increase trade liberalization in both developing countries and industrial nations.

29. Regional trade agreements have grown since World War II. They have taken the form of (a) common markets, (b) custom unions, and (c) free trade agreements.

30. *Common markets* provide for free trade, common tariffs, and free movement of capital and labor. *Customs unions* provide for common tariffs and free trade. *Free trade agreements* provide only for free trade.

31. The future of free trade clouded by (a) the growth of regional trade agreements and (b) the re-emergence of state-directed trade.

32. Major free trade arrangements include the European Union-European Free Trade Association (EU-EFTA) Agreement and NAFTA (North American Free Trade Agreement).

33. Policy makers today must face a major question: Can international trade provide the primary basis for the economic development of poor nations? In the 1960s, 1970s, and 1980s, growth of the newly industrialized countries (NICs) seemed to suggest yes.

34. Views differ as to the relation between trade and development. Classical economists (Adam Smith, David Ricardo) felt that comparative-advantage trade was essential to increasing output and maximizing the wealth of a nation.

35. Much of the debate over the relation between trade and development involves the distinction between the static principles of comparative-advantage and the dynamic principles of growth.

36. One can show that, in a static sense (that is, at a point in time), a nation can maximize its output if it allocates all its resources to their most productive uses. However, there is no certainty that if a nation does this, the growth of its output over a period of time will be greater than it would have been if it had departed, selectively, from comparative-advantage trade.

37. Those who argue for restricting comparative advantage, as the basis for trade, argue on the basis of: (a) *Factor costs.* Imperfections in the factor markets of underdeveloped nations cause their factor costs not to reflect their real relative cost. (b) *Export markets.* Comparative-advantage specialization on the part of the poor nations may result in unstable economies. Low income and price elasticities of demand for raw-material exports may turn the terms of trade against the nation that specializes. (c) *Productivity changes.* In an economy based on manufacturing, the skills of labor and management increase and diversify more rapidly than they do in an economy based on agriculture. (d) *Dynamic external economies.* Several investments—a whole package of them—may have to be made simultaneously in order to make them succeed, or pay off. This is more likely to happen in an industry-based economy than in an agriculture-based economy. (e) *Uncertainty and flexibility.* A diversified economy is more flexible, and can adjust more readily to changes in supply and demand, than an economy that specializes in a few raw-material exports. Thus, it can better resist the effects of worsening terms of trade.

38. Economists generally discount points (a) and (b) as reasons to abandon comparative-advantage trade. However, they must take into account factors (c), (d), and (e) when they are working out trade policy.

39. Deviations from free trade seem often to give rise to bureaucratic red tape in LDCs and to monopoly grants and corruption. These impediments to productivity growth raise prices and make LDC exports less competitive in world markets

40. Faced with rising import (especially fuel) prices in the 1970s and falling primary commodity prices, LDCs and some NICs borrowed heavily in world capital markets. Where the capital was not wisely invested, a "debt crisis" has arisen in which threats to default or limit payments have created serious problems in financial markets.

41. For years LDCs and NICs have argued for a "new international economic order" with restrictions on free trade involving guaranteed export prices, easier access to markets, and below market interest rates for capital.

42. Economists generally espouse free trade. Many, probably most American economists, argue that free trade is preferable as a means to create productivity growth and minimize the distortions of bureaucracy and corruption. Some, however, argue that free trade is stacked against LDCs and NICs and that trade preferences should be considered.

KEY TERMS

Absolute advantage, comparative advantage
Autarky
"Beggar-thy-neighbor" argument
Burden of a tariff (consumer burden, producer burden)
Cheap foreign labor argument
Commodity balance of trade
Common markets
Customs unions
Exports, imports
Free trade agreements
General Agreement on Tariffs and Trade (GATT)
Infant-industry argument
National security argument
Net foreign trade
Open economy, closed economy
Protectionism
Rational ignorance
Tariffs, quotas, embargoes
Terms of trade
Visible items, invisible items of trade
World Trade Organization (WTO)

QUESTIONS

1. What is meant by the term "open economy?" "Closed economy?"

2. What imported goods do you often buy? How would you be affected if the U.S. restricted international trade or stopped trading with other nations entirely?

3. Why are most production-possibilities curves *not* straight lines? What happens to international specialization when such curves are truly curves?

4. Consider the following hypothetical production-possibilities schedules for the U.S. and Honduras:

United States		Honduras	
Units of Tractors	Units of Bananas	Units of Tractors	Units of Bananas
50	0	0	100
40	5	5	80
30	10	10	60
20	15	15	40
10	20	20	20
0	25	25	0

   a. Plot the production-possibilities curves.
   b. Is there a basis for mutually beneficial trade between the two countries?
   c. What will determine the terms of trade that are established between the two countries?

5. Based on the arguments advanced in this chapter, why, in your opinion, did the beggar-thy-neighbor tariff (Smoot-Hawley tariff) of 1930 perhaps slow the American recovery between 1930 and 1934?

6. What happens to the trade from either developed or under-developed nations when monopoly export and import agencies are set up? Why?

7. Evaluate the following statements:
   a. "Free trade forces domestic producers to pay attention to consumer tastes and needs."
   b. "Free trade would be desirable, but we can't afford to rely on the Russians, or the French, or even the British, for our military hardware."
   c. "High tariffs to create more jobs will work for the U.S. because other, less powerful nations wouldn't dare retaliate."

d. "In several recent years, the U.S. has run a large commodity trade deficit. What we should do to counteract this is to buy less from abroad."

e. "In several recent years, the U.S. has run a large commodity trade deficit. We don't need to worry, though, because exchange rate changes will eliminate the deficit."

8. In the graph below, we see the demand for and supply of an imported good. D_d is the domestic demand, S_d is the domestic supply. S_{ft} is the supply with free trade of both domestic producers and imports, and S_{at} is the supply after a tariff is imposed.

a. What is the price and quantity of the good without trade? With free trade? After a tariff is imposed?

b. Who bears most of the burden of the tariff, consumers or importing firms? What is the burden of each?

c. Who benefits from the tariff? What is the price benefit?

9. What are the differences between common markets, customs unions and free trade agreements? Which of these is the most comprehensive form of trade agreement.

10. What was the basic role of GATT? What is the basic objective of the WTO?

11. What are the major threats to further world trade liberalization?

12. What are the differences between the static view of comparative advantage and the dynamic view of growth?

13. If you were recommending economic policy to a developing low-income country, at what point would you recommend that it follow a policy of comparative-advantage trade, and at what point would you

recommend that it sacrifice a certain amount of efficiency in the use of its resources in order to achieve more growth?

14. Consider an underdeveloped country (for example, Chile), and suppose that it primarily exports one raw material (for example, copper). How can low price and income elasticities of demand for copper affect Chile's export earnings, its ability to import other necessary goods, and its terms of trade?

SUGGESTED READINGS

Baldwin, Robert E., and David Richardson, Jr. (eds). *International Trade and Finance Readings*. 2nd ed. Boston: Little Brown, 1981.

Baldwin, Robert E. "The Political Economy of Postwar United States Trade." Reprinted in Baldwin, Robert E., and J. David Richardson (eds), *International Trade and Financial Readings*. 2nd ed. Boston: Little Brown, 1981.

Bergsten, C. Fred. "Reform Trade Policy with Auction Quotas." *Challenge*. May/June, 1987.

Brandt, Willy, et al. *North-South: A Program for Survival*. Cambridge: MIT Press, 1980.

Brown, Wilson B. and Jan S. Hogendorn. *International Economics Theory and Context*. Reading, MA: Addison-Wesley, 1994.

Cameron, Rondo. "Some Lessons of History for Developing Nations." Reprinted in Dennis R. Starleaf (ed), *Economics: Readings in Analysis and Policy*. Glenview, IL: Scott, Foresman, 1969.
Caves, Richard E., and Ronald W. Jones. *World Trade and Payments, An Introduction*. 4th ed. Boston: Little Brown, 1985.

Chenery, Hollis B. "Comparative Advantage and Development Policy." *American Economic Review*. 51:1. March, 1961.

Cline, William R. (ed). *Trade Policy in the 1980s*. Cambridge: MIT Press, 1983.

Council of Economic Advisers. International Economic Report of the President. Washington, D.C.: G.P.O., 1995.

Culbertson, John M. "The Folly of Free Trade." *Harvard Business Review*. September/October, 1986. Reprinted in Don Cole (ed), *Economics 88/89*. Guilford, CT: The Dushkin Publishing Group, Inc., 1989.

Dolan, Edwin G., and John C. Goodman. "Restricting Automobile Imports." *Economics of Public Policy*. Ch. 13. 4th ed. St. Paul, West Publishing Co., 1989.

Dornbusch, Rudiger, and Jacob A. Frenkel (eds). *International Economic Policy, Theory and Evidence*. Baltimore: Johns Hopkins Press, 1979.

Drucker, Peter J. "Low Wages No Longer Give Competitive Edge." *The Wall Street Journal*. March 16, 1988.

Friedman, Milton. "Outdoing Smoot-Hawley." *The Wall Street Journal*. April 20, 1987.

Gould, David M.; Roy J. Ruffin; and Graeme L. Woodbridge. "The Theory and Practice of Free Trade." *Economic Review*. Federal Reserve Bank of Dallas. Fourth Quarter, 1993.

Harberger, Arnold C. (ed). *World Economic Growth: Case Studies of Developed and Developing Nations*. San Francisco: Institute for Contemporary Studies, 1984.

Hirschman, A. O. *The Strategy of Economic Development*. New Haven, CT: Yale, 1958.

Hufbauer, Gary Clyde and Kimberly Ann Elliot. *Measuring the Costs of Protection in the United States*. Washington, DC: Institute for International Economics, 1994.

Johnson, Harry J. *Economic Policies Toward Less Developed Countries*. Washington, D.C.: Brookins Institution, 1967.
Jones, Steven, and Ralph Pura. "Indonesian Decrees Help Suharto's Friends and Relatives Prosper." *The Wall Street Journal*. November 24, 1986.

Krugman, Paul R. and Maurice Obsfeld. *International Economics*, Second Edition. Harper Collins, New York, 1993.

Lindert, Peter H., and Charles P. Kindleberger. *International Economics*. 9th ed. Homewood, IL: Richard D. Irwin, 1993.

Meier, Gerald M. *Problems of Trade Policy*. NY: Oxford University Press, 1973.

Michaely, Michael, Demetris Papageorgiou, and Armeane M. Choksi (eds). *Liberalizing Foreign Trade: Lessons of Experience in the Developing World*. Cambridge, MA: Basil Blackwell, 1991.

Pincus, John. "Trade Preferences for Underdeveloped Countries." Reprinted in *Economics in Action* by Shelley M. Mark. 4th ed. Belmont, CA: Wadsworth, 1969.

Safire, William. "Smoot-Hawley Lives." *The New York Times*. March 17, 1983.

Singer, Hans W. "The Distribution of Gains Between Investing and Borrowing Countries." Reprinted in Theodore Morgan and George W. Betz (eds), *Economic Development: Readings in Theory and Practice*. Belmont, CA: Wadsworth, 1970.

Smith, Adam. "Restraints on Foreign Imports" in *The Wealth of Nations*. Vol. I. Reprinted in John R. McKean and Ronald A. Wykstra (eds), *Readings in Introductory Economics*. NY: Harper & Row, 1971.

World Bank. *World Development Report*, 1994.

CHAPTER 15

International Trade: Exchange Rates and the Balance of Payments

If the value of the dollar doesn't begin to decline dramatically against major foreign currencies, American farmers, manufacturers and most allied industries dependent on export trade will be out of business and nearly six million people will be out of work.

OBJECTIVES

After studying this chapter you will be able to:

- Explain how the value of the dollar is determined on international markets.
- Discuss the pros and cons of freely floating exchange rates versus fixed exchange rates.
- Explain how a devaluation or revaluation affects the U.S. business sector and the consumer sector.
- Explain how and why our government devalued the dollar in 1985.
- Have a working knowledge of the following terms and concepts:

Balance of payments	Gold standard
Bretton Woods Conference	International monetary fund (IMF)
Dirty float	Rate of exchange
Equilibrium exchange rate	Reserve transaction account
Fixed exchange rate	Special drawing rights
Freely floating exchange rate	

International Trade: Exchange Rates and the Balance of Payments

We have developed the logic of international trade and have seen why, based on comparative advantage, nations that engage in trade are better off than those that practice autarky. As a part of that same argument, we saw further evidence that the freer trade is, the greater are its benefits when compared with protectionist trade practices. Now we will examine the role of money in international trade.

It is true, of course, that nations can engage in barter or, in other words, exchange goods for goods. If they do so, there is no need for money. Occasionally, this practice is still carried out, usually when trade between two governments is involved. Like domestic exchanges, however, nearly all international exchanges of goods and services require an exchange of money. A key difference, though, is that international exchanges involve more than one currency. For international trade to move smoothly requires not only markets to price the goods and services that are exported and imported, but also markets that establish the exchange values of the different currencies used in that trade. The latter are called **foreign exchange markets**, or markets in which the exchange values of different domestic currencies are established. Let's now see why these foreign exchange markets are so important to world trade. Then we will see how they work to establish exchange rates.

Foreign Exchange Markets
International money markets in which the exchange values of domestic currencies are established.

An Example of Trade Involving Different Domestic Currencies

Suppose that the American Steel Company agrees to sell $500,000 worth of rolled steel to the Japanese Automobile Company. Suppose also that the *rate of exchange*, the price at which Japanese yen can be exchanged for American dollars, is 100 yen per dollar. (Later we will see how this rate is established.) The Japanese importer, in other words, owes 50 million yen (500,000 x 100) to the American Steel Company. Let's follow this transaction through the banking system in both countries:

1. Japanese Auto writes a check on its Tokyo bank for 50 million yen, and mails the check to American Steel.

2. American Steel cannot pay its workers and creditors in Japanese yen; it needs dollars. Therefore, it sells the check to a New York bank that has a correspondent relation with a Japanese bank.

3. Now American Steel has a $500,000 deposit in the New York bank. The New York bank deposits the check from Japanese Auto in its correspondent bank in Tokyo and becomes the owner of a claim to 50 million Japanese yen.

Note. Nearly all of this is now accomplished by electronic transfers.

In other words, an American company's exports of a commodity create a demand for dollars. When this demand is fulfilled, more foreign currency is available to people in the U.S. who will demand it to pay for their own (Japanese) imports.

When a U.S. company imports something, the process is reversed. The American company must obtain a supply of the currency of the country from which it is buying the goods. The supply comes from foreign currencies that American firms have earned through their exports. Thus, Japanese yen are available to pay for U.S. imports of Toyotas because Americans have exported wheat (and many other commodities) to Japan. In other words, *in order to be able to pay for its imports, a country must also export or sell its goods to other countries*.

A Workable International Monetary System

This two-country illustration, although it is correct, makes the financing of international trade seem simpler than it is. Financing trade is quite complex, and involves intricate relationships between the domestic economies of more than a hundred independent nations, each with its own domestic currency, that exchange goods and services. In short, it involves an elaborate international monetary system.

Let's examine the characteristics of a workable money system in an *international* economy. One feature that is absolutely essential is that the system expedite the trading of goods and services. (After all, barter, as we noted earlier, is no more feasible in international trade than it is in domestic trade.) By what criteria is a workable system of payments judged?

1. *The system must strike a reasonable balance between stability and growth in international trade and stability and growth in the individual nations that engage in it.* The economy of the U.S. (or

Britain, or any other nation) should not have to absorb large shocks to its own employment and investment situation in order to accommodate changes in its international trade position, or that of other nations. This doesn't mean that nations need not make long-term adjustments in their domestic economies as their trade positions change, only that these adjustments should be gradual and not overly disruptive. The present set of monetary arrangements, although it is a great improvement over the gold standard in these respects, may still force some countries, especially those with large external debts denominated in other currencies, to make major adjustments in their internal economies in order to handle their international payments. This is a problem for many less-developed countries (LDCs) and newly industrialized countries (NICs).

Essential to this requirement of reasonable balance is consistency of action. Once the rules for international financial transactions have been made, all the participating nations must play by the rules. The system may force a nation to make adjustments that conflict with its political and economic objectives, or even threaten the political survival of its government. (For example, it may have to raise interest rates, lower investment, and create unemployment.) If the system demands too many adjustments of this sort, nations may not adhere to it consistently. Then the system may become unstable.

2. *The system of payments must be seen to be equitable.* It is hard for nations to agree on how the costs and benefits of a system are to be distributed so that there is equity for all. Many nations, especially the developing ones, feel that present international financial arrangements are inequitable. They claim that they do not have enough control over decisions about the availability of capital and credit, and about who is to bear the costs of financing. At the same time, the system must facilitate the repayment of capital whose movement is essential to the finance of exports and imports. Proposals for further capital flows to the LDCs and even some NICs must incorporate this principle.

3. *The system of payments must be efficient,* just as any other system of markets must. The efficiency of an international system of payments is measured in terms of the effect of that system on the cost of trade. An efficient system encourages trade by making the means of financing exports and imports readily available and low cost, and by reducing the risks of trade (unanticipated changes in exchange rates, for example).

Let's now look at how foreign exchange markets work. Fundamentally, they work like other markets to establish equilibrium or market clearing results. Like other markets, their results depend on their competitiveness or lack of competitiveness.

Foreign Exchange Markets: Determining Equilibrium Exchange Rates

An **equilibrium exchange rate** is the rate of exchange between two currencies that clears the market or eliminates excess supply or demand. This rate will change only as the supply of or demand for the currencies changes. Like any other price, the exchange rate may be established in one of two ways: (1) It may be freely floating, that is, established by impersonal market forces (competition), or (2) It may be fixed, that is, administered (determined by certain individuals or agencies). We will illustrate both approaches in this section.

Freely Floating Exchange Rates

Let's take as an example the exchange rate between the dollar and the deutsche mark (the currency of the Federal Republic of Germany). With a **freely floating exchange rate**, the exchange rate is established through the interplay of supply and demand. Figure 15-1 illustrates this interplay.

Figure 15-1
Foreign Exchange Market with a Freely Floating (Competitive) Exchange Rate (dollars versus marks)

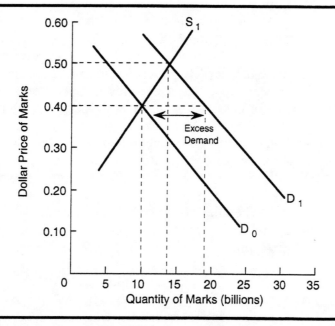

In Figure 15-1, D_0 represents the initial American demand for marks. It is derived from the American demand for German goods and services. The supply of marks is S_1 and slopes upward because, as the mark/dollar rate rises, American goods are cheaper in Germany and more marks are supplied to pay for these German imports. With a competitive exchange rate market, the equilibrium (market clearing) rate is 0.40 where the quantity supplied of marks equals the quantity demanded of marks. Ten billion marks are exchanged. If a disequilibrum occurs, a new equilibrium exchange rate must be established. An increase in the demand for marks (D_0 to D_1) leaves excess demand at a rate of .40 dollars to the mark (2.5 dollars per mark); to eliminate the excess, demand requires a new exchange rate of .50 (2 dollars to the mark). At the new exchange rate, there is no excess demand or supply.

The curve D_0 is the American demand for marks. It slopes downward because as the dollar price of marks falls (as a dollar buys more marks), German goods (Volkswagens, Rhine wine, cameras, binoculars, and so on) become cheaper for Americans to buy. When that happens, the quantity demanded by Americans of German goods increases and Americans demand more marks, so they can pay for those goods. The demand for marks, in other words, is a *derived demand*, a demand derived from the demand for German imports. The curve S_1 is the supply of marks. It slopes upward because as the dollar price of marks rises (as marks buy more dollars), American exports become cheaper for Germans to buy. When that happens, Germans increase the quantity demanded of imported American goods and demand more dollars, so they can pay for those goods (cars, computers, wheat, and so on). The Germans pay for their purchases with checks drawn on German banks.

Since the exchange rate is free to seek its market level, the equilibrium level is the one at which quantity supplied equals quantity demanded. We see in Figure 15-1 a foreign exchange market, the market in which exchange rates and exchange rate charges are established. Here, equilibrium is established at 0.40, which is 2.5 marks to the dollar ($1/.40 = 2.5$). In other words, a mark will buy four-tenths of a dollar. The equilibrium quantity of marks in Figure 15-1 is 10 billion.

Now what if a disequilibrium—a variation in supply or demand that throws things off balance—develops in this market? Suppose that Detroit auto makers, in a surprise move, announce a big increase in prices. (If the price increase had been anticipated, it would have been reflected in D_0—the original demand for marks.) Higher prices for Detroit-made cars mean that German cars are now cheaper by comparison. As a result, the demand for marks shifts upward (people want to buy more Volkswagens and Mercedes Benzes). But now there is disequilibrium. At the present exchange rate (0.40), only 10 billion marks are supplied, but foreign-exchange buyers now want nearly 20 billion.

When the exchange rate is freely floating, the excess demand of 10 million marks is taken care of by dealers in foreign exchange markets who bid up the dollar price of the mark. (There are foreign exchange markets and dealers in nearly every major city in the world.) The mark then costs more to buy. When the rate of exchange rises to 0.50 ($1/.50 = 2$ marks to the dollar), excess demand is eliminated. Remember that the additional quantity of marks supplied is forthcoming because, as the mark appreciates in value, Germans buy more of relatively cheaper American goods (ironically, they even buy more of the now relatively cheaper American cars if exchange rate changes more than offset the original price increases), thus creating claims to marks by American exporters.

Advantages and Disadvantages of Floating Exchange Rates

Let's look at the advantages and disadvantages of allowing the value of currencies to float freely. The *advantages* are those of a competitive market: (1) The system responds quickly to changes in supply and demand. (2) Disequilibria in payments are readily resolved; for example, the excess demand that appeared when Americans wanted to buy more German goods (Figure 15-1).

The *disadvantages* of the system are as follows: (1) The rate of exchange may be very unstable. This instability may inhibit trade, because a buyer who orders an imported article will soon stop buying if large changes in the exchange rate make the article cost more when it is delivered than when it is ordered. (2) Some countries depend heavily on international trade to provide jobs and investment capital (especially the LDCs and NICs, in which the foreign-trade sectors dominate the economies). In these countries, wide swings in exchange rates can cause very destabilizing changes in exports and imports. (3) A nation's financial terms of trade can change quickly and sharply. The terms of trade, recall, refer to the ratio of export prices to import prices. In a sense, they measure the value of exports a nation must have in order to maintain a given level of imports. Wide variations in the values of currencies can cause either variations in imports or disruptive efforts to adjust exports. In either case, destabilization may result.

Freely floating exchange rates have been common since 1971 and President Nixon's decision to "float" the U.S. dollar. Some economists have reservations about such fluctuations. Arthur Burns, former chairman of the Federal Reserve Board, gave four reasons for his skepticism: (1) Freely floating rates are an academic dream that cause people to demand protection through government controls or government intervention in the money market. (2) Floating rates may lead to political friction. If other nations suspect that the rates are being manipulated, they will take retaliatory steps. (3) Floating rates increase people's uncertainty and thus inhibit both commodity trade and capital flows. (4) Floating rates make it harder for the government to implement suitable domestic fiscal and monetary policies.

Arbitrage
A practice under which exchange dealers buy currencies in one market and sell it at a higher price in another.

Other economists (such as Milton Friedman) believe that fears such as these about the dangers of floating rates are exaggerated. They say the following: (1) Where the policy of floating rates has been tried, there have not been enormous swings in rates. The apparent reason for this is that speculators in foreign exchange, those who engage in **arbitrage** or who buy and sell currencies in different markets to make profits, stabilize the market. (2) Although freely floating rates do increase business uncertainty, this is thought by many economists to be a price worth paying in exchange for the above-mentioned benefits of the system.

Fixed Exchange Rates

*Fixed Exchange
Rates*
A system in which the
rates of exchange
between currencies
are established by
government and not
allowed to vary with
changing currency
market conditions.

By contrast with floating exchange rates, some rates of exchange between currencies are based on **fixed exchange rates,** a system of payments involving agreed-upon relationships between the world's currencies. Even today, some nations fix the rate at which their currencies exchange. Some have a two-tiered system with fixed rates for some transactions and flexible rates for others. For much of the post-World War II period fixed exchange rates prevailed. To see how a fixed rate system works, refer again to Figure 15-1. Suppose that at the fixed rate of 2.5 marks to the dollar, there is an excess demand of 6 billion marks. The U.S. and German governments (perhaps dealing through an international agency) are committed to maintaining the 2.5:1 rate. The additional marks come from somewhere. Since the market will not supply them at the fixed rate, governments or international agencies must. (Note that this is hypothetical: the dollar/mark exchange rate is, in fact, not fixed and has not been since 1971.)

*International
Reserves*
Assets available to
central banks and
other agencies that are
accepted in payment
of international debts.

The additional marks can come only from **international reserves,** assets available to central banks and other agencies that are acceptable in payment of international debts. (In the past it was gold.) It is possible, of course, that the German central bank (the Deutsche Bundesbank) might lend the marks to the Federal Reserve (Fed) System. The Fed, in turn, would make them available to American commercial banks. Alternatively, there might be an international agency such as the *International Monetary Fund (IMF)*, which has reserves of dollars, deutsche marks, Swiss francs, British pounds, claims to gold, and all other major currencies. The IMF makes loans to the Fed and through the Fed to our commercial banks.

Note: Fixed exchange rates require large currency reserves. In the face of growing world trade, they require *increasing reserves,* if banks are to be able to take care of fluctuations in demand for currencies.

The chief advantage of fixed exchange rates is that they lend stability to world trade. Fixed rates reduce uncertainty about international prices. If you want to buy a German car or import German machinery, and you know that the banking system is committed to a 2.5:1 exchange rate, you can plan your purchase even if the goods are not actually delivered to you until months later. This stability provides a favorable climate for the growth of trade, especially for long-term capital flows.

Even fixed exchange rates are not necessarily fixed forever. For example, the German government may decide that subsidizing German exports to the U.S. is not in Germany's best interests. The U.S. government may decide that at the 2.5:1 rate its exports to Germany are too low. The international reserves needed to finance this trade imbalance may run dangerously low. The countries, by mutual agreement, may change the rate to 2 marks to the dollar (which will equilibrate the exchange market shown in Figure 15-1).

Exchange Rate Market Intervention

We have posed the exchange rate policy choice of governments as either: (1) allow exchange rates to float freely (flexible rates) or (2) fix rates and adjust them occasionally by mutual agreement (fixed rates). For both political and economic reasons, governments, including that of the U.S. have not been willing consistently to follow one path or the other. When they have not, they have choosen to intervene but only selectively in exchange markets. In doing so, they have created a system of managed exchange rates on what is often called the **managed or "dirty" float**. Essentially, it means that the Fed allows the dollar to float but only within certain "pegs" or limits. While these pegs are rarely clearly defined, their expectation does send a (poorly defined) signal to exchange rate dealers about the limits of rate changes.

Managed or "Dirty" Float
A system in which exchange rates are "pegged" or allowed by central banks to move within certain limits.

Why, in the absence of fixed exchange rates, do governments intervene in this way? It is sometimes said that nations intervene out of national pride to keep their currency high and stable in value against other currencies. There is no evidence to support this and it seems that there are much stronger reasons that can be shown for intervention. Consider the case of the U.S. dollar, which is a key currency in international finance. Much of the reserves of America's trading partners (reserves of their central banks) consist of holdings of U.S. dollars. Thus, when the U.S. dollar declines sharply, so do the value of the assets of those banks (Bank of Japan, Deutsche Bundesbank, etc.). The Fed then, perhaps under pressure from our allies, may intervene if the dollar drops too sharply. The U.S. dollar is sometimes the only currency accepted in payment for certain international transactions. OPEC, for example, accepts only U.S. dollars in payment for its oil exports. If the U.S. dollar rises sharply against the pound sterling or French franc, those countries must spend more to buy the dollars to pay for their oil imports. Again, the Fed may intervene to moderate the growth in the exchange value of the dollar.

Market intervention by different governments may, of course, be contradictory. When the dollar falls against other currencies, U.S. exports become cheaper and the Fed may do nothing to support its currency. This was generally the case in the late 1980s, because stimulating export growth was U.S. national policy. Other nations such as Japan, however, saw the dollar falling against their currencies and their own exports becoming more expensive. To avert a decline in its export industries, Japan intervened at times to buy dollars and keep the yen from falling further against the dollar. It is not surprising in view of the potential for conflicting interventionist policies that there are numerous meetings and other efforts by central banks to agree on exchange rates.

Adjusting Economies to Fluctuations in the Exchange Rate

One can trace the origin of an exchange-rate disequilibrium (such as the excess demand in Figure 15-1) to changes in economic conditions in the exporting and importing nations. Figure 15-2 gives you the situation at a glance.

Suppose that the dollar-mark exchange market is initially in equilibrium. The demand for marks is D_0, supply is S_1, and the exchange rate is 2.5:1 (that is, the mark is equal to 0.40 dollars). Ten billion marks are exchanged. Now, suppose that inflation hits the U.S. The rapidly rising prices of American goods make German imports relatively cheaper. As a result, American demand for marks to finance purchases of German goods rises to D_1. At the old exchange rate, there is an excess demand of 6.5 billion marks (16.5:10). If the dollar-mark rate is *not* freely floating, and if there is no system of international reserves to finance the payments deficit at existing exchange rates, two things may happen.

Figure 15-2
Exchange-Rate Equilibrium Maintained Through Macroeconomic Adjustment

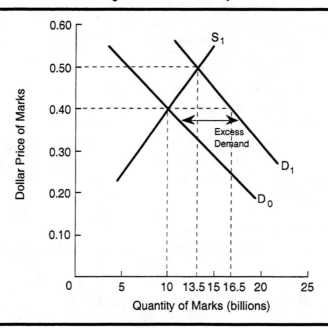

In Figure 15-2, the dollar-mark exchange rate is in equilibrium with demand D_0 and supply S_1. The equilibrium exchange rate is 0.40 dollars per mark (or it takes 2.5 marks to buy a dollar). As a result of U.S. inflation, rising domestic prices make German imports cheaper and the demand for marks increases to D_1 to finance additional imports. At the new demand D_1 there is excess demand for marks at the old rate of 0.40. With a freely floating rate, the exchange rate would rise to 0.50 where quantity demanded of marks would equal quantity supplied. To maintain the old (fixed) exchange rate of 0.40, governments would (1) have to ration the exchange available (10 million marks) to prevent the excess demand (6.5 million marks) from raising the rate, or (2) deflate the American economy, reducing the total demand for imports and reducing the demand for marks again to D_0.

Means of Adjustment

Exchange Controls
A system by which a nation rations foreign currency when there is excess demand for that currency.

1. Excess demand may be treated as a rationing problem. People demand more marks than the amount of marks available at the going exchange rate. So to "ration" marks, a nation might set up a system of **exchange controls** (perhaps an agency acting through its central bank). The agency could establish priorities to determine who should get the available marks. In effect, this would mean determining what kinds and quantities of German goods could be imported into the U.S. (perhaps Volkswagens, but no Mercedes Benzes, or perhaps machinery, but no cars at all). Presumably, these priorities would reflect certain national goals.

The main advantage of this approach to managing fluctuations in the exchange rate is that it enables countries to hold to a fixed exchange rate (with the aforementioned stability of trade), while at the same time ensuring that national import priorities are consistent with domestic economic priorities. The main disadvantages are that it does not allow the market to work, and that it imposes public tastes and preferences in place of private ones. (No matter how much you might like to import a Mercedes, you cannot, because the government regards it as more important to the country to import farm machinery.) It can also lead to corruption through granting special access to foreign exchange on the part of those favored by the government.

Neither the U.S. nor other major trading nations use exchange controls, although many LDCs do. Low-income countries must import much of their capital. They do not have the domestic markets to provide it, and their governments do not wish to import expensive consumer goods at the same time.

2. The deficit in payments (or the excess demand) shown in Figure 15-2 may be taken care of by adjustments in income and employment in the economy of the country that is demanding "too much" foreign currency.

Deflation
A general lowering of prices in an economy.

In this case, inflation in the U.S. is causing the excess demand for marks. To counter this demand, the U.S. may use the the macroeconomic adjustment of **deflation**, which is a general lowering of prices. To accomplish this, the government may reduce aggregate demand by increasing taxes. It may also reduce government spending and raise interest rates. Or it may adopt any of the combinations of means that you will/or have already learned in your Macroeconomics course. (Of course, a tax on imports could correct the relative imbalance in prices between the two countries, but this would be at the price of free trade.)

If the U.S. follows a deflationary policy and aggregate demand does decrease, money incomes will certainly decrease also. Now let's assume that the demand for imports has a strongly positive income elasticity. (Americans, like many people, have a strong taste for imported goods.) Demand for imports, and for German marks, will fall. If the decline is strong enough, D_1 in Figure 15-2 may shift back to D_0, and the dollar-mark ratio may again find its equilibrium at 2.5:1.

The main advantage of tying a nation's economy to its exchange-rate position is that it practically guarantees stable rates of exchange. (Remember that stable exchange rates are desirable because they enhance trade and make possible longer term planning for trade.) The main disadvantage of such a policy is that the nation has to pay a price for this stability of exchange rates and equilibrium of payments. Most economists believe this price is out of proportion to its worth. It is truly letting "the tail wag the dog." In the example here, the U.S. would have to deflate its economy deliberately—with all the effects it would have on income distribution, jobs, savings, and investment. Even if the U.S. had been at full employment before the government introduced the fiscal and monetary measures necessary to bring about deflation, there would soon be some significant changes in prices, incomes, and employment. But suppose that the U.S. had been suffering significant unemployment coupled with inflation, as it did in the early 1980s, and the government came along and put through these measures. Then, deflating the economy would just add to the unemployment problem, thus curing an external problem by worsening an internal one. Few countries would be willing to pay such a price for stability of exchange rates, though some LDCs and NICs have done so as part of a program to lower inflation and refinance external debts.

Gold Standard
An international system under which currencies are valued in terms of gold content. Nations are obligated to exchange their currencies for that amount of gold.

The Gold Standard

During the nineteenth and much of the twentieth centuries, the system of fixed exchange rates was tied to the **gold standard**. The gold standard provided for the rates of exchange of most of the world's currencies for about 50 years before World War I, in varying degrees until the Great Depression of the 1930s and, to a lesser extent, to 1971. Under the freely convertible gold standard, nations could be sure of two things:

1. Each trading nation permitted unrestricted exports and imports of gold.

2. Each nation defined its own currency in terms of a specific quantity of gold, and guaranteed to convert any claims to that currency into gold at the defined rate.

Under the gold standard, each currency was defined to be worth so many grains of gold. For example, the German mark might be defined as 10 grains of gold and the American dollar as 25 grains of gold. Therefore, the dollar would be worth 2.5 marks. No one would pay more than 2.5 marks to get $1, or sell a mark for less than 40¢, because the dollars (or marks) could always be converted into gold at the official rate. People could take their dollars or marks down to the bank and get gold for them. (Here we are ignoring the cost of moving gold—actually physically moving it—from one nation to another: transporting, insuring, and handling it.)

Suppose that the U.S. was operating on the gold standard with an initial equilibrium at demand D_0, supply S_1, and a dollar price of marks of 0.40 (point A in Figure 15-3). A disequilibrium of payments (see Figure 15-3). Demand increases first to D_1 and then to D_2. The U.S. is committed to exchanging dollars for gold at 25 grains of gold per dollar. But it is *not* bound to keep the dollar-mark exchange rate constant. At first, therefore, the excess demand for marks at 40¢ apiece (distance AB, or 10.5 billion marks) causes the dollar price of marks to be bid upward (depreciating the dollar). At some price—let's say 40¢ per mark plus the cost of transferring gold (shown arbitrarily as 45¢ to the mark)—it becomes cheaper to buy gold in the U.S., at

Figure 15-3
Exchange-Rate Equilibrium Under the Gold Standard

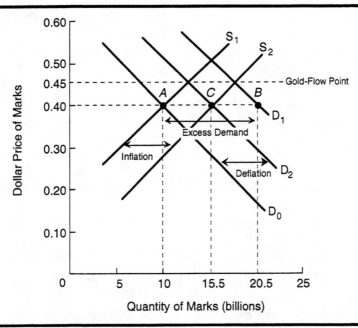

Under the gold standard, gold may move if an exchange rate is significantly different from the official (gold-determined) rate. In Figure 15-3, there is an initial equilibrium at point A where demand D_0 and supply S_1 intersect. Because of demand increases (D_0 to D_1, D_1 to D_2) there is ultimately a disequilibrium or excess demand for marks at the old exchange rate (0.40) of 10.5 billion marks (AB). At some exchange rate (0.45) the gold-flow point is reached and gold moves to Germany from the U.S. As this happens, the U.S., with less gold to back to its currency, must reduce the money supply and *deflate* the economy. This in turn reduces the demand for marks. The influx of gold into Germany increases the supply of marks and *inflates* the German economy, enlarging the demand for U.S. goods and shifting the supply of marks to S_2. In a new equilibrium with demand for marks (D_2) and supply of marks (S_2) the old equilibrium of 0.40 is established at B.

the fixed price, and ship it to Germany to pay for imports than to buy marks with dollars to pay for the imports. This price is called the **gold-flow point**.

Let's suppose that the dollar price of the mark (Figure 15-3) rises beyond the gold-flow point. Gold begins to flow from the U.S. to Germany. Under the gold standard, the U.S. government backs its dollars by gold and must redeem them for gold. Since there is now less gold to back the currency, the money supply in the U.S. must be reduced.

The contraction in the money supply leads to a decline in the volume of transactions. Banks call in their loans, refuse to renew loans, and tighten credit. In effect, there is a deflation. Assuming a positive income elasticity of demand for German goods, the demand for imports (and German marks to pay for them) diminishes. The American demand for marks (D_1) will shift to the left to D_2.

Now let's switch to Germany, where the gold is flowing in. More gold means a larger supply of money (M). Either prices (P) will rise, or quantities of goods sold (Q) will rise, or both. In either case, the German economy is inflated toward full employment. This will increase German demand for American imports, and thereby increase the supply of marks available to the U.S. The supply of marks (S_1) shifts to the right to S_2 in Figure 15-3.

In the long run, equilibrium is restored. The changed supply of marks again intersects the demand, at the previous exchange rate of 40¢ to the mark. The equilibrium quantity of marks exchanged must be between *A* and *C*: in this instance at *B* (15.5 billion marks).

The U.S. and other leading trading nations have not, in any strict sense, used the gold standard since the 1930s and have not used it at all since 1971. Yet there are still those, including some economists, who advocate its return. In the 1970s, the government of France came out in favor of it. The gold standard thus remains a source of controversy, particularly among those who believe it would restore discipline not only to international trade, but also to domestic economic policies.

The advantages of the gold standard are the following: (1) It is automatic; any imbalance in relations between currencies sets in motion corrective gold flows. (2) It stabilizes exchange rates, and thereby makes possible long-term planning for trade. (3) Some economists maintain that gold flows make a nation practice economic self-discipline, live within its own (gold-determined) means, and refrain from forcing other nations to subsidize its consumption of goods.

The disadvantages of the gold standard are the following: (1) It causes domestic economic policy to be tied to international trade (the tail-wagging-the-dog argument). (2) It causes the volume of trade to be tied to the supply of an exhaustible resource, gold, which is in inelastic supply.

Postwar International Exchange Arrangements

Most present-day arrangements for financing trade stem from a meeting that the allied nations (the U.S., Britain, and France) held at Bretton Woods, New Hampshire, in 1944. There were many other nations present as well, however, Britain and the U.S. dominated the meeting. The Bretton Woods conference set up two basic trade features: (1) a system of adjustable pegs for exchange of currencies, a system that lasted until the 1970s, and (2) the **International Monetary Fund (IMF)**, an intergovernmental agency designed to administer the post-World War II monetary system and enhance its stability. It administers the operation of the *adjustable-peg system*, a system of exchange in which currencies are pegged, or are not allowed to change in value by more than a specific percentage. It can use its capital to make bridge loans to nations experiencing exchange-rate disequilibrium problems.

The nations that met at Bretton Woods sought to create relatively fixed exchange rates, which could be maintained. Each currency was to be valued in terms of both gold *and* U.S. dollars. Currencies could vary from these parities by no more than 1 percent. Exchange rates could be changed, however, when countries found that there was a "fundamental disequilibrium" in their payments position. But the Bretton Woods conference failed to define the term *fundamental disequilibrium*.

So, beginning in the 1950s, countries such as the U.S. began to run long-term deficits in payments, with no changes in exchange rates. They did this by drawing on gold reserves—reserves held by the IMF—and by borrowing from the central banks of other countries. Thus, they were without the automatic, self-correcting, adjustment mechanism that had existed under the gold standard (a good feature, for all its other flaws). This went on until 1971, when President Nixon devalued the dollar and set it free from the pegged rate.

During the 1960s, pressure for change in the international money system began to develop. The countries that had to absorb the excess dollars created by U.S. balance-of-payments deficits began to be dissatisfied with the terms of the Bretton Woods agreement—and with good reason: Speculators in the late 1960s were moving huge amounts of money out of dollars and into strong currencies such as German marks.

One modification of the system was the creation by the IMF of **special drawing rights (SDRs)**. By using SDRs, countries with deficits could borrow so-called paper gold from the IMF to finance their imbalances of payments. This made it possible for the exchange system itself to finance trade. But it did nothing to establish equilibrium relations between the world's major currencies.

A second modification was to allow currencies to establish a supply-demand equilibrium through freely floating against each other. The dollar, as you know, led the way in doing this in 1971.

The system of freely floating rates, even if it is accompanied by the managed or "dirty" float, that is presently in force seems to work reasonably well. It does not satisfy those who want more stability in the exchange rate for dollars. Other people, who want a competitive exchange-rate system, praise the system.

The Managed or "Dirty" Float: Whither the Future?

There are some economists who say the Bretton Woods exchange-rate system with its fixed but adjustable pegs died in late 1971 with the floating of the dollar against other major trading currencies. That assessment is warranted at least to the extent that there is no longer a governmental or intergovernmental agreement on the ratios at which (or even within which) international currencies will be allowed to trade.

The present international monetary system is a hybrid version of those (gold standard and fixed exchange rates with adjustable pegs) that preceded it. SDRs in some measure have provided the liquidity that might have been supplied by gold flows. The managed (dirty) float seems to be workable in the face of multi-country central bank cooperation. Dissatisfied with a dollar subject to wide swings in price, efforts have been made to create alternatives to it as *the* international currency. Some European nations have formed the European monetary system under which they value their currencies against each other. This group has also created a new unit of money called ECU (European currency unit), which the countries hope will become a rival to the U.S. dollar in international trade and finance.

For the near-term, it seems unlikely that there will be major changes in the present system of international finance. The managed or "dirty" float seems likely to continue. What long-term effect the 1992 integration of Europe and the expansion of free trade areas, such as NAFTA, will have on the system of international payments is, at this juncture, impossible to assay. The IMF seems likely to increase in importance as industrial nations, LDCs, and NICs alike attempt to come to grips with debt crises, threats of repudiation, and balance-of-payments problems that, for some nations, threaten domestic economic growth.

The Mexican Peso and the December 1994 Debt Crisis

An illustration of how the international financial system may work in crisis was provided in Mexico in December 1994. During the 1980s, Mexico's economy moved toward becoming more free-market. Under the regime of President Carlos Salinas, government ownership of industries was reduced (banks, for example, were reprivatized), import restrictions were lifted, foreign capital investment was encouraged, and a stable Mexican peso was promised.

For much or the 1980s and in the first years of the 1990s, the Mexican economy boomed, enjoying one of the highest growth rates and lowest inflation rates in the western hemisphere. The peso, pegged at .29 to the U.S. dollar, was stable until December 1994. Although Mexico ran substantial deficits in its current account, foreign (especially American) capital inflows permitted their financing with little inflationary threat. Although the peso was thought by some to be overvalued, it remained strong throughout the period.

In late 1994, Mexico's political and economic situation changed dramatically. A combination of a peasant uprising in Southern Mexico and two major political assassinations (including that of the nation's presumptive next president) produced pessimism and uncertainty not only among Mexicans, but among foreign investors as well. As a result, what had been a strong inflow of foreign capital became a net outflow, putting great pressure on the exchange rate between the Mexican peso and other currencies (especially the U.S. and Canadian dollars).

In late December 1994, Mexico's new president, Ernesto Zedillo, unexpectedly devalued the peso by 13 percent and allowed the currency to float freely in foreign exchange markets. As a result, the value of the peso fell to about 18 pesos to the U.S. dollar. The results were predictable: (1) Foreigners with investments in Mexico (those holding securities, or those whose mutual funds had invested there) took huge losses; (2) U.S. exports to Mexico were drastically reduced; (3) Many Mexican firms faced bankruptcy (Mexico raised domestic interest rates to reduce capital outflows); (4) A "spread effect" to other Latin American countries (their stock markets, for example) occurred as far south as Argentina and Brazil).

What could stop the free fall of the (floating) Mexican peso? Political decisions were taken at the highest levels of the U.S. and Canadian governments to provide Mexico with large quantities of U.S. and Canadian dollars. Mexico's central bank (Banco de Mexico) intervened with those dollars, together with a large loan from the International Monetary Fund (IMF), to stop the free fall, finally stabilizing the peso.

While the rescue (critics called it a bailout) of the Mexican peso remains controversial, it was, in retrospect, predictable. Earlier, we said that trade policy is based as much on political considerations as on economic ones. A decision to intervene by Mexico's trade partners was surely impelled by considerations of political instability as much as by calculations of the effects on trade among three countries. Those considerations were probably influential with the IMF, as well. Though some said Mexico should have solved its problems alone through macroeconomic adjustments (drastic spending cuts, and the like), would Mexico's political system have survived this economic medicine?

The Balance of Payments

Up to now, we have dealt with trade as a process of exporting and importing goods and services and paying for them directly with currency, but there is more to international trade. Not only goods and services move between nations. There are capital flows as well as other movements.

Balance-of-Payments Statement
An annual monetary statement by a nation of its exports, imports, and reconciliation and payments.

Each nation puts together an annual accounting of all its trade transactions (including trade in goods and services). This is called its **balance-of-payments statement**. This national statement is like a firm's profit-and-loss statement. It reveals not only what is bought and what is sold, but also how any difference between the two is financed. Table 15-1 shows a recent balance-of-payments statement for the U.S.

By definition, the balance of payments must balance (be equal to zero). A nation, like a firm or a person, must somehow find a means to pay for everything it buys. Let's look at these accounts to see how the U.S. paid for all the things it bought (imported) in 1994.

The Balance-of-Payments Statement

A. Current account. The current account is like a family's calculation of current income and expenses. It includes both visible items (exports and imports of merchandise) and invisible items (services, including financial services). The biggest item, a visible item, is merchandise exports (1) and imports (2). In 1994, the U.S. exported

Table 15-1
The United States Balance of Payments, 1994 (billions of dollars)

Item	Debits (-)	Credits (+)	Balance
A. Current Account			
1. Merchandise Exports		+502	
2. Merchandise Imports	-669		
3. Trade Balance (1+2)			-167
4. Service Exports		+199	
5. Service Imports	-139		
6. Goods and Services Balance (3+4+5)			-121
7. Net Unilateral Transfers	-36		
8. Net Investment Income	-19		
9. Current Account Balance (6+7+8)			-152
B. Capital Account			
10. Outflow of U.S. Capital	30		
11. Inflow of Foreign Capital		252	
12. Capital Account Balance (9+10+11)			+121
C. Basic Balance (A–B)			-31
D. Official Reserve Transactions Account			
13. Decrease in U.S. Official Assets Abroad		+5	
14. Increase in Foreign Official Assets in U.S.		+39	
15. Statistical Discrepancy	-14		
16. Official Reserve Balance (13+14+15)		+31	
United States Net Total (Balance) (9+12+16)			0

Sources: *Survey of Current Business*, June, 1995

$502 billion and imported $669 billion worth of merchandise. This means that imports of merchandise were greater than exports by $167 billion. Thus, the U.S. had a large *balance-of-trade deficit*[1] (3). (Remember, though, that this is only a part of the balance of payments.)

Other items in the current account include service exports (4) and service imports (5). Since we sold more export services than we bought, but imported more goods and services than we exported, the goods and services balances (6), like the trade balance, is negative (-$121 billion). Net unilateral transfers (7) consist of dollar claims transferred to foreigners by governments (foreign aid), by individuals (e.g., social security payments to Americans retired abroad), and charitable donations. As in every year since World War II, these transfers were negative (Americans earned fewer such transfers than we transferred abroad) by $15.1 billion. Net investment income (8) is the difference between investment income repatriated to other countries by firms in the U.S. and investment income repatriated to the U.S. by firms abroad. In 1994, this was a negative $19 billion. The **current account balance** (9) is obtained by adding exports of goods and services minus imports of goods and services plus net unilateral transfers. The current account balance need not balance (be zero) and for 1994, the U.S. had a deficit on the current account balance of $152 billion.

Current Account Balance
A statement for a nation of its annual balance of exports of goods and services minus its imports of goods and services together with net unilateral transfers.

The deficit on the current account must, of course, be paid for, and we see how the U.S. financed that deficit in item B which reflects capital flows.

B. Capital account. Note that $130 billion of capital flowed out (10) of the U.S. in 1994. We are referring here to financial capital flows, purchases of assets abroad such as stocks and bonds. In the same year, $252 billion of foreign capital flowed into (11) the U.S. in the form of purchases of U.S. assets by foreigners. For most of the 1980s and the 1990s, America has enjoyed this net inflow or surplus in its capital account. There are two major reasons why this has happened. First, interest rates have been relatively high in the U.S., resulting in investors buying U.S. assets for interest returns. Second, in contrast with many countries, the U.S. is a relatively "safe" place to invest without threat of nationalization, exchange controls to limit repatriation of funds, and other constraints that raise the risk of owning assets, especially in the LDCs.

Basic Balance
The balance shown in the nation's current account plus its capital account.

C. Basic balance. The combination of a nation's current account and its capital account is often referred to as its **basic balance**. In 1994, the basic balance of the U.S. showed a deficit of $31 billion. This amount had to be financed.

---

[1]We referred to this as the commodity trade balance earlier.

Official Reserve Transactions Account
An account of those sources such as borrowing from other official agencies that finance the basic balance.

D. Official reserve transactions account. The account labeled **official reserve transactions account** shows how the U.S. met its payments to the rest of the world that remained on its basic balance. For 1994, this difference (A + B = -152 + 121 = $31 billion). Mainly, it met its obligations by borrowing from official agencies (usually central banks), by persuading them to hold more dollars ($39 billion more). Also, the U.S. sold some government debt ($5 billion). It is thought that much of this statistical discrepancy is due to secret or unreported movements of capital into the U.S., especially from countries where such movements are either limited or prohibited on an official basis. The offical reserve balance (13 + 14 + 15) was $30 billion.

The Balance of Payments in Summary

As you can see, there is a lot of detail in the balance of payments. For an overview of it, let's put it in capsule form (Table 15-2). The 4 major accounts are shown again, without the previous detail. A, the current account, shows a deficit of $152 billion. To this is added B, the capital account, which has a surplus of $121 billion. Together (A + B) they form the basic balance (C), which shows a deficit of $31 billion. The balance to be financed is D or $31 billion. The balance (again, there *must* be one) comes from the official reserve transactions balance. The balance of payments (C + D) equals zero. In other words, the U.S. in 1994, as in every other year, financed all its international trade.

Deficits to be Financed: Current and Capital Account Balances

Figure 15-4 shows that, since the early 1980s, the U.S. has had deficits (amounts to be financed) in its current account balances. The problem in recent years seems to be primarily in the merchandise export-import position, Because the dollar's exchange rate is free to float (at least a "dirty" float), and because American goods, between 1980 and 1985, became relatively more expensive and difficult to export (at least until 1985), the trade (merchandise) deficits from 1980 to 1985 grew rapidly. Since 1985, however, the dollar has fallen against the yen and other currencies, and, as we saw earlier,

Table 15-2
The United States Balance of Payments, 1994, Summary Form
(billions of dollars)

Item	Credits (+) Debits (−)
A. Current account	−152
B. Capital account	+121
C. Basic balance (A + B)	−31
D. Official reserve transactions balance	+31
Balance of payments (B + C)	0

Figure 15-4
Balances on the U.S. Current and Capital Accounts, 1981 to 1994

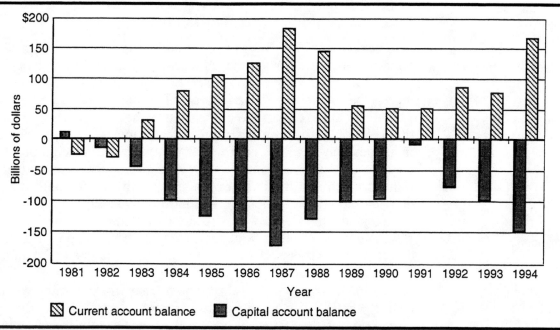

Sources: *Economic Indicators* , June 1995

In 1981, the U.S. had a very small surplus in its current account and a small deficit in its capital account. In 1982, both accounts showed small deficits. Since 1983, it has had consistent deficits in its current account and surpluses in its capital account.

America's exports have grown substantially. We see that the large deficits in the current account are partially offset by substantial surpluses in the capital account.

The deficits to be financed since 1980 have largely been accommodated, as we have seen, through capital inflows into the U.S. that are reflected in the capital account surpluses. While some people have seen this as the "buying of America," these inflows of capital have not only financed America's taste for imports but also, through enlarging the supply of financial capital, have permitted credit markets to be equilibriated at what otherwise might have been higher interest rates. In this sense, they have stimulated the domestic American economy through encouraging domestic investment.

If the dollar continues to fall against other currencies and the deficits to be financed decline, "trade" deficits may decline or even disappear. This will require major readjustments in trade patterns and flows of capital. Financing trade deficits with the U.S. will again become a problem for many nations. At this juncture, any such forecast is difficult to make with confidence. Whether the deficits are eliminated and whether trading relationships will continue to be essentially free are political as well as economic questions as we will see in the following application.

APPLICATION:
Politics and the Balance-of-Payments Problem

Reasons Behind Import Restraints

Whenever the U.S. buys more goods and services from other countries than they buy from us there is a deficit in our balance of trade, (current account or goods and service's balance) and a resulting cry to "buy American!" Various people, union leaders and business executives alike, exhort the citizenry to either buy products made in the U.S. or to impose restrictions on imports. In fact, firms or industries may urge this at any juncture, whenever foreign producers begin to take away any sizable share of domestic sales from American industry. In the mid 1980s for instance, lobbyists for both the steel and automobile industries worked hard in Washington trying to get Congress to impose import restrictions on European and Japanese steel and cars. (Detroit watches with gloom the import figures on Toyotas and Nissans, Volvos and Saabs, Renaults and Peugeots, Hyundais and Hondas.)

From early years of independence to the mid-twentieth century, the U.S. ran deficits on its current account. Up until the Great Depression of the 1930s, however, there was rarely much attention paid to the buy-American slogan. A country's nervousness about excessive imports usually comes out when some if not most of its industries are enduring hard times. But as we have seen, since the early 1980s, there have been large deficits in U.S. goods and services and U.S. current account (including U.S. government grants). The U.S. has had such continuing deficits in its balance of trade only twice since 1893 (also in the early 1970s).

In the early 1980s, the cries for protectionism, which had been muted since the mid 1970s, again became loud. In apparent response to the threat of protective legislation, the executive branch of the government negotiated "voluntary" export agreements with some foreign manufacturers, especially with Japanese auto makers. Like quotas, these restraints limited imports but, unlike quotas, were imposed or at least agreed to by foreign manufacturers. While such firms (Nissan, Toyota, etc.) may have agreed to the export limitations to prevent more restrictive action by U.S. Congress, they may also have agreed because they benefit from the higher net price on automobiles in the American market that resulted from the reduced supply.

Voluntary export agreements, alone, did not seem to satisfy the proponents of protectionism including those who believed that America should work more aggressively to open the markets of other nations to its exports. Many argued that the U.S. should retaliate against those who engaged in "unfair" trading practices such as **dumping** goods in its markets. Dumping is the practice of selling goods in foreign markets at prices below their cost of production. Indeed the Trade Agreements Act of 1979 provides for severe anti-

Dumping
The practice of selling goods in foreign markets at prices below their costs of production.

dumping penalties. The Trade and Tariff Act of 1984 did little to allay the fears of those who have argued for "fair" as opposed to "free" trade. The act extended the Generalized System of Preferences (GSP) adopted in 1974, which provides duty-free access to U.S. markets for many "non-import sensitive" items from the LDCs and NICs. In a policy statement in 1985, the AFL-CIO argued that such preferences, especially for many of the successful NICs (Korea, Taiwan, Singapore, Hong Kong) are no longer necessary, and argued as well that they have even been extended to some Communist countries. The 1984 act authorized the President to negotiate bilateral free-trade agreements with other nations, with NAFTA the recent free trade agreement with Canada and Mexico being the first major fruit of that activity.

The trade-offs between trade policy and policy toward the LDCs and NICs promise to be difficult. As distinguished economist Bela Belassa has argued: "The more advanced developing economies would, thus benefit from liberalizing their imports in exchange for reductions in the trade barriers of the developed countries." Perhaps such bilateral "free trade" agreements will become a more prominent feature of U.S. policy. The 1984 act also extended the authority of the President to negotiate further voluntary export agreements, especially with foreign steel producers and these, too, may become a more prominent feature of our trade policy.

Protectionism: Costs and Benefits

Restrictions in the form of tariffs or quotas have usually been imposed for the purpose of saving the jobs of workers in the U.S. In 1985 the AFL-CIO put it this way:

> "...positive governmental action is needed to reverse the erosion of America's industrial base—(between 1982 and 1985) it is estimated that more than 3 million jobs have been lost or not created due to America's continued trade decline."

In the mid 1970s, a major labor leader in the U.S. argued that the costs of free trade ("low-wage imports") were borne by American workers but that "international operators" not U.S. consumers got the benefits. Economists, on the other hand, have estimated that the cost of both tariff and nontariff restrictions (including voluntary export controls) is between $20 billion and $45 billion per year. This figure reflects the consumer burden of higher prices resulting from import duties (for example, there is a 12 percent import tax on cars). It also reflects the higher prices resulting from a lowered supply and a less competitive market in the U.S. for cars, steel, cattle, meat, dairy products—and all the other goods protected by high tariffs. For example, economist William Albrecht says:

Between 1969, when the quota system was first introduced, and 1972, steel companies increased their prices 5 times as much as they had in the preceding 8-year period, despite the fact the industry was experiencing declining demand and had unused capacity of 25 to 50 percent.

To the extent that this heightened price structure may be generalized to apply to many industries, one could say that it is indeed the American consumer who suffers as a result of import restrictions. Even a consumer who has lost a job because of competition from cheap imports is worse off. After all, the jobless consumer, who very much needs bargains, cannot buy cheap shirts made in Taiwan or cheap shoes made in Korea or low-price beef from Argentina.

America's Trade Problem: The Myths

Murray Weidenbaum, a former chairman of the Council of Economic Advisers, argues that much of the rhetoric surrounding our trade problems is based on misconception. Weidenbaum identifies five myths that he believes are fairly common:

1. *Japan is the problem, and if it would only open its markets, much of the problem would disappear.* As Weidenbaum points out, our trade deficit extends to Canada, Mexico, Europe, and almost every non-communist nation in the world. It must be "our problem," not a "Japanese problem."

2. *The U.S. is alone in practicing free trade.* In fact, says Weidenbaum, we have an elaborate system of preferences, even apart from quotas (sugar, beef, etc.); only 30 percent of our imports are allowed in duty free (though NAFTA will eventually raise this percentage).

3. *Imports depress the American economy, especially in terms of manufacturing jobs.* Imports, says Weidenbaum, have little to do with the structural decline in relative importance of manufacturing; services have been larger than manufacturing in the U.S. since 1929. Manufacturing production, in an absolute sense, has never been as high as it is today.

4. *The way to save American jobs is through trade protection.* On the contrary, says Weidenbaum, "protectionism is the most inefficient welfare program ever devised." Saving a job in the steel industry, for example, may cost 3 to 4 jobs in steel using industries (due to higher costs).

5. *Workers in import-sensitive industries deserve better treatment than other workers.* As Weidenbaum says, "I know of no reason why the one group is more meritorious than the other."

Protectionism: Will It Triumph or Fail?

It is not difficult to imagine some form of protectionism triumphing in the political arena. After all, NAFTA passed with the smallest of margins in the U.S. Congress. If it does, a likely explanation is that offered by Weidenbaum who says that "Protectionism is a politician's delight because it delivers visible benefits to the protected parties while imposing the costs as a hidden tax on the public." This public choice explanation, seems compelling. After all, a higher tariff or a quota on automobiles, for example, will clearly and significantly benefit a particular industry (its owners and managers) as well as particular groups of American workers (the members of the United Automobile Workers Union). The costs, on the other hand, will be spread over many millions of would-be automobile buyers in the form of higher automobile prices. Which group has the more intense and intensely expressed preferences: The protectionists or the free traders?

Before we too hurriedly proclaim the likely demise of freer trade, however, let us remember the following:

1. For more than 50 years, America has moved toward lower tariffs and freer trade as reflected in Reciprocal Trade Agreements Acts and other forms of legislation as well as through bilateral agreements, the recent renewal of GATT, the creation of the WTO, and the extension of NAFTA. Many industries and workers in this country are well served by lower priced imported goods and services. In addition, many industries and jobs depend on American exports and would surely suffer in the retaliation that American protectionism would engender. Resistance to protectionism may be strong from those with preferences for freer trade.

2. The push for increased protectionism has stemmed in large measure from U.S. balance of trade deficits since the early 1980s. If the dollar continues to decline against the currencies of its major trading partners in the late 1990s, we are likely to see a growth of American exports, and decline in imports; some even predict, trade surpluses in the early years of the next century. Historically, when this has happened, the push for protectionism has abated, and we may see this happen again.

Lessons to Be Learned

There are several things one can learn from the recent unusual balance-of-trade situation. First, the U.S. should not formulate foreign economic policy on the basis of short-term variations in its trade position. This position can change so quickly, and the changes are so hard to forecast, much less control, that the situation may change by the time the policy is implemented. Second, protectionism is nearly always self-defeating. If the U.S. enacts a drastic import-quota system, Western Europe and Japan assuredly will retaliate. They will put import quotas of their own on the things the U.S. wants to sell to *them*. U.S. exports will decline and the projected balance-of-trade turnabout will never take place. Tariffs and quotas have a way of boomeranging.

In general, then, economists rarely espouse the cause of protectionism. When industries find that they can no longer maintain a competitive cost position with respect to foreign suppliers, economists' advice is usually "Retrain labor! Reallocate resources!"

SUMMING UP

1. Very little international trade is carried out by means of barter. Nearly all of it requires a means of monetary payment, a money exchange system. *Foreign exchange markets* provide the essential function of establishing exchange rates, the rates at which different domestic currencies exchange.

2. The conversion of currency of one nation to that of another is carried out by the international banking system and by specialized dealers. For example, a person importing a pair of shoes from Italy can mail a check to the Italian exporter. The exporter deposits it in a bank in Italy and gets a certain amount of lire for it. The Italian bank gets a claim to dollars from its correspondent bank in the U.S.

3. The money exchange system enables exporters and importers to end up with the kind of national currency (dollars, marks, yen, and so on) that they need.

4. Exports by the U.S. create a demand overseas for dollars to pay for them. When a French firm imports American goods, for example, it creates a supply of claims to francs with which Americans may pay for their imports from France. In other words, *a country that wishes to export must import, in order to create the claims to currency necessary for it to trade.*

5. A workable international monetary system has the following characteristics: (a) It establishes a balance between stability and growth in international trade and stability and growth in each of the trading nations. (b) It is equitable and ensures that each nation will have access to foreign exchange, and that each will help bear the costs of operating the exchange system. (c) It is efficient and thus lowers the cost of trade and enhances the growth of international trade.

6. Exchange rates established in foreign exchange markets may be of two basic types of systems: (a) freely floating exchange rates and (b) fixed exchange rates.

7. A *freely floating exchange rate* is determined by the supply of a currency and the demand for it. The *equilibrium exchange rate* is the rate at which quantity supplied and quantity demanded are equal. This means that there is no excess demand or excess supply.

8. The advantages of a freely floating rate are that (a) the rate responds quickly to changes in supply and demand, and (b) imbalances or disequilibria in payments are readily resolved. The disadvantages are that (a) there can be great instability in rates, (b) there can be great instability in savings, investment, and prices in countries that depend heavily on foreign trade, and (c) there can be sudden changes in *terms of trade,* requiring a country to make a reallocation of resources so that it can export more, in order to continue to import.

9. Economists differ on the merits of freely floating exchange rates, though most favor their competitive characteristics. For the time being, the U.S. seems committed to letting the dollar continue to float within certain ill defined limits.

10. *Fixed exchange rates* mean that the currency of a country keeps the same value with respect to the currencies of other countries. The main advantage of fixed rates is stability; they permit longer term planning for trade. The main disadvantage is that supply and demand are not allowed to work freely. Also, fixed exchange rates require a system of *international reserves* to fill excess demands.

11. Most governments do not consistently follow the principle of freely floating or that of fixed exchange rates. They intervene selectively in what is called a *managed or "dirty" float.*

12. Fluctuations of exchange rates derive from changes in economic conditions in the exporting and importing nations. Excess demand can be handled by (a) introducing *exchange controls* (rationing of currencies) or (b) by adjusting the economy of the country suffering the disequilibrium so that the domestic cause is eliminated.

13. LDCs often use exchange controls. They determine who shall have access to the limited foreign exchange available. The advantage is a stable exchange rate; the disadvantage is that exchange controls impose a set of public tastes on what would be the private tastes for imports. The government decides what is best for the country to import. Such controls may also give rise to corruption or favoritism in access to foreign exchange.

14. Adjusting a country's domestic economy to eliminate excess demand for foreign exchange means adjusting domestic prices, incomes, and employment. Although a nation may use such means to establish exchange-rate equilibrium, it is a drastic solution. Most economists feel that it creates a major problem (unemployment) in order to solve a lesser problem for which other solutions exist.

15. Under the freely convertible *gold standard,* which has not been used since the 1930s, currencies are valued in terms of grains of gold. Each currency has a value in terms of gold as well as in terms of other currencies. In order for the gold standard to work, the exchange value cannot deviate much from the gold value. If it does, people buy gold and ship it overseas to pay for traded goods, rather than using currencies to pay for them.

16. The *gold-flow point* is the exchange rate at which it is cheaper to ship gold in payment for traded goods than to buy currency.

17. The advantages claimed for the gold standard are that (a) it operates automatically, (b) it stabilizes exchange rates, and (c) gold flows impose an economic self-discipline on nations. The disadvantages claimed for the gold standard are that (a) it ties a nation's internal economic policy to the balance of its foreign payments (the tail wags the dog), and (b) it ties the world's volume of trade to the inelastic supply of an exhaustible resource.

18. The Bretton Woods Conference in 1944 established (a) an *adjustable-peg system* for international currencies, and (b) and the *International Monetary Fund (IMF)* to administer the system.

19. The system of pegging currencies meant that they could change in value by no more than 1 percent. The world no longer uses this currency-pegging system. However, the IMF still exists. It administers a system of *special drawing rights (SDRs), (*or *"paper gold")* through which countries with balance-of-payments problems can borrow from the IMF.

20. The debt crisis of Mexico in late 1994 illustrates how (1) economic trade policy is driven by political considerations, and how (2) nations (U.S., Canada) and international organizations (IMF) will intervene to prevent the continued free fall of a floating currency (the Mexican peso).

21. The freely floating exchange rates now in use appear to work reasonably well. Actions of private speculators, who buy and sell currency (arbitrage), may have helped to prevent exaggerated fluctuations.

22. Each nation annually prepares a *balance-of-payments statement,* an accounting of its international purchases and sales, plus an explanation of how it has financed any deficit payments.

23. A balance-of-payments statement lists (a) current account (visible and invisible items of trade), (b) current account balance (balance on current account including unilateral transfers), (c) capital account which shows both capital outflows and capital inflows (d) balance to be financed, and (e) *official reserve transactions balance* (what the

nation borrows from other nations, changes in its gold holdings, and so on). A nations' official reserves change when it has a payments deficit or surplus. The balance of payments *must* balance.

24. Since the late 1960s, the U.S. has usually had a deficit to be financed in its balance of payments. Recently (after 1980), this deficit has been due mainly to a *balance-of-trade deficit* (merchandise exports minus imports), and partly to military commitments abroad and our foreign aid program. Our export position since the late 1980s has improved somewhat. Prices of things we exported fell relative to prices of other nations' export items. Even so, the deficit in our balance of payments continues. Some, however, forecast an end to the deficits within 5 years but such forecasts are extremely difficult to be made precise.

25. When any nation experiences a deficit in its balance of trade (that is, when it exports less than it imports), citizens are urged to buy locally made products, and people call on the government to impose either voluntary or mandatory controls in order to limit imports of foreign goods.

26. A strong push for protectionism has reemerged in the 1980s and 1990s. To head off protective legislation, "voluntary" export agreements to limit foreign sales, especially of Japanese autos, were negotiated. The AFL-CIO, however, argued for a new trade policy including the elimination of many of the preferences given to the LDCs and NICs. The Trade and Tariff Act of 1984, however, authorized more voluntary export agreements and other bilateral trade agreements which may become an increasing feature of American trade policy. Under this 1984 law, agreements between Canada, the U.S. and Mexico have led to the creation of the North American Free Trade Association (NAFTA).

27. Labor leaders maintain that protectionism is necessary to guard American workers against competition from low-wage areas of the world. They also claim that low-priced foreign imports do not benefit American consumers; they benefit international (multinational) manufacturers. Economists, however, estimate that direct and indirect controls cost American consumers between $20 and $45 billion per year. They maintain that such import controls not only add to the costs of goods, but also enhance the monopoly power of domestic producers.

28. Support for protectionism seems in part to be based on some myths about America's trade problem. These include: (a) Japan and its protectionism are the problem. (b) Only the U.S. practices free trade. (c) Imports have caused the decline of manufacturing industry in the U.S. (d) American jobs can be saved through protectionism.

(e) Workers in import-sensitive industries deserve better treatment than other U.S. workers.

29. One can learn two things from the recent U.S. balance-of-trade experience: (a) The U.S. should not base its foreign economic policy on short-term changes in its trade position, because its trade position can change dramatically and is difficult to predict. (b) Protectionism is almost bound to be self-defeating, since it invites retaliation by foreign customers for U.S. exports.

30. Economists rarely support protectionism. Most feel that retraining of labor, plus reallocation of resources, is the way out for an industry that cannot compete with cheaper imports from low-wage areas of the world.

KEY TERMS

Balance-of-payments statement
Basic balance
Current account balance
Deflation
Dumping
Equilibrium exchange rates
Exchange controls
Fixed exchange rates
Foreign exchange markets
Freely floating exchange rates
Gold standard
Gold-flow point
International Monetary Fund (IMF)
International reserves
Managed or "dirty" float
Official reserves transactions account
Special drawing rights (SDRs)

QUESTIONS

1. What are foreign exchange markets? Why are they essential to a modern system of international trade and finance?

2. Do you think the U.S. should continue to let the American dollar float against other currencies, or should it go back to some sort of pegged or fixed exchange rate system? Why?

3. Evaluate the following statement: "A nation cannot for long export (sell its goods to others) unless it imports (buys from others)."

4. What were the problems associated with the gold standard? What were its advantages?

5. Why is it correct to say that a nation's balance of payments *must* balance even though its balance of trade need not? What are the main balancing items?

6. What is the managed or "dirty" float? Why do nations try to manage their exchange rates?

7. What are the advantages and disadvantages of fully floating exchange rates? What is the role of arbitrage in such a system?

8. In the figure below, the exchange rate between the U.S. dollar and the Japanese yen is initially in equilibrium with demand for yen D_0 and supply of yen S_0 at 120 yen = 1 dollar. An increase in the demand for yen D_1 occurs to finance imports from Japan:

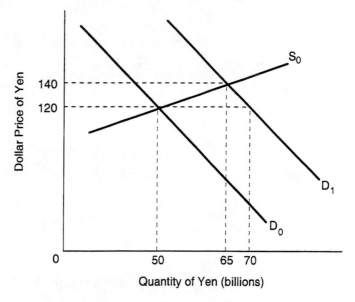

a. If the exchange rate of the dollar to the yen is freely floating, what will be the new equilibrium exchange rate?

b. If the U.S. and Japan want to restore the old equilibrium rate (120), how many yen will have to be supplied to eliminate excess demand?

c. If the excess demand is treated as a rationing problem, what might be the solution?

d. If the U.S. sought to reduce demand for yen by deflating the economy, what might it do?

9. What are the advantages and disadvantages of fixed exchange rates?

10. Suppose that the Secretary of the Treasury calls you in and says, "I have to go before the Joint Economic Committee of Congress and present a good argument for why the dollar should not be allowed to float on world currency markets. What's the best argument I can make?" What would your response be?

11. From the standpoint of value, the U.S. has a greater volume of international trade than any other nation. In the face of this, why would a protectionist policy with respect to imports almost certainly cause other nations to retaliate?

12. Evaluate this statement: "American workers earn high wages. The government must protect them against the imports of goods that are from low-wage countries."

13. What is the role of the IMF in international trade and finance? What are SDRs?

14. In what ways does the Mexican debt crisis of 1994 illustrate the likely future of international financial relationships?

15. What is dumping?

16. What groups are likely to pay the bill for protectionism?

17. In what ways is a policy of retraining workers and reallocating resources preferable to a policy of protecting (by tariffs and quotas) a firm or an industry that is inefficient, relative to foreign firms or industries?

18. What are some of the myths about America's trade problems?

SUGGESTED READINGS

Adams, John (ed). *The Contemporary International Economy*. NY: St Martins Press, 1985.

Balassa, Bela. "The Importance of Trade for Developing Countries." *Banca Nazionale Del Lavoro Quarterly Review*. No 163. Rome, December, 1987.

Baldwin, Robert E., and J. David Richardson (eds). *International Trade and Finance Readings*. 2nd ed. Boston: Little Brown, 1981.

Battles, Deborah. "Trade Theory and Comparative Advantage: Is the Real World *Really* Like That?" *The Margin*. March/April, 1989.

Caves, Richard E., and Ronald W. Jones. *World Trade and Payments, An Introduction*. 4th ed. Boston: Little Brown, 1985.

Cline, William R. (ed). *Trade Policy in the 1980s*. Cambridge: MIT Press, 1983.

Economist. "Pulling Mexico Back Together Again." February 4, 1995.

Erceg, John J., and Theodore G. Bernard. "Productivity Costs and International Competition." *Economic Commentary*. Federal Reserve Bank of Cleveland. November 15, 1989.

Gordon, David M. "Do We Need to Be No. 1?" *The Atlantic Monthly*. April, 1986. Reprinted in Annual Editions 87/88, John Pisciotta, ed. Sluice Dock, CT: Dushkin Publishing Co., 1987.

Gould, David M.; Roy J. Ruffin; and Graeme L. Woodbridge. "The Theory and Practice of Free Trade." *Economic Review*. Federal Reserve Bank of Dallas, Fourth Quarter, 1993.

Hickok, Susan. "Recent Trade Liberalization in Developing Countries: The Effects of Global Trade and Output." *Quarterly Review*. Federal Reserve Bank of New York. Autumn, 1993.

"International Trade and Investment." *The National Economy and Trade*. Report of the Executive Council of the AFL-CIO. October, 1985. Reprinted in Peter D. McClelland (ed), *Introduction to Macroeconomics*. 1986-1987. NY: McGraw-Hill, 1986.

Lindert, Peter H., and Charles P. Kindleberger *International Economics*. 9th ed. Homewood, IL: Richard D. Irwin Co., 1993.

Maskus, Keith E. "Rising Protectionism and U.S. International Trade Policy." *Economic Review,* Federal Reserve Bank of Kansas. July/August, 1984. Reprinted in *Annual Editions 87/88*. John Pisciotta, ed. Sluice Dock, CT: Dushkin Publishing Co., 1987.

Porter, Michael. *The Competitive Advantage of Nations*. New York, Free Press, 1990.

Rezvin, Philip. "As Trade Gap Closes, Partners of U.S. Face End of the Gravy Train." *Wall Street Journal*. April 3, 1988.

Stein, Herbert. "Don't Worry About the Trade Deficit." *The Wall Street Journal*. May 16, 1989.

Stone, Charles F., and Isabel V. Sawhill. "Trade's Impact on U.S. Jobs." *Challenge*. September/October, 1987. Reprinted in Annual Editions: *Economics 88/89*. Don Cole, Editor. Guilford, CT: The Dushkin Publishing Group, 1989.

"The Politics of Trade: Five Ways to Choke off Imports." *Business Week.* October 7, 1985. Reprinted in *Annual Editions 87/88.* John Pisciotta, ed. Sluice Dock, CT: Dushkin Publishing Co., 1987.

Torres, Craig. "Mexico's Central Bank Struggles as Reserves Reach Lows." *The Wall Street Journal.* February 3, 1995.

Weidenbaum, Murray L. *Foreign Trade and the U.S. Economy: Dispelling the Myths.* CATO Policy Report. January/February, 1986. Reprinted in Peter D. McClelland (ed), *Introduction to Macroeconomics.* 1986-1987. NY: McGraw-Hill, 1986.

Williamson, John. *The Open Economy and the World Economy.* NY: Basic Books, 1983.

Yeutter, Clayton. "Protectionism. Competition in the World Marketplace." *Readings in Introductory Macroeconomics.* Peter D. McClelland (ed). NY: McGraw-Hill, 1988.

CHAPTER 16

Economic Systems - How Many In the Twenty-First Century

"The Economic system that the world finally embraces is the one that meets every ones' needs."

N.A. Iyere

OBJECTIVES

After studying this chapter you will be able to:

- Explain Dialectical materialism and Historical materialism.
- Sketch the main points of Max's model of history and explain why Marx's prediction about the collapse od capitalism has not come true.
- Why has planned socialism largely lost out in the contest with market capitalism?
- Have a working knowledge of the following terms and concepts:

  Command economy
  Dynamic efficiency
  Economic system
  Market capitalism
  Property rights
  Static efficiency
  Surplus value

Economic Systems—How Many in the Twenty-First Century?

Economic System
The institutions a society establishes to deal with choices imposed on it by scarcity.

As we saw at the outset of our introduction to the study of economic societies, scarcity—the inability to satisfy all human wants with limited resources—imposes on every society the necessity to create institutions that result in choices about how to use those limited resources. As well, decisions about *which* wants to satisfy must be made. These institutions created to bring about these choices are called an **economic system**.

Throughout history, economic systems have competed against one another, both intellectually and politically. Those judged inferior, especially in terms of efficiency and growth, have given way to those judged superior on one or both grounds. In perhaps no period of history was that competition more intense than in the twentieth century. The two main rival systems from the mid to the late twentieth century were planned socialism and market capitalism. We will look at each in turn, but let us first look again at the kinds of choices all societies throughout history have been forced to make because of scarcity.

Basic Economic Choices: A Reminder

Let's remind ourselves of the choices imposed by scarcity. Regardless of the philosophical or ideological preferences of a society, these are the questions about using resources that *must* be answered. By way of quick review, these choices are:

1. *What* shall be the composition of output? Since everything that is desirable cannot be produced in the quantities desired, choices, often difficult ones—must somehow be made about allocating resources to produce one good as opposed to another. Shall these choices be made by individual consumers or shall government planners make the decisions? Whose tastes and preferences, in other words, shall dominate the choice about output?

2. *How* shall goods be produced? At any particular time, there is a menu of choices about producing goods. Shall we, for example, produce information for making economic decisions with typewriters and telephones or with computer hardware and software? An answer to this question is necessary; shall it come from individual managers and entrepreneurs or from central planners?

3. *Who* shall receive the output (real income) of the society? This question of distribution is perhaps the most difficult and potentially divisive one for all nations. Shall markets, responding to productivity signals, ration output on the basis of (market-earned) incomes and tastes or shall planners set prices and factor incomes according to some set of "social" objectives? What is equitable or fair? Since, as we have noted at various points, there is no unique definition of distributive equity, each society must not only find a means or process to distribute income, but must also agree on the results of that process.

Evaluating an Economic System

There are many dimensions to the evaluation of an economic system and economic, along with moral and political criteria may be used. An economic criterion inevitably used is that of efficiency in resource usage. Rich society or poor, socialist or capitalist, the ability to provide solutions to economic problems now and in the future depends heavily on efficiency. We shall look at efficiency questions in two dimensions.

Static Efficiency
At a point in time, using resources in ways that produce the most desired mix of output.

Static Efficiency
Since resources are scarce, they must, to be used efficiently, be allocated to produce that mix of goods and services that the society prefers. While the answer to what is preferred depends on whose preferences are considered, no society in a static (timeless) sense is efficient if it produces one good (for example, pet rocks) where doing so causes it to produce less of another good (microcomputers for example) that is more preferred.

Dynamic Efficiency

Dynamic Efficiency
Over a period of time, using resources in ways that maximize the long-term benefits from their employment.

Dynamics involves looking at a process over time. Present uses of resources will have consequences for the future and for future consumers. Efficiency over time requires that scarce resources be used in ways that maximize the stream of long-term benefits from their employment.

Whether from the standpoint of static or of dynamic efficiency, the successful use of resources critically involves control over those resources or, in other words, the location and security of property rights.

Property Rights: Should They be Vested in Individuals or in the State?

Property Rights
The rights to own, control, and profit from the use of resources.

Property rights, the rights to own, control, and profit from the use of resources, must be vested somewhere in any society. Without property rights and the control they carry with them, choices about resource usage would be impossible. There are two basic ways these rights may be assigned in an economic system:

Private Property Rights

Property rights in resources may be assigned exclusively to individuals who not only control their use but also have the right to transfer control to others through a process of exchange. In such a system, the individual owns not only his own labor, but also any other real or financial assets to which title is held. Homes and land, for example, are owned by individuals and families who are free to sell them, rent them, or make any other lawful use of them.

Public Property Rights

Public property rights are not assigned to individuals but are held in some kind of communal ownership. Though individuals own their own labor, other resources including land and housing are not individually owned and cannot, therefore, be sold or rented to others by their occupants. Collective ownership of resources implies that the state through some means must decide who shall have access to a society's resources.

No society today assigns property rights entirely in one way or the other. In the U.S. there are some goods such as parks as well as many schools that are collectively owned. There are also public goods such as military weapons that have indivisible benefits. In the former Soviet Union, there were some goods, such as automobiles, that were privately owned, and much agricultural output came from privately controlled plots of land. In addition, there was a large informal or "underground" economy. Still, each present society has a *emphasis* about the location of property rights with some such as the United States emphasizing private property rights and others such as Cuba emphasizing public property rights.

Why Do Property Rights Matter?

Property rights are important to an economy in two separate but interrelated ways. To begin with, such rights or their lack, create incentives or disincentives on the part of individuals to supply effort and to create innovations. If I do not own the home in which I live, what incentive have I to keep it up or improve it? If I cannot patent a new process, what incentive have I to develop it? A society with secure widespread private property rights is, therefore, one in which individuals will be likely to supply effort voluntarily and one in which innovation is likely to be forthcoming.

Property rights also heavily influence the distribution of income in a society. Those who own more resources or more productive kinds of resources will be likely to receive a greater part of the income and real product of the economy. If individuals such as inventors or innovators are given exclusive use to their new processes, they will enjoy monopoly returns and incomes. If, on the other hand, individuals are completely denied such ownership rights, disincentives to effort and innovation are created. Trade-offs, thus, are created in all societies when property rights choices are made.

Housing may well be one of the best examples of these trade-offs. If privately owned, incentives exist to maintain and improve it. At the same time, the best housing will go to those with the most income, while those with lesser incomes will have less desirable housing. Some may actually be homeless. If housing is publicly owned, disincentives exist for individuals to maintain and improve it but there may be more widespread access to it (assuming enough of it is produced).

With this background in mind, let us turn to look at each of the two major twentieth century benchmark economic systems— market capitalism and planned socialism—in turn. First, we will examine market capitalism, a system whose detail has been examined throughout this book. Now, however, we want to examine its systemic fundamentals.

MARKET CAPITALISM

Market Capitalism
An economic system characterized by (1) private assignment of property rights and (2) decision making about uses of resources is expressed through a system of product and factor markets.

A system of **market capitalism** has two *essential criteria*:

1. Most of the means of production are privately owned. Property rights are vested in individuals. As a result, economic decision making is relatively decentralized, and

2. Economic decisions about uses of resources are expressed through a system of interrelated product and factor markets.

By private ownership of the means of production, we mean that the legal owners of real capital (machines, buildings, and so on) used to produce goods and services in an economy are *individuals* in that society. This definition allows for the existence of corporations, since they are owned by stockholders. In addition, it allows for some government ownership. But the amount of capital owned by the government is a small percentage of the total means of production. The fact that, in the U.S., governments own some schools, hospitals, parks, and so on, does not, therefore, mean the U.S. economy is not *capitalist*.

Markets in a capitalist economy may be organized in many ways ranging from highly competitive to monopolistic in structure. The key feature of capitalism, though, is not the structure of these markets, but the fact that *markets exist*. Market capitalism is not necessarily the same thing as a competitive-free-enterprise market system. Nor, in the political realm, does capitalism *necessarily* translate into a representative, democratic system of government. We will come back to this point later.

Necessary Legal Features of Market Capitalism: (1) right of private ownership, (2) legal enforceability of contracts.

For a capitalist economy to function well, two **necessary legal features of market capitalism** must exist. The two basic elements of this legal framework are (1) *the right of private ownership or, in other words, secure private property rights* and (2) *the legal enforceability of contracts.*

Economic Advantages of Market Capitalism

Because choices about what to produce and what to buy are made by private individuals, choice making under capitalism, as we noted, is relatively decentralized. This is true even in a capitalist economy in which significant elements of monopoly may exist in product and factor markets. Voluntary exchange based upon mutual advantage is perhaps the most important distinguishing characteristic of capitalism. The role of government in such an economic system, while important, is relatively limited.

As noted before, a principal advantage of a capitalist economy lies in the incentives to efficiency created by private property rights. Because private owners of resources keep the gains of their use and have the right to sell their property, there is a strong incentive to maximize the value of those rights by using resources efficiently. Those who take risks receive whatever profit is created; to use the term economists prefer, there are no "**free riders**," individuals who can lay claim to the benefits from resource usage for which they bore none of the costs.

Free Riders Individuals who can lay claim to the benefits of using resources while bearing none of the costs of their usage.

A second advantage of capitalism is that the costs of decision making are likely to be low relative to societies without private property rights. The administrative costs of firms and private decision makers in general may be sizable but there is an incentive to minimize them since profit is the residual after subtracting costs from revenue flows. In a centrally planned economy, on the other hand, the planning mechanism must be relatively large and costly. Those who manage it have less clear incentives to minimize its costs since they have no property rights in the resources and must share any productive gains with numerous "free riders."

Economic Criticisms of Capitalism

Even though a capitalistic system allocates resources with efficiency, its critics argue that it has two drawbacks:

1. The tastes of some consumers, those with greater incomes; are given more weight than those of others in determining what to produce. Output is rationed, therefore, on the basis of how much money each consumer has to spend. For those in poverty, who have needs but less purchasing power, the market does not readily supply goods. These output results trouble those who regard them as inequitable and frequently lead to arguments in capitalist societies "for income transfer programs."

2. Business firms, in setting output and prices, fail to include in their calculations the external costs (and benefits) that result from production but that are not part of the private costs or benefits of production or consumption. The most notable of these external costs are pollution and other forms of damage to the environment. *Note:* Socialist countries are by no means untarnished in this respect. The same kinds of externalities appear to occur in socialist economies such as the former Soviet Union as was seen in the nuclear plant disaster at Chernobyl in 1987 and in the pollution of many of that nation's major lakes and waterways.

In order to deal with the problems of poverty and ecological damage, societies—often acting through governments—must devise means of interfering with or supplementing market decisions. Inevitably, such interferences involve abridgments of private property rights.

PLANNED SOCIALISM

Because of the diversity of socialist theory, it is difficult to give a precise definition of socialism that can encompass all its forms. Here we will describe the most important one in modern times: all forms of planned socialism.

What is Planned Socialism?

Planned Socialism
An economic system in which property rights are largely held publicly, and choices about resource usage are made by central planners.

Of the many varieties of socialism found in the late 20th century, **planned socialism** is the one with most direct ties to Marxist thought. Property rights are largely held publicly and choices about resource usage are made centrally by a group of planners. If one created a spectrum of economic systems, this one would be at the opposite end in terms of resource decisions and rewards from the pure form of market capitalism discussed earlier.

Advantages of Planned Socialism

Unlike the results of pure capitalism, planners in socialism can create any distribution of real income desired. By allocating resources and by setting prices, all distributional "inequities," at least in theory, can be eliminated. By planning, all externalities (theoretically) can be incorporated into those prices and resource allocations.

Criticisms of Planned Socialism

The major disadvantage of planned socialism is that with public property rights, there are, as indicated earlier, disincentives to individual effort. If all laborers, for example, are to be paid the same, why would one work harder than any other? Distribution, in other words, can be made more "equitable," but there may be less to distribute since productivity differentials are not rewarded. The second major disadvantage of planned socialism is more technical. Since there are no private markets to guide the allocation of resources (no "market tests"), how do the planners figure out where financial capital and other resources should go? All must be done by plan, an enormously more difficult and costly task than the "invisible hand" direction of capitalism. If to this is added the fact that managers who actually produce goods are given quotas, the incentives to quality as opposed to quantity may be low as well. Resource wasteage may be high.

Marx and Socialism

Just as Adam Smith created much of the foundation for capitalist thought, Karl Marx is responsible for the foundation of planned socialism. Marx's theory of history sought to explain the evolution of socialism and, for that reason, we will briefly examine the principles he set forth. This is true even though Marx wrote mostly about Capitalism rather than socialism. Indeed, his most important work, *Das Kapital*, is an analysis of capitalism and a forecast by Marx of its ultimate demise.

Dialectical Materialism

Dialectical Materialism
A view that material things are the subject of all change and that technology, and the natural environment are the causes of that change.

The philosophical foundation of Marxism is **dialectical materialism**, a philosophy that views material things as the subject of all change and technology, and the natural environment as the main forces that cause human society to change continually. Let's examine this philosophy one step at a time.

Dialectics emphasizes that all phenomena, natural and human, involve processes of development. The seed grows into the plant. The infant grows into the child, the child into the youth, the youth into the adult. (Darwin's theory of evolution is another example of this dialectical process of reasoning.)

Marx analyzed this process of development of human society, and used it, as he came to understand it, as the scientific basis for socialism. The first law of this argument is that the foundation of society is materialistic. Technology and the natural environment (climate, resources, geography) are the dominant forces in society's development. The rest (culture, institutions, social classes, and the relations between them) are linked to the economic (materialist) base, and are shaped by that base.

Historical Materialism
The view that human society undergoes a continual process of change from one form to another.

Dialectical materialism is the basic idea behind Marx's concept of **historical materialism**, which holds that human society throughout history has undergone a continual process of change, or development from one form to another: this change results from conflict between classes in a society. In ancient times, there was slavery; in medieval times, serfdom; then came handicraft and cottage industry, which gave way to factory-oriented capitalism. The guiding factors in this process are changing technology and the natural environment.

Figure 16-1 illustrates this process of social change or class conflict for the transition from feudalism to the beginnings of capitalism. The *thesis* (the class system that is dominant at a given time) is feudalism, in which the ruling class is the landed aristocracy. The *antithesis* (the class that is the main force in changing the thesis) is the emerging commercial class. The *synthesis* (the system that evolves after the antithesis has forced changes) is mercantile capitalism, in which the commercial class replaces the landed aristocracy as the dominant class.

Class Conflict

Marx, as we indicated before, believed that the most dramatic feature of this process of change was the conflict of classes at each stage of development. In ancient Rome, the slaves were in conflict with their masters. In medieval Europe, the serfs and the emerging merchant class were in conflict with the landed aristocracy. With

Figure 16-1
An Example of Marxian Analysis

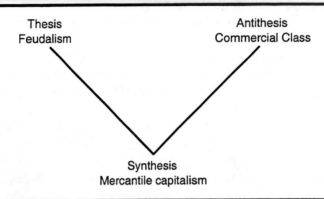

Another example would be: thesis = industrial capitalism; antithesis = the proletariat, or laboring class; synthesis (what Marx predicted would occur) = socialism.

Labor Theory of Value
The Marxist argument that the entire value of a product is made up of its labor cost.

Surplus Value
In Marxist theory, the difference between the value created by labor and its wage payments.

the development of factories, a new class, the *proletariat* (the workers in the factories), came into conflict with the capitalists, the owners of the factories. The basis of these conflicts is the effort of one class to dominate and exploit other classes. A basic tenet of Marxism is that as long as there are private property rights classes will continue to exist, and conflict will result. Marx argued for a **labor theory of value**, that is that all value is created by labor, but that wages under capitalism tend toward a subsistence level. The difference between the value of products created by labor and the wage payments to labor constituted what Marx called **surplus value**.

Falling Profits and the Reserve Army of the Unemployed

According to Marx, competition between firms and the increasing scarcity of profitable investment opportunities would cause profits in a capitalist economy to fall. Capitalists could counter this fall in two ways: (1) They could get employees to work longer hours, and in this way increase surplus value and the degree of exploitation of labor. But the opportunity to do this was limited. (2) They could invest more and improve technology further, thus increasing output per worker and surplus value. However, improving technology meant that more and more machines replaced more and more workers, and this increased unemployment.

Reserve Army of the Unemployed
Marxist idea that capitalist societies displace labor in favor of capital and create a growing number of unemployed workers.

The rising number of unemployed caused by increased use of capital and improved technology was called the **reserve army of the unemployed**. This reserve army, Marx said, competed with the employed workers, and this competition had the effect of keeping wages down.

Recurring Business Cycles

Marx also maintained that as capitalists increase investment to ward off falling profits, the productive capacity of the economy expands and output increases. But because wages are kept low, workers do not have the ability to buy this expanded output. So, although the economy expands for a while, eventually industry's ability to produce output far outstrips consumers' ability to buy that growing output. (If you tool up your factory with all the latest equipment, so that you can make 10,000 washing machines a month, but the public has enough purchasing power to buy only 5,000 of them, you will eventually go broke.) Excess capacity is generated, which causes economic crisis and then collapse. Along comes a depression, and firms are forced out of business. Eventually, enough firms are forced out of business so that capacity contracts to a point at which expansion can be renewed, and the process repeats itself. Marx identified the business cycle and the exploitation of labor as the two hallmarks of the capitalist system. Marx was one of the first to introduce the idea of recurring business cycles, and his theory of them constituted a significant contribution to economic theory.

Marx's Prediction: The Collapse of Capitalism

Marx concluded that capitalism (the thesis) contained within it inherent contradictions (capitalism's antithesis) that would bring about its end and a movement toward the next stage of development, socialism. He predicted that economic crises would recur, and would become progressively more serious. With more investment and continuing technological change, the reserve army of the unemployed would become larger and larger. Because of their increased investment and ever-greater need to compete against others, firms would get bigger. As this occurred, those among the bourgeoisie who owned smaller firms would be forced into the proletariat and into the reserve army of the unemployed.

Eventually, Marx predicted, economic crisis and unemployment would become so large that revolution would take place, and capitalism would be overthrown. The proletariat would come to realize that capitalism was against their self-interest; the wastes of resources due to recurring crises would become apparent. The proletariat would therefore seize political power and establish a socialist society which would ultimately evolve into a classless communist society.

What Happened to the Collapse?

Marx argued that the overthrow of capitalism would take place in the most advanced countries. Marxist socialism, however, was established almost entirely in economically backward societies. In addition, in the late 20th century, many Marxist economies have moved toward the establishment or reestablishment of capitalist economic institutions. Has history proved Marx wrong?

Whether the Marxist prediction would have ever been fulfilled had capitalist economies remained unchanged is unclear. What is evident is that since Marx's prophesy, there have been four fundamental influences at work in capitalist societies that have increased their vitality and made their predicted collapse fundamentally wrong.

1. Contrary to the labor theory of value, labor's wage depends, in a market economy, on its productivity. As more capital is employed, labor's productivity rises as does its wage. Indeed, labor's (wage-salary) share of national income, at least in the U.S., has grown to 60 to 70 percent and has been remarkably steady since World War II. The Marxist view of increasing exploitation seems unwarranted. The very (labor) theory of value on which it was based has been repudiated.

2. Since the 1930s, governments in market economies have taken an active role in trying to stabilize their economies. To many economists, this seems to have reduced the severity of recurring business crises. Also, it is not at all clear that crises in such economies were becoming ever more severe.

3. Modern capitalist states have developed extensive social welfare programs to redistribute real income. Whatever its growth effects and incentive effects, redistribution is seen by some as having taken the "sting" out of pure market capitalism.

4. Many workers have themselves become capitalists in a small way. In the U.S., 67 percent of the population either own or are buying their own homes, and about 40 percent own stocks or bonds, either as individuals or through pension and retirement funds. In other words, larger numbers of workers are sharing in the property rights of capitalism.

Efficiency of Central Planning: The "Fatal Conceit" Problem

Over time, centrally planned economies in the twentieth century ultimately seem to have suffered from "economic sclerosis." Some of these economies, especially that of the Soviet Union, experienced substantial growth during periods in which they were building basic industries such as steel. As they matured, however, an inability to reallocate resources to their most productive uses became increasingly severe. As we know, in market economies, this process of reallocation depends on a myriad of changing supply and demand signals that emanate from both consumers and producers. The market pricing system, thus, provides generally reliable information to resource owners about the most profitable uses of those resources in the face of changing consumer tastes as well as changing technology.

In a centrally planned economy, on the other hand, such flows of information do not "bubble up" from the interaction of buyers and sellers. Rather, central planners, in deciding on uses of resources, their prices, and the prices of both producer and consumer goods must try to estimate all that information. A Nobel Laureate, Frederick Hayek, referred to the presumption by planners that they could generate and efficiently use this information without allowing markets to exist as the "fatal conceit" of centrally planned economies. It led Hayek to conclude that, ultimately, centrally planned economies would grow less and less efficient and would fail. This remarkable insight by Hayek occurred decades before the collapse of the Soviet Union.

The End of Planned Socialism?

Ironically for Marxists, by the late 1980s, it was the planned socialist states that were on the brink of collapse. In the amazingly brief period of less than a decade following 1989, the Soviet Union collapsed (1991) and split into ten independent republics, most of which moved in varying degrees to try to create capitalist economies. In addition, all the planned socialist states of Eastern Europe moved to recreate capitalist economies with Eastern Germany becoming a part of a reunited German capitalist society. In Asia, in the 1980s, China, the world's most populous society, began a steady movement toward a capitalist economy. While proclaiming its devotion to socialism, the nation began basic economic reform first in agriculture where private property rights were restored and then to create private firms and private stock ownership throughout special economic zones. In 1997, a decision was made to either privatize or close many of the huge, inefficient state-owned firms in basic and consumer goods industries. As we enter the twenty-first century, there are few economic societies left that can be called planned socialist. North Korea and Cuba are two that cling to a rejection of markets in favor of central planning, Even Cuba, though, is experimenting with limited market reforms though seeking to find ways to do so while maintaining its commitment to a socialist economy.

Has history proved Marx wrong? Impressive evidence suggests that the answer is Yes. In recent years, some writers have argued that we are witnessing an "end to history," a termination of the contest among competing economic systems. We are skeptical of this argument, for systems evolve and the future, by definition, is unknown. What seems clear at the end of the twentieth century, however, is that the contest between economic systems based on markets and those based on central planning has been resolved in favor of markets.

Transition from Planned Socialism to Market Capitalism: How Long and How Difficult?

Major questions exist about how to accomplish a transition from planned socialism to market capitalism and about the length of time required for such a transition. Even in Eastern Europe, which had market economies until the 1940s, major problems of transition occurred. While it might seem relatively simple to privatize a socialist economy, in fact, it has proved complex even in Poland, whose pace of reform has been among the most rapid in the region.

Key Reforms

There is no simple "recipe" of reforms in the transition from planned socialism to market capitalism. Nonetheless, there is widespread agreement, based especially on the experience of Eastern Europe, that among the most important key reforms are:

1. Creation of private property with secure property rights

2. Creation of a system of prices that reflect relative scarcity

3. A monetary system that permits price stability and the achievement of the price goals in (2) above

4. A system of institutions, both economic and political, that facilitates the first three reforms

Command Economy
An economy in which the problems created by scarcity are dealt with by a central planning bureaucracy.

Market Economy
An economy in which the problems created by scarcity are dealt with by market signals that allocate and reallocate resources.

Let's look at each of these four interrelated reforms to see why they form a package of changes necessary to transform a **command economy**—*one in which the problems created by scarcity are dealt with by a central planning bureaucracy*—into a **market economy**—*one in which the problems arising from scarcity are dealt with by market signals*. These signals allocate and reallocate resources to their (changing) most productive uses.

Secure Private Property Rights

A key feature of a market economy is the ability of private individuals—acting on the incentive to maximize the value of their property rights—to choose how to use resources, including financial capital, under their control. As we said before, secure private property rights minimize free rider problems and permit an expectation on the part of property owners that they will be able to appropriate the benefits of their maximizing efforts. Under planned socialism, this type of private gain was officially discouraged, if not prohibited. Today, in some former socialist states, especially the former Soviet Union, private property rights remain restricted. As an example, Russia has yet to permit unrestricted private ownership of land. Partially, as a result, agriculture remains a major problem in terms of productivity.

Prices that Reflect Relative Scarcity

Under planned socialism, prices were set by central planners to accomplish "social" objectives. Heavily subsidized prices, particularly of basic staples such as bread, electricity and housing were seen as "equitable." The two main problems that resulted, however, were that (1) not nearly enough of the goods were produced to clear markets, thus creating unfilled demand (long waiting lines, in many cases), and (2) the distorted prices created perverse incentives to use goods that were produced. As an example, in the 1980s, administered bread prices were so low in Poland that farmers reportedly fed bread, rather than more expensive grain, to their cattle and hogs! Many formerly socialist states have reformed prices (it was a first action of the democratic Polish government in 1990), but Russia has yet to undertake the politically painful rationalization of its entire pricing system.

A Monetary System that Permits Price Stability

Price reform and monetary reform go hand in hand. When prices are reformed and subsidies eliminated, governments in newly-forming market economies are tempted to expand the money supply to "take some of the sting" out of price reform. The result in Russia in the mid 1990s, for example, was an inflation rate of over 1,000 percent per year. A currency of determinate and stable value is also necessary for foreign trade and as an incentive to attract long-term foreign capital to the former socialist states. Still, the temptation to ease the pain of price reform with increased supplies of money is intense. Russia's central bank announced in 1999 that it planned to do just that.

Institutional Reform

The economic and political institutions created by a society are nothing less than the set of means by which all economic activities are governed. These institutions determine the cost of economic transactions. If the institutions are reliable and efficient, the volume of transactions increases and the size of the economy is enhanced. If the institutions are unreliable and inefficient, the reverse happens and economic growth slows. Where institutions are unreliable, economic activities are subject to corruption and many are diverted to an "underground economy." The institutions created by long-standing market economies took long to create. It remains to be seen whether they can easily be transferred to some formerly planned socialist economies. This is especially true of such economies that had never been fully evolved market societies.

Mixed Economies: A Third System?

There is no economy in the late 20th century that falls neatly into one of the two systems that we have outlined. Private property rights are dominant in some, public property rights in others; almost all have a mixture of the two assignment methods. In some economies choices about using resources are very decentralized; in others, central planning of those choices continues; in almost all there is some mixture of these levels. Nations at this time are, thus, **mixed economies**, those that combine elements of private and public property rights along with centralized as well as decentralized choice making about resources.

Mixed Economies
Economic systems that combine elements of private and public property rights and centralized as well as decentralized choices about resource usage.

Many Western European economies have evolved what is known as *democratic socialism*. Sweden, Belgium and other economies come to mind. One may question whether such modern "welfare states" are really a distinct economic system. Almost all, though, rely, in practice, on private property rights to create incentives for resource usage while permitting decentralized private markets to allocate resources. Democratic socialism, in other words, seems more a political than an economic system, one in which the state has distributional goals which it achieves through political means while relying on a decentralized market economy for the resources with which to achieve those goals.

The End of Socialism: A Disclaimer

Does the end of the Cold War mean that capitalism has won out over socialism and that the latter will disappear as an economic system? The argument *has* been advanced that ideological contest and the evolution of economic systems is over. Contrary to Marx's prophecy, say proponents of this view, capitalism has proved to be the ultimately successful economic system. Others, such as the well known American socialist economist, Herbert Gintis, conclude that "reports of the death of socialism are premature." Gintis concedes that "markets work because they are disciplinary devices," thus they avoid shirking, reveal price information and produce high-quality goods under the threat of losing buyers. In turn, managers have incentives to invest in profitable activities and employees incentives to work hard to avoid loss of jobs.

Nonetheless, says Gintis, Eastern Europe (including the Soviet Union) was never the socialism envisioned by its philosophical founders. Nor, according to Gintis, are modern capitalist economies, the models envisioned by Conservatives because they have "incorporated socialist goals and structures into their institutional fabric." Both systems, he argues, must continue to evolve and incorporate the features of each that have merit.

Economic and Political Freedom: Are They Related?

As planned socialist economies began their transition to market capitalist economies, a question that became common was: *Will the increased freedom associated with capitalism lead to faster growth as well as greater political freedom?* These are, in fact, two *interrelated* questions. One appears to have a fairly clear answer, the other is more arguable.

Faster Growth

Recent studies seem to confirm the view that greater economic freedom is associated with higher levels of GDP and faster growth. In a 1994 study by the *Heritage Foundation*, free and mostly free nations (relatively free of government economic controls), such as Hong Kong, the U.S., and the U.K., dominated the list of nations with high per capita GDP. Mostly unfree and repressed nations, such as Vietnam, Cuba, and N. Korea (all of which remain planned socialist economies), dominated the list of nations with low GDP per capita. GDP growth rates continued this pattern. It would seem, thus, that as economic freedom increases in formerly planned societies, their growth rates will increase. But, will this, in turn, lead to greater political freedom as well?

Political Freedom: Does it Follow from Economic Freedom

In the 1994 article in *The Wall Street Journal*, Kim R. Holmes argues that policy makers have paid inadequate attention to economic freedom while concentrating on political freedom in the movement away from planned socialism. She suggests a change of emphasis not only because "a free economy can lift itself—and its people—out of poverty," but also because "economic freedom is a breeding ground for political freedom." Should we expect, then, that economic liberalization, with its increased freedom of choice, will be accompanied by political liberalization and increased freedom to choose political leaders.

Proponents of this economic-political liberalization argument feel that as consumers and producers exercise economic freedom they will press for freer political choice as well. This is especially true, argue some political scientists, as a middle class develops and grows with faster growth in per capita GDP. Those skeptical of the argument counter that economic and political freedom are not that well correlated. Skeptics point, for example, to Singapore and Hong Kong as examples of high income countries with great economic freedom that have significantly lesser levels of political freedom.

China: A Test Case?

Nowhere has the argument about economic and political freedom crystallized more than in arguments about U.S. economic policy toward the People's Republic of China. Though China still is not among the World's most free economies (it ranked 87 of 101 nations in the 1994 Heritage Foundation Study), it has moved in the 1990s *toward* creation of the requisites of a market economy. Nonetheless, China, at least at the national level, remains politically monolithic. Only the Communist party is permitted to exist. In 1999, dissidents who attempted to form a new political party were imprisoned. Critics of the "economic-freedom-leads-to-political-freedom argument" cite this as evidence, not only of the incorrectness of the argument, but also of the need to change U.S. economic policy toward China. Proponents, on the other hand, point to increased political freedom at local levels in China and argue it will ultimately translate into political liberalization at the national level.

Who is right? At this point, there is no clear answer. In the twenty-first century, however, China may well be the clearest test case of the arguments about the relationship between economic and political freedom.

SUMMING UP

1. An economic system consists of the institutions created by a society to deal with the problems created by scarcity.

2. The basic questions that all economic systems must address because of scarcity are: (a) What to produce, (b) What shall be the technology of production, and (c) Who shall receive the real income of the society.

3. Any economic system can be evaluated in terms of its (a) static efficiency, (does it produce what is desired?), and (b) dynamic efficiency, (are resources used to maximize the long-term stream of benefits from their use?).

4. The placement of the *property rights*, rights to own, transfer and profit from the ownership of resources, may be public or private. All societies have some mix of these two assignment methods.

5. Property rights are important to societies in two ways: (a) they create incentives innovation and (b) they heavily influence the distribution of income.

6. A system based on *market capitalism* has two essential criteria: (a) The means of production are privately owned and property rights are vested in individuals. (b) Economic decisions are expressed through a system of interrelated markets and are

Cartoon Feature Syndicate

"I forget whether he calls himself a conservative radical or a radical conservative."

decentralized. The two legal features necessary to achieve these essentials are (a) the right of private ownership and (b) the legal enforceability of contracts.

7. Two major economic advantages of market capitalism are (a) the incentives to efficiency by private property owners seeking to maximize the value of their rights along with the absence of *free riders*—those who benefit from using resources but bear none of their cost, and (b) incentives to minimize decision-making costs.

8. The criticisms of market capitalism are: In a society in which there is pure capitalism, the needs of poor people who have less purchasing power are given less weight in establishing market demand. In addition, firms may fail to consider external costs and benefits, especially the costs to the populace of pollution and other forms of environmental damage. The economic advantages of capitalism include: (a) the efficiency that private property right incentives creates, and (b) the low costs of decision making that decentralized decision making creates.

9. *Socialism* has various forms but there is a common belief in each that resources other than labor should be socially owned and there should be few private property rights.

10. *Planned socialism* involves public property rights with centralized choices about using resources. Theoretically, it can create any distribution of real income chosen and can incorporate externalities. However, it creates disincentives to efficiency and lacks an appropriate and low-cost way to allocate resources. It is also far from clear that planned socialism in practice leads to the incorporation of externalities.

11. Karl Marx, the intellectual father of modern planned socialism wrote about capitalism and predicted its ultimate demise. *Dialectical materialism*, the basic principle behind Marx's concept of *historical materialism*, holds that human society throughout history has undergone a continual process of change or development. The social structure evolves from one form to another; the guiding factors in this process of evolution are changing technology and the natural environment.

12. It is basic to Marxist thought that as long as there is private ownership of the means of production, there will be differing classes. As long as classes exist, conflict will exist, as one class exploits another.

13. According to Marx, surplus value, the difference between the value of products created by labor and its wage payments will create a problem of inadequate demand for growing output under

capitalism. A declining rate of profit will lead to recurrent depression according to Marx.

14. Marx argued that the falling profits would lead capitalists to increase their investment to improve technology, and this in turn would increase unemployment. The result would be a *reserve army of the unemployed,* with the effect of keeping wages down.

15. Because Marx based his theory of value on labor, he failed to see that labors' payment depends on its productivity. As more capital, and other factors are used that productivity rises and so does labor income; He also failed to foresee that (a) governments in market economies, would step into the picture and reduce the severity of business cycles by manipulating interest rates, taxes, and government spending, (b) that modern capitalist states would develop extensive social welfare programs and, (c) that many workers would themselves become capitalists, through ownership of property or stocks and bonds.

16. Most economies today are mixed economies. They involve various mixes of property rights and levels of resource usage decision making. *Democratic socialism* seems to be a system in which private property rights exist but in which states intervene after decentralized choices about resource usage are made to achieve distributional goals.

17. Over time, planned socialist economies suffered from the "problem of fatal conceit," a term of Frederick Hayek. Hayek predicted the ultimate failure of such economies because of their inability to generate the information necessary to reallocate resources in the face of changing tastes and technology.

18. By the late 1980s, planned socialist economies began to fail. Many, including the former Soviet Union and the People's Republic of China, began to create or recreate market capitalist institutions.

19. In the 20th century contest between market capitalism and planned socialism, it appears that planned socialism has lost out.

20. The four main reforms necessary in the transition from planned socialism to market capitalism are (a) creation of secure private property rights, (b) creation of a system of prices that reflect relative scarcity, (c) a monetary system that produces price stability and relative scarcity prices, and (d) political and economic institutions that facilitate (a), (b), and (c).

21. Arguments continue about the relationship between economic freedom and political freedom. Some argue that in the transition

from planned socialism to market capitalism the greater economic freedom of capitalism will engender greater political freedom. Studies indicate that economically freer societies grow more rapidly than planned societies. Arguments continue about whether greater political freedom will accompany increased economic liberalization.

22. Arguments remain about the continuing viability of socialism in the post-cold war era. Some conclude that ideological evolution has ended and that capitalism has been proved the only viable economic system. Others, such as Herbert Gintis, argue that a new socialism true to its intellectual origins will evolve and that each system will adopt the best features of the other.

KEY TERMS

Command economy
Dialectical Materialism
Dynamic efficiency
Economic System
Essential Criteria of Capitalism
Free riders
Historical Materialism
Market capitalism
Mixed economies
Planned Socialism
Property rights
Reserve Army of the unemployed
Static efficiency
Surplus Value
The problem of "Fatal Conceit"

QUESTIONS

1. What is an economic system?

2. As a reminder, what choices *must* any economic system create answers to? Why must it do so?

3. As a student of economics, what arguments would you advance for market capitalism as a desirable economic system?

4. What is *planned socialism*? What are its main differences from market capitalism?

5. Sketch the main points of Marx's model of history and explain why Marx's prediction about the collapse of capitalism has not come true.

6. What is meant by the Marxist term, "surplus value"? What is the labor theory of value on which it was based?

7. How is the "free rider" problem resolved in a market capitalist economy?

8. Why do property rights and the level at which choices about using resources occur matter to an economic society?

9. What seems to be the explanation for the fact that most economies in the late 20th century are "mixed economies"?

10. What is the problem of "fatal conceit" that has afflicted planned socialist economies in the 20th century? What causes the problem?

11. Why has planned socialism largely lost out in the contest with market capitalism?

12. What are the major reforms necessary in the transition from planned socialism to market capitalism?

13. What is the argument of Herbert Gintis about the future of socialism?

SUGGESTED READINGS

Beichman, Arnold. "The Returns Are In and Socialism Is Out." *The Wall Street Journal.* September 16, 1989.

Buchanan, James. "Socialism Is Dead; Leviathan Lives." *The Wall Street Journal.* July 18, 1990.

Farney, Matt. "China's Democratic Experiment Hits Its Limits." *The Wall Street Journal,* January 10, 1999.

Friedman, Milton. *Capitalism and Freedom.* Chicago: University of Chicago Press, 1972.

Gintis, Herbert. "Is Socialism Dead?" *The Margin.* March/April, 1991.

Holmes, Kim R. "In Search of Free Markets." *The Wall Street Journal,* December 12, 1994.

Maddison, Angus. "Poor Until 1820." *The Wall Street Journal,* January 11, 1999.

Mann, Martha Lindberg. "Warsaw Diary: The Long Road to Capitalism." *The Margin.* March/April, 1991.

Marx, Karl. "Capital," reprinted in Charles W. Needy (ed) and Owen, Robert. "A New View of Society." In *Masterworks of Economics,* edited by Leonard D. Abbott. NY: McGraw-Hill, 1946. Volume II.

Mellvan, George. "Examining the Engine of Economic Growth." *The Wall Street Journal,* January 12, 1999.

Schnitzer, Martin C. *Comparative Economic Systems.* 5th edition. Cincinnati, OH: Southwestern Publishing Co., 1994.

Seldon, Arthur. *Capitalism.* Cambridge, Mass: Basil Blackwell, Inc. 1990.

Glossary

Ability-to-pay principle A principle of taxation under which those who have a larger income are deemed capable of paying not only a larger tax but a larger percentage of their income in taxes.

Absolute advantage The ability of a given nation to produce all commodities more cheaply (that is, using up few resources per unit of output) than any other nation with which it might trade.

Abstinence theory of interest A theory that people prefer to consume goods and services now, rather than later; therefore, people will save (postpone consuming) only if they are given a reward. That reward is called interest.

Accelerator principle The general rule that changes in the rate of change of consumer demand cause much larger changes in induced investment. The accelerator is positive if a change in the increase in consumer demand causes induced investment to increase. It is negative if the change in induced investment decreases.

Accounting profit The difference between total revenue and total explicit cost.

Adaptive expectations hypothesis The view that decision makers form their inflationary expectations on the basis of events of the recent past.

Adjustable-peg system A system of exchange in which currencies are pegged, or are not allowed to change in value by more than a specific percentage. The pegs themselves, however, may be changed from time to time.

Administered-price inflation A kind of inflation that occurs when firms with some control over price use that power to raise prices more rapidly than cost increases.

Administered pricing A term used by some economists to refer to prices that are set by the administrators of firms rather than established by independent influences of supply and demand.

Age-earnings profile A profile that shows the relationship between annual incomes and age for groups with various levels of education.

Aggregate-demand-equals-aggregate-supply approach (Keynesian) An approach to the problem of finding equilibrium income in a simple economic model without government and foreign trade. According to this approach, the equilibrium is at that level at which *aggregate supply*—consumption plus savings (C + S)—is equal to *aggregate demand*—consumption plus intended investment (C + II).

Aggregate-demand-equals-aggregate-supply approach (General) An approach that holds that equilibrium real income is established where aggregate quantity demanded equals aggregate quantity supplied.

Aggregate demand shock A term used to describe a shift in aggregate demand.

Aggregate production function The relationship in physical (nonmonetary) terms between output and employment for a given economy (at a specific time). A "receipe" for output.

Aggregate supply shock A term used to describe a shift in aggregate supply.

Allocative inefficiency The tendency for monopoly firms to set prices above marginal costs and to allocate fewer resources to producing their products than consumers prefer.

Antithesis In Marxist theory, the force arising from a social contradiction that compels a change in the existing theses (or set of social arrangements).

Arbitrage The practice of buying international currencies at low prices and selling them at high prices.

At factor prices Method of computing national income using the prices paid in the factor markets. This measuring practice excludes indirect business taxes.

At market prices Method of computing national economic accounts using the prices paid in the markets for goods and services. This measuring practice must utilize all market costs incurred in production.

Autarky Economic self-sufficiency.

Automatic stabilizers Structures built into the U.S. economy that have a moderating influence on recessions and inflations. They are automatic in that they operate without being invoked by government policy makers. They are not considered strong enough to prevent, by themselves, the occurrence of business fluctuations. The progressive personal income tax is an example.

Autonomous investment Investment that is not affected by changes in the nation's overall level of income and consumption.

Average propensity to consume The percentage of their incomes that people at a given level of income tend to consume:

$$APC = \frac{C}{Y}$$

Average propensity to save The percentage of their incomes that people at a given level of income tend to save:

$$APS = \frac{S}{Y}$$

Average revenue Total revenue divided by output.

Average total cost Average fixed cost plus average variable cost.

Backward-bending labor supply curve A graphic illustration of a situation in which the quantity of labor supplied decreases as the wage increases beyond a certain level.

Balance-of-payments statement The annual accounting statement disclosing the status of a nation's foreign trade, including its capital transactions. The statement reveals what was bought and sold, and how any difference between the two was financed. (The balance-of-payments account must balance.)

Balance of trade The monetary value of exports minus imports:

$$X - M.$$

Balance to be financed In the balance-of-payments statement, the combination of the basic balance plus the short-term capital account.

Balanced-budget multiplier The multiplier that makes itself felt when a balanced-budget change in government expenditures and taxes (that is, government expenditures and taxes moving in the same direction and by the same amount) causes the level of national income to change in the same direction and by the same amount as the expenditure-tax change. *See also* Multiplier effect.

Bank holding companies Corporations that own one or more banks.

Barriers to entry Factors that prevent other firms from entering monopolist's market.

Barter A system of exchange that does not involve money; the trading of goods directly for other goods.

Basic balance In the balance-of-payments statement, the balance in the current account plus the balance in the long-term capital account.

Benefits-received principle of taxation The theory of taxation according to which people pay taxes that are commensurate with, or in line with, the benefits they receive from government services.

Bilateral monopoly A market situation in which a single seller bargains with a single buyer.

Bonds Instruments of debt, guaranteeing payment of the investment (face value) plus interest by a certain date. Interest on bonds is a cost of production to a business firm that raises capital by selling bonds.

Break-even point or price Occurs when a firm just covers its opportunity costs. A price that equals average cost and marginal cost is a break-even price.

Bretton Woods Conference International monetary conference held in 1944, which established the International Monetary Fund (IMF) and the International Bank for Reconstruction and Development (IBRD).

Budget restraint The limits on purchases of goods imposed by a consumer's income and by the prices of the goods bought.

Business cycles Variations in a nation's general economic activity; fluctuations in output, income, employment, and prices.

Capital account The account, in a nation's balance-of-payments statement, that is made up of long-term and short-term capital flows.

Capital broadening (constant capital-to-labor ratio) The situation in which capital instruments grow at the same rate as the amount of labor employed.

Capital consumption allowance *See* Depreciation.

Capital deepening The situation in which a nation's employers use more capital relative to the amount of labor used, thus raising the capital-to-labor ratio for the economy.

Capital gains tax A tax placed on the increase in the value of an asset, which is realized on sale of the asset. It is considered a tax loophole because the tax rate on such gains tends to be lower than on other forms of income.

Capital-intensive process A production process that uses relatively more capital than labor or land.

Capitalism An economic system with two essential ingredients: (1) the private ownership of the means of production, and (2) the expression of economic decisions through a system of interrelated markets.

Capture hypothesis The view that regulatory agencies are often captured by the industries they regulate and serve industry interests rather than those of the public.

Cartel A group of producers who join forces and behave like a monopoly with respect to price and output.

Ceteris paribus In economic analysis, the practice of holding certain variables constant and permitting other *key* variables to change.

Change in demand A shift in a demand curve (by which more or less of a good is bought at all prices) that results from a change in (1) income, (2) tastes, (3) prices of other goods, (4) number of consumers, or (5) consumers' expectations of future prices.

Change in quantity demanded A movement along a demand curve that results from a change in the price of that good.

Change in quantity supplied A movement along a supply curve that reflects a change in the amount of a good offered for sale as only the price of that good changes.

Change in supply A shift in a supply curve that reflects that more or less of a good is offered for sale by a firm at all prices.

Check An order to a bank from the holder of a demand deposit to transfer money from that demand-deposit account and pay it to someone else.

Checking accounts *See* Demand deposits.

Closed market economy A market economy consisting of interrelated product and factor markets that does not trade products, services, or resources with other economies.

Closed shop An employment situation in which workers *must* join a union in order to get or hold a job.

Coins Metal tokens minted by the Treasury and issued through the Federal Reserve Banks; the smallest component of the supply of money.

Command economy An economy in which the problems generated by scarcity are solved by a system of central government planning.

Commercial bank Any bank that holds demand deposits.

Common property resources Those that are open to use by everyone. They have, thus, no individual owners (also called common access resources).

Common rent *See* Quasi-rent

Common stock Instruments of ownership of a corporation. People who own shares of common stock can vote on all matters requiring stockholders' consent, and there are no limitations on the amount of dividends they can receive. However, they receive dividends only after all prior claims against the company (interest on bonds, and so on) have been paid.

Comparable worth A proposal under which wages would be based on the intellectual and physical demands of various jobs. Points would be created for each job and jobs with the same numbers of points would receive equal wages.

Comparative advantage A situation in which a nation is relatively more efficient at producing some goods than at producing others, compared with the production capabilities of other nations with which it trades.

Compensatory fiscal policy *See* Functional finance.

Competing interest laws Those in which special interest groups on both sides of a legislative issue vie for favor in order to obtain concentrated benefits.

Competition The market form in which no individual buyer or seller has influence over the price at which she or he buys or sells. *See also* Pure competition.

Complementary investment An investment that increases the productivity of other investments.

Complements Products used in conjunction with each other.

Concentration ratios A measure of the combined market shares of an industry's largest firms.

Conscious parallelism A practice in which a dominant firm sets its prices and other firms set theirs in a way that parallels those of the price leader.

Constant capital-to-labor ratio *See* Capital broadening.

Constant-cost industry An industry in which the cost curves of individual firms remain the same as the output of the industry varies.

Constant GNP *See* Real GNP.

Constant returns to scale The condition for a firm when total costs increase at a constant rate and long-run average costs are constant.

Consumer choice A theory of demand that rests on four assumptions about consumers: (1) Consumers buy competitively. (2) Consumers have limited money incomes and full information. (3) Consumers are rational. (4) Consumers maximize their utility or satisfaction.

Consumer price index An index that measures price changes for a certain market basket of goods likely to be purchased by a family of four living in an urban area. Compiled and published monthly by the Bureau of Labor Statistics.

Consumers' surplus The difference between what consumers would be willing to pay for a good and what they actually pay for it.

Consumption function Schedule of the quantities that people are willing and able to consume at different levels of income during a given time period.

Contestable market One in which there are no significant losses from entry or exit due to sunk costs.

Contraction phase That part of the business cycle in which the level of economic activity falls.

Control through the ruble Control that the Soviet Union exercises over business firms through the medium of the Gosbank (central bank). A business firm's account at the Gosbank is credited with the value of its assigned production goal. As the firm uses resources, it pays for them by checks on its account. If the firm uses up its account before it achieves its assigned goal, it fails in its assignment.

Corporate profits The return to entrepreneurship in firms that are incorporated. Corporate profits equal dividends plus retained earnings (undistributed corporate profits) plus corporate taxes.

Corporation A legal entity or form of business enterprise, created by the process of incorporation, which functions separately from its owners.

Cost-plus pricing A form of administered pricing in which a firm first computes its variable cost, then its overhead or fixed cost, and finally adds its expected profit per unit. The result is the price it charges to consumers.

Cost-push inflation The kind of inflation that occurs when suppliers of resources increase their prices faster than productivity of manufacturers increases. Costs of production then go up, which forces prices up.

Countervailing power The idea that monopoly power often exists on both sides of a market. The monopsony power of buyers is counterbalanced by the monopoly power of sellers.

Coupon economics The system by which a government rations the output of the economy by issuing ration coupons to consumers, which consumers must redeem in order to buy rationed products.

Covert collusion A situation in which representatives of various firms in the same industry meet and decide on prices, shares of the market, and other conditions of the market.

Creeping inflation A kind of inflation in which there is a moderate rise in prices that continues for an extended period of time.

Criticism and self-criticism program A program in the Soviet Union that requires individual citizens to identify and report deviations from the government's economic plan.

Cross price elasticity of demand The percentage change in the demand for one good divided by the percentage change in the price of another good.

Crowding theory A theory that explains the effects of discrimination by tracing the impact that discrimination has in forcing women, blacks, or other minorities into certain kinds of employment and out of others.

Cultural Revolution A mass social movement that took place in the People's Republic of China in 1966-1969, supported by the Chinese government and aimed at rooting out bourgeois and antirevolutionary thought and action.

Currency in circulation Currency (both paper money and coins) that is actually in use, not in the vaults of banks or in the Treasury.

Current account An account in the balance-of-payments statement that is like the income and expense statement of a nation. It includes all current transactions, but excludes short-term and long-term movements of capital.

Current account balance The balance in the interpayments accounts obtained by adding exports of goods and services minus imports of goods and services plus net unilateral transfers.

Customer discrimination Job and wage discrimination resulting from tastes of buyers (for example, diners in restaurants preferring to be served by men or whites).

Cyclical deficits component That part of the federal deficit which arises from automatic stabilizers.

Deadweight loss of monopoly A welfare loss to society of consumers' and producers' surplus that results from monopoly. It is a loss not captured by someone else.

Decreasing-cost industry An industry in which external economies cause costs of all individual firms in the industry to fall as the output of the industry as a whole increases.

Deflating current GNP The act of decreasing current GNP to take into account a rise in prices; expressing GNP in terms of dollars of constant purchasing power.

Deflation A general lowering of prices in an economy.

Deflationary gap The increase in aggregate demand necessary to make aggregate demand equal to aggregate supply at full employment.

Demand A set of relationships representing the quantities of a good that consumers will buy over a given range of prices in a given period of time.

Demand curve A graphic plotting of the demand schedule, or a set of relationships between various prices of a good and the quantities of it that the public will buy at each of those prices in a given period of time.

Demand deposits Deposits in commercial banks that can be withdrawn "on demand" by one who presents a check.

Demand-pull inflation A rise in prices that occurs when demand for goods exceeds the ability of the economy to supply these goods at existing prices. The result is that the market rations this short supply through the medium of increased prices.

Demand schedule Indicates the quantity demanded at each of several prices.

Democratic socialists Those who believe in using democratic procedures to gain political power and curtail capitalism.

Dependent variable The factor in a two-variable system that changes as a result of changes in the independent factor.

Deposit multiplier That formula for determining the multiple that demand deposits may be of the required reserve ratio.

Depreciation An account allowance for the capital that "wears out" (either through use or obsolescence) while being used to produce the final goods and services of an economy in a given period of time.

Derived demand A demand for one thing that depends on the demand for something else. (For example, the demand for labor depends on the demand for the goods produced by labor.)

Dialectical materialism A philosophy in which material things are viewed as the subject of all change, and technology and the natural environment as the main forces that cause society to change continually.

Diminishing marginal utility of income The theory that people get less and less satisfaction from each increase in their incomes.

Diminishing rate of transformation The idea that the rate at which one good may be traded off, or transformed, into another decreases.

Direct The relationship between the independent variable and the dependent variable is direct if the dependent variable changes in the same direction as the independent variable.

Direct democracy A governmental system in which citizens directly choose the rules under which they will be governed.

Dirty float A system of managed exchange rates in which exchange rates are "pegged" or allowed by central banks to move with certain limits.

Discommunication The problems that a large organization encounters in trying to communicate in order to achieve effective decision making; due in part to large size.

Discount rate The rate of interest that the Federal Reserve charges depository institutions when it discounts acceptable short-term debt at the Federal Reserve, to enable the institutions to obtain reserves.

Discretionary fiscal policy Day-to-day fiscal policies established by government officials, designed to cope with changing economic conditions.

Diseconomies of scale The disadvantage a firm may encounter when it increases the size of its plant and increases its output, only to find that the cost of each unit produced is greater than before.

Dissavings Consuming more than is produced, or consuming more than one's income.

Double coincidence of demand In a system of barter exchange the requirement for a mutuality of needs; each party to a transaction must want what the other has.

Double taxation A situation that arises when a corporation pays taxes on its gross receipts. Then it distributes its dividends from these receipts to its stockholders, who must then pay income tax on the previously taxed money.

Duopoly An industry with two interdependent major sellers, although there may be a number of fringe firms as well.

Durable goods Commodities (such as automobiles) that are used up at a very slow rate; that is, it takes a long time to use them up.

Dynamic efficiency Over a period of time, using resources in ways that maximize the long-term benefits from their employment.

Dynamic framework A concept or set of relationships by which one can explain the way certain things change through time.

Economic capacity The level of long-run production that is achieved with the lowest per-unit cost of the optimal plant.

Economic determinism Assuming that all actions are reactions to changing economic reality.

Economic development The long-term process by which the material well-being of a society's people is significantly increased.

Economic dualism The coexistence within a society of two or more different economies (frequently, one with markets and cash incomes and the other with barter).

Economic imperialism A Marxist concept according to which capitalists ward off a fall in profits and lessen the severity of economic crises by exploiting the underdeveloped countries. Supposedly, capitalists do so by using the underdeveloped countries as a source of demand for their output and supply of cheap raw material and as places to invest capital.

Economic integration The degree to which an economy's resources are employed in their most productive uses.

Economic institutions Social institutions through which economic decisions are made (for example, the Federal Reserve System).

Economic loss The excess of total costs over total revenues.

Economic loss with production A situation in which a firm's short-run total revenue is less than its total costs, but greater than its total variable costs. The firm minimizes its loss by continuing to produce.

Economic loss with shut down A situation in which a firm's short-run total revenue is less than its total costs, but greater than its total variable costs. The firm minimizes its loss by continuing to produce.

Economic loss without production A situation in which a firm's short-run total revenue is not only less than its total costs, but also less than its total variable costs. The firm loses less by closing down altogether.

Economic profit Profit that is above normal profit. When there is economic profit, total revenue is greater than total cost (including the opportunity cost of entrepreneurs).

Economic rent The payment made to a resource whose supply is perfectly inelastic.

Economics The social science that deals with the analysis of material problems, how societies allocate scarce resources to satisfy human wants.

Economies of scale Achieved by a firm when the cost of each unit produced falls as output increases with larger plant size.

Effective demand The total aggregate demand for commodities and services in an economy.

Elasticity of (product) supply A measure of the rate of change in quantity supplied divided by the rate of change in price.

Elasticity of resource demand The rate at which the quantity of a resource demanded changes as its price changes:

$$\frac{\Delta Q}{Q} \div \frac{\Delta P}{P},$$

where Q = quantity of the resource demanded, P = price of the resource, and Δ (Greek delta) = "change in."

Elasticity of resource supply The rate of change in the quantity of an input supplied as its price changes:

$$\frac{\Delta L}{L} \div \frac{\Delta W}{W},$$

where L = amount of labor, W = wage rate, and Δ (Greek delta) = "change in."

Elasticity of supply of labor The rate of change in the quantity of labor supplied divided by the rate of change in the wage or:

$$\frac{\Delta Qs}{Qs} \Big/ \frac{\Delta W}{W},$$

where W equals the wage rate.

Embargo An absolute prohibition against importing certain goods.

Employment The situation in which a unit of resource (labor, land, capital, entrepreneurship) is used in some economic activity.

Entrepreneurship The function of organizing labor, land, and capital into a firm capable of producing and marketing a commodity or service.

Entry limit pricing The practice by monopoly and oligopoly firms of setting prices below profit maximizing levels in order to deter entry of new firms.

Equation of exchange MV = PQ, where M = supply of money, V = velocity of exchange (number of times M changes hands), P = price level, and Q = number of transactions.

Equilibrium exchange rate The rate of exchange between two currencies that clears the market or eliminates excess supply and demand.

Equilibrium income The level of income that results from the central tendency of a model. This level will be maintained as long as the factors in the model (savings and investment) remain the same.

Equilibrium price The market-clearing price, or the price at which quantity demanded equals quantity supplied.

Equity stock *See* Common stock.

Ex-ante investment The amount of investment firms plan to make.

Ex-post investment The investment that firms actually undertake (not simply plan to undertake).

Excess demand The excess of quantity demanded over quantity supplied at a price lower than the equilibrium price.

Excess reserves Assets that depository institutions hold in the form of reserves, but which are over and above that required by Federal Reserve regulations.

Excess supply The excess of quantity supplied over quantity demanded at a price higher than the equilibrium price.

Exchange controls Devices governments use to ration foreign currencies or eliminate excess demand for those currencies.

Exclusive unions Bargaining agents that agree to restrict union size and maximize the wage gains of their members.

Expansion The process by which a society's output grows as it uses more and more resources.

Expansion phase That part of the business cycle in which economic activity rises.

Expenditure approach A method of computing national income accounts that is concerned with the kinds of goods people buy, with what kinds of expenditures they make.

Explicit costs Those costs of a firm that result from contracting for resources in the markets.

Exploitation In neoclassical economic theory, a payment to a resource that is less than its value of marginal product.

Exports Commodities and services sold to other nations.

External diseconomies of scale An increase in a firm's costs caused by changes in the output of the industry as a whole.

External diseconomy A cost increase originating outside of the individual firm.

External economies of scale A decrease in a firm's costs caused by increases in the output of the industry as a whole.

External economy A cost decrease originating outside of the individual firm.

Externalities The differences between privately expressed (market) costs and benefits and publicly expressed (nonmarket) costs and benefits. *See also* Spillovers.

Factor markets Those in which the prices of resources like land, labor, capital, and entrepreneurship are established and in which these resources are allocated.

Fascism An economic system combining private property rights with centralized choices about what to produce.

Featherbedding A practice in which unions require a certain number of jobs for the production of goods or services.

Federal funds market The market in which banks lend their excess reserves to each other at the federal funds rate.

Fiat money Money that has greater value as a monetary instrument than as a commodity. It is money because the government issued it and says that it is money, and because people accept it as such.

Final goods and services Goods and services sold to the ultimate user.

Final-value method Method of computing GNP that sums up the prices to final buyers of all goods and services produced by the economy. Avoids double counting by eliminating intermediate production, and leads to the same statistical result as the value-added method of computing GNP.

Financial capital Capital in the form of money; savings that are available for investment in physical capital.

Fine tuning Discretionary changes in fiscal and monetary policy leading to counterchanges in the state of the economy.

Fiscal policy Manipulation of the expenditures and taxes of the federal government to achieve certain economic goals.

Fixed costs Costs that do not vary with output.

Fixed exchange rates A system of international exchange in which the currency of each nation has a certain fixed relationship to the currencies of other nations that is established by government decision. Rates are not allowed to vary with changing market conditions.

Foreign-trade multiplier effect (FTM) The change in GNP resulting from a change in net foreign trade:

$$FTM = \frac{\Delta GNP}{\Delta(X-M)},$$

where X = exports, M = imports, and Δ (Greek delta) = "change in."

Fractional reserve requirement The percentage of demand deposits that depository institutions must hold as reserves. As a result, such institutions can lend out amounts that are a multiple of their reserves.

Free good A good with a price of zero. Supply is greater than demand at any price above zero.

Free rider problem Refers to the fact that once public goods are produced, they are available for consumption by individuals who may have contributed nothing to the cost of producing them.

Freely-floating exchange rate A competitive system of international exchange in which the currencies of the various nations are valued according to supply and demand in the international money market. The exchange rate is free to move up or down to eliminate excess supply or excess demand.

Frictional unemployment Short-term unemployment resulting from workers moving from one job to another.

Full capacity A situation in which a firm or industry is at the low point on its long-run average-cost curve.

Full economic integration When all resources of a society are employed and used in their most productive uses.

Full employment A situation in which everyone in the labor force is employed except those who are frictionally unemployed.

Full-employment budget The budget that balances government expenditures against the level of receipts (taxes) that the government would receive if the economy were at full employment.

Functional distribution of income An approach to the distribution of income that emphasizes the *sources* of income: wages, interest, rent, and profit.

Functional finance A policy that aims at compensating for changes in aggregate demand in the private sector by varying the public sector's expenditures and taxes.

General powers of the Federal Reserve System Powers that enable the Federal Reserve to increase or decrease the amounts of excess reserves that commercial banks need in order to make loans.

General price index Index construction by the Commerce Department to convert current GNP to constant GNP.

Giffen goods Those inferior goods with an income effect that moves in the same direction as price and for which the income effect is larger than the substitution effect.

GNP gap The difference between potential GNP at four percent unemployment and actual GNP achieved.

GNP implicit price deflator *See* General price index.

Gold-flow point The disequilibrium exchange rate at which it is cheaper to buy and ship gold in payment for trade than to buy currencies.

Gold standard The system of international exchange used up until the 1930s, according to which currencies were valued in terms of gold and were convertible into gold, and each nation was obligated to exchange its currency for gold.

Gold tranche position The amount of gold a member nation can borrow from the International Monetary Fund (IMF).

Gosbank The state bank in the Soviet Union, used to control and audit individual firms' activities. All firms have accounts with Gosbank, and all their purchases and sales go through the bank.

Gosplan An agency in the Soviet Union that translates overall goals into a comprehensive plan for the economy. Gosplan is the central planning committee of the Soviet Union.

Government expenditures In the national economic accounts, the measure of all government purchases of goods and services.

Great Leap Forward Second 5-year plan of the people's Republic of China (1958-1962). Execution of the plan was such a disaster that it was abandoned in 1960.

Gross national income (GNI) Total income at market prices generated in the production of all final goods and services during a specific time period. GNI = wages and salaries + rent + interest + proprietors' income + corporate profits + depreciation + indirect business taxes.

Gross national product (GNP) Total dollar value of all final goods and services produced in a given time period. GNP = consumption + gross investment + government expenditures + net foreign investment (export - imports).

Gross private domestic investment Investment including depreciation or capital consumption allowance. *Private* means counting only nongovernment investment; *domestic* means counting only investment made in the U.S.. Investment is the act of creating capital, manufactured producer goods that aid in producing consumer goods and other capital goods.

Growth The intensive process by which the productivity (output per hour of labor employed or income per capita) increases.

Hedonism A philosophical school that argues that self-satisfaction is the primary goal of individuals.

Hedonist One who argues that people act to achieve self-satisfaction.

Herfindahl index A measure of market concentration obtained by summing the squared percentage market shares of firms in an industry.

Historical materialism The view that society throughout history has undergone a continual process of change and development from one form to another. The guiding factors in this process are the natural environment and changing technology.

Historical period A period of time in which technology changes.

Homo communista Communist or communal man.

Homo economicus A term meaning "economic man."

Homogeneous product A product so standarized that buyers do not differentiate between the output of different firms.

Horizontal mergers Those between firms in the same industry.

Human capital The improvement in labor skills (marginal physical product) attributable to education or other training, innate ability and acquired skills.

Implicit costs Those costs associated with using self-owned resources.

Import duties *See* Tariffs.

Imports Commodities and services bought from other nations.

Inclusive unions Bargaining agents that seek to expand the number of jobs offered, and thus, the size of the union.

Income approach Computation of the national income accounts based on measuring the kinds of income generated in producing the output of the economy.

Income effect In demand analysis, the change in the quantity of a good that consumers demand as a result of a change in its price and thereby the consumers' purchasing power, or real income.

Income elasticity of demand An estimate of the rate at which the demand for a good varies as consumer incomes vary.

Income-inferior goods Those goods that consumers tend to buy less of as their incomes increase, and more of as their incomes fall.

Incomes policy A policy that frequently involves wage and price controls by the government. In general, a cooperative effort of labor, management, and government to find mutually agreeable goals for the economy and the means to achieve these goals.

Increasing-cost industry An industry in which individual firms experience external diseconomics (increasing costs) caused by increases in output by the industry as a whole.

Increasing marginal utility of income The assumption that people get more and more satisfaction from each additional increase in their incomes.

Increasing opportunity cost The assumption that as a nation chooses to produce more of one good, it must (ultimately) give up increasing amounts of the other good.

Incremental capital-output ratio The additional capital needed to produce additional output.

Independent variable In a set of relationships, the variable that changes first.

Indicative planning The kind of planning one finds in France, where the government draws up targets for the economy and brings together employers and unions to discuss and modify the proposals. Firms and workers, with government support, move to implement these plans.

Indirect business taxes Taxes on goods and services passed on to consumers in the form of higher prices (for example, excise and sales taxes).

Induced investment Investment generated by changes in income and in quantity consumed. An increase in income leads to greater quantities consumed. Then there is an increase in investment to expand capacity in order to satisfy the new demand.

Inferior goods A general case of goods for which there is a weak income related taste. As price rises, quantity demanded decreases because the substitution of goods outweighs the tendency to buy more with reduced real income (in contrast with Giffen goods, a special case of *very* income-inferior goods).

Inflating current GNP Increasing current GNP to take into account a fall in prices; expressing GNP in terms of dollars of constant purchasing power.

Inflationary gap The excess demand at full employment that causes prices, rather than output, to increase.

Innovation Introduction of new products or processes.

Input-output relationships The complex set of interrelated requirements for inputs needed by the economy to produce various combinations of output (arranged by industries).

Instantaneous multiplier A multiplier effect that takes place without an intervening period of time. *See also* Multiplier effect.

Interdependency A situation in which economic actions depend on each other (for example, when firms in an industry act on the assumption that their price and output policies are dependent on the actions of other firms in that industry).

Interest The return to the owners of capital. Only interest paid by businesses is included in gross national income. (Interest on the national debt or interest on consumer loans is not included.)

Interlocking directorates A practice in which individuals serve on the boards of directors of more than one firm in the same industry.

Internal economies of scale Decreasing costs from a firm's increased output in the long term.

Internalizing costs and benefits The process through which the prevention of spillovers or externalities is accomplished by having all costs, private and public included in the price of a good.

Internal rate of exchange The rate at which a nation gives up one good in order to produce another.

International monetary fund (IMF) An organization set up at the Bretton Woods Conference in 1944 to facilitate international trade, especially to assure the financing of such trade and to administer the adjustable peg system of post-World War II exchange rates.

International reserves Assets available to central banks and other agencies that are accepted in payment of international debts.

Inverse The relation between independent and dependent variables is inverse if the dependent variable changes in the opposite direction from the independent variable.

Investment function A schedule of the quantities that people are willing and able to invest at various levels of income during a given period of time.

Invisible hand argument The idea attributable to Adam Smith that self-interest based voluntary exchanges can make all those involved in the exchanges better off.

Invisible items The services, including financial services (as opposed to physical commodities), that are exported or imported by a nation. Items not normally reflected in merchandise exports and imports.

Involuntary additions to inventory *See* Unplanned additions to inventory.

Involuntary reductions to inventory *See* Unplanned reductions in inventory.

Jawboning The use of persuasion on the part of the government to get business and industry to comply with wage and price guidelines.

Job discrimination A situation in which workers are employed on the basis of some consideration other than their productivity, such as race or sex.

Kibbutz A community that operates on the principle of complete income equality. In Israel in 1973, there were 240 kibbutzim, with more than 85,000 members.

Kinked-demand curve A demand curve that is based on the assumption that firms in an oligopoly follow suit when competitors' prices decrease, but ignore other firms' price increases.

Labor-intensive process A production process that uses relatively more labor than capital or land.

Laffer curve A theoretical association between various tax rates and the tax revenues collected at each rate.

Law of demand The general rule that consumers buy more at low prices than they do at high prices; that price and quantity demanded are inversely related.

Law of diminishing marginal utility The general rule that as more of a particular good is consumed in a given time period, the additional utility of each additional unit of the good will ultimately decrease.

Law of diminishing returns *See* Law of variable proportions.

Law of supply The general rule that the quantity supplied rises as price rises, and falls as price falls; that price and quantity supplied are directly related.

Law of variable proportions (diminishing returns) The general short-run rule that as a firm uses successive equal units of a variable input in conjunction with a fixed input, additions to output (marginal output) derived from the variable input begin to diminish beyond some point.

Leading indicators Certain kinds of economic activity that lead the business cycle by increasing or decreasing before the rest do. Measurements of these indicators are "weather vanes" for the economy.

Leakages Factors in the multiple creation of demand deposits that reduce the ability of depository institutions to expand the supply of money or demand deposits.

Legal tender Anything that the law requires be accepted in payment of a debt.

Limited liability A legal term that means that those who own the corporation (stockholders) are not responsible for its debts. Stockholders' liability (or the amount stockholders are liable for if the firm goes bankrupt) is limited to the purchase price of their stock.

Liquid assets Assets, such as savings accounts or government bonds, that can be quickly converted into money with little risk of loss.

Liquidate To sell a firm or to convert its plant capacity to producing other goods.

Logrolling The practice of trading votes or trading support for one issue in order to obtain support for another.

Long-run period A planning period of a firm or industry, in which all inputs are variable. During this period, the firm can choose any plant size permitted by present technology and by its financial limitations.

Lorenz curve A curve that shows the degree of inequality in the distribution of income for a specific year. The percentage of people in different groups is shown on the horizontal axis, and the percentage of income going to each group is shown on the vertical axis.

Loss minimization *See* Profit maximization.

M1 money A measure of the money supply that consists of currency, coin and checking deposits.

M2 money A measure of the money supply that consists of all components in M1 plus savings deposits, small time deposits and money market mutual funds.

M3 money A measure of the money supply that consists of all the components of M2 plus large value certificates of deposit.

Macroeconomics The study of the forces that determine the level of income and employment in a society.

Malthusian specter The nineteenth-century view, advanced by Thomas R. Malthus, that the supply of people (increasing at a geometric rate) would outrun the supply of food (increasing at an arithmetic rate), and that widespread starvation would result.

Margin requirements Regulation by the Federal Reserve of the percentage of the selling price of stock that a purchaser must put down in cash in order to buy a stock. The purchaser may borrow the rest from a bank or a stockbroker.

Marginal cost The cost of producing an additional unit of output.

Marginal efficiency of capital The expected rate of return on capital; the stream of income a business expects to obtain over the life of a piece of capital in relation to the price of that capital.

Marginal physical product The additional amount of product that a firm can produce as a result of hiring an additional unit of input (labor, capital, and so on).

Marginal private cost or benefit Cost or benefit that individuals derive from producing or consuming an additional unit of a good.

Marginal propensity to consume The percentage of any change in income that people tend to spend:

$$MPC = \frac{\Delta C}{\Delta Y},$$

where C = consumption, Y = income and Δ (Greek delta) = "change in."

Marginal propensity to save The percentage of any change in income that people tend to save:

$$MPS = \frac{\Delta S}{\Delta Y},$$

where S = savings, Y = income and Δ (Greek delta) = "change in."

Marginal resource cost The amount it costs a firm to hire one more unit of a resource or factor.

Marginal revenue The change in total revenue due to a small or one-unit change in output.

Marginal revenue product The addition to total revenue attributable to using an additional unit of a resource. One finds it by multiplying the marginal physical product of the resource times the marginal revenue from selling the additional units of product it produces.

Marginal social cost or benefit Cost or benefit to society caused by producing and consuming an additional unit of a good.

Marginal tax rates The rates on additional taxable income.

Marginal utility The additional satisfaction derived from the consumption of the last unit (or additional unit) of a good purchased.

Marginal utility of income The change in satisfaction derived from a change in income.

Marginal utility of leisure The change in satisfaction derived from a per-unit change in leisure time.

Market period The period of time in which a firm has already produced its output. All costs are fixed costs.

Market system The set of means by which exchanges between buyer and seller are made.

Marxist socialism A system of philosophy of government and economics that grew out of the writings of Karl Marx in the nineteenth century.

Materials-balance approach An explanation of environmental problems based on the amount of input used in production and the disposal of waste products created in the consumption of that output.

Means of deferred payment The function of money that is concerned with facilitating lending and the repayment of loans.

Medium of exchange The function of money that deals with exchanging goods for money and money for goods.

Mercantilism A system of economic thought, at its peak from the sixteenth to nineteenth centuries, according to which governments were responsible for the welfare of the economy.

Microeconomics The study of disaggregated economic activities or how a market economy allocates resources through prices.

Midpoint formula A device for calculating the price elasticity of demand by dividing the average rate of change in quantity demanded by the average rate of change in price.

Mixed economies Economic systems that combine elements of private and public property rights and centralized as well as decentralized choices about resource usage.

Model A device economists use to create a systematic analogy to actual economic behavior.

Monetarism An approach to economic policy that emphasizes the dominant role of the supply of money. It calls for a fixed and appropriate increase in the money supply each year as the basic policy for economic stabilization.

Monetary policy A government's manipulation of the money supply and the rate of interest to achieve economic goals.

Money Anything that performs the functions of a medium of exchange, standard of values, store of value, and standard of deferred payment.

Money (current) GNP Output of a given year valued at the prices of that year. Data on GNP before being adjusted for price changes.

Money income The number of dollars received in income; does not reflect purchasing power.

Monopolistic competition A market situation with three main characteristics: (1) many firms, (2) differentiated products, and (3) relative ease of entry into and exit from the market.

Monopoly power A firm's ability to influence the price of its product.

Monopsony A market situation in which there is only one buyer.

Monopsony profit *See* Technical factor exploitation.

Moral suasion The use of persuasion by the Federal Reserve to get depository institutions to do what it wants.

Multinational corporations (MNCs) International firms that buy raw materials, sell finished products, and have production facilities in many countries.

Multiplier effect The multiple change in income due to a given initial change in aggregate demand. *See also* Balanced-budget multiplier.

Multiplier formula

$$M = \frac{1}{1-MPC} \quad \text{or} \quad M = \frac{1}{MPS},$$

where MPC = marginal propensity to consume and MPS = marginal propensity to save.

National banks Commercial banks chartered by the federal government.

National income (NI) Net income of a country using factor prices generated in the production of all goods and services in a given period of time. NI = wages and salaries + rent + interest + proprietors' income + corporate profits.

National income at factor prices Net income of a country obtained by using only market prices of factors rather than market prices of finished commodities or sales on the commodity markets.

Natural monopoly A market situation for an industry in which there are economies of scale up to the output rate that fills the market. A single firm is more efficient than any larger number of firms.

Natural rate of unemployment The difference between full employment and a zero level of unemployment. Explained by frictional unemployment.

Near money Assets that have all the characteristics of money except that they are not used as a medium of exchange.

Negatively sloped Sloping downward, as in a curve.

Negative net investment A situation in which gross investment is less than depreciation. In such a case, the capital stock of the economy is contracting.

Negative savings *See* Dissavings.

Negative sum game When losses exceed the winnings in a game.

Neoclassical economics School of economic thought developed during the late nineteenth century. Many aspects of this thought are considered valid today, and many others have been changed and expanded. For example, Keynesian economics (named after John Maynard Keynes) evolved from a basic change in one aspect of neoclassical economics.

Net foreign trade (NFT) The difference betwen exports and imports:

$$NFT = X - M,$$

where X = exports and M = imports.

Net national income (NNI) A nation's net income at market prices generated in the production of all final goods and services during a given period of time (excluding depreciation) NNI = wages and salaries + rent + interest + proprietors' income + corporate profits + indirect business taxes.

Net national product (NNP) The net value of all final goods and services a nation produces during a given time period (excluding depreciation), NNP = consumption + net investment + government expenditures $\pm$ net exports.

Nomenklatura The term used to describe the Soviet elite whose special entitlements increase their real incomes.

Nondurable goods Commodities, such as food, that are used up fairly quickly.

Nonprice competition Forms of competition between businesses that do not involve price. May include competition in styling, services, advertising, and quality.

Normal goods Those that consumers buy more of as their real incomes rise and less of as their real incomes fall.

Normal profit A profit just large enough to keep the firm producing in the long run. Normal profit equals the entrepreneur's opportunity cost (what entrepreneurship could earn in other uses). A normal profit is included in total cost.

Normative economics Economic discussions that make judgments about the way things should be.

Official reserve transactions account An account of those sources such as borrowing from other official agencies that finance the basic balance.

Official reserve transactions balance In a nation's balance of payments, the account showing how a payment deficit is financed.

Oligopoly An industry characterized by (1) the existence of several firms, each of which can affect the actions of others in the industry; (2) either homogeneous or differentiated products; and (3) significant barriers to entry.

Oligopsony A situation in which there are few buyers in the market.

OPEC An acronym for the Organization of Petroleum Exporting Countries, an international oil export cartel that sets the price of (most) exported oil.

Open market economy A market economy that does exchange products, services, or resources with other economies.

Open-market operations The buying and selling, by the Federal Reserve, of highly liquid, short-term, low-risk government debt.

Opportunity cost The alternative goods one gives up when one chooses to produce a certain thing.

PACs or political action committees Organizations that channel funds from special interest groups to the election campaigns of politicians.

Paradox of thrift An ironic situation in which, during a recession, if people all try to increase their savings, the equilibrium level of income of the nation and the actual quantity saved decrease.

Paradox of value That some goods have great total utility in use (e.g.; water) but little in exchange while other goods have relatively little value in use (e.g.; diamonds) but great value in exchange. The price we are willing to pay for a good is based on its value in exchange.

Pareto optimal A rule change that makes at least one person better off while making no one else worse off.

Parity A level for farm-product prices, maintained by governmental support and intended to give farmers the same purchasing power for each product sold as they had in some designated base period.

Partnership A business arrangement in which two or more individuals combine to operate an unincorporated business enterprise.

Per capital real GNP The figure obtained by dividing real GNP by the size of the population.

Per se rule A rule in law that certain acts are illegal in and of themselves, no matter what their intent.

Perfect economic integration The situation in which units of a resource are paid the same amount in all uses of that resource.

Perfect elasticity The situation in which price elasticity of demand approaches infinity. This means that as the quantity demanded changes, there is no change in price. The demand curve is horizontal.

Perfect inelasticity The situation in which price elasticity of demand equals zero. This means that as price changes, there is no change in quantity demanded. The demand curve is vertical.

Perfect integration The situation in which units of a resource are paid the same amount in all uses of that resource.

Perfect price discrimination The situation in which a firm charges the same consumer a different price for each unit sold. The price is the maximum that the consumer will pay for each unit.

Perfectly contestable market One in which there are no losses from entry or exit due to sunk costs.

Periodic multiplier A multiplier effect that takes place over time. *See also* Multiplier effect.

Personal disposable income The portion of personal income that people may either spend or save. PDI = personal income - personal taxes.

Personal income All income received by people, whether from production or from transfer payments. PI = national income + undistributed corporate profits + corporate taxes ± net transfer payments.

Phillips curve A curve that shows the tradeoff between unemployment and price changes. If employment increases, prices will increase; if unemployment increases, price increases will go down.

Physical capital Capital in the form of tools and instruments of production.

Pigou effect An economic reaction whereby, as prices fall, people with savings have greater purchasing power; therefore, savers increase their demand for goods and services.

Positive economics Economic discussions that consist of pointing out what *is*.

Positive net investment A situation in which gross investment exceeds depreciation; this means that the capital stock of the economy is expanding.

Positive sum game When winnings exceed losses in a game.

Positively sloped Sloping upward, as in a curve.

Precautionary purposes One reason why people want to hold money; they want cash in hand in case of emergencies.

Preferred stocks Stocks that have preference status when it comes to receiving dividends and assets of a given corporation, in case the corporation should have to liquidate. Preferred stocks usually do not carry voting privileges, and the amount of dividends is usually limited.

Present discriminatory activity Basing jobs and wages on goods other than productivity.

Price discrimination The charging of different prices for a good to different consumers. A situation in which the price of a unit of some good, divided by the marginal cost of that unit, is not the same for all customers. The seller of the good discriminates against some customers.

Price elastic A term describing a market situation in which the quantity of a good demanded changes at a faster rate than the price of the good:

$$\frac{\Delta Q}{Q} > \frac{\Delta P}{P} \, ,$$

where Q = quantity demanded, P = price, Δ (Greek delta) = "change in, " and > = "greater than."

Price elasticity of demand (E_d) An estimate of the rate at which the quantity demanded of a good varies in response to its price:

$$E_d = \frac{\Delta Q}{Q} / \frac{\Delta P}{P} \, ,$$

where Q = quantity demanded, P = price, Δ (Greek delta) = "change in."

Price elasticity of supply An estimate of the rate at which the quantity demanded of a good supplied changes as the price of the product changes:

$$\frac{\Delta Q}{Q} / \frac{\Delta P}{P} \, ,$$

where Q = quantity supplied, P = price, Δ (Greek delta) = "change in."

Price floor A target price, usually established by government, below which the market price is not allowed to move.

Price index A measure of changes in a price level.

Price inelastic demand A term describing a market situation in which the quantity of a good demanded changes at a slower rate than the price of the good:

$$\frac{\Delta Q}{Q} < \frac{\Delta P}{P} \, ,$$

where Q = quantity demanded, P = price, Δ (Greek delta="change in," and < = "less than."

Price leadership In an oligopoly, a form of implicit collusion in which a leader firm sets prices that are observed and followed by others in the industry.

Price rivalry The contest in which sellers watch what prices others charge and then react to those prices.

Price seeker A firm that must set the price of its product(s) as well as determine its most profitable output rate.

Price taker A firm which acts on a price that is beyond its control.

Primary demand Demand for a commodity (such as cars or refrigerators) by those who have not owned that commodity before: first-time owners.

Private equilibrium The *market* equilibrium between the buyer's privately and noncollusively determined benefits from the sale of a commodity and the seller's privately determined costs (including the profit necessary for entrepreneurship).

Private rates of return Rates of return on investment that do not take into account indirect social costs and benefits (called external costs and benefits).

Producers' surplus The difference between the actual selling price of a good and the marginal cost of producing it.

Product differentiation The preference of consumers for the products of one firm over those of other firms.

Production-possibilities curve A useful device derived from the production-possibilities function. *See also* Production-possibilities function.

Production-possibilities function A relationship expressing those combinations of goods that the full-employment use of a society's resources can produce during a particular period of time (using the best available technology).

Profit A return or payment to the entrepreneur.

Profit maximization Profit is said to be maximized or loss minimized when production is at the level at which marginal cost is equal to marginal revenue.

Profit-push inflation *See* Administered-price inflation.

Profits of unincorporated businesses. *See* Proprietors' income.

Progressive tax A tax with a rate that increases as the tax base increases.

Proletariat Workers in the factories of the industrial societies developed since the eighteenth century.

Property rights Rights of ownership to use, to transfer, and to benefit from the employment of factors of production.

Proportional tax A tax with a rate that remains the same as the tax base changes.

Proprietors' income The return to entrepreneurship in firms that are not incorporated.

Protectionism The government's effort to protect domestic firms or industries from free (competitive) international trade by imposing tariffs or quotas on imported commodities.

Public goods Goods that can be used by a person without reducing the amount available for other people to use.

Pure competition A market form that has the following characteristics: (1) No single firm can influence price. (2) There is no collusion. (3) Products are homogeneous. (4) There are no barriers to entry or exit. (5) Prices are flexible. (6) Buyers and sellers have full information.

Pure economic determinism The assumption that the actions of people and institutions are reactions to changing economic reality.

Pure economic rent The payment to a resource whose supply is perfectly inelastic.

Pure monopoly A market form in which (1) there is just one firm, and (2) the firm's product has no close substitutes.

Pure monopsony A labor market situation in which there is one employer that sets wage rates.

Pure number A number that is independent of the units of measure of the factors involved in compiling it.

Quantity adjuster A firm that has no control over the price at which it sells its product. It decides only how much to produce.

Quasi-rent or common rent The difference between the actual payment to a resource in relatively inelastic supply and its opportunity cost.

Quotas Restrictions on the quantities of goods that may be imported into, or exported from, a country.

Random variations Variations that cannot be accounted or planned for, since they do not follow any regular pattern.

Rational expectations hypothesis The view that decision makers form their inflationary expectations on the basis of current and recent past events and thus anticipate future events.

Rate of exchange The price at which one nation's currency is exchanged for that of another.

Rate of transformation The rate at which one good is traded off for another.

Rational ignorance The argument that when the benefits of a public choice are highly concentrated and its costs highly diffused, it is rational for those who bear its costs to ignore them.

Real GNP The output of a nation for a given year, adjusted for price changes between that year and given base year.

Real income The value of what one can buy with one's money income.

Regressive tax A tax with a rate that declines as the tax base increases.

Regulated monopoly A market situation in which one firm usually has a franchise from government, but a government regulatory commission sets prices and other conditions that the firm must follow.

Regulation Q A government regulation that empowered the Federal Reserve to set the maximum interest rates that commercial banks can pay on savings accounts and demand deposit (checking) accounts. This regulation was abolished in the early 1980s.

Regulations X and W Government regulations that empowered the Federal Reserve to set minimum down payments and maximum length of loans for consumer lending and real estate lending; expired in the 1960s.

Relative rent Differences in rent payments to a resource in different uses.

Rent (national income measures) In the calculation of gross national income, the payments to owners of land. Includes an estimated rent on homes occupied by their owners.

Rent (resource market payments) A payment to resource owners above that which would just induce them to employ resources in a particular use.

Rent seeking activities Those activities undertaken by special interest groups to obtain privileges from governments that will raise their return above opportunity cost.

Replacement demand *See* Secondary demand.

Representative democracies Systems of government in which voters choose elected representatives to make public choices.

Required reserve ratio The percentage of depository institutions' demand deposits that the Federal Reserve requires these banks to keep in the form of assets called reserves.

Reserve army of the unemployed A Marxist term denoting the number of people who are unemployed in capitalistic societies because of the increased use of capital and improved technology (that is, machines replacing labor).

Reserves Eligible assets (their eligibility determined by the Federal Reserve) that must be held by depository institutions.

Resource externalities Changes in the costs of resources that are not attributable to the actions of a single firm but are due to changes in the industry, or in the natural or political environment.

Resources The inputs (land, labor, capital, entrepreneurship) used to make consumer and producer goods.

Results of historical discrimination The effects on present patterns of jobs and wages attributable to previous economic discrimination.

Retained earnings Undistributed corporate profits.

Rule of reason A rule under which there is a broad judicial determination of the reasons for a firm's conduct and the effects of that conduct on restraint of trade.

Sales maximization hypothesis The argument that firms seek to maximize sales or the size of the firm rather than the firm's profit.

Satisficing A decision to seek an acceptable or satisfactory level of profit as opposed to a maximum level of profit.

Savings-equals-intended-investment approach An approach to the problem of finding equilibrium income—in a model without government and foreign trade—according to which the intended investment curve is placed above the x axis (measured income) in relation to the savings function (S = II).

Savings function Schedule of the quantities that people are willing and able to save at different levels of income during a given period of time.

Say's law Supply creates its own demand

Scarcity The relation between limited resources and unlimited wants which results in the inability to satisfy all human wants for goods and services.

Seasonal variations Fluctuations in employment, money supply, and cash flows that occur regularly at certain periods each year.

Second degree price discrimination The practice of charging different prices to different groups of buyers.

Secondary demand Demand by consumers for commodities to replace consumer goods.

Secular trend The expansion or contraction of an economy over very long periods of time. The long-term trend in any time series.

Services Those products of an economy (haircuts, medical attention, and so on) that are not commodities. The value of services is included when GNP is computed.

Short-run period The period of actual production, in which some resources used by a firm are fixed and at least one resource is variable.

Shut down point or price The rate of output that corresponds to a price equaling average variable cost. Total revenue equals total variable cost and the firm's loss is no greater with than without production.

Signaling The idea that employers pay higher wages to more educated workers because the education is a signal of other aspects of productivity increasing behavior.

Single-tax movement A school of thought in the late nineteenth century, led by Henry George, which proposed taxing away all land rents and using the revenues to fund governments.

Social costs Private costs plus spillovers (externalities). *See also* Externalities; Spillovers.

Socialism A social system in which there is collective or governmental ownership of the means of production and distribution of goods. There are many brands of socialism, encompassing many gradations of political and economic thought. Common to all of them is the idea that control of the means of production should be in public, not private, hands.

Sole proprietorship A form of business enterprise in which one person is the owner, and is solely responsible for that enterprise.

Special drawing rights (SDRs) A system of international reserve assets, the so-called "paper gold"; a market basket of currencies established by the International Monetary Fund (IMF). Nations that are members of the IMF may borrow these SDRs to ease currency crises.

Special interest laws Those that confer concentrated benefits but impose diffused costs on voters.

Specific powers of the Federal Reserve Powers of the Federal Reserve to regulate particular areas of lending, such as margin requirements on stock purchases; Regulation Q, W, and X were part of these powers.

Speculative purposes One reason why people wish to hold some of their assets in the form of money: they want to be able to take advantage of unforeseen opportunities to invest, to buy bargains, and so forth.

Spillovers Differences between *private* costs and benefits and *public* costs and benefits. *See also* Externalities.

Standard of value The function of money that enables people to place values on goods and services.

State banks Commercial banks chartered by the various state governments.

Static efficiency At a point in time, using resources in ways that produce the most desired mix of output.

Stationary state A condition in which a given society has reached the upper limit to its growth in per capita income.

Store of value The function of money that enables holders of money to save by a process of transferring value from the present to the future.

Structural deficits component That part of the federal deficit that arises from discretionary fiscal policy.

Structural unemployment A kind of unemployment caused by changes in the structure of the economy, either in the composition of demand or in technology. Either one of these types of changes may cause changes in the composition of the demand for labor.

Substitutes Products that may be consumed in place of each other.

Substitution effect An effect that appears when there is a change in the quantity of a good demanded resulting from a change in its price relative to other goods' prices. This effect comes to light during analysis of demand in a given market. A relatively cheaper good is substituted for relatively more expensive goods.

Sunk costs Outlays on resources that have already been made. Also called fixed costs.

Superior goods Those whose consumption varies in the same direction as but at a greater rate than real income.

Supply A set of relationships representing the quantities of a product that a firm (or all firms in an industry) will offer for sale at each possible price in a given period of time.

Supply curve A graphic plotting of the supply schedule, or a set of relationships between various prices of a good and the quantities of it that a firm supplies.

Supply of M_1 money All demand deposits in commercial banks, plus all currency and coin in circulation.

Supply of resources The quantities of a resource offered for sale at various prices in a given period of time.

Supply side economics Efforts and incentives to stimulate growth in aggregate supply.

Surplus value Marxist term for the differences between the wages paid to workers and the market value of what workers produce. Surplus value, to Marxists, measures the degree of exploitation of the proletariat (working class).

Synthesis In Marxist theory, the system that evolves after the antithesis has forced social changes.

Tariffs Taxes on imported goods.

Tax avoidance The process by which tax obligations are minimized by lawful use of the provision of tax laws.

Tax evasion The illegal process by which tax obligations are either not reported or incorrectly reported in order to evade payment.

Tax rate With respect to income, the percentage of income a citizen must pay annually in taxes. With respect to property, the percentage of the value of property the owner must pay to the government annually in taxes.

Technical factor exploitation In factor markets, the failure of a monopsonistic employers to pay resources their value of marginal product or marginal revenue product (also called monopsony profit).

Technocrats Term used by John Kenneth Galbraith to describe those who hold power in large corporations (also used to apply to those who would "manage" the economy).

Technological change Growth in knowledge or advances in techniques that result in more productive capital goods and more efficient organization.

Technostructure Term used by John Kenneth Galbraith to describe the many interlocking committees of people with technical expertise in large corporations, who make the essential corporate decisions.

Terms of trade Relationship between a nation's export prices and its import prices:

$$T = \frac{P_X}{P_I},$$

where P_X = prices of exports and P_I = prices of imports.

Thesis In Marxist theory, the set of social arrangements existing at a given time.

Tight money policy A policy of a nation's central banking authority that aims at reducing aggregate demand by decreasing the supply of money and increasing interest rates.

Time deposits Savings accounts for which depository institutions can require prior notice before the account holder can withdraw the funds.

Total cost Total fixed cost plus total variable cost.

Total utility The entire satisfaction from consuming a good.

Transactions purposes One reason for holding some assets in the form of money. People do not receive their income at exactly the same time that they need to pay out money. Thus, they want to hold money to be able to meet these day-to-day payments.

Trust An organization that controls the voting shares of an industry and thus can set output rates and prices like a multi-plant monopoly.

Turnover tax A tax on goods as they pass through the various stages of production. The Soviet Union uses turnover taxes to increase prices so that the quantities of goods available (quantity supplied) will be equal to the quantities demanded. It is also employed in some Western European countries.

UNCTAD United Nations Conference on Trade and Development.

Underemployment An employment situation in which units of resources are not employed in their most productive uses.

Unemployment A situation in which a unit of a resource is unable to find use as an input.

Underground economy Transactions that occur and give rise to taxable income but are not reported for tax purposes.

Union shop A labor market in which individuals who are employed by a firm must then join the union.

Unions Organizations formed by employees for purposes of collective bargaining with employers.

Unit elastic demand A term describing a market situation in which quantity demanded of a good changes at the same rate as its price:

$$\frac{\Delta Q}{Q} = \frac{\Delta P}{P},$$

where Q = quantity demanded, P = price, and Δ (Greek delta) = "change in."

Unit of account *See* Standard of value.

Unlimited liability A situation in which there is no differentiation between the assets of the business and the personal wealth of its proprietor. If the business suffers reverses, the owner is personally liable for all its debts.

Unlimited life A situation in which a corporation can continue to exist no matter who owns its stock.

Unplanned additions to inventory A situation in which a business firm produces more of its product than the public is willing or able to buy, which must then be added to inventory. The result is that the business acts to reduce supplies and reduce amounts produced; income moves toward equilibrium.

Unplanned reduction in inventory A situation in which a business firm does not produce as much of its product as the public is willing and able to buy. The result is that the business acts to increase its orders and increase the amounts produced; income moves toward equilibrium.

Utility theory A theory of demand that assumes that consumers buy things on the basis of their evalution of the satisfaction to be derived from various combinations of goods, and of their effort to maximize that satisfaction.

Value-added method A method of computing GNP in which one adds all additions to the value of a product made at each stage of production; the total of these additions for a given product equals the final value of that product.

Value of marginal product The value to consumers of the output produced by using an additional unit of a resources. One computes this value by multiplying the marginal physical product of the resource times the price of the good produced by the resource.

Variable costs Costs of factors of production (such as labor, raw materials, and so forth) that vary according to variations in the firm's output.

Veblen good A good whose appeal is greater at higher prices than at lower prices.

Velocity of exchange The number of times the supply of money changes hands in a given period of time.

Vertical mergers Those between firms in different industries.

Visible items Those commodities (such as cars, food, and machinery) that are exported or imported by a nation.

Wage and price controls Mandatory limits on wages and prices established by a regulatory authority and enforced by law.

Wage and price guidelines Suggested rules for levels of wages and prices. The government suggests these rules, but compliance with them is voluntary.

Wage discrimination A form of price discrimination in which employers use, as criteria to determine the wages they pay to their employees, certain characteristics that have nothing to do with the productivity of the employees, such as race or sex. They may pay lower wages to blacks than to whites, to women than to men, and so forth.

Wages and salaries The money income, including social security taxes, that is the return to labor; figured into the computation of gross national income.

Waste of monopolistic competition The failure of monopolistically competitive firms to produce at minimum long-run average cost or, in other words, the tendency to product with excess capacity.

Wholesale price index An index that measures change in wholesale prices.

Zero economic growth (ZEG) The idea or belief that an economy's GNP should not increase. ZEG is usually based on a concern for preserving or improving the physical and cultural environment.

Zero population growth (ZPG) The slogan advanced by people who feel that the birth rate should equal the death rate so that population will not increase.

Zero sum game When winnings are equal to losses in a game.

Index

A

(EWOT) 31
Account balance
    Capital 508
    Current 508
Accounting profit 129
Adding Up To Market Supply 63
Adjustable-peg system 503
Advertising 271, 302-307
    Pros and cons of 302-307
Age-earnings profile 379
Aggregation 63
Agricultural Act 214
Agricultural Adjustment Act 209
Agricultural economic problems 210-214
Agricultural Marketing Agreement Acts 351
Agricultural Reform Act 353
Agricultural support program 214-216, 219-220
Agriculture and Consumer Protection Act 217
Air pollution
    Enforcing limits on 170-171
Airline mergers 258
Albrecht, William 511
Allocative inefficiency 244
American democracy
    Public choice in 340-342
Antitrust
    Government and 331
    Mergers and 332-333
    More or less? 334-335
Antitrust laws 294, 295, 337
Arbitrage 495
Autarky 451
Average rate of change 102

B

Backward-bending labor supply curve 391
Balance of payments 506-509
    Politics and the 510-514
Balance-of-payments deficit
Balance-of-payments statement 506-508
Balance-of-trade deficit 507
Barriers to entry 232-234, 259
Basic balance 507

Baumol, William 256, 308
Beggar-thy-neighbor argument 465
Belassa, Bela 511
Benefit
    Internalizing of 163
    Social 40
    Spillover 162
Bergmann, Barbara 431, 433, 434
Bilateral monopoly 406-408, 409
Black Market 73
Break-even point 192
Break-even price 192
Buckley, William F. 13
Budget restraint 95
Bumpass, Donald 412
Business cycles
    Recurring 533
Butler, Samuel 15

C

Caesar's Column (Donnelly) 230
Capital 424-425
    Financial 424
    Physical 424
Capital account 509
Capital goods 33
Capital market
    Government and the 425
Capitalism 21, 23
    Characteristics of 27
    Collapse of 533
Capture hypothesis 256
Carlyle, Thomas 2
Cartel 293
Celler-Kefauver Act 295
Ceteris Paribus 51, 54, 59, 60, 62, 78
Chamberlain, Edward 269
Change
    Technological 214
Cheap-foreign-labor argument 465
Chenery, Hollis 473, 477
Clayton Act 230, 295, 354
Closed market economy 364
Closed shop 406
Command economy 536
Commodity balance of trade 447, 448, 477
Commodity exports 447, 477

Commodity imports 447, 477
Common access resources 164-165
Common market 469, 480
Common property resources 164-165
Common rent 422-424
Communism 32
Comparable worth 429, 431-434
Comparative advantage 455-456
    Trade and 451-452
Competing interest laws 346
Competition 48, 78
    in the Product market 398-401
    Monopolistic 269-270, 281
    Nonprice 301-307
    Pure 191-193
Competitive equilibrium 204-205
Competitive Market 49, 58, 60, 65, 66, 78
Competitive wages 390-393
Complements 51, 79
Concentration ratio 332
Congress 513
Conscious parallelism 314
Constant returns to scale 140
Constant-cost industry 197-198
Consumer Demand 54
Consumer Goods 7, 40
Consumer Income 79
Consumer sovereignty 29
Consumers' surplus 202-203
Contestable market 256
Costs
    Economic 127
    Explicit 127
    Fixed 131, 133, 139
    Implicit 127
    Marginal 136
    Marginal resource 369
    Opportunity 35, 39, 40, 63, 70, 127
    Psychic 127
    Real 39
    Social 162
    Spillover 162
    Sunk 131, 133
    Total 181
    Variable 133
Cross price elasticity of demand 114-115
Crowding
    Consequences of 414-415
Crowding theory 414
Current account 509
Current account balance 507

Curve 10
    Demand 51, 53, 56, 57, 58, 62, 65, 78, 101
    Production-Possibilities 36, 37, 38, 39, 41, 48
    Supply 61, 62, 63, 72, 79, 142-143
Customer discrimination 417
Customs union 469, 480

D

Deadweight loss of monopoly 254
Decrease in Income 57
Decreasing-cost industry 198-199
Deficit 508
    Balance-of-payment 509
    Balance-of-trade 507
Deflation 499
Demand 9, 49, 50, 51, 53, 55, 57, 58, 59, 63, 65, 66, 69, 70, 78, 79, 80, 88-89, 210-211
    Change in 56, 64, 79
    Computing price elasticity of 102-103
    Consumer 54
    Cross price elasticity of 114-115
    Derived 365, 494
    Determinants of 50-51
    Determinants of the elasticity of 105-106
    Differing elasticities of 103-105
    Effect of illegality on 146-147
    Elasticity of 101, 236-237
    Excess 65, 66, 69, 79, 80
    Factor 366-369
    Income elasticity of 112-114
    Kinked 299-301
    Law of 54, 55, 56, 57, 78, 79, 88
    Market 51, 58, 64, 99-100
    Price elastic 101
    Price elasticity of 101, 106-107
    Price inelastic 101
    Resource elasticity of 371-372
    Shift in 64
    Theoretical exceptions to the law of 90-92
    Total 51
    Unit elastic 101
Demand curve 50, 51, 53, 56, 57, 58, 62, 65, 78, 101
    Deriving a 97-99
    Movements along 58, 64
    Shifts in 64
Demand Effect 71
Demand Schedule 53, 57, 58, 65

Democracy
  Direct **340**
  Representative **343**
  Representative versus direct **343-344**
Democratic socialism **538**
Denison, Edward **381**
Dependent Variable **10, 11**
Deregulation **257**
  Long-run **258**
  Reconcentration **258**
  Short-run **257-258**
Derived demand **365, 494**
Dialectial materialism **531**
Diminishing marginal productivity **367**
Diminishing marginal utility **99**
Diminishing returns
  Law of **133-134**
Direct democracy **340**
Dirty float **497, 504**
Discommunication **141**
Discrimination
  Customer **417**
  Economic **413-414**
  Price **148-149, 250, 253**
  Results of historical **413**
  Understanding **414**
  Wage **395, 413**
Diseconomies of scale **140**
Diseconomy
  External **196**
Disequilibrium Price **80**
Distribution of Income **6, 116-117, 372**
  Governments and **117-118**
Dumping **510**
Duopoly **317**
  Edgeworth model of **317-319**
Dynamic efficiency **526**

E

Economese **13, 16**
Economic Activity
  Domestic **446**
  International **446**
Economic Analysis **7**
Economic capacity **200**
Economic costs **127**
Economic Determinism
  Pure **43**
Economic Development **43**
Economic Goods **39**

Economic Growth **38**
Economic Integration **42**
Economic liberty **22**
Economic loss **129**
Economic loss resulting in shut down **184**
Economic loss with production **182, 189-190**
Economic loss with shut down **190-191**
Economic Model **41**
Economic policy **476, 502**
Economic profit **128, 181-182, 186-188, 426**
Economic rent **419**
Economic systems **524**
  Evalutating **525-526**
Economic trade policy **516**
Economics **2, 4, 15**
  Normative **12, 16**
  Positive **11, 12, 16**
Economics and the Public Purpose
  (Galbraith) **245**
Economics Normative **11**
Economics of Public Issues, The (North and
  Miller) **377**
Economies of scale **140**
  External **142**
  Internal **142**
Economists **13, 16**
Economy **446**
  Closed market **364**
  External **196**
  Market **80**
  Mixed **538**
  Open market **364**
  Underground **349**
Econospeak **13**
Edgeworth model of duopoly **317-319**
Edgeworth, Francis **317**
Efficiency
  Dynamic **526**
  Static **525**
Efficient market **27**
Elasticity **100-115**
  Perfect **104**
  Total revenue and **107-108**
Elasticity of demand **101, 236-237**
  Determinants of the **105-106**
  Differing **103-105**
Elasticity of resource demand **371-372**
Elasticity of supply **131, 143**
Elasticity of supply of labor **393**
Embargo **463**
Employment **6, 41**

Full 36, 38, 39
Entrepreneur 33
    Creating 419
Entrepreneurship
    and Profit 426-427
Entry
    Barriers to 232-234
Entry limit pricing 308
Environmental pollution 168-171
Equilibrium 66, 69, 80, 96
    Competitive 204-205
    Private 160
    Public 163
    Social 161-162
Equilibrium exchange rates
    Determining 493-496
Equilibrium Price 65, 71, 79, 80, 158-160
Equilibrium Pricing 65
Excess Demand 65, 66, 69, 79, 80
    Total 71, 80
Excess Supply 66, 69, 79, 80
Exchange controls 499
Exchange Rate 505, 514
    Floating 495
Exchange rates 490
    Equilibrium 493-496
    Fixed 496
    Fluctuations in 498-500
    Freely floating 493-495
Excise Tax 8, 110-111
Exclusive unions 408
Explicit costs 127
Export quotas 463-464
Exports 219-220, 446, 449, 453
    Commodity 447, 477
External diseconomy 196
External economies of scale 142
External economy 196
Externalities 162
    Effects of 162
Externality 28
    Negative 28
    Positive 28
    Resource 370

F

Factor demand 366-369
Factor markets 364-376
Farming mess 178, 220
Featherbedding 409

Federal Equal Pay Act 428
Federal Tax 9
Federal Trade Commission Act 295
Feudalism 21, 23, 32
Financial capital 424
Fixed costs 131, 133
    Role of 139
Fixed exchange rates 496
Food and Agriculture Act 217
Food Security Act 217
Foreign exchange markets 490, 492, 514
Foreign-aid program 217
Free goods 420
Free Lunch 39
Free Market 69
Free rider problem 167
Free riders 528
Free To Choose (Friedman) 230
Free trade 22, 469, 470, 476, 504
Free trade agreement 469, 480, 511
Freely floating exchange rate 493-495
Friedman, Milton 302, 418, 495
Full Employment 36, 38, 39

G

Gains from trade 453
Galbraith, John Kenneth 245, 311, 427
General Agreement on Tariffs and Trade
    (GATT) 468, 480, 513
Generalized System of Preferences 511
George, Henry 421
Giffen goods 55, 56, 92
Giffen, Sir Robert 55, 92
Gintis, Herbert 539
Gold standard 500, 502
    Advantages of 502
    Disadvantages of 502
Gold-flow point 502
Goods
    Capital 33
    Consumer 7, 40
    Economic 39
    Free 420
    Giffen 55, 56, 92
    Illegal 145-146
    Income-Inferior 79
    Inferior 56, 92, 114
    Normal 56, 91, 114
    Producer 40
    Public 167

Superior 91, 114
Veblen 54, 55, 56, 79, 90
Government
    and Antitrust 331
    Role of 349-350
Government Intervention 69, 80, 166-167, 217
    Efforts to reduce direct 217
    on the Demand side 217-219
    Origins of 209
    Spillovers and 167-168
Great Depression 470, 500, 510
Gross Domestic Product (GDP) 6
Growth
    Economic 38
    Market 42
    Population 43

H

Harberger, Arnold 476
Hawley-Smoot tariffs 466
Herfindahl index 332
Historical materialism 531
Historical period 132
Homogeneous 41
Homogeneous product 180
Horizontal mergers 332
Human capital 377
Human resources 33

I

Illegal drug market 150
Illegal goods
    Pricing 145-146
Imperfect Competition (Robinson) 269
Implicit costs 127
Import embargo 462
Import quotas 462-463
Import restraints
    Reasons behind 510-511
Imports 446, 453
    Commodity 447, 477
Inclusive unions 408
Income 6, 7, 8, 12, 51, 54, 57
    Change in 57, 58
    Consumer 79
    Decrease in 57
    Distribution of 6
    Real 2, 54, 69
Income distribution 116-117, 372

Governments and 117-118
Income Effect 54, 79, 89-90
Income elasticity of demand 112-114
Income Tax 8
Income, the growth of output and .iB.Real
    Income 2
Income-Inferior Goods 79
Increasing Opportunity Costs 39, 40, 42
Increasing-cost industry 195-197
Independent utility 99
Independent Variable 10, 11
Industrial Unions 419
Industry
    Constant-cost 197-198
    Decreasing-cost 198-199
    Increasing-cost 195-197
Inelasticity
    Perfect 104
Infant-industry argument 464
Inferior Goods 56, 92, 114
Inferiors goods 56
Inflation 2, 8
Inquiry into the Nature and Causes of the
    Wealth of Nations, An (Smith) 22
Interdependency 291
Interest rates 424-425
Interlocking directorates 295
Internal economies of scale 142
Internalizing of benefits 163
International Monetary Fund 496, 503
International Monetary Fund (IMF) 505
International monetary system 491-492
International reserves 496
International Trade 6, 38, 509
    Gains from 453
    Terms of 453-455
International trade policy 468
Inverse 10
Investment
    Foreign 504, 505
Invisible hand 29
Invisible items 447

J

Jewkes, J. D. 311
Job discrimination 395

K

Keynes, John Maynard 3
Kindleberger, C. P. 474

Kinked demand 299-301
    Relevancy of 301
Kohn, Robert E. 169

L

Labor
    Competitively priced 395-397
    Noncompetitively priced 397-398
Labor market
    Monopsony in the 398-406
Labor markets
    Monopsony versus competitive 412
Labor theory of value 532
Laissez-faire economics 22
Land 33
Law enforcement
    Strict 149
Law of Demand 54, 55, 56, 57, 78, 79, 88
    Exceptions to the 54-55
    Theoretical exceptions to the 90-92
Law of diminishing marginal utility 94
Law of diminishing returns 133-134
Law of Supply 60, 62
Law of variable proportions 133-134, 367
Limited Resources 6
Linneman, Peter 412
Liquidate 182
Local Tax 9
Logrolling 341-342
Long-run period 132
    Costs and supply in the 139-142
Long-run supply 212, 213
Loss
    Economic 129

M

Macroeconomics 6
Macroeconomics-employment argument
    465-467
Malthus, Thomas 25
Malthusian Theory 25
Mansfield, Edwin 311
Marginal cost 193-194
Marginal costs 136
Marginal physical product 133, 367
Marginal private benefit 161
Marginal private costs 161
Marginal Rate of Transformation 41
    Diminishing 41
Marginal resource costs 369

Marginal revenue product 366
Marginal social benefit 161
Marginal social costs 161
Marginal utility
    Diminishing 99
    Law of diminishing 94
Market
    Black 73
    Competitive 49, 58, 60, 65, 66, 78
    Contestable 256
    Free 69
    Illegal drug 150
    Perfectly contestable 256
Market Capitalism 527-529
    Economic advantages of 528-529
    Economic Criticisms of 529
    Necessary legal features of 528
Market classifications 179
Market Demand 51, 58, 64, 99-100
Market Economy 80, 446, 536
Market efficiency 27
Market failure 28-29
Market Growth 42
Market period 130-131
    Costs and supply in the 133
Market Supply 60, 64
Marshall, Alfred 15
Marx, Karl 31, 32, 530, 533, 534
Material Resources 4, 16
Materialism
    Dialectical 531
    Historical 531
Materials-balance approach 169
Median-voter model 340-341
Mergers
    Airline 258
    and Antitrust 332-333
    Horizontal 332
    Vertical 332
Microeconomics 6
Midpoint formula 102
Miller, Roger Leroy 146, 377
Minimum-wage laws 409-412
    Past and future of 411-412
Mixed economic system 32
Mixed economy 538
Model 8, 16
    Economic 41
    Production-Possibilities 42
Monetary system
    International 491-492

Monopolistic competition 269-270, 281
    Conclusions about 283-284
    Excess capacity argument of 279-281
    Long-run 277-278
    Short-run 273-277
    Waste of 280
Monopolistic Competition (Chamberlain)
    269
Monopoly 230, 475
    and the Creation of technology 245-246
    Bilateral 406-408, 409
    Deadweight loss of 254
    in the Product market 402-406
    Natural 245
    Price discriminating 255
    Product 375-376
    Pure 230-232, 234-235
    Regulated 234, 248-250
Monopoly Capitalism (Baran and Sweezy)
    230
Monopoly power 231, 426-427
Monopsony
    in the Labor market 398-406
    Professional sports and 405-406
    Pure 397
    versus competitive labor markets 412
Monopsony profit 401
Morrison, Steven 259

N

NAFTA trade agreement 50
National security argument 465
Natural monopoly 245
Natural Resources 44
Negative externality 28
Negative-sum game 339
Net foreign trade 448
Noncompetitive wages 390-393
Nonprice competition 301-307
Normal Goods 56, 91, 114
Normal profit 128, 182, 188-189
Normative Economics 11, 12, 16
North American Free Trade Association
    (NAFTA) 511, 513, 517
North, Douglass C. 146, 377

O

Occupation
    Choice of 430
Official reserve transactions account 508

Oligopoly 310-311
    Behavior of 292
    Behaviors of 311-319
    Class I 293-295, 311-314
    Class II 295-298, 314-317
    Class III 298-301, 317-319
    Defintion of 290-292
    Efficiency effects of class I 294
    Efficiency implications of class II 296-298
    Social reaction to class I 294-295
Open market economy 364
Opportunity Cost 35
Opportunity costs 35, 39, 40, 63, 70, 127
    Increasing 39, 40, 42
    Positive 39
    Real 40, 41
    Zero 39

P

Panzar, John 256
Paradox of value 99
Pareto optimal 339
Parity 215
Payment-in-kind program 217
Per se rule 295
Perfect elasticity 104
Perfect inelasticity 104
Perfect price discrimination 251
Perfectly contestable market 256
Physical capital 424
Planned Socialism 529, 530
    Advantages of 530
    Criticisms of 530
Political action committees 348
Pollution
    Air 170-171
    Environmental 168-171
Population (Consumer) 51, 59
Population Growth 43
Positive Economics 11, 12, 16
Positive externality 28
Positive-sum game 339
Present discriminatory activity 413
Price
    Break-even 192
    Disequilibrium 80
    Equilibrium 65, 71, 79, 80, 158-160
    Shut-down 192
Price discrimination 148-149, 150, 250, 253
    Conditions necessary for 251-252

Perfect **251**
Reverse **148-149, 150**
Second degree **251**
Price elastic **103**
Price elastic demand **101**
Price elasticity of demand **101, 106-107**
Computing **102-103**
Product differentiation and the **271-273**
Price elasticity of supply **143**
Price floors **351**
Price inelastic **103**
Price inelastic demand **101**
Price leadership **296**
Price Rivalry **48**
Price seeker **185**
Price taker **180**
Private benefit
Marginal **161**
Private costs
Marginal **161**
Private equilibrium **160**
Private ownership **30**
Private property rights **526**
Producer Goods **40**
Producers' surplus **203-204**
Product differentiation **270**
Forms of **281-283**
Price elasticity of demand and **271-273**
Sources of **270-271**
Product market
Competition in the **398-401**
Monopoly in the **402-406**
Product monopoly **375-376**
Production **33**
Continuity of **213-214**
Factors of **419-427**
Production Possibilities Curve **36, 37**
Production Possibilities Table **36**
Production-Possibilities Curve **36, 37, 38, 39, 41, 48**
Production-Possibilities Function **36**
Production-Possibilities Model **42**
Profit **128**
Accounting **129**
Economic **128, 181-182, 186-188, 426**
Entrepreneurship and **426-427**
Monopsony **401**
Normal **128, 182, 188-189**
Profit maximization **184-191, 307-310**
Rule for **184**
Progress and Poverty (George) **421**

Property rights **527**
Government and **165-166**
Importance of **527**
Private **526**
Public **526**
Protectionism **457, 458-467, 513**
Costs and benefits of **511-512**
Psychic costs **127**
Public choice **337-338, 350**
in American democracy **340-342**
Public equilibrium
a Tax to create **163**
Public goods **167**
Public property rights **526**
Pure competition **191-193**
Advantages of **199-205**
Characteristics of **179-181**
Disadvantages of **206-207**
in the Long run **194-199**
in the short run **181-194**
Relevance of **207-208**
Static **333-334**
Versus pure monopoly **241-244**
Pure Economic Determinism **43**
Pure economic rent **419**
Pure monopoly **230-232, 234-235**
Long-run **241**
Short-run **237-241**
Versus pure competition **241-244**
Pure monopsony **397**
Pure number **101**

Q

Quantity adjuster **126, 185**
Quantity Demanded **51, 53, 54, 57, 65, 70, 71, 79, 80**
Change in **56, 57, 64, 66, 79**
Quantity Supplied **60, 61, 62, 63, 65, 66, 70, 71, 79, 80**
Change in **61, 64**
Quasi rent **422-424**
Quotas
Export **463-464**

R

Rate of change
Average **102**
Rate of exchange **490**
Rational ignorance **344**
Real Costs **39**

Real Income 54, 69
Real Opportunity Costs 40, 41
Reciprocal Trade Agreements Acts 513
Regulated monopoly 234, 248-250
Regulation
    Industry under 256
    Transportation 256
Relative rent 422
Rent 346, 419-424
    Common 422-424
    Economic 419
    Quasi 422-424
    Relative 422
Rent seeking activities 346
Representative democracy 343
Reregulation 259
Reserve army of the unemployed 532
Reserves
    International 496
Resource externality 370
Resources 5, 33, 36, 38, 39, 40, 41, 42, 43, 49,
    62, 63, 69, 73, 80
    Common access 164-165
    Common property 164-165
    Human 33
    Limited 6
    Material 4, 16
    Natural 44
    Specialized 40
    Supply of 390
Results of historical discrimination 413
Revenue
    Total 107-108, 181
Ricardo, David 471
Ridker, Robert 169
Rights
    Property 165-166, 527
Robinson, Joan 269
Robinson-Patman Act 230, 295
Role of government 28-29
Rule of reason 331
Rustbelt 467-468

S

Sales maximization hypothesis 308
Satisficing 308
Scarcity 4, 5, 6, 42, 69
Schumpeter, Joseph 246, 334, 427
Scully, Gerald 406
Second degree price discrimination 251

Self-interest 22, 29
Shepherd, William 335, 336
Sherman Act 294, 295
Sherman Antitrust Act 230
Short-run period 131-132
    Costs and supply in the 133-139
Short-run supply 134-137, 211-212
Shut-down point 192
Shut-down price 192
Signaling 380
Smith, Adam 14, 15, 21, 22, 27, 28, 29, 42, 99,
    471, 530
Social Benefit 40
    Marginal 161
Social costs 162
    Marginal 161
Social equilibrium 161-162
Socialism 32
    Democratic 538
    Marx and 530
    Planned 530
Special drawing rights 503
Special interest laws 346
Spillovers 162
    and Government intervention 167-168
Standard Oil Trust (Loyd) 230
Static efficiency 525
Static pure competition 333-334
Strict law enforcement 149
Substitutability 41
Substitutes 51, 57, 79
Substitution Effect 54, 79, 89-90
Sunk costs 131, 133
Superior goods 91, 114
Supply 9, 49, 59, 61, 63, 65, 66, 69, 70, 78, 79,
    80, 126, 144
    Change in 61, 64, 66
    Determinants of 59
    Effect of legalization on 147
    Elasticity of 131, 143
    Excess 66, 69, 79, 80
    Influence of time on 130-132
    Law of 60, 62
    Long-run 212-213
    Market 60, 63, 64
    Price elasticity of 143
    Shift in 64
    Short-run 134-137, 211-212
    Total 60
Supply curve 60, 61, 62, 63, 72, 79, 142-143
    Backward-bending labor 391

Competitive firm's short-run 193-194
    Movements along 61, 64
    Shifts in 64
Supply Data 62
Supply Effect 71
Supply of labor
    Elasticity of 393
Supply of resources 390
Supply Schedule 60, 61, 65
Surplus
    Consumers' 202-203
    Producers' 203-204
Surplus value 532

T

Tariff 470
Tariff of Abominations 466
Tariffs 458-462
Tax
    Excise 8, 110-111
    Federal 9
    Income 8
    Local 9
Tax avoidance 349
Tax evasion 349
Technical factor exploitation 401
Technological change 214
Technological unemployment 366
Technology
    Dynamic versus static 246-247
    Monopoly and the creation of 245-246
Terms of trade 453-455
The Law of the Market 24
Theory of Moral Sentiments, The (Smith) 22
Theory of the Leisure Class, The (Veblen) 54, 55, 90
TINPEA 50-51
TIPET 59
Total Costs 181
Total Demand 51
Total Excess Demand 71, 80
Total revenue 181
    Elasticity and 107-108
Total Supply 60
Total utility 93
Trade 446
    Comparative advantage and 451-452
    Free 470
    International 446, 477, 490, 502, 509
    Net foreign 448

Trade Agreement Act 467
Trade and Tariff Act 511
Trade policy 468, 470, 505
    Economic 516
    International 468
Trade Unions 419
Transportation regulation 256
Tregarthen, Timothy 257, 258, 259, 318, 319, 353
Trust 293

U

Underground economy 349
Unemployment 4
    Technological 366
Union shop 406
Unions 74, 406, 419
    Exclusive and inclusive 408
    Industrial 419
    Trade 419
Unit elastic 104
Unit elastic demand 101
United Nations Conference on Trade and Development 476
Utility 93-96
    Independent 99
    Total 93
Utility theory 89, 93
Utils 93

V

Value of marginal product 368
Variable
    Dependent 10, 11
    Independent 10, 11
Variable costs 133
Variable proportions
    Law of 133-134
Veblen goods 54, 56, 79, 90
Veblen, Thorstein 54, 55, 90
Vertical mergers 332
Visible items 447
Volstead Act 146

W

Wage discrimination 395, 413
Wages
    Competitive versus noncompetitive 390-393

Wants **4**
Waste of monopolistic competition **280**
Wealth of Nations **14, 42**
Wealth of Nations, The (Smith) **99**
Weidenbaum, Murray **512, 513**
Weisbrod, Burton A. **377**
Weiss, Leonard **281**
What Is Competition **48**
What is Demand? **88**
Williams, Walter **431**
Willig, Robert **256**
Winkler, Donald **380**
World Trade Organization (WTO) **468, 480,
    513**

Z

Zero-sum game **339**